T0399059

THE OXFORD HANDBOOK OF

HIP HOP DANCE STUDIES

THE OXFORD HANDBOOK OF

HIP HOP DANCE STUDIES

Edited by

MARY FOGARTY

and

IMANI KAI JOHNSON

OXFORD

UNIVERSITY PRESS

OXFORD
UNIVERSITY PRESS

Oxford University Press is a department of the University of Oxford. It furthers
the University's objective of excellence in research, scholarship, and education
by publishing worldwide. Oxford is a registered trade mark of Oxford University
Press in the UK and certain other countries.

Published in the United States of America by Oxford University Press
198 Madison Avenue, New York, NY 10016, United States of America.

Library of Congress Cataloging-in-Publication Data
Names: Fogarty, Mary, 1978- editor. | Johnson, Imani Kai, editor.
Title: The Oxford handbook of hip hop dance studies / edited by Mary Fogarty, Imani Kai Johnson.
Other titles: Handbook of hip hop dance studies
Description: New York, NY : Oxford University Press, 2022. |
Series: Oxford handbooks series | Includes bibliographical references and index. |
Identifiers: LCCN 2021054127 | ISBN 9780190247867 (hardback) |
ISBN 9780190247881 | ISBN 9780190247898 (epub) |
ISBN 9780190247874
Subjects: LCSH: Hip hop dance.
Classification: LCC GV1796.H57 O84 2022 | DDC 793.3—dc23/eng/20211206
LC record available at https://lccn.loc.gov/2021054127

DOI: 10.1093/oxfordhb/9780190247867.001.0001

Printed by Sheridan Books, Inc., United States of America

CONTENTS

Acknowledgments   ix
List of Contributors   xi

Introduction   1
    MARY FOGARTY AND IMANI KAI JOHNSON

PART I. HIP HOP DANCE LEGACIES AND TRADITIONS

1. Foundation: Context and Components of Breaking Fundamentals   13
    KENNETH "KEN SWIFT" GABBERT WITH YARROW "OSOFLY" LUTZ

2. The Camera in the Cypher: High Times and Hypervisibility in Early
Hip Hop Dance   32
    VANESSA FLEET LAKEWOOD

3. The Technical Developments in Breaking from Conditioning to
Mindset   58
    NIELS "STORM" ROBITZKY

4. Connecting Hip Hop History and Heritage   80
    E. MONCELL DURDEN

5. Kung Fu Fandom: B-Boys and the Grindhouse Distribution
of Kung Fu Films   97
    ERIC PELLERIN

6. What Makes a Man Break?   116
    MARY FOGARTY

PART II. HIP HOP DANCE METHODOLOGIES

7. Learn Your History: Using Academic Oral Histories of
   NYC B-Girls in the 1990s to Broaden Hip Hop Scholarship   131
   MiRi Park

8. Hard Love Part 1: Corporealities of Women Ethnographers of
   Hip Hop Dances   149
   Imani Kai Johnson

9. Framing Hip Hop Dance as an Object of Sociological and
   Cultural Research   171
   Andy Bennett

10. Through Sound and Space: Notes on Education from the
    Edge of the Cypher   188
    Emery Petchauer

11. The Vault: Collecting and Archiving Streetdance Footage   204
    Marc "Scramblelock" Sakalauskas

12. Critical Hiphopography in Streetdance Communities
    (Hard Love Part 2)   217
    Imani Kai Johnson

PART III. *OVERSTANDING IDENTITIES IN HIP HOP STREETDANCE PRACTICES*

13. Breaking in My House: Popular Dance, Gender Identities, and
    Postracial Empathies   243
    Thomas F. DeFrantz

14. Globalization and the Hip Hop Dance Cipher   260
    Halifu Osumare and Terry Bright Kweku Ofosu

15. Asian American Liminality: Racial Triangulation in
    Hip Hop Dance   280
    Grace Shinhae Jun

16. Breakin' Down the Bloc: Hip Hop Dance in Armenia   292
    Serouj "Midus" Aprahamian

17. Twerking and P-Popping in the Context of the New Orleans Local
Hip Hop Scene   308
MATT MILLER

18. Is She B-Boying or B-Girling? Understanding how B-Girls
Negotiate Gender and Belonging   326
HELEN SIMARD

PART IV. BREAKING WITH CONVENTION

19. Streetdance and Black Aesthetics   347
NAOMI MACALALAD BRAGIN

20. Living in the Tension: The Aesthetics and Logics of Popping   365
ROSEMARIE A. ROBERTS

21. Staging Hip Hop Dance: Fly Girls in the House   384
LEAH "McFLY" McKESEY, DIANA "FLY LADY DI" REYES,
AND MARY "MJ" FOGARTY

22. Battles and Ballets: Hip Hop Dance in France   408
ROBERTA SHAPIRO, TRANSLATION BY DAVID LAVIN,
ROBERTA SHAPIRO, AND IMANI KAI JOHNSON

23. Negotiating the Metaspace: Hip Hop Dance Artists in the
Space of UK Dance Theatre   430
PAUL SADOT

24. Make the Letters Dance: A Hip Hop Approach to Creative Practice   457
ANTHONY "YNOT" DeNARO AND MARY FOGARTY

PART V. HIP HOP HEALTH: INJURY, HEALING, AND REHABILITATION

25. Hip Hop Dance and Injury Prevention   477
TONY INGRAM

26. They Come for the Hip Hop but Stay for the Healing   497
STEPHEN "BUDDHA" LEAFLOOR

27. Can Expert Dancers Be a Springboard Model to Examine
Neurorehabilitation via Dance?   516
    REBECCA BARNSTAPLE, DÉBORA RABINOVICH, AND
    JOSEPH FRANCIS XAVIER DESOUZA

Afterword: Dance, Hip Hop Studies, and the Academy   534
    JOSEPH SCHLOSS

Index   559

Acknowledgments

We thank all of our contributing authors for putting in the hard work that made this handbook happen. A big shout-out goes to UC-Irvine's Jennifer Fisher for setting things in motion. Thank you to the team at Oxford University Press, including Norman Hirshy, Lauralee Yeary, Karthiga Ramu, and Kayalvizhi Ganesan. We appreciate Serouj "Midus" Aprahamian's contributions as an additional editorial assistant, as well as the anonymous peer reviewers for their helpful suggestions. We are also grateful to Rob Bowman, Naomi Bragin, Tommy DeFrantz, Moncell Durden, Murray Forman, Simon Frith, and Michele Byrd McPhee for their generous comments and feedback on specific chapters.

To these extraordinary people in our lives, thank you for your impact and inspiration: Mariano "Glizzi" Abarca, Caerina Abrenica, Amanda "Lafotographeuse" Adams-Louis, Tim "DJ Timber" Armstrong, Gina Arnold, Melissa Avdeeff, Tyrell Black, Melissa Britt, Anna Buonomo, Jesse "Jazzy Jester" Catibog, Melad Charkhabi, Greg "Flex" Chee-A-Tow, Robin "Rocabye" Coltez, Andy "Leg-o, Blacktop" Recardo Connell, Jonzi D, Marcel "Frostalino" DaCosta, Martha Diaz, Sami Elkout, Troy Feldman, Don Geraghty, Kevin "Renegade" Gopie, Robby Graham, Sean Graham, d. Sabela Grimes, Paula Guerra, Rachael Gunn, Xena Jayne Gusthart, Emma "Ready" Hamilton, "Lil Tim" Hamilton, Scott Henderson, Joseph "J-Rebel" Hersco, Robert Hylton, Elon Höglund, Rebecca "Sparkles" Horton, Vicki Uchenna Igbokwe, Lance "Leftelep" Johnson, Melissa Kastern, Deanne Kearney, Kwende Kefentse, Anthony Kelly, Gloria Kim, Emily Law, Tim Lawrence, Jooyoung Lee, Emmanuelle LePhan, Nadia Lumley, Michelle Lo, Judi Lopez, François Lukawecki, Shay Lyons, House Magana, Peter Maniam, Eric "Zig" Martel, Sideshow Maule, Shelltoe Mel, Jacqueline Melindy, Karou Mendy, Natasha Lea Mills, Ruby Morales, Andy Moro, Michèle Moss, Shirley Mpagi, Jason Ng, Nkechi Njaka, Jason "J-Sun" Noer, Kevin Ormsby, Jillian Osier, Ashley "Colours" Perez, Poe One, Marius "M4RS" Pleniceanu, Brian Polite, Lindsay Rapport, Jon "Drops" Reid, Geoff Reyes, Sabra Ripley, Raquel Rivera, Krystal Riverz, Eve Robertson, Sean Robertson-Palmer, Luis Sanchez, Kerrie Sauce, Kate Scanlan, Alesandra Seutin, Helen Simard, Keith Smith, Kevin Smith, SA Smythe, Victor Sono, Soupy Souphommanychanh, Lynanne Sparrow, Andrea "Firefly" Stockburn, Joshua Swamy, Tammy Theis, Beebee Thomas, Carla Trim-Vamben, Tree Turtle, Pablo Herrera Veitia, Matthieu "Knoxander" Walker, Marsali Wallace, Charlotte Whelan, Roger White, Laura Wiebe, Steve Willick, Claire Wootten, Lauren Worth, Richard Worth, Andrea Wrigley, and Mike Zryd.

MF: Thank you to my coeditor, Imani, and all of our contributing authors for the conversations and company. Shoutouts to Breaking Canada, the Toronto B-Girl Movement, the Albino Zebrahs and the Flyin' Jalapenos.

IKJ: I especially thank my coeditor Mary for her hard work and support. Though we stepped up for each other at different stages of the anthology (corresponding to different points of our lives), she carried this project home. I truly appreciate you for it!

List of Contributors

Serouj "Midus" Aprahamian is a longtime practitioner of breaking, popping, and underground hip hop dance styles. He is currently pursuing a PhD in dance studies at York University, with a focus on hip hop history, and his writings have appeared in the *Journal of Black Studies*, *Oxford African American Studies Center*, and *Dance Research Journal*.

Rebecca Barnstaple is a postdoctoral researcher at the intersection of dance and neuroscience at York University, Toronto, Canada. Her primary projects involve developing new methods in dance research, and applications for dance in health and well-being across the life span.

Andy Bennett is Professor of Cultural Sociology in the School of Humanities, Languages and Social Science at Griffith University in Queensland, Australia. He has written and edited numerous books, including *Popular Music and Youth Culture*, *Music, Style and Aging*, and *Music Scenes* (coedited with Richard A. Peterson).

Naomi Bragin teaches performance and cultural theory at the University of Washington. Her article "Shot & Captured" links Turf dancing in Oakland to the policing of blackness. She's a former NYC Hip-Hop Theater Future Aesthetics Artist and danced to deescalate militarization in Seattle streets during the 1999 WTO protests. Her book *Black Power of Hip-Hop Dance* studies hip hop/streetdance aesthetics.

Thomas F. DeFrantz believes in our shared capacity to do better. Evidence: Hip Hop. Checking @ www.slippage.org.

Anthony "YNOT" DeNaro explores the design, sustainability, history, and community of Hip Hop. Through a futurist lens, his work manifests in dance, typography, music, and architecture. Currently, his classes can be found on a workshop basis internationally, as well as online and in person through the University of Wisconsin–Milwaukee and Arizona State University.

Joseph FX DeSouza is an Associate Professor in the Department of Psychology & and Graduate programs in Biology, Interdisciplinary Studies and Neuroscience Graduate Diploma Program at York University's Centre for Vision Research. His lab aims to show how, when, and where brain networks change as a function of neurorehabilitation.

E. Moncell Durden is an active dancer, historian, ethnographer, author, and documentarian. Durden is an Associate Professor of Practice at the University of Southern

California Kauman International School of Dance, specializing in the pedagogical practices of what he calls the Morphology of Afro-Kinetic Memory.

Mary Fogarty began Breaking in the early 2000s and is an Associate Professor in the Department of Dance at York University, Toronto. She is coediting an issue of *Global Hip Hop Studies* about Breaking and the Olympics. Her recent writing about Breaking appears in *We Still Here* (2020), and *The Oxford Handbook of Dance and Competition* (2019).

Kenneth "Ken Swift" Gabbert is a second-generation Bboy from New York City and is recognized worldwide for his contributions educating and preserving Breaking and Hip Hop culture for over forty years. Currently, he judges Breaking competitions and teaches at universities and schools around the globe.

Tony Ingram is a researcher, entrepreneur, and dancer based in Halifax, Canada. He has an MSc in kinesiology, an MSc in physiotherapy, and is pursuing a PhD in neuroscience. Prior to his current focus of running a medical-device company, he practiced physical therapy and taught injury prevention to dancers.

Imani Kai Johnson, PhD (Critical Dance Studies, UC Riverside) is founder and chair of the Show & Prove Hip Hop Studies Conference Series. Her book *Dark Matter in Breaking Cyphers: The Life of Africanist Aesthetics in Global Hip Hop* is forthcoming from Oxford University Press.

grace shinhae jun, PhD, MFA, is a mother, wife, mover, scholar, and organizer, who creates and educates on the unceded territory of the Kumeyaay Nation. She is a founder and director of bkSOUL performance company, and a cofounder of Asian Solidarity Collective. She teaches dance at the University of California, San Diego and at San Diego City College.

Vanessa Fleet Lakewood is a writer, educator, and photo-historian. She is a Vanier Canada Graduate Scholar and a Ryerson Image Centre Doctoral Research Fellow and currently a Lecturer in the graduate program in Film + Photography Preservation and Collections Management at Ryerson University. Her doctoral research examines the life and work of the American documentary photographer Martha Cooper.

Stephen "Buddha" Leafloor cofounded the Canadian Floor Masters. He has danced for James Brown, GrandMaster Flash, George Clinton and worked as a consultant for Cirque du Soleil. Buddha was appointed an Ashoka Fellow in Canada as a changemaker and awarded the Meritorious Service Cross from Canada's Governor General. He has an MA in Social Work and has worked for 35 years in Child Protection, Probation, Street Work, and Group Homes.

Yarrow "Osofly" Lutz has been a multimedia artist, educator, and program director at numerous organizations, schools, and youth programs for over twenty years. She holds a Masters in Arts Education from the Pratt Institute and has worked with Precita Eyes Mural Arts Center, Urban Arts Partnership, Hip Hop Film Festival, and H2Ed.

Carlos Mare is a renowned artist from the first generation of Hip Hop culture. A respected and celebrated artist/lecturer/scholar of New York's Golden Age of Graffiti Art, his works push the boundaries of contemporary urban art, academia, and technology. Designer of the annual BET Award, and the first Hip Hop artist to earn a Webby Award, he was also a founding member of the Museum of Graffiti in Miami. His work is in the permanent collection of the Museum of Modern Art and he exhibits in galleries and museums globally.

Leah "McFly" McKesey is an eclectic creator, performer, and choreographer. She has danced for such artists as Kool Herc, Wu-Tang, and Kaytranda; worked on music videos, television, and commercials; and won competitions. Leah has curated events and, for over fifteen years, has offered her skills as a youth mentor, guidance counselor, and motivational speaker in schools from primary to university.

Matt Miller is an independent scholar and musician based in the Atlanta metro area. He is the author of *Bounce: Rap Music and Local Identity in New Orleans*, published in 2012 by the University of Massachusetts Press.

Terry Bright Kweku Ofosu is an Assistant Lecturer and a pioneering popular dance scholar in the Department of Dance Studies, University of Ghana. He is the 1989 National Dance Champion of Ghana and currently a PhD candidate at the Institute of African Studies, University of Ghana.

Halifu Osumare is Professor Emerita of African American and African Studies at the University of California, Davis. She published *The Africanist Aesthetic in Global Hip-Hop* (2007) and *The Hiplife in Ghana: West Africanist Indigenization of Hip-Hop* (2012), and was a 2008 Fulbright Scholar to Ghana. Her recent *Dancing in Blackness, A Memoir* (2018) won the 2019 Selma Jeanne Cohen Prize in Dance Aesthetics and a National Book Award.

MiRi Park is a b-girl, choreographer, performer, producer, scholar, teacher, and mother based in Southern California. She reps New York City where she spent her formative adult years and learned the art of b-girling and other underground dance forms.

Eric Pellerin is Assistant Professor and Librarian at Medgar Evers College, City University of New York. His research interests include hip hop history, authorship in film, and Hong Kong cinema.

Emery Petchauer is a scholar, teacher, DJ/turntablist, and cultural organizer. He works as an Associate Professor in the Departments of English and Teacher Education at Michigan State University. He has over twenty years of experience as a DJ in hip hop dance community spaces under his artist name, DJ ILL Literate.

Débora B. Rabinovich graduated with honors from the University of Buenos Aires, Argentina, in 1988, and now works as a clinical psychologist. She holds an MSc. in Experimental Medicine from McGill University. Rabinovich has lectured at UBA

Faculties of Medicine and Psychology. Her research integrates dance into the field of neurological rehabilitation and wellbeing.

Diana "Fly Lady Di" Reyes is a multidisciplinary artist from Toronto, known as a street dance artist, DJ, and painter. McGill University educated and Elite Force/Dance Fusion NYC trained, Reyes has worked with industry greats like Jason Derulo, Ciara, and Director X. She is currently investigating her Filipino heritage.

Rosemarie A. Roberts is a Professor of Dance at Connecticut College whose artistic and scholarly work blend history, dance, and theater in order to investigate Afro-diasporic dance as embodiments of difference, knowledge, and resistive power. Her book project, *Baring Unbearable Sensualities: Hip Hop Dance, Bodies, Race and Power* is forthcoming from Wesleyan University Press.

Niels "Storm" Robitzky, started Breaking, Popping, and Locking in 1983 in North Germany. He is a choreographer for dance theater, researcher, author of the book, *From Swipe to Storm* (Backspin Verlag 2000), and considers himself a B-Boyologist.

Paul Sadot, PhD, is a Dance/Theatre practitioner, a practice researcher and a Visiting Research Fellow at the Centre for Interdisciplinary Performative Arts (CIPA), Royal Birmingham Conservatoire, UK. He is a Capoeira Professor and works internationally as a Movement Director and Choreographer.

Marc "Scramblelock" Sakalauskas is a practitioner of b-boying (1998) and locking (2000). He has learned from many originators in the locking scene and has won several international competitions. He organizes various events and is focused on building the Canadian locking community. He travels worldwide and continues to develop new teaching formats for locking.

Joseph Schloss is an interdisciplinary scholar specializing in the cultural politics of music and dance. He is the author of *Foundation: B-Boys, B-Girls and Hip-Hop Culture in New York* (Oxford University Press, 2009) and *Making Beats: The Art of Sample-Based Hip-Hop* (Wesleyan University Press, 2014), and teaches at the City University of New York and Princeton University.

Roberta Shapiro is a sociologist with a special interest in art, work and social change. She coauthored *Cultural Sociology: Special Issue on Artification* (Vol. 13: 3, Sept. 2019), and *De l'artification. Enquêtes sur le passage à l'art* (Paris, EHESS, 2012). She works at the Ecole des hautes études en sciences sociales and the Centre do l'emploi et du travail in Paris.

Helen Simard is a choreographer, dance researcher, and retired b-girl based in Tiohtiá:ke/Montréal, Canada. Her interdisciplinary artistic research examines the musicality of the dancing body in improvisational practices. Her most recent work, *Papillon*, premiered via live stream in November 2020. She holds a BFA and an MA in Dance.

INTRODUCTION

MARY FOGARTY AND IMANI KAI JOHNSON

THE announcement that Breaking is to be an official part of the 2024 Paris Olympics is one more pivot in Hip Hop dance studies' expanding repertoire of moves. As the diverse dance styles grouped together under the rubric, "Hip Hop dance," migrate from street and club, into film and video, book and university, conservatory and studio, and beyond, what remains constant is how these embodied expressions of social identity have <u>always</u> mattered. Irrespective of institutional recognition or disregard, Hip Hop dance has long offered a site where pleasure and politics arise in tandem. Taken seriously by its practitioners and dedicated followers, in the past few decades Hip Hop dance has entered more traditional—and at times problematic—spaces of acknowledgment and contemplation. As an intervention in this more traditional form of recognition, this Oxford Handbook seeks to honor practitioners by foregrounding their voices and stories, accompanied by insights from critical dance studies researchers. In so doing, it hopes to help set the stage for future work, by showing what can be done when practitioners, practitioner-scholars, dance scholars, and community workers from around the world get together to chronicle, contemplate, and at times criticize where Hip Hop dances have been so far, and where they may be going.

In this introduction, each of the co-editors outlines key aspects of the field of Hip Hop dance. Imani Kai Johnson sets up some of the political and social issues of our times. Mary Fogarty then looks at how researchers working both inside and outside the academy have crucially shaped scholarship about Breaking, the original dance of Hip Hop culture. She also provides an overview of the content of the anthology. Further reflection on the content of individual chapters can be found in the Afterword by Joseph Schloss. The respective authors of each section are indicated by initials (IKJ) for Imani Kai Johnson and (MF) for Mary Fogarty.

* * *

A Love Letter of Sorts (IKJ)

This is not a *roses are red / violets are blue* kind of love letter, but it is a love letter nonetheless. It is written for those who think deeply about the streetdances affiliated with Hip Hop[1] and who write about them with both curiosity and care. We share your desire to strengthen the field because, like you, we recognize that Hip Hop streetdance cultures are a wellspring of underexplored knowledges. Mary and I dedicate this book to students both inside and out of academia, because this kind of collection is most valuable to those who recognize such sentiments. *The Oxford Handbook of Hip Hop Dance Studies* is intended to serve as a compendium of topics, approaches, theoretical influences, histories, and perspectives that demonstrate the possibilities of a field in formation.

I met my co-editor, Mary Fogarty, through researching Hip Hop dances. I read and cited Mary's MA thesis as a doctoral student; and she then assigned parts of my dissertation to her students. When we finally met in person, we began an exchange that has been ongoing for years, learning from each other and shaping each other's ideas. We first plotted this anthology in 2012, walking down New York City streets, excitedly brainstorming about the types of research such a collection could include. It felt palpably important for us as junior scholars positioned across multiple disciplines (including music, dance, African diaspora, American, and performance studies), to assemble a collection informed by Hip Hop culture and with an eye toward our varied audiences— from Hip Hop heads and practitioners to new students and seasoned scholars. We sought to create a collection that we would have wanted when we were students, one that attended to the interests of practitioners themselves.

Such an approach matters precisely because there is a dearth of scholarship on Hip Hop streetdances in both Hip Hop studies and dance studies. Very little of the published research on Hip Hop over the last approximately forty years has focused on dance, (and little of what has been published goes beyond breaking). Dance studies does not frequently prioritize social, popular, battle, or competition dances,[2] which characterize most Hip Hop streetdances. That they are doubly overlooked signals the ways Hip Hop dance challenges both fields to shift their respective perspectives (i.e., from the proscenium stage to cyphers and clubs, or from textual analysis to embodiment), to discard outmoded ideas (e.g., high-low culture divides, or the mind-body split), and to trouble value systems that disregard non-Western epistemologies, oral cultures, and embodied knowledges. Hip Hop dances are an incredibly rich yet neglected area of research that can add critical insights to both fields.

Those walks in 2012 solidified a certainty that Hip Hop streetdances not only add to a body of knowledge; they contend with some of the ideological assumptions that invisiblize or exploit the peoples and sensibilities that grow out of them. Since the academy and its hierarchies play a significant part in the development of a field, the institutional contexts and hurdles contributing to this neglect merit attention. Consider, for example, how the approval process for fledgling dissertation projects shapes future research. In *Black Noise: Rap Music and Black Culture in* Contemporary America, Tricia Rose (1994) writes that her dissertation committee was initially "worried . . . that rap would disappear before I finished my research, I wouldn't have enough material to write about, and I might be unmarketable as a job candidate" (xii). At the outset, Rose clearly had to convince the committee that rap music warranted attention despite their concern that it was a flash in the pan fad that could undermine her career. Some students looking to break new ground by studying emerging or little-known cultures are still told that their research is "too niche" to be worthy of sustained intellectual attention.[3] Others alter their projects beyond recognition to fit disciplinary expectations or abandon them altogether if they do not. Yet, though it was inconceivable to her committee at the time, Rose's work was formative of a field. The book was so impactful that I have often wondered, had they not approved the project, just where Hip Hop studies would be over twenty-five years later.[4]

Our efforts to support research on Hip Hop dances extends beyond scholarship to the vulnerable and essential workers within the corporatized university whose labor is also invisiblized and exploited. Not long after our decision to make this a love letter, education strikes around the world hit close to home. In January 2020, graduate students at multiple University of California campuses (some already engaged in a grading strike) stepped up their demonstrations in support of a cost-of-living salary adjustment. By February, seventeen protestors at UC Santa Cruz had been arrested and eighty-two graduate student workers were fired, which (temporarily) eliminated their health insurance.[5] Yet the demonstrators marched on.

It should not be seen as an extravagance that graduate-student workers, some of whom were living out of their cars, want to pursue their studies while being able to afford groceries. The degree of economic precarity they experienced is an example of structural inequalities within the university. As a result, the stakes are incredibly high for students, and their sacrifices are not always evident. For us to vision toward a field, and in support of research yet to come, we must recognize the unreasonable sacrifices that people are forced to make now and "leverage our complicity"[6] with these institutions so as to not perpetuate them down the line.

As future-minded as we tried to be, by March 2020 the global pandemic that had been spreading worldwide for months became undeniable in North America, where we both reside. As much of the world began dealing with the uncertainty of COVID-19, sheltering-in-place, and the economic disparities it amplified, there was, too, a growing longing to be together. Hip Hop DJs began saving our spirits in nightly "live" sessions; rappers and singers competed or just shared music in live Verzuz[7] battles featured in apps like Instagram; and dancers the world over fostered community by sharing their art online to cultivate embodied social exchanges in the face of physical distancing practices. The joy of dancing "together" to "live" music energized the spirit in the face of the virus, with Hip Hop illuminating hopeful strategies for living under the COVID-19 restrictions.

Within two months, though, following viral footage of an eight-minute clip featuring a Minneapolis police officer asphyxiating George Floyd,[8] weeks of protests and public demonstrations ensued around the world against antiblack policing and state-sanctioned violence. Demands for action were distilled into calls to defund and/or abolish the police, tear down monuments to racist and colonial histories, and mounting pressure to hold institutions accountable for their continuing racist, and specifically antiblack practices and legacies. Empty statements were called out, and various organizations made public commitments to change, including academic ones like the Dance Studies Association.[9] What Mary and I hope is that Hip Hop Dance studies becomes a medium to study these various conditions through a streetdance lens, and be responsive to demands for the academy to reckon with racist legacies in thought and training.

We thus dedicate this handbook to students of all levels, within and outside institutions, because we share your enthusiasm and still need you to keep going. We call on you to follow your curiosities because perhaps they will offer clues to surviving, thriving, and cultivating new ways of living.

It's Been a Long Time Coming. . . (MF)

This Handbook represents a practitioner-based turn in the emerging field of Hip Hop dance studies. As someone who was a b-girl before she became a researcher into Breaking culture, I have always looked to dancers for insight as well as inspiration. While some of the chapters here take a more theoretical approach, much of the content addresses Hip Hop dance explicitly as a lived practice. Alongside the important work of scholarly researchers, the Handbook includes the insights of internationally recognized dancers who have made considerable contributions to Hip Hop dance scholarship, through their teaching as well as through their careers as artists.

The chapters share a number of common interests, including the outlining of teaching methods, the questioning of legacies, the exploration of how cultural traditions that matter are passed down from generation to generation, and of how vocabularies are codified. Unsurprisingly, the chapters in this anthology do not always use terms consistently; both practitioners and scholars seek to define and label their terms, sometimes being at odds with each other. While b-boys Ken Swift and Storm, for example, show considerable agreement in vocabulary, shared historical understanding, and concern about passing down knowledge and traditions, some of the authors in our anthology will deeply disagree with each other on terminology, history, and analysis. We believe it is useful for students to encounter these incongruencies and differences. We hope these chapters will not only map out the current stage of knowledge but, in particular, will also help to identify what future research is needed. Moreover, our inclusion of the insights of multiple practitioners from Hip Hop dance scenes not only offers counterpoints to scholarly orthodoxy, but equally helps to reimagine research agendas. In so doing, it is also our intention to highlight those contradictions that inform Hip Hop and its endlessly shapeshifting, fragmented, competitive yet collaborative energies.

This Handbook serves as a resource for students wanting to study different dance styles and their distinctive histories. Dances such as House, Popping, Locking, or Twerking, to name but a handful of the many styles, grow out of Afro-diasporic communities where music provides a central source of inspiration and solidarity. As the beloved, iconic, and late Tyrone "The Bone" Proctor said, "The best choreographer is music." Although we are advocating here for more dance practitioner-based accounts, I also want to honor the crucial contributions of Hip Hop researchers who brought Breaking into the scholarly conversation. I have long advocated for more crossover conversation between popular music studies and dance scholarship. For example, the three 'Rs,' Tricia Rose (1994), Raquel Rivera (2003), and Rachel Raimist (1999), all provided early accounts of Hip Hop that considered dance important enough to conduct interviews with dancers. Their scholarly contributions helped create space for the work that would follow. I can still remember picking up Rivera's *New York Ricans in the Hip Hop Zone* (2004) and being thrilled to discover that she had devoted ten pages to a discussion of Breaking. When Raimist's documentary filmwork not only showed one of my favorite rappers, Medusa, but also the iconic b-girl Asia One, I felt seen as a b-girl, further validating a movement that mattered (an overview of the earliest scholarship on Breaking is found in Fogarty 2006).

Some of the contributors to this anthology wrote some of the earliest monographs about Breaking, such as Halifu Osumare (2007) and Joseph Schloss (2009). Schloss offers an overview of the field in his 'Afterword', while Osumare extends her earlier thinking about the globalization of Afrodiasporic dances by collaborating with dancer and scholar, Terry Bright Kweku Ofusu. Their chapter captures the broader spirit of this project, and the ethos of working together, passing along knowledge, and centering dancers' perspectives in the academy.

The Oxford Handbook of Hip Hop Dance Studies consists of five parts. Part I addresses the first few decades of Hip Hop, its legacies and traditions, with chapters by Ken Swift and Yarrow Lutz, Storm, and E. Moncell Durden. Speaking more generally of legendary dancers, Durden asks "what happens when their personal truth is romanticized and passed on as fact?", suggesting that the key is to keep on asking questions. Like Storm and Ken Swift, Durden is known internationally as a Hip Hop dance practitioner and mentor. Durden was part of the influential Hip Hop dance group, the Mop Top Crew, as well as being a dancer for Rennie Harris' Puremovement; Durden has consistently emphasized Hip Hop dance as Afrodiasporic tradition and heritage, a fact too often obscured as Hip Hop dance becomes more and more globalized. In my chapter, I discuss transformations that happen within the lifecycle of an individual's performance. I also explain for the uninitiated why Frosty Freeze and Ken Swift are so damn fresh.

Alongside this work by well-known figures in the global Hip Hop dance community, we also introduce new research by emerging scholars in the field. Vanessa Lakewood identifies the power of the media in shaping discourses about Breaking through a case study of early Hip Hop photography, including works by Martha Cooper that accompanied some of the very earliest writing in the press about Breaking by Sally Banes (1981). In Eric Pellerin's chapter, he interviews second-generation B-Boys in New York City who were heavily influenced by kung fu aesthetics, considers how kung fu films were distributed, and highlights the impact of cross-cultural, mediated exchanges.

Part II addresses Hip Hop methodologies. Miri Park, B-girl-scholar-mother, compares oral historical traditions in Hip Hop to academic oral history methodologies. She takes as her case in point the history of New York City B-girls of the 1990s who went on theatrical tours. B-girls Rokafella and Honey Rockwell reveal the ambiguities and tensions of professional life as a B-girl. Imani Kai Johnson examines the challenges and complexities facing women ethnographers working in Hip Hop dance spaces. Andy Bennett then examines Hip Hop dance as an object of sociological and cultural research. He introduces key interdisciplinary frameworks from adjacent fields of youth, subcultural, leisure, and popular music studies to expand the toolbox available to Hip Hop dance scholars. DJ Emery Petchauer's approach is rooted in Hip Hop pedagogy, and centers on the experience of music when one is learning how to Break. Marc "Scramblelock" Sakalauskas presents a personal account of establishing and maintaining his archive, describing how he collects material, how he catalogues it as he does, and why. In the process, he lays out some of the terrain of locking as a dance style. In her second chapter for the anthology, Johnson explores the term *hiphopography*, a method that builds on other critical ethnographic, decolonial, and Black feminist epistemologies and methodologies.

Part III, "*Over*standing Identities in Hip Hop Practices," includes academic-practitioner-artists who analyze Hip Hop identities. Thomas DeFrantz asks if Breaking can belong to House, placing the spiritual meaning of dance at the center of his analysis. Halifu Osumare and Terry Bright Kweku Ofusu then compare Hawaiian and Ghanaian popular culture and dance, offering an *over*standing of the translocal, Africanist aesthetics of Hip Hop dances and their cooptation and corporatization in the circulation of popular culture, in the process, showing how "the Ghanaian class divide played right into the snare of American pop cultural hegemony." Serouj "Midus" Aprahamian's chapter builds on the earlier work of Osumare to provide a historically informed ethnography of Hip Hop dance in Armenia (a former Soviet Republic), where it becomes a globalized resource for youth seeking alternative ways of being in the world.

As a powerful point of comparison, grace shinhae jun's chapter examines the development of Asian Hip Hop dance teams in Southern California, and through them, the exponential growth in Hip Hop dance competitions. She argues that these Asian American dancers embrace Black culture, in part, as a means of being seen as more fully "American." Matt Miller's chapter explores the grassroots trajectory of twerking and P-Popping in New Orleans and, through thick ethnographic research, expands the definition of what counts as Hip Hop in the local culture. Finally, Helen Simard asks what happens when B-girls navigate an already-gendered space, initially emulating men, and then figuring out whether what they are doing is to be considered 'B-boying' or 'B-girling.'

In Part IV, we head to the stage, television set, and the studio. Naomi Bragin approaches Hip Hop aesthetics as Black aesthetics, considering the diminishing of authenticity that may occur when dancers learn Hip Hop dance in the studio rather than the street or club. Dance scholar and artist Rosemarie Roberts interviews Mr Wiggles, one of the most influential Hip Hop dancers internationally, and considers the political impulse of Popping's physicality.

Switching gears, Leah "McFly" McKesey, Diana "Fly Lady Di" Reyes, and I rehearse the influence of the Fly Girls, the dance troupe on the syndicated television show *In Living Color*. The Fly Girls get their shine in this chapter via a recorded oral history of their influence on dance practitioners. The questions about professionalization raised in the Fly Girls chapter lead us back to discussions about Hip Hop on the proscenium stage. In the next two chapters, Roberta Shapiro and Paul Sadot cover the development of Hip Hop theatre in France and the United Kingdom, respectively. Shapiro begins with questions about how Breaking moved onto the theatrical stage and into contexts of art and curation, while Sadot problematizes the development of Hip Hop theatre within UK institutional frameworks. The institutional contexts of the art school and art career also figure in the last chapter by Anthony "YNOT" DeNaro and I, where we explore the aesthetics of Breaking within writing (i.e., "graffiti"), music, and movement.

In Part V, the concluding section of *The Oxford Handbook of Hip Hop Dance Studies*, Tony Ingram surveys the scientific research on dance injuries from Breaking. As a B-Boy himself, he wades through the vague, if not insulting, terminology of "break-dancing" used by scientific researchers, to argue that it matters whether researchers are looking at Breaking, Locking, Popping, or other dance styles, since they each require very different assessments when it comes to injury diagnosis and prevention. Rebecca Barnstaple, Débora Rabinovich, and Joseph DeSouza discuss ideas about dance and the brain, including a study I co-authored in which Ken Swift agreed to have an fMRI scan of his brain conducted while listening to music. Although it is perhaps unconventional to place neuroscience articles in a Handbook such as this, the chapter provides a provocation for future research in this area. Finally, Stephen "Buddha" Leafloor shares some of his insights as a social worker providing Hip Hop–inspired programming to Indigenous communities in Canada.

In the 'Afterword,' Joseph Schloss calls attention to how dancers position themselves in both Hip Hop culture and scholarly research, ending our anthology with movement as the central metaphor for thinking about how Hip Hop dance scholarship shapes, and is shaped by, practitioners' positionalities in the world.

The different sections of *The Oxford Handbook of Hip Hop Dance Studies* seek to place the voices of practitioners in dialogue with scholarly concerns. Some of the chapters are polemical; others are more tentative. Some are written with undergraduate students in mind and are intended to empower new or marginal voices who are just entering the academy, while others challenge orthodoxies, guide graduate students, or provide facts for future history books.

ABSENCE AND PRESENCE (IKJ)

The *Oxford Handbook on Hip Hop Dance Studies* is a beginning conversation, not an exhaustive representation of a field. We have gathered scholarly and practitioner-based studies and accounts in a collection that indicates its possibilities. Although there are absences in this collection (e.g., material expanding the geographic scope and analytical depth of Hip Hop dance), due to conditions beyond our control, it is important to acknowledge that what we bring together here is still in conversation with *that* material. There is so much more research that *is* and *can happen* beyond what is here. *The Oxford Handbook of Hip Hop Dance Studies* is first and foremost an introduction.

Absence is palpable in the text by way of another register: the OGs, the teachers, legendary practitioners, respected scholars, friends, and family who have passed away, several of whose deaths were immediate to the drafting of this introduction. The unexpected twist of a global pandemic is that collective losses, especially without our usual collective means of paying respect and celebrating lives, have made the urgency of this project even clearer. Those of us who study Hip Hop streetdances already know this urgency because in Hip Hop's fifty-year existence we were fortunate to experience and learn from so many of those legends while they were alive. In many cases we can still talk to the people who were "there," when and wherever "there" is. Getting their stories into the annals of history is essential, not simply to develop the field but because their lives do not end when they die. But rather than present an inevitably incomplete list of names that falls short of honoring the countless contributors to Hip Hop dance histories and cultures who have passed on, some we might not know but whose impact we nonetheless feel, we want to recognize that this collection strives to feature people and practices that have captured their lessons and legacies. We honor the dead because they live on in those they have taught, mentored, schooled, and battled. Thus, we end where we started: with appreciation for those students who carry the legacies of these figures in their bodies, their practices, and their writing.

NOTES

1. The term *Hip Hop streetdances*, or streetdances that fall under the umbrella of Hip Hop, acknowledges the range of practices that are affiliated with or related to Hip Hop culture in broad terms, while respecting that such genres have distinct histories beyond the ways Hip Hop gets narrativized and thus cannot be totally subsumed under that header. For a discussion on the capitalization of Hip Hop, see Johnson's "Hard Love Part 1" in this volume.
2. Including party, club, and combat dances.
3. Within the academy, getting such research greenlit can be its own challenge, but on the flip side, many Hip Hop practitioners are especially sensitive to Ivory Tower elitism and anything that reeks of exploitation and are wary of academics who dabble in their communities, take from them, and leave. Hence, the importance of care and respect.
4. In November 2019, the American Studies Association Annual Conference in Honolulu, Hawaii, featured a panel titled "Black Noise at 25" to commemorate the twenty-fifth anniversary of its publication.
5. See UC Santa Cruz Wildcat Strikers (2020), "The University of California Strike Enters Its 4th Month," *The Nation* (online), April 6. Last accessed December 19, 2020. https://www.thenation.com/article/society/the-university-of-california-strike-enters-its-fourth-month/.

6. I borrow this phrase from Fred Moten, who used it in a conversation with Stephano Harney during a talk titled, "The University: Last Words" on July 9, 2020, which was part of the Action Network's FUC series on labor movements, decommodified knowledge, and the university. See https://www.youtube.com/watch?v = zqWMejD_XU8& feature = youtu.be.

7. "Verzuz, also known as Verzuz TV, is an American webcast series created by producers Timbaland and Swizz Beatz. Verzuz was introduced during the COVID-19 pandemic as a virtual DJ battle, with Timbaland and Swizz Beatz facing off in its first iteration through an Instagram Live broadcast in March 2020." Wikipedia, s.v. "Verzuz," n.d. https://en.wikipe dia.org/wiki/Verzuz.

8. George Floyd was an African American man from Minneapolis who was stopped by police after allegations of using a counterfeit $20 bill to buy cigarettes. Officer Derek Chauvin was eventually charged with murder after kneeling on Floyd's throat for several minutes until he died. See "George Floyd: What Happened in the Final Moments of His Life," *BBC News*, US and Canada (online), July 16 2020. Last accessed 20 December 2020. https://www.bbc.com/news/world-us-canada-52861726.

9. See their letter addressed to the entire field of dance studies, titled, "DSA Strongly and Unequivocally Condemns Global Anti-Blackness and White Supremacy," June 16, 2020, available on their website. Last accessed December 20, 2020. https://dancestudiesassociat ion.org/news/2020/the-dance-studies-association-strongly-and-unequivocally-conde mns-global-anti-blackness-and-white-supremacy. The group followed up on August 21, 2020, with a letter to individual departments titled, "Departmental Call-to-Anti-Racist-Action." Last accessed December 20, 2020. https://dancestudiesassociation.org/news/2020/departmental-call-to-anti-racist-action.

References

Banes, S. (1981). "To the Beat Y'all: Breaking is Hard to Do." *Village Voice*. April 10.

Crawley, A. (2017). *Blackpentecostal Breath: the Aesthetics of Possibility*. New York: Fordham University Press.

Fogarty, M. (2006). " 'What ever happened to Breakdancing': Transnational B-Boy/B-Girl Networks, Underground Video Magazines and Imagined *Affinities*." MA thesis dissertation. Available online: https://dr.library.brocku.ca/bitstream/handle/10464/2826/Brock_Fogart y_Mary_2007.pdf?sequence=1&isAllowed=y

Fogarty, M. (2019). "Why Are Breaking Battles Judged? The Rise of International Competitions." In *The Oxford Handbook of Dance and Competition*, edited by Sherril Dodds, 409–428. New York: Oxford University Press.

Fogarty, M. (2020). "*Following the Thread: Toronto's Place in Hip Hop Dance Histories.*" In *We Still Here: Hip Hop North of the 49th Parallel*, edited by C. Marsh and M. V. Campbell, 97–115. Montreal: McGill-Queen's University Press.

Johnson, I. K. (2012). "Music Meant to Make You Move: Considering the Aural Kinesthetic." *Sounding Out* (blog), June 18. https://soundstudiesblog.com/2012/06/18/music-meant-to-make-you-move-considering-the-aural-kinesthetic/.

Moten, F. (2003). *In the Break: the Aesthetics of the Black Radical Tradition*. Minneapolis: University of Minnesota Press.

Osumare, H. (2007). *The Africanist Aesthetic in Global Hip Hop: Power Moves*. New York: Palgrave.

Raimist, Rachel. (1999). *Nobody Knows My Name.* Featuring Medusa and Asian One. Distributed through Women Make Movies.

Rivera, Raquel. (2003). *New York Ricans in the Hip Hop Zone.* New York: Palgrave MacMillan.

Rose, T. (1994). *Black Noise: Rap Music and Black Culture in Contemporary America.* Middleton, CT: Wesleyan University Press.

Robitzky, N. (2000). *Von Swipe zu Storm: Breakdance in Deutschland.* Hamburg, Germany: Backspin.

Schloss, J. G. (2009). *Foundation: B-Boys, B-girls and Hip-Hop Culture in New York.* New York: Oxford University Press.

PART I

HIP HOP DANCE LEGACIES AND TRADITIONS

....

FOUNDATION

Context and Components of Breaking Fundamentals

....

KENNETH "KEN SWIFT" GABBERT
WITH YARROW "OSOFLY" LUTZ

INTRODUCTION

....

IN 1977, I was eleven years old, growing up on the Upper West Side of Manhattan. My friend Dante[1] and I were walking by a record shop on 98th Street and Broadway while "Back in Love Again" by L.T.D.[2] played on the speakers. Dante did a top spin into a split, and it was the first time I saw someone drop and touch the floor in person, not on TV. It felt daring and radical. I was blown away that he didn't care what people thought as he reacted to the music right there on the sidewalk.

"This is what B.Boys do," said my friend Doze Green[3] the following year, 1978, as he dropped to the floor and did a little knee shuffle. Doze lived a floor above me on 97th St. and Amsterdam Avenue, Manhattan, and his cousin Tee, a DJ from the Bronx, had taught him how to DJ. Doze got a mixer and turntable, and we started practicing. Tee also showed him how to *go down* and do a few dance moves on the floor. It was the style of *going off*, which started in the Bronx at parties and jams in the early to mid-1970s. Because these moves were quick and precise, Breaking instantly made an impression on us as something fresh and new. It wasn't on television yet, or in the schools, and our parents didn't know about it. All of this made it something underground and intriguing. At that young age, creativity and physical daring came naturally to me. And it was easy to imitate and experiment with my body. There was a concrete path in Central Park at 100th St. next to a playground, where on the weekends a group of Black kids would run fast, do back handsprings for thirty feet straight, and then finish with high somersaults, some with twists and other impressive tricks. I was inspired by how talented and fearless they were.

At that time, the city had summer carnivals at night with rides and games in the big school park on W. 100th St. This is when I first saw kids my age and older dancing and "getting down" in a circle. As I watched one kid do some crazy movement with his body, it blew my mind. I later found out that his name was Greggo and that he came with other B.Boys from the East Side of Manhattan to this park on the West Side to get down. I was really excited, but at first, I felt I should just watch and check it out, because it was intimidating and different, and they were all Black, so I didn't know if it was only their thing, if I was allowed since I'm not Black, but Puerto Rican and Cuban American. At the time, my older brother, Speedy, started hanging out with a crew called the #1 Sure Shot Boys, which included Raul, aka "Kid Terrific," and Markie D. They were Puerto Rican, and when I saw them Rocking and Breaking, it made me feel a bit more comfortable, so I started practicing.

I started to Break in circles at church jams—Holy Name on W. 96th St. and St. Gregory's on W. 90th would throw parties with music and dancing for the community— and also at block parties, where local residents would get a permit to close the street to play music, cook food, and socialize. There would be jams from 80th up to 104th Street, Amsterdam Ave. to Columbus Ave. The Douglas Projects had DJs like Mike D and The Untouchables, DJ Sherlock of the Shamrock Crew, and others bringing their music equipment out into the courtyard to throw jams. When specific songs were played, like "Apache"[4] or "Dance to the Drummers Beat,"[5] that's when people would start breaking. Breaking at these jams is how I gained confidence, attention, and notoriety. It was also where I started meeting more local B.Boys, even some that were in that first circle I saw on 100th St. I discovered that some of those "Black" B.Boys were a mix of African American, Afro Latinos, Dominicans, and Puerto Ricans. Race, ethnicity, and nationality meant less than the fact that we all shared the same living conditions, were all poor and lower class. And we all shared something else: it was also a dance that took some courage, so anybody who dared try to Break had to be willing to show what they could do with their skills, personality, and style.

It was said that Breaking was dying out in some areas of the Bronx in the late 1970s, when many original B.Boys were moving on from their late teens and adapting to adulthood. But breaking was strong and picking up on the Upper West Side, and in many other neighborhoods.[6] The original dancers from the Bronx had developed the "rules" and structure, and these were passed down to a second generation of dancers in my neighborhood and throughout the boroughs of New York City. It was during the late 1970s that the initial form took on new life, and a larger movement of dance and culture was created, all based on those original foundations of the traditions of the first B.Boys and B.Girls. It was a pivotal time that both solidified the dance and advanced it to another level. We had no idea that in just a few years, it would move across the whole country and quickly become an important popular culture around the world.

Over the last forty years, Breaking has evolved and grown into an international movement, with many schools and dance studios, as well as high-level competitions around the world. The dance has been seen in music videos, films, commercials, on theatrical stages, and with the advent of YouTube and other social media platforms, it is now everywhere. Even with minimal access to electronic media, people across the globe have seen the dance, whether on their screens or in the streets.

But often, those watching the dance do not understand what they are seeing. Even many who actively break do not understand the form's basic foundations. And though they can perform some of the dance's elements, they know little of its complexities or its history. I am writing this chapter to pass down what was passed down to me regarding Breaking's foundation as I learned it. My aim in doing so is to keep the art form true to its traditions and history. Breaking is always evolving but, like other art forms, those who know where it comes from are best situated to bring it into the future.

I will describe the general context and aesthetics of Breaking in New York City in the late 1970s and early 1980s. During this period, Breaking consisted of six main components: *top rock*, *go downs*, *footwork*, *spins*, *air moves*, and *freezes*. These traditional elements kept the dance grounded and moving forward as an art form where creativity, innovation, and improvisation were highly valued. When Breaking was in its developmental stages, these components were already central to the dance, and they remain so today. They are the starting points and glue that holds Breaking together as it contemplates the infinite possibilities of its future, and I will describe some of their particular movements based on my own experience on the Upper West Side of Manhattan and the Bronx.

I have italicized the names of key Breaking moves to help readers identify and understand the dance's terminology. I have also chosen to use the term "B.Boy/B.Girl" when describing a dancer who breaks. There were a few B.Girls, but I acknowledge the vast majority of dancers in the 1970s and 1980s were male, and the term "B.Boying" was popular. The term "Breaker" came out in the 1980s, and when the media caught on, they started using the term "Breakdancer," which wasn't used in the streets. I also commonly refer to the dance as Breaking because it seems the most accurate description, one that stays true to the dance's history and is still in common use today. However, it is also important to keep in mind that much of the terminology of the dance and its movements varied depending on one's neighborhood. In that time, a move had completely different names in different parts of the city since the dance developed largely off the grid, in very local contexts.

For the more experienced dancer or dance scholar, some of what follows may seem too basic or overexplained, but I want to accurately document the fundamentals of the dance. These fundamentals make up the form's foundation and are also what make the dance unique. Understanding them is just as valuable to today's dancers as it was to those of my generation. To me, foundation is not about having an "old school" style or dancing like people did in the late 1970s. It is simply the starting point from which this art form has developed, and it still provides a platform to build on. I will leave it to others to conclude how the dance's fundamentals are present in their own work.

THE CONTEXT OF BREAKING: JAMS, PARTIES, CREWS, AND BATTLES

Like other dancers from the 1970s, I was introduced to Breaking by seeing it in person. There was no media coverage or documented information to explain Breaking back then. House parties, park jams, community centers, block parties, schoolyards, and roller-skating rinks were where one was most likely to see the dance. Local family gatherings also helped expose young people to elders or siblings who danced, which further contributed to their inspiration and exploration and spread the dance throughout various New York City neighborhoods.

A park jam or block party was especially important because it provided music and did not restrict attendance according to age. It brought out families and friends together in one place, and many practitioners first experienced Breaking in these situations. The DJs at park jams played different genres of music—both the newest hits and lesser known songs not heard on the radio. Each musical genre presented different opportunities to do a specific social dance, such as Rocking, the Freak, the Hustle, the Bump, the Gigolo, and the Bus Stop. The songs that had the most exciting breaks were recognized immediately by the audience, and B.Boys would get ready to show off their moves and excite the crowd. Some would develop a routine in advance, and when particular songs came on, the circle would form for B.Boys and B.Girls to perform in. "Some B.Boys would take a favorite song they liked and practice a routine at home," as Grandmaster Melle Mel put it, "and then when the song would come on at a jam or party they throw the routine they made up in the dance circle."[7]

Breaking wasn't always competitive, but practitioners often wanted to demonstrate that their skills were better than those who came before them in a circle. As each dancer took turns trying to outperform another dancer and show off their individual variations of moves, the dance took on characteristics of a challenge and became known as a *battle*. In turn, the crowd would express who they liked better in a circle by vocally responding to their movements. This winning over of the crowd was an essential part of a battle in a party or park jam, whereas formal dance contests were a bit more organized, often with official judges; but even then, the crowd played a big part in determining the final winners, as well.

The individuality of a dancer was also expressed in their B.Boy or B.Girl name or "alias," which was sometimes given to them by others or chosen by the dancer him- or herself. Such names tended to be descriptive of the dancer's dancing abilities or unique characteristics. For instance, I first chose "Kid Zoom" as my alias because I was known for having very quick moves. That name later evolved into Ken Swift. Other B.Boys chose to use the name they had as writers or aerosol artists, because they liked the word or its letter combinations. Sometimes a dancer's name would be preceded with a Lil or Junior because they were a student or had been inspired by another dancer.

First-generation B.Boy Sondance[8] said, "You can tell immediately who was a B.Boy by how he was dressed"; this was due to the fact that there was a distinct fashion style. From top to bottom, there was style intention, a full outfit from sneaker to hat, including shell toe Adidas sneakers, track suits, athletic gear, PRO-Keds, Puma Clydes, ski hats, Lee jean matching suits, Graffiti jackets, mock-neck shirts, BVD Nylons, Kangol hats, mesh baseball hats, and British Walkers. It was all about dressing with style, with matching colors to look good and stand out.

Many B.Boys and B.Girls would also either start a *crew* or become a part of one. These crews tended to be made up of people who lived in the same neighborhood, while some groups also were formed around the way they danced or some other mutually shared interests. Like individual dancers, crews would come up with a unique name to represent themselves—such as the Zulu Kings, The Smokatrons, The Bronx Boys, Rockwell Association, Floor Masters, Rock City Crew, or The Executioners—and these names were commonly displayed on their clothing. A typical approach would be to put the crew's name on the back of a T-shirt and the individual alias on the front, either using iron-on letters or acrylic paint. Such names would also be featured in stylized letters on the back of a jean jacket or pant leg. A crew could be small, about three or four people, or it could branch out to more than fifteen or twenty. However, not everyone would be immediately accepted into certain crews. You had to either be skilled in the dance or battle someone to get in. This was to ensure that everyone in the group could hold their own weight and bring in their individual skills.

Crew battles would also occur, either spontaneously or at a set place and time decided in advance. Individuals that had more experience or skills would usually be at the forefront of these battles but everybody in the crew contributed however they could. Initially, the battle might go back and forth with solos to prove which dancers had superiority in a particular move or style. For example, most groups had a person who specialized in spins, flips, or flexibility. There was a buildup process in these battles, as well, so solos tended to be short, quick, and to the point. Usually, though, the battle would lean toward crew routines as the battles moved on. These routines showcased a group's overall skills, using more of a storytelling approach that was attuned to the audience and geared toward making them react to a narrative. It was also common for crews to weave individual dancers' specialties together within a routine, while at the same time creating a skit or story. Such routines displayed a sense of group confidence, teamwork, and camaraderie, as well as strong individualism.

Among the many crew routines performed citywide during this period, some particularly stood out for their creativity and popularity. For instance, there was one where a pair of B.Boys would face each other and *top rock*. Then one turns and faints while the other catches him from behind and throws him back up as he hits a *drop move* to the floor. Another common routine was known as the *throw back flip*, where one B.Boy would clasp his hands while the other stepped into his clasped hands and was thrown into a back flip. Other common routines involved two or more B.Boys transitioning in unison from top rock into *footwork* and then into a *freeze* (most times, a *baby* or *chair*)—or just top rock into a fast *spin* and then into a freeze. The *shoeshine* routine was also very popular. It consisted of one B.Boy taking a knee while the other would put his foot up to get his shoe shined, act as if he was paying money, and then both would transition into a move and freeze. In the *heartbeat*, a B.Boy would break then just stop, as if he had died or fainted. Then another B.Boy would resuscitate him by miming that he had electric pads. The "dead" B.Boy would get "revived" and would go into fast, sporadic footwork to finish his solo. A classic full-crew routine would involve members doing the *spider*, *turtle*, and *bridge* moves to create a scenario: the turtles would crawl under the spider as the spider walked back and forth under someone in the bridge position. Crews worked together to create and perform these choreographic routines, which included both stage blocking and showmanship.

Foundational Styles of Breaking: Rocking, Freestyle, Burning, and Breaking

Rocking—also known as *Freestyle, Burning,* or, later, *Uprock*—is a New York dance style that existed prior to and was a central influence on Breaking. Rocking consisted of side-to-side steps, turns, and drops, akin to the dances of the funk, disco, and soul eras. It also included signature *jerks* (big back and forth movements) and *burns* (competitive gestures). The aggressive gesturing in burns included mimicking the shooting of a gun, or bow and arrow and other creative ways to humiliate your opponent. Dancers would often act out the lyrics of a song or play imaginary instruments in tune with the music. Whereas the posture of Breaking is more hunched down and focused on the floor, Freestyle, or Rocking, was more upright, with a confident posture, and it involved a different kind of finesse and class.[9]

Rocking was also an improvisational dance that had a competitive component to it, where dancers took turns going against each other in pairs or in a line of multiple pairs. These contests were also referred to as *Burning,* where you would take out your opponent with aggressive moves and body language.[10] In formal contests, held in discos or clubs, a group of judges would decide who the winners were, but in many informal underground battles, the audience would determine who won.[11] Much as in Breaking, practitioners of Rocking had aliases and were part of "crews" (groups of friends) in neighborhoods throughout New York's five boroughs. At that time, Latinos mostly did Rocking. As Sundance remembers, "That's what the Latino brothers did."[12]

In the 1970s, Rocking and Breaking were performed to a lot of the same soul, funk, rock, and disco records, but not in the same way. Rock dance was performed for the entire duration of a song, from start to finish, whereas Breaking maintained a fast, short dance-and-rest process, and was almost exclusively done to specific songs, which featured "breaks"—sections of the song when the band would "break down" to just the drums or to the drum and bass. During the songs that facilitated breaking, it was common for DJs to "cut up" and elongate the break of these songs, alternating back and forth between two copies of the same record. These songs included "Apache," "Scorpio,"[13] "Take Me to the Mardi Gras,"[14] "I Can't Stop,"[15] "Scratchin',"[16] "Shangri La,"[17] and "Dance to the Drummers Beat." Some of the songs of this time period were up to fifteen minutes long, so Rocking was about endurance and being familiar with a song's structure and progression, while Breaking was a high-energy expression that was specifically danced to the break of a record that B.Boys and B.Girls would anticipate from knowing the song. This exciting section of the song is where Rock dancers would do their better moves, too, and was also referred to as the time when you would "Break."[18] Rocking involved upright movement, performance, skits and acting out lyrics, while Breaking was a quick moment to show off, to *go off*, and to *break it down*. These moments in rocking show its breaking roots, whatever the distinct differences.

In New York in the late 1970s, both Rocking and Breaking would happen on any given night at a jam, at house parties or block parties, where most of the music being played was current and popular, with a few underground songs now and then. During a typical party, people would dance with each other most of the night, and when these songs were played, usually only one or two times during the course of an evening, it would be the moment to Rock or to Break. Specific songs would dictate the moment when spectators would create a circle around the B.Boys to watch what was happening, as different people went in to show their skills and challenge one another. But it was always the music itself that would get breaking started.

Components: Top Rock

Top rock is an evolution of the opening, upright dance movements of rocking before going down to the floor. It is the starting place of Breaking, and a time to introduce oneself to an audience and other dancers.

When I first began to break, I was told by Doze that you have to top rock before going down into floor-based moves. It was a very simple rule that I followed from that point on. At first, I was not truly interested in top rock, because it seemed like a boring prerequisite to me, and going down to the floor was more exciting. In the late 1970s and early 1980s, Breaking was still relatively unknown and the innovative moves we did on the floor were the center of attention—for both the dancers and the audience. This is why most footage of Breaking from that time period features relatively brief moments of top rock. In those days, 5 percent of what I did was on top, and the other 95 percent was *footwork* and moves on the floor.

Top rock is a major, valuable, and mandatory component of Breaking as we know it today. I still do it because it is part of being a B.Boy, and I'm following a tradition that I feel obliged to continue. Top rock is also an opportunity to showcase one's character and dancing ability. As I grew as a dancer, I came to see its importance in developing my style and personality. Sometimes, in a battle or showcase, top rock gives a dancer valuable time to plot their next moves or to strategize against an opponent. Even so, top rock should not be separated from Breaking; it must be combined with going down to the floor or it isn't complete. Though you can borrow moves from Rocking, or any dance form, in top rock, you cannot top rock in Rock because top rock is only done prior to doing floor movements in a Breaking set.

The performance of top rock consists of bouncing, rhythmic movements, and the main side-to-side step central to freestyle and Rock dance. Top rock has evolved from the earliest versions of that side-to-side step and was turned into more of a spring step, or even a lunge. Moving from side to side, with twisting bounce steps, top rock steps can repeat, move in a circle, or be executed with very high leg kicks. Some B.Boys are aggressive within their top rock; others have moments that are smooth, dancers even laugh while doing them as a ploy to pull the opponent and audience in to win. The confidence is an attack in itself, at times done with a smile to clown around and make it look easy. This I learned from watching what Frosty Freeze[19] and other early B.Boys/B.Girls did. In contrast to the posture of early Rock dance—supremely confident, with dancers standing upright—Top Rock was more aggressive and hunched over. It is performed almost the way a boxer like Muhammad Ali or a martial artist like Bruce Lee moves, with a pivot on the ball of the foot, bouncing, almost floating, moving around, and being in complete control.

Each person would then change those basic steps little by little, helping to showcase their skills and flexibility before going down to the floor. For example, a dancer might keep their upper body straight while twisting their hips and lower body, creating a noodle-like illusion, or rubber-band effect. Many dancers crossed and uncrossed their arms before stepping, announcing that they were coming in and presenting themselves. These simple movements could express who you were as a dancer, how you related to the song or to the people present, and a wide range of other emotions with style.

In certain neighborhoods, names were associated with some of these top rock steps— for example, the *truck driver*, where you acted as if you were turning a big steering wheel as you did your steps.[20] But it was more common to develop an individual approach to top rock without specifically naming a step. The top rock of Lenny Len, an older B.Boy from RCA Freakmasters and the Rock Steady Crew, was just kind of crazy and different; you could recognize the basic moves, but he was flexible and creative in how he turned and twisted in a way that stood out and reminded me of salsa. Frosty Freeze's top rock was also particularly *fresh* (unique). Those of us deeply involved in the dance also noted specific individual influences. For instance, one of the older guys in my neighborhood named Charlie Rock was a mentor of Frosty Freeze, and we could see the former's influence on the latter's top rock. This influence was so pervasive that one style of top rock was known simply as the *Charlie Rock*.

As practitioners, we expanded the creative journey by inspiring each other and taking inspiration from all that was around us, as well. We were inspired by Kung Fu movies, comedies, cartoons, animals—whatever we thought would be cool to include in our dance. One example is the *python style* top rock, which was inspired by the hand and arm movements of a fight segment in the Shaw Brothers film *Mad Monkey Kung-Fu* (1979). I added these hand and arm movements into my right-to-left lunges, leading with opposite arm and leg while doing the step. Importing moves from such sources, combined with our youthful imaginations, greatly increased the vocabulary of Breaking. It also helped us to develop our character, as our B.Boy or B.Girl names and repertoire of moves started adding up to fully formed personas and styles that were integral to communicating our narratives and emotions.

COMPONENTS: GO DOWNS

Dropping or doing *go downs*—two terms used interchangeably to describe transitioning to the floor—were also integral to Breaking. Some of the main go downs, described below, included *drops*, *sweeps*, *spin downs*, *parachutes*, and *corkscrews*. Most B.Boys had these go downs in their repertoire and, in keeping with the individual and character-based nature of Breaking, adapted them in their own unique ways. One's approach and flow in top rock was used to set up certain go downs, and importance was placed on style, speed, and creativity.

The *drop* move is self-explanatory: you squat directly into footwork or go right into a floor-based freeze. The *sweep* is a move that happens at the same time you go down to the floor, sweeping your straight leg around in a circular motion and jumping over it with your opposite leg. Popping back upright after executing a sweep was a single move but also a kind of tease that would allow you to continue back up into top rock, and then go down again. A *spin down* was a rotating move that created the illusion that you were drilling into the floor, but it was also an opportunity to use hand movements and gestures. Some of the most common spin down hand movements included folding the arms, putting one's fists on the hips, pointing while covering one's eyes, rolling the wrists, and shooting two imaginary guns while in motion. The go down known as the *spin down* could be executed rapidly, with aggression and precision, or calmly, with finesse and personal style. It was ideal to have both approaches, because both could go right into a *freeze* or *footwork*. The most common and traditional variation of this move was to spin into a freeze, which was also prevalent in freestyle and rock dance. However, Breaking gave you more options for movement following the spin. In the *parachute*, you would use your arms to imitate throwing a parachute, and you would drop slowly to the ground, as if meeting some wind resistance. The *corkscrew* is when you tuck your foot behind your knee and drop to the floor and then spin up into your freeze. All of these moves allowed you to transition to the ground to either freeze or begin footwork and other floor-based moves.

COMPONENTS: FOOTWORK

Footwork is the primary element of Breaking—the distinctive component that separates the dance from any other. It was the first step in the evolution of the dance from the top down to the floor. It was radical at the time—no other dances in New York spent as large a percentage of time on the floor, and none used dancers' bodies in this way. Having very fast and/or smooth and fluid footwork was the prime indicator that you had skills as a B.Boy or B.Girl.

Footwork involves quick rotating and twisting motions on all fours, and the dancer controls most of the energy with the upper body. Some of the movements pause and repeat, which some people described as *legwork*. Quality footwork would often look as if a person was going off, or careening out of control, but at the same time being smooth and making it look easy, despite the physical challenge. A sharper, choppier type of footwork was done with raw power, aggression, and speed, involving less finesse and control but more energy. The range of physical flexibility among different B.Boys would also help make the delivery of their footwork unique and create more options for expressing their creativity.

Being able to stop a footwork rotation demonstrated one's control, and highlighted certain moves. Sometimes, a B.Boy would stop in a position where their legs were in front of them, as in a right-to-left drop, or with their legs behind them, as in a *shuffle*, where you kick your knees up alternately. Single moves were often repeated on each side to show that a dancer had the skills to do moves on both sides of their body. Doing moves in both directions, left- and right-handed, was also an appreciated skill that expanded a B.Boy's repertoire of moves. Another technique was using body parts aside from the hands and feet to hold up one's footwork, like in *knee rock* or *elbow rock*. It was common to see B.Boys repeat a pattern with a small change or addition to make sure people saw their subtle skills.

These techniques and adaptations were also used to develop new moves within the dance. For instance, B.Boys began to show their ability by repeating a single sweep, and then adding more speed and repetition to the move, eventually leading to the *helicopter sweep*. Showing how you "rocked" (performed) a move with your own personal signature was also one way to take out another dancer in a battle. For instance, doing helicopter sweeps backward or forward with one hand, while holding your hat in the other hand, could make your performance stand out against a competitor. In addition, everyone sought to expand on what they could do with footwork because, at first, our collective vocabulary was extremely limited. Despite the challenge of coming up with a new move, the object in footwork was to pull out something extra, such as doing a move with one hand—or even no hands. A good example of this is a move known as *backrock*, where one basically performs a footwork move but, on their back, with no hands, and with right-to-left twisting of the legs. In *The Russian*, B.Boys would kick their legs out with no hands, like a Russian folk dancer. *Around the worlds* or *Zulu Spins* in footwork consist of tight, small, balled-up fast spins low to the ground, using the hands and feet, but some people can catch a few spins even without their hands. It was these little things B.Boys had to invent and perfect that made the dance a creative and innovative process.

Footwork is also where many ideas for other aspects of the dance originated. For instance, the leg movements in footwork created a base from which one could go in the air, using jumps and twists. Spinning existed in many aspects of the dance but, in footwork, it soon evolved into doing spins on various parts of the body. Freezing existed in all elements of the dance also, but it was particularly common in footwork, as a way to signal the end of a solo.

COMPONENTS: SPINS

Spins are a true highlight in Breaking and allow for a huge amount of individual inspiration and inventiveness. We have seen spins in almost every form of dance, so, visually, an upright spin in top rock or a descending spin in a go down may seem similar to those in other disciplines. But spins in Breaking have, from the beginning, been continually evolving. To try to spin on every possible part of the body truly challenged B.Boys, and sped up the evolution of the dance tremendously. Common spins back in the day included the *shoulder spin* and *butt spin to back spin*. A shoulder spin is set up with a sweep first or comes right in from footwork. The sweep to a shoulder spin is a common combination and usually ends in a freeze. The spin matches the direction of the sweep to keep its circular motion and flow. The number of rotations depends on a dancer's flexibility, technique, the flooring material, and even the type of clothing they are wearing. When the spins were about to end, a dancer would keep the same motion and roll from one shoulder to the other (almost on the neck) into a freeze. When doing shoulder spins from footwork, the circular motion of the footwork helps increase power and momentum, since the spin has to come from the same circular direction of the footwork and starts with a single shoulder dive. Some use the term *neck move* when describing this footwork to shoulder to spin move.[21]

Another common type of spin back then was the *butt spin to back spin*. This spin gets its power from the circular upper body motion, generated by whipping the leg around like a propeller. The energy comes from pulling the leg up by the thigh to get momentum. The force needed for this could come straight from top rock or from footwork. From top rock, one drops with one hand reaching to grab the floor as the leg generates motion. It is common to see top rock that drops right into this move, catching as many spins as possible, and then finishing with a freeze. The straight leg acts like a propeller at first, to get the speed up, but then is retracted to ball up the body as tightly as possible after spinning from the butt to the back. Balling up creates a visual where the dancer looks almost like a spinning top. A person's flexibility in the waist and back plays a big part in being able to bring the knees closer to the chest to improve the quality of this spin. Some people rotate in one place, and others might move sideways, but the most impressive technique is to make that spinning transition from butt to back in one place and as fast as possible. The same technique applies when the dancer transitions to this spin from footwork; one just needs sufficient circular momentum from the footwork. The bigger circular motion transforms into a very small, fast spin that enhances the visual effect. The butt spin to back spin also often culminated in a freeze, such as the *chair freeze*, *baby freeze*, or *bridge freeze*—the most commonly used for ending spins back then. For more skilled B.Boys, however, it was also an option to pop up from these spins right into a *head spin*.

There was also an early spin, which some call the *California backspin*, where you roll back from sitting down, use your legs as propellers, and grab the floor with both hands to direct your rotation. A similar technique was the *stomach roll to backspin*. This basic movement—rolling backward onto your back and then popping up into a standing position—was common in Kung Fu films in the late 1970s, as well, but without the long spinning effect. As the early 1980s came in, the *single-hand pushing backspin*, the *continuous backspin*, and the *windmill* brought spinning to its peak. The *single-hand pushing backspin* generated more power than the previous spins, using a balanced burst of upper body strength and lower flexibility at the same time. The *continuous backspin* involved continuing the spin by restarting the initial one-arm push at each rotation. The *windmill* utilized flexibility, good technique, and, most importantly, momentum to spin up onto the shoulders and upper back.

In all of these spin categories, it was common to use different leg positions to create different visual effects. Keeping the knees tucked in and parallel while spinning created one type of look, and gradually crossing the legs while spinning was also a common adjustment. Mastering spins in both directions added to your versatility and opened up other options for combinations. In Breaking, to spin on every possible part of the body was one of the more intriguing challenges, and most B.Boys at that time developed one or two individualized spins as their specialty. Other common spins during that time were the *knee spin, hand glide spin*, and *head spin*.

The *head spin* was, at the time, the most radical, unpredictable, dangerous, and challenging move to do. The *one-shot head spin* was the most common, and could come from many different body positions and combinations. The name *one shot* is self-explanatory—you have one shot, or one push, to start and finish. There were also many other names for this move in different neighborhoods throughout New York, like *drill, pencil, burner*, and *sizzler*. Early *one-shot head spins* were done on concrete or asphalt, which limited the number of rotations—three to six was the average, and eight was extraordinary. A hat, or even a full head of hair, helped by cushioning weight and decreasing friction. Each dancer's body positioning varied; some would use different leg and arm angles while spinning. Spinning with the body completely straight showed good control and balance. Unlike the discontinuity of the one shot, the *pushing* or *tapping head spin* made it possible to prolong the spin by repeating the push after a rotation.

Integrating these spins into combinations was also a common technique. For example, one could execute the knee spin, go into a back spin, then a shoulder spin, and then into a head spin. The idea was to connect these movements while keeping one's speed and momentum steady. It is important to note that B.Boys throughout New York City did their own unique variations and alterations on these spins.

Again, spinning takes place in almost every dance form, but spinning in Breaking was radical due to its daring, unique, and experimental quality. Trying to spin on any and every part of the body challenged an individual's creative and physical possibilities. Some of these larger, more dynamic moves are still among the most widely recognized aspects of Breaking today.

COMPONENTS: AIR MOVES

All of the elements of Breaking enhance one another. Although the core of Breaking remains on the floor, both the going-into-the-air and mid-level moves are important visual aspects of the dance. Because the battle is an essential part of the culture and practice of Breaking, dancers had a real incentive to be creative and experimental, taking inspiration from any source as long as the basic core elements of the dance were involved. The experimental push of the dance made going into the air a natural progression, and once it did, you always wanted to jump higher, try the same move bigger, do something that made the crowd excited, or something to intimidate other dancers.

Flipping and acrobatics were easy inspirations for B.Boys to adopt, and because of the wow factor, they were seen in the streets on a regular basis. In Uptown Manhattan, guys would often line up, run, and then round off into three or four back handsprings, followed by a somersault, an Arabian, or even a full twist. Back and front versions of handsprings and flips have always been visually exciting, so when people started Breaking, they used various flips in their dance if they could do them. Such moves got an immediate response and, when showing off or simply entering a circle, breakers incorporated many moves with similar effects. Many of these larger, acrobatic, and gymnastic moves were also executed in the air. I will never forget seeing The Light Brothers in the park at 100th Street and Amsterdam Avenue. They were clearly partners in that they were dressed alike. They had sweatshirts with the name "Light Brothers" in iron-on letters on the back. They also had matching train conductor hats and train gloves, and they wore hard denim Lee jeans, freshly dipped with the permanent crease sewed in on the front, thigh to bottom. They had these crazy flip routines that would rock the crowd. I saw them only once, but the impression remains magical to this day.

The competitive nature of battling pushed the limits of these exciting moments within the dance, and opened up an enormous number of new possibilities. The *helicopter sweep* is a prime example of this evolution, creating a visual that looked as if you were floating in the air. Going backward and forward with the helicopter was a skill move, and even though it was circular, it was not technically footwork because it was performed in the air. The helicopter was a move that you can also see in many of the older Shaw Brothers and Golden Harvest Kung Fu films from the late 1970s and early 1980s.

A move that pushed things further in Breaking was the *high swipe*, which I first saw executed directly from top rock. It was a daring move that required a twisting leap, throwing the legs in the air and twisting half of the body in the opposite direction while reaching for the floor with the hands. Once the hands touched the floor, the lower body (which is still in the air) twists again and comes down to the floor. Delivering this move from top rock has to involve a quick, forward-moving skip step to create the power needed for an effective execution. The high swipe is an original move that requires flexibility and quickness. In the best high swipes, the waist is very high, almost like a bridge. In my neighborhood, we were told that B.Boy Spy from the Bronx was the first person to execute the move within Breaking. This move also had a floor-based version called the *baby swipe*, which consists of a small hop or jumping twist from the sweep. The difference is the position of the waist: in the baby swipe, the waist is low to the ground. Either swipe can be done as one move, back-to-back, in place, or repeated in a circular motion.

Another prominent air move with a lot of variations was called the *suicide*. In one version, a dancer does a front flip with no hands and lands on their back, usually with knees up and feet flat on the ground. The higher a B.Boy did it, the more impressive it was. And if it was used from a surprise perspective, people respected the technique and inventiveness. Another form of suicide, which was not done by many dancers, was the *back breaker*. In this move you jump straight in the air, legs out in front of you, then straighten out your whole body and come down flat on your back. Frosty Freeze was known for this type of suicide, which he did in the movie *Flashdance* (1984). Both moves had to be done in a precise and careful way so that a B.Boy would not hurt himself but still give the shock value intended.

Some moves, such as the *donkey*, were also combined with flips to keep the feel of being in the air. The *donkey*, also referred to as a *bronco*, is a move that requires an initial dive in the air, then landing on both hands with the back bent, and snapping the feet back to the floor again. When repeating this motion in succession, the move looks like a bucking animal. Donkeys are more effective visually when they also contain a sort of springboard-like bounce at the start. Adding a backflip or even a front somersault to donkeys was pretty common to see in B.Boy solos during that time. *Nipping up*, or *kipping up*, is another move that had an air effect. The gymnastic version of the *kip up* move was done by springing up from the back, but in Breaking, the kip up was executed in different ways. For instance, it could come after a fake back handspring that would go straight into the high shoulders and then *kip up*, coming fully up, back to the feet, and then repeated—almost doing the *donkey* backward. The *turtle*, also an air move, consisted of propelling the body forward, backward, or circularly on two hands while facing the floor, with elbows as the brace pressed in the stomach. The hands are the only things that touch the floor in this move. The circular style, which was the most common, was also known to some as *floats*. It was performed in many ways, with different leg positions. Turtles were also done by some with a noticeable circular jump between each two-hand push, which gave it a floating visual.

Although some springy-type footwork that requires the legs to elevate could make it look as if a B.Boy was in the air at certain times, the most commonly considered air moves in the Breaking community are swipes, flips, spins, and, soon after, *flares*. A flare is an acrobatic move in which one alternates the balance between either arm while swinging the legs in continuous circles; it was originated by gymnast Kurt Thomas.[22] Nevertheless, there are a lot of different times in a solo that you are actually in the air, making the category of air moves much larger than is often realized.

COMPONENTS: FREEZES

The *freeze* is another very important category. The freeze is the moment when a dancer's movement stops abruptly, and the body freezes in a specific way. Stopping suddenly in rock and freestyle dance existed both on the floor and on top before Breaking, but the dancing would often continue right after it happened. To pause within dancing could be a personal gesture, showing the mood and attitude of the dancer, usually prompted by the music. The freeze emphasized not just the dancer's attitude of but the physical challenge and surprising nature of the pose. To stop motion in top rock was a way to have fun and work the circle while going in and out of floor moves. Some would stop in a position and gesture, for example, with one leg folded, holding the visor of their hat, or hands together on the side of their face as if they were sleeping, or one arm folded and the other arm with the hand holding the chin, like posing for a picture. Most of the time, however, a freeze would be the ending of a go down, set, or solo. The freeze was a highlight and, although there were many common freezes, the challenge was to come up with something unique. Again, creativity was important, but it was equally important to stop completely and cleanly, to finish with style and skill.

Some of the freezes performed involved an arrogance or showing a humorous side (or both). For example, B.Boys would do combinations of moves, and then end up in a comfortable, relaxed position, almost like a model posing on the floor. You might see a B.Boy go up high on their shoulders after a backspin, then fall flat on their stomach and not move, like in the *dead man freeze*. It could bring an immediate, desired reaction from the crowd when completing a set.

A freeze can be a physically challenging body position and animated gesture at the same time. For instance, the *baby freeze* went from a sort of skit of pretending to be a baby on the floor with a thumb in the mouth, to its evolution of moving like a baby with half of one's body held up in the air. The *chair freeze* was also one of the most utilized freezes. Here, the arm positioning was key: balancing the side of the body on the elbow, the arm from wrist to elbow being used as a brace, with one hand flat on the ground. The B.Boy is holding up the weight of his body while the bottom half of the body is twisted in a leg-folded position, as if sitting in a chair. The back corner of the head is resting on the floor while he gestures primarily with the free hand. The common hand gestures included reaching the floor over your head, putting the hand on the forehead as if looking into the distance, and also putting the fist on the side of the hip. These gestures were confident and comedic. The most intriguing and raw chair freeze involved grabbing one's crotch with the free hand while in that position. There was a macho, arrogant, and hardcore side to hitting that freeze, so it usually caught positive attention in circles, and allowed a B.Boy to outshine other dancers. The *chair freeze* was at its best when the B.Boy, no matter what gesture he did, looked completely comfortable and relaxed in that contorted position. As can be seen, the *chair freeze* centered on flexibility, so capabilities with the waist allowed some to do it with special flavor. To be able to change the folded-leg position was a useful skill to have, as was being able to freeze from the right to the left arm while switching the folded leg. The same movement from the left to right arm was used in executing the baby freeze, as well. As such, the chair and baby were the most common freezes coming from footwork, combinations, and spins. So, again, having the versatility of being able to use both arms and legs gave you more options to choose from.

If an ending movement was not stable, or a dancer swayed in their freeze—even if balanced in place—it would not be considered a good freeze. Even though one could stop and go while in footwork, a freeze had to be held for a solid second and a half or more. The freeze signified the dancer's ability, and signaled the feeling or personality they wanted to express, solidifying their character. Freezes could be either preconceived or spontaneously improvised. At times, a freeze would even happen by accident. For instance, one can overdo a move with too much energy or excitement and get momentarily stuck.

When a B.Boy or B.Girl came up with an original freeze, it was common for them to give the freeze a name and to make people aware that they had made it up. It would become a sort of trademark, a way to get recognition for their personal creativity, and a claim to fame that built notoriety and reputation. Taking someone else's move, or *biting*, was looked down upon in the community. You would be called a *biter* by other B.Boys and B.Girls, and your reputation would be damaged. This could also easily result in a confrontation or even a fight. Due to how difficult it was to be original, and the work and discipline that it took to develop unique skills and ideas, many people took biting very personally. The dance vocabulary of Breaking in the late 1970s was very limited. The individual's character had to be more interesting than the moves themselves, and it was imperative to have your own way of doing things that represented who you were as a person. Doing a freeze by stopping on a dime from top rock, footwork, air moves, or a spin was an important moment that not only showed command of your skills and body but also provided a striking moment to display your individuality, creativity, and character.

OTHER CONCEPTS IN BREAKING

These general components—top rock, go downs, footwork, spins, air moves, and freezes—were combined with each other and with other techniques in Breaking performances. B.Boys and B.Girls tried to use them in ways that demonstrated the breadth and depth of their skills, and that entertained and wowed the circle or audience. One essential way to do this was to *represent* the previously noted character and personality within Breaking. This was done with attitude, and drew on many different sources, such as movie roles, cartoon characters, neighborhood characteristics, or other cultural understandings. Also, as discussed earlier, certain moves—the helicopter, chair freeze, and so on—represented different entities in the real world, including animals like the turtle and donkey. These representations were constructed from different components within the dance—a chair by using a freeze, for instance, or the helicopter as a floor move or an air move. These forms of imitation or representation were very quickly an essential part of a dancer's repertoire, and the character they presented through their dance.

In imitating insects or creatures, B.Boys also developed a physical language that has continued to evolve. Early techniques included the development of moves like the *spider*. The *spider* required good flexibility and technique, and involved a practitioner squatting and reaching both arms under the legs and behind the body, with the hands flat on the floor. The triceps of both arms brace both quadriceps, with arms behind and feet forward. From that point on, the idea was to make small, quick movements back and forth, both circular and sideways, in the sporadic way of a real spider, or crazy like a cartoon character. As the move evolved, it began to include rolling forward or hopping on the hands while remaining in the *spider* position. But not all B.Boys could pull off these difficult moves. Representing creatures with moves like these was a creative challenge, as was trying to make the imitation convincing.

Other examples of such moves included the *roach*, the *crab*, and even a forward-to-back pushing of knees while on all fours called the *dog* or *walking the dog*. These moves were like skits—they can be thought of as a form of storytelling. Rock and freestyle dancers had already incorporated this theatrical dance-acting into their performances, and it appealed to the crowd. There were times when B.Boys would imitate specific actions, as in the case of sitting down and miming rowing across the floor in a *rowboat*. Or lying on the stomach, banging the floor with the hand, and humping the floor as in the *headache*. The *Russian* and the various borrowings from martial arts films demonstrate how this mimicry took inspiration from other art forms. In some ways, these were classic vaudevillian moves, and they made the audience laugh and react. Such performative displays are part of the endless evolution of Breaking, and an important element of the youthful exploration of mind and body that took place within the dance.

CONCLUSION

All of these general components and concepts of Breaking came together to create the full system of the dance as it exists today. All the current moves can be traced back, in one way or another, to these fundamentals. All B.Boys and B.Girls need to have these components somewhere within their dance vocabulary, and to have a good balance of these skills. With the incredible evolution of Breaking over the last forty years, it is important not to lose sight of the foundations of the art form.

Breaking has drawn inspiration from many other dances and many other performance genres over the years, but at its core, it has always been about the freestyle combination of these elements with style flowing through them. The sporadic, often abstract running around the body on the floor, the use of footwork, spins, air work, freezes, and top rock was unique in its time and place and content in NYC at that time. Especially, the specific forms of circular motion footwork down on the floor—the stuff that made the news and was featured in movies—changed dance in NYC from the rock, freestyle, and funk styles that had existed previously. Footwork became the circular twisting and moving start-up process that created options for the evolved moves that came after, that is, windmills, halos, flares etc. When connected to all the other components, the dance becomes truly unique.

Early on, people drew from musical artists, athletes, movie stars, Kung Fu movies, acrobatics, gymnastics, and cartoons. As this dance has evolved, we have also infused it with inspiration from different underground dances such as African, capoeira, house, popping, locking, waacking, vogue, salsa, the hustle, swing, original jazz, Lindy Hop, and tap. While the dance has grown and evolved in communities around the world, one sees local cultural traditions, folk dances, and other artforms being incorporated, with these new contexts resulting in new movements and techniques. Personal style in Breaking, as in any art form, is key. Making sure that the foundation stays visual and strong is very important, as is maintaining the components that have built the dance as it has evolved. Some movement was purely about parody and making fun of other dance forms, animals, or pop culture to get a reaction from the audience. The context of the musical breaks of the DJ, the combining of the traditional fundamentals of Breaking with improvisational movements, and the emphasis on creativity and personal style all connect it to the elements of Hip Hop culture, and so the foundation of the dance is both a constraint and a source of endless ingenuity.

In my own journey, music has always been the main source of inspiration for me. The thing that helps me express myself and gets me to push further and try harder. When I heard the DJs cut the breaks back-to-back in my youth, I got excited. It made me want to go off to match the intensity of the drums. It challenged me to sustain my energy and push through what I had assumed were my limits. The music has always carried me beyond where I thought my abilities stopped and, through intuitively trying to connect with the mood, attitude, and emotional power of a song, I have had many happy accidents, expanding my dance vocabulary and suggesting new directions. You never know where the music can bring you, so it challenges you, in real time, to reflect back whatever feeling the music provides.

Theoretically, you can break to and be inspired by any kind of music. But, for Breaking, the beat and the break are the original and central contexts. All types of music have breaks, and we danced to it all in the 1970s and 1980s. But it was always the beat, not the melodic, harmonic, or lyrical aspects of a song (although those were important, too) that provided the groove and the energy needed for the physicality of Breaking.

We should all expect an innovative dance like Breaking to change and grow, but foundation is the definition, the master plan, and the manifesto of this dance. From this perspective we can preserve the early traditions and intention as this dance continues to evolve. Doing it your own way is actually the tradition, so you can make up your own rules and moves as long as you understand the basics. You can borrow from every other art form, dance, or sport, but style and context are the glue that brings it back to Breaking; otherwise, it is just the inspiration. Personal expression and creativity will keep the dance alive, so I encourage experimentation and personal style as motivators in practice and theory. It is also a way to honor African American and Latino cultures by respecting the rules that were set out at the beginning of the form. Hip Hop is a full, multi-elemental artistic culture, and often "Hip Hop dance" is an umbrella term for many street dances. However, Breaking is the original Hip Hop dance, so it is important to understand the components and context to better understand how it relates to the other elements and other Hip Hop dance forms.

NOTES

1. Dante was my best friend, member of my first crew Young City Boys, and later became my business partner, who helped open Breaklife Studios in 2005.
2. L.T.D., "Back in Love Again," A & M Records, 1977.
3. Doze Green is a fellow member of Rock Steady Crew, and now a world-renowned visual artist.
4. Incredible Bongo Band, "Apache," Polydor Records, 1973.
5. Herman Kelly and Life, "Dance to the Drummers Beat," T. K. Disco, 1978.
6. Lenny Len (RCA Freakmasters/Rock Steady Crew), interview with the author, Rock Street Studios, Brooklyn, NY, September 2010.
7. Grandmaster Melle Mel (Furious 5 MCs), interview with the author, Pro-Am Event, Osaka, Japan, September 2006.
8. Sondance (Baby Spades/Rock City Crew), interview with the author, Rock Street Studios, Brooklyn, NY, March 2009.
9. Noel Angel (Latin Symbolics), Mike Dominguez "The Club Kid," Danny Rodriguez, Papo, Enoch, Biscocho (INDs), Jose (J&R Dancers), Ron (J&R Dancers), interviews with the author, Rock Street Studios, Brooklyn, NY, September 2009– April 2011.
10. PHASE 2 interview with the author, Breaklife Studios, Brooklyn, NY, February 2006.
11. Mike Dominguez "The Club Kid," interview with the author, Rock Street Studios, Brooklyn, NY, May 2010.
12. Sondance (Baby Spades/Rock City Crew), interview with the author, Rock Street Studios, Brooklyn, NY, November 2009.
13. Dennis Coffey and the Detroit City Guitar Band, "Scorpio," Sussex Records, 1971.
14. Bob James, "Take Me to the Mardi Gras," CTI, 1975.
15. John Lewis and the Monster Orchestra, "I Can't Stop," Sam Records, 1976.
16. The Magic Disco Machine, "Scratchin'," Motown, 1975.
17. La Pregunta, "Shangri La," GNP Crescendo, 1978.
18. Lil Dave (Lil Dave Rockers), interview with the author, Rock Street Studios, Brooklyn, NY, September 2009.
19. Frosty Freeze was a legendary breaking pioneer and the co–vice president of Rock Steady Crew.
20. Grandmixer DST, interview with the author, the New York City Rap Tour, November 1982.
21. Mr. Freeze (Rock Steady Crew), interview with the author, Rock Steady Park, Manhattan, 1981.
22. Kurt Thomas was an American Olympic gymnast and part-time actor from the late 1970s.

CHAPTER 2

THE CAMERA IN THE CYPHER

High Times and Hypervisibility in Early Hip Hop Dance

VANESSA FLEET LAKEWOOD

COVER STORY: BREAKING MEETS THE MEDIA

WHEN the underground cultural phenomenon of breaking first surfaced in the mass media, its arrival was accompanied by a jarring visualization that conflated aesthetics with criminality. In the issue of April 22–28, 1981, the *Village Voice* published the first-ever article on the dance, written by performance critic Sally Banes and illustrated with photographs by Martha Cooper (Banes, 1981, 31–33). The story's lead image features "Frosty Freeze" (Wayne Frost), a member of the Rock Steady Crew and gifted b-boy then in his late teens, rehearsing for a battle. Masking was used in the editing process to selectively hide and reveal specific elements of the picture. The background rehearsal space appears indistinct and transparent, and the wood floors had been dodged out of the frame so that the dancer appears suspended in mid-air. But the figure of Frost pops from the page in dynamic contrast to the hazy graffiti painting behind him; the dark ink of the image reveals the texture of his clothing, his concentrated expression, and the outline of his hair. Pictured in profile, Frost is in a forward lunge with his left leg extended straight in front of him, sneakered toes flexed upward, arm thrust out at shoulder height, fingers curled into a fist (see Figure 2.1). In the context of the other elements on the cover, the bold aesthetic action of this dancer takes on a slightly different meaning—one that is far less suggestive in Cooper's unedited version of the image (see Figure 2.2). It looks like he could be fighting

Appearing just below the paper's main headline, "Revolt in Reagan's Backyard," the picture of Frost conjures a potentially threatening image of insurgency. The headline

FIGURE 2.1. Frosty Freeze on the cover of the *Village Voice*, April 22–28, 1981. Courtesy of Martha Cooper.

FIGURE 2.2. Frosty Freeze with graffiti backdrop by TKid, April 1981. Common Ground studio. Courtesy of Martha Cooper.

echoes this sentiment, the word "backyard" evoking an image of enclosure, out of public sight, suggesting a boundary between the dominant order and those who are excluded from its communities.

While the cover conveys a visual message that seems to play on a mixture of readers' assumptions and expectations, Banes's article inside resolves the tension between physical aggression and performative action suggested in the image (see Figure 2.3). On page thirty-one, where it begins, we see four black-and-white photographs by Martha Cooper

Crazy Legs flips (left); Ty Fly, too.

Breaking Is Hard To Do

To the Beat, Y'All

By Sally Banes *Photographs by Martha Cooper*

Ty Fly and Freeze team up.

Crazy Legs shows Lil Crazy Legs a move.

VOICE ARTS

Chico and Tee and their friends from 175th Street in the High Times crew were breaking in the subway and the cops busted them for fighting.

"We're not fighting. We're dancing!" they claimed. At the precinct station, one kid demonstrated certain moves: a head spin, ass spin, swipe, chin freeze, "the Helicopter," "the Baby."

An officer called in the other members of the crew, one by one. "Do a head spin," he would command as he consulted a clipboard full of notes. "Do 'the Baby.' " As each kid complied, performing on cue as unhesitatingly as a ballet dancer might toss off an enchainement, the cops scratched their heads in bewildered defeat.

Or so the story goes. But then, like ballet and like great battles (it shares elements of both), breaking is wreathed in legends. "This guy in Queens does a whole bunch of head spins in a row, more than 10; he spins, stops real quick, spins . . ."

"Yeah, but he stops. Left just goes right into seven spins, he never stops."

"There's a 10-year-old kid on my block learned to break in three days."

"The best is Spy, Ronnie Ron, Drago, me [Crazy Legs], Freeze, Mongo, Mr. Freeze, Lace, Track Two, Weevil . . ."

"Spy, he's called the man with the thousand moves, he had a girl and he taught her how to break. She did it good. She looked like a guy."

"Spy, man, in '78—he was breaking at Mom and Pop's on Katona Avenue in the Bronx; he did his footwork so fast you could hardly see his feet."

"I saw Spy doing something wild in a garage where all the old-timers used to break. They had a priest judging a contest, and Spy was doing some kind of Indian dance. All of a sudden, he threw himself in the air, his hat flew up, he spun on his back, and the hat landed right on his chest. And everyone said, 'That was luck.' So he did it once more for the priest, and the hat landed right on his chest. If I didn't see it, I would never have believed it."

The heroes of these legends are the Break Kids, the B Boys, the Puerto Rican and black teenagers who invent and endlessly elaborate this exquisite, heady blend of dancing, acrobatics, and martial spectacle. Like other forms of ghetto street culture—graffiti, verbal dueling, rapping—breaking is a public arena for the flamboyant triumph of virility, wit, and skill. In short, of style. Breaking is a way of using your body to inscribe your identity on streets and trains, in parks and high school gyms. It is a physical version of two favorite modes of street rhetoric, the taunt and the boast. It is a celebration of the flexibility and budding sexuality of the gangly male adolescent body. It is a subjunctive expression of bodily states, testing things that might be or are not, contrasting masculine vitality with its range of opposites: women, babies, animals, illness and death. It is a way of claiming territory and status, for yourself and for your group, your crew. But most of all, breaking is a competitive display of physical and imaginative virtuosity, a codified dance form cum warfare that cracks open to flaunt personal inventiveness.

For the current generation of B Boys, it doesn't really matter that the Breakdown is an old name in Afro-American dance for both rapid, complex footwork and a competitive format. Or that a break in jazz means a soloist's improvised bridge between melodies. For the B Boys, the history of breaking started six or seven years ago, maybe in the Bronx, maybe in Harlem. It started with the Zulus. Or with Charlie Rock. Or with Joe, from the Casanovas, from the Bronx, who taught it to Charlie Rock. "Breaking means going crazy on the floor. It means making a style for yourself." In Manhattan, kids call it rocking. A dancer in the center of a ring of onlookers drops to the floor, circles around his own axis with a flurry of slashing steps, then spins, flips, gesticulates, and poses in a flood of rhythmic motion and fleeting imagery that prompts the next guy to top him. To burn him, as the B Boys put it.

Fab Five Freddy Love, a graffiti-based artist and rapper from Bedford

Continued on next page

FIGURE 2.3. Rock Steady Crew rehearsing at Common Ground. Sequence printed in the *Village Voice*, April 22–28, 1981. Courtesy of Martha Cooper.

that add context to Frost's potent freeze on the cover. These orient us more clearly inside a studio—a SoHo loft space called Common Ground—where bodies were expected to move more freely than in most public environments.

Cooper's photographs were taken at a dress rehearsal for *Aspects of Performance: Graffiti Rock*, a multifaceted exhibition and performance event that would feature a graffiti slide show and live breaking, music, and rapping. It had been organized by the artist Henry Chalfant, the photographer behind the slides, who had invited members of the Rock Steady Crew, artist/MC Fred Braithwaite (Fab 5 Freddy Love), and artist/DJ Rammellzee to participate (Lawrence 2016, 174). It was to have been, as Chalfant later claimed, "probably the first time that graffiti, breaking, rap, and DJing were connected under one roof" (quoted in Cooper 2004, 163). Such early performances and demonstrations of breaking, which were often recorded in lens-based media and involved the display of visual material, helped affirm the conceptual ties being formed between the distinct communities of breakers and graffiti writers in the movement that became known as hip hop—however artificial these ties may have been in reality (e.g., being an aerosol artist didn't automatically make one interested in rap music).

But if Cooper's rehearsal pictures positioned the reader visually and imaginatively in the Common Ground studio, the first line of Banes's (1981) article took us elsewhere, to a transit police station in the Washington Heights neighborhood of Upper Manhattan in January 1980: it is a sentence about criminal profiling: "*Chico and Tee and their friends from 175th Street in the High Times Crew were breaking in the subway when the cops busted them for fighting*" (31; emphasis added). Conjuring the kids' words, "We're not fighting, we're dancing!" Banes describes how the boys demonstrated dance moves to police officers to ostensibly prove their innocence. Together with Cooper's cover image of Frosty Freeze, Banes's secondhand account of the crew's arrest was myth-making. Narrating the illicit character of breaking, these framing devices wove a story of youthful aggression and outlawry into the origins of early hip hop dance.

Cooper, reflecting later on the significance of the *Voice* article in *Hip Hop Files: Photographs 1979–1984*, her magnum opus of hip hop photography, published some twenty-four years after the incident, rightly points out that though Chalfant played an important role as an organizer putting together a hip hop package her photos "were important in sending that out to the world" (Cooper 2004, 163). Yet the power of Cooper's photographs, their interaction with Banes's words, and the way they shaped early conceptions of the dance—as well as broader visions of a hip hop imaginary—have not been fully explored.

HIGH TIMES AND HYPERVISIBILITY

The circumstances and events leading to breaking's publicization and mediatization warrant further study. It is well-known that Cooper was present the night of the High Times Crew's arrest and saw some of the aftermath at the police station. She also photographed the crew demonstrating the dance, producing the earliest known photographs of breaking.

It is important to note that those pictures—taken about fifteen months before Rock Steady's rehearsal at Common Ground—were not the ones chosen to illustrate the *Voice* article.. Nevertheless, soon after the *Voice* story broke in 1981, audiences seemed to already have a picture in their minds of young breakers being arrested, evoked by the anecdote narrated by Banes, and accompanied with a vision of Wayne "Frosty Freeze" Frost on the *Voice's* cover). Cooper's photographic record, as well as her written and oral accounts of this history, constitute formative documents of breaking's arrival into public discourse. This chapter aims to unpack the significance of Cooper's role in early conceptions of hip hop dance through an analysis of what her images revealed and where they were circulated. It also explores the broader social circumstances and photo-historical conditions that surrounded the surfacing of hip hop dance into the public discourse and mass visual media.

In considering this history and the ephemeral archive produced by its agents, this chapter will analyze themes of visibility, racialized perception, and aesthetic judgment as they align with issues of media and state power (Muñoz 1996, 16). What were the historical conditions that mediated our ability to visualize early forms of hip hop dance? And how were these historical conditions reactivated in mass-mediated discourse and hip hop's early visual forms? To answer these questions, I examine Martha Cooper's influence on how breaking was initially defined for outsider audiences. Starting with that night in January 1980, this chapter examines the broader circumstances that led to breaking's emergence as visual news, as well as the impact the media had on the shaping the image of a dance once considered too violent to be an art form. In so doing, I attend to the slippages occurring between documentation, historicization, event, and experience—and the need to include the voices of subjects who appear in the research archive. I argue that lens-based media both illustrated and helped to fashion the aesthetics of outlawry that defined breaking's early cultural formation. Tracing the diffusion and multiplication of Cooper's images in print—as well as in the cult films *Wild Style* and *Beat Street*—the chapter explores her critical and complex role in shaping early hip hop visions.

"No Riot, No Story": Martha Cooper's Story and Pictures of January 21, 1980

In *Hip Hop Files*, Cooper recalls the night of the alleged subway riot. She was working for the *New York Post* as a staff photographer, and her editors sent her to a transit police station, where, she was told, a group of about twenty-five boys—some as young as ten or eleven—had been arrested for fighting.[1] In the station's cramped holding area, an officer explained to Cooper that she would not be taking any pictures that night. Being minors, he said, the boys were entitled to have their identities protected. But Cooper was coming from a daily tabloid newspaper culture, where "they didn't care if you did anything illegal or not" to get the shot, and so she made a furtive move.[2] Angling the camera upward from her hip, she managed to "squeeze off [a] single frame without looking through the viewfinder," capturing some of the boys' downcast faces as they sat under the watchful eye of a policeman (Cooper, 2004, 70).

The black-and-white picture Cooper covertly snapped was published in the section on b-boying in Hip Hop Files. It is hard to tell just what is going on in the grainy, uncomposed picture. The subjects appear fractured and disorganized. A fluorescent light fixture cuts diagonally across the frame, reminding us of the awkward angle at which Cooper held her camera. Eclipsing the right side of the image are the blurred head and sweater-clad shoulders of a boy facing the officer in charge, who is pictured in profile, looking down at the group of youngsters barely captured in the scene. The boys appear very young, still wearing their winter jackets, waiting, and looking anxious and bored. Most of them look down, their chins tucked into coat collars or resting on their hands, and none of them watch as another officer leads one of their crew out of the room.

The story is that, eventually, some of the boys were released—the ones who had not been caught with weapons or graffiti paraphernalia. On a subway platform outside the transit police station, members of the High Times Crew demonstrated their moves for Cooper's camera (see Figure 2.5). In the pictures, the boys stand in a semicircle and take turns getting wild on the platform floor, which is coldly illuminated by electric white light. A tiny kid in a knit sweater spins on his head and his friends break out in huge grins (uncropped versions of these photographs reveal a transit officer keeping watch on the group, smiling from behind a door).

In Cooper's book, these images are positioned opposite a full-page photograph captioned "Cops with Confiscated Items": a frank portrait of two White officers standing behind a table displaying paraphernalia: Marks-A-Lot and Marvy brand markers, cans of spray paint, switchblades, and a small gun (See Figure 2.4). The police had prohibited Cooper from using her camera in the holding area, but in this room, they pose willingly, holding up small weapons they had seized from the kids. One officer holds a pair of knives and stares sideways toward something beyond the frame; the other smiles slightly as he gazes into the lens, holding a pair of nunchucks. The iconography is indisputable. The White officers present themselves in their professional capacity, standing erect in crisp dark uniforms, facing the camera, projecting ease, confidence, and pride in a job well done fighting crime. The table of paraphernalia in front of them is at waist-level— a superficial extension of their bodies, displaying items seized from other bodies.

Cooper explained to her readers that when her editors at the *Post* learned there had been no riot, they were no longer interested in running the piece. "I thought this was a great story," she explains, "so I called the *Post* editors and said, 'They weren't having a riot, they were having a dance contest.' But the *Post* didn't like that idea. No riot, no story" (Cooper 2004, 70). Although print media outlets can be powerful and fast ways of transmitting and broadcasting images, the speed at which pictures are released into the public eye will depend on "the social investment in either their dissemination or

FIGURE 2.4. Cops with items confiscated from kids. Washington Heights transit police station, January 1980. Courtesy of Martha Cooper.

occlusion" (Hill and Schwartz 2015, 8). That a group of young Latinx and Black kids were stopped and arrested because their activities were perceived as threatening was not considered unusual or even newsworthy, and so her editors were not interested in pursuing the story.

In 1980, the *New York Post* was still in the dawn of its takeover by Rupert Murdoch, a shift in leadership that had transformed the paper into a tabloid. Cooper was adamant about the paper's decline: "[The new *Post*] was really a horrible paper, a rag of a paper,

FIGURE 2.5. Kids breaking in a Washington Heights subway station, January 1980. Courtesy of Martha Cooper.

but it had a really good staff, because it had been a really *good* paper" (Cooper interview). Things had changed with the introduction of Murdoch's ethos of daily reporting. The newspaper began featuring more sensationalized content, headlines, and visuals, and devoting less "grey space" to text (Pasadeos and Renfro 1988). "The [new] *Post* was heavily about crime, and celebrities. Those were the two main assignments" (Cooper interview). People left or got squeezed out. Her favorite photo editor, Susan Welchman, was fired—and after that, "the assignments were terrible." Despite the good pay and benefits from her unionized position, Cooper would end up resigning later that year.

HORIZONS OF THE PUBLISHABLE

In the early 1980s, hip hop performance and dance entered the broader public sphere via a series of historical processes and permissions. These affected the way its aesthetics were defined for audiences and publics outside its community of practitioners and spectators. How would such images have been received? What was thought possible to publish about the subjects and communities that came together around hip hop's early cultural formation?

Publishing is "a set of processes and relations," Rachel Malik (2008) states in her important theoretical contribution to publication studies. These processes and relations combine to form what the author terms "horizons of the publishable, which govern what is thinkable to publish within a particular historical moment" (709). The question of what does and does not get published, documented, and archived in the public record inevitably leads historians to consider the limits of how certain acts and actions get recorded. These questions are even more salient for historians of performance and dance, whose interpretations of bodily expressions and experiences are bound to be mediated through various spheres of public distribution and reception: in photographs, television, videos, newspaper accounts, reviews, and books, as well as in oral testimonies.

Photography historians Thierry Gervais and Gaëlle Morel (2017) have noted the ways news photography evolved through various visual styles combining words and images, arguing that twentieth-century American photojournalism was deeply shaped by an editorial model imported from Europe. For instance, Black Star, an international picture agency, was formed in 1935 in New York City by a group of photographers and publishers who had fled Germany following Hitler's rise to power (115–116). As the field of journalism and photo-reportage professionalized, Black Star linked the services of picture editors with those of picture takers dispatched worldwide, creating a network that included Time Inc., the Associated Press, and *Life* magazine and setting the tone for news whose subjects were brought to life by innovative journalistic practices and a recognizably snapshot aesthetic of pictures taken in the field (116). As Gervais and Morel write about this period, "Producing visual stories became the goal of magazines and photographers alike" (127).

The historical developments in the professional field of photojournalism are important to consider, not only for their influence on Cooper's training and eye, but also as a set of circumstances that made it possible for her to move her pictures into wider circulation. Born in 1943, the daughter of a camera-store owner and journalism teacher in Baltimore, Maryland, Cooper had been absorbing picture stories from an early age and began entering her own photographs in Kodak camera competitions as a teenager. She wanted to work for *Life*. To this end, after earning an art degree from Grinnell College, she got a competitive photography internship in the 1960s at *National Geographic* (the magazine's first female intern). She then received further training at the Maine Photographic Workshop under John Loengard, the picture editor at *Life* (Cooper interview). Her mentors repeatedly emphasized that "newspapers were the way in" to more prestigious magazine work, and so Cooper started shooting for weekly papers in Rhode Island before finally making the move to New York in the 1970s, to try for "the big time." The city, she said, "was the center of public things—everything was out of New York" (Cooper interview). Hoping to eventually work for the *New York Times*, Cooper accepted the job at the *Post* in 1977, when the paper was looking for a woman to add to its all-male photo staff. At a time when it was hugely competitive for any photographer to get a job at a daily paper, this gave Cooper an edge. As a woman, it was easier to get close to the action and gain the trust of her subjects. People never saw her as threatening (Cooper interview).

But in the mid-1970s, general news magazines were in crisis, and opportunities for jobs at mainstream publications were starting to disappear (Gervais and Morel 2017,

178). The creative energy devoted to making dramatic visual essays in glossy magazines like *Life* became downturned with the economic decline of the illustrated press. Tabloids and television broadcasting were starting to take over. Professional photographers responded to the changes by diversifying, seeking alternative forms of publication, working in various streams of visual media, and trying to publish their pictures in photographic books. . The rise of the photo-book author, "a new figure in photography," attracted both newspaper and magazine photographers to the book market. This was the context in which Cooper worked: she was thinking and maneuvering in picture stories, with an eye to eventually publishing her own book.

Between 1977 and 1980, when she was still on staff at the *Post,* Cooper would walk the boroughs of New York City between daily assignments. She would use up her leftover roll of film by snapping photos of children playing among "abandoned buildings and rubble-strewn lots," which, she wrote provided "raw materials and open space for improvised play" (Cooper 2006, 3). Cooper began documenting and collecting the elemental traces of young people's vibrant street life, and this period became life-changing for her. The relationships she built with her young subjects were catalysts for her introduction and emergence into the underground art movements of graffiti writing and breaking, both of which captivated her and would remain the focus of her creative output for years. Defining her photographic practice in opposition to dominant channels of imagery in the popular press, Cooper was committed to discovering subject matter she had "never seen before" (Cooper interview), and she wanted to make the illicit actions of her young subjects *seen* as something other than an urban problem.

Later recalling her time at the *Post,* Cooper talked about the long and pointless hours she spent stationed outside a courthouse or a police station, waiting for officers to parade a suspect in front of a line of news photographers. It was boring and demotivating, and she hated standing around with other journalists instead of being out in the streets, on the hunt for pictures. "I just couldn't be enthusiastic about the assignments anymore. I felt like I couldn't do it." Mid-way through1980, Cooper eventually decided to quit her job so she would have more time to photograph the trains (Cooper interview).

On her last day, Cooper recalled, she packed up all her contact sheets, prints, and negatives, knowing their artistic and historical value. There is no question that everything started to move for Cooper after she left the *Post,* and that she became a better photographer, creating pictures for which there was no aesthetic precedent.

Cooper met Henry Chalfant in September 1980 at his solo exhibition at the OK Harris Gallery, *Graffiti in New York.* What may have started as a semicompetitive dynamic between them—they were aware of one another's work but moved independently—evolved into a fruitful collaboration. Appreciating the challenges of the publishing market, they decided to try coauthoring a book on graffiti, rather than come out with two separate books on the same subject. Cooper and Chalfant shared a fascination with "art transit" (initially considering the term as a title), which resulted in their explosive 1984 publication *Subway Art*(Cooper and Chalfant, 1984). The historical significance of the book cannot be overstated. For their work collecting material and publishing a photo book on graffiti at such an early time, music critic Bill Adler (2006) dubbed the pair the "mother and father" of hip hop photography (102).

While Cooper and Chalfant would not collaborate on another book project again, they remained friends and close colleagues, supportive of one another's work. Looking through the pages of *Subway Art*, it is clear that, while Cooper and Chalfant had graffiti in common, their aesthetic leanings were not the same. Chalfant took close-up pictures of subway paintings in expressive detail, while Cooper took a longer view with her camera, catching whole-car murals on trains in good light, in places where the trains move above ground. As much as possible, Cooper wanted to capture subway murals in their full context, revealing the energy of the graffiti movement alongside the rush of the trains amidst street scenes and city scapes.

BREAKING IS HARD TO WRITE

In the fall of 1980, around the time she met Chalfant, , when she was already freelancing, Cooper contacted Sally Banes, a PhD student in New York University's Department of Graduate Drama. A mutual friend had put the two in touch. Cooper asked Banes if she would be interested in writing an article on a new kind of dance.

The *Village Voice*, a left-leaning, alternative weekly paper, would be the outlet for the article. It was a different kind of paper than the *Post*, the once-decent daily tabloid. For instance, the same year Cooper got her start in New York, the *Voice* hired Bill Bernstein (who also worked for Black Star) as a staff photographer, later sending him on assignment to Studio 54 and opening the channels of mainstream journalism to his iconic and transgressive images of the city's nightlife and club scenes. The *Voice* is also where Michele Wallace started publishing her early Black feminist criticism and writing in the 1970s. The *Voice* prioritized more diverse, creative, and experimental forms in its coverage of the city's events, and was a fitting venue for the breaking story.

Working with Banes as the writer of the piece made sense to Cooper, who was not confident in her own writing. She found the dance difficult to describe, telling her collaborator that it featured "solo performance with wild acrobatics and poses" (Banes 1986, 11). They got right to work. Using the names and phone numbers Cooper had collected from the High Times members in January, the two women tracked down some of the boys for an informal interview and demonstration. They were now reluctant to dance (claiming to have moved on to roller disco), but they were willing to talk about the art form they had been a part of creating: "Breaking means going crazy on the floor. It means making a style for yourself" (Banes 1981, 31). During this exploratory conversation, Cooper managed to snap some photographs of their moves. However, the pictures were awkward and aesthetic failures, and she needed more visual and contextual material to round out the story she and Banes were writing. The challenge would be to find a community of breakers who might open up their circle to this pair of aesthetic outsiders.

It was breaking's connection to the graffiti art scene that made this possible. In Steven Hager's book *Hip Hop: The Illustrated History*, Henry Chalfant remembers that he and Cooper had been comparing notes on graffiti for some time, when "one day she showed me a photo she'd taken of a break dancer" (quoted in Hager 1984, 86). Cooper had been talking about her old *Post* days and recalling her encounter with the High Times group. Chalfant had not seen anything like it before. His interest was especially piqued by the graffiti paraphernalia the police had found on the boys. As a result, he began probing the writers who would come by his studio about the dance. Promising to deliver the best, a young writer and breaker named Take 1 brought Frost, Crazy Legs, Ty Fly, and Lil Crazy Legs of the Rock Steady Crew into the studio. This facilitated Cooper's formal introduction to the breakers. Cooper had directed Chalfant's attention to breaking's underground existence, and his connections to the graffiti community would help move the dance into a wider public view.

Together, Chalfant and Cooper, along with Banes, acted as both documentarians and organizers of early expressions of hip hop. Their introduction to the Rock Steady Crew led to the planning of the *Graffiti Rock* event at Common Ground featuring the projected slide show exhibition of Chalfant's graffiti photographs and the staged battle by the dance crew. The boys divided themselves into two fictional crews and dressed in coordinating t-shirts displaying their names in iron-on lettering. In this way, *Graffiti Rock* can be understood in the context of other contemporary events and performances that sought to define a unified vision of what hip hop culture was and who was part of it. Some organizers and promoters, such as Michael Holman—who credits himself for putting on the first downtown show assembling all-live hip hop elements—acknowledged the potential artifice in such performances, suggesting, "We were toying with evolution" (quoted in Lawrence 2016, 177). While there was an element of fabrication to the work of Banes, Chalfant, and Cooper in the *Graffiti Rock* staging, it is also true they were following the aesthetic expressions of the young people involved in creating the culture.

In Banes's article, *Graffiti Rock* "was written up as something you could go to," Cooper explained (quoted in Holman 1984, 142), and it was scheduled to open on Sunday May 3, 1981, with two additional dates. But then Chalfant's show was suddenly canceled by the venue's owner, who feared that escalating tensions between Rock Steady and other neighborhood groups at the time would erupt into "gang warfare." But even though the event never happened, Cooper's photographs of the dress rehearsal would have a long public life as illustrations to the foundational article.

The piece in this history around gang violence is almost hard to believe, given the general wholesomeness of Cooper's images, which show members of Rock Steady practicing flips, windmills, and top rocking as their friends look on. Shooting from a low angle near the floor, Cooper captured the experience of spectating near the action of the dancers while also revealing the bright open surroundings of the rehearsal space. Visually speaking, she helped the esoteric and sometimes bewildering movements of breaking look appealing to a broader public, presenting the dance as accessible and fun, with a raw street edge.

The title of Banes's article in the *Voice*, "Physical Graffiti: Breaking Is Hard to Do," relates breaking's stylistic imperatives to those of graffiti—whose negative associations with vandalism, a deteriorating transit system, and ghetto culture—would have resonated for contemporary readers. Yet the article itself was the first to center the experiences of breakers, or "B Boys," as Banes called them. She did more than simply explore what breaking is and who does it. Like Cooper, she was enthusiastic about the dance and serious about its analysis, offering insights into movement vocabulary, musical influences, and ethnic and cultural references. Banes also connected breaking to historic freedom practices, writing that "the Breakdown is an old name in Afro-American dance for both rapid, complex footwork and a competitive format." Cooper and Banes completed the article with interviews of young practitioners and aerosol artists who were involved in hip hop, such as Fab 5 Freddy and Rammellzee.

The *Village Voice* article is important for many reasons, yet there are pieces around it that are confusing and appear inconsistent. From a framing standpoint, it made sense for Banes to write about the night of the High Times Crew's arrest—and it would keep the narrative faithful to Cooper's experience as an outsider called to the scene expecting to meet and report on a gang of young people involved in social disruption and unrest. But apart from a credit for her photographs of the Common Ground rehearsal, Martha Cooper's name is not mentioned in Banes's article. This is a strange omission, given that the former's work as a photojournalist is widely acknowledged elsewhere in the history.

Although the pictures Cooper took that January night were not used in Banes's article, they gained currency and mythic status through their retelling and reconstruction in hip hop history and its broader imaginary. For instance, Holman's (1984) recounting of the events erroneously suggested that the pictures of the arrested boys are the ones featured in the piece:

> Sally Banes' article in *The Village Voice* in 1981 [was] about photographer Martha Cooper covering breakdancers in the subway who were arrested, then released when Martha Cooper identified what it was they were doing, not fighting but break-dancing. Martha Cooper's photographs which were meant for the Post were rejected but were picked up by the Village Voice and gave new light and new life to break-dancing in spring of 1981. (69)

Despite Holman's mischaracterization, his account is noteworthy for how it closely follows the initial rejection of Cooper's story by the *Post* and the subsequent hook that "gave new light" to the dance once the article finally surfaced, written in collaboration with Banes and published by the *Voice*. Steven Hager (1984) was also impressed by how a single quote in the article—"not fighting, but dancing"—seemed to break through the publishing barrier that had excluded early forms of hip hop arts:

> Although it was still nearly impossible to publish articles on graffiti and rap music, both of which seemed to be universally hated by magazine editors, breaking had an immediate appeal for the national press, possibly because a quote in the *Voice* credited the dance with replacing fighting as an outlet for urban aggression . . . The

statement was not entirely accurate … *but it was just the sort of quote that makes good newspaper copy.* (87; emphasis added)

In his book *Can't Stop Won't Stop*, historian Jeff Chang discusses the dynamic interplay between violence and aesthetics as narrated by Banes in the *Voice*. He quotes from the article:

Breaking isn't just an urgent response to pulsating music. It is also a ritual combat that transmutes aggression into art. "In the summer of '78," Tee [of the High Times Crew] remembers, "when you got mad at someone, instead of saying, 'Hey man, you want to fight?' you'd say, 'Hey man, you want to rock?' " (Banes (1981), quoted in Chang 2005, 157)

The transformation of outlawry into art, according to Chang, was the element of the story that most captivated the *Voice*'s liberal readership: "Rocking instead of fighting—the idea would become one of the most enduring myths of hip hop" (157). Chang is correct to acknowledge this. However, he and other historians have not fully explored the piece of the history about the *presumption* of criminality and the misreading of aesthetic action as deviant behavior. This phenomenon was projected into outlaw visions, culminating in what cultural scholar Richard Iton (2008) called "the omnipotent and spectacular but faceless and threatening b-boy" (129).

Ultimately, Banes produced a ground-breaking story that has been referenced and repeated in much of the historical literature on hip hop. A hungry market for hip hop would soon develop, fueled by a desire for its musical and performative elements as well as its *look* and aesthetics. Cooper also played a role in organizing and documenting other early performances by the Rock Steady Crew—notably, at the Conference on the Folk Culture of the Bronx, May 15–17, 1981, and their infamous battle against the Dynamic Rockers at Lincoln Center on August 15, 1981, among others. As Banes recalled in a later article, between the fall of 1980 and the spring of 1981, breaking was a waning dance form, "a fad that had appeared and already disappeared" (1986, 11). The public attention brought by her and Cooper's efforts helped revive and make visible a dance that had been losing momentum. If her first feature pictures of breaking were ambiguous, her later photographs have the quality of magic. Cooper's image of Frosty Freeze at the Lincoln Center battle, executing a move called the Suicide (the one he is, perhaps, best known for), catches the dancer mid-flight, hovering at a seemingly impossible angle before executing a death-defying drop (see Figure 2.6).

"RITUAL WARFARE" ON ABC'S *20/20*

A few months after Banes's article in the *Voice* was published, the pictures Cooper took at the 175th street transit police station in Washington Heights were used as still

FIGURE 2.6 Frosty Freeze of Rock Steady Crew battling at the Lincoln Center Out of Doors Festival, Rocksteady Crew versus Dynamic Rockers, August 1981. New York City. Courtesy of Martha Cooper.

images in a special report by correspondent Steve Fox on the American Broadcasting Corporation's *20/20*, titled "Rappin' to the Beat"(*20/20* 1981).[3] ABC aired the program in early July 1981, making it the first national televised news program to cover the hip hop movement. In it, Fox interviews the syndicated rock columnist Lisa Robinson and asks her about the increasing public presence of boom boxes blaring rap music over loud beats. "It is very Black, and very urban, and people are scared of that," she replies. Fox linked the aural aggression of African American rap music to the physical competition it inspires in breaking, noting that some of the dancers' movements "have occasionally been misinterpreted by the authorities as gang warfare." Fox's commentary is presented alongside a bird's-eye view of Wayne Frost on his back, knees pulled up close to his chest, spinning like a turntable. The camera then cuts to Fox's interview with a New York transit police officer, Lieutenant John Englert, who tries to explain how his men responded to and subdued a "riot-in-progress" in January 1980 that had turned out to be just kids breaking. Englert says the police arrested thirty-seven kids that night, out of fear they were involved in "ritual warfare." As he speaks, the camera cuts to Cooper's still photographs of the High Times Crew demonstrating their moves in the subway outside the transit police station. The camera then zooms in on the face of one of the officers in the picture *Cops with Confiscated Items*. Whether Englert is one of the men Cooper photographed is not known with certainty, however he does resemble the officer on the right (see Figure 2.4).

WE SEE THAT WE ARE IN TROUBLE

Historians of race in contemporary culture often consider blackness in popular media as a site where disciplinary narratives play out. The cultural work of the white-dominated visual media, which tends toward representations of race that contain, commodify, and reproduce negative stereotypes about culture, results in a particular kind of subjection of racialized people. Ronald Jackson (2006) proposes "scripting" as a way to think about this, noting that the US popular media's "scripting" of the Black body with signifiers to histories of racism, reinforces destructive myths and stereotypes, while also compelling subjects to participate in their creation and positive reception. Scripting envisions limited pictures of and possibilities for Black life, particularly in representations of the poor. Cultural theorist bell hooks (1992) writes: "There is a direct and abiding connection between the maintenance of white supremacist patriarchy in this society and the institutionalization via mass media of specific images, representations of race, of blackness, that support and maintain the oppression . . . of all black people" (2). Just by flipping through books and magazines, looking at the daily news, or going to the movies, hooks observes, Black people experience "a collective crisis" in the realm of the image—"*we see that we are in trouble* [original emphasis]" (6). And Michele Wallace (1990), observing a link between the stories that get told about Black life in the news and a white-dominated art world that does not usually see minoritized subjects as legitimate cultural producers, has addressed the impact of mass media on the institutional acceptance of Black artists.

Hip hop scholars also often recall the disturbing news images of Black and Latinx communities in the Bronx—the home and heartbeat of hip hop culture—that proliferated in the media after the late 1970s. A number of factors worsened the decay of already impoverished neighborhoods and intensified the socioeconomic devastation of that period: the completed construction of the Cross Bronx Expressway and other public works projects, wide deindustrialization and loss of manufacturing jobs, a growing youth unemployment rate. Moreover, the racial make-up of the neighborhood had shifted with the influx of African American, Caribbean, and Puerto Rican immigrants, who took up residence in public-housing projects while many Jewish and Irish Americans moved to the suburbs. The stories and pictures of this time and place that endure in the imagination are of arson and gang violence, a devastated inner city made up of ruined buildings and yards of rubble, symbols of social decay and unrest. The first chapter of Hager's (1984) influential *Hip Hop: The Illustrated History* features images taken by Black Star photographer Michael Abramson in 1973 for an in-depth documentary project on the Savage Skulls and Black Spades gangs of the Bronx. Abramson's photographs of teenagers in embellished vests and jackets, roughhousing and embracing on the street and in their clubhouses helped solidify a problematic gang origin narrative around hip hop's prehistory (see Aprahamian 2019).

Reflecting on the pictures of the Bronx that fixed themselves in public consciousness through news stories and popular films, Tricia Rose (1994) observed that the popular media joins the American public school system and the police in the disciplinary perception and construction of "young African Americans as a dangerous internal element in urban America; an element that, if allowed to roam freely, will threaten the social order; an element that must be policed" (126). Rose and other scholars, such as Naomi Bragin (2014), Simone Browne (2015), and Mark Anthony Neal (2004), root this perception in deeper historical concerns about Black social congregation in public spaces, tracing how the reactions of the press and law enforcement construct and contribute to racial paranoia in American society.

In his expansive study of this subject, Neal (2004) suggests that the changing urban landscape of New York and the erection of public housing projects were factors in the conflation of the private and public realms, as pathological stories of African American social "dysfunction" entered the public discourse. Although dysfunction exists in any communal setting, the script of Black dysfunction "was mass mediated and commodified for mass consumption via network news programs, Hollywood films like *Fort Apache*, and television programs like *Starsky and Hutch* and *Baretta*." Neal concludes, "The black poor or underclass as human spectacle became a standard trope of mass culture" (422). Such misrepresentations were showed up in the rhetoric of conservative politicians like Ronald Reagan, who famously supported racist stereotypes by referring to single Black mothers as "welfare queens" and opposed spending on social programs (432). Given this context, it is not surprising that there was tension between the pictures Cooper was creating and the type of picture stories it was possible to tell about Black experience.

PERFORMANCE UNDER ARREST

The night of the High Times Crew's arrest and release contained three separate performances, all saturated with visual significance. Two of them occurred without cameras present. The first was the dance-battle-turned-stop-and-arrest in the Washington Heights subway station: an improvised performance that began when police officers and transit authorities failed to find legibility and meaning (in the form of recognizable dance steps) in the bodies of the dancers.

The second performance occurred out of public sight, behind the walls of the police station, when the boys were called upon to give a sort of show to the officers—a performance under arrest—listing and then executing a series of moves to demonstrate their innocence, to prove they really were just dancing. Banes (1981) writes:

> An officer called in other members of the crew, one by one. "Do a head spin," he would command as he consulted a clipboard full of notes. "Do 'the baby.'" As each kid complied, performing on cue as unhesitatingly as a ballet dancer might toss off an enchainment, the cops scratched their heads in bewildered defeat. (31)

It is difficult to imagine how this scene would have taken place in real time. Banes's account injects an element of comic relief into what must have been an uncomfortable and physically intimidating situation. But there is much we don't know about this second performance. Did the cops really make all the boys dance on cue, isolated from their friends? How long did it take to round everyone up, process them at the station, and then assess their dance moves?

"The important thing to remember about this story is that the night was January 21st," former High Times member Hector Ortiz told me.[4] Ortiz, who was fifteen when Cooper took his picture and is now a Grammy-winning DJ and producer performing under the name Hex Hector. When I interviewed him, he didn't know about the 20/20 segment and had no idea his picture had been shown on national television. He joked about the iron-on letters he and his brother wore on their t-shirts, spelling out their name, but this is partly what enabled a friend of his to identify him in Cooper's (2004) book *Hip Hop Files*. Hector explained that the temperature was freezing that night, and he and his crew had gone into the subway station to keep warm.

Hector described the Washington Heights neighborhood of his youth as "a safe and fun place for a kid to grow up." That night, the boys were doing what a lot of kids did for fun back then: they laid some cardboard on the ground, started up some music on a portable boombox, and got crazy on the floor. They favored a rarely used corridor near the end of the station, where the music would be amplified by the empty subway tunnel. Hector estimates they had practiced between forty-five minutes and an hour, surveilled by transit cops, who maintained their distance at first, and then decided to swarm the group He wanted me to understand the crew had been profiled. I asked if he knew that Lieutenant Englert claimed on 20/20 that they had arrested thirty-seven boys during the "riot-in-progress." Hector could hardly believe it. He clearly remembered the group was small—no more than eight or so individuals—and described the experience of arrest and the conduct of the officers as intimidating. Of Cooper, Hector remembered that she was approachable and kind, and seemed genuinely interested in what he and his friends were doing. He never met her again after that night. Hector and his friends got back on the train and went home.

Projections

The conflation of aesthetics and criminality that animates the visual forces at work in Cooper's early breaking images were diffused and multiplied in a series of semifictional and documentary films that embraced this bourgeoning outlaw aesthetic. In 1981, American director and artist Charlie Ahearn began work on the cult film *Wild Style* (1982), which featured performances by real-life graffiti writers, rappers, and b-boys. It was the first in a handful of "breaksploitation" films made around that time. The film included a small role for the no-wave actress and gallerist Patti Astor, who played an intrepid reporter who travels to the Bronx to do a story on hip hop artists. Whether Ahearn's vision of her character was an oblique reference to Cooper is not known, although the latter was the still photographer on the film (see Figure 2.7).

Wild Style opens with a dramatic scene that narrates the force of hypervisibility on the bodies of young men of color: the lead character, Zoro, played by real-life graffiti artist Lee Quiñones, scales a graffiti-covered wall to break into a train yard at night. The scene invokes lynching-related imagery. Lee lowers a rope down the wall—where it hangs for a moment—before descending himself, gripping the rope with both hands while he tries to find his footing. He drops to the ground, then stands. Dressed entirely in black, with a do-rag around his head, he advances into the train yard, climbing over another chain fence. In this unedited shot, the camera remains motionless, giving the viewer the experience of watching surveillance footage. As Lee approaches the camera, his face becomes partially illuminated by a harsh white light. His eyes search the scene. He is looking to see if he is being watched.

Similarly, *Beat Street* includes a famous scene that compels us to reflect on the pathological scrutiny of the bodies of young men of color, whose mere presence in the public sphere is misapprehended as dangerous or deviant. It also effectively reimagines the break battle of Hector's past, only this time, the stakes are higher and more stylized. Two rival crews who previously had an encounter in a nightclub engage in a brazen dance-off in an empty corridor in the subway before being swarmed by police officers. A White cop is shown using his baton to hold down the talented young b-boy Lee, played by Robert Taylor. Yet *Beat Street* also rehearses and reimagines the possibilities for resistance to a scripted narrative of police domination. At the station, where the kids are shown inside a chained-off holding area, the commanding officer is confronted by Lee's mother, who has come to take him home. She reprimands the cop, calling on him to consider the deviancy of the criminal justice system in the profiling of young people.

DARK MATTERS

These images and projections offer examples of what Simone Browne (2015) articulates as "moments of living with, refusals, and alternatives to routinized, racializing surveillance" (82). In her book *Dark Matters: On the Surveillance of Blackness*, Browne asserts that, historically and in the present, "cultural production, expressive acts, and everyday practices" can resist such techniques by allowing us to think otherwise about "the predicaments, policies, and performances constituting surveillance" (82). The predicaments and practices that concern Browne take place in the mid-nineteenth century in New York City, yet she traces how the historic regulation of Black life is felt over two hundred years later. Arguing that "the potentiality of being under watch" is a cumulative effect of technologies of surveillance, micro-regulation, and restrictions stemming from transatlantic slavery, Browne considers visual and printed media, such as

FIGURE 2.7. The cast from *Wild Style* posing for photos in Riverside Park, Manhattan, August 1983. *Left to right*: (row 1) Doze, Frosty Freeze, Ken Swift; (row 2) Patti Astor, Fab 5 Freddy, Lady Pink; (row 3) Lil Crazy Legs, Revolt, Sharp Revolt. Sharp painted the mural. Courtesy of Martha Cooper.

fugitive slave posters and printed news advertisements, as among numerous sites of invasion and the scrutiny of Black life. However, she also understands that these channels play a role in bringing performances of freedom into fuller view.

Browne (2015) historicizes the apparatus of watchfulness of Black life through laws that forbade enslaved people to assemble, including gathering in groups of three or more to talk or play sports, or to make loud noises. She points to the Lantern laws, which required individuals and groups of enslaved people to carry candles and lanterns after

dark so they could be "plainly seen," their mobility regulated, "made knowable, locat-
able, and contained within the city" (78–79). Browne locates this in the larger project
of racialized surveillance of Black, mixed-race, and Indigenous subjects. Illuminating
the possibilities for unsupervised leisure and socializing that persisted despite such
conditions, Browne turns to "spaces of sometimes interracial and cross-class commerce and socializing" and to "black performative practices of drumming, dancing
and chanting" (80). Browne offers published descriptions of "public negro dances," including one eyewitness account of the Catherine Market breakdown. (80). Various styles
of competitive dance were performed for market spectators—but the historical account
describes how the breakdown was danced on a wooden board while participants kept
the rhythm by tapping their feet and clapping their hands against the sides of their
legs (81). Browne claims that the performative sensibilities of these dances can be felt
"200 years later, through the emergence of hip hop in the Bronx" (80), and that the remains of these performances linger "in the cardboard, turntables, b-girls, and b-boys of
the breakdancing cypher" (82).

THE CAMERA IN THE CYPHER

In their unsanctioned forms of public dance and occupations of space, breakers in the
1980s continued to attract the attention of law enforcement and news reporters alike.
In the years following the publication of the *Voice* article, newspapers reported more
arrests of Black and Puerto Rican dancers for "disturbing the peace" and "attracting un-
desirable crowds in the malls" (Rose 1994, 50). A newspaper story announced that the
city council of San Bernardino, California, was introducing fines of $100 for breakers
performing in public without a designated permit: "City Council to Dancers: Break It
Up!" the headline read.[5]

But even as breaking was being actively policed, the dance was becoming a popular
craze across the United States and overseas. As hip hop expanded into the visual field,
its aesthetics became "violently public" in the late 1980s, coming into view with greater
ubiquity and intensity. Iton (2008) has argued that this, combined with technological
developments such as handheld video recorders and surveillance cameras, would bring
about a "heightened performative sensibility" or "expectation that one is always potentially being watched" in response (105).

Of course, breakers sought to dance and compete in front of other people; but there
is a difference between being observed by members of one's aesthetic community and
being looked at by outsiders. Hager (1984) observed that the visual force of the media
attention on the breaking phenomenon coincided with the appearance and rise of rap
music and hip hop celebrity culture in nightclubs such as Negril, where it was a priority
to have "plenty of Bronx boys on hand to give the place an authentic flavor" (89). And
Rose (1994) noted that dance schools hired breakers to give lessons oriented to the "'hip'
middle class whites" who were the main partygoers at the downtown clubs and in private

venues where breakers were recruited to perform (50). She quotes Crazy Legs recalling this period of notoriety: "We weren't making no money . . . all these white people coming in . . . we were pretty much on display, and we didn't even know it . . . . Now I realize we were on display. People were paying $8 and $7 whatever it cost . . . to watch us" (50).

It is important to acknowledge the presence of cameras in the context of breaking cyphers—and the effect they had on the way the dance was performed and made visible to its own practitioners and to wider audiences. The mediatization of breaking battles both translated and affirmed the outlaw aesthetics of the dance's practitioners. Visual and printed media tended to play to mainstream white America's fascination with the "news" of the breaking craze and its supposed gang origins. A surge of still photographs, videos, television, and film, helped move breaking from marginality in the 1970s to public visibility in the 1980s.

The presence of the camera compounded a shift in the way hip hop's performing arts were created and consumed. Breaking's journey from cypher and street to still and moving image carried with it a new emphasis on a frontal orientation and predesigned composition—at the expense of the raw energy and improvised vernacular that defined its indigenous forms. This was a necessary outcome of the logistical needs of television camera crews, reporters, and film crews who needed room to record the quick maneuvers of their subjects. Thus, the dance itself evolved and changed as crews made room for and engaged with people holding cameras. Banes (1986) reports an anecdote about Crazy Legs at a battle, repeating the words of a camera person who earlier had instructed them to "open up the circle" so they could film. The dancer told everyone to "open up the circle," and they moved (16).

The anecdote comes from a piece Banes (1986) published titled "Breakdancing: A Reporter's Story," with pictures by Cooper, in which she looked back on the "telescopic story of breaking," reflecting on the experience of reporting on the breakdancing "craze" and the "wildfire popular diffusion" of media attention that came in the wake of the *Voice* article. Pointing out that breaking "was invented by a generation of kids raised on television, movies, radio, and videogames," Banes acknowledged that the dance's relationship with the media is "densely layered, beginning with the use of pop culture imagery and with brevity of format, and evolving with the succession of responses to media coverage and dissemination" (20). In part because of this relationship, she argued, early observers and reporters (among whom she included herself) were active participants in early hip hop dance, having had "such an enormous effect on its meteoric history" (10).

CONCLUSION

Hip hop performance and dance has not been fully explored as a hypervisible phenomenon: one that is the product of the hegemony of what Fred Moten terms the visual

(2003, 197). Even as the commodification of hip hop aesthetics toward auditory and performative experiences has accelerated over time—acquiring widespread acceptance, celebration, and economic success in terms of record sales, music downloads, and live concerts—it has generated considerable visual material (Iton 2008, 105). Early in this history, Cooper contributed images to several books and other publications that built formative understandings of breaking as a dance and hip hop as a cultural movement. Picturing the complex, imaginative, and dynamic actions and gestures of breakers, her photographs appeared in how-to manuals and "definitive guides" to hip hop— giving small bursts of color and life to the more static and serial imagery these types of books tended toward. Within a framework of looking in which increased visibility is linked with commercial exploitation, Cooper's early breaking pictures offer counter-documents to this narrative of success.

The presence of Cooper's camera in the High Times Crew's breaking cypher heightened the experience of spectatorship and extended the parameters of the visual field to viewers beyond their immediate circle. Like a subway-car mural moving beyond the borough limits, the photographic image—by participating in a circulating image economy that brings subjects into relation with one another—expands the cultural (and temporal) space in which practitioners of hip hop operate. The historical anecdote about the High Times Crew's arrest tells us how particular bodies, histories, and creative forms of expression are affirmed or denied in public discourse. As the first published witness, spectator, and photographer of breaking's emergence in New York City, Cooper's accounts of this history constitute a powerful record that both accompanied and set the conditions for the art form's arrival above ground. To come into more meaningful contact with this history, however, it is necessary to pivot our perspective from her published account and speculate into territory that is difficult to see. Cooper was creating photographs for which there was no aesthetic precedent. Working at a historical moment when the elevation of Black performance was not fully seen in white-dominated media, Cooper's contribution to hip hop and visual culture—while not uncomplicated—is significant.

ACKNOWLEDGMENTS

I gratefully acknowledge Martha Cooper for sharing her experiences and recollections in an interview and in anecdotes and conversation, for providing me access to her archives and collections, as well as permission to use her photographs in this chapter. The research for this work would not have been possible without her participation and generosity. I am also grateful to Hector Ortiz for agreeing to be interviewed for this work. Research for this chapter was supported in part by a Ryerson Image Centre (RIC) Doctoral Research Fellowship. I am grateful to my colleagues at the RIC for their time, energy, and assistance during my fellowship.

NOTES

1. The exact number varies between sources. In an interview with Michael Holman (1984) for his book *Breaking and the New York City Breakers*, Cooper estimated the number of boys who were stopped and arrested to be around forty-five or fifty (142). A televised news clip from 1981 reported the number to be thirty-seven.
2. Martha Cooper, interview with the author, February 6, 2017, New York City, New York. Unless otherwise indicated, the quotations from Cooper in the chapter are from this interview, cited in the text as "Cooper interview."
3. I gratefully acknowledge Serouj Aprahamian for sharing the clip and alerting me to Cooper's connection.
4. Hector Ortiz, personal interview, April 26, 2018.
5. "SB Council wants to bran breakdancing," *Desert Sun*, No. 184, March 6, 1984.

REFERENCES

20/20. 1981. "Rappin' to the Beat." Directed by American Broadcasting Corporation. Aired July 1981 on ABC. (Youtube 2009). https://www.youtube.com/watch?v=onRKOcsfiJo.

Adler, B. (2006). "Who Shot Ya: A History of Hip-Hop Photography." In *Total Chaos: The Art and Aesthetics of Hip-Hop*, edited by J.. Chang, 102–116. New York: Perseus Books.

Aprahamian, S. (2019). "Hip Hop, Gangs, and the Criminalization of African American Culture: A Critical Appraisal of Yes Yes Y'All." *Journal of Black Studies* 50 (3): 298–315.

Banes, S. (1981). "Physical Graffiti: Breaking Is Hard to Do." *Village Voice*, April 22–28, 31–33.

Banes, S. (1986). "Breakdancing: A Reporter's Story." In *Folklife Annual 1986*, edited by A. Jabbour and J. Hardin, 8–23. Washington, DC: American Folklife Center, Library of Congress.

Bragin, N. (2014). "Shot and Captured: Turf Dance, YAK Films, and the Oakland, California, R.I.P. Project." *TDR: Drama Review* 58 (2): 99–114.

Browne, S. (2015). *Dark Matters: On the Surveillance of Blackness*. Durham, NC: Duke University Press.

Chang, J. (2005). *Can't Stop Won't Stop: A History of the Hip-Hop Generation*. New York: St. Martin's Press.

Cooper, M. (2004). *Hip Hop Files: Photographs 1979–1984*. Cologne: From Here to Fame Publishing.

Cooper, M. (2006). *Street Play*. Berlin: From Here to Fame Publishing.

Cooper, M. and H. Chalfant. (1984). *Subway Art*. New York: Holt, Rinehart and Winston.

Gervais, T., and Morel, G. (2017). *The Making of Visual News: A History of Photography in the Press*. London: Bloomsbury Academic.

Hager, S. (1984). *Hip Hop: The Illustrated History of Break Dancing, Rap Music, and Graffiti*. New York: St. Martin's Press.

Hill, J., and Schwartz, V. (2015). *Getting the Picture: The Visual Culture of the News*. New York: Bloomsbury Academic.

Holman, M. (1984). *Breaking and the New York City Breakers*. New York. Freundlich Books.

hooks, b. (1992). *Black Looks: Race and Representation*. Boston: South End Press.

Iton, R. (2008). *In Search of the Black Fantastic: Politics and Popular Culture in the Post–Civil Rights Era*. New York: Oxford University Press.

Jackson, R., II. (2006). *Scripting the Black Masculine Body: Identity, Discourse, and Racial Politics in Popular Media*. Albany: State University of New York Press.

Lawrence, T. (2016). *Life and Death on the New York Dance Floor, 1980–1983*. Durham, NC: Duke University Press.

Malik, R. (2008). "Horizons of the Publishable: Publishing in/as Literary Studies." *ELH* 75 (3): 707–735.

Moten, F. (2003). *In the Break: The Aesthetics of the Black Radical Tradition*. Minneapolis: University of Minnesota Press.

Muñoz, J. E. (1996). "Ephemera as Evidence: Introductory Notes to Queer Acts." *Women and Performance: A Journal of Feminist Theory* 8 (2): 5–16.

Neal, M. A. (2004). "Postindustrial Soul: Black Popular Music at the Crossroads." In *That's the Joint: The Hip-Hop Studies Reader*, edited by M. Forman and M. A. Neal, 417–446. New York: Routledge.

Pasadeos, Y., and Renfro, P. (1988). "Rupert Murdoch's Style: *The New York Post*." *Newspaper Research Journal* 9: 25–33.

Rose, T. (1994). *Black Noise: Rap Music and Black Culture in Contemporary America*. Middletown, CT: Wesleyan University Press.

Wallace, M. (1990). *Dark Designs and Visual Culture*. New York: Duke University Press.

....

CHAPTER 3

THE TECHNICAL DEVELOPMENTS IN BREAKING FROM CONDITIONING TO MINDSET

....

NIELS "STORM" ROBITZKY

INTRODUCTION

....

I started Breaking in 1983 and have actively participated in the dance's evolution ever since. I published a book on the history of Breaking in Germany titled *Von Swipe zu Storm* (Robitzky 2000), and also produced the first tutorial DVD, *Footwork Fundamentals* (2004), on a specific aspect of the dance known as Footwork. In this chapter I discuss how the moves in this dance were created and how they developed, drawing on a few key examples. There is currently not much literature available that covers this topic. My assertions are based mainly on my personal experience, and most of my theories stem from practice. Although the chapter reveals information about the technical development of Breaking, it does not replace the experience of being a B-Boy or B-Girl.

TRENDS

....

Certain moves became fashionable at certain times. It would be impossible to list all the moves that are relevant in the development of the dance. The few that I shed light on here are all part of the Foundation.[1] Without these inventions, entire branches of the art form would not exist. They are used as rudiments and had a multiplying function in the evolution of the dance.

I also list some conceptions and misconceptions that were relevant to the coming into being of the dance. The dance has changed many times over the years and has gone through different phases. Each era experienced the dance differently. The sociopolitical conditions of different times have influenced the paradigms people lived in. This dance culture and its technical developments were formed by a group of people who were receptive to new ideas only to a certain degree. Whether something could become a trend or not happened according to the sociopolitical paradigms in effect. A person could have done the most incredible movement that was technically well connected to Breaking, but if that person or move was not part of the Breaking paradigm, B-Girls and B-Boys would not accept or even notice the idea. For example, moves like the Thomas Flare that came from gymnastics became part of the dance quite late, even though the move fit perfectly. It was not the move itself, but what it stood for that hindered its full integration at the beginning. B-Boys and B-Girls wanted to distance themselves from the point-toed, straight-legged, rigor of Gymnastics and the establishment. Certain Capoeira moves on the other hand, as part of the African diasporic heritage and a style of fighting, were embraced very quickly. Here is a taxonomy of some of the best-known moves in the development of Breaking.

The Six-step

Keeping in mind that the dance was and is mainly performed inside a circle of bystanders, there was one combination of aligned steps that changed the style of dance more than anything else that came after. It is the most well-known foundational footwork concept and is called the Six-step. In the initial position, the dancer sits on the heels. Both feet are on the ground. Now the dancer has to imagine a circle in which the head and the shoulders mark the center. The rest of the body moves around this center, and the legs and feet are doing the pattern of six steps around that circle. The arms support and balance the body while it swings, depending on its position in the process. The Crazy Commandos, one of the earliest crews from the Bronx, New York, used to do a very extended version of this move, reportedly to open the circle.

The exploitation era of Breaking in the early to mid-1980s serves us very well with all its referential videos. One of the earliest clips features Ken Swift and Crazy Legs in 1983 on the *David Letterman Show*. In their solos, we can see how they execute a Six-step each time they dance. The combination must be ingrained to the point where all the patterns were "at one's fingertips" so that small, improvised parts could be added on at all times and in all positions. When the dance spread across the globe in the mid-1980s, the Six-step versions of different New York icons were analyzed and named after each one. They vary mainly in rotation. For example, the way Crazy Legs of the Rock Steady Crew did his Six-step has partly evolved into what is known as the Atomic style today. It is significant for its spin of the body in one direction and the step pattern orbiting into the other direction. The advantage of the Atomic-style Six-step is mostly that it can be danced much faster and, therefore, looks wilder. Another one is the Icey Ice Six-step, named after a dancer from the New York City Breakers, in which the upper body turns in the same direction as the footwork pattern and the circular body swings. The Six-step is the most important foundational move of Breaking today. Most of the current circular footwork patterns are variations derived from this concept.

The Stab

The Stab was established by a dancer trying to support his body on one arm in a horizontal or a diagonal position with the head touching the floor. It is not a dance move but a supportive addition that helps the dancer by economizing movement. The elbow is tucked into the belly and is stabilized by the ribcage and the hipbone that surrounds the area it stands in. The lower arm and the hand build a pillar down to the ground on which the entire body can be balanced.

The Baby Freeze and Chair Freeze

The Stab also played an important role in the evolution of the two most common foundational freezes: the Baby Freeze and the Chair Freeze. When the Baby Freeze first appeared, it was an imitation of a baby lying on the ground in a fetal position, with a thumb in its mouth. The version of the Baby Freeze that is taught in classes today, however, does not resemble this first version at all. The Freeze was altered many times and presented an obvious challenge for balance—it was too easy to just end up on one's back, so its difficulty was enhanced and with greater play in difficulty came more respect. Since the 1980s, it has been done with the dancer standing on a tripod made with the head and both arms. One elbow is "stabbed" and the other one becomes a resting point for the opposite knee.

The Stab also helped the family of power moves to develop. Most moves in which the body is held in a horizontal position utilize the Stab position in their basic appearance. A spin on a Stab, in which the rest of the body does not touch the ground, is called a Handglide, and a walk from a Stab on one hand to another Stab on the other is a Turtle.

The Windmill

The invention of the Windmill opened a new dimension within the dance, to the point that it became the main object in a Breaking performance during the 1980s. The Windmill marked the birth of power moves in Breaking, and a practitioner that did not know how to do the move was looked at as a beginner—or even as unworthy—at that time. Combining the Windmill with other rotational moves, like the Head Spin, Turtles, Flares, or an Elbow Spin, where the feet would never touch the ground, became the main purpose of the dance. It became possible to perform a solo during this period simply by spinning. Power moves became a new subset of Breaking from that moment on.

In a YouTube video of the US President Ronald Reagan's inaugural gala in 1985, we see the New York City Breakers performing the Windmill repeatedly. The crew consists of eight members, and Flip Rock and Mr. Wave (who was the Boogie-Boy in the group) were the only members who did not perform a version of a Windmill in their solos. As much as this performance demonstrated the prevalence of this move in Breaking, it also marks the end of New York City's influence on the dance, since it is the last TV show aired after the big hype of Breaking.[2]

A New Beginning into Autonomy

From the mid-1980s on, the few remaining Breakers started working together more closely and documenting their knowledge for future generations. Their epistemic loneliness made them realize how valuable it is to have people that share the same passion. The New York heritage served as the foundational knowledge base for a new cultural beginning. But the continuation of the culture happened in new places that adopted the culture. Whether the B-Boys that were far away from the dance's birthplace had good or bad technique was not the question. Their commitment to the dance gave it the stronghold it needed for a continued, steady growth. Their perseverance in times when the dance was called a fad, and their struggle to search for information and inspiration was a burden they shared. When these B-Boys met for the first time, their passion created a bond immediately. New ideas were cultivated, and resulted in visible changes in style. At times, misinformation creates new paths. For example, Gabin from the Aktuel Force crew in Paris never heard of the Six-step until 1993. When he saw Breaking for the first time in the early 1980s, he developed something that closely resembled the Six-step but was based on a different idea. He had a massive impact in spreading his version of that similar footwork concept, which was embraced by the community.

Bigger metropolitan areas slowly matured into autonomous scenes and got connected with one another. Hip Hop jams were getting organized, and well-known Breakers were invited as guests. Breakers generally started to travel for weeks to get new inspiration and learn more. The enthusiasm before a jam helped motivate training immensely. Furthermore, it increased the impact of all the newly seen moves after a jam. Traveling became the most important source of information and motivation in a scene that, at the time, barely had access to video cameras. One still had to be there in person to experience what the dance was about. I would call this decade the "journeymen era" in Breaking. It was not like in New York, where one took the subway home after a "throwdown." Rather, travel to other places had to be well organized. It was normal for B-Boys to stay abroad as guests and share their passion for several days. This was different from the relatively hostile New York environment of rival crews and gangs of the 1970s and 1980s.

At the beginning of the 1990s, New York finally got back into the Breaking picture and became a part of its growing global dance network. A handful of B-Boys and B-girls who understood the cultural relevance of the City as the capital of the dance slowly started to pull other dancers out of retirement to speak about the history of Breaking and show their skills.

THE 1990S

The Battle as a Format of Organized Competition

In the 1990s, another stage in Breaking history opened up. The International Battle of the Year event began in 1991 and would become, over the years, the biggest Breaking event in the world, with qualifiers from every continent. Breaking crews would organize themselves to perform a showcase together to represent their country. A group of selected judges decided which were the best performances, and then chose those crews to battle against each other for first place. For many years, Battle of the Year—including the national qualifiers in all the different countries and the finals in Germany—was also a place where people exchanged information. And as crews had to perform and then battle together on a huge stage, new graphical ways of utilizing space were also cultivated. For example, staging techniques like the "Pick Up" or the "Revolver," which are now common ways to switch soloists, were developed. By getting together on an international stage, dancers made new contacts and exchanged skills with other dancers.

Other international Battle events in the 1990s included the Pro-Am in Miami and Freestyle Session in Southern California. These competitions set off new trends, and the dancers who attended them grew up in the period when these organized battles were the main events to go to. As the number of people in the audience grew, the expectations and anticipations for action, but also the stage fright of performers increased.

DRAMATURGY

The threefold performance strategy of Breaking—Top Rock, Down Rock, Freeze— builds the common, dramaturgical "three-act structure" of a B-Boy or B-Girl solo. From the late 1970s until the mid-1990s, Top Rock consisted of two basic steps that are most frequently called the Indian Two-Step and the Crossover Step. Every B-Boy had a few personal signature moves, but typically there was not much to them compared to the floor-based moves. Breaking principally took the form of ground moves in those early two decades.

However, from the late 1990s on, along with the research about the origins of Breaking, Rocking started to have a renaissance. A lot of dancers from the Rock era reappeared or came out of retirement. They started teaching their skills to a vast B-Boy and B-Girl community worldwide that was hungry for steps done on top.

The evolution of upright dancing in Breaking during this period can also be seen in the footage of International Battle of the Year events in Germany. This contest is a useful reference point for finding out what happened in Breaking throughout those decades, and their videos are easily found online or available on DVDs. We can see, for example, that crews in the 1990s kept mixing their Breaking skills with Popping, Locking, Hip Hop Freestyle, and House dance when they were choreographing their shows. Battle Squad did a Hip Hop Freestyle dance routine in their winning showcase in 1991, as well as a Popping skit in 1992. Flying Steps from Germany performed a Locking routine in their winning show in 2000, as did the Spartanic Rockers from Japan, their opponents in the final battle. There was not much variety in Top Rock, and the few steps at hand did not provide a good enough contrast for a dynamic, choreographic build-up. After 2000, however, these dance forms appeared less and less, due to the fast development of Top Rocking. Old school Rockers started teaching their skills to a hungry generation of Breakers.

Thus, in the post-2000 period, after about ten years during which Breaking was developing autonomously in different parts of the world, every B-Boy and B-Girl had to look at New York again. Practitioners started seeking out the missing history and vocabulary of the Rock to connect it with their Top Rock. The knowledge they gained was mainly spread by videos, DVDs, and the Internet. As the International Battle of the Year event evolved, this meant that all the other dance styles that were performed alongside Breaking became redundant. They were treated as placeholders, because they were coming from another dance lineage. For the ordinary audience, the shift might mean a loss of spectacle, but for a B-Boy and B-Girl it is a gain of purity within the art form.

Theater Productions

When Breaking returned, it came back as an emancipated dance form, with strong arguments and that it deserved a place in the art world. An advance into theater also began in the early 1990s. Companies like Ghettoriginal in New York and Aktuel Force in St. Denis and Accrorap in Lyon, France, worked hard to establish the dance in the field of contemporary dance. The trend had mainly started in France, where companies such as Black, Blanc, Beur worked with dancers from an urban environment in the postmodern theatrical network. The annual festival "Cité Danse" in Suresnes, which is dedicated to urban contemporary performing arts, was the first of its kind when it opened in January 1993. By choreographing and performing entire dance pieces on large stages, B-Boys and B-Girls began learning more about theatrics. The center of expression tried to get away from the dominant agonistic approach. One technique-expanding aspect was that theatre work made it possible to dwell in subtleties. Concepts that had to be dealt with in seconds in a Battle could now be expanded into themes in a longer dance piece. "Portrait of a Freeze," for example, was a piece by the Ghettoriginal Dance Company in which the main subject was the Freeze.

Instead of looking at moves as inferior or superior weapons, they now became legitimate, useful forms of expression in the dramatic composition of the production. Until this point, it wouldn't have occurred to anyone to perform one round of a Windmill in a two-minute time frame—in a jam, Battle, or Cypher that would have been inappropriate. But when an audience sits down and is ready to watch a performance for ninety minutes, it could work. In a Battle or a Cypher nobody would have dreamed of showing a loss of composure. In a play, that effect can be a good trigger for a different sort of emotion. Moves that could simply be overlooked due to their modest appearance can proliferate.

Through the chance it was given to invade contemporary theater houses, Breaking enlarged its performance spectrum. Here, the art of Breaking developed into a more individual expression, outside the traditional format. It could unfold in countless free and expressive ways. That these are all part of Breaking culture, or not, shows in the audience and its reactions. Being able to perform one's own artistic creations, even if they are based on notions that were adopted from a foreign culture, also helps to assess that they are a part of one's own culture. By approaching the art world, Breaking advanced in a more poetic direction, in which the original raw, Bronx approach seems to have been subordinated.

Another important effect that we can attribute to the effort to create choreographies through these avenues is the professionalization of the scene. To make a living doing something one has passion for gives one the freedom to pursue their dreams without the distraction of worrying about paying the rent. A greater number of B-Boys and B-Girls could now devote themselves to Breaking full time. The time factor also plays an important role in learning a craft. The more I can dedicate myself to a skill, the more thoroughly I can analyze it, and the more I can experiment.

The Heart of Practice

Craftsmanship

When we look at how to learn technique within Breaking, it is helpful to look at the craftsmanship and at how skills are acquired. First, we receive instruction, and then we imitate or try to follow those instructions. By going through the necessary working steps carefully and slowly, while we try to realize the move physically, we start to cultivate the motion. Every discouraging error makes us try again. Once we develop a slow, steady rhythm, we can loop the movement without breaking it up. Now we can also accelerate. But we want to assure the quality of our movements, so, sometimes we might have to slow down again.

Here, we reach the second stage of skill acquisition, when we can adjust our own natural rhythm to the beat of music that is playing. In time, we do not have to think about the how to do the moves anymore, and they become automatic. This is the moment when most dancers would say they "feel it." The facility is ingrained into our body and the technique becomes a habit, always at the dancer's disposal. Lightness occurs and the entire body is subject to a metamorphosis in skill. That means that a change of posture and conduct becomes inevitable.

The third and most important stage for artists is the research stage, in which one learns to apply new moves to the already learned and existing technique. Compared to the other two stages, this process takes the longest. With every new idea applied to the move, the dancer must start the ingraining process over again. Every new move becomes subject to empirical evaluation. After a while, the moves become more complex and the dancer develops more variations, establishing a repertoire of techniques. In other words, the dancer's competence increases not just by knowing how to address a problem, but by knowing alternatives if their first choice does not suffice. A dancer becomes successful by developing and mastering many different skills, not just through sheer instinct.

Individuality

Creativity is one of the main objectives in Breaking. Technical command also produces individuality. Creating "signature" movements is one of the prime tasks of the dancer. In time, a practitioner will learn how to stamp their individual character on a guiding foundational move and make it their own. To be creative without any foundational references, however, is like floating in space, with no coordination and nothing to hold on to. That is why foundational moves are important to build on.

Sometimes students copy what they see and leave it at that. This might be enough to make one a good technician or find work for choreographer, since they mainly look for dancers that execute well and follow orders, but will not gain the dancer much respect in the B-Boy world. Indeed, the negative term for people who just copy and profit from the creative work of others is "Biter." It is not just that one gets a reputation as a copier; it also means that one is not able to express himself by using his own thoughts and technique. Trying new ways to do the dance therefore becomes a source of pride if the skill is successfully acquired. By working on new ideas and different techniques from the first hour of practice on, we can develop transversally and discover many possible ways to interpret the movements. By doing so, the participant becomes the "author of one's own object" and creates his individual way of expression.

One example of this process is Poe One's invention of the Airchair. In an interview from 2015 with B-Boy Focus from Finland, Poe One revealed how he came up with the move, called it the "Cobra attacking the eagle," and then it developed further. For a long time, nobody dared to copy his signature move since he is quite famous in the scene. Nobody wished to be called a biter. Then some B-Boys in Florida used the Airchair, not as a Freeze but as a position one can dance in.

In the regular Chair Freeze, there would be three or four pillars: the head, one foot, and one or both hands are on the ground to stabilize the body while it is in a horizontal position. In contrast, the Airchair position is a Stab (explained below) into the back, where the kidneys are. As long as the elbow stabs into the back, and the body is turned upward and the head and feet are in the air, this move will be called an Airchair. It is extremely difficult to move and balance in this position at the same time. The fewer the pillars to support the body from falling, the more difficult it is to balance. Again, in contrast to the regular Chair Freeze, which only has one position (the leg rests on the opposite knee), the Airchair has varied possibilities. Threads, in which a dancer holds his foot or knee and moves the other leg through the loophole that is created, have especially become a great way to utilize this more dynamic position. This has made the Airchair a lot more popular today. The regular Chair Freeze still serves a purpose for all the B-Boys who specialize in Footwork. Yet, for most power movers, the Airchair is the preferred freeze, since in their philosophy it is a nightmare when a foot is touching the ground.

Musicality

It is of paramount importance today for a B-Boy to be able to connect with the accompanying music. Only by embodying its rhythm, velocity, melody, timing, and atmosphere is it possible for a dancer to interpret a song successfully. One must school one's musical receptivity to develop creativity. "Music" itself is a very broad term. Here we can start with a beat as an indicator for movements and their coherence within the rhythmic grid. The more complex a move or a combination of moves is, the more difficult it becomes to execute them in time with the music. The ability to adjust and drive a movement from its natural cadence into the cadence of the music thus represents a level of mastery. You and others become the music in physical form, and you are on the way to becoming one with it.

It should also be remembered that Breaking got its name partly from the "breaks" in Funk songs. A break was when most of the instruments were pulled out of a song and the percussion took over. Breakers responded by improvising and filling up that musical emptiness with their bodies, in a visual and kinesthetic expression. In the early days of the dance, this was called "Going Off," which says a lot about the mental state of dancer. Back then, it seems, the mood was much more important than dancing on the beat. In most of the rare old footage, we can see that the B-Boys were mainly off rhythm. If the music was getting a dancer so hyped that he felt it was okay to ignore the music, this is understandable. Or maybe a performing at a high creative and athletic level was more important than dancing on beat. If technique is more created than ingrained, and if the courage to do new moves is higher than the desire to be in unison with the rhythm, then of course that makes sense too. The goal of most B-Boys today is to create a virtuoso performance within musical rules, as if playing a visual instrument.

Nevertheless, we realize that in Going Off the music can easily change our mental state. The sound of the music does something to the mind. It creates a mood, which can boost the work output. The drive to achieve one's goals increases, and it distracts the dancer from the pain. One gets ready for action and the rhythm engages the sympathetic nervous system and prepares a person for developing variations in movement (Fenske 2012). That the New York Marathon banned music in 2007 because of its performance-enhancing qualities should give us enough proof that music is a natural steroid (Bradford 2013). Thus it is not just that certain music is part of the cultural heritage of Breaking. Music is a great aid that helps dancers to get into the right mindset to execute a demanding, extreme performance.

Consistency

If we learn a technique in just one "right" way, we cannot discover new possibilities by doing it the "wrong" way. What might be wrong in one situation can be stimulating in another. In other words, evolution makes it possible to transform something that is seemingly wrong into something that is right.

It is also vital to accept that difficulty is part of being a B-Boy or B-girl. If things aren't difficult enough, our sense of curiosity will no longer be animated, and we can easily lose interest in learning. The teacher suggests the basic movements one can build on. We will have to adjust our dancing based on different conditions, such as a different surface or faster music. Otherwise, our moves may not serve their purpose in the composition of a danced set of moves. For all these reasons, learning the craft of Breaking takes time.

Breaking requires rigorous physical training. The fact that the shaping has to stay within the cultural codes of the dance presents a practitioner with multiple challenges *and* multiple opportunities to find solutions and put their personal touch into every move. Dancers will eventually begin to express themselves and communicate through their personally developed movements. This is why the motto in the dance is that if there is a will, there is a way. Furthermore, the work isn't done if the motion is perfectly executed just once. It has to come out well consistently.

The Mission in Rehearsals

Once a B-Boy or B-Girl has developed a repertoire of moves, he or she can rehearse with others. A crew needs to find a common movement vocabulary for the dance passages they performed together. This means they have to design a choreography. Because almost every move has a name, even before the actual physical training, dancers can find out what techniques they have in common and what elements they can focus on. But when dancers want to explain something, they "show" rather than "tell" it. Analysis and interpretation are left to others.

The skill of making a clear statement becomes as important as the skill of watching closely. Its main importance lies in picking up concrete details. Each B-Boy has their own expressive habits, which need to be pointed out. In rehearsal, it is up to each participant to decide whether it is okay to share these habits. If so, the others not only must decide whether to accept them as material that can be used, but also whether they will be able to adjust their skills to the moves. Then the dialectic method is used to establish a common ground, and the play with opposites gradually builds up to a synthesis. There is a great side effect that comes with sharing movements for choreography in this fashion: fellow dancers get to see many different variations of the existing technique. The act of showing and explaining one's personal achievements can inspire others, and new ways are opened up. If a B-Boy suggests dancing a personally invented technique with others, it may lose its exclusiveness but may gain in general value. If it proliferates in the community, it can easily become a part of the foundation and serve as a new reference point.

ATHLETICISM

The more physically complex a movement is, the more chance that it might become a "Burner."

This term describes the negative effect a move can have on an opponent's self-esteem. The term circulates in the same way as "dropping bombs" does in Hip Hop culture; or, a person's loss is described as "somebody got smoked." In a Battle situation, an audience compares two dancers, and if dancer A has stronger moves in her arsenal than dancer B, it will take a lot of strategy and finesse for dancer B to counter that.

The competitive tradition in Breaking that has inspired dancers to challenge their own expectations about the physical limits of the human body. The chance of getting hurt is greater when one pushes their body's limits while experimenting. Toward the end of the empirical testing, when the only thing missing is a steady execution, one is left to hope that one's fantastic visions are shared with others and the move will be accepted. Nobody can know for sure that their newly developed idea will be recognized by the community.

In addition, as mentioned, the chance of a positive result in Breaking is greater if the move is executed to the music. If not, it is often condescendingly referred to as a "trick." However, some people who are working on a very high acrobatic and athletic level are not necessarily following the music. Some may not want to be part of the broader Breaking community; others may not have a clue about the essence of the dance. Nevertheless, they have pushed their physical ability to new limits and are respected for becoming specialists. It is because of these specialists that the rest of the community has the chance to witness and learn. Each time a B-Girl or B-Boy raises the bar, their technique becomes referential for all the others. There are countless directions this process can go in, and at the end, they are all at the limits of known physical possibilities

The One-Hand-1990

An example of a specialist pushing the limits of the dance, which I often use in my seminars, is B-Boy Cico from Italy. He became famous for his execution of the One-Hand-1990, a move that involves spinning in a one-handed handstand. This power move is considered the king of all spins, because it is the most vertical maneuver possible in Breaking, and even a small tilt or shift in a dancer's center of gravity can have grave consequences. It also requires a lot of core strength to even hold the position stable during a spin.

In the early 1980s, the maximum number of rotations a Breaker would be able to execute in a One-Hand 1990 was three. Although a few B-Boys back then are said to have performed it for up to ten rotations (such as German from the Incredible Breakers crew in New York), these performances were never captured on film. Thus they became legends that subsequent generations would only hear about but not witness. However, by 2004, Cico and a few other Breakers worldwide had evolved the technique to such a high level that they could spin for more than twenty rounds. Indeed, today Cico still holds the record for the One-Hand 1990 of twenty-eight spins. Although he has never won a major solo Breaking competition, he has more worldwide recognition for this accomplishment than most B-Boys have received throughout the history of the dance. Given that it is such an influential power move, it is also worth providing a bit more historical context about its development.

In the early 1980s, Ken Swift of the Rock Steady Crew originally performed the move from a handstand position, in which he indicated a spin on one of his wrists. While spinning, he descended further down to his elbow, and then further down to his shoulder until the spinning motion finally resulted in a Backspin. At the time of its creation, Ken Swift considered it a futuristic move, so he called it the One-Hand 1990. Pretty soon, more dancers were taking part in its development. After some time, the main emphasis of the training in the move resulted in a spin in a one-handed handstand. In other words, the transitory notion of spiraling down to a backspin was forgotten by most B-Boys.

Today, the question remains of whether the original move Ken Swift created or the subsequently developed spin on one hand should be called the One-Hand Spin. On one side is the argument that due to the drastic change of the concept—and out of respect for Ken Swift, who also invented its terminology—the original way of performing the move should carry the name. On the other side is the reality that most Breaking practitioners today do not use Ken Swift's approach. They want to show their gratitude to him by recognizing the spark that he started, and so they keep calling the spinning version of the move the One-Hand 1990. Other spins in a handstand position clearly follow this same discourse. For example, spinning on the opposite hand in a handstand is called the Reverse 1990; spinning on both hands in a handstand is called a "2000"; and spinning on a wrist in a handstand is known as the "2001."

The Invention of the Airflare

Toward the end of the 1990s, a new power move opened a new dimension in Breaking. During this period, the California scene was developing quickly and producing new creative talents at an incredible pace. One amazing result was the creation of a move known as the Airflare. The predecessor of this technique is what we know as the Thomas Flare, from gymnastics. The big difference between the two moves lies in the angle of the body toward the floor. In the Thomas Flare, the body hangs and is swung around between the arms In the Airflare, it is executed in a diagonal stance, and is pushed rather stiffly. There is a moment in the Airflare where the body-supporting hands change from one to another, and the back starts turning toward the ground. Now, a whip from the legs and hips creates a little hop. This is the moment when one is suspended in the air (hence the move's title), and it is necessary to arrive back on the other arm to continue the move.

From 1998 until 2000, at around the same time that the One-Hand 1990 was being advanced, many of the same B-Boys worked on the innovation of this ground-breaking Airflare move. It became clear, once again, how important it is in Breaking to have friends that inhabit the same realm of ideas and possibilities, and who are willing to share information. What the Windmill was in the 1980s, including all its ensuing technical variety, is what the Airflare became in the 2000s.

It was also around this time that Breaking began to take off in South Korea. The scene in Seoul benefited from some American Koreans who imported DVDs from the United States, as well as from the development of new technologies. The Internet assured the flow of information about moves such as the Airflare and ensured quick and strong growth. The B-Boy community there grew and prospered as fast as their economy, and South Korea has dominated development in Breaking ever since.

Adjusting to the Medium

When performing a spin, one has to understand that a parquet floor reacts differently than marble, concrete, or metal surfaces. In some cases, the fabric of one's shirt can make a difference. For example, nylon or polyester is more slippery than cotton; and especially in the mid-1990s, lubricants like furniture polish, car wax, or silicone spray were used on garments and surfaces to facilitate a better spin. Similarly, a floor can be uneven, or wobbly, or very slippery. Depending on the stability of the ground, I will use my hands to support my body. If the floor is stable, I can execute my Down Rock on my fingertips to make it look light and gracious. If the floor tends to shake, or if it is slippery, I use my full hands in order not to fall down and to make sure my Down Rock is solid. Thus a Breaker needs to be able to adjust to the medium, just as a craftsman needs know how to work with different materials. Sometimes the music is faster or slower, the shoes are heavy, the pants are tight, the dance space is narrow, and so on. There are thousands of possibilities that need the same number of solutions, and each of these solutions makes way for a new version of a move.

Once one achieves mastery, a dancer can be confident in their technique, though reaching the level of mastery does not mean the learning process has reached an end. On the contrary, knowledge is infinite, and every new situation requires new solutions. The moves have to stay sharp, and the dancer needs to keep up with all the new developments to stay competitive. The learning process never stops. To stay current, one needs to continue on one's path.

Fashion and Uniformity

The easiest way to project a warrior image is through fashion. Wearing certain clothes and accessories that were once or are now worn by a seemingly powerful group of people leads other people to associate the dancer with that group. This is how combat army clothes or martial arts gear became part of the Hip Hop fashion. Looking at rap groups like Public Enemy, with their "98 Posse" in army uniforms; DJ-Gestapo, whose name speaks for itself; or the Wu-Tang Clan, who named themselves after a Hong Kong martial arts movie, underlines this fact. Generally, a person wearing loose-fitting clothes looks bigger than he is and can hide weapons in his garments. Their biggest advantage is that they leave plenty of for moves—a person has more flexibility and can obviously fight better in loose clothes than in tighter clothes. For the same reason, sports clothes were getting popular for everyday wear. The idea that you are ready to B-Boy at any time during the day is necessary for full productivity. Fashion does not just serve to categorize people based on into their specific looks but also supports the mind and body to serve them in doing their tasks. By wearing a gang vest, one would be treated like a gangster. By looking like a B-Boy, one would be challenged as a B-Boy. If the uniform did not fit the person inside there would be trouble. Anybody wearing a certain uniform just for show would easily be spotted as an impostor. That is why it is necessary to *be* and not just to *do*. Fashion in Breaking has to be a lifestyle.

TERMINOLOGY

Adopted Terms

Before the name Breaking came around, most of the moves were adapted or borrowed from other performing art forms, and the original names were often kept in naming the moves and dances based on them. The Russian Taps, for example, were borrowed from the Kasatschók, and the technique of the sweep derives from Shaolin Kung Fu. The Flare comes from gymnastics, and the name Salsa-Step or Salsa-Rock simply implies its origin.

It was only when the moves developed into something different and their origin became obscure, that the terminology changed. So, the Sweep, for example, became the Coffee Grinder or the Helicopter when done continuously, and the Kip-Up, from gymnastics, became the Pop-Up when done out of a backspin.

A Dance Called Breaking

The neologism Breaking only occurred because its creators shaped and twisted preexisting moves and influences so much that their origins could no longer be recognized as being from one dominant source. These moves were merged and cultivated into this new concept. After some time, the main stimulus for new movements came from the dance's vocabulary itself.

Here are a few obvious examples that we can see in the spins category. At first, there was a move called the Turtle, which developed into the UFO, and then into what some people called the Wolfe. These newly molded moves inspired other new moves, and a large vocabulary of moves arose.

Character

In Breaking, character is developed through cultivating a person's natural ability and talent. Indeed, there are similarities between how B-Boys and superheroes develop their powers and learn how to control them over time. For example, if someone is double-jointed or extremely flexible, this will become apparent in the dance style, and very often in the nickname the person earned. A comic book superhero with those abilities might be called "Elastigirl." In Breaking there are B-Boys like "Flex," "Rubberlegs," or "Spaghetti." Anybody who is incredibly strong might be called "Superman: The Man of Steel" in the world of superheroes. The equivalent in Breaking is "Ivan: The Urban Action Figure." If one is looking for somebody fast, one finds B-Boys like "Ken Swift" or "Kwikstep." The entire Breaking game is a meritocracy. The players are valued for their skills, and B-Boys need to live up to their names and status, which they earn in confrontational dance challenges called Battles, or in dialogical dance circles called Cyphers.

Reasons for Terms

Generally, inventors name their own creations. Sometimes a movement becomes notorious as a person's signature, and it is named after the B-Boy or the B-Girl who is known for the move. For instance, there was a B-Boy named Spider in Dynamic Rockers and a Swipe in Da Funky Style in Siberia, where both names are also the names of well-known tricks. There is a special entry into a Windmill that derives from a Back Swipe that is only called the Icey Ice, after Corey "Icey Ice" Montalvo from the New York City Breakers.

Very often, a term simply describes what is done, such as the Head Spin, the Backspin, or the Hollowback Freeze. In many other cases, names of objects that resemble the movements are used, like in the Windmill, the Helicopter, or the Turtle. Some moves were named were for the traces they leave on the floor after execution, like in the Donut or the Pretzel. Once we are aware of the concrete jungle philosophy and the fact that B-Boys and B-Girls are dancing warriors, it is not surprising to find moves with names like the Apache in Top Rock, and the Ninja Freeze in ground moves, as well as exaggerated terms like the Nazi, the Stab, or the Suicide, which emphasize that mentality.

The development of names for moves can also go together with their technical development, as the more complex and sophisticated a move becomes, the more difficult it is to describe. But if one word can describe the entire move, it facilitates the naming process. For example, let's say I find a new way to go from Swipes into Halos. Then I only need to describe this new way, and not the two moves Swipe and Halo. If the term diffuses through the community fast enough, and spreads as quickly as people can copy its technique, it becomes a new reference point, and if I document it, I have a chance to make the term universal.

However, there is always a chance that language barriers, ignorance, or a person who claims the same movement and labels it differently hinder the distribution of a term, and so it might be changed into something else. Unfortunately, this has happened quite often in the history of Breaking. The result is a general confusion in even basic terminology. The reason lies in the fact that, until recently, the culture's origins were mainly spread orally. If the originators of moves had written their ideas down during the creation process of, there would be enough evidence for a righteous name. But that did not happen often enough, and so the community will continue to debate and deal with the ambiguity of its terminology. Only by cross-referencing and comparing can we find our way through the confusing jungle of names.

Lost Knowledge

With a great influx of students globally, there is more demand for knowledge today. However, on the flip side, now anybody who thinks they know something about this art form can also teach it. There is no committee or council with the authorities to award degrees, and, as noted, we have yet to agree on terminology or a common history. Even though a lot of teachers can demonstrate a move, they might not know its original name. Sometimes, people confuse it with another move by mistake, or give it their own term to use with their students. In the worst case, they will fear losing authority by admitting they do not know the correct term. The few researchers in the field of Breaking have not been able to provide new historical facts as fast as those who have spread false and misleading half-knowledge. This has had significant consequences for the vocabulary used today.

The first generation of B-Boys outside the United States often came up with terms on their own (not knowing what the original terms were). They also often used their mother language if they didn't speak any English. The best examples are the Francophone countries, which seem to have a different name for every move that was ever invented. Swipes became *Envolé*; Footwork is *Pass-pass*; a Halo is a *Couronne*; an Airflare became a *Vrille*; Baby Mills are *Coupole allemande*,' and a Head Spin Drill is called a *baguette*. The need to tag moves, styles, and other creations gains importance when they become part of a curriculum.

In the first years after 1984 there was a huge decline in the number of B-Boys, and a lot of information was lost for many years. Nevertheless, the people who continued dancing showed great appreciation for any information they could get hold of, and they started archiving. By the time an international network emerged, around 1991, famous B-Boys had not only started teaching but were also pulling old school B-Boys out of retirement to spread their knowledge. Dance classes and workshops have been organized more frequently since 2000.

In my opinion, it is important to discover who came up with a move, as well as when and how. The history of a move gives us information about the mindset of the originator and the conceptual path during the creation process. Even if a move was invented by accident, there must have been something that led to the occurrence. The names of moves are only important so that we are able to communicate clearly with others.

People often have different opinions about the origin or interpretation of a move, and the names vary too. Sometimes an origin story turns out to be a myth. If that myth became accepted as part of the common knowledge of Breakers, it also changed their reality and thereby changed the dance. For example, before videos became widely available, one had to rely on the memories of people who and had witnessed moves, and their stories about what they had seen sometimes turned out to be too sensational. We wanted to believe what they told us, so we tried hard to get close to what we imagined they had seen. I personally remember how Emilio Sgalambro from my crew, Battle Squad, used to talk about an imaginary Windmill, in which only the head touched the ground. We worked on this move for a long time but never perfected it. The closest we got to it was touching the ground with our necks after two rounds around our heads. Then, we tipped off for the next two rounds. We called the move "Twinmill" because we could never do more than two turns around the head. The story had triggered our imagination and inspired us. Even though that move never existed, we heard from many people that Chino from Incredible Breakers spun so high and fast that it appeared as if he did that Windmill, which we had tried so hard to do. By believing the story was true, we pushed each other emotionally to practice the physically impossible. We had a shared bliss and inspired others, and a new move evolved from it.

CONCLUSION

Breaking and the acquisition of skills it requires should be regarded as a form of craftsmanship. When starting the journey of learning the style, one is advised to commence with the movements of the foundation. The most common way of to pass on knowledge is in an "each one teach one" fashion. Movements are developed and embodied through empiric testing. As a result of drilling the rhythmic rudiments, these moves get cultivated in all sorts of expressive ways. Here it is necessary to also transcend one innovation to put a personal imprint on the technique. Individuality is also necessary to express oneself freely. Therefore, that a large amount of time for research is needed must be taken into account.

Almost every technique in Breaking has its own proper name, which facilitates verbal communication. New innovations with high developmental potential can easily become part of the general expressive repertoire of the majority of B-Boys one day. Concepts like the Six-step or moves like the Windmill, Airflare, or Airchair were game changers in their day, and offer good examples of how personal concepts can become part of the broader foundation of Breaking. Whether a move will be accepted, praised, further developed, and diffused—or simply left with its originator—depends on its technical and physical difficulty and possible variations.

In the fashion realm, the uniform a Breaker wears serves their artistic purposes. To be spiritually and physically on track at all times and to try different surfaces, fabrics, lubricants, music, and occasions for performing enhance one's knowledge of how to adjust to any media. In turn, the most frequent performance media and prolific Breaking events are the dialogical Cyphers and the combative Battles, which can happen spontaneously anywhere, but also serve as theatrical spaces for audience ranging from a few bystanders to the thousands that fit inside a stadium. The general audience finds access mostly by watching organized competitions, which are battles in most cases. Numerous dance companies also perform the art of Breaking by presenting dance pieces on theatrical stages. Choreographers with postmodern ideas often reconfigure and recontextualize Breaking according to own concepts. Even though the entertainment industry, the press, and other forms of media have exploited Breaking, they also played a major role in its proliferation.

Certain moves that have existed since the early New York days are still evolving. Breaking is accessible to and can be practiced by anybody. Every person in the game has the freedom to adjust any movement to their physical abilities and interpret any move in any way that feels comfortable. That alone gives the art form the great capacity to stay current with its latest developments in society and can also serve as an inspiration for our contemporary society to look at its value system and its developmental ways.

FIGURE 3.1. Storm demonstrating the six-step sequence.

FIGURE 3.2. The Stab.

FIGURE 3.3. Baby Freeze.

FIGURE 3.4. Chair Freeze.

FIGURE 3.5. Airchair.

FIGURE 3.6. Airflare.

NOTES

1. I don't describe foundations and New York City history here as they are accounted by Ken Swift. See chapter 1 of this volume.
2. See https://www.youtube.com/results?search_query=new+york+city+breakers+inaugural+gala (accessed November , 2021).

REFERENCES

Bradford, M. (2013). "Music and Exercise: Tunes Are a Natural Steroid." *Dialogues @ RU* 9: 17–28. https://dialogues.rutgers.edu/journals/149-music-and-exercise-tunes-are-a-natural-steroid/file.

Fenske, M. (2012). "Why Does Music Motivate Us?" *Globe and* Mail, February 1. https://www.theglobeandmail.com/life/health-and-fitness/health/conditions/why-does-music-motivate-us/article542629/.

Interview Poe One on the origins of the airchair. https://www.youtube.com/watch?v=Q3BC14m_vGQ.

Robitzky, N. (2000). *Von Swipe zu Storm: Breakdance in Deutschland*. Hamburg: Backspin.

Robitzky, N. (Dir.). (2004). *Storm's Footwork Fundamentals*. Instructional DVD. USA. CypherStyles.com.

....

CHAPTER 4

CONNECTING HIP HOP HISTORY AND HERITAGE

....

E. MONCELL DURDEN

INTRODUCTION

....

IN 2004, I was on tour with Rennie Harris's production *Legends of Hip Hop*. The show featured some of America's pioneering dance crews and founding practitioners of funk and Hip Hop dance: the Rock Steady Crew, Mop-Top (of which I was a member), Don Campbell (the creator of locking), Greg "Campbellock Jr." Pope (an original member of Don's group), and the Electric Boogaloos. Our soundtrack was provided by Philadelphia DJs Razor Ramon and Evil Tracy and London's Kevin "DJ Renegade" James Gopie, along with the New York–based human beat boxer, Anointed S. During a two-week engagement at Queen Elizabeth Hall in London, I began to cogitate on the word *legend* through observations of the dancers I was on tour with, those I had looked up to for years and who had inspired me to dance professionally. I wondered, "Am I now a legend because I was in a show called *Legends of Hip Hop*? What does it mean to refer to someone as or be called a legend? Have I earned that label? And what value does it hold in the Hip Hop community? Does that value shift now that I have taken a scholarly journey in dance?"

The word *legend* is widely used as part of the global Hip Hop lexicon. For example, it is common to hear Hip Hoppers say, "She is a legend" or "That event or time period was legendary." The influential b-boy Ivan "the Urban Action Figure" has suggested that being called a legend is to "respecognize" an individual's or a group's contributions to the culture or community. In the general context of the English language, the word *legend* evokes stories like "The Legend of Sleepy Hollow," a pop-culture tale of its time, which was not based on fact, and is just a well-told mythical story. Here we run into some incongruity: the word *legend* can describe a historical figure, or it can describe a story spun through years of retelling. Legends in Hip Hop are more than just popular or well-told stories. They are human beings, each with their own truth. But what happens when their personal truth is romanticized and passed on as fact?

Pioneering b-boy and president of the Rock Steady Crew, Richard "Crazy Legs" Colon, addressed the concept of mythology in a video he posted on social media ("Hip Hop Meeting" 2016), where he suggested—after a "meeting of the minds" between Afrika Bambaataa, KRS-One, and Amad Henderson (former member of the Black Spades and member of the Zulu Nation)—that he and others may have romanticized some of the experiences of being in park jams back in the day. He was not suggesting that those events did not happen, but pointing to a discrepancy between memory and history in their recollections.

HIP HOP HERITAGE AND APPROPRIATION

History often refers to dates, times, events, and places, but *heritage* speaks to the continuum of a cultural legacy. It is the connective tissue that becomes the groove between Hip Hop's present and its forgotten past. Many researchers have agreed that Hip Hop began in the 1970s (Chang 2005; Charnas 2010). The available narratives, however, do not always address the particular influences and cultural phenomena that helped to construct and characterize the movement practices, those demonstrated throughout the Afro-diasporic continuum, making them narratives that are inadvertently contemptuous of the people who came before.

This may be a debate over semantics, but it is similar to the introduction by Nelson George to the book *Fresh*, wherein he stated, "Fresh was as important a word as groovy in the late 1960s, fresh signified something good, exciting, positive, different and new; it represented a culture that celebrates innovation and rejects blatant imitation and stagnation" (George et al. 1985, xviii). This description is no different than any of the earlier generations of African American expressive practices. The elders of Hip Hop culture are adamant about passing down knowledge, claiming that it is imperative to acknowledge those who made significant contributions to the culture. This chapter continues that work by centering my account of cultural heritage and lineage beyond the emergence of Hip Hop culture in the 1970s.

When speaking about the progenitors of Hip Hop culture, referencing these names is widely accepted: DJ Kool Herc, Afrika Bambaataa, Grandmaster Flash, and DJ Hollywood, to name a few. However, no one or two people created Hip Hop. I argue that Hip Hop is an unfolding and expansion of Afro-diasporic communication practices spanning hundreds of years. As a dance, Hip Hop is just the contemporary name given to a practice that traces back to African roots and traditions predating the Atlantic slave trade. Hip Hop is a part of this living, evergreen continuum, just as gospel, juba, ragtime, jazz, blues, rock 'n' roll, soul, and funk are all names that highlight Afro-diasporic expression. In no way is this meant to nullify early pioneers' contributions to Hip Hop. It is, rather, a critique of what gets erased when one or two names are cited as the beginning of Hip Hop's genealogy, and the lineage of styles they say influenced their movements gets downplayed. For example, early generations of b-boys often mention that they watched

Soul Train and *American Bandstand* and tried other dances before breaking, and even incorporated moves like the Charleston into their routines.

ADJUSTING THE APPROACH

How, then, do we begin to discuss Hip Hop as a continuum of cultural heritage that expands beyond the fragmentation of a subculture during a particular era? First, let me suggest that we include more dialogue that addresses the longer histories of the migration of Afro-diasporic people, exploring their thought processes, lived experiences, and cultural identities. These aspects illuminate their ways of being in the world and supply context. Let me also suggest that we stop using such terms as "urban" or "street" when referring to Hip Hop, or ideas that give a place equal or more power than is given to the people who gave the landmark any significance. These terms take away from the fact that the movements and expressions of Hip Hop are culturally rich and are based on Afro-diasporic people, their cellular memory, cultural heritage, and modes of communication. Pioneering Hip Hop practitioner Buddha Stretch has said, "Hip Hop is and will always be an urban thing" (Durden 2007). But when considering the words *urban* and *street*, it is important, particularly to the global Hip Hop community, to reinforce that they are not synonymous with "Black," nor are they specific to the United States. Urban and street merely describe an area of a city and are not specific to Black or American communities. Every country in the world has an urban community and, in the United States urban areas are not homogenous. While I understand Stretch's claim that Hip Hop is associated with the construct of "urban" in America, I would offer that Hip Hop is not an urban form but rather a cultural (re-)creation that exists from the experiences of Black and Brown people over time.

Let us imagine, for example, that Black and Latinx people no longer live in urban areas but now reside in what we know as the suburbs. Would Hip Hop still be considered an urban thing? Many famous rappers, including Run DMC and Public Enemy, came from the suburbs. The environment may contribute to the expression of self, but culture comes from people, and wherever you find the people, you will find the preservation and practice of their cultural heritage. The literal definition of *street* is simply "a public thoroughfare, usually paved, in a village, town, or city, including the sidewalk or sidewalks" (http://www.dictionary.com). However, based on conversations I have had in Japan, Poland, Sweden, Switzerland, Russia, and Ukraine, I feel that the global Hip Hop community does not fully grasp this connotation. "Street" has its own meaning among Black people in America—a meaning that does not translate properly to all international audiences.

Each community and its subcommunities can develop its own sociocultural identity, which may contrast with the national identity—especially on an international scale. Do African American phrases such as "out in them streets," "hitting the streets," "the streets are watchin/talkin," "ear to the streets" or "putting ones business in the streets," hold the same context or value systems globally? Without Hip Hop, these colloquialisms probably would not exist in other countries. Especially the phrase "out in them streets," which is clearly a grammatical phrase born out of Black American English. These phrases are not ascribed solely to the Hip Hop community. They can also be heard in multiple subcultures, such as gang culture, ball culture, battle culture, hustle culture, and so on. I wonder if the words *street* and *urban* oversimplify, or even trivialize, the very people and characteristics dancers around the world try to emulate through their language and movement practices.

THE RHYTHM IN THE RHYME

Rhymin was a fad in the days of my dad.

—Ep Rock X

Anthony "DJ Hollywood" Holloway has boasted that he was the first to start talking or rhyming on the mic, with phrases like, "If I was snow I would be cold. / If I was a jug of wine I would be old. / But since none of this is true / And I'm right here with you, / Passing the time / With the baddest jams I could find, / Without further time wasted / Or another drink tasted, / Let's go!" (quoted in Charnas, 2010, 9). Meanwhile, DJ Hollywood and others may have been rhyming over a recording as a separate but accompanying component of a prerecorded song played at local parties in their community. Yet DJ Hollywood was influenced by on-air radio personalities like Frankie Crocker, Douglas "Jocko" Henderson, and Hank Spann, who also rhymed over recordings as they introduced the records they played (Pore and Lawrence, 2014). He was also equally influenced by the Jamaican toasting of emcees such as U Roy and I Roy.

The Dozens or "playing the dozens," an insult game of verbal graffiti played by two or more people, which may be in the form of a rhyme, is another influential verbal practice. The objective is to outwit your opponent with an exceptional, prodigious succession of epithets, which many people today refer to as "mama jokes" (Wald, 2012). During the ragtime and jazz eras, you could hear musicians sing in this style, such as Trixie Smith; Lucille Bogan; and Speckled Red, in his 1929 song "The Dirty Dozen." Hep cats like Cab Calloway, Louis Armstrong, and Count Basie are also, then, predecessors of Hank Spann and DJ Hollywood. What can be discovered by injecting Hip Hop with these histories of music?

Whereas Hip Hop DJs used two turntables to keep the music going so people did not leave the dance floor, the Savoy Ballroom used two bands so that the music never stopped (Manning and Millman, 2007, 63). Jazz artists sometimes went into rhyme to set off a dance contest. Count Basie can be seen rhyming in the movie short *Air Mail Special* (1941), "Listen everybody / here's a boogie woogie solid beat / come on you dancers, on your feet / the winner gets the prize as you all know / and we pick 'em by the speed and the class they show / let's go." Award-winning playwright Charlie Russell also wrote the

1969 off-Broadway play *Five on the Black-Hand Side*, which was adapted into a movie in 1973. In the movie, Frankie Crocker lays down a series of rhymes as he portrays the numbers runner "Fun Lovin," who says, "I'm imp the dimp, the women's pimp / women fight for my delight"—which may sound familiar, as it was used in the 1979 hit rap record "Rapper's Delight."

Brooklyn emcee KC the Prince of Soul was also influenced by Hank Spann. Spann was known for saying a phrase from a 1972 Bill Withers song titled "Kissing My Love." The phrase went "Put your foot on the rock and pat your foot don't stop / put your foot on the rock" (Pore and Lawrence, 2014). In the Black church, "rock" stands for faith. In Withers's song, the word *rock* speaks to the faith in love. KC was the emcee for another Brooklyn DJ named Grandmaster Flowers. Brooklyn DJ James Gilmore takes credit for giving Grandmaster Flowers his name, and party promoter M. Morton Hall suggested that DJ Grandmaster Flash adopted the "Grandmaster" title from Grandmaster Flowers (Pore and Lawrence, 2014). Crocker and Henderson also had their own recognizable catch phrases on the air.

These examples all demonstrate a popular way of communicating. Rhyming is nothing new. Such forms of rhyming were not exclusive to musicians, either. In fact, rhyming, tone, and pitch are just some of the vocal stylizations that represent continuity in Africanist aesthetics. These linguistic practices are found in everyday speech, from the entertainer, schoolboy, working man, writer, and even preacher (Asante 1998 Holt, 1999).

CORPOREAL ORATORS

Linguist Dr. Ernie Smith once posed the following question when looking at linguistic connections among peoples of African descent: "What are the common kinds of experiences and common intersecting events of Afro-diasporic people?" Let's consider that whether we are speaking about linguistics, music, or movement, we are talking about some systematic rule of governed patterns that relate to African practices and traditions, which distinguish our expressions from those of other cultural aesthetic values here in the United States. Languages of the world do not all use the same systems or patterns of sound to shape and form thought; but is there a diasporic root structure?[1]

According to neuroscientist Daniel Levitin, "Our brains learn a kind of musical grammar that is specific to the music of our culture, just like we learn to speak the language of our culture" (Levitin 2006, 106). If our brains learn a kind of musical grammar, is it not possible that our bodies learn a kind of movement grammar, as well? Ethnomusicologist Kyra Gaunt (2006) suggests that the dexterity of Afro-diasporic people in dance is not simply innate, but that those codes are strengthened through rhythmic play: "For example, patting juba (an embodied practice of hand-clapping), finger snapping, thigh-and-chest slapping, and foot stomping accompanied by a rhymed pattern known as juba rhyming, was an improvised nineteenth-century practice shared among enslaved peoples of African descent" (21). Hand-clapping games often feature a melodic tune or chanted lyrics that resemble an approach to rapping that not only is prominent in Hip Hop culture but also has existed in African American music-making since slavery.

In the oral tradition, Patting juba shares kinship with the traditional Jola body-patting dance called the Pat-Pat, of the Casamance region of Southern Senegal. This form also gave way to a style of patting called Playing Spoons or Playing Bones, games that were played using a repeated rhythmic pattern. It is also the forerunner to *hambone*, a form of patting currently associated with the dance Campbellocking, or locking,[2] created in 1970 by Don Campbell. Although hamboning was played before the twentieth century, it was in this century that the game gained prominence through a number of hand-clapping games and songs. These games would develop rhythmic complexities after hours of playful competition (Gaunt, 2006).

In Bessie Lomax Hawes's short film *Pizza, Pizza Daddy O* (1968), young girls are on a playground in Oakland, California, and the games they are playing speak to the experiences and functional integration of adolescents who are expressing an array of emotional highs and lows. These expressions are also an act of imitating the world around them. In one game called "A Biscuit," the girls break into a dance called "The Boogaloo."[3] In other games, they demonstrate dances such as the Jerk, the Swim, the Freak, and the Mess Around. The consistency in how the literal body is positioned aligns across genres and generations, and is/ reflects the corporeal language of social value and cultural belonging in the African diaspora. More-current Hip Hop dances also incorporate elements of older dances and often resemble them (see "Social Dance Addendum" at the end of the chapter). In this way, Hip Hop continues to follow Afro-diasporic traditions.

EUROCENTRIC DANCE HIERARCHIES

Eurocentric hierarchies have taken their toll on African and African American culture. A single example of this can be found in the social backlash sparked by ragtime, a music structure derived from African drumming, Afro-Caribbean dance rhythms, and patting juba. *Ragtime* can also be described as a musical era that included specific dances known as "animal dances," which mimicked the movements of animals and carried names like Fish Tail, Snake Hips, the Chicken Scratch, and the Kangaroo Dip. All of these dances stemmed from African concepts and traditions (Stearns and Stearns 1968, 95).

These animal dances were considered "suggestive" and, according to Vernon and Irene Castle, popular dance instructors who catered to New York high society (Jonas 1935, 175), they needed to be tamed. An article in the *New York Times* circa 1914 stated that "the 'rag' [was] a dance of the most primitive peoples and of the most ancient times" (Knowles 2009, 61). The Castles viewed African dance through a Eurocentric lens, instructing their students:

> Do not wriggle the shoulders. Do not shake the hips. Do not twist the body. Do not flounce the elbows. Do not pump the arms. Do not hop—glide instead. Avoid low, fantastic and acrobatic dips. Drop the Turkey Trot, the Grizzly Bear, the Bunny Hug, etc. These dances are ugly, ungraceful, and out of fashion. (Knowles 2009, 98).

This is a prime example of Eurocentric ideals promoting the notion of a dance hierarchy. European cultural traditions that advance such values as an erect posture built on fixed positions is not more meaningful or elegant than African or Afro-Caribbean dance traditions in which dancers bend forward from the waist, and that focus on the importance of improvisation, spontaneity, call-and-response patterns, elegance, and control (Dixon Gottschild 2003; Jonas 1935; Knowles 2009; Malone 1996; Stearns and Stearns 1968). Likewise, it is important to note that, although this dance hierarchy or ethnocentrism still runs deep in the classical and traditional dance studios and universities today, the fact remains that these are just different aesthetic choices. Our sociocultural differences are just that: differences. No one cultural form is inherently more valuable than the other.

This idea of hierarchy in dance practice owes its beginnings to Western European colonizers and the lack of cultural sensitivity in our current social and dance societies. For example, Rachel Straus (2007), a lecturer in dance history at the Juilliard School, wrote in her blog that dancer Eugene Louis Facciuto, professionally known as Luigi, considered his choreographic approach to be the first codified jazz technique. I would argue that Tap, Lindy Hop, and solo jazz dances like the Charleston and Boogie Woogie are not only true jazz dances—especially the latter two forms because they were created for jazz music—but were codified in practice long before Luigi or Gus Giordano and Matt Mattox (also written about by Straus) came around.

LINEAGES OF MUSIC AND MOVES

> There was something about either what we seen through our parents that became an involvement to a different culture of dance through our heritage, and it took this music and this cultural aspect for it to be showcased all over again, but with a different interpretation.
>
> —Trac 2

At the 2006 "Unity and Respect" dance event in Boston, I sat down with Steffan "Mr. Wiggles" Clemente to discuss growing up in the Bronx in the 1970s. While we talked, I showed him some footage of the performance of the dance trio the Third Generation on the *Mike Douglas Show*, circa 1974. In it, seventeen-year-old Terry Criner, nineteen-year-old Cindy Notz, and twenty-one-year-old Ivery Wheeler performed an array of tap steps, splits, and flips that were reminiscent of the Four Step Brothers and Tip, Tap & Toe, two amazing Tap acts from the 1940s. In fact, the group ended their performance with Criner displaying some of his best flash steps: he slides across the top of an oval stage, lands on the floor in a split, then jumps up on the platform to complete a few two-legged pirouettes, followed by jumping straddle splits and then rotating splits on the floor. Criner then lands on his back, grabs his ankles, rocks back onto his head, and, with only his feet and head on the floor, hops around on the platform. He then does a kip-up to a squat to demonstrate a few kick-outs into two legged swipes, then two half-rotating head turns, followed by two front flips using his head instead of his hands. To end, Criner does a front tuck off the platform into another split, where Notz and Wheeler join him. Mr. Wiggles reacted with such joy, all he could say was, "That's it, that's it. That's how the cats did the swipes."[4]

Ken Swift, who is recognized by many b-boys and b-girls as the quintessential b-boy, mentioned that on the way to developing or innovating what became known as breaking, youth in his community were inspired by gymnastics and martial arts films: "The Nuyorican kids of the South Bronx saw what their parents were dancing."[5] Dance is deeply ingrained in the cultural identity of Afro-Caribbean people. Dances like Rumba, Samba, Salsa, Mambo, and Merengue were born and practiced among Afro-Caribbean people, and their aesthetics were also injected into breaking. What I learned as an open Indian Step, which is similar to a basic Cuban Rumba performed with a bounce, is a popular step with b-boys. Movements from the early twentieth-century jazz movement are also found in Breaking and Hip Hop dances, suggesting the possibility that previously innovated dance steps culminate in multiple dance forms within Hip Hop culture.

I use these two distinct terms, *Breaking* and *Hip Hop*, because—although I recognize that breaking was Hip Hop's first dance—these forms carry two different legacies. Breaking emerged during Hip Hop's infant stages and was danced to funk, soul, and electronic and rock music of the 1960s and 1970s. It relies heavily on the "break" of the music, which is an important aspect of the dance because it gives reason and information to the dancer concerning how to execute certain movements. Most Hip Hoppers usually refer to this musical era as the funk and soul period. In most cases, b-boys and b-girls preferred dancing to the breaks of older records over dancing to Hip Hop songs. Rock Steady Crew's Crazy Legs has stated, "I like the records before they were sampled," and that "there aren't a lot of records within the Hip Hop world that cater to a b-boy."[6]

LOCKING AND THE MUSIC BUSINESS

The lineage of locking moves was informed by relationships built in the music business. Charles "Cholly" Atkins, of the classic tap act Coles and Atkins, was a choreographer and director at Motown Records, where he used to work with acts like Gladys Knight and the Pips, Smokey Robinson and the Miracles, and the Temptations. As described by Gladys Knight, "Atkins was our everything . . . He taught us how to walk onstage, how to walk offstage, how to move" (Atkins and Malone 2001). The Jacksons were also signed to Motown when they went on the *Ed Sullivan Show* and performed the Drop Charleston, as well as other old dances like the Boogaloo, the Camel Walk, and the Hitch-Hike. The latter inspired Greg "Campbellock Jr." Pope to create a Hitch-Hike variation in locking.[7] Atkins said that the Jackson Five "used to stand in the wings during performances, and at Motown they would sit on the stairs and watch me rehearse the other groups" (Atkins and Malone 2001, 171). Besides Atkins, the Jacksons learned dance steps by watching famous acts like James Brown and Jackie Wilson. The importance of these entertainers, and the fact that Atkins was teaching dances from the 1920s, 1930s, and 1940s to these popular groups, meant that young people would surely copy what they saw their favorite groups doing, and maybe create their own variations to keep the continuum alive. Indeed, Frank Rojas, a Bronx native who was a freestyle and hustle dancer in the 1970s, suggests that the Jackson Five's performance on the Ed Sullivan show December 14, 1969 probably had an impact on their ideas for new steps to stylize.

As an example of the music industry's influence on dance, we can also look at James Brown's famous "James Brown" dance step, which is a combination of the Mashed Potato and the Slop (popular dances from the 1960s, derived from the Charleston and the Apple Jack of the 1940s). Brown's 1968 song "There Was a Time" mentions some of the dances he did throughout his life: the Mashed Potato, the Jerk, the Boogaloo, and the Camel Walk. Brown is noted as a prominent influence on Hip Hop culture, through both his music and dancing. In fact, in 1988 rap duo Super Lover Cee and Casanova Rud paid homage to Brown by recording the song "Do the James," which was a staple dance among Hip Hoppers.

The Camel Walk has a very interesting history of making its mark on Hip Hop dance, particularly in locking. The Camel Walk is a ragtime animal dance said to have been popularized in the late 1890s, during the Vaudeville era, that was initially created by African American kids and danced by college students and flappers during the early jazz period (Knowles 2009; Stearns and Stearns 1968). The Camel Walk can be characterized as a kind of flat-footed, traveling hop step. The earliest record we have of this step on film was shot by Thomas Edison in 1894 (see Hill 2010, 23), when he filmed Joe Rastus, Denny Tolliver, and Walter Wilkins of the Passing Show. The beginning of the clip shows Rastus doing the aforementioned traveling hop step. Dance scholar Ama (Sheron) Wray suggests that the Camel Walk has its origins in the Ghanaian people of the Republic of Ghana, in their traditional dance called the Adowa.

In 1924 the song of choice to dance the Camel Walk to was "See, See Rider" by Ma Rainey, known as the Mother of the Blues.[8] The step had a variation that called for placing the straight leg behind the bent leg as you walked forward. In 1957, rhythm and blues singer Chuck Willis had a number one hit on the R & B chart with his remake of "See, See Rider," for which he changed the lyrics and the title to "C.C. Rider." Black teenagers at the time were still doing the Camel Walk, adding a sustained movement by dragging one of their legs and renaming it the Camel Walk Stroll, or simply the Stroll. Recognizing that this dance did not have a particular song associated with it, American radio and television personality Dick Clark reached out to songwriters Clyde Otis and Nancy Lee to write a song by the same name for the Canadian group the Diamonds to record. This song and the Stroll dance were captured on a local teen show in Idaho in 1958. Thirteen years later, when thinking about a signature movement for his dancers, Don Cornelius remembered the Stroll from his teenage years and adopted its formation, renaming it the Soul Train Line (Broven 2009, 417–419).

This account of the evolution of the Camel Walk is important because it shows how dancers in Hip Hop pull material from the dances and music that preceded them. As a consequence, they are able to develop or to innovate based on those steps to create new forms. This allows an influx of new vocabulary, which is then used as the backbone of the dance's development. In short, Hip Hop in its entirety has a lineage that, if acknowledged, proves its long-standing roots. This signifies that the dance itself is a continuum of movements, vocabulary, and music that are part of a deep cultural structure.

CULTURAL IDENTITY AND MIGRATION: MOP-TOPS IN JAPAN

> Dance is a sort of hand-me-down art form; you learn it from someone else.
> —Sammy Davis Jr.

As discussed, many dances of the current Hip Hop generation have a direct lineage to dances dating further back, and many of these can be traced back even further, to the West Indies, Europe, Africa, and perhaps even to the Indigenous peoples of the Americas. Diffusion of information, or, in our case, expression, can be direct or indirect. We live in a time when cultural and subcultural expressions are diffused through digital media, so we no longer have to wait for an individual or group to bring a dance to our community to access it. This can be dangerous to the authenticity of a dance because meanings and messages may get lost in translation without a practitioner there to properly communicate the physical and historical context of a form.

Elite Force Crew offers an example of the rise of Hip Hop's international influence, and the connection it has to the learning of Hip Hop expression by indirect diffusion. In 1992 the Brooklyn dance group Elite Force Crew (then known as Mop-Top) was featured in a PBS documentary directed by Diane Martel titled, *Reck n' Shop Live from Brooklyn*. Mop-Top stands for **M**otivated **O**n **P**recision **T**owards **O**utstanding **P**erformance and was a reference to the "locks" or "dreadlocks" hairstyle that most of the members in the group wore. In the documentary, which also featured the extended Mop-Top dancers "Mystidious Misfits," the group's dancing abilities and social and environmental background are captured in footage of them performing in a studio, on a playground, in front of their houses, and in a circle at a club. Other segments focused on their social and environmental status, camaraderie, and dialogue, giving attention to their sense of fashion, which at the time was represented by their affinity for Polo and Guess clothing. These televised images of Hip Hop culture influenced dancers in Japan to emulate the style and movements of dancers from New York, in particular.

In 1994, because of the popularity of Hip Hop, Elite Force was invited to judge and perform at Dance Delight, one of Japan's largest streetdance events. However, Dance Delight was not Japan's first or only Hip Hop dance influence. Other groups who had previously made an impact on the country included Rock Steady Crew, Electric Boogaloos, and the Soul Train Dancers. Japanese dancers emulated the dance styles, gestures, hairstyles, jargon, and clothing of these groups. Some would even go to hair salons to get special perms so that their hair could lock—a process that would take up to four or five hours. Adopting clothing styles is one thing; but changing one's hairstyle to emulate a different cultural group may spark serious debate about cultural appropriation in a place like Japan. According to Kozo Okumura, Japanese-born film director of the documentary *Far East Coast in the House* (1998), people in Japan do not usually have to consider ethnic awareness because Japanese society is almost completely racially homogeneous. The influence of Elite Force Crew on dance communities in Japan, Canada, California, and France led to their dance style being called Nu-Style, short for New York Style. Nu-style or "freestyle" Hip Hop, as described by Elite Force Crew, would mix all the dance forms under the Hip Hop umbrella, drawing on influences from the local environment and, of course, being moved by music.

Stretch, one of the original dancers of Elite Force Crew, describes how, during the group's first trip to Japan,[9] two members of the crew were standing outside a convenience store when they noticed a group of Japanese kids walking toward them. The kids were dressed in baggy jeans, sneakers, Timberland boots, hoodies, and baseball caps—the typical and popular fashion of the crew's Brooklyn neighborhood at the time. What was unsettling, however, was the way these kids were walking with a *ditty bop* (or "strolling with a dip in one's walk," as they say) and had a type of dead stare on their faces based on the neighborhood "survival" codes of Brooklyn. Ditty bop and this and facial expression helped Brooklynites to navigate the calamitous streets that made crew members feel the need to be prepared to defend themselves at all times. As the account goes, however, when the group of kids reached the crew members, they bowed and extended their hands in the Japanese greeting, "Stretch-son, Hajimemashite, Yoroshiku onegai shimasu," which means "how do you do" or "nice to meet you." What the Japanese kids saw in Martel's documentary was based solely on an aesthetic perception of how they felt they should act, dress, walk, and what their overall demeanor should be. What they did not understand was the neighborhood and the surrounding environmental influences in which one is raised (Schloss 2009). None of the concepts of Hip Hop are based on a single monolithic approach.

CONCLUSION

History would be an excellent thing if only it were true.
                                        —Leo Nikolaevich Tolstoy

Hip Hop is the continuum of African and Afro-Caribbean aesthetics in transition. It is rooted in those concepts and traditions, with some European influences. Hip Hop represents not only an intangible cultural heritage, but also how it has grown and continues to grow into a multicultural expression, teaching and liberating a global subculture. It also challenges and encourages the exploration of aesthetic values and concepts of communication that have existed for hundreds of years among African, Afro-diasporic, and Indigenous peoples of these lands we call North and South America.

When I speak about Hip Hop dance, I define it from a cultural base, as something that was conceived out of African and Afro-diasporic experiences and then recontextualized, redefined, inspired, and born in American economic, sociopolitical, and environmental circumstances. By understanding Hip Hop culture in its entirety and taking into account the people and the individual elements of these forms, we can clearly see that the importance of vocabulary is not just as a teaching tool. It is important to note that names add substance and resources to connection and expression. They define intrinsic values that speak to time, space, and place. The accurate use of Hip Hop dance names, concepts, and movement principles may seem inconsequential to an outsider, but correct comprehension of the movement grammar holds great meaning to practitioners. Word association is part of our learning process—in language, in dance, and in life. These descriptors connect the dancer to social and environmental time periods involving community and heritage. The vocabulary grounds them in authentic terminology and solidifies their ability to pass down knowledge as practitioners or teachers, while acknowledging the people, thoughts, and concepts the dancers represent.

I suggest that it might be calamitous to the cultural lineage and heritage of its practitioners when we give the wrong kind of power to "spaces" and "places" where Hip Hop was experienced, like park jams, clubs, or, more specifically, the building at 1520 Sedgwick Ave in the Bronx, the suggested birthplace of Hip Hop. These locations are part of the history of Hip Hop, not its heritage. Hip Hop may have been born in the Bronx, but it was conceived of through the mixing of African, Caribbean, and Indigenous peoples of North and South America. It was also mixed and influenced by European people hundreds of years earlier. Born out of the deconstruction and reconstruction of cultural retention, for example, much of the Latin music we hear today has its origins in Cuba, Haiti, the Dominican Republic, and Brazil, blending African drums with Spanish guitars to create a variety of music and dances. The "Black" lexicon of today consists of intrusions, reflexivity, or, more properly, "transfer phenomena" in African speech. Meaning that Africans changed much of their lexicon when they learned

Spanish, French, or English words, without changing their African known grammatical, morphological, or syntactical rules (Rickford 1999; Smitherman 1977).

At some point you, they, we have to repudiate the illusion of hierarchy in dance and illuminate our sociocultural differences. Even if we do not agree with the concepts and principles of a culture, we must learn to appreciate the concepts that society, culture, and even subculture find essentially valuable. It is not that one has to discard the opinions and approaches of one traditional value over another; rather, we must illuminate our social and cultural diversity, appreciating those values that diverge from our own beliefs.

Hip Hop is a continuum of the organic phrasing of the African diaspora. It is the stylization, dancing, music, lingo, gestures, call-and-response patterns, improvisations, polyrhythms, and so on, that are deeply rooted in our characteristics of behavior and responsible for creating, not simply a move, but a whole movement grammar and cultural identity. And this identity is not bound by time and geography, nor is it simply a surface structure for others to claim. We are the manifestation of our ancestors. We stand on their shoulders, and we must continue to honor them and our lived experience and manage our cultural heritage—because as the legend becomes fact, others will indoctrinate the legend.

SOCIAL DANCE ADDENDUM

Parallel steps from jazz and Hip Hop vocabulary:

The *Twist* of the 1960s, first performed by Hank Ballard's background singers, the Midnighters, is said to have been influenced by a similar step in Lindy Hop called the Twist Step, also sometimes referred to as the Harlem Twist. It is thought to have been invented by dancers George "Twist Mouth" Ganaway and Edith Mathews in the 1930s. The Hip Hop dance Walk It Out is nothing more than the Twist in a forward motion. The Twist was also one of the influences for Sam "Boogaloo Sam" Solomon's "Hip Rolls" in the dance forms of Popping and Boogaloo. It is also behind such steps as the Twist-o-Flex.

The *Jerk* from the 1960s finds roots in the Jamaican Ska dance Rocksteady. The Jerk was also an influence for Sam's arm placements in Popping. And it also gave birth to the American dance the Monkey.

The *Chicken Scratch* of 1912 is seen in the Hip Hop dance known as the Jerry Lewis of the 1980s.

The *Drop Charleston* from the 1930s is the same as the Charlie Rock in breaking in the 1970s. The influence of the Latino communities changed the quarter notes from 1-2-3-4 to a more Latin triple step of 1 2-3, 5-6-7 as in Salsa/Mambo and Cha Cha Cha.

The *Scissor Kick Charleston*, circa the 1930s, is the same as the Party Machine dance, circa 1980, and the Sponge Bob. The Scissor Kick and Party Machine focus on the step kicking away from the body, while the Sponge Bob, circa 2000, emphasizes flexing the kicking leg instead of extending it.

The 2007 *Rack Daddy* of the American South is the same as the Shorty George step of the 1930s.

Much of *Top Rockin'* in breaking is directly from Salsa, Samba, Merengue, Rhumba, Hustle dance, other Latin dances, and the Lindy Hop.

Parts of steps in the *Irish Hornpipe* are the same as the 1980s Roger Rabbit (R.R.). The Hornpipe is pulled up and tight, whereas the R.R. is slightly down and stretched out. Many Irish Jigs, Hornpipes, and Reels are also found in original social jazz-dance steps, with just a change in the aesthetic and movement principles.

The dance *Milking the Cow* from early 1918 can be seen in the Rocksteady of 1971.

The *Backslide* has its lineage in a step called the Essence, which was popular during the height of Minstrelsy in the 1840s. In the 1940s it was a popular tap step known as the Get Off, also referred to as the Buzz. Michael Jackson first saw the movement in 1978 on *Soul Train*, performed by Jeffrey Daniels. Jackson then learned the step from Gerome "Casper" Candidate, a friend of Daniels. Tap dancer Bill Bailey can be seen doing the step in "Show Time at the Apollo" in the 1950s and in the 1943 movie *Cabin in the Sky*.

The *Charleston Basic* was the influence for the Kid n' Play Kickstep of the 1980s. Kid n' Play's version was originally called the Funky Charleston, credited to one of their dancers named Nadine "Hi-Hat" Ruffin. There are over ten different variations of the Charleston, a step believed to have reached North America by way of the Middle Passage, having roots in a West African dance called Yankadi from the Republic of Guinea. Of course, other African countries have similar dance steps that may play a role in the genealogy of this step. Dancers Asadata Dafora from Sierra Leone and Geoffrey Holder from Trinidad, West Indies, who were interviewed by scholars Marshall Stearns and Jean Stearns (1968) for their book *Jazz Dance: The Story of American Vernacular Dance*, mention that the Charleston was similar to an Obolo Dance of the Ibo tribe in West Africa and the King Sailor dance in Trinidad.

The *Hitch-Hike* from 1962 was modified by Greg "Campbellock Jr." Pope and is performed in the 1970s dance form of locking.

Patting Juba, also known as Hambone, is still practiced today in locking. Patting Juba has its roots in the Pat Pat dance of the Jola people in Southern Senegal.

The *Boogaloo* movement of Sam Solomon is equal to the eccentric movement of Earl "Snake Hips" Tucker, who danced from the 1930s to the 1940s.

The *Samba* shows up in the Hip Hop dance Heel Toe.

The *Gaze Afar* of the 1930s shows up as the Popeye in the 1960s and as the Seek in locking.

The *Shimmy* from the early twentieth century is the same as the Shimmy in locking, and in Hip Hop, it is related to the Harlem Shake (it is important to note that I am speaking of the real Harlem shake dance, not the song that went viral with people dressed in costume flailing about). Dafora said the American shimmy was the beginning of the Shika dance of Nigeria. This step began in the shoulders and moved down the body until the whole body was shaking. After Dafora demonstrated it, New York jazz dancers Al Minns and Leon James commented, "You're doing our Shake Dance!" In Hip Hop, we refer to this movement as a *vibration*.

The *Wing* step in House is the same as one of the many wing steps in Tap.

The *Farmer* in House is said to come from the Hip Hop dance East Coast Stomp, which can be seen in the instructional DVD "The Hip Hop House Dance Classic" by Sekou Heru.

The *Cakewalk*, a prominent African American dance performed from 1850 to the 1940s, can still be seen on American football fields when a majorette prances across the field. It can also be seen in the Harlem Lite Feet dance step Chicken Noodle Soup and in the Chicago dance known as Footwork.

Tutting has a lineage in traditional Cambodian dances like Apsara or Khmer, and is also influenced by the God Kahli; hieroglyphs; and, for some, the Bugs Bunny cartoon "Ickity Ackity Oop," which the animators based on real Hindu movements.

The *Tacky Annie*, a step that is part of the Shim Sham created by Lenard Reed and Willie Bryant in 1927, was inspired by Jack Wiggins's step called the Pull It. The movement structure of the Tacky Annie is the same as the 1960s popular dance called the Dog and the 2015 Nae Nae.

The *Bop* dance, as seen in the Whip Nae Nae, can be seen in the 1980s Pac-Man and even back to the early 1900s, when it was called the Uncle Willie.

Motown artists the Temptations helped to popularize a step called the Skate in the 1960s, which they learned from Cholly Atkins, who took it from a movement in the Shim Sham known as the Pushes.

NOTES

1. Ernie Smith, personal interview, 2014.
2. *Locking* is a direct but fluid movement based on 1970s social dances such as the robot shuffle, rocksteady, and the breakdown. It uses gestures such as looks, hand-slaps, points, and the Lock, a type of pause or momentary freeze in an asymmetrical posture standing on one straight leg and one bent leg, with the ribcage forward over the waist, shoulders down and arms extended forward in a slight curve and the palms facing each other.
3. The *Boogaloo*, or *bugalu*, is a music made popular by Latin artists Joe Bataan, Johnny Colon, and others. There is also a popular African American dance performed to the song "Boogaloo Down Broadway" by the Fabulous Johnny C, as well as by the dancing of James Brown (Kempton 2003). *We Like It Like That*, dir. Mathew Ramirez Warren, Prod. Mathew Ramirez Warren and Elena Martinez, 2015.
4. Mr. Wiggles, personnel interview, 2006.
5. *From Mambo to Hip Hop*, documentary, 2006.
6. B-boy YNOT, interview, 2005.
7. Greg Pope, personal interview, 2005.
8. Frankie Manning, personal interview, October 2, 2002.
9. personal interview, July 26, 2006.

REFERENCES

Atkins, C., and Malone, J. (2001). *Class Act: The Jazz Life of Choreographer Cholly Atkins.* New York: Columbia University Press.

Broven, J. (2009). *Record Makers and Breakers: Voices of the Independent Rock 'n' Roll Pioneers.* Urbana: University of Illinois Press.

Chang, J. (2005). *Can't Stop Won't Stop: A History of the Hip-Hop Generation.* New York: St. Martin's Press.

Charnas, D. (2010). *The Big Payback: The History of the Business of Hip Hop.* New York: New American Library.

Dixon Gottschild, B. (2003). *The Black Dancing Body: A Geography from Coon to Cool.* New York: Palgrave Macmillan.

Durden, E. M., dir. (2007) *Everything Remains Raw.*

Eliot, L. (1999). *What's Going On in There? How the Brain and Mind Develop in the First Five Years of Life.* New York: Bantam Books.

Gaunt, K. D. (2006). *The Games Black Girls Play: Learning the Ropes from Double-Dutch to Hip-Hop.* New York: New York University Press.

George, N., Banes, S., Flinker, S., and Romanowski, P. (1985). *Fresh: Hip Hop Don't Stop.* New York: Random House.

Hill, C. V. (2010). *Tap Dancing America: A Cultural History.* New York: Oxford University Press.

Holt, G. S. (1999). "Stylin' Outta the Black Pulpit." In *Signifyin(g), Sanctifyin', & Slam Dunking: A Reader in African American Expressive Culture,* edited by G. D. Caponi, 331–347. Amherst: University of Massachusetts Press.

Jonas, G. (1935). *Dancing.* New York: Abrams.

Kempton, A. (2003). *Boogaloo: The Quintessence of American Popular Music.* New York: Pantheon.

Knowles, M. (2009). *The Wicked Waltz and Other Scandalous Dances: Outrage at Couple Dancing in the 19th and Early 20th Centuries.* Jefferson, NC: McFarland.

Lane, L. (1946). *How to Become a Comedian.* London: Frederick Muller.

Levitin, D. J. (2006). *This Is Your Brain on Music: The Science of a Human Obsession.* New York: Penguin.

Malone, J. (1996). *Steppin' on the Blues: The Visible Rhythms of African American Dance.* Urbana: University of Illinois Press.

Manning, F., and Millman, C. R. (2007). *Frankie Manning: Ambassador of Lindy Hop.* Philadelphia: Temple University Press.

Pore, H., and Lawrence, R. (2014). "Founding Fathers: The Untold Story of Hip Hop-Narrated by Chuck D." Video documentary, April 7. YouTube. https://youtu.be/1G13bRoBo-8.

Rickford, J. R. (1999). *African American Vernacular English: Features, Evolution, Educational Implications.* Malden, MA: Blackwell.

Roach, J. R. (1996). *Cities of the Dead: Circum-Atlantic Performance.* New York: Columbia University Press.

Schloss, J. G. (2009). *Foundation: B-Boys, B-Girls and Hip-Hop Culture in New York.* New York: Oxford University Press.

Smitherman, G. (1977). *Talkin and Testifyin: The Language of Black America.* Boston: Houghton Mifflin.

Stearns, M. W., and Stearns, J. (1968). *Jazz Dance: The Story of American Vernacular Dance.* New York: Macmillan.

Straus, R. (2007). "Luigi, Gus Giordano, and Matt Mattox: Jazz Masters." *Rachel Straus* (blog), July 7. http://rachelstraus.com/2007/07/luigi-gus-giordano-and-matt-mattox-jazz-masters/.

Thompson, R. F. (1984). *Flash of the Spirit.* New York: Vintage Books.

Sam Sam Music. (2012). "Tielman Brothers: Rollin Rock (Best Rock 'n Roll/ Indo Rock) Live TV Show 1960." September 8. YouTube https://www.youtube.com/watch?v=muKkVufg kAE&feature=youtu.be.

"Hip Hop Meeting of the Minds with KRS One Crazy Legs and Afrika Bambaataa." (2016). YouTube, January 6. https://www.youtube.com/watch?v=X4min5ePFHQ&feature=youtu.be.

Wald, E. 2012. *The Dozens: A History of Rap's Mama.* New York: Oxford University Press.

Welsh-Asante, K. (1998). *African Dance: An Artistic, Historical, and Philosophical Inquiry.* Trenton, NJ: Africa World Press.

CHAPTER 5

....

KUNG FU FANDOM

*B-Boys and the Grindhouse Distribution
of Kung Fu Films*

....

ERIC PELLERIN

INTRODUCTION

....

JOSEPH Schloss (2009) has speculated that the series Black Belt Theater might be "the single most influential unacknowledged influence on New York City's Hip Hop culture" (161). But instead of focusing on a TV series, I will address some of the specifics of kung fu films, their distribution and reception in Breaking culture. From 1973 until approximately 1984, kung fu films were a regular staple of New York City's Times Square grindhouse circuit, and the predominant audience for these films was young African American and Latinx males (Desser 2000, 25).

After kung fu cinema's highly successful first year of importation, in 1973, the films continued to be shown on grindhouse screens throughout New York, oftentimes sharing the bill with other exploitation genres. B-boys would make the journey to Times Square to watch kung fu films, and second-generation b-boys that I interviewed were inspired to incorporate some of the kung fu movements they'd seen on the screen into their dance. The b-boys were especially attracted to the exciting choreography and dynamic physical action of kung fu because it was so close to what they were already doing in their dance. The place where they watched the films also had its charms in framing that experience.

The kung fu film as a genre celebrates the extraordinary physical feats of the actors, showcasing a complex choreography that has been carefully designed for the screen. Even more than the swordplay film, the kung fu film centers on displays of the human body in action, and inspires viewers to have an actual physical response to the action they have witnessed on the screen. In *Kung Fu Cult Masters*, Leon Hunt (2003) writes: "At one level, the kung fu film can be seen as what Steven Shaviro (1993) and

Linda Williams (1991) call a 'body genre' (although neither one include it as one) along-side pornography, horror and the 'weepie'" (2). Positioning the kung fu film as a body genre sets up an understanding of its dynamic physicality and visceral impact on the audience. "Visceral" relates to the nervous system, and although I don't explore it fully in this chapter, I suspect affect theory might provide even more specificity to describe an audience's responses to Hip Hop performances.[1] Likewise, Stephen Teo (2013) makes the connection to body genres in his essay "The Female Kung Fu Chop," stating that he believes "this is 'real history' that is communicated through bodies in a certain fashion—and, in my opinion, the martial arts cinema is really one of the great 'body genres' in world cinema" (84). Although one could easily suppose that body genre implies a body-mind split or, more accurately, a limbs-brain split, I would suggest that the body genre read indicates the possibility of incorporating listening practices and their impacts on the body as well. The context of kung fu films' distribution and reception gives shape to the meanings of the films, for a general audience as well as for the b-boys who are the focus of this chapter.

I start from the premise that kung fu films are the most logical addition to Williams's (1991) three body genres of *melodrama*, *horror*, and *pornography*. The logic is twofold. First, the emphasis in kung fu films on the spectacle of the human body and their power to elicit a physical response to the action in the viewer are related. Much has been made of neuroscience studies of mirror neurons, especially in regard to dance. I don't address that here, but I do recognize that the spectacle presented in these films addresses the human body and movement, where temporality and gravity are brought to fantastic heights. The second reason is that when kung fu films were distributed in the United States, they shared the bill with two of Williams's focus genres, horror and pornography, in the grindhouse theaters of inner cities like the ones on New York City's 42nd Street, in double and triple features (Chute 2003, 5; RZA and Norris 2005, 58–60). Kung fu films were billed with horror or pornography because their themes of violence and revenge fitted with the transgressive nature of that material, exploiting the desires of audiences to experience actions and events that were outside socially accepted norms. The grindhouse theaters on 42nd Street focused on exploitation films because they were cheap to acquire, and without a recognizable Hollywood star or expensive production values, these films focused on violence and sex to sell tickets (Church 2011, 20–22). Again, this is a whole-body experience of watching films in these contexts, from the sticky seats to the quips from the crowd.

Studying a dance culture, and interviewing influential b-boys directly impacted by their kung fu fandom, provides a unique case study for both film and dance studies. In this chapter, I will discuss the marketing of films through trailers, and the impact this also had for the reception of the films among subaltern audiences who create art. For a brief period in 1973, Hong Kong martial arts films actually outsold Hollywood films at the box office (Desser 2000). This did not last, but kung fu films were still distributed in the grindhouse circuits until the mid 1980s, when the rise of home video was one of the factors that led to the eventual demise of grindhouse theaters (Church 2011, 22).

Later in the chapter, I will describe how Ken Swift and I were invited to Hong Kong when the Shaw Brothers kung fu films were digitally remastered. In doing so, I highlight b-boy fandom of kung fu films and demonstrate how the embodied knowledge transmitted through these films contributed to cross-cultural affinities and a symbiosis between kung fu in cinema and the cinematic aesthetics of Hip Hop culture. Like Paul Willis's (1978) early subcultural studies of 1950s British motorbike boys, some b-boys express a preference for music that is exciting and encourages speed, like a car chase. Similarly, the sound effects of kung fu films captured the speed and comedy of young b-boys out on the streets, playing at manhood.

VISCERAL BODILY RESPONSES TO KUNG FU FILMS

For an online article I wrote, "Challenge of the B-Boy Masters" (Pellerin 2003), I interviewed members of New York City b-boy crews, and asked them about their experience watching kung fu films, and the influence that those films had on their dancing. As a practitioner myself, I had already seen connections because of what dancers talked about, but I wanted more on their perspective. The b-boys I interviewed included Ken Swift from Rock Steady Crew, Lil' Lep from Rock Steady Crew and the New York City Breakers, Trac 2 from Starchild La Rock, KWON from Swift Kids, and Ras AKA Ray from Floormasters Dancers (Brooklyn). They all noted the similarities between kung fu and breaking (see Pellerin 2003).

Kung fu films provided inspiration for the creation of new dance moves because the moves were so similar to kung fu moves to begin with. Ras AKA Ray from the Floormasters Dancers (Brooklyn) said, "Kung fu played a part in my life. You see the styles they had, they spin on their heads, like b-boying, they had windmills, they were doing the helicopter, which is the swipe. We looked at these things, we used it as dance" (Pellerin 2003, 3). KWON from Swift Kids explained the influence these moves had on breaking, "As far as the martial arts goes, that gave a lot of b-boys ideas as far as doing things on the floor and expanding their ideas for movement and bringing out their character" (Pellerin 2003, 2). Kung fu films and b-boying have a lot of parallels, and part of their popularity with the b-boys is that the dancers had already been doing movements in their dance that were very similar to the movements in kung fu films, before they had even seen any of the movies. This gave the b-boys a unique position in being able to identify with the action they saw on the screen, and contributed to their fandom of the films.

Kung fu films elicited visceral reactions, not only for dancers, but for many of the people watching the films. It's the presentation of the body in the film that binds us as spectators, inspiring artists and everyday audience members to leave the theater feeling pumped up. Influential film scholar, David Bordwell (2000) does not claim to be moved to imitate the action on screen the way b-boys like Ken Swift are, but he has talked about feeling a bodily response to Hong Kong films:

> When this quality is captured in vigorous, strictly patterned movement, in nicely judged framings and crackling cutting, with overwhelming music and sound effects, you can feel yourself tensing and twitching to the rhythms of the fight. (8)

Bordwell (1998) has written about the Hong Kong martial arts film and its relation to the theories of early filmmaker Sergei Eisenstein. Bordwell (2000) explains that Eisenstein believed that actors, through their gestures, could cause the spectator to imitate the action seen on screen, although on a smaller scale (244). Here, he couldn't have predicted that b-boys would take this up on a larger-than-life scale, enhanced by their fantasies of a kung fu lifestyle. In "Aesthetics in Action," Bordwell (1998) examines how Hong Kong filmmakers constructed their films through an analysis of editing and other formal techniques. He ties the success of Hong Kong films to their ability to make the audience feel something through an engagement of the senses while watching them. He says that many Hong Kong filmmakers intended to make the audience, quoting Yuen Wo Ping, "feel the blow" (Bordwell 1998, 410). This refers to the ability of a kung fu film's action design to create a bodily reaction in the viewer, however diminished it might be from the original action portrayed on screen. Bordwell explains how Hong Kong filmmakers made this reaction possible through pro-filmic performances by the actors, the framing of shots, and editing.

Bordwell's examination of Eisenstein's theories of expressive movement in relation to the Hong Kong martial arts film is also related to Linda Williams's (1991) body genres. In addition to celebrating the excess of the human body, she says, "what may especially mark these body genres as low is the perception that the body of the spectator is caught up in an almost involuntary mimicry of the emotion or sensation of the body on the screen" (4). As I have suggested so far, Kung fu films can go beyond producing the smaller bodily response of muscles twitching, as Bordwell has described, to performance strategies of dancers (watching the films for ideas and studying the moves) and, later, in the case of the New York City b-boys, appropriation of certain pedagogical principles that are as much about disciplining the mind as they are a bodily response.

Joseph Schloss (2009) suggests that b-boys such as Alien Ness have a whole approach to pedagogy rooted in their fandom of kung fu films. Frances Gateward (2009) also suggests that many moves in breaking were inspired by kung fu movements, noting the important connection with kung fu films and early Hip Hop where a practitioner like a DJ would take the title of "Grandmaster" (63), the most prominent example being the pioneering DJ Grandmaster Flash. This is further compounded by Ken Swift, who describes, in the documentary *Iron Fists and Kung Fu Kicks* (Ou 2019), how the b-boys were calling themselves Grandmasters, living out their childhood fantasies and fandom.

RENDERING THE SOUND OF KUNG FU

The sound design of kung fu films is just as important to the viewer's experience as the visual images are, and the Shaw Brothers studio created their own sound design for each film, in house. I can see Michel Chion's concept of sound "rendering" specifically in the kung fu films made by the Shaw Brothers studio (see Chion 1994). The kung fu films made by the Shaw Brothers studio from 1972 to 1985 all have a unified look and sound that is the product of the vertically integrated studio system they employed, based on the old Hollywood studios, such as Warner Bros. The Shaw Brothers controlled every aspect of production, from the actors and directors they put under exclusive contract; to processing the film in labs that they owned, located on the studio lot; to showing their films in their wholly owned cinema circuits in Hong Kong and Southeast Asia. The sound effects the Shaw Brothers created for their martial arts films are distinct from the ones made by rival studios like Golden Harvest. The making of these foley effects can be seen in the French documentary on the studio *Citizen Shaw* (1980).

A silent print of a Chang Cheh kung fu picture is screened in the sound room, as a group of eight workers "render" the sounds of martial arts by hand. One man renders the sound of forearms blocking by banging two sticks together. An elderly man smoking a cigarette bangs small metal weapons together to make the sound of steel clashing against steel. A woman shakes cloth and slaps her lap to make the sound of clothing flying through the air. The star of the sound team is a young man who vigorously swings a bamboo whip through the air, with one hand on his hip, to create the sound of a sword cutting through the air. A group of voice actors will later make the *kias*, the yells made by the kung fu actors while they fight. The finished soundtrack is then matched up with the silent film and shown, and we can see how much it adds to the picture. The sound is foregrounded in the mix; it is loud and immediate. It helps to produce the same effect that Bordwell describes in discussing Hong Kong action films. The combination of the sounds and the action is what makes the films really work to create the spectator's enjoyment and, in some cases, spontaneous imitation of the film's scenes.

As Ken Swift (quoted in Ou 2019) has described, the sounds of the audiences in the film house also provided a comedic soundtrack. This echoes Mary Fogarty's (2016) argument that "the film being exhibited always encounters the possibility of external sounds, especially those created by the cinema audience itself, resulting in the co-creation of an event" (43). I suggest that the soundtracks of kung fu films also gave rise to some of the cinematic expressions in breaking battles. Like car-chase scenes in movies translated to music soundtracks for breaking, kung fu films have sound effects that focus and amplify the onscreen action, and these soundtracks contribute to the larger-than-life performances of b-boys known for their character. Hunt (2003) suggests that the impact of kung fu films on the spectator has a lot to do with their sound design and the exaggerated kung fu fighting noises. Here, crucially, Hunt suggests that kung fu films can be understood by the effect they have on spectators wanting to imitate what they have seen on the screen and says that the Hollywood musical is the body genre that comes closest to the Hong Kong kung fu film in being able to capture the pro-filmic skill of the actors (22).

Because the distribution of kung fu films in the West was limited to grindhouse theaters and to kung fu theater television packages that were available in major metropolitan areas, and because the translations of the dramatic dialogue were poor, the genre became more about the displays of the human body and comedic sound effects. This was different from what was experienced by the original Hong Kong and Southeast Asian audiences. Thus, the films took on a different meaning for the target audience of Black and Latinx youth. This demographic of viewers missed some of the historical or mythical Chinese history that was being represented on the screen in the original Mandarin or Cantonese Hong Kong prints of these films for the Southeast Asian audiences. Gateward (2009) points out that the kung fu film was being marketed specifically to a Black audience, in Black newspapers like the *Chicago Defender* and the *New Amsterdam*, as early as March 3, 1973 (55–57).

There is some scholarship on the marketing of kung fu films to an African American audience, but there is a lot less scholarship on how these films were targeting Latinx audiences. One example of targeting Latinx audiences is given by Desser (2000), who says, "To attract inner city audiences in Los Angeles, it was not uncommon to find English-dubbed kung fu films with Spanish subtitles in neighborhood or downtown theatres" (35). My interviews with many Puerto Rican b-boys, including Ken Swift and an examination of their relationship with kung fu films suggest similar reasons for the appeal of the same films to a Latinx audience at the same time.

GRINDHOUSE DISTRIBUTION AND HIP HOP AESTHETICS

The kung fu film had a big impact on Hip Hop culture as it emerged from New York City in the mid 1970s, the same time kung fu films were playing at the grindhouse theaters at 42nd Street Times Square in New York. The films by Shaw Brothers director Lau Kar Leung, in particular, would influence Hip Hop culture, most prominently in the creation of the rap group the Wu-Tang Clan, who would take their name from a film Lau ghost-directed for Gordon Liu under the name Kung Fu Leung, *Shaolin and Wu Tang* (1983) (Teo 1997, 107; RZA and Norris 2005, 60). The b-boys would be inspired by the dynamic choreography they saw in Lau's films, and by the kung fu genre in general.

The genre's focus on training the human body and the discipline aspect of the martial arts would have a major impact on the b-boys and the Wu Tang Clan. Another reason for the inner-city audience's identification with kung fu films was the genre's focus on stories of underdogs, and the appeal of identifying with non-White heroes (Desser 2000, 38). Amy Abugo Ongiri (2005) suggests a more complex explanation for the popularity of the kung fu genre with African American audiences, contending that African American audiences identified with the kung fu films' stories of justice and empowerment, and the fact that the films "condensed thematic and visual concerns . . . into narratives that chronicle the transformation of a protagonist through a regime of physical discipline and rigorous training" (254). She also highlights the importance of broadcasting kung fu films in TV packages like Black Belt Theater, and suggests that these programs were just as welcome in Black households as broadcasts of Black athletes like Dr. J and Kareem Abdul Jabbar were (252). Ongiri points out that the African American audiences not only watched these films, but also used them to "remake" what to Western critics was a "trash" cinema (250–259). This of course fits in with Hip Hop culture's practice of appropriation and sampling, as we will see.

The first kung fu film craze in America started in 1973. David Desser goes into great detail about how this phenomenon came about in America, and he explains the role that the Warner Bros. studio had in beginning the importation of Hong Kong films for American audiences. Desser (2000, 22–23) has pointed out that the whole reason for the initial kung fu craze was the success of Bruce Lee's Hong Kong films. In fact, Warner Bros. made the biggest contribution to the initial kung fu craze by producing Bruce Lee's *Enter the Dragon* (1973) in Hong Kong. The film was the first true co-production between a Hollywood studio and a Hong Kong studio, Bruce Lee's own Concord Productions, a satellite company of Golden Harvest (Lee 1989, 135). The film was a huge success, premiering in August 1973 shortly after Lee's tragic death on July 20, 1973. The film was distributed worldwide by Warner Bros. and introduced kung fu and Hong Kong kung fu films to the world.

After the enormous success of *Enter the Dragon* (1973), Shaw Brothers rushed to make co-productions with Western studios, including Warner Bros, but none of them would match the success or quality of *Enter the Dragon*. Another important connection between Warner Bros. and the kung fu phenomenon in America is that the studio realized the link between the genre's popularity with Black audiences and its relationship to blaxploitation films, such as the hit *Superfly* (1972), which Warner Bros. also distributed. A specific reason for the affinity between *Superfly* and the kung fu genre is that the hero of the film, Priest, is shown learning Asian martial arts in a gym (Desser 2000, 25). Priest later uses this skill to defeat the main villain, a White man who controls the drug trade Priest is trying to escape.

Another reason for the connection between both genres is the way these films celebrate non-White heroes, something not seen often in mainstream Hollywood films. Suidiata Keita Cha-Jua (2008) sees the relation between the genres in the narrative structures of the films, when he notes, "Finally, the narrative structure of blaxploitation was so similar to that of kung fu films that it preconditioned African Americans for violent tales of retribution, especially the violent racial and class-based revenge sagas pioneered by Shaw Brothers but perfected by Bruce Lee at Golden Harvest" (219). Desser (2000) points out that Warner Bros. picked up on this connection and distributed its kung fu imports along with its own blaxploitation films and other exploitation films in downtown theaters (25).

In my research, I interviewed Trac 2 from Starchild La Rock, a second-generation Latinx b-boy from the Bronx. He remembers that the first kung fu film to be released in New York was *Five Fingers of Death* (1973), and he used to go to Times Square with his friends to watch double and triple features for $1.50. He recalled that, in addition to viewing martial arts films, many early b-boys practiced karate, and that he himself practiced Shotokan for two years (Pellerin 2003). It was during the first wave of kung fu films being imported to the United States that the New York City street gangs were at their peak.

A key component of Hip Hop culture is the concept of competition by battling another practitioner to see whose style is the best. Rappers battled each other to see who had the best rhymes, and b-boys battled each other to see who had the better style. One of the parallels between Hip Hop and kung fu films is the idea of battling an opponent using your specific style, and the aspect of discipline and training to improve your skill. The influence of kung fu appears throughout Hip Hop, but most directly through dance and rap. There have been a few articles written about the connection between Hip Hop and kung fu movies (Gateward 2009; Wilkins 2008), but they primarily focus on rap music's appropriation of kung fu films, and do not go into depth about how the b-boys were influenced by the focus on the body and choreography in kung fu films.

Gateward (2009) notes the similarity between competition in battling and plots in kung fu films that pit one style, like Tiger, versus another, like Crane. Crazy Legs from Rock Steady Crew has likened the battling aspect of b-boying to the challenge of styles seen in kung fu films. In the documentary *The Freshest Kids* (Israel 2002), Crazy Legs related, "When you hung out with people, they might know someone that might be breaking in another area, OK, cool, and I would battle them. It's like the martial arts films, where its like [imitating dubbed kung fu voice] 'I heard your style is good! But mine is better!' And you go there and you test their style."

TRAILERS AND MARKETING OF KUNG FU FILMS

The original American theatrical trailers for kung fu films are interesting in relation to the exploitation model they were distributed on, which focused on the films' revenge-driven plots and celebrations of ritualized violence. These trailers for kung fu films can be seen on a VHS tape called *Bruce Lee and Kung Fu Mania* (1993). This tape has clips of Bruce Lee's films, and the original trailers for the dubbed Hong Kong kung fu imports. One thing that becomes clear from watching the first set of trailers is that the link to Black audiences and blaxploitation films was used very heavily in the marketing of the films. The trailer for *The Black Dragon* (1974), an independent film starring an African American martial artist Ron Van Clief and directed by Shaw Brothers director Lu Chin-ku, uses Black slang heavily throughout. The voiceover proclaims,

"Introducing Ron Van Clief, the Black Dragon, rougher, tougher, stronger than any-thing you have seen before! . . . With catlike speed, you know he takes care of business real quick." As Van Clief chops a fat Asian stuntman to the ground, the voiceover says, "The Black Dragon, big mothers are his specialty. Don't miss it. It will be exploding in this theater soon!"

The use of 1970s jive slang would continue in other trailers, which clearly marks them as being marketed primarily to a Black audience. The trailer for *Shadow of the Dragon* (1973), a cheap Hong Kong independent kung fu film, even more heavily leans on the jive talk to sell the film. The voiceover says, "Hey dudes and foxy ladies, look out. Here comes the meanest mother in town, Shadow of the Dragon." The music used in the trailer is 1970s funk, despite the film's setting in early Republican China. The voiceover continues, "Not since Bruce Lee has the screen seen such skull-busting action. He tears them apart, piece by piece. He comes on strong, like King Kong. He's rough, tough, and hard to bluff! See him get down and do it in Shadow of the Dragon." Despite the trailer's claims, the action is not that inspired, and does not come close to the level of Bruce Lee's films in any way. The trailer relies on the target audience's supposed appetite for violence and the hope that they might be seeing a blaxploitation film in the same theater.

It is through these trailers, and the pairing of the kung fu films with other grindhouse genres like blaxploitation, spaghetti westerns, horror, and, eventually, pornos on 42nd Street that the kung fu film would come to take on new meanings for an inner-city audi-ence. The audience for these films would include the same Black and Latinx youth who would create Hip Hop as we know it, beginning in the mid 1970s. American studios like Warner Bros. had a hand in distributing kung fu films and pairing them with blaxploita-tion films in downtown theaters, as we have seen. The grindhouse theaters were concen-trated on 42nd Street in the 1970s and 1980s, which was a dangerous place during those years. Times Square was riddled with prostitution, drugs, robbery, and violence, and to watch a kung fu film, the viewer would have to negotiate this world. It was a world that was not accommodating for many female audience members, and the grindhouse be-came a space inhabited primarily by men. This world is described by Kevin Esch (2012) who, in his article "Grindhouse and Theatrical Nostalgia," quotes Landis and Clifford, authors of the *Sleazoid Express*, at length for their description of the Anco theater across the street from the Port Authority bus terminal,

> The Anco was the raunchiest, most dilapidated grindhouse of them all . . . At the Anco you'd base your seat choice on avoidance—a hellhole for decades, its filthy, broken chairs were a haven for a host of area criminals . . . Professional Black Deuce criminals—men who stole credit cards, pickpocketed wallets, and burned suburbanites with phony drug deals—also hid out, knowing no tourist would ever lead the cops in here. (2)

Esch feels that the authors might be slightly exaggerating, but even if they were, the conditions of the theaters were run down, and they were being used for all sorts of il-licit activities that would not be sanctioned in mainstream theaters. This description fits with ones given to me by Ken Swift, and as the RZA described in an interview he gave for the Dragon Dynasty DVD release of Lau's *The 36th Chamber of Shaolin* (2007). Ken Swift, a b-boy from the Rock Steady Crew, told me that in 1978, he and his friends, who were only teenagers at the time, would head down to 42nd Street from the Upper West Side and go wild in the theaters watching kung fu films. Ken remembers, "I mean we did it every weekend . . . So we would get our little Ballantine ale, throw it in the pocket, a little bag of weed, and go down there and just get nice, either in the theater or outside because everyone and their mother was smoking in the theater, and just bug out on these flicks" (interview with the author, January 2001). It was a wild scene; people would be yelling and fighting in the aisles during the films. He said that he can only remember parts of the films he watched, because they would be so high during the second half of the films. They would leave the theater hyped off the energy they had seen on the screen, and immediately try out the moves they had just seen on the streets, against each other or on innocent bystanders (interview with the author, June 2013). The RZA made similar comments about the 42nd Street theaters, "If I think back on it, there was dope fiends, sniffers, I definitely was a little dude in the middle of all this slime just to watch these movies man. And after 42nd Street went downhill, pornos started taking over and they had the 24-hour theaters, and to see a real kung fu movie, you had to go to the bummiest theaters" (Liu 2007).

As early as 1974, film scholars discussed the medium of kung fu films as a challenge to accepted traditions: "A primary difficulty reviewers, critics and some adults have in dealing with the Kung Fu films is that their performance is based upon violence, destruction and death, not musical expression" (Kaminsky 2013, 132). Likewise, the first generation of b-boys to be celebrated in the media also found it difficult to be taken seriously by academics as non-White, marginalized men who dance (Fogarty 2016).

ROCK STEADY CREW AND CHOREOGRAPHY

The Rock Steady Crew would be the ones to take breaking to the outside world beyond New York City, with their appearances in movies like *Flashdance* (1983), *Wild Style* (1983), *Style Wars* (1983), and *Beat Street* (1984). Subsequently, they became the most famous b-boy crew in the world, and they introduced a lot of new moves to the dance. The Rock Steady Crew was formed by Jimmy Lee and Jimmy Dee, in 1977, as a young breaking crew that wanted to keep the dance alive, at a time when many older b-boys were moving on to other things and retiring from dancing (Fricke and Ahearn 2002, 112–118; Cooper 2004, 86). It was the next generation of Rock Steady, including Crazy Legs, Ken Swift, Frosty Freeze, Doze, Buck 4, Kuriaki, Baby Love, and others, who would take breaking to the world stage.

In an article called "Power Moves," Doze Green from the second generation of Rock Steady is also quoted as saying that Chinese kung fu had "seeped into B-Boy consciousness":

That was basically an inspiration for floor moves-the sweeps and swipes. And when they got on their head and killed a whole army and shit. We came up with the eggroll and all these different maneuvers because we used to see them on their shoulders with their legs up in the air kickin' niggas. (quoted in Mare 139 1996, 28)

Doze subsequently mentioned the Shaw Brothers, in particular, as an influence on Rock Steady, telling journalist Jeff Chang (2005), "Every Saturday, me, Legs, Frosty and Kenny spent all day in the movies in Times Square. Three dollars for ten movies, some crazy shit! Just watch Shaw Brothers movies and just bug out. And so we started incorporating those moves into the dance" (137). Although power moves in breaking like the windmill are very similar to a scissors kick seen in kung fu movies that actors use to defend themselves when they are on their backs, and to get up off the ground, the creation of the windmill can, in fact, be traced to Crazy Legs, who has explained, "I didn't set out to evolve the backspin, I was practicing a chair freeze and I over-rated and spun fast. And then I over-rotated again on another time, and went into a continuous backspin and kept doing it" (Chang 2005, 138). The continuous backspin is another name for the power move that became known as the windmill.

When I asked Ken Swift if certain moves had come from kung fu films, he said, "I have no clue. I'm going to tell you right now, if we saw that happen in a movie, that's what we would try. You know, we would kip up or nip up, a lot of that was happening in kung fu movies" (Swift interview, January 2001). He told me that they would try to remember the moves they had seen in the kung fu films and try them out in practice. Because they would watch the films in the theater, they were not able to rewind or watch scenes in slow motion to really dissect the movements. They would have to attempt the moves from memory, which led them to be incorporated in a slightly different way. Ken said that they would try to emulate moves, but change them too, to put their own twist on them, because originality was prized in breaking and Hip Hop culture (Swift interview, June 2013).

Lil' Lep, a member of the Rock Steady Crew and, later, the New York City Breakers (NYCB), recalled that one aspect from kung fu films that really influenced b-boys was the choreography. When asked about the choreography he had to do with the NYCB, he said, "If we didn't do it right, we would have to do it over and over until we got it right, you know that is part of being a professional dancer" (Pellerin 2003, 3). This is also how the kung fu films they watched were made; sometimes there might be forty takes of single shot before the choreography is executed correctly in a kung fu film. The elaborate choreography seen in films like *Mad Monkey Kung Fu* (1979) inspired the b-boys to choreograph two-man routines with more precision. They had already been choreographing their own routines, but the kung fu films inspired them to do it better. Trac 2 also said that choreography from kung fu films was a big influence on the routines in breaking, as well as the disciplinary aspects of the training scenes (Pellerin 2003).

Ken Swift said that Lau Kar Leung's *Mad Monkey Kung Fu* really impacted them, in particular the scene of Lau teaching Hsiao Ho side by side, which is the scene singled out by Hong Kong critic Roger Garcia (1980) as the example of Lau in the act of physical pedagogy (132). The scene again took on a pedagogical role as the young b-boys watched Lau teaching Monkey boxing to Ho on the screen, and it inspired them to choreograph similar routines. Ken told me, "I remember being very impressed by the side-by-side stuff because it reminded me of b-boy routines. It was the way we would do routines. To see such synchronicity, we wouldn't say we need to look like this, but we knew this looks good, so I think, internally, we pushed ourselves to really have that link, in sync, in unison" (Swift interview, June 2013). Another reason for the affinity with *Mad Monkey Kung Fu* is that Monkey kung fu is very similar to breaking, with the practitioner rolling around on the ground, and utilizing sweeps and windmill-like kicks. The Monkey kung fu stylist will stay close to the ground, using his hands on the ground to support his body while executing a kick to his opponent (Chow and Spangler 1977, 66–69).

KUNG FU FILMS REMASTERED AND THE MEETING OF TWO LEGENDS

Ken Swift said that, back in the 1970s and 1980s, what attracted the b-boys' attention about a kung fu film was its name on the marquee outside. He said they liked to go to 42nd Street to watch movies because it was cheap and they could drink, smoke, and talk inside the theater. If the film had an interesting title like *Mystery of Chess Boxing* (1979), or *Crippled Masters* (1979), it would attract them to the films. He said that Lau Kar Leung's film *Mad Monkey Kung Fu* (1979) had a cool-sounding name to him and his friends (Swift interview, June 2013). They were drawn to the titles of the films, and to the stars they had seen in previous films. In Hong Kong, the trailers would advertise Lau Kar Leung as the director and choreographer, but in America he was an unknown, so the trailers would highlight the star of his films; and after Bruce Lee, one of the biggest stars for the b-boys and RZA was Gordon Liu, the star of *The 36th Chamber of Shaolin* (1978), AKA *Master Killer*. RZA felt that the Shaw Brothers films held a special place among the hundreds of other kung fu imports shown on 42nd Street. He said, "When you knew it was Shaw Brothers, you knew it was dope. Its like the sound effects, the acting, you know there's a lot of great kung fu movies, don't get it twisted, but their movies were of the highest standard, highest quality" (Liu 2007).

The young Black and Latinx audiences that went to see kung fu films by the hundreds in Times Square would recognize the Shaw Brothers studio by the distinctive SB shield that announced every film before the credit sequence, but mostly they were all just kung fu movies to the young kids who went to the theaters to bug out on whatever was showing that day. Going to Times Square to watch kung fu movies became a ritual for the youth of New York City, and the b-boys watched so many of these films, kung fu moves started to appear in the dance when they would practice in the street and the parks (Pellerin 2003; Chang 2005).

While I was living in China in 2004 and 2005, I sent my online article, "Challenge of the B-Boy Masters," to Celestial Pictures, the company that remastered and released the Shaw Brothers films on DVD. After reading the article, Celestial invited me and Ken Swift to perform at the Shanghai Tang Yong Kung Fu Collection clothing line launch party on May 4, 2005, in Hong Kong. The Shanghai Tang Yong Kung Fu Collection featured a selection of clothing and accessories called "Shaw Brothers Icons of Kung Fu" that featured artwork from the Shaw Brothers films. I had become a student of Ken's after interviewing him, and now we were asked to give a lecture, and perform a two-man breaking routine for the attendees, who included Shaw Brothers stars Gordon Liu, Chen Kuan Tai, and Hsiao Hou. We were thrilled to be able to meet our kung fu heroes, but then we found out that Hsiao Hou couldn't make it that night. We explained to the audience that breaking had been influenced by classic Shaw Brothers kung fu films, and I gave the example of Gordon Liu jumping his own leg in *The 36th Chamber of Shaolin* as the type of movement b-boys were inspired by.

I showed them the basic sweep from *Mad Monkey Kung Fu*, and Swift followed me and showed how they incorporated the sweep into the dance. Then we did our four minute two-man routine. The end featured the two of us dancing in sync, similar to the scene in *Mad Monkey Kung Fu*. We were able to meet and talk to Gordon Liu and Chen Kuan Tai after the performance. Ken was in awe of Liu, who had been a superhero figure to him growing up. We were both disappointed that Hsiao Ho couldn't make it, but the next day Celestial Pictures called us and told us to come to the Shaw Brothers studio at Clearwater Bay, because Hsiao Ho was willing to meet us.

We arrived at the old Shaw House, the former office of Run Run Shaw, and Hsiao Ho greeted us inside. We went to take pictures with him outside the Shaw House building, and when Ken and I went into Mad Monkey style poses, he instinctively did so without being asked, with Ken leaning against him, just like he did with Lau in the film. I put my arm around his, and his back felt like hard marble. Despite being fifty years old at the time, all the years of kung fu filmmaking had left his body in great shape.

I asked Ho, with his son interpreting, if he could still do the acrobatics he used to do in Lau's films, and he got up on the two-foot planter, and with just a roll of his hips, did a huge aerial and went into the film's Mad Monkey routine on the concrete. Ken and I were blown away. I asked Ho more questions when we went to lunch in the studio cafeteria. Ho wanted to know how many people in America had seen *Mad Monkey Kung Fu*. I told him millions had seen the film in the theater and on TV, as well as on home video. I think he didn't realize how popular the kung fu films Lau Kar Leung had made were outside Hong Kong. Because the actors were paid a standard salary and lived on the studio lot, they did not benefit from the films' popularity, especially in America, where Run Run Shaw no doubt kept the distribution money for himself.

We had a banquet-style feast at lunch in the old Shaw cafeteria, where the actors used to eat every meal, and Ho told me they filmed the final fight scene for *Mad Monkey Kung Fu* in the studio right across from the cafeteria. Ho recalled that Lau's troupe was the number one troupe in Hong Kong. They were in direct competition with Golden Harvest and Sammo Hung's troupe, and later Jackie Chan's troupe, but they really felt they were the best, and this competition drove them to excel. We all went into the Celestial offices in the old Shaw House, and then Ken, Hsiao Ho, his son, and I took a cab down to the MTR (Mass Transit Train) station. Ken told me in the taxi that if I had told him when he was a 13-year old kid watching kung fu movies on 42nd Street that twenty years plus later, he would be sitting in a taxi with the star of *Mad Monkey Kung Fu* in Hong Kong, driving down from Shaw Brothers studio, he would have thought I was crazy.

This story exemplifies Ken Swift's fandom of kung fu films and the embodied knowledge of the form that Ken and I carry in our bodies from having mimicked the moves that we saw in the films. The story also demonstrates the kinesthetic understanding that we shared cross-culturally, and how it brought us into a meaning-making exchange with a legend of a different kind. In other words, if kung fu is a "body genre," it's as much about the relationship between bodies interacting. In other words, it's a *bodies* genre for dancers and kung fu stars alike. Although Ken Swift wasn't one of the earliest generations of b-boys and b-girls, he was part of the first generation that experienced their own images circulating around the globe as breaking pioneers. He became a legend in his own right, and, thus, understood what it was for this kung fu cinema to share in arts that center body knowledge and discipline in their practices, before celebrity and status mediate their face-to-face interactions.

BREAKING AND KUNG FU FILMS
GO UNDERGROUND

The release of films like *Flashdance* (1983), *Wild Style* (1983), and *Beat Street* (1984), which featured New York City b-boys like the Rock Steady Crew, and the New York City Breakers, made breaking enormously popular across the United States and the world. Breaking's popularity reached a peak in 1984, appearing on the cover of *Newsweek*, and numerous television shows, and spawned how-to breakdance books, videos, and records. It was no longer an underground culture, and because of the mass media exposure, now every suburban kid in the United States could try their hand at breaking (Banes 2004, 13). In 1984, kung fu films were still being shown on 42nd Street and in their original Chinese language versions in Chinatown theaters. In Hong Kong, traditional kung fu films were reaching the end of their dominance, which had started in 1971 with Bruce Lee's first smash hit, *The Big Boss* (1971). Audiences were growing tired of kung fu due to oversaturation—thousands of movies had been made to satisfy the local Southeast Asian audience, as well as some made just for overseas markets like the United States (Lau 1980, 145–146).At the beginning of 1986, the Shaw Brothers studio closed its filmmaking branch to concentrate on making television programs for their TV station TVB (Chung 2003, 14). This was due in large part to the dwindling demand for the period kung fu films that they had specialized in. Competing studios like Golden Harvest, and their stars like Jackie Chan and Sammo Hung, had started making more contemporary films that Hong Kong audiences wanted to see, and which were enormously successful and shifted the industry to more contemporary filmmaking (Bordwell 2000, 70–71).

The end of traditional kung fu moviemaking in Hong Kong coincided with the end of breakdancing in the eyes of the media and the public, also due to overexposure. In 1984 breakdancing was everywhere, in TV commercials and a range of products, but in 1985, it was now perceived as a fad, and overnight it seemed that no one was doing it anymore, with the exception of some diehard b-boys (Strange 1996, 65). One of the new modern films made in Hong Kong was a breakdancing kung fu comedy starring Donnie Yen titled *Mismatched Couples* (1985), directed by Yuen Wo Ping. Yen had been raised in Boston, and he'd had a hand in incorporating breakdancing into his second starring film role. The dance was now directly influencing Hong Kong cinema and kung fu choreography, but it was made at the end of breaking's mass popularity, and did not perform well at the box office (Leeder 1999, 42). This film does not seem to have been distributed outside of Southeast Asia, and the grindhouse theater chains were coming to an end, due in part to the rise of home video (Church 2011, 22). Viewers could now watch exploitation films in the comfort of their homes, rather than brave the conditions of 42nd Street (23). Black Belt Theater would continue to show kung fu films, but the screenings were dramatically scaled back in 1985. Breaking and kung fu films would both remain underground for the remainder of the 1980s. Kung fu films found a cult following on VHS in the late 1980s through the 1990s. Breaking would also find a new life on video in the 1990s, with the emergence of b-boying VHS tapes released by Rock Steady Crew and others (Fogarty 2012, 450).

CONCLUSION

The kung fu film had a large impact on the development of Hip Hop culture, inspiring an aspect of the breaking aesthetic. The Black and Latinx youth were drawn to the films because of the concentration on the dynamic expression of the human body, but also because the films gave them movie stars they could look up to that were not White (Desser 2000, 38). The English dubs, which most filmgoers see as a marker of the films' poor quality, became a source of entertainment to the inner- city audiences, but they also became a source of appropriation in the case of the music of the Wu Tang Clan. The kung fu films were incredibly popular, and were viewed widely in the inner city, having been marketed specifically to this audience by studios like Warner Bros. who double-billed them with blaxploitation movies. The themes of discipline and training, and achieving mastery in a specific discipline, appealed to the creators of Hip Hop culture, who watched hundreds of kung fu films on 42nd Street and on television. The aspect of kung fu styles being pitted against other styles was a theme in kung fu films, and in the Hip Hop community, battling each other to see whose style is the best has been part of Hip Hop since the beginning.

FIGURE 5.1. Hsiao Hou and Eric Pellerin. Mad Monkey style, May 5, 2005. Shaw Brothers Studio, Hong Kong.

Due to overexposure and oversaturation, breakdancing and kung fu movies each had periods when they were perceived as unfashionable and no longer relevant. Both had comebacks in the 1990s; breaking could be viewed and traded worldwide with the advent of b-boying videos (Fogarty 2012), and Hong Kong had a cycle of new-wave kung fu films beginning with Jet Li's *Once upon a Time in China* ([1991]; Bordwell 2000, 152). B-boying is now practiced worldwide; it is no longer a subculture practiced solely in New York City. There is a large Asian b-boying community, and major competitions are held within China itself. Hong Kong kung fu films from the 1970s and 1980s by studios like the Shaw Brothers and Golden Harvest are available for streaming on multiple platforms such as Netflix, Amazon, and iTunes. These films have been digitally remastered and look better than they ever did when they had their first runs in grindhouses in NYC, or on cropped pan and scan prints made for television and VHS. Kung fu films are a part of Hip Hop's shared cultural history during its creation in New York City. Viewers can now watch those films in the comfort of their own homes, and because they have the power to create a bodily response, kung fu movies can still inspire b-boys today. However, the "body genre" is at its peak when it's a *bodies* genre, about relationships and b-boys bonding over their love of kung fu films and their proximity to each other in kinesthetic response.

FIGURE 5.2. Hsiao Hou, Eric Pellerin, and Ken Swift, Mad Monkey and B-boying, May 5, 2005. Shaw Brothers Studio, Hong Kong.

FIGURE 5.3. Hsiao Hou and Ken Swift, Mad Monkey style, May 5, 2005. Shaw Brothers Studio, Hong Kong.

NOTE

1. See Pilkington (2012) for a comparative study of the visceral effect of Russian punk band performances on the crowd.

REFERENCES

Banes, S. (2004). "Breaking." In *That's the Joint: The Hip-Hop Studies Reader*, edited by M. Forman and M. A. Neal, 13–20. New York: Routledge.

Bordwell, D. (1998). "Aesthetics in Action: Kung Fu, Gunplay and Cinematic Expression." In *Poetics of Cinema*, 395–412. New York: Routledge.

Bordwell, D. (2000). *Planet Hong Kong: Popular Cinema and the Art of Entertainment*. Cambridge, MA: Harvard University Press.

Cha-Jua, S. K. (2008). "Black Audiences, Blaxploitation and Kung Fu Films, and Challenges to White Celluloid Masculinity." In *China Forever: The Shaw Brothers and Diasporic Cinema*, edited by P. Fu, 200–223. Urbana: University of Illinois Press.

Chang, J. (2005). *Can't Stop Won't Stop: A History of the Hip Hop Generation*. New York: St. Martin's Press.

Chion, M. (1994). *Audio-Vision: Sound on Screen*. New York: Columbia University Press.

Chow, D., and Spangler, R. (1977). *Kung Fu: History, Philosophy and Technique*. New York: Doubleday.

Chung, S. P. (2003). "The Industrial Evolution of a Fraternal Enterprise." In *The Shaw Screen: A Preliminary Study*, edited by A. L. Wong, 1–17. Hong Kong: Hong Kong Film Archive.

Church, D. (2011). "From Exhibition to Genre: The Case of Grind-House Films." *Cinema Journal* 50(4): 1–25.

Chute, D. (2003) Introduction to *Heroic Grace: The Chinese Martial Arts Film*, edited by D. Chute and C. S. Lim, 5–8. Los Angeles: UCLA Film and Television Archive.

Cooper, M. (2004). *Hip Hop Files: Photographs 1979–1984*. Cologne, Germany: From Here to Fame Publishing.

Desser, D. (2000). "The Kung Fu Craze: Hong Kong Cinema's First American Reception." *The Cinema of Hong Kong: History, Arts, Identity*, edited by P. Fu and D. Desser, 19–43. Cambridge: Cambridge University Press.

Esch, K. (2012). "Grindhouse and Theatrical Nostalgia." *Jump Cut: A Review of Contemporary Media* 54. https://www.ejumpcut.org/archive/jc54.2012/EschGrindhouse/index.html.

Fogarty, M. (2012). "Breaking Expectations: Imagined Affinities in Mediated Youth Cultures." *Continuum Journal of Media & Culture Studies* 26 (3): 449–462.

Fogarty, M. (2016). "From Beat Street to Step Up 3D: The Sound of Street Dance Films." In *Movies, Moves and Music: The Sonic World of Dance Films*, edited by M. Evans and M. Fogarty, 43–60. Sheffield, UK: Equinox.

Fricke, J., and Ahearn, C. (2002). *Yes Yes Y'all: The Experience Music Project Oral History of Hip-Hop's First Decade*. Cambridge, MA: Da Capo Press.

Frydland, M. (Dir.) (1980). *Citizen Shaw*. France: France 3 (FR 3).

Garcia, R. (1980). "The Autarkic World of Liu Chi-Liang." In *A Study of the Hong Kong Martial Arts Film: 4th Hong Kong International Film Festival*, edited by S. Lau, 121–134. Hong Kong: Urban Council.

Gateward, F. (2009). "Wong Fei-Hung in Da House: Hong Kong Martial Arts Films and Hip-Hop Culture." In *Chinese Connections: Critical Perspectives on Film, Identity and Diaspora*, edited by T. See-Kan, P. X. Feng, and G. Marchetti, 51–67. Philadelphia: Temple University Press.

Hunt, L. (2003). *Kung Fu Cult Masters.* New York: Wallflower Press.

Kaminsky, S. M. (2013). "Kung Fu Film as Ghetto Myth." *Journal of Popular Film* 3 (2): 129–138.

Lau, S., ed. (1980). *A Study of the Hong Kong Martial Arts Film: 4th Hong Kong International Film Festival.* Hong Kong: Urban Council.

Leeder, M. (1999). "A Yen for Success." *Inside Kung-Fu*, August, 38–42.

Lee, L. (1989). *The Bruce Lee Story.* Santa Clarita, CA: Ohara.

Liu, L. C. (Dir.). (2007). *The 36th Chamber of Shaolin: Special Collector's Edition.* DVD. USA: Dragon Dynasty.

Mare 139. (1996). "Power Moves." *Rap Pages* 5(8): 15.

Oliveri, S. (Ed.). (1993). Bruce Lee and Kung Fu Mania. VHS. USA: Good Times Home Video.

Ongiri, A. A. (2005). "Bruce Lee in the Ghetto Connection: Kung Fu Theater and African Americans Reinventing Culture at the Margins." In *East Main Street: Asian American Popular Culture*, edited by S. Dave, L. Nishime, and T. G. Oren, 249–261. New York: New York University Press.

Ou, S. (Dir.). (2019). *Iron Fists and Kung Fu Kicks.* Documentary film. Netflix.

Pellerin, E. (2003). "Challenge of the B-Boy Master: The Impact of Kung Fu Movies on Breakdancing." Kung Fu Cinema. http://kungfucinema.com/articles/2003-11-24-01.htm.

Pilkington, H. (2012). "Mutants of the 67th Parallel North": Punk Performance and the Transformation of Everyday Life." *Post & Post-Punk* 1 (3): 323–344.

RZA, and Norris, C. (2005). *The Wu-Tang Manual.* New York: Riverhead Freestyle.

Schloss, J. (2009). *Foundation: B-Boys, B-Girls, and Hip-Hop Culture in New York.* New York: Oxford University Press.

Strange, A. (1996). "Battle Cry." *Source Magazine*, February, 64–66.

Israel. (Dir.). (2002). *The Freshest Kids.* Motion Picture. USA: QD3 Entertainment.

Teo, S. (1997). *Hong Kong Cinema: The Extra Dimensions.* London: British Film Institute.

Teo, S. (2013). "The Female Kung Fu Chop." In *Golden Harvest: Leading Change in Changing Times*, edited by P. Fung and L. Yam, 78–95. Hong Kong: Hong Kong Film Archive.

Wilkins, F. C. (2008). "Shaw Brothers and the Hip-Hop Imagination." In *China Forever: The Shaw Brothers and Diasporic Cinema*, edited by P. Fu, 224–245. Urbana: University of Illinois Press.

Williams, L. (1991). "Film Bodies: Gender, Genre and Excess." *Film Quarterly* 44 (4): 2–13.

Willis, Paul E. (1978). *Profane Culture.* Boston: Routledge and Keegan Paul.

CHAPTER 6

....

WHAT MAKES A MAN BREAK?

....

MARY FOGARTY

MANY years ago, as an aspiring B-Girl in my early 20s, I had the privilege of watching
Honey Rockwell rehearse at Ken Swift's studio in New York. I was inspired in many ways,
and not least by the fact that both Honey and Ken were dancing into their 30s and 40s,
refuting early views of Breaking as an exclusively male youth culture. This helped me
grasp some of the paradoxes of Breaking--or, rather, some of the dominant conceptions
and contradictions in the form: on the one hand, a highly-localized and racialized youth
subculture dominated by a masculinist aesthetic, while on the other, a globalized multiracial culture, with some dancers continuing to dance well into middle-age, and a practice that has featured women breaking from the 1970s onward.

In fact, the growing scholarly work on gender in Breaking turns out to be dominated
by studies of B-Girls (see Raimist 1999, Ogaz 2006, Jones 2010, Gupta-Carlson 2010,
Simard 2014, Johnson 2014, Gunn 2016a and 2016b, Salmivuori 2017, Fogarty, Cleto,
Zsolt & Melindy 2018, Jones 2018, Dodds 2018, Chew & Mo 2019, Aprahamian 2020,
Gunn 2021, Dodds 2022). So, despite the stereotype of Breaking as a singularly masculinist form, there is in fact a plurality of work on women Breaking. And yet the relative dearth of work specifically on masculinity in the form contributes, in its own way,
to ongoing misconceptions (for an important exception see Sara LaBoskey 2014). This
chapter thus seeks to help complicate views of Breaking as a singularly masculinist
youth (sub)culture by looking more directly at that very masculinity.

As an Afro-diasporic artform that took shape in the New York of the 1970s, Breaking
followed global pathways echoing those laid out by Brenda Dixon Gottschild (1996; see
also Gaunt 2006, Osumare 2016). The almost instantaneous circulation of mediated
images of Breaking in the 1980s, via "Breaksploitation" films (see Banes 1994, Fogarty
2016, DeFrantz 2014), helped make global stars of second-generation practitioners like
the Rocksteady Crew--a predominantly New York Puerto Rican, male-dominated crew
with a sole female member, Daisy "Baby Love" Castro (her fellow crew members included Ken Swift, Crazy Legs, and Frosty Freeze, among others). As Breaking took hold
in various countries around the world, its participants tended overwhelmingly to consist

of B-Boys and to a lesser extent B-Girls (despite the presence from the very outset of women breaking; for e.g., see Rivera 2003, Jones 2010, Fogarty 2010, Aprahamian 2020).

Joseph Schloss (2009) argues that Breaking is about identity and being true to oneself, yet insists that if women break, then they are B-Boying. Ansley Joye Jones (2018) disagrees, contending instead that B-Girls who play with androgyny and mix gender performances in liminal spaces actually expand the vocabulary of Breaking in crucial ways. Yet a patriarchal sensibility has restricted the potential for performances by women involved in the dance as B-Girls to be deemed "authentic" by the larger culture. What many view as Breaking's masculine aesthetic had been formed in a particular historical crucible of race, gender and age. Even as bodies and contexts changed dramatically, key aesthetic features of the dance persisted alongside fantasies of a singular identity as definitive of what Breaking was all about. Challenging that singularity is the goal of this chapter.

MEN BREAKING

Breaking emerges into a world already historically structured by patriarchy (Rivera 2003). For example, as children, one of the first lessons that boys may learn is that the worst thing that can happen is to lose to a girl. This will then inform not only how dancers feel in battles, but how audiences and media interpret the meaning of winning and losing, based on the respective genders of the practitioners. When scholars first wrote about breaking, for example, they often sought to understand the dance in terms of a "masculine aesthetic" (cf. Steve Cohan on Gene Kelly's TV show Dancing: A Man's Game). Breaking performances have indeed been frequently described in terms of 'machismo', or a 'masculine aesthetic'. Machismo is a derogatory, racialized term "that presumes to be a concept" (Ramirez 2008). It forcefully evokes the kinaesthetics of Breaking conceived as a racialized, masculine, hetero-normative dance practice (including gestures, body language, attitudes and insinuations).

There are two dominant ways in which this perceived aesthetic in breaking has been thought about in relation to gender performances working across a gender divide. On the one hand, B-Boys are frequently framed as expressing a particular type of masculinity, linked to lower-class bravado and status seeking on the street--a more traditional image of "macho" (Banes 1981). On the other hand, the performances of B-Girls, using a similar, learned aesthetic, are interpreted as self-reflexive and empowering, engendering new notions of femininity and resistance (Ogaz 2006, Johnson 2014).[1] Jones (2018 p. 197) argues that B-Girls can aspire to what she calls "the unrecognizable" to underscore liminal possibilities and thus expand Breaking's vocabulary beyond binaries.

The link across these conceptions is, of course, "power," read through bodies. Breaking offered marginalized peoples a public space to wield power, but since its medium was the body, different bodies were read as articulating power differently, not least in terms of preexisting notions of gender specificity. Both Johnson (2014) and Aprahamian

(2020) argue that those preexisting notions were white, Western sensibilities about masculinities and femininities, sensibilities that Black and Brown performers didn't necessarily conform to yet were presumed to be organized around. Moreover, Johnson sees performances of B-Boys as "steeped in clichéd masculinity" and an "outlaw" aesthetic. Yet there is also within this a complexity of distinctions and nuances; a series of different choices, intentions, and agencies within the gender performances of B-Boys. As it turns out, B-Boys are often both more playful and creative than stereotyped interpretations might suggest.[2]

It is important, then, to help make those nuanced and resistant performances legible, because dance continues to be undervalued as a form of knowledge in its own right. That is not to say that we need to focus on the intentions of the artists per se, but that watching many performances closely (see Gottschild 1996), and having some understandings of the historical transformations within the dance, can aid greatly in interpretations of the significance of performances, especially for audiences with some degree of subcultural capital (Thornton 1996). This makes the histories of the dance form a vital and critical component of its practices. Also, performances of dancers from different class, ethnic, and cultural backgrounds do carry different meanings and interpretations. Further to that, dancers from similar class, ethnic, and cultural backgrounds articulate very different ways of being in the world through their choices as performers, teachers, and human beings (Fogarty 2012).

Both for youth and the adults that they grow into, Breaking provides ways of organizing the world that are complicated and creative. I approach the study of gender through an acknowledgment that dichotomous conceptions of genders are constructed (Butler 1990) and learned (Young 1980), underpinned by the exigencies of the human life cycle as these exist in particular socioeconomic and cultural conjunctures. In this context, dancers' performances of gender are also about the agency of art related to a social group, the crew, and beyond that, to the social groups of other crews, as they battle in both formal and informal competitions. B-Boys and B-Girls have typically been able to sign up to compete regardless of level, age, or experience, to go head-to-head against each other. Only recently have competitions divided themselves into B-Girl and B-Boy categories that exclude based on ascribed gender identities.

Competition is a key moment in Breaking culture, and one also deeply implicated in conventional notions of the masculine (Driver and Bennett 2015). This is matched by clichés that circulate widely in popular culture about B-Girls supposedly being more collaborative and "better dancers," and about B-Boys being more aggressive and individualistic. These ideas are rooted in racialized and gendered stereotypes mapped onto the performances and baked into practices by dancers in the global circulation of the dance. For example, a major point I have seen made by expert B-Boys and B-Girls from New York City when teaching their global classes is to tell students to refrain from doing movements in someone's face, feigning toughness, and/or pretending to be violent towards their opponents. Such actions would not have been taken lightly in New York City performance contexts, despite the misguided fantasies of student dancers. Ken Swift would describe instead projecting his eyes downward and beating other dancers simply with his Breaking skills. In these pedagogical moments, what is revealed are the stereotyped performance ideas that students often bring to the dance--in imagining themselves to be "outlaws," performing stereotypically racialized street codes of "toughness". And these indeed resemble minstrelsy more than they do actual performances in the earliest documented footage of the dance (on minstrelsy's painful endurance, see Dixon Gottschild 1996 and Hartman 1997).

Those with many years of experience may become experts and professionals performing at very high levels. This is where "legendary" status really starts to get cemented for some dancers. Conferred by others in the scene based on recognition and consensus (even if it is rarely experienced as a full consensus), one ages into the status and carries it with them. I suggest that this blurring of ability and skillset, from enthusiasts to experts, was an absolute necessity for the sustained growth of the scene and the development of an international network of players who could cultivate the continued practice of the dance. In other words, as other researchers have noted when it comes to music and theatre (Finnegan 1989), dancers, similarly, begin as amateurs, doing it for fun and because they love it, and some then go on to do some work professionally or become professionals, or contribute to the channels of professionalization that allow generations after them to more easily become professionals themselves. The name of an important annual event in Miami (since 1997), the "Pro-Am," captures this blurring of lines between professional and amateur, expert and novice. By the twenty-first century, the sheer number of years some B-Boys and B-Girls had put in to honing their craft contributed not only to their status in the community but also to important changes in the shape of the dance, to which I now turn.

SEXUALIZED GESTURES

Now I am able to take a critical stance on certain elements of a heteronormative masculine aesthetic, in relation to the shifting ecology I have just outlined. Performances of masculinity are neither fixed nor self-evident; rather, they are complex and always in a process of becoming. This is not about "fluidity," but about affordances and agencies[3] and how this impacts on the notion of self. Gender also is not just a performance. It's a powerful idea lived through the body, something believed in, as well as felt. The creative and dynamic force of the dance is informed by the channeling of such affective intensities.

Another element of performances of masculinity, as they have been thought about in regard to breaking, has to do with particular gestures that are read as a form of masculine, competitive sociability—that is, basically any sexual gesture indicating male anatomy. I want to put this into some particular social contexts to begin my unpacking of how masculinity has been thought about, and the processes through which masculinity is assigned or ascribed to this particular dance form. When breaking started in the 1970s, most B-Boys stopped practicing by the age of sixteen (Fogarty 2012). The dissemination and sustainment of the form through media interest allowed for B-Boys such as Ken Swift and Crazy Legs to grow into manhood while still practicing the form. If you had told them at fourteen that they would still be doing the dance at forty, they likely would have laughed--and that spirit lives on in their dance.

However, those early sexual gestures that they enacted were the gestures of boys coming into manhood. They were the kind of gestures that, in the words of Ken Swift, "if your mom saw you do, she would grab you by the ear and take you home." This wasn't so much about male dominance, as it was about trying on masculinity and sexuality, as one grew from boyhood to adulthood through acts of play--and that is how Breaking was at one time thought about, not as a dance but as a part of street culture and games. And B-Girls of the first generation had paved the way for that.

Ansley Joye Jones (2010) and Serouj Aprahamian (2020) have discussed how B-Girls were influential in the earliest stages of the development of the form, and would often challenge B-Boys on the dance floor. Jones suggests that the 1970s African American B-Girls' "burns" or "burners"--slang for moves to attack or dis an opponent symbolically through gestures--were not construed as a "masculine" performance at all, at least in the beginning; however, by the 1990s the same gestures would be organized in the global Breaking community as somehow inappropriate for women. In one battle I attended in Leeds in the 2010s, for example, B-Girl Roxy even mocked other B-Girls for doing phallic, masculine gestures. In doing so, she animated a strength of character (refusing to mimic others) and critical thinking manifested through movements, before annihilating her opponent with powerful skills. Notably, any sexual gestures are banned in the rules and regulations for Breaking's debut as a competitive sport at the Paris Olympics in 2024.

KEN SWIFT: THE "EPITOME OF THE B-BOY"

At this point, the elephant in the room is the classification of "B-Boy," which is a complex allusion to race/racism, masculinity, and youth. "B-Boy" seems somehow to preclude the "B-Man." And yet, in the 1990s, breaking witnessed a new sort of (mature) masculinity, one, I would argue, that was in many ways *defined* by Ken Swift's performances in this decade and beyond. Ken Swift was by then older, in his thirties, a man battling up-and-coming, younger crews, such as Style Elements or K-Mel from the Boogie Brats. Swift was also repping with B-Boys who had wanted to be mentored by him, most memorably, Flo Master. Unlike some of his earlier contemporaries, who were seen to embody past eras[4] (insofar as their style of dance had not changed much since their peak time as performers in another historical moment), in the nineties Ken Swift refreshed his style in significant and globally influential ways. He began to add new endings to his movements, and just as importantly, his body changed. He was now a man with commercial gigs, theater choreographies, and world tours behind him, which presented differently in the space of Breaking culture. Read against his celebrity in that culture and amplified by his swiftness and speed on the floor, his refreshed style became an ideal of the dance for many B-Boys. In how he would move, how he would listen to the music and express concepts, and how he would exit the space, Ken Swift had become the "epitome" of what a B-Boy was.

Ken Swift was well past the typical "prime" of B-Boys of that time, who were mostly quite young adults. My claim here is that, in the sorts of performances that he began to do at events in the 1990s, he created (artistically) a different type of masculinity. While staying true to the "classic" form, he also showed how a somewhat older male body could look in performing this supposed "youth" dance, thereby refreshing the form. This offered the culture new possibilities, not only around ideas of longevity but in one's significance as a dancer, mixing what we might call "classic" and "modern" approaches. Take B-Boy Summit 3 (1996): here a young crew, Style Elements, would make a name for themselves (they had already won at Radiotron) by battling Rock Steady Crew. What is evident is that Ken Swift was absolutely a contender and one of the strongest members battling that day. He did more rounds than most, with more self-assuredness and confidence, energy, and craft than his younger competitors.

He could thus hold his own against the generation coming up and make them question their mastery of the dance through his ability to dance longer, have more material, be more on the music, and have cleaner endings (in how he exits the space, Ken has really exciting go downs and getups). In other words, his performance in many ways relates directly to his younger self and movement vocabulary even as he was redefining the form. Feeling unable to compete directly with new developments in the dance, with younger bodies more capable of acquiring newer difficult moves, he used this strategy to not only stay in the game but also to take out those younger B-Boys in battles. At the same time, he wasn't alone in this. Notably, Mr. Wiggles was doing the same for popping and locking, among others.

Perhaps most significantly, Ken Swift's performance of masculinity was perceived differently now that he was an adult male in his thirties. What was once the performance of a teenager and young man trying out masculinity in form and gesture now could be read as a man with a less playful sense of power and energy. Younger B-Boys who came up against him definitely began to question their own authority in the face of his physical and verbal responses to their battle strategies. So, if B-Boying continued to be portrayed as a predominantly masculine aesthetic, it was Ken's aesthetic, a particular way of presenting masculinity, embodied in his perseverance with the form, his continued participation as an aging and able competitor, and his particular character, that challenged the dominant, even as he worked to reshape the form. As his influence grew, there were B-Boys of this time that were called out for looking too much like Ken.

Ken, of course, had himself been influenced by other dancers. The third of the three icons of breaking to emerge from the Rock Steady Crew alongside Ken Swift and Crazy Legs, was Frosty Freeze. In the underground scene he was looked up to by many B-Boys in different neighborhoods in NYC, getting along with and bringing together diverse people and crews. Frosty Freeze was famous for his "freeze to please," entertaining style that captured the hearts of audiences and academics alike with the clarity of his homages to other dances, such as the Charleston, and his pursuit of making the audience laugh.

Frosty Freeze's death in 2011 was devastating for the scene, and I would argue that Ken Swift's style changed again during this period. If Ken Swift's refreshed style of the 1990s was one defining articulation of what masculinity could look like in breaking, with his swiftness and seemingly infinite combinations and go downs, the transformation in his style in the 2010s had a more playful aesthetic. His performances now seemed to be telling stories of youth, relating memories and love of music that are so clearly articulated that his style has sometimes been called "traditional". In other words, Ken Swift's dancing now also embodied the memory and performances of Frosty Freeze, in a homage that is as breathtaking in its craft as it is powerful in its message.

Finally, in a performance of Ken Swift dancing in 2015, you can see the impact of an injury (he is leaning more heavily on one leg). It is also evident in the time he takes to set up his dancing, to set his character. Yet the iconic speed at which he spins to the ground, the use of comedy and play were new elements in his performance, juxtaposed neatly with the old. An archaeology of embodiment would suggest not that performances necessarily "evolve" over time, but that they are layered. In this later incarnation, aspects of Ken Swift's earlier performances and those of his peers get recycled and repeated and reworked. Elements of humor, play, and clowning exist throughout and over time, depending on circumstances, on who got down before him, on whether it's a battle or a cypher, whether he feels connected to the person or not, what the music is, what the crowd is like. There is also the most recent "layer," the leg injury that alters the aesthetic choices (putting younger body and older body in a different sort of dialogue, perhaps). Performances, then, are not necessarily singularly "masculine" and, even within that aesthetic, will be complicated by contexts that are always changing. Even hearing a particular song, the meaning changes over time, from novelty to familiarity, and this scaffolds the meaning for artist and audience alike. As Breaking became more and more of a global artform, Ken Swift's layered style not only became canonical, it entered into ongoing and productive dialogue with other innovators and definers, who in turn help refresh the culture.

"Conclusion: Cosmopolitan Masculinities"

Mark Anthony Neal (2013) reframes notions of masculinity in a useful way in his work on "cosmopolitan masculinities". Here he refers to the masculine as multiple, rather than singular. He draws from the experiences of Black men from the 'block' or 'hood' who are exposed to different classes, countries, and neighbourhoods, and are transformed through these interactions. These experiences cultivate unique senses of selfhood, drawn from the intersection of the core principles and values of different worlds. Neal acknowledges that this awareness does not necessarily guarantee any sort of social mobility or points of access to other realities. Within Breaking practices, these levels of awareness become embedded in the aesthetic choices of B-Boys in battles, in response to each other, and frame B-Boy experiences in foreign countries where they teach in environments where their bodies may be objectified, exoticized, and emulated. Thinking through the trajectory of performances of aging masculinities that are expressed through the dance, as well as the consequent production and construction of norms over time, such a "cosmopolitan" identity comes out of a longer process, akin to invention: it is not static but, rather, in a perpetual state of becoming.

There have always been many different forms of masculinity,[5] different performances, a wealth and variety of position-taking within the ecology of ordinary and art worlds, different roles and engagements, different strategies toward equality, different complications. For example, B-Boy Midus explains: "I was never a fan of the concept that breaking had to be this tough guy, gangster approach dance where you grab your nuts every 10 seconds. We would clown that when we started dancing in the 90's" (personal correspondence, July 2015). "Clowning" here is a sort of irony and sarcasm that can also provide an alibi. This resistance to a particular type of masculine aesthetic performed by other dancers crucially challenges the intentions, articulations, and creativity of one's peers, and though one is just playing around, everyone also knows they really mean the critique. In these exchanges, values are being both challenged and enacted. By taking a position about choices in the ways one's sense of style will be framed, there are also, implicitly and sometimes explicitly, contested and negotiated thoughts about one's sense of self, of what it means, for instance, to be a young male, adult and, ultimately, human.

Early on in Breaking, performances invoked highly gendered forms of street politics. As the dance moved into institutions, art worlds, and new social contexts, an archaeology of embodiment and cosmopolitan masculinities reveal that this embodiment is now being framed inside legitimating institutions—the institutional codification of Breaking changes the historical situation of this embodiment.

Globalization has increased cosmopolitanism's importance as the key attribute of the professional-managerial class. However, through the destruction of neighborhoods, austerity's undermining of communities, and what Habermas (1984) calls the colonialization of the social by the instrumental, capitalist logics are all reducing the spaces of subcultural solidarities, resulting in the homogenizing of experience through the multinational corporatization of our world. With the rise of the World Wide Web, by 2014, six-year old B-Girl Terra can spectacularly win battles viewed by millions. What's at stake for society is revealed in the headlines and comments that accompany this sort of instantaneous uploading and international circulation of her victories over B-Boys. Yet society at large continues to teach young boys that the worst imaginable fate is to lose to a girl. But we can do better.

Multiple masculinities exist in relationship with different understandings of equity and equality, and different hopes of what B-Girls might bring to performances. This we know. What we have not been afforded is the same potential of position-taking for female participants. B-Girls continue to be assessed on a characteristic (or caricature) called "feminine energies," which is essentialist and remains relatively unchallenged.

Instead of being perceived according to the multitude of possible narratives, emotions, or relationships to music that they express through their dance, old ideas persist. B-Girls are capable of the same (as well as different) varieties and distinctions, from playful jests to aggressive taunts, as any other dancers, in knowing and expressing their varied experiences. If performances of masculinities transform over time, so do possible interpretations of performances. Time puts the dance practice, training, technique, and style into the bodies of performers, forever changing their experiences of their world. With age and cultural transformation, so, too, do the discourses we employ change. The frames and references are also altered as we strive to make sense of the shifting environment around us and the dynamics involved.

Finally, if the multiple masculinities operating in Breaking, as I have argued, are enacted by individuals in performance, and these performances change over time, then the "expert" aging body may also help to reconfigure Breaking's cultural imaginings. In other words, the notion of the "expert" itself means something different in 1984, 1996, 2004, and 2022. There have been visible growing pains around this question when it comes to who gets to judge international events, for example. In the beginning, the legendary dancers of the past were asked to judge as a sign of respect; now, in 2022, judges are expected to be current with recent global developments in the dance and to track who is coming up with new moves, to grasp the difficulties involved in various combinations of power moves that didn't even exist in past decades, and to be accountable to explain the basis of their judgments. This is a totally different category of expertise, now.

This will likely also develop through the validating of LGBTQ+ participants, in such a way that they, too, can be acknowledged as experts and authorities. It is one thing to allow women to become "students of the dance," who can prove that they too have skills, often required to overcompensate and demonstrate excessive seriousness on their part. It is quite another to attribute to women and LGBTQ+ practitioners the authority to judge, to develop their own frameworks, to produce and name them not only as influential but as game changers. To create a culture where dancers do not have to hide their sexual orientations in order to have a career. It is not so much about the recognition that women, queer dancers and non-gender-conforming people participate fully, but more about acknowledging that their involvement has, indeed, already changed the game. And further to that, to acknowledge and accept that losing to them in a battle is no calamity but just a part of life, is a reality that everyone will experience regularly and then grow from. When that happens, the aesthetic labeling of the dance as "masculine" will sound odd and incomprehensible to future generations of people who go off when they hear the break of the record.

ACKNOWLEDGMENTS

Thank you to the KISMIF conference for inviting me to be a keynote speaker in Porto, Portugal, in 2015, where I presented an earlier version of this chapter. Thank you to

Frosty Freeze, Ken Swift, and Honey Rockwell for the inspiration, conversations and insights.

NOTES

1. Although Jones (2010) complicates this empowerment model.
2. See Fogarty (2020) for a local history of how Toronto B-Boys created their own style of threading that addresses the playfulness inherent in the aesthetic itself.
3. What Anthony Giddens (1991) would articulate as *reflexive modernity*.
4. This movement-focused methodological approach references the influential work of Michel Foucault (1969) in *Archaeology of Knowledge*. See Diana Taylor's (2001) work, *The Archive and the Repertoire: Performing Cultural Memory in the Americas*, for an engaged discussion of how performances store and archive memories from earlier times. Borrowing from Taylor's framework, one could argue that the performances of B-Boys today, those that danced in the late 1970s and early 1980s, shape our cultural memory of what we think the dance is and what it's about.
5. See Gilroy (2004) for a critique of "cosmopolitanism" as a concept.

REFERENCES

Aprahamian, S. (2020). "'There Were Females That Danced Too': Uncovering the Role of Women in Breaking History." *Dance Research Journal* 52 (2): 41–58.

Banes, S. (1981). "Breaking Is Hard to Do: To the Beat, Y'all." Village Voice, April 22–28, 31–33.

Banes, S. (1994). *Writing Dancing in the Age of Postmodernism*. Hanover: Wesleyan University Press.

Bennett, A. (2013). *Music, Style, and Aging: Growing Old Disgracefully?* Philadelphia: Temple University Press.

Butler, J. (1990). *Gender Trouble: Feminism and the Subversion of Identity*. New York: Routledge.

Chew, M.M. and Mo, S.P.S. (2019). "Towards a Chinese Hip-hop Feminism and a Feminist Reassessment of Hip-hop with Breakdance: B-girling in Hong Kong, Taiwan and China." *Asian Studies Review* 43(3): 455–474.

DeFrantz, T. (2014). "Hip Hop in Hollywood: Encounter, Community, Resistance". *The Oxford Handbook of Dance and the Popular Screen*. Eds. M. Blanco Borelli. N.Y.: Oxford. pp. 113–131.

Dodds, S. (2018). "The brutal encounters of a novice b-girl." *Choreographic Practices* 9(2): 233–252

Dodds, S. (2022). "B-Girl at 50." *Dancing Across the Lifespan* Eds. Musil, P., Risner, D. Karen Schupp, K. London: Palgrave Macmillan. pp 97–112.

Driver, C., and Bennett, A. (2015). "Music Scenes, Space and the Body." *Cultural Sociology* 9 (1): 99–115.

Finnegan, R. (1989). *The Hidden Musicians: Music-Making in an English Town*. Cambridge: Cambridge University Press.

Fogarty, M. (2006). "'Whatever Happened to Breakdancing?' Transnational B-Boy/B-Girl Networks, Underground Video Magazines and Imagined Affinities." Unpublished MA thesis, Brock University.

Fogarty, M. (2011). "Dance to the Drummer's Beat: Competing Tastes in International B-Boy/ B-Girl Culture." Unpublished PhD diss., University of Edinburgh.

Fogarty, M. (2012). "'Each One Teach One': B-Boying and Ageing." In *Ageing and Youth Cultures: Music, Style and Identity*, edited by A. Bennett and P. Hodkinson, 53–65. London: Bloomsbury.

Fogarty, M. (2016). "From *Beat Street* to *Step Up 3-D*: The Sound of Street Dance Films." in *Movies, Moves and Music: The Sonic World of Dance Films*. Eds. M. Evans and M. Fogarty. Sheffield: Equinox. pp. 43–60.

Fogarty, M. (2019). "Why Are Breaking Battles Judged? The Rise of International Competitions." In *The Oxford Handbook of Dance and Competition*, edited by S. Dodds, 409–428. New York: Oxford University Press.

Fogarty, M. (2020). "Following the Thread: Toronto's Place in Hip Hop Dance Histories." In *We Still Here: Hip Hop North of the 49th Parallel*, edited by C. Marsh and M. V. Campbell, 97–115. Montreal: McGill-Queen's University Press.

Fogarty, M., Cleto, E., Zsolt, J. & Melindy, J. (2018) "Strength In Numbers: B-Girls, Gender Identities and Hip-Hop Education." *Journal of Popular Music Education* 2(1–2): 115–132

Foucault, M. (1969). *The Archaeology of Knowledge*. London: Tavistock.

Gaunt, K. (2006). *The Games Black Girls Play: Learning The Ropes From Double-Dutch To Hip-Hop*. N.Y.: NYU.

Giddens, A. (1991). *Modernity and Self Identity: Self and Society in the Late Modern Age*. Cambridge, UK: Polity.

Gilroy, P. (2004). *After Empire: Melancholia or Convivial Culture?* London: Routledge.

Gottschild, B.D. (1996). *Digging the Africanist presence in American performance: Dance and Other Contexts*. Westport: Praeger.

Gunn, R. (2016a). "Don't worry, it's just a girl!. Negotiating and challenging gendered assumptions in Sydney's breakdancing scene." *Journal of World Popular Music*, 3(1), 54–74.

Gunn, R. (2016b). "The 'systems of relay'in doing cultural studies: experimenting with the 'Body without Organs' in b-girling practice. *Continuum*, 30(2): 183–194.

Gunn, R. (2021). "Where the #bgirls at? Politics of (in)visibility in breaking culture." *Feminist Media Studies* Feb. 19: 1–6

Gupta-Carlson, H. (2010). "Planet B-Girl: Community Building and Feminism in Hip-Hop." *New Political Science* 32 (4): 515–529.

Habermas, J. (1984). *The Theory of Communicative Action*. Vol. 1. Boston: Beacon Press.

Haenfler, R. (2014). *Subcultures: The Basics*. London: Routledge.

Hebdige, D. (1979). *Subculture: The Meaning of Style*. London: Routledge.

Hodkinson, P., and Bennett, A., eds. (2012). *Ageing and Youth Cultures: Music, Style and Identity*. London: Bloomsbury.

Johnson, I. (2014). "From Blues Women to B-Girls: Performing Badass Femininity." *Women & Performance: A Journal of Feminist Theory* 24 (1): 15–28.

Jones, A. J. (2010). "A Battle of Repression: Hip Hop Bgirls, Burns and Gestural Languages 1970 to 2010." Unpublished MA thesis, Florida State University.

Jones, A.J. (2018). "Bgirls as Drag Kings." *Perspectives on American Dance: The New Millenium*. Eds. J. Atkins, S.R. Sommer, and T.H. Young. Gainesville: University Press of Florida. pp. 190–207.

LaBoskey, S. (2001). "Getting off: Portrayals of Masculinity in Hip Hop Dance in Film." *Dance Research Journal* (33)2:112–120.

Neal, M. A. (2010). "'A Man without a Country': The Boundaries of Legibility, Social Capital and Cosmopolitan Masculinity." *Criticism* 52 (3–4): 399–411.

Neal, M. A. (2013). *Looking for Leroy: Illegible Black Masculinities*. New York: New York University Press.

Ogaz, C. (2006). "Learning from B-girls." *Feminism in Popular Culture*, edited by J. Hollows and R. Moseley. New York: Berg. pp. 161–182.

Osumare, H. (2002). "Global Breakdancing and the Intercultural Body." *Dance Research Journal* 34.

Osumare, H. (2016). *The Africanist Aesthetic in Global Hip-hop: Power Moves*. N.Y.: Springer.

Rivera, R. Z. (2003). *New York Ricans from the Hip Hop Zone*. N.Y.: Palgrave Macmillan.

Salmivuori, R. (2017). "Breaking Through: B-Girls' Journey Towards a Stronger Sense Of Self." Unpublished M.A. thesis, Department of Social Research, Helsinki University, Finland.

Schloss, J. G. (2009). *Foundation: B-boys, B-girls, and Hip-Hop Culture in New York*. New York: Oxford University Press.

Shapiro, R. (2004). "The Aesthetics of Institutionalization: Breakdancing in France." *Journal of Arts Management, Law, and Society* 33 (4): 316–335.

Simard, H. (2014). "Breaking Down the Differences Between Breakdancing and B-Boying: A Grounded Theory Approach." Unpublished Master of Dance thesis, Université du Québec à Montréal.

Taylor, D. (2001). *The Archive and the Repertoire: Performing and Cultural Memory in the Americas*. Durham, NC: Duke University Press.

Thornton, S. (1996). *Club Cultures: Music, Media, and Subcultural Capital*. Middletown, CT: Wesleyan University Press.

Young, A. A., Jr. (2006). *The Minds of Marginalized Black Men: Making Sense of Mobility, Opportunity and Future Life Chances*. Princeton, NJ: Princeton University Press.

Young, I. M. (1980). "Throwing like a Girl: A Phenomenology of Feminine Body Comportment Motility and Spatiality." *Human Studies* 3 (1): 137–156.

Movies

Lyne, A. (Dir.). (1983). *Flashdance*. USA: Paramount Pictures.

Latham (Dir.). (1984). *Beat Street*. USA: MGM.

Raimist, R. (1999). *Nobody Knows My Name*. Women Make Movies.

YouTube

Style Elements V.S. Rock Steady Crew B-Boy Summit#3. https://www.youtube.com/watch?v=7JR7QNLLX6Q (accessed July 11, 2015).

Ken Swift vs K-Mel Boogie Brats | 90s Battle. https://www.youtube.com/watch?v=EBZcpG6RQvM| 90s battle: https://www.youtube.com/watch?v=EBZcpG6RQvM (accessed July 11, 2015).

Swift/Flow Master Routine B-Boy Summit#2 After Party: https://www.youtube.com/watch?v=KQN5O5wBNcs (accessed July 11, 2015).

Wild Style Coldcrush Brothers and Rock Steady Crew. https://www.youtube.com/watch?v=v2DmZKm6pIU (accessed July 11, 2015).

Bboy Physicx Korea Focus Finland Ken Swift USA | 2015 Dragon Styl Chins. https://www.youtube.com/watch?v=JmMBTwoEoGo (accessed July 11, 2015).

PART II

HIP HOP DANCE METHODOLOGIES

CHAPTER 7

....

LEARN YOUR HISTORY

Using Academic Oral Histories of NYC B-Girls in the 1990s to Broaden Hip Hop Scholarship

....

MIRI PARK

INTRODUCTION

WHEN I first started breaking, in 2001, I attended various events where b-boy elders constantly lectured us new jacks[1] to "learn your history!" I heard this mandate ad nauseum at the jams I attended in New York City (NYC). We were told to learn about who created what moves, who started what style, where things "went down,"[2] and so on. As most of us waited around (not so) patiently for the DJ to start playing the beats again, the message sank in eventually. How could it not? At nearly every event, at least one person, if not two or three people, would grab the mic and go on and on about how we needed to "learn your history!"

Naturally curious, I heeded the call and started asking the older generation of members in my crew, Breaking in Style (BIS), led by Richard "Breakeasy" Santiago, and its affiliate Dynasty Rockers, led by Ralph "King Uprock" Casanova, about their experiences. These conversations usually took place after practice sessions at McCarren Park, local gyms, hip hop jams, late-night *cuchifritos*[3] joints under the Williamsburg Bridge, people's homes, or in parking lots. I learned a great deal about breaking, as well as a dance that predated it called *rocking* (or *uprocking*), which was popular in the Williamsburg and Bushwick sections of Brooklyn from the late 1960s through the 1980s (Rivera 2003). I also learned about a Manhattan-based form called *lofting* through these informal conversations[4].

About a year after I started breaking, I was on a commercial shoot, where I met members of the all-female dance group Tru Essencia Cru (TEC): Ereina "Honey Rockwell" Valencia, Colleen "Miss Twist" Moore, and Deena "Snapshot" Clemente. At the time, Miss Twist was a b-girl known for her physical agility in power moves, and she had scored a tour with recording artist Missy Elliott. As a result, the crew needed a replacement for her for their upcoming gigs. After I got over the shock and honor of them asking me to step in, I continued my education in hip hop and b-boy/b-girl culture through TEC.

In this crew, I was in the presence of b-girl elders for the first time, whose dance lineage was completely different from the members of my home crew, BIS. For example, Snapshot's older brother is Stephen "Mr. Wiggles" Clemente, and Wanda "WandeePop" Candelario also grew up with both him and Jorge "PopMaster Fabel" Pabon, two of the most recognized dancers of their generation due to their membership in the Rock Steady Crew (it is worth noting that Mr. Wiggles credits his older sister Wanda—not to be confused with WandeePop—for inspiring him to dance[5]). Four of the five members of TEC had also been involved in *Jam on the Groove* (*JOTG*), the widely recognized first hip hop musical, and were closely affiliated with members of the Rock Steady Crew, Electric Boogaloos, and others prominent groups in the hip hop dance scene.

Through these two crew experiences, it wasn't long before I came across conflicting accounts of hip hop history and people who disagreed with each other's origin stories. Some people actively tried to discredit others in a thinly veiled attempt at self-preservation. Everyone spoke with authority, so it was difficult to draw a definitive conclusion. Was there an absolute truth in this situation? What affected the way the stories were told to me, specifically, versus the way the stories were told to someone else?

On one occasion, I had a conversation with PopMaster Fabel after an event in Los Angeles. I'd practiced and performed with him before in New York, as part of training with TEC, so while catching up with him, I told him that I was about to start graduate school with the goal of researching the roots of rocking/rock dance in Brooklyn. He listened to what I had to say, and then said that we can go over the dance's history right then and there, in the parking lot, and that everything can be and has been passed down orally. I wasn't sure if he meant that I didn't need go to graduate school to study the history, but his statement echoed in my mind.

While in graduate school, I came across oral history as an academic methodology I could use in my ongoing quest to "learn your history." I appreciated that this methodology was a way to hear everyone's story, and so I added to the lessons I had learned from my b-boy/b-girl elders before commencing my formal research. I found that oral history also coexisted with and extended the practices of the griot in (primarily West) African culture (Asante 2001). The griot is responsible for passing on histories via the oral traditions of storytelling, which often incorporate song and dance, helping these histories become their own forms of creation. As hip hop dance is rooted in Afrodiasporic practices, so too should attempts to capture its history be. Dance scholar Halifu Osumare (2009) writes:

> B-boying/b-girling is embodied text just as rap music is oral poetry. Dance in hip-hop culture, as a part of the African diaspora, can be likened aesthetically to a Sene-Gambian village bantaba circle, where a griot, or oral historian, sings the genealogical

> lineage of the people along with symbolic gestures and often spontaneous dance by
> the people that serve to focus the expressive energy of the entire event. (263)

When it came to interviewing dancers, specifically, I also found that oral history helped capture the gestures and songs practitioners used to fully relive their personal experiences and share their narratives.

Oral historian Alessandro Portelli (1998) writes: "Oral history has no unified subject; it is told from a multitude of points of view, and the impartiality traditionally claimed by historians is replaced by the partiality of the narrator" (73). To that end, academic oral history is a collaborative work between interviewer and interviewee to create a living history: a co-created document. It is an attempt to capture the recollection of stories, helping bridge the gap between the oral traditions of the past with present Western practices.

As part of my master's thesis project, I applied such an oral history method when conducting interviews with b-girls who came up in New York City in the 1990s, a time of regrowth for breaking following its mass commercialization and subsequent decline in the 1980s. Due to time and space constraints, I could not interview all of the b-girls who were active during this time period,[6] so I focused on the oral history of five specific practitioners: Colleen "Miss Twist" Moore, Pauline Sherrow, Ana "Rokafella" Garcia, Ereina "Honey Rockwell" Valencia, and Tara "big tara" Crichlow. I selected these women based on the definition of a "b-girl" as "the term for a girl who breaks" (Ana "Rokafella" Garcia-Dionisio, interview by author, January 15, 2008), as well as their contributions to the breaking scene while performing, organizing practices, teaching, battling, or judging in the 1990s. Also, since so much of this dance is about showing up and staying relevant, these b-girls continued to affect the scene by simply maintaining their involvement in the dance.

This chapter focuses on the oral history interviews I conducted with Rokafella and Honey Rockwell, the two women who inspired me and, I believe, a new generation of b-boys and b-girls locally in NYC and worldwide. When I asked Breakeasy and other people at practice who some other b-girls in the scene were, the names of these women were usually the first mentioned. In fact, the first b-girl I met in my career was Rokafella. We met on a photo shoot for *Dance Spirit Magazine* when I was researching an article about b-girls. I also met Honey Rockwell on a commercial shoot for the Oxygen network and subsequently became a part of her dance group TEC. Centering their histories as the focus of this time period complicates the common narrative of hip hop history, due to their participation in and around the production of *Jam on the Groove*. Whether or not they were aware of it at the time, they set standards and became role models in a time when stars were made more accessible, and at a faster rate than any other time in breaking history, thanks to the circulation of videotapes (Fogarty 2012), and the beginning of Internet use. Their stories provide links between the previous generation of b-boys and b-girls, and these women played a central role in preserving the art of breaking. Their perspectives on dealing with gender, femininity, and race provide insight as to how their life decisions filter into a larger consciousness about plural identities.

Each oral history interview I conducted lasted between one and two hours, and was conducted separately. I cite long passages from these interviews so that the reader can begin to feel the cadence of the interviewee's voice, with the intention that each woman speaks for herself in her own words. Before and following these quotes, I will provide context and significance to their stories, threading the individual stories through the needle holes of existing breaking history and elements of breaking culture.

Both women evoked the voices of others they interacted with, a storytelling technique known as "marking" (Mitchell-Kernan 1999), which I noticed was standard in the accounts of breakers. In this technique, the narrator would not only convey what was said but also take on the physical embodiment of how a person said something to tell you more about that person's character. During practice sessions or after rehearsals, I sat through many storytelling sessions, in order to understand the background for a move or a particular routine, or just to gossip and get filled in on why certain personal relationships were the way they were. Hearing these accounts taught me the value of storytelling, witnessing, marking, and naming in the breaking scene. Such stories helped define one's legacy and preserve personal histories.

Many b-girl battle stories are told in this manner to convey the excitement, disappointment, anger, or other emotion experienced by a participant or witness. As with any story, some were deliberately told in a way to alter perceptions or rewrite history in a favorable manner. I heard things about these people whom I thought had been around forever and was surprised to find out that their legacy had been created after one definitive battle or event. As they recalled their histories, I sometimes heard stories that were extremely deep and personal. Some chose to be more explicit than others to describe their stories more fully. In this sense, I found the oral history methodology of allowing my sources to help shape what would be made public to be the most appropriate.

When Honey Rockwell begins her story, she uses her "government-name," Ereina Valencia, signaling that her starting point in dance was her life prior to hip hop. More often than not, people in hip hop culture have aliases they become known by. It's only been recently that I've learned the "government names" of b-boys and b-girls I've known for years, because Facebook requires usage of one's given name. Prior to social media, it was unusual to know someone's real name unless you developed a rapport or friendship with them. It is not only a matter of pride but a type of protection. While this practice developed as an extension of affectionately identifying someone, it developed into a standard practice for b-boys and b-girls.

> I went from Ereina Valencia to Honey Rockwell in '94, and I've had it since. And this is how *this* happened. I had another name, which I dunno if I should say [*laughs*]. Okay, I'll say it. It's horrible, whatever. I thought of it myself, okay and it was right after I got back from doing the movie also. This is the name I wanted to be called, and that's the time I started doing bar mitzvahs, so we would all have [names] ... My name was "Rainbow," and the reason why I chose Rainbow was because, number one, my name is "Ereina," and it sounded like "rain," and I liked that ...

Right before that though, I didn't even know if I should get a name, but I did want one after Anita[7] got a name. She had told me one day, she goes, "I got a name!" I's like, "What's your name?" and I was *so* mad, because I was like, "*I* wanted to get a name." And she told me her name, and I thought—she was like, "It's Rokafella," and I was like, "That is sooo fresh!" And I was *so* jealous that she had a name. I was like, "Rock . . . a . . . fella . . . [*tsk*] . . . DAMN, I WANT A NAME!" So then I was thinking and writing things down, and I was like, "Rainbow!" because I do back handsprings, and my name is "REIN-a, " so it could be "Rainbow!" So, I did my first performance with Ghettoriginal/Rock Steady, and I have Wiggles, if, somebody may have that on tape, and I have Wiggles introducing me as, "Let's give it up for RAAAINBOW!" And at the end of that performance, he tells me, "I ain't eva callin you that name ever again." I'm like, "Whyyyy?" He was like, "You need a new name." And I was like, "Rainbow-Rock," "Rainbow-Rules," "Rainbow-One-er." I was tryin' to think of everything, and I couldn't [*laughs*] . . . So a lotta people knew me as Rainbow, because I would make sure that everybody . . . I was like, "Rainbow! I'm Rainbow." So Kwikstep was like, "No. We ain't callin you Rainbow, heh-HEH!" I was like, "Fine!"

So one time . . . we went to this practice in Jersey . . . It was me, Kwikstep, Gremlin, Smerk, Rokafella . . . And then we were comin' back, Gremlin would call me "honey" sometimes, he be like, "C'mere, honey." And there was a "Honey" in Rock Steady already, "Honey Dip," and she lives in California, she has her own store . . . she's the coolest girl. But you know, she had that name, so he knew her, he's from California. So I guess he would call me "honey," jus whatever, "Hey hon," you know, "What's up," he would always say "honey." So then, we were dropping off somebody in the Bronx, near, there was a street corner sign, and it was called "Rockwell Avenue," and Kwikstep said, "Yo, your name should be Honey Rockwell." He put it together, and Gremlin was like, "Yeah." So he started writing it down. He was like, "Yeah. Honey Rockwell." So the both of them . . . and I was like, "Honey Rockwell, yeah, I like it! Yeah." So that's it. And back then, at the time . . . my hair was kinda like, honey-colored so that's why in little rhymes, I would say, "Cuz my hair's like honey, and I rock real well." (Ereina "Honey Rockwell" Valencia, interview by author, October 15, 2006)

Rokafella saw her naming process start during her time in the clubs, when she went from being called "Ana" to being called "Anita," which she felt was somehow more freeing than her proper name.

When I started to dance on the street, I turned into somebody else. It just happened, because if I was nice and let myself get run over, I was gonna get runned over, so I had to change. I couldn't be the polite type of sweetheart, that maybe I was in the club, when I was dancing and tryna be pretty, and do some moves, even though they were tight and tough moves, I was still smiling, and still happy-go-lucky in the club. When I danced on the street it was different. Especially when I made the change from skirt to pants and all that. It was just like, "I need a name that's gonna be hard, because this is hard. This is not glamorous. It's not like a dance studio." So I think I just picked "Rokafella" because of Rockefeller Center, because people would say, "Yo, she be rocking people." I felt like that was the name that would typify who I had to be when I was in this realm. So that's how that name came up.

And I don't think anybody had that name yet. I think Redman had had a song called "Rockafella,"[8] and I believe that Jay-Z was up and around that time too. He was nowhere *near* who he is now,[9] but I felt like it was good. Granted, back then, I didn't know all the bullshit about the Rockefellers, I didn't know anything about the ... Rockefeller drug laws. I didn't know a lotta things, so I think the name was cute. I had spelled it differently, and it stuck. And it stuck, and it made me feel like, "Yeah man. I'm the ROKA. You can *build* on me. Like, what I'm gonna set down, y'all can really stand on it cuz it's gonna be solid. It's not gonna be some fluff-type shit." And so I think that's where it happened. It might have happened in '94, when I was going the whole rehab change, I think that's when I was really startin' to feel like "Roka-fella." I think maybe before then, I was playing with the name, and even cocaine and crack, "Rock" you know? So I was kinda like just playin with it. I didn't know if it would stick, and it wasn't until I started to break, that I got with GhettOriginal, that I was like, "Yo, I'm Rokafella. Call me Roka." And it stuck. (Rokafella interview)

For reference, here is a list of other dancers named in the oral history passages:

- Ken Gabbert, aka Ken Swift, or "Kenny"
- Gabriel Dionisio, aka Kwikstep, or "Kwik"
- Jorge Pabon, aka PopMaster Fabel, or "Fabel"
- Steffan Clemente, aka Mr. Wiggles, or "Wiggles" or "Wiggz"
- Adesola Osakalumi, aka D'Incredible, or "Des"
- Jerry Randolph, aka Flo Master, or "Flo" or "L.A." (Legs Almighty)
- Steve Roybal, aka Zulu Gremlin, or "Gremlin"
- Louis Torres, aka Louie New Wave
- Masami Kimihara, aka Masami

In his history of hip hop from 1968 to 2001, author Jeff Chang (2005) describes how the culture grew out of the ashes of the burnt-out buildings in the South Bronx in a post–Civil Rights, post–Malcolm X, post-Vietnam, pre–crack era, at the hands of Afrika Bambaataa and Kool DJ Herc. He also describes sculptor Henry Chalfant, photographer Martha Cooper, and dance historian Sally Banes as being the earliest documentarians of the scene. The commonality between the elements of what was to become hip hop—breaking, MCing, DJing, and writing—lay in their emphasis on marking your territory, either by original innovation, style, flavor, or technique. According to Rivera (2003), in the Bronx of the mid-1970s, former Black Spades gang member Afrika Bambaataa brought together the elements under the umbrella term "hip hop" and was the founding father of the Zulu Nation. People passed on knowledge of each element through personal contact at block parties, and technological developments also expedited growth and transmission of the practices of each element, spreading the popularity of hip hop.

In recent years, scholars such as Joseph Schloss (2009) and Halifu Osumare (2002) have focused on the history and issues related to breaking specifically, a tricky feat considering that the evolution of the dance is somewhat contested within the b-boy/b-girl community. In my own research and experience, as well as in Schloss's research, some trace the history of breaking back to Bushwick, Brooklyn, in the 1960s when a dance among Latino and White outlaw gangs developed from slam-dancing to a form now called "uprocking" (Richard "Breakeasy" Santiago, interview by author, April 15, 2007). This dance took place on street corners, parties in churches or dance halls, and bars. If a funk, rock, or soul record played at a function, people (usually men) created an Apache line[10] and gestured like they were attacking their opponent when dancing (Schloss 2009, 136). Such aggressive dancing was not necessarily a substitute for real violence. Many battles ended in actual fights or sometimes homicide (137; Chang 2005, 157–158). Often, the stakes of what could be won or lost became high. One could lose his name, colors (shirts or jackets that showed what gang you belonged to), sneakers, or even girlfriends. In the informal history sessions with my mentors, I only ever heard about women in this context of being prized possessions to be won or lost. In my time training with BIS/Dynasty, the only female rocker mentioned to me by name was Diana of the Dynasty Rockers, who is one of the women interviewed by Rivera (2003) in her book *New York Ricans from the Hip Hop Zone* (74). Rivera also names b-girls from before my time, such as Headspin Janet, Mamma Maribel, Sunkist Evie, Bunny Lee, and Lady Doze. She also profiles b-girls I had met or knew of, like Rokafella and Honey Rockwell.[11]

Sally Banes (1981) wrote the first article about breaking for the *Village Voice*, with accompanying photos by Martha Cooper. Banes (1984) noted in a follow-up article that the media had affected the development of breaking in the three years since she had first covered it. The older dancers had honed their skills and understood how to open up the circle to become more presentational; new dancers learned and copied from media sources instead of creating their own style. B-boys were used in the marketing of everything, from Burger King and McDonald's hamburgers to shoes and designer clothing. Soon, the scene in New York started to feel the negative effects of a fickle advertising industry that no longer thought hip hop and "breakdancing" would sell their products. This, coupled with the natural attrition[12] for the same reasons, in mid-seventies with the Black b-boys, and in the late-seventies with the first Latino b-boys, the New York scene went through another transition.

In a 2002 follow-up interview for the documentary *Style Wars* (1983), b-boy Frosty Freeze recalled how the scene shifted: "[In] 1985, the breaking scene was fading away, and I was struggling. One year, I didn't know what a $20 bill looked like. But I think the *Jam on the Groove* play, which happened in '94 to '96, I think that started it. That uplifted it again. And then the Rock Steady Anniversary, more b-boys started coming to the event" (Chalfant and Silver 2003).

By 1990, Fabel and Mr. Wiggles of Rhythm Technician, along with Crazy Legs and Ken Swift of the Rock Steady Crew (RSC), had parlayed their movie fame into performance careers. Under the auspices of GhettOriginal Productions, they put together their own show called *So What Happens Now?*, inspired by the death of RSC crewmember Buck4 earlier that year. They performed the piece at PS 122, a downtown performance space on 1st Avenue and 9th St., garnering critical praise from the downtown dance community and eventually winning a Bessie Award.[13]

They kept developing their theatrical work and, in November 1995, *JOTG* opened an off-Broadway run at the Minetta Lane Theater, produced by Gindi Theatrical Management. The show's mission was to educate people on how the performers used hip hop to survive, a message that would resonate with theatrical audiences. In May 1996, *JOTG* started touring, with its first international shows in Israel and Brazil and its last show in 1999 (Figure 7.1).[14]

In the process of developing the show, the members of *JOTG* ran practice sessions that became a touchstone for out-of-town b-boys looking to connect with NYC practitioners. This included German b-boys like Niels "Storm" Robitzky and Italian b-boy Maurizio "The Next One" Cannavó. The practice sessions also served to recruit and train new dancers: Honey Rockwell was then a twenty-three-year-old former gymnast and new mother, and Rokafella was a twenty-two-year-old street dancer with the Breeze Team–Transformers Crew and recovering drug addict. Thus, *JOTG* practice sessions not only gave life to this new stage show, but also to the b-girls who would go on to inspire a new generation of breakers.

FIGURE 7.1. Jam on the Groove reunion panel at the 30th Rock Steady Crew Anniversary at the Canal Room, July 24, 2007. *Left to right*: Rokafella, Kwikstep, Doc, Adesola, Honey Rockwell, Crazy Legs, SugaPop, unknown. Rokafella and Kwikstep were not extended a formal invite to participate in the panel but were added to the table because they showed up that day.

Rokafella came to the session after spending a few years hitting with her boyfriend Robert "Zen," and supporting a drug habit he had introduced her to. After entering that scene bright-eyed, she'd quickly learned that being the only woman in the crew came with massive challenges. People made assumptions about her relationships with the other members of the crew, who all made passes at her regularly. She went from dancing in cute outfits to dancing in baggy clothes that covered up most of her body. After all was said and done, Rokafella fought for her piece of the floor.

Only a few guys in the other crews, such as United Street Artists (USA) and the Float Committee, had one or two guys who were breaking. Rokafella admired one b-boy who never seemed to get dirty while dancing. On the sporadic occasions that she saw Kwikstep, she listened attentively as he told her about hip hop history. To Zen's chagrin, Rokafella learned that she was part of something more than just getting high and dancing on the street for money. When she decided to get clean in 1994, she ran into Kwikstep on the subway, on her way to church with her parents. He had just returned from Europe, touring with *So What Happens Now?* Knowing Rokafella as a street dancer, he told her about a dance audition for "girls who could do floor moves."

> So I told my parents, "Peace!" and I went [*laughs*] and I went to the audition, and I didn't have any shoes so, cuz I had like heels or something, I think I was tryna be the church-girl, and I had shoes. Yeah, so I auditioned barefoot. I did what I knew how to do, the knee spins, the popping, I learned the choreography, and I beat all the girls out, and I made it. In that batch of girls who auditioned was Deena, Wandee, Honey Rockwell, and a couple other girls, but somehow I made it. I made it, and they were only looking for one girl to go to France, to take Wiggles's wife's[15] place cuz she was pregnant at the time. So I got that gig, and that gig was the turning point. (Rokafella interview)

Both Honey and Rokafella came to the *JOTG* sessions with a hunger to learn everything thrown at them, but the ways they approached the sessions were on opposite ends of the spectrum. Rokafella was a natural when it came to picking up the challenging choreography. She had endured enough sexism from fellow street dancers and audience members, and hoped that working in this capacity, she would be respected and seen as equal to others in the room. Honey worked just as hard, but learning choreography was a challenge for her, so she happily accepted her place in the room. By the early 1990s, she had worked her first professional gig, as a dancer in the film *Mannequin 2* (1991). While on the set, she befriended dancer Louie New Wave, whom she ran into after having her first child. He later told her about practice sessions and encouraged her to attend to get active again. She went in the hopes of getting back in shape and having fun.

> So I went, you know I met up with Louie, I went over there and I see [*pauses*] I'm gonna cry[16]—I see these guys doin' routines, I see them, like, goin' crazy, I see Anita on the floor, learning *something*, with Kenny or somebody, and I see these other girls you know, CHOO CHHH [*gestures popping moves*], practicing doing their popping, and I'm like, "WOOOOW, this is, this is dope." You know? And I'm like . . . so

I start, they were like, "Go ahead. Go warm up," Louie was like, "Go warm up on the side or whatever," and I'm like, "Alright." So I warm up on the side and I start doing handstands and doing flips. So I see Anita looking at me out the corner of her eye and she's like, "Go 'head, mama . . . you know you wanna do that, go ahead, do your flips. Do it." So I was like, "Alright!" [*laughs*]. So I went in, I started doing aerials, and back handsprings, I's like "SHYAAAAA!" I was going crazy, and then, THEN, once I did that, Legs comes up to me. He's like, "Hey, what's up . . . oh you know howta break?" and [I was] like, "Yeah, sure." He's like, "Lemme see some footwork." I was like, "OK." I started doin' the MC Hammer-dance, the running man. He started crackin' up. He's like, "Yo, what are you doing?" I's like, "You said footwork," you know? So I started doing Running Man.[17] He was like, "Nah—YO, L.A. (Legs Almighty)! Help her." (L.A. is now Flo Master. His old name was Legs Almighty, and the reason why he changed it is because he didn't want everybody to call him Legs . . . Crazy Legs is who I'm talking about.) So, Flo Master took me on the side, first one person to teach me six-step, and to this day, I teach the way I was taught: Squat, right foot over left, watch the arms, and I mimicked his exact same movement and from then on, they would just drill me, all the time, and I would meet them, and . . .

I didn't really talk to the other girls, not that much, I didn't hang out with them. I was a mom. I had to—I would bring my daughter wit me in the carriage, you know, Amanda (my daughter) and you know, it was like really quick, in and out, and I was always with Louie. Louie'd come and I'd also . . . everybody had their own little people, in the dance studio, who they would connect with, but they would always tell me, "Go 'head, learn the routines," you know, like, cuz Anita was like, getting them all super-fast. I was like, "Man, I can't . . . I'm not gonna be able to learn that you know, it's gonna take me awhile." They were like, "Go 'head they got shows coming up, you know, in the school." So I's like, "Damn." So I would tryta practice. You know, either you went in, and you mimicked and got it, or you know, it was hard to like, they WOULD, they would show you, but I didn't wanna go up to them. I didn't want to interrupt nobody's flow or nothing, so I would just try to practice on the side and try to get it, but I didn't have the knack of getting choreography like that, it was really hard for me. In order for me to get it, I had to have someone really drill it into my head and teach it to me and me do it a thousand times. Oh, Masami was there too, my bad. Masami was there, Japan.

So then they started getting . . . you know, the girls who are called Deena and Wandee—it was Deena, Wandee and Brendy. Those were the three girls and then, wow, Deena, Wandee, Brendy, Masami, and Anita. The real hungry one was Anita. Always hungry, both of us, back-to-back learning chairs,[18] like, sweating profusely, and just like [*mimics holding a chair-freeze*], "JsHoldit! A little longer!" (Honey Rockwell interview)

Although *Jam on the Groove* presented the positivity of hip hop culture, the production was fraught with drama. For reasons unbeknownst to the cast, the management fostered an atmosphere of distrust and turned cast members against each other,[19] not a difficult task since dancers constantly tested each other's limits anyway. Rokafella and Masami were the first girls on tour to Austria with GhettOriginal, before *JOTG* opened at the Minetta Lane Theater, but things did not remain calm. Rokafella consistently came up against some friction when dealing with the guys in the cast, who would try to get involved personally with her. She had already dealt with this when she was hitting, and gotten kicked out of her crew, and had no mind to deal with the issue again.

It was fun, but it was also hard because I think the guys there, who were these pioneers, had a hard time, I think, dealing with me, because by the time I got to them, I was already kind of hardcore in my heart and in my mind, about who I was and what I was gonna be. And I think they were kinda like, "No, there's no girls like that. We're the kings, and breaking is for guys . . . I'll have sex witchu, but other than that, no." So I definitely was a thorn in their side when I got with them . . . Fabel, Kenny, Crazy Legs, Adesola, Doc, Gremlin (Zulu), Messiah came in and out (Soul Messiah). Those were the guys.

I think when I first came in, everybody was excited, cuz I think I looked and felt hardcore, like I was gonna fit what they were looking for, but then when I would open my mouth, or whenever I would turn down any of their stupid advances, I think they were kinda like, "Fuck you!" You know? [*laughs*] Like, "Who are you?" or, like, I would make a suggestion like "Shouldn't there be more women in that piece?" They were kinda like, "Okay, you're a new jack, and you're a *woman*, so . . . " And that's just saying it nicely. There was a serious perception of what women could or should do, made or solidified by the other women who were in the company. So you know, me being the way I was, really made me the enemy because those other women who were in the company were kinda like, "Oh, don't say nothin', don't rock the boat. We're guests in this house. I'm happy with crumbs. Not the b-boy [Crumbs].[20] I mean, happy getting crumbs from the table . . .

Yeah so, I was just the enemy. I think what I was doing was a little bit ahead of, ahead of the curve, you know? And I'll admit that I coulda been more, I dunno, more tactful with it, but at the same time like, fuck no, you know? It's just, the time had to just change, and I wanted to just feel free for a change to just say things and have them be well-received, you know? On the street, it was nothin' but like, you know, resistance and conflict, and you know, shit, I got kicked out of one crew because I *wouldn't* give up the panties, you know? . . . and here I am in a crew, in a theater troupe, that I thought would be different, but they were just more subtle . . . like, it was still there, but it was a little more polished. But I was still reacting the same, like, "No. I'm not havin' it. I don't want you, I don't want it. I wanna learn howta dance." And so because that was my stance, you know, the other girls got to go away a lot more than I did. And they got all the hype, and they got all the glory, whereas I was kinda like chucked away to the side, even though I was getting way better than they were. So, I didn't care because when it came down to doin' it in the circle, or on stage, you could, you could see me.

Even if you couldn't see me in the poster, or see me in the interview, or on tour,[21] you know. So I just kinda relied on that. I put my nose into the training thing. And luckily, because I was so into breaking and learning the history and learning the dance, I didn't need to go to rehab, because *this* was the rehab. So it was really like I picked up a dance instead of going to meetings all the time, and I was actually feeling like, "If I stopped smoking cigarettes and all this other stuff, I can dance longer. And look at these DANCES that I'm doing!" So now I could try to merge that with house and everything else that I did. You know, I didn't wanna do anymore drugs. That was over, you know. Of course, I relapsed a couple of times cuz I would run into my ex at clubs, or outside, or whatever, and he'd always get the best of me, because that was six years, you know? And I was *just* crawling away from him. I was just getting into a flow. So I did relapse a couple of times, for old time's sake, you know. But um, once I got with Kwikstep, he was like, "Yeah, I'm gonna be there with you. I'll train you, and I *do* have feelings for you." Then that door for drugs and Rob was shut so I was pretty happy about that. So I went clean, you know? . . .

And you know, I got kicked out of GhettOriginal, fuck it. And you know, they wanna say that the producers said I didn't have what it take, okay, but that was their explanation, which is fine. You know, if it makes them sleep better at night, [*laughs*] but I knew what it was. It was just becoming too much of, of a rif[t]. (Rokafella interview)

While Rokafella and Masami were in Austria, Honey used the time in New York to keep learning the routines for the show. Having had a different set of experiences leading up to the GhettOriginal practices, her perspective differed from Rokafella's. Crazy Legs put her down with the Rock Steady Crew and she opened *JOTG* at Minetta Lane and went on to tour with the show from 1995 to 1997.

Anita would—she liked to speak her piece all the time. If something was wrong, she'd come right out and say it, which I envy her for that, that she was able to do that, and I would talk to her about it. Being a girl, we'd talk and stuff. But I couldn't, I couldn't say anything because I felt it wasn't my place. I'm here for other reasons. I wasn't there to make a movement, or to . . . label myself as anything. I was there to practice. It was my outlet. It was something I did for fun, because I had a child. You know, I needed to make money, and these were *my* reasons. It wasn't about—and I was down with a good crew, and I just wanted to help continue to keep the crew, you know, together and do shows and routines and whatever we wanted to do at the time, and those were my reasons. And Anita . . . didn't want that. I dunno, Anita was just always standing up for women's rights and, she was right. I just wasn't ready for that yet, and she got kicked off the tour. And she said alotta things she shouldn't have said; she said certain things I didn't agree with, that I wasn't there with her, but she got kicked off the tour, so it just became me and Masami. Masami, she's Japanese, she didn't really know the language or what was being done at the time . . . the tour was difficult. (Honey Rockwell interview)

Upon opening at the Minetta Lane Theater, a mostly positive review of the show ran in *Variety*, highlighting the dancing of Mr. Wiggles, Ken Swift, Kwikstep, and Flo Master. In what looks like to be a calendar-listing summary that appears below the cast list, there is a mention of Honey's participation, but no mention of Rokafella. It stated:

With b-boys and fly-girls showing their moves everywhere from subway stations to "In Living Color" to the Kennedy Center Honors, potential ticket-buyers might doubt the need to shell out $35 for a hip hop stage show. They'd be wrong: In the live, intimate setting of the Minetta Lane Theater, the spins, pops and gyrations that make up hip hop dancing seem vibrant and new, and the dancers—a fifteen-member troupe called GhettOriginal Prods.—are splendid down to a man (although four women are included in the mix, their contributions seem secondary to what remains, like it or not, a male-dominated, even macho, form).[22]

The reviewer feels obligated to parenthetically mention the women in the work, and refers to them, not as the female counterpart to a "b-boy," but as "fly-girls."[23] After interviewing Honey and Rokafella, we see that two of the most-well respected b-girl elders in the current scene had only begun their breaking training while practicing with the cast members of *JOTG*. Each fought for her place the way that she thought best. Ultimately, their divergent views led them on different paths, and both had a significant impact on the breaking scene, starting in the mid-nineties. While on tour with *JOTG*, Honey inspired people all over the world to start breaking; back in New York, Rokafella helped build the NYC scene back up.

Honey started dating someone in the company, causing more controversy within the show. I should note here that in her oral history interview, Honey deliberately did not disclose details about this, and I chose not to ask for clarification. Before we began the interview, I made clear to her that we were co-creating a record of her life history and that she could share as much or as little as she cared to. Beyond that, the process of oral history interviewing also allows interviewees to redact information from their transcripts for as long as they feel necessary. In this case, Honey chose not to disclose the identity of the person in the company, and, therefore, I did not ask. Despite the scrutiny she got for having a relationship with another cast member, Honey had a few moments to realize the importance of the show she was a part of.

> I remember doing the shows and doing question and answer wit people and them saying, you know, and listening to the guys and what they would were saying. They would talk how this dance is not respected and, "We need to, you know, we're trying to teach the world," you know, all of you in the theater audience we would be in, "We want all of you to recognize this dance as a *dance*, and it is not a fad and this, what we live, is our culture, and it is not what you see on TV, what they are portraying hip hop to be." And at the time when we toured, it was the big things of Tupac and Biggie,[24] when they were goin' through all their stuff, all gangsta violence this, and seeing the hoochie videos and all of this stuff, and here we are, 1994–1997, here we are, *Jam on the Groove: A Hip Hop Musical*. People see "hip hop" [as a] new word at the time,[25] people see that word and would literally get scared. And I'm telling you the honest truth, we were sitting eating dinner one time, me, Kenny, Wiggles, an old grandpa, right at the end of a show, whatever, an old grandpa couple, come up to me, and they were like, "God bless you. You did such a wonderful performance today. At first, I'm gonna tell you, we were a little nervous coming to see a show like this, but we got tickets, we're part of the theater's mailing list or whatever, and at first we were scared, but we are going to recommend our entire family to come see your show. It's incredible." See?

We were making differences then that we didn't even know. And I really think now because of the guys that ran it and got, I love them . . . Fabel and all them, but I think because they were so caught up in the business end of it, they couldn't be a part of their creativity and art, that they missed—I bet you *they* don't realize how much of an influence or impact they have on the world! You know, they just go ahead with their duties, and they're continuing to do their duties today as being hip hop spokesmen, ambassadors for everyone, and I don't even think they realize it. And that's why I always feel it's important for me, too, because I feel I'm the last one to learn from the guys that made it up and I feel it's important for me to speak now. Now is my time, like when Anita wanted me to speak, I couldn't. I didn't *know* anything about it,[26] but being, living, and experiencing everything I've done, *now* I feel like I can talk about, you know, keeping kids outta trouble, and, you know, I know nobody's perfect, I'm not perfect, you know, I do my thing or whatever, but having that outlet just for them to know, as long as you have something and live your dream and think of something you would ever wanna become, it helps, it helps. It helped me, it helped a lotta people get out of their situations. So, show closes up, or no, show didn't close up, I was asked—Wiggles was asked to do a show in Las Vegas.[27] He had gotten the people for it, and I wanted out of *Jam on the Groove* so bad. I was done. It was too much hecticness for me, too much controversy, I couldn't take it anymore. It was killing me, the relationship I was in was terrible. (Honey Rockwell interview)

Meanwhile, in New York, Rokafella was busy trying to find her own way outside the affiliation of GhettOriginal. She and Kwikstep had started dating soon after she joined the GhettOriginal practices, and even though Kwik opened the show in New York, he quit the tour because of the excessive drama between the dancers and management. They started their own production crew called "Full Circle," with the mission of reviving the careers of old b-boys. Since they started presenting work that covered some of the same ground that *JOTG* did, they experienced some backlash from their former castmates but kept on with their goal. Full Circle started holding practice sessions at Ferretta's,[28] providing space for the old schoolers to practice, while also training newer dancers. Rokafella had the painful realization that, even though their efforts were reviving the New York scene, once she and Kwikstep retrained the old school b-boys and trained the new jacks, people started to defect to *JOTG*.

Our first members were Speedy-D from the Bronx, Shakey-Shake the DJ from the Bronx, Simey from the Lower East Side, and Bam-Bam from the Lower East Side. That was our first crew . . . It was fun, it's just that when we started to pick up a little bit of momentum and a little bit of notoriety, the egos clashed again, you know, and everybody kind of splintered off, and went to GhettOriginal. So it was kinda like, "I don't need this, I'll make my own shit. Oh, hey wait. I'ma go and work with GhettOriginal," you know? And Kwik was still with GhettOriginal, so Kwik did the *Jam on the Groove* thing when it was at the Minetta Lane, but there was so much *shit* happening with GhettOriginal and everything there that he didn't go on tour with them. He was like, "I'm *not* traveling. There's no way, you know . . . I'm not going to a country where I can't just leave and go to my house. When I'm stuck in the same hotel room, or with you guys . . . " So he made that decision at that point. And it wasn't for me. He was like, "I'm not leaving because of Roka," he was leaving because, "I can't deal. This was really just going to implode." Which it did, sadly. And that was I think, '98? No, '96. Then they toured without him, and we were kinda pickin' up the pace a little bit with our company too, even though a lot of our company members ended up there. Bam-bam did it . . . Shakey-Shake was a DJ for them for a while. Speedy-D rocked with them for a while. Speedy-D went with New York City Breakers, which was experiencing a comeback.

It was hard, because I think b-boying, in New York, was really starting to wake up, and people were coming out of the woodwork, talkin 'bout, "Oh, *I* was there," "Oh, *I'm* the shit," and then because me and Kwik were startin' to make headway, people were like really projecting their like, negative energy towards me and Kwik, like, "*Y'all* weren't there, and who the fuck are *you*, a girl, blablabla." It was just, people would tell me, "Well, you're not even uprocking, right? and I'd be like, you know, "Are you crazy? Were you there with me? I wasn't around your way. I'm not questioning you. Do you *want* me to question you? Like, does that make you feel relevant?" You know? So it was really difficult. Between '96 and 2000, it was *really* hard in New York City because everybody was like scrutinizing everybody, like, "Y'all ain't the shit," or "Y'all ain't doin' it right," or "I don't charge for practice sessions," or . . . It was just bananas. It was the rebirth I think, of b-boying in New York City. (Rokafella interview)

Despite the negativity that Rokafella and Kwikstep faced while holding their own sessions, their efforts opened the floor for people to come back to breaking and to foster new dancers. Their sessions extended the tradition of free or low-cost local practices that *JOTG* presented. In 2001, a dancer invited me to a free practice session in McCarren Park in Williamsburg, Brooklyn. When it was too cold to practice outside, we would dance at a community center in the Bushwick Houses, a housing project, a spot procured by Breakeasy. In 2016, these sessions continue, with the addition of house dance (Cricket's *Househead Session*, all-women house dance crew MAWU's *M.U.D. sessions*), and popping (*Pop Shop*) practices at various dance studios for $5 per person.

Given the growing number of b-girls in the world, it's not only a restorative practice to recount these women's life experiences, but a necessary one. The practice of oral history provides a dynamic space for difference and equality to coexist, allowing for all identities and voices to be heard in the same space. The stories are at once reconciliatory, conflicting, and reformative. In this chapter, we have seen that hip hop as a craft, a culture, an identity, and a lived experience that is tremendously nuanced. The range of experiences in just these two women's life stories shows that they do not encompass a straightforward trajectory. In exploring these women's stories, we see that there's less difference in the physical act of breaking or the performance qualities of b-boying and b-girling. Rather, the differences emerge in the lived experience, or the performative qualities of being a "b-girl" or a "b-boy."

Of course, the story doesn't end there. Honey Rockwell has since moved to Georgia, and opened the Rockwell Dance Academy with her husband, b-boy Roger "Orko"

Romero. Rokafella also continues to train new dancers with her husband, Kwikstep, in New York City as part of Full Circle, and she also teaches hip hop dance at the New School, a university in NYC. Both women serve as judges in local, national, and international breaking competitions.

As standard oral history practice goes, it may be necessary to conduct more interviews with them, along with further analysis of breaking history and culture. These women's lives show how hip hop and breaking exist in multiple horizons of time, space, and cultural identity. Oral history methodology has the capability to give us a way to explore stories that add to an existing narrative, in order to complicate history as it's written in scholarship, presented in media, and as it is told socially. In hearing these two women's stories, we learn about the challenges women faced navigating a dance culture dominated by men, and the relationship they had to each other that was one of sisterhood with all of the complexity that comes with familial relationships. In their stories, we see the struggles, sacrifices, and decisions that characterize the difference between a b-girl's experiences as opposed to that of a b-boy's. I am hopeful that this methodology will allow us to hear the multiple voices of the many people who make up the breaking and hip hop dance communities.

NOTES

1. Slang for "newcomers."
2. Slang for "happened," both in actions and words.
3. Puerto Rican and Dominican restaurants in primarily Latino neighborhoods of NYC that serve fried foods, soup, rotisserie chicken, rice, beans, *yúca, plátanos, espaguetí*, fresh juices, and coffee, among other food items.
4. Lofting refers to dancing that took place at David Mancuso's Loft in the East Village. There is debate as to whether or not lofting is its own dance form/discipline or what some dancers talk about as "a feeling." Breakeasy spoke about lofting as a foil to the characteristically aggressive nature of rocking. He also discussed about lofting gear (fashion) differed from rocking gear.
5. In an interview in a documentary, Wanda stated:

    Stevie [Mr. Wiggles] says that he always used to watch me . . . I didn't have a problem uprocking wit my heels on, you know? And Stevie could tell you some stories that I wouldn't even remember on my own. But he says that he remembered seeing me one time passing by, with a bag or something, I think I was shopping for my mom, and I'm in my heels and stuff, and they're uprockin in the middle of Fox Street and 156th. And all of the sudden outta nowhere, I put down my bag and I started burning the guy. He says, 'I'll never forget that, Wanda. You just started uprockin, you had your heels on, and you just burned the guy. From that day on, I was like WOW, that's what I wanna do.' You know?" (Samantha Marie Prior [2005], "Women in Battle," videorecording, DVD, Project Amazon Films)

6. I'd like to acknowledge the other b-girls active in New York scene in the 1990s whom I did not interview but hope to in a larger iteration of this project: A-B girl (formerly of Problemz Kru, now with Domestic Apes Crew); PattiDukes; Bonnie (Supreme Beings);

Mega and Renegade (now with Rock Steady Crew); Melissa and Cat (formerly of Power Femalia); and Nez (Breaks Kru). I also would like to point out that there were women active at the time who were hip hop dancers but specialized in other forms, such as popping, locking, waacking, party dances, or freestyle. Some of these women are Deena "Snapshot" Clemente, Wanda "WandeePop" Candelario, Lenaya "Tweetie" Straker, Robin Dunn, and Marjory Smarth.

7. This is the familiar name of "Ana" (Rokafella).
8. He had an album on Def Jam called *Rockafella*, released in 1994.
9. Jay-Z started Roc-a-fella Records in 1996.
10. Two lines of men facing each other. It is a variation on a gang initiation, where an initiate must make it through the two lines of men assaulting him with bats, fists, chains or other weapons (Chang 2005, 42). For a longer explanation see Schloss (2009, 135–138).
11. It should also be noted that among the few articles written specifically about women's contributions, Nancy Guevara (1996) profiles Baby Love, one of the first b-girls down with the Rock Steady Crew.
12. People leaving the scene for reasons ranging from settling down with a family, moving away from the City to getting locked up, going to college, etc.
13. A New York Dance and Performance Award, the downtown dance equivalent of the Oscars. The awards ceremony is held annually at the Joyce Theater and co-presented by Dance Theater Workshop and Danspace Project. The award is named in honor of Bessie Schonberg.
14. "Jam on the Groove" panel discussion, Rock Steady Anniversary, New York, NY, July 24, 2007. Panelists included Rokafella, Kwikstep, Doc, Adesola, Honey Rockwell, Crazy Legs, and Suga Pop.
15. Zoraya Clemente aka "Zee Boogie" or "Zee."
16. Honey's voice is full of emotion as she recalls the first time she saw this practice. I, too, get a little cloudy-eyed because I was transported back to before I knew anything about breaking or the scene. We share the sentimentality and significance of our first-practice experience, because we've now become a second family with the people we first practiced with.
17. Popular '90s hip hop party dance where a dancer appears to be running in place. It is, however, not anything close to breaking.
18. Chair Freeze, or "Chair," for short—a foundational b-boy freeze, or pose, where one elbow is tucked into the lower abdomen and the corresponding hand and head are on the floor, with the corresponding foot completing the support of the body on one side. The free leg is typically bent and crossed over the supporting leg. The free arm is usually placed akimbo on the free side. A basic move, but difficult for a beginner to master.
19. "Jam on the Groove" panel discussion.
20. She says this to distinguish from a b-boy named "Crumbs." She was talking about "crumbs" as in the bread pieces.
21. This is an attitude shared by many underground dancers who do not "go commercial," either by choice or by consequence (of not getting hired).
22. Evans, George. "Jam on the Groove." *Variety*. 10 December 1995. http://variety.com/1995/film/reviews/jam-on-the-groove-1200444135/ (accessed April 25, 2016).
23. The "Fly Girls" was the name of the group of interstitial dancers from the TV show *In Living Color*. They were led and choreographed by Rosie Perez, and included Jennifer Lopez and Carrie Ann Inaba, before each went on to mainstream acting, singing, and producing success and fame.

24. Rap stars Tupac Shakur and Biggie Smalls (see George 1998, 47)
25. The term "hip hop" was coined in the 1970s but wouldn't become popular in mainstream vernacular until about a decade later, after the media blitz; but the term was virtually unknown to theater-going audiences.
26. It's interesting to note here that Rokafella was "hitting" (breaking in public spaces for money) in the 1980s and 1990s, effectively making her "older" than Honey.
27. A show called *MADhattan* opened at the New York-New York Hotel and Casino in Las Vegas on June 12, 1997 (Marks 1997).
28. Located at 651 Broadway, above Houston. The building also housed Dance Space Center, and Leslie Roll 'n' Skate.

References

Asante, K. W. (2001). "Commonalities in African Dance." In *Moving History/Dancing Cultures*, edited by A. Dils and A. C. Albright, 144–151. Middletown, CT: Wesleyan University Press.

Banes, S. (1981). "Breaking Is Hard to Do: To the Beat Y'all." *Village Voice*, April 22–28, 31–33.

Banes, S. (1984). "Breaking Changing." *Village Voice*, June 12, 82.

Chalfant, H., and Silver, T. (2003). *Style Wars*. New York: Plexifilm.

Chang, J. (2005). *Can't Stop Won't Stop: A History of the Hip-Hop Generation*. New York: St. Martin's Press.

Fogarty, M. (2012). "Breaking Expectations: Imagined Affinities in Mediated Youth Cultures." *Continuum: Journal of Media & Cultural Studies* 26 (3): 449–462.

George, N. (1998). *Hip Hop America*. New York: Penguin.

Guevara, N. (1996). "Women Writin' Rappin' Breakin'." In *Droppin' Science: Critical Essays on Rap Music and Hip Hop Culture*, edited by W. E. Perkins, 49–62. Philadelphia: Temple University Press.

Marks, P. (1997). "They Took Manhattan and Gussied It Up for Las Vegas." *New York Times*, July 14. https://www.nytimes.com/1997/07/14/theater/they-took-manhattan-and-gussied-it-up-for-las-vegas.html?pagewanted=all.

Mitchell-Kernan, C. (1999). "Signifying, Loud-Talking and Marking." In *Signifyin(g), Sanctifying, and Slam Dunking: A Reader in African American Expressive Culture*, edited by G. D. Caponi, 309–330. Amherst: University of Massachusetts Press.

Osumare, H. (2002). "Global Breakdancing and the Intercultural Body." *Dance Research Journal* 34 (2): 30–45.

Osumare, H. (2009). "The Dance Archaeology of Rennie Harris: Hip-Hop or Postmodern?" In *Ballroom, Boogie, Shimmy Sham, Shake: A Social and Popular Dance Reader*, edited by J. Malnig, 261–281. Urbana: University of Illinois Press.

Portelli, A. (1998). "What Makes Oral History Different." In *The Oral History Reader*, edited by R. Perks and A. Thompson, 63–74. New York: Routledge.

Rivera, R. Z. (2003). *New York Ricans from the Hip Hop Zone*. New York: Palgrave Macmillan.

Schloss, J. G. (2009). *Foundation: B-boys, B-girls and Hip Hop Culture in New York*. New York: Oxford University Press.

CHAPTER 8

HARD LOVE PART 1

Corporealities of Women Ethnographers of Hip Hop Dances

IMANI KAI JOHNSON

INTRODUCTION

HIP HOP studies has always been shaped by women conducting on-the-ground research among practitioners. Whether we are talking about Tricia Rose and her field-establishing *Black Noise: Rap Music and Black Culture in Contemporary America* (1994), or dance journalist Sally Banes, whose 1981 cover story in the *Village Voice* (April 22–28 issue), titled, "To the Beat Y'All: Breaking Is Hard to Do," featuring shots from famed photographer Martha Cooper, how Hip Hop gets talked about has their mark on it (Banes 1994, 121–123; Cooper 2004; Cooper and Chalfant 1984). This chapter focuses on the dance element of Hip Hop, and thus provides an opportunity to explore the experiences of women ethnographers, most of whom are, incidentally, practitioner-researchers. By documenting how our experiences shape the questions we ask, we have a better understanding of where Hip Hop studies and Hip Hop dance studies are and can go. I offer this exploration as a contribution to broadening the field's areas of inquiry.

Though I grew up with Hip Hop and felt its ubiquitousness in my daily life, research offered a way both to deepen my relationship to the culture and even contribute something back, despite not being a practitioner. I spent over ten years researching breaking culture, specifically the epistemological implications of the embodied Africanist aesthetics embedded in the ritual cypher (the dance circle) and in global Hip Hop. My research situated me in a circuit of breaking and streetdance events across the United States, in parts of Europe, and in Toronto, during which time I crossed paths with an array of women ethnographers. Perhaps they were especially noticeable to me because my focus on breaking meant attending events where women were frequently a numerical minority. Initially, my interest in other researchers was to see if there were correlations in our experiences, and personally to explore the forms of participation others have carved out for themselves. Eventually I came to appreciate both the commitment of a cadre of researchers that I had inadvertently joined, and the critical analytic lenses that they offer.

The overlap in our experiences began to give my analysis some direction. For example, one shared struggle, even for practitioner-scholars, is dealing with the tendency of streetdancers to distrust researchers, and specifically academics, for reasons rooted in past misrepresentations and exploitations, which are known and shared orally throughout the community. To research streetdances necessitates navigating spaces wherein you are held at arm's length by many until you "show and prove"—a foundational, competitive demand to demonstrate one's skills and knowledge of Hip Hop cultural imperatives. One practitioner-scholar described the feeling of attempting to join a new breaking scene alongside researching it as "a kind of hard love where you had to prove yourself, but they were paying attention to let you know that you had to prove yourself." She articulates a trial by fire that any breaker could experience in the beginning, but her comments must be contextualized by the reality that earning their attention is already experienced in gendered ways—that being ignored or not taken seriously has particular connotations for women in those scenes, as will become clear in the following discussion. Those conditions in turn magnify the challenges any researcher faces when entering those scenes, even as a practitioner. "Hard love" speaks to the labor involved in researching under these conditions; of showing and proving that they can be trusted and respected. The experiences of the researchers featured here give insight into the nature of doing fieldwork in Hip Hop dance spaces, all while doing the unrecognized labor that comes with navigating our corporealities (or corporeal realities) as women.

The "love" part of hard love is evident in what Hip Hop feminists write about as the contradictory positionality of women in Hip Hop that coexists with the "oppositional consciousness" that Hip Hop nonetheless arms them with to challenge those very conditions (see Pough 2007; Durham et al. 2013). Hence my spelling of Hip Hop with capitals and no hyphen. A hyphen might imply a compound word, but Hip Hop is a meaningful noun on its own. Moreover, Hip Hop is a culture, a sensibility, and for many, a way of life; therefore it is irreducible to a genre of music or dance, as lower-case "hip hop" tends to represent.[1] The dynamism of Hip Hop rests on internal logics that allow it to adapt and make room for those who help to shape it on *its* terms. That is a very special kind of love to me, one that amplifies the culture as much as it challenges it to move differently. As I have written elsewhere, "Love is both a modality through which to build community, and a resource for changing that community such that it is more receptive to alternative grounds that challenge existing forms of control" (Johnson 2014, 26). Put more simply, as Tricia Rose has said, "love is an incredibly political act," (quoted in Schwartzapfel 2009, n.p.). The experiences of the ethnographers featured here contextualize real-world applications of methodological approaches that have been honed over time. Their investigatory possibilities are ultimately in service to contributing back to those at the center of their research. That, too, is the hard love of their work.

This study of women ethnographers of Hip Hop streetdances draws on interviews I conducted about their experiences navigating their fields, which I have anonymized to respect the sometimes candid nature of our conversations. The chapter asks: How do women ethnographers prepare themselves for the field, and then navigate it in service of shining a light on the contributions of the people they observe, consult, and connect with? How do they deal with the demands of ethnographic research in a culture wherein "issues of sexism, misogyny, and homophobia [are] still excluded" in visions of Hip Hop, as Shana Calixte (2009, n.p.) notes? How do these women ethnographers balance their personal connections and participation in the life of the communities they are researching with the demands of their professions?

METHODOLOGICAL APPROACH

I approached this project in two ways. From December 2014 through Summer 2015 I conducted in-depth, one-on-one interviews via Skype with seven women who have done substantial ethnographic research in Hip Hop dance communities.[2] These interviews lasted one to three hours each. I started by interviewing women I already knew and had relationships with, and soon branched out to others I encountered informally, through mutual colleagues or during fieldwork. It goes without saying that the countless other conversations I have had over the years about successes and failures in fieldwork, and everything in-between, also inform this project.

Secondly, in 2015 I opened a private Facebook group page called "Women Documenting Hip Hop Dance Cultures." At first, participation in the group was by invitation, and then the group expanded by word-of mouth to include others, some of whom had just begun their research. I never pursued trying to develop the Facebook page into a more official site for the exchange of ideas (and it eventually fell out of use), but at its peak there were a dozen members, including graduate students, photographers, professors, journalists, and oral historians. The page revealed that the vast majority of the women I am in contact with started out as Hip Hop dancers, and those who did not were dancers in other genres. While the page largely served as a place of making introductions and sharing details about how we came to research Hip Hop dances, it confirmed a predominance of practitioner-scholars or other folks who had dual roles as artist- researchers. Many of their comments spoke to that duality.

Because the women I interviewed are all at different stages in their careers and have varying degrees of ongoing participation in their respective scenes, it is important that their participation in this chapter "causes no harm," as one informant phrased it. My close relationship with several of the people featured here resulted in particularly candid interviews about their lives and the lives of their research subjects, making the use the interviews possible only if I anonymized their quoted remarks. Protecting them is essential to my investigation. I omit time, place, and dates, and offer only select identifying information when relevant to the context of their statements.

My study includes cis women and a trans woman, and features contributors of various races, ethnicities, ages, marital statuses, and professions. Since most of the scholarship on Hip Hop dances focuses on breaking, most of the ethnographers featured here do too, but not all of them. Each person interviewed studies genres that can fall under the umbrella of Hip Hop, including but not limited to locking, popping, waacking, breaking, voguing, turfing, house, and Hip Hop party and social dances.[3] Thus I use the term *Hip Hop streetdances* broadly, not to extract them from their particular histories but to explore dance research experiences that become evident when we consider Hip Hop dance in its most generous of definitions. Thus the material products of their research vary: books, academic articles, journalism, photographic exhibits, archives, and more. That said, this work does focus on North American women, which has bearing on their comments, notwithstanding that most of them have spent significant time abroad over the course of their lives or careers. I offer this exploration to begin a conversation with the hopes of recognizing what echoes in our experiences across our differences, and without erasing the particularities of our stories.

Unsurprisingly, I define *ethnography* broadly as well. In this work, ethnography encompasses participant-observation and in-depth interviews alongside spending sustained time in Hip Hop dance communities, cultivating social networks as a necessary part of producing various materials. As a result, I use the words "researcher" and "ethnographer" interchangeably to capture how their various on-the-ground and culturally embedded research approaches might fall outside of discipline-specific definitions of ethnography in the academy. My broad approach is an expression of Hip Hop's foundational recognition that expertise comes from living, doing, and being, which tends to get more respect than degrees. It is worth stating, then, that not all of those interviewed identify as academics, but they all contribute to Hip Hop dance studies.

While "dancers as embodied researchers" is not a new concept, the notion that streetdancers are in fact sophisticated researchers who study movement over time and in contemporary contexts is, arguably, less valued. Yet they study and analyze dance in an embodied way. As one ethnographer explained:

> I really argue in my work that streetdancers are scholars. Of course, I'm not trying to say that what we do as academic scholars is the same as what we do as practitioners of streetdance. But I think it's very important to understand that the structures of the dance styles themselves offer opportunities to study, and that what we are doing, for example, when we enter a dance cypher is studying movement.

Unlike how we study in classrooms or studios, participating in the culture (for example, in a cypher) is a deep study of moving bodies in relation to the music, onlookers, other practitioners, and one's own approach. Moreover, practitioners already value the preservation of Hip Hop streetdance's oral histories. Their sense of duty is most evident in the urgency they attach to documenting aging pioneers. Thus, there is a research-drive embedded in streetdance cultures that might account for why so many ethnographers of Hip Hop dances were practitioners first.

Finally, this chapter presents autoethnographic accounts of research experiences. Communications scholars Carolynn Ellis, Tony Adams, and Arthur Bochner begin their article "Autoethnography: An Overview" with a clear definition: "Autoethnography is an approach to research and writing that seeks to describe and systematically analyze (*graphy*) personal experience (*auto*) in order to understand cultural experience (*ethno*)" (Ellis, Adams, and Bochner 2011, n.p.). The dialogic between personal and cultural experience they propose is deeply layered in meaning. In a talk titled "Home with Hip Hop Feminism," media studies scholar Aisha Durham (2018, n.p.) speaks to that dialogic in her approach to autoethnography, which seeks to "bridge lived experience with living memories that are encoded in signs and symbols that allow us to craft creative, or critically engaged, community-centered, and culturally relevant research using democratic writing and presentation practices that can live in and transcend the academy." One of the ways that they transcend the academy is captured in feminist sociologist Elizabeth Ettorre's (2016) *Autoethnography as Feminist Method*, which asserts that it is critical not to effectuate an inauthentic sense of methodological distance or false objectivity, but instead to name the ways that our lives and even our bodies are implicated within our research projects. Autoethnography magnifies the fact that I share a closeness, interrelatedness, and differences with the women featured here that I wish to highlight instead of downplay. Indeed, this chapter argues that our shared experiences and our differences are essential for understanding our corporealities.

Corporealities in dance studies captures the meaningfulness of our physicality within a given space. Our bodies in dance spaces are "meaning-filled," as dance scholar Susan Foster (1996, xiii) writes. While the nature of that meaning is relative to any given experience, corporeality reminds us that "the body [acts] as mediator between physical reality and larger social contexts" (O'Shea 2019). One of the women I interviewed articulated this particularity as follows:

> I think that, at the risk of sounding essentialist, and that's not what I'm going for . . . I think that because we are in touch with the assumptions about gender, about race, about sexuality, about class, there's a certain sensibility because of our own location that gives us a really important lens through which to understand Hip Hop culture, [and] Hip Hop dance given its roots . . . It facilitates a level of expertise that I think is not really quite understood but [it] is really important that we continue to do this work.

She began by referencing an obvious assumption: that speaking about women broadly ran the risk of being misread as essentialist or reductive. By naming it though, she infers a purposeful "strategic essentialism," a term coined by Gayatri Chakravorty Spivak (1988) to identify an embodied understanding that does not gloss over our variances, and instead promotes our differences as our strengths. Returning to the quote, I especially appreciate her use of the word "facilitate," which suggests that an experiential understanding of being subjected to assumptions about race, gender, and sexuality gives one an acumen in navigating community-based Hip Hop spaces. "A certain sensibility" is an appropriately imprecise way of articulating insights informed by our corporealities. It is not some prior analytical awareness that makes women "experts." Rather, it is that our existences enable an understanding of Hip Hop spaces, which are also subject to racist, sexist, and classist assumptions. Although in this example, her unstated "we" might also speak to the fact that *we* are both African diasporic women, the "we" in this chapter is broader. By extension, "a certain sensibility" is more nebulous in my use, but nonetheless important to highlighting a strategically essentialist grouping whose overlapping, but particular, experiences lend themselves to greater insights about the research side of streetdance.

Thematic Analysis

I organize my analysis into three overlapping themes: (a) self-presentation and identity in the field; (b) strategies for establishing boundaries in the context of informal social dance spaces; and (c) the corporealities at the intersection of race, gender, age, and nationality in the field. I will present several perspectives on these themes to draw out the similarities and differences of our experiences. I add my own to provide another layer of comparative and contrastive analysis. These themes also allow me to pinpoint the challenges that we face, and the hard love of our decision-making in the field.

Self-Presentation, Identity, Boundaries, and Intimacy

What kinds of concerns do women ethnographers of Hip Hop streetdances consider before they enter the field and interact with research subjects? Dress and attire play a significant part in the initial efforts to do fieldwork. Hip Hop streetdance events have their own demands, too. Interviewees shared that they considered different kinds of preparatory work related to self-presentation, identity, personal boundaries, and intimacy, before entering the field. Interviewees were concerned about how they cared for their bodies in anticipation of fieldwork, the functional particulars of the space that impacted how they engaged with subjects, and how their bodies would be interpreted in those spaces as a result.

The women I consulted raised matters that reminded me of my own efforts to prepare for eight-hour days of standing, squatting, sitting on grungy floors and maneuvering for the best view while carrying a digital camera, a mini-dv video camera, a notebook, and a pen (before my phone could handle it all). Ultimately, I started wearing my own kind of utilitarian research uniform: cargo pants, a comfortable T-shirt, some kind of easy-to-remove sweater with pockets, and sneakers. I attempted to keep my style at least a little Hip Hop, but more so, was mindful of not standing out too much.

For others, preparing for the field meant preparing the body. In particular, it meant dressing in anticipation of how they would be received in streetdance scenes. One choreographer and dance scholar acknowledged that her mature age factored into her preparations: "On the age level, I would always have to take a nap in the middle of the day because, like I said, things wouldn't jump off until midnight, and I'd be going up until two or three in the morning, and I would always have to have had a nap and then drink some coffee before I go to the club . . . because there's no way I could go all day long and then go to the club." Though the process of preparation focused on the body and its needs, she goes on to suggest that her attire represented who she was in the eyes of potential research informants. Where age and gender intersected, she paid attention to whether her clothes would undermine her research interests: "On the gender level, I would always be aware that I couldn't be trying to look cute and be taken seriously . . . I wouldn't be trying to look younger for that generation, but I would just come maybe with some athletic shoes on, some jeans, and just to kind of fit in." One of the underlying connotations of "looking cute" is dressing youthfully. Another dance scholar researching younger generations of dancers concurred: "I was very aware of the clothes that I chose to wear . . . I'm of a certain age so I wasn't trying to be a 16-year-old." Both alluded to the idea that dressing younger would feel more like costuming and read as inauthentic, which would absolutely work against their interests. As one woman stated plainly, "I find that in general, most Hip Hop circles are conscious of accepting people who really seem, quote, 'authentic' as a part of the culture."

"Dressing cute" also connotes dressing in a manner that might draw romantic interest, and avoiding that is something many of us did. I did not dress in a way that might sexualize my body, and tended to minimize accessories, makeup, and cleavage in favor of more gender-neutral clothing. In contrast, since I am not a practitioner, I also purposefully avoided dressing like a b-girl, though at times I was encouraged to try to pass as one. I also did not want to misrepresent myself, nor did I want possibly to draw the ire of actual b-girls laboring on those dance floors. I learned early on that wardrobe choices also matter when one has to adapt to unexpected changes in circumstances. For example, during my very first sit-down interview I picked a fairly quiet café for a late lunch, and wore jeans and a weather-appropriate wool sweater. After the interview, though, my interviewee suggested we visit a small salsa club that happened to be right next door, which I had not known about. It was one of several moments throughout my research when (I suspected) someone wanted to see if I could dance, even if I did not break.[4] So we danced for a couple of hours, while I pretended that I wasn't burning up in my wool sweater, too embarrassed to reveal the short, semitransparent undershirt beneath—which was never meant to see the light of day. Instead, my refusal to remove my sweater likely made an equally embarrassing impression because I was sweating profusely through it. This incident, my very first foray into the field, taught me the importance of comfort and adaptability. I quickly learned from my mistake and created my "uniform" as a result.

For another streetdancer, scholar and artist, fashion was more than utilitarian because of its more pointed ties to identity and community:

> Dress is a huge thing for me. I think it's kind of a signifier. Clothing and fashion is a huge signifier of your ability to . . . be readable or recognizable as a member of the community. I always give a lot of thought to how I present myself, just as an academic does . . . I'm very careful about making sure how I present myself will telegraph my interest in the work that I'm doing, and my position and how I see my position in the community.

Dress signaled both her interests and that she belonged there, rendering her recognizable as a community member before she even spoke about her research. She specified the distinctions: "I'm not going in and pretending to all of a sudden [be] putting on a costume, basically. I just dress the way I would dress. But I don't dress in my little academia-type, you know, what I might wear at, like, at a conference . . . I'm going to dress informally. I'm going to dress with more of a Hip Hop flavor."

Since her situatedness within the community has immediate bearing on how she was treated, balancing being both a scholar and practitioner also meant signaling in ways other than dress: "I will kind of, I guess, code switch, if you want to call it that, between more slang within our community— like slang that we all commonly know and that does signify, okay, I'm a part of this community. But then, on the other side, I might also speak in more, not like fully scholarly terms, but in more academic language." With both dress and speech, the goal was to project a sense of who she is: "I'm not pretending to be something I'm not, but that I'm also showing that I'm also a part of something that I am." That she code-switches reminds us that the balance she attempted to strike between the two roles is an ongoing kind of labor, going back and forth between strategies to "telegraph" her interests at any given moment.

The impact of attire on how one is received is felt in research as well. For one scholar-practitioner, re-entering her own dance scene meant choosing what to wear in a new role as researcher. After a hiatus due to injury, her clothing choices prompted a near identity-crisis: "When I was breaking hardcore, my gear was very specific, you know. I had a reason to be rocking certain footwear, or shirts, or whatever . . . I feel a little bit of a loss of identity since I stopped hardcore, because then I was like, 'Oh, I can wear dresses or grown woman shoes!'" This posed some challenges to her sense of self within the scene and how she might be sexualized:

> Because I didn't want to be perceived as a groupie in any way, shape, or form. Because when I came into the scene in the beginning of the 2000s, like 2001, it was, like, the worst insult was that, "Oh, you're just a groupie? Whatever. I'm not going to pay any attention to you. I'm not going to take you seriously." So that mentality just stayed with me. And I did feel like I was sort of staying in this zone to a certain degree by keeping my research focused on b-girls . . . I didn't have to go through the initial sort of hazing that might happen. I just was like, let me deal with the people who know who I am and what my intentions are.

A general pressure for women practitioners and researchers to distinguish themselves from so-called groupies has bearing, then, on attire and research. By extension, the judgment attached to being a "groupie"—a reductive, controlling image that figures women's participation to be merely a front for getting into romantic or sexual relationships—position women who are subjected to that label in breaking spaces as lacking seriousness about the culture. It also denigrates certain kinds of sexual relationships, primarily shaming women. Rejecting the groupie label was a kind of cultural sensibility that shaped how she presented herself both as a dancer and a researcher. Simply put, she was quite aware that if she dressed in conventionally feminine ways, it *could* have worked against her as a researcher. Something seemingly simple, like how to dress to enter the field, ultimately illuminates the choices she made as a researcher, going so far as to shape her decision to focus on women practitioners she already knew.

Dressing in a way that avoids a groupie label also gestures toward issues of personal safety. In one instance, another ethnographer not only avoided sexualizing attire but dressed in an intentionally desexualized way. She took preemptive measures that, in retrospect, felt extra to her: "Yeah, I'm going to someone's hotel room to meet up with X, they're on tour and whatever. I'm wearing a wrinkly big black t-shirt. You know what I'm saying? That is not sexy, right? I'm specifically . . . dressing in a way that was communicating 'Can you like, iron your clothes?'. Do you know what I mean? I took it to an extreme." While she recounted this story with humor, she recognized in hindsight that her slovenly presentation—from unkept hair to a shirt that she later described as "gross"—might have inadvertently made comment on her personal hygiene.

At the same time, her presentation is also a defense mechanism to mitigate unwanted sexual advances. Ethnographer Esther Newton (1993), in "My Best Informant's Dress: the Erotic Equation in Fieldwork," elaborates on the roles that the dress and appearance of subjects and researchers play in managing safety and risk when considering the possibility of erotic advances in the field. An interview alone in a man's hotel room is a delicate situation that this researcher agreed to in the early stages of her research, a move she would not make today. Through attire, she made a performative effort to ensure that she was received solely as a researcher, and not as a potential sexual conquest, an especially important maneuver when in a situation where she is alone in a private space with a man or group of men without protection or backup.

While dress is an especially impactful dimension of entering the field, mental preparation matters too. One ethnographer and dancer noted that comfort and practicality were key, as was balancing functionality alongside any formal dress codes determined by the various underground club scenes at the center of her research (e.g., rules about sneakers, heels, etc.). "Physically, if I'm going to a club, it's dressing so that I'm able to dance, able to photograph, and able to move through the club." Over time though, she noted that, "because I've been a part of the underground dance community for nearly a decade now, it doesn't really matter how I physically am dressed, or whatever. How you are able to talk to people and explain what you're doing makes a difference. And also, I find with any of the dance communities, it's really about becoming a part of that community." The questions she followed up with are thus about community belonging: "Do people trust you? Do people recognize you? Do they know what you're there for? Have they seen what you produce? Do they respect it? . . . I think it's more of a principle of embedding than presentation." These questions signal the deeper work of being in a field site. To get to that stage of work, she asked a series of questions to prepare her mind for the work at hand: "Mentally, I always ask myself, what's my story? Why am I here? What's the purpose of me being here? What do I want to capture? What do I wanna show?" Answering these questions sharpens her approach and clarifies her intentions, helping to better shape the course of the evening's work and whatever else might happen. She noted that, "the beautiful thing about streetdancing is the spontaneity. I do know on a certain level amazing shit will happen that I had no planning for."

Setting Boundaries

The informality of Hip Hop social dance spaces can foster an atmosphere of openness, fun, and possibility (i.e., "amazing shit"). This means that the cultural and social dynamics around personal boundaries are informal and open as well, since, for the community it is about life, not a job. While major reports by *PLoS ONE* (Clancy 2014) and *REIF: Respect and Equality in Fieldwork* (Woodgate 2018) make clear that fieldworkers have begun to survey and set guidelines for assessing the risk of sexual advances and possible transgressions in ethnographic research,[5] for my purposes I am concerned with how the women that I consulted make quotidian determinations of the presence or absence of risk while setting boundaries in their relationships with their research subjects. Researchers thus employ strategies that reinforce personal boundaries as they negotiate spaces wherein romantic or sexual advances are a dimension of their engagement with research subjects. Though not all advances are problematic or even unwanted, individuals have cultivated various strategies to ensure their personal boundaries remain uncrossed.

Intimacy is not simply a matter of romantic or sexual relationships; a connection might not entail erotic intentions at all. Researchers inevitably can form close relationships with and feelings about informants, which can inevitably shape a researcher's project overall. One scholar-practitioner told me that participant-observation in dance scenes often entails building relationships that combine personal ties with research obligations. She explained that valuing those "very, very close friendships" she formed with some of the dancers—relationships that were intimate without ever becoming sexual because of her own beliefs and boundaries[6]—meant respecting that relationship because "friendship is also important," and one's research should, above all, "cause no harm."

Setting boundaries is important precisely because intimacies in field research can be murky. For example, in reference to a particular connection with a research subject, one scholar-practitioner recounted "intimacy with someone that I was, like, I would never consider in any kind of way, *in any kind of way* being in a relationship with." The repetition and emphasis on there being no possibility that anything would come of their relationship put in stark relief the potency of their connection, which developed out of "working together, dancing together, and talking about the history and the culture and things that we love together, and just appreciating this person . . . [T]hat's part of what you do as an ethnographer." Essentially, just by doing her job and getting a great interview out of it, questions of intimacy came to the fore. She concluded her story by telling me the importance of "celebrating the fact that we can talk on these kinds of levels, and talk intimately without it having to go there," meaning toward anything romantic or sexual. Her clarity though comes partly by way of an explicit decision to keep her personal life very separate from her research.

While fieldwork can provide new strategies, the skills women deploy to establish their boundaries are not new. The women I interviewed made it clear that they have already been socialized to set boundaries in everyday life. Reflecting on the practices she has cultivated over time and in response to her everyday experiences, one practitioner-scholar described it in this way: "We are women. There's a certain preconceived notion of how we're supposed to act and move through the world." Another ethnographer stated that, "I just feel, like, it's one of those things that women have to deal with. There's no getting around it." For example, being offered "free dance lessons" or "hanging out" might be less an invitation to train or socialize platonically than an invitation to hook up or date. One scholar-practitioner noted, "Obviously, there's people who are like, 'Oh, I'll talk to you if that means that we're going to *hang out,*'" with a wink to indicate that there was more to it than just talking. Yet this goes beyond Hip Hop, as the same researcher recalled a parallel situation when being taught how to play guitar: "I remember I hung out with someone who thought that I really wanted to, like [*lifts eyebrows and smiles suggestively*]. And I'm like, 'No. I really just want to learn how to play the guitar. Seriously . . . That wasn't code for anything else.'" Part of ethnography, then, is balancing the need to develop close bonds to subjects, alongside the need to set boundaries where few otherwise exist. Many heavily stressed that they did not wish to disparage consensual romantic relationships. Every researcher must consider the gravity of her relationships in fieldwork, and gauge the ethical obligations and research protocols in her affiliated disciplines and/or professions.

At the same time, protecting their reputations (from, for example, a "groupie" label) and ensuring their own physical safety are clearly concerns, making boundaries all the more important. Sometimes these strategies demand that researchers adjust their own personal traits because of the ways that such traits might misrepresent their interests. For example, one scholar-practitioner stated, "I have a flirtatious energy and I recognize that about myself, but I also know how to be very clear with my boundaries." To do this, she told me that one of her approaches is respectfully to emphasize her credentials.

Others have opted to "shut down" unwanted advances in more personalized ways. One described her approach in the following manner:

> If I felt like there was a weird energy of, "Yeah, I'm going to talk to you because I want to get in your pants," I'd be very clear about who I am: at that point I am a graduate student; this is what I'm writing this particular paper on; and I'm from the scene, so I know about this, this, and this. I'd also establish who my anchors were within the scene so they know that I'm not just some rando [random person] off the street, that they couldn't just be, like, "Alright, now I'm going to hit it [have sex], right?" I don't

know what that is . . . establishing a family almost. Because you know with some of my mentors, I considered them parental figures. It's just like, "You wouldn't mess with this person's kids, would you?" To sort of let them know where I stood within the scene . . . It's like, once you've established that boundary, it's okay. . . . It's very few and far between that I've ever come across someone who tried to step beyond the boundary.

Noting that this was a dimension of being a practitioner too, she told me that highlighting her academic credentials alongside her dance lineage set a clear tone that most people respected. By positioning herself simultaneously as a student, a practitioner, a researcher, and extended family, she articulated a set of relations that not only minimized the degrees of separation between herself and another, but also demarcated that they might be messing with "this person's kid." She told me that a slight shift in demeanor also communicated to her subjects that an advance was unwanted: "If I didn't smile as much, just being straight-faced. This is my serious face. Like, I'm speaking to you seriously. And I'm a very laugh-y, smiley person, but if I'm serious, I'm not smiling." Accordingly, she employed multiple strategies at once to clearly and swiftly establish her boundaries, suggesting that this is an ongoing effort.

Within Hip Hop dance spaces, family is a regularly invoked trope. A dance family tree clearly does a certain kind of work in the context of the social relationships at the center of streetdance research. "Daughter" can work as a means of establishing boundaries because it serves as a mechanism for recognizing or determining relationships, connections, and boundaries. "Daughter" invokes a gendered, familial positionality wherein protection and concern are at the center. One scholar-practitioner acknowledged how, with older dancers, she was often treated as a daughter, "because I'm young, younger. And they pretty much probably think I'm even younger than I am." Her perceived youthfulness relative to the older dancers in her scene perhaps contributed to their protective, mentoring relationship.

Another dance scholar also felt like she was positioned within a kind of family trope, which also seemed to help. During a period of concentrated field research wherein this particular scholar-artist interviewed several practitioners, one holdout—someone known to outright reject academics ("He was very concerned about someone stealing his shit, which has happened to him")—changed his mind after she became legible to him through a family trope. Here is how she described this development:

We got to talking and we realized that we were from the same neighborhood . . . His older sister and I probably knew each other, even though I wasn't sure, but we were contemporaries. I think there was something about that moment where he then started to relate to me as his sister. He started to say, "You're my sister." It was almost like he could place me in a role that was then the bridge role for him . . . The very next day, "Oh yeah, sister, you can be in my class, whatever you want." Now we went from doors being completely closed to doors being completely open . . . My take on it was that he was used to dealing with women in a particular way. It was clear that I wasn't giving off that vibe [of], "I'm interested," so I think that that was part of what was the thing. . . He was trying to figure out where to place me. I wasn't quite clear for him until he was like, "Okay, got it. Same age as sister? Sister . . . "

The confluence of age, gender, ethnicity, and geography was a marker that allowed him to situate her within a familial trope, and in doing so, she became legible in terms other than a researcher and potential thief. She referred to the family trope as the "bridge" that allowed them to cross that dividing between them as a dancer and academic-practitioner.

Family is a trope of recognition, positioning, and respect in each of these examples. It becomes a shortcut, facilitating interactions that better suit research-based social relationships rather than obstructing them. This way of identifying and situating oneself in the scene is not uncommon. Breaking crews sometimes espouse a family narrative to contextualize their relationships to each other (Johnson 2009). Most notably, queer ball houses organize themselves into kinship groups, identifying each other as surrogate family members, such as mother, father, sister, and brother (Abeni 2002; Bailey 2013). It is worth noting that the invocation of family as a form of protection happened particularly in the context of women's interactions with cis-heterosexual men. The interactions shifted when the context was a queer and trans one.

In the voguing community, surrogate family ties are profoundly important. One ethnographer was cautioned not to trade on her biological ties to her actual cousin, a prominent founding member of the community. She recounted that her research subjects "did not want me to trade on my associations in order to get my work out there," perhaps warning against taking shortcuts rather than earning their respect. She clarified that earning trust was key to becoming "family" or "one of the children," regardless of one's biological ties with individual community members. The overall implication, though, persists: that in the context of Hip Hop streetdances, the family we choose is as prioritized as literal blood ties.

While a distrust of academics places pressures on most researchers to show and prove their intentions, at the same time, that pressure is relative to the people with whom we interact. The same researcher who was once rejected by a pioneering male practitioner had a quite different dynamic with a prolific woman practitioner: "We were *here*, right away [*gestures being on the same level*]. The playing field was even right away . . . There was rapport right away and that sense of—the researcher identity wasn't one down because I was a woman researcher, like often happens with men." When her presence as a researcher was not questioned, their mutual recognition led to her feeling an evenness between them. She demonstrated this by holding up both hands, palms down and middle fingers near touching, creating an even plane to demonstrate their being "*here, right away,*" in contrast to waving her hands up and down at contrasting levels to demonstrate an uneven playing field. As another interviewee put it, "I don't feel like the male researchers have to justify who they are and what they do as much. Or why they're doing it or that I am quote-unquote 'authentic.'"

This is not to suggest, though, that women ethnographers necessarily have an easier time when they are dealing with other women. Gender alone does not make for easy relationships. For one scholar-practitioner, being young and single complicated her so-cial interactions with women and men. For example, while doing fieldwork in a close-knit small town outside of her home country, she confronted a particular challenge as a young, unpartnered woman:

> I was really excited to talk to some guys, and in a few cases their girlfriends felt un-comfortable. . . [O]ne of my best friends now, I have notes about not knowing that they were a couple and . . . her boyfriend being one of the older dancers . . . and I'm like, "Oh my God. Let's talk!" And being quite excited to talk to him [and] him being cool [receptive] the first time I talked to him; but then being *really* cold, and her being really cold with me for a year. Until, coincidentally, I got a boyfriend. And my access to the scene definitely improved then.

The groupie narrative is an implied yet unstated influence here (one that might have mattered less had an injury not prevented her from dancing—another means of qualifying her reasons for being there). She told me a few variations of this story in our interview, instances acknowledged in her fieldnotes and her memories in which, immediately after interviews with her, straight couples would openly argue *about* her. Subsequently, someone accused her of flirting to get interviews. "A week later," she explained to me, someone else suggested that she flirt *more* to get interviews. Mixed messages and suspicion seasoned this time in her fieldwork regularly enough that, "The year when I was with a partner, shit just got easier." Being part of a couple established boundaries around her, undoubtedly influenced by assumptions that being partnered took her out of romantic competition. Assumptions aside, being partnered opened the door to more convivial relationships. She thought of these experiences in the early stages in her fieldwork as having paid her dues as an ethnographer, because she really felt like an outsider despite also being a practitioner. And likely, too, age and employment status played a part; she noted that when she moved to a bigger city and got institutional affilia-tion, "It was way easier to not be a student in people's eyes, but to be someone who could possibly get them a job. And I was getting people jobs."

Another ethnographer doing research advised that women needed to "set up the parameters that you want to deal within from the very beginning." On an eight-month research trip outside of her home country, she set those parameters in part by bringing her partner with her for the first month, "to establish the fact that I was taken, and that he was going to be a phone call away. And almost everybody who was around in that first month, they got a chance to meet him to know who he was. . . So, I had established that I was a part of the unit." Again, the "unit" tempered unwanted advances, eased concerns about romantic competition, and established her as being a researcher first and foremost.

As complicated as these dynamics can be for women, some nonetheless speculated that it might actually be more difficult for men researchers because, as one dancer and scholar stated, "I don't even know how, if I was guy, I think it would be hard to navi-gate . . . I think it's probably easier for women in some ways." Specifically, "I think that attractiveness is definitely a measure." Insofar as women are judged by their looks, someone else's attraction to them can help secure research subjects. Another streetdance scholar-practitioner detailed her advantages in soliciting interviews:

> I definitely think that being a woman has been an advantage to me in a male-dominated scene, just because I think sometimes it's just like, "Okay, well . . . she's cute. Yeah, let's do that interview." You know? It's not even necessarily lurid . . . It's just more like we're dealing with streetdancers. They're a little bit more on the gangster side of things, and they're not really shy about, "Oh, you're cute. Yeah, let's hang out. Whatever." You know what I mean? It doesn't necessarily mean anything. But there's that kind of casualness. Then, it sometimes is easier to connect with people and stuff. But, on the other side of things, I feel like I always want to really assert my seriousness in the work that I do . . . All of a sudden, it's like business, you know?

Reminding us again of the casual and informal nature of streetdance scenes (because most people are there in a social, not professional capacity), her words capture how being the object of someone else's attraction created opportunities to secure interviews, after which she shifted gears in order to make clear the seriousness of her work. Again, reasserting boundaries is necessary. She further speculated that the sociocultural codes that shape how straight men of color interact with one another might also hinder male researchers' access to the type of interviews that she obtained: "Because of the male thing, and that kind of . . . Especially because we're also dealing with folks of color, there's issues of power and control that are specific to that dynamic, and I think with men, it's more difficult in some ways." Her speculation about the social dynamic among men of various races, which could entail barriers that hinder the forms of intimacy that were impactful in her research, reveals additional points of analysis for future work on Hip Hop–based research methods.

She added, though, that she took the "easy route" by focusing on practitioners who were already open to being interviewed, not unlike the practitioner-scholar who focused on b-girls. I have done the same thing, focusing my efforts on those who already seemed open to speaking with me, and being strategic in pursuing those more-difficult-to-get interviews. Ultimately, the path of least resistance looks different for everyone.

Corporealities of Identity in the Field

The term *corporealities* highlights how bodily realities are tangible, substantial, and convey meaning. As women ethnographers move through the social spaces of Hip Hop dance, issues of identity in the field touch on how race, age, and nationality qualify gendered experiences, ultimately shaping researchers' fieldwork. As a result, despite carefully crafted efforts to "telegraph" who we are, our physicality and mobility prompt interpretations that we cannot control.

Our corporealities signify differently based on context, which complicates experiences of being in community. For this Asian American ethnographer, being in a Hip Hop community was largely validating:

> I never felt quite comfortable in my skin until I started going to practices. And it was like, Oh, everyone needs to be here right now. Everyone was *meant* to be here right now ... I got more attention because, I feel like, Asian women of a certain size within the Asian community, you have to be really skinny. You had to have perfect skin. My legs, for example, growing up, they're, like, "Oh, you have what people call tree-trunk legs." And I don't have tree-trunk legs. I just have a lot of muscles in my legs because I've been dancing my whole life! [IKJ: *Right.*] Where that was a bad thing within just the [Asian] community, in the scene, they're like, "Oh, she got legs!" And so, I got much more positive attention, even if it was a little bit extra attention, because I was Asian and because I was female.

Even though this experience was rooted in her practitioner life, and was not a research-based one, her corporeality in streetdance spaces allowed her to experience her body in a more positive and self-affirming way. Streetdancers appreciated physical qualities that were belittled in the Asian community. In the end though, she also hinted at being fetishized, getting that "little bit extra attention" that wanders into the creepy. She follows this statement by stating, "I did not like to play into it as a [dancer]. I did not take advantage of it. I really was very clear that I wanted to be accepted for my skill." From the perspective of "a certain sensibility," she is thus aware that unsolicited attention can get interpreted as unearned recognition *because* she is an Asian woman.

Her decision to go to graduate school and pursue Hip Hop research resulted in an argument with a friend, who questioned her commitment, and wondered whether she was taking advantage of any privilege she had as a middle-class, Asian American college student to profit off of the culture in a way that was not accessible to him. The immediate distrust is evident. Again, for practitioner-scholars, they risk community when transitioning to academia, which can erode hard-earned respect.

One biracial scholar-practitioner told me that her body and appearance get read in multiple ways, allowing people of various racial and ethnic backgrounds to identify with her:

> Honestly, I have to be really honest with you. I feel like, generally, people kind of read me how they want to read me. Obviously, I'm mixed race. I feel like people, if they want to read me as Black because they want me to be Black—because they want me to be more connected to them—they'll think I'm Black, or that I have Black in me. Or they'll think I'm Latina. I get more of this, "Oh, you're like me in this way," which is an advantage.

In any context, conversations about race, gender, and sexuality can be quite sensitive. Since people assumed or perhaps found comfort in a sense of connection or shared identity, this lent itself to the possibility of people speaking to her in the kind of shorthand typically reserved for "in group" conversations. Since her project addressed race, a re-search subject's sense of connection to her can foster communication. At the same time, it is important to acknowledge that, while she did not intentionally mislead people, she did not always correct them either; this can lead into ethically murky territory, which the researcher must interrogate fairly and with appropriate self-reflexiveness in the write-up. Nonetheless, assumptions of shared identity can produce opportune re-search moments. Although no one has ever confused my race, I have had experiences with dancers of various races and ethnicities who offered commentary that felt possible only because of their sense that we shared an understanding or politics because I am Black despite our different races. In this case, as a strategy for navigating how her body is read in the public sphere, my interviewee has turned what might otherwise be a per-sistent point of confusion about what she is (which consequently can be a persistent microaggression that many multiracial people bristle at) into an advantage.

Location also impacts how racialized bodies signify. One African American ethnog-rapher, researching at a US site with few Black people, remarked that her age and race often "overshadowed issues of gender." In her research sites, blackness signaled "know-ledge" and "authenticity," and her age helped her be taken seriously. In another example, a Black artist-researcher working in Europe also felt that her blackness conjured stere-otypical notions of "authenticity": "I remember when I did a panel, the entire staff that hired me was shocked because they're like, 'But you're not Hip Hop. You don't act Hip Hop.' And I was like, 'What is act Hip Hop?' They basically meant ghetto." Her reception by white Europeans was often shaped by how they thought she should act because she is Black American. When asked specifically about how Black Europeans received her, she replied, "Very cool. It's like, 'Oh, you're my cousins from across the Atlantic. Yay.' And then there's also, sort of, the American stereotypes, but because I do speak European languages and because I have a sense of geography and geo-politics, that's, I guess, not what they normally expect of Americans . . . I don't think it's personal." While it is not personal, there is something telling in how these two examples demonstrate the impact of assumptions tied to race in general, blackness in particular, and the ways that nation-ality, age, and gender inflect those assumptions.

How one speaks is also a means of determining a person's "authenticity" in streetdance spaces. Another African American woman ethnographer told me that her speech and natural tendency *not* to speak colloquially seemed to disrupt expectations of what her research subjects deemed "authentic." For example, she learned that some of her interviewees called her by the nickname "The White Woman," in reference to her manner of speech, which she described as with "a certain care and fidelity and re-spect and compassion." The nickname, with its racialized assumption of privilege, belied her actual identity and upbringing. Instead of accusing her of "being ghetto," the com-munity she studied—comprising primarily Black and Brown gay men—questioned whether she was putting on airs. Community members were concerned that her speech was inauthentic or incongruent to who they knew her to be. Her concern was less about the nickname itself than what it implied about how she was perceived. Put simply, being called "The White Woman" was infused with critiques about her identity in terms of gender, race, and class:

> And that, that term comes with a sense of suspicion, a sneaking sense of suspicion around . . . around presenting yourself in a way that does not, does not hew to authenticity to where you came from. Here you are, you didn't come with a silver spoon in your mouth, you know.

I am especially drawn to her delivery, which was precise and tactful. The repetition of certain words builds a kind of layered emphasis that qualifies and expands the meaning of every additional phrase. Each modification clarifies its meaning, ending with the silver spoon image, steeped in whiteness and wealth— a far cry from her upbringing in the foster-care system.

On the surface, the unwanted nickname was a form of signifying, a Black American expressive cultural practice wherein implied and explicit critiques are couched in humorous teasing. "It was a ribbing," she explained. "It was a way of, you know, of, uh, teasing . . . It wasn't a chronic, community-wide thing but, but it was . . . I certainly wasn't referred to as a white man! . . . But it did worry me." Though she eventually took this in stride, the occasion repeated a dynamic of being misread that she had experienced many times as a Black trans woman: "But see, this is something that's been a part of my life from since as a child, in the beginning. I was a nerd, a reader, and a person who cared about how I phrased language . . . And so, in the environments I was in I was always suspect. So, the way the ball world [voguing community] treated me, the way the [Hip Hop] street cultures treated me was, is no different." Her frustration echoes similar forms of being misread. She went on to draw links between Hip Hop's "pretty damned vexed" relationship to openly trans people, and similar challenges in the dance world at large: "Trans is different in the dance world. Very, very different." Earlier in the interview, she recounted stories from her youth about the repeated ways in which she stood out in the dance world. Whether it was ballet as a youth, or modern dance as a graduate student, her physical body was always the locus of criticism and difference from the normative expectations within what she called the "power structures of dance."

Ultimately, the idea that one should simply be "authentic" to be accepted does not hold in her example. So much so that her years of living and being in these communities are not enough to secure her authority and knowledge of streetdance. She explained,

> As a feminist and as trans, it's very hard for me to even have a voice within that [Hip Hop]. I know, from my observation just recently, quite a bit about popping, for example, but being able to share that knowledge in terms of your authority? Remember when I said earlier that [in] dance, the problem is that "who you are" is often assessed by "how much you fit you in"? The same with Hip Hop worlds, too. And as a teacher, someone who for a while taught these forms, it's also very hard to get that.

The perception that she had no authority in the forms she studied and taught was a dimension of her corporeality. It was a more pronounced expression of a frustration shared by other scholar-practitioners who, too, have had their expertise questioned because of their gender.[7] Ultimately, the body is a problematic authenticator of Hip Hop belonging. In addition to perpetuating the exclusionary discourse—reducing complex histories to one-dimensional caricatures like "acting ghetto," or the implied "sneaking suspicion" used against trans people—"authenticity" also fails to distinguish between *who I am* and *who you think I am*. Not all bodies are readily accepted in Hip Hop dance spaces as a result.

Despite the limitations of "authenticity" in academic discourses, this same interviewee goes on generously to point out that suspicion also signals concern about researchers' capacity for and history of imposing harm. She explained it in the following way:

> It's a hallmark of how people in the community, the suspicion they have of people coopting or problematizing the oppression that really is, that really does come against members of the community. So that, that when you say suspicion, that suspicion, it's . . . it's merited. 'Cause of people, white people, who have mistreated members of the community. Or traded off of them! Right? You know, or who have sort of parachuted in[to] the community to do their work, and parachuted out . . . So, the suspicion is warranted. But when the suspicion is turned on someone like me, who came from different circumstances, and who has a different—and did not come in as a researcher? Although. . . I tried to be respectful of that and not use that as a calling card and everything.

It is challenging to be held accountable for the actions of prior researchers who may have exploited community oppressions or misrepresented those experiences, which then required her to be especially sensitive about emphasizing her shared background as a way of overcoming the hostility directed at researchers. There are very real concerns among people whose lives have been directly affected by researchers parachuting in and out of the community. With suspicion comes a quite purposeful effort to manage or mitigate the potential for discursive violence from outsiders who do not otherwise fully grasp the stakes. Thus, suspicion is warranted under certain circumstances because of past harms that have been done. At the same time, when we factor in the ways that this researcher was discouraged from trading on family ties to do the work, we begin to see just how confining it can be to maneuver in a community. An underlying and otherwise unresolved conundrum persists: feeling unrecognized in one's own community on multiple fronts (for her authority, gender expression, speech), yet still being of the community.

Although authenticity is more often written about in relation to rap music and the veracity of certain lyrical claims relative to personal history, authenticity still matters in streetdance research because who you are perceived to be and how you present yourself are central to bodily forms of communication within dance worlds. That is precisely because we are talking about communities of people with a heightened collective capacity to read moving bodies, study them, and value how embodiment conveys meaning.

Though self-presentation for researchers is carefully constructed with respect to a multitude of motivating factors, the body still signifies on one's behalf, ultimately creating opportunities in some instances and foreclosing opportunities in others. Thus, a key part of negotiating one's place in the field is negotiating the expectations and assumptions placed on our bodies before we even speak a word. This truly is part of the hard love of these women's research on Hip Hop dances.

CONCLUSION

The corporealities of women doing research on Hip Hop dances shape how we move through streetdance worlds as diverse bodies. Our corporealities mean grappling with how our bodies signify in those spaces. Women ethnographers employ various strategies—including dress, deportment, verbal cues, shifts in tone, and invocations of family relationships—to establish boundaries when first entering a research site. Boundaries are important, precisely because how the body is read has direct bearing on how one might be treated in a dance environment, and which doors are opened or closed. Ethnographers who, for varying reasons, do not conform to others' expectations have to then negotiate the assumptions projected onto on their bodies as a necessary part of fieldwork.

My goal in analyzing these reflections about research practices is to share little-known information about how women ethnographers of Hip Hop dance navigate these sites. Ultimately, these complications serve to empower future Hip Hop dance ethnographers of varying identities to break through unworkable norms, and to find culturally responsive and culturally sensitive methods that meet the demands of the people and the practices in the field (see my chapter twelve, this volume). My hope is that clarifying and analyzing what we do, how we do, and why such approaches matter will foster awareness of the roles we play in the distribution of knowledge about Hip Hop streetdances, and be supported by our comrades in the community and the academy. And as the interest in Hip Hop streetdances expands, I hope that even more women and gender nonconforming people know that they, too, have spaces for involvement, critique, and support as both practitioners and scholars of Hip Hop dances.

NOTES

1. The lower-case and (sometimes) hyphenated spelling of Hip Hop is standard in the publishing industry. Changing how publishing spells Hip Hop has been of interest to others who bristle at alternative spellings like *hip hop* or *hip-hop*. Dr. Tasha Iglesias and Dr. Travis Harris have solicited the Merriam-Webster Dictionary and the American Psychological Association to amend their spelling style, and called for collective action from the Hip Hop community to help in a July 2019 Facebook post, tracing the lower-case and hyphenated spelling to "a mainstream White media source" rather than the people who identify as Hip

Hop. They did so on behalf of the *Journal of Hip Hop Studies*, whose publisher enforced the APA spelling "hip-hop," as the standard and used Merriam-Webster's spelling as their justification. See https://www.facebook.com/49erfanbam/posts/2260877864028180, and https://www.facebook.com/49erfanbam/posts/2244672652315368 for these discussions.

2. I solicited interviews from several other women ethnographers who either did not or could not participate.

3. Locking, popping, waacking, breaking, voguing, Hip Hop party and social dances, house, and turfing are distinct genres of dance, each with their own histories and aesthetic elements. Hip Hop, a term with roots in mid-1970s New York City, does not adequately represent all the dances discussed in this chapter. Yet in practice, the term itself actually acts as an umbrella for those genres at the same time. While some prefer the term *streetdance*, I specify Hip Hop, in part because it captures both shared histories of post–Civil Rights, working-class, urban environments across the United States and roots in Black vernacular expressive cultural forms. Thus, "Hip Hop dances" and "Hip Hop streetdances" are terms that capture a body of originating dances of a particular era that are fundamentally informed by African diasporic aesthetic traditions as they manifest in the United States.

4. When I asked a white male colleague about such tests, he spoke to the opposite experience, where it was not expected that he could dance, and it was appreciated that he did. I suspect that, as a Black woman studying dancers, had I no rhythm it would have made me questionable in a way that did not seem to have bearing on my white male colleague's reception.

5. In "Signaling Safety: Characterizing Fieldwork Experiences and Their Implications for Career Trajectories," Robin Nelson (2017) examines the impact of these matters on researchers' professional standing and concomitant perceptions of their work.

6. Specifically, she states that as an ordained Buddhist, "sexual relationships don't really play a role in my life in that manner, in *that* kind of manner."

7. As one scholar-practitioner of breaking pointed out, "You need to treat them [practitioners] like they're the authorities. There's not a space for me to be an authority . . . The only thing I can do is be a collaborator who just appreciates what other people do and bring." I discuss this example further in chapter twelve of this volume, "Critical Hiphopography in Streetdance Communities (Hard Love Part 2)," where I touch on relinquishing authority in the context of Hip Hop community that nonetheless perpetuates a gendered dimension to women being denied expertise and relegating her to a position of helper.

References

Abeni, C. (2002). "The Social World of Voguing." *Journal for the Anthropological Study of Human Movement* 12 (2): 26–42.

Bailey, M. M. (2013). *Butch Queens Up in Pumps: Gender, Performance, and Ballroom Culture in Detroit*. Ann Arbor: University of Michigan Press.

Banes, S. (1994). *Writing Dancing in the Age of Postmodernism*. Middletown, CT: Wesleyan University Press.

Calixte, S. (2009). "A Feminist Call to Radical Hip Hop Heads." *Upping the Anti: A Journal of Theory and Action* 7(13). https://uppingtheanti.org/journal/article/07-a-feminist-call-to-radical-hip-hop-heads. Accessed November 16, 2020.

Clancy, K. B. H., Nelson, R. G., Rutherford, J. N., and Hinde, K. (2014). "Survey of Academic Field Experiences (SAFE): Trainees Report Harassment and Assault." *PLoS ONE* 9 (7). https://doi.org/10.1371/journal.pone.0102172.

Cooper, M. (2004). *Hip Hop Files: Photographs 1979–1984*. New York: From Here to Fame.

Cooper, M., and Chalfant, H. (1984). *Subway Art*. New York: Thames & Hudson.

Durham, A. S. (2018). "Aisha Durham Presents 'Home with Hip Hop Feminism.'" The University of Tampa Institutional Repository, May 4. https://www.youtube.com/watch?v=w3YGNCY5pM8.

Durham, A., Cooper, B. C., and Morris, S. M. (2013). "The Stage Hip-Hop Feminism Built: A New Directions Essay." *Signs: Journal of Women in Culture and Society* 38 (3): 721–737.

Ellis, C., Adams, T. E., and Bochner, A. P. (2011). "Autoethnography: An Overview." *Forum Qualitative Sozialforschung / Forum: Qualitative Social Research* 12 (1): Article 10. http://nbn-resolving.de/urn:nbn:de:0114-fqs1101108.

Ettorre, E. (2016). *Autoethnography as Feminist Method: Sensitising the Feminist 'I'*. New York: Routledge.

Foster, S. L., ed. (1996). *Corporealities: Dancing Knowledge, Culture, and Power*. New York: Routledge.

Johnson, I. K. (2009). "Dark Matter in B-Boying Cyphers: Race and Global Connection in Hip Hop. PhD diss., USC Dornsife College of Letters, Arts and Sciences.

Johnson, I. K. (2014). "From Blues Women to B-Girls: Performing Badass Femininity." *Women & Performance: A Journal of Feminist Theory* 24 (1): 15–28.

Nelson, R. G. (2017). "Signaling Safety: Characterizing Fieldwork Experiences and Their Implications for Career Trajectories." *American Anthropologist* 119 (4): 710–722.

Newton, E. (1993). "My Best Informant's Dress: The Erotic Equation in Fieldwork." *Cultural Anthropology* 8 (1): 3–23.

O'Shea, J. (2019). "Strange Bedfellows? Academic Disciplines in an Age of Right-Wing Populism." Looking Forward Looking Back: Commemorating the 25th Anniversary of the PhD in Critical Dance Studies at UC Riverside, February 9. Culver Center of the Arts, Riverside, CA.

Pough, G. D., ed. (2007). *Home Girls Make Some Noise: Hip Hop Feminism Anthology*. New York: Parker.

Rose, T. (1994). *Black Noise: Rap Music and Black Culture in Contemporary America*. Middletown, CT: Wesleyan University Press.

Rose, T. (2008). *The Hip Hop Wars: What We Talk about When We Talk about Hip Hop—and Why It Matters*. New York: Civitas Books.

Schwartzapfel, B. (2009). "It's All About Love." Interview with Tricia Rose. *Brown Alumni Magazine*, July–August. https://www.brownalumnimagazine.com/articles/2009-07-22/its-all-about-love

Spivak, G. C. (1988). "Subaltern Studies: Deconstructing Historiography." *In Other Worlds*, 197–221. New York: Routledge..

Woodgate, R. et al. (2018). White Paper for the REIF: Respect and Equality in Fieldwork, January. University of Washington Committee.

CHAPTER 9

FRAMING HIP HOP DANCE AS AN OBJECT OF SOCIOLOGICAL AND CULTURAL RESEARCH

ANDY BENNETT

INTRODUCTION

HIP hop dance is a multifarious term covering a range of styles and techniques. Although "breakdance" is the style most readily associated with Hip Hop, largely because of breaking's brief spell in the global spotlight during the mid-1980s, the longevity of Hip Hop has generated a rich cultural legacy that encompasses a range of interwoven practices linking dance with music, spoken word, art, writing, photography, and so forth. Another important feature of Hip Hop, and something that is highlighted through Hip Hop dances, is the way in which it situates the embodied subject in space and place. Although Hip Hop and Hip Hop dance are now ostensibly global cultural forms, they each retain strong ties to the "local," a quality that reflects Hip Hop's origins as a vernacular form of street culture. Significantly, however, if Hip Hop dance has been a focus for a number of academic disciplines, among them dance studies (Fogarty 2012a, 2012b; Hazzard-Donald 2004; LaBoskey 2001), sports science (Ojofeitimi, Bronner, and Woo 2010), health studies (Beaulac, Olavarria, and Kristjansson 2010), contemporary history (Rajakumar 2010), and globalization studies (Huntington 2007), it has been less of a focus in sociology and cultural theory. The purpose of this chapter, therefore, is to offer the reader a series of frameworks through which to consider and analyze the everyday significance of Hip Hop dance using established conceptual approaches applied in sociological and cultural theory scholarship.

The chapter is divided into four main sections, each of which focuses on a key conceptual theme that can be applied to Hip Hop dance to examine its sociocultural significance using perspectives commonly applied in sociological and cultural theory. The first theme examined in the chapter is "space and place," a term now commonly used by sociological and cultural theorists to describe the situatedness of human action and collective cultural practices in relation to their local, translocal, and global contexts. This leads to a discussion of the significance of scene and its value as a means of analyzing how Hip Hop dance, within the broader matrix of Hip Hop culture, is perceived by practitioners as a shared form of practices with its own discourses and tropes of belonging and inclusion. The next part of the chapter considers how sociological renderings of identity (both individual and collective) can be useful in framing Hip Hop dancers as cultural beings whose dance practices must be contextualized within the broader lifeworlds that they inhabit. The chapter concludes with a discussion of recent work on the sociology of the body and what it can offer us in the way of understanding how Hip Hop dancers, through their embodied subjectivity, contribute to the articulation of Hip Hop as a translocal culture as their bodies move in space and time.

Space and Place

> Even as today's rappers revise and redirect rap music, most understand
> themselves as working out of a tradition of style, attitude and form which
> has critical and primary roots in New York City in the 1970s.
> —Tricia Rose (1994, 73)

Although Hip Hop is not exclusively city-based (see, e.g., Warren and Evitt 2010), many Hip Hop practitioners continue to regard it as a primarily urban cultural form with historical roots in the inner-city ghettos of North American cities, in particular New York City. Indeed, the fact that many iconic Hip Hop artists, including Hip Hop dancers, emerged from New York and continue to have significant connections with the city is a telling indication of New York's significant place in the history and heritage of Hip Hop and continuing "iconicity" (Alexander 2008) among successive generations of hip hoppers. If New York is considered by many to be the critical point of origin for Hip Hop culture in its manifest forms, then this widely shared belief among hip hoppers has also done much to promote the global spirit of Hip Hop as something organically linked to the flow and churn of urban life, and inextricably bound up with the spaces and places of urban existence. It is, arguably, this understanding of Hip Hop, rather than any necessarily racial or ethnic claims to Hip Hop "authenticity," that bonds hip hoppers around the world and forges the sense of connection and cohesion many Hip Hop practitioners believe to be the lifeblood of what they consider a "global" Hip Hop community.

During its emergence in the 1970s and rapid development as a high-profile youth cultural form during the following decade, what set Hip Hop apart from previous and existing youth cultures and youth musics was its highly participatory quality (Bennett 2001). Although punk had previously claimed to break down the barriers between artist and audience (see Laing 1985), eschewing rock's emphasis on musicianship and professionalization, many of rock's trappings remained, notably, the drums, bass, and guitar-driven sound of punk and its preservation of rock's classic four-piece band structure typically featuring an all-white, usually male, line-up. Hip Hop sidestepped such conventions in a wholesale manner, emphasizing and giving sonic space to the expression of the spoken voice and reinventing a music playback device—the vinyl record turntable—as a musical instrument in its own right. Similarly, in opposition to the whiteness of rock, Hip Hop, though commonly represented in its early years as an African American cultural form, was characteristically multiethnic (see Lipsitz 1994). Hip Hop's other critical point of departure from rock and, indeed, from most other previous youth cultural scenes, was the equal emphasis it placed on music, dance, and art. Moreover, while each of these expressions of Hip Hop culture would later be commodified to a greater or lesser extent, in Hip Hop's early days they were explicitly articulated as DIY (do-it-yourself) forms of cultural practice and typically situated at the level of neighborhood, utilizing the same communal spaces and places where local Hip Hop crews had grown up. Again, this facet of Hip Hop gave it a quality distinct from many previous youth cultural styles and musics in that, even as it grew in significance as a global form, Hip Hop retained distinct discourses of neighborhood and community, the latter being made and remade as Hip Hop was appropriated by youth in cities and regions around the world (see, e.g., Mitchell 1996; Bennett 2000).

That the global spread of Hip Hop has been accompanied by practitioners' understanding of it as a cultural form grounded in issues of space and place is illustrated by the sheer number of studies that emphasize Hip Hop's significance as a form capable of instilling in its followers a global sense of belonging, while at the same time providing them with tools to address themes of locality in their creative works. Studies conducted on Hip Hop cultures in various locations across the world, ranging from Europe (Bennett 2000; Bjurström 1997; Huq 1999) to Africa (Ntarangwi 2009), Asia (Bodden 2005), and Oceania (Mitchell 1996), have mapped the strongly articulated, spatially grounded discourses of local Hip Hop culture that exist in these dispersed and diverse regions. Although the ghetto connotations that partly propelled global youth's fascination with Hip Hop in its early years do not universally translate to those many other local spaces in which Hip Hop has assumed cultural resonance since the mid-1980s, its importance as a street form with a capacity to spectacularly unfold in public, urban space has remained a centrally defining characteristic of Hip Hop, one that Hip Hop dance, as a highly physical and visualized form, has done much to articulate. In discussing the dynamic and ever-changing character of urban space, social geographer Doreen Massey (1993) has observed: "If it is now recognized that people have multiple identities, then the same point can be made in relation to places. Moreover, such multiple identities can be either, or both, a source of richness or a source of conflict" (65).

From its very early days, the interface between Hip Hop dance and the street setting was highly evident and served to set this style of dance apart from many other dance forms, including an established history of youth-based dance styles, from jive and Lindy Hop to disco, styles that were primarily dance hall or, in the case of disco, nightclub based (see Dodds 2011). Indeed, though its emphasis on the appropriation of open public spaces for exhibitions of dance that rely on high levels of energy and physical stamina, Hip Hop dance can be seen as historically interwoven into a rich sartorial tradition of conspicuous display among urban youth. Such displays have, in one way or another, been concerned with and reliant upon a collective marking out and symbolic appropriation of physical space. From Thresher's (1927) work on the street gangs of Chicago's Southside in the 1920s, to Jefferson's (1976) study of the turf wars engaged in by British Teddy boys during the 1950s, to more recent research on activities such as skateboarding (Borden 2000) and flash mobs (Bird 2014), there is a long tradition of academic scholarship that engages with youth's ongoing struggle to win space for itself in the urban landscape. The extreme physicality of Hip Hop dance, combined with its unorthodox use of urban spaces, such as pavements (sidewalks) and other pedestrianized zones, positions it as another facet of youth's spatialized relationship to the city. Bennett (2000) has theorized youth's symbolic appropriation and inscription of urban space in this way as core to what he describes as the collective narrativization of space and place, a facet of urban existence that can invariably lead to struggle, contestation, and conflict as different social groups (informed by particular lifestyle politics, aesthetic sensibilities, and relationships of power) impose different spatial narratives on the same physical space. Thus, argues Bennett (2000):

> In referring to the "local," we are in effect speaking about a space which is crossed by a variety of different collective sensibilities each of which imposes a different set of expectations and cultural needs upon that space. In doing so, such sensibilities also construct the local in particular ways, a process which ensures that terms such as *locality* and *local identity* are always, in part at least, subjective elements which begin by utilising the same basic knowledges about the local, its social and spatial organisation, but supplement such knowledges with their own collectively held values to create particular narratives of locality. From the point of view of the young, one of the key resources in the facilitation of such narratives is popular music and its attendant stylistic resources. (66)

Massey (1993) suggests that, through engagement in such processes of spatial contestation regarding the places where they live, work, and play, individuals create what she refers to as "power-geometries," which enable the exertion of power and control over urban landscapes, even if in some cases, this amounts only to a temporal level of power and control. Such a process can be clearly seen in the efforts of Hip Hop dancers to temporally weave their cultural practice into the urban narrative. In a similar way to graffiti art, which, according to MacDonald (2001), also provides an avenue for the appropriation and inscription of space, Hip Hop dance produces its own narrative of spatial positioning for those participating in it (see, e.g., Pabon 2006). Through their practice, Hip Hop dancers can temporally claim and reinscribe urban space with their own meaning, one that subverts the more regulated definition of that space assigned by state and local authorities and re-zones it through dance as an unregulated space of carnivalesque (Bakhtin 1984) fun, play, and spectacle.

Although Hip Hop dance has been far less exposed to the level of commodification and formalization that has accompanied rap's rise in global popularity, this is not to suggest that it has remained an exclusively grassroots form of practice either. Thus, as Fogarty (2012a) observes, in the wake of rap's transformation into a global cultural form, Hip Hop dance also received a temporarily elevated public profile through its marketing and exposure as "breakdance" (see also Banes 1985), and by the inclusion of breakdancing scenes in mainstream films such as *Flashdance* (1983). Although the global "craze" for breakdancing quickly faded, Hip Hop dance continued as a largely underground scene perpetuated by devotees. As Fogarty (2012a) notes, however, in more recent times, Hip Hop dance has once again acquired a broader public profile owing to its incorporation into the world of professional dance, including tours subsidized by funding bodies such as arts councils, and an increased emphasis on formal instruction (in many cases, from those same aging denizens of Hip Hop dance who first helped to make the form popular as a street dance in the 1970s and 1980s). Hebdige (1979), in his seminal study of punk, has noted how incorporation of this and similar forms of initially DIY culture into more mainstream and institutionalized systems of cultural production and consumption has created tensions regarding threats to the authenticity and integrity of the resulting product. In this context, it is useful to consider the work of Benjamin (1973), particularly his concept of "aura" as an inherent quality of a cultural object—or, by definition, a cultural practice—which can survive the process of mass reproduction and dissemination.[1] Obviously, the reproduction of streetdance for a global audience cannot be said to constitute a form of "mass reproduction" in the same way, although some parallels are evident in that the success of each dance show depends on the dancer interpreting the choreographed steps in a broadly similar way each time. Nevertheless, threaded through the production and reception of each performance is a shared understanding on the part of both dancers and the audience of the symbolic significance of the dance—grounded in its street origins—and the cultural continuities that prevail when Hip Hop dance is performed in a theater context. To put this another way, when dancers perform for an audience, the aura of the dance as a form of cultural practice tied to place and locality, and as a vernacular expression of that experience, remains present.

SCENES

The discussion of Hip Hop dance's relationship to space and place leads into a consideration of its connections with the concept of scene. Indeed, many aspects of Hip Hop, including Hip Hop dance, can be said to constitute significant cultural scenes at local, translocal, and, indeed, virtual levels. As will presently be illustrated, in the case of Hip Hop dance, its established global character is, importantly, embedded in the intersections that exist between its local, translocal, and virtual manifestations.

The concept of "scene" was first introduced into academic work as a conceptual framework by Straw (1991). In what was to become a highly influential position paper, Straw took issue with the existing and, at the time, dominant theoretical frameworks such as "community" and "subculture" (see also the next section of this chapter, "Identity"), as presenting too limited a perspective on the relationship between music, place, and social bonds. According to Straw, the critical value of scene as a counter-concept was its depiction of musical communities as entities that might share common experiences in terms of things such as class, ethnicity, and neighborhood, but could equally extend across and beyond such structural factors to connect people dispersed across translocal, aesthetically linked configurations "reflect[ing] and actualiz[ing] a particular state of relations between various populations and social groups, as these coalesce around particular coalitions of musical style" (379).

Straw's conceptualization of scene's translocal qualities has been used in a highly effective way in work on a variety of different musical genres, including goth (Hodkinson 2002), alternative (Stahl 2004), hardcore (Haenfler 2006), and metal (Kahn-Harris 2007). By contrast, in much of the existing work on Hip Hop, little attention has been focused on the relevance of scene—or on competing concepts such as subculture and community—for our understanding of Hip Hop as a collective cultural practice in either a local or a global context. Arguably, this is to some extent due to the associations of such conceptual terminologies with white youth cultures, their associated styles and musics. Nevertheless, and for reasons already alluded to in the "Space and Place" section of this chapter, the concept scene, in both its local and translocal applications, has clear resonances for our understanding of Hip Hop as well. For example, there are clear similarities between Kahn-Harris (2007) description of the translocal qualities of contemporary metal styles and the global connections that exist between hip hoppers. Thus, as Kahn-Harris explains, beyond the professionalized, and quite limited, sphere of high-profile metal bands with major record company backing, metal's global reach is highly reliant on the interconnected nature of local scenes through activities such as the touring of bands from different local scenes throughout different regions of the world and the translocal exchange of music that is produced in specific local scenes on the Internet.

Similarly interconnected, translocal forms of activity can also be seen to underpin Hip Hop. Indeed, it could be argued that Hip Hop was, in fact, one of the first style-based youth cultures to feel this sense of global connectedness, as a relatively early example of a scene that embraced DIY (do-it-yourself) qualities of cultural production, dissemination, and consumption. As already noted, if Hip Hop has established roots in New York and other North American cities, then it quickly transformed into a highly vibrant global youth culture as myriad Hip Hop cultures sprang up in cities around the world. In this respect, Hip Hop dance has played a majorly significant part. Early Hip Hop artifacts, such as Stan Lathan's (1984) film *Beat Street*, became important sources of inspiration for globally dispersed Hip Hop fans, and prospective buyers often joined waiting lists to buy mail order copies of the film. Similarly, US Armed Forces Radio networks and American GIs stationed overseas played their part in exposing new audiences to Hip Hop music, dance, and style during the early 1980s (see Bennett 1999).

As more research utilizing the scenes concept has emerged, so the range and application of scene have been finessed and broadened. Indeed, since the publication of Straw's (1991) original article on scene, something that has had a considerable impact on the nature of music scenes has been the arrival of the internet. An important innovation in scenes research that attempts to map the ways in which the Internet has influenced the nature of music scenes is Peterson and Bennett's (2004) introduction of a three-tier model of music scenes. This consists of the established terms "local" and "translocal" scene, augmenting them with a new category—the "virtual" scene. As this term suggests, virtual scenes have emerged due to music fans' use of Internet communication technology to communicate with each other, one significant facet of this being that geographically dispersed music fans can now interact with each other online. Thus, as Peterson and Bennett observe:

> Whereas a conventional local scene is kept in motion by a series of gigs, club nights, fairs, and similar events, where fans converge, communicate, and reinforce their sense of belonging to a particular scene, the virtual scene involves direct net-mediated person-to-person communication between fans... This may, involve, for example, the creation of chat-rooms or list-serves dedicated to the scene and may involve the trading of music and images online. (11)

The "virtual" scene category facilitates new ways of conceptualizing music scenes and their memberships, not as exclusively reliant upon face-to-face interaction but as forms of interaction that can be enacted primarily, if not exclusively, online. As Bennett (2013) notes, through the presence of virtual scenes,

> the internet becomes an important new medium for forms of musicalised association, the physical, face-to-face forms of interaction that characterise the local scene being replaced with [or joined by] new forms of interaction that centre primarily on articulations of knowledge, taste and authority that go along with a pro-longed commitment to a particular genre or genres of music. (57)

This process of online connection and exchange can also be seen in relation to Hip Hop, including among Hip Hop dancers. This is saliently illustrated in Fogarty's highly instructive research on the way that Hip Hop dancers across the world have learned moves and techniques from each other through the exchange of self-made video footage. Indeed, as Fogarty (2012b) explains, this practice, though it has become more prominent because of the Internet, actually began in the predigital age:

> Many of the b-boys who were featured in films, documentaries and television shows made in the early 1980s began to produce their video artefacts in the 1990s that were exchanged and circulated across the world. These creative acts are historically significant to the shaping of local breaking practices within an international configuration of scenes. (450)

Fogarty's observations here support the earlier observation that Hip Hop (and within it, Hip Hop dance) in many ways qualifies as an example of a scene that developed a mature sense of its global connectedness some time before this began to apply in the case of other scenes, such as metal and punk. Moreover, if much is now made of the DIY nature of such global scenes, based on the fact that a significant amount of the cultural activity they engage in sidesteps the mainstream cultural industries (through a mixture of ideological ethos and necessity), then again Hip Hop can lay claim to being an early forerunner in this respect. This is particularly so in the case of Hip Hop dance. Thus, as noted earlier, while Hip Hop dance experienced a mid-1980s moment of global exposure and popularity in the immediate wake of rap's commercial success, for much of its history it has existed as a more niche practice, situated within its own subscene of Hip Hop. Largely unassisted by the global commercial trappings of rap, Hip Hop dance has, often by necessity, been forced to resort to other means of effecting an ongoing sense of connection between the global community of dancers.

Indeed, in this respect, the historical trajectory of Hip Hop dance helps forge another important point in relation to the validity of scene as a concept for understanding local-global connections in contemporary cultural life. An often mooted criticism of the tripartite model proposed by Peterson and Bennett (2004) is its apparent supposition that the different manifestations of scene outlined in its framework—local, translocal and virtual—exist in isolation from each other (see, e.g., Tarassi 2012). Indeed, in a later study, focusing on music scenes in a specifically Australian context, Bennett, Stratton, and Peterson (2008) address this particular point, suggesting that in studying scenes it is important to bear in mind that "many, perhaps most, scenes today have [local, translocal and virtual] characteristics" (595). Thus, as Fogarty's (2012b) work cited above cogently illustrates, in relation to Hip Hop dance, it can be clearly seen how these different articulations of scene overlay each other in that Hip Hop dance scenes are locally situated in physical space and simultaneously connected with each other through the global mobility of scene members, the exchange of artifacts, and online communication. Indeed, as Fogarty explains, the early, predigital exchange of video material between Hip Hop dancers provided the basis for more instantaneous online exchanges in the digital era as well as a platform for other translocal links that flourished as dancers traveled internationally to compete in dancing competitions in each other's countries.

IDENTITY

Conceptualizations of identity have undergone significant change since the "cultural turn" of the early 1990s (see Chaney 1994). Up until that point, the dominant tropes for explaining identity in sociology and cultural theory were premised on the idea that identities were produced through the specific structural circumstances—class, race, gender, community, and so on—through which individuals were socialized. Before the publication of Straw's (1991) work on scenes and subsequent work on what was to become known as post-subcultural theory (Muggleton 2000), such a perspective on the origins of sociocultural identity was also prevalent in studies of youth cultures and music. Thus a centrally defining characteristic of the classic subcultural studies, produced by the Birmingham Centre for Contemporary Cultural Studies (CCCS) during the 1970s and early 1980s (see Cohen 1972; Hall and Jefferson 1976), was that style-based youth cultures of post–Second World War Britain personified the class struggles that had persisted since the industrialization of Britain in the mid-eighteenth century. Indeed, for the CCCS, while the so-called working-class youth subcultures of postwar Britain were stylistically spectacular and invoked "moral panics" (Cohen 1987) within the British media and general public, the reality of the situation was that the patterns spectacular resistance they engaged in merely reinforced a situation of frustration and entrapment. Thus, as Clarke et al. (1976) observe:

> There is no "subcultural solution" to working-class youth unemployment, educational disadvantage, compulsory miseducation, deadend jobs, the routinisation and specialisation of labour, low pay and the loss of skills. Sub-cultural strategies…"solve," but in an imaginary way, problems which at the concrete material level remain unresolved. (47–48)

Elements of the CCCS subcultural theory also made their way into North American sociology and cultural studies via the work of writers such as Weinstein (1991) and Epstein (1998). Like their British counterparts, North American theorists who adopted the concept of subculture argued that through the collision of repressed working-class youth with the spectacular youth styles produced by the fashion market, new collective identities of resistance were fashioned, identities that only made sense when they were placed within the context of the structural processes that dominated these young people's lives.

On the face of it, Hip Hop would appear to share many of the qualities that subcultural theorists identified among white, working-class youth, except that the everyday circumstances of hip hoppers were often more extreme in terms of the poverty and social exclusion they experienced, the latter being accentuated through exposure to other social maladies such as institutional racism, racial harassment, and police brutality (see Rose 1994). And yet, in many ways it is arguably another chapter in the academic conceptualization of youth culture that more vividly depicts the emergence of Hip Hop and its significance for youth as a form of individual and collective identity. Indeed, as Lipsitz (1994) explains, in the Bronx and other socioeconomically depressed areas of New York City in the early 1970s, Hip Hop assumed critical significance as a form of expression for young people and as a community-wide means of addressing and negotiating the extreme socioeconomic circumstances that characterized everyday life of youth in these neighborhoods.

Notwithstanding the importance of music and associated cultural practices as a means of engaging with aspects of socioeconomic oppression, during the early 2000s, a series of studies began to appear that took issue with the straightforward association of youth culture with class, social structure, and socioeconomic environment that prevailed among subcultural theorists. Muggleton (2000), in his book *Inside Subculture: The Postmodern Meaning of Style*, draws elements of Weber's work on consumption and status together with postmodern notions of historical rupture and affect. In doing so Muggleton argues that previous incarnations of youth culture that were tied to closely integrated subcultural groupings have given way to a new, reflexive form of youth consumer, whose stylized identity was based around a mixing and matching of style in a creative project of the self. Muggleton and other exponents of the post-subcultural approach (notably, Bennett 1999; Miles 2000) have been criticized for an alleged focus on style over substance; a focus on consumerism that excludes from consideration those not able to participate in consumption due to socioeconomic hardship (Shildrick and MacDonald 2006). Similarly, Blackman (2005) has argued that post-subcultural theory takes no account of the ongoing politicized concerns of youth in the so-called post-subcultural era. Bennett (2005, 2011), taking on board these criticisms, has argued that a reduction of emphasis on the relationship between youth culture and the structural circumstances of youth does not necessarily connote a wholesale dismissal of the latter. Rather, he suggests, through invoking a post-subcultural perspective it is possible to disentangle youth culture from the rigidly deterministic perspective to which it is subjected in the work of CCCS era theorists. For Bennett, the post-subcultural perspective allows for the repositioning of youth cultures, not as largely inarticulate rehearsals of class and related structural constraints (Waters 1981), but as fully articulated, fully conscious attempts to engage and subvert their everyday situations. Bennett (2005) also suggests that an ongoing emphasis in criticisms of post-subcultural theory on consumption as connoting the purchasing of objects (and thus being related to economic power) is to downplay other qualities—related, for example, to the consumption of music on the radio or a sound system, or the experience of engaging in street dance while simultaneously watching others performing and learning new moves from them. Also absent from such critical ideas about consumption is the way that this, in turn, can lead to creative forms of engagement with cultural commodities that foster opportunities for grassroots forms of cultural production.

The emergence of Hip Hop onto the global youth cultural landscape marked a significant point of departure from previous youth cultural manifestations in a number of important ways. First, and as previously noted, Hip Hop was initially (though not exclusively) associated with African American street culture, but it quickly became a very multiethnic, multicultural, and transnational form of youth culture. Indeed, Hip Hop's very emphasis on the "local" rendered it a youth cultural form that, while respectful of the origins Hip Hop, did not attempt to slavishly recreate these but looked for ways to creatively remake and refashion the Hip Hop text to respond to local circumstances. Aligned with this was the fact that, whereas previous youth cultures (with the notable exception of punk) had been primarily driven by the youth market and its mass-produced youth commodities (Chambers 1985), a key element of Hip Hop was centered upon the production of cultural resources—notably music, dance and art—for consumption within the wider Hip Hop scene. In this sense, Hip Hop was an early example of what has become commonly referred to as "prosumer" culture, a reference to the way in which individuals can simultaneously be both producers and consumers of culture (see, e.g., Ritzer and Jurgenson 2010). From its earliest origins, Hip Hop was a dynamic, evolving youth cultural form that sought, through the creative practices of music, dance, and art, both to interpret and engage with the socioeconomic environments in which Hip Hop practitioners found themselves. Indeed, Hip Hop's mission in this respect, and its emphasis upon "creative solutions" that enabled disadvantaged youth to understand and attempt to rise above the everyday social problems with which they were faced, was definitively cast by the Universal Zulu Nation, an early Hip Hop collective whose self-ascribed mission was to channel the energy of street youth away from violence and aggression towards more creative, meaningful, and self-fulfilling activities (see Lipsitz 1994).

Such examples of Hip Hop's origins and its cultural mission indicate that it was, from the outset, a highly engaged and reflexive form of cultural practice that set great store on the possibilities of positive transformation of space and place and, of equal importance, of the identities of Hip Hop practitioners themselves through giving them expressive tools with which to empower themselves. Inasmuch as these transformative qualities of Hip Hop have been acknowledged, much of the attention of academic researchers has been focused on rap. As this chapter, and indeed the rest of the chapters in this handbook, aims to illustrate, however, Hip Hop dance has also played a fundamental, if often less readily acknowledged, part in mobilizing the progressive and transformative qualities of Hip Hop. If rap is interpreted in academic work as a highly participatory and inclusive form, shunning the formalism of many musical approaches, then the same can be said of Hip Hop dance, which continues to promote a grassroots, bottom-up approach to the acquisition of a performative skill and its dissemination in the global Hip Hop dance scene. As was noted in the previous section (see "Scenes") Hip Hop dance has been subjected to a significant degree of professionalization and cultural commodification because of its reclassification (Janssen, Verboord, and Kuipers 2011) as a quasi-high art form; however, at the other end of the spectrum the Hip Hop dance community remains committed to engaging with local communities and drawing young people together through using dance as a highly participatory form of self-expression and individual development (Fogarty 2012a).

The ongoing significance of Hip Hop dance as a medium for the transformation and empowerment of identity is perhaps most clearly demonstrated through the intergenerational Hip Hop dance communities now seen around the world. Within these communities, young, upcoming dancers take their lead and inspiration from older dancers whose acquired experience of the dance as young people has inspired them to move into teaching, often as a means of making a living but, equally, as a means of contributing to the development of Hip Hop dance and its preservation as a cultural form. As Fogarty (2012a) observes, typical among older Hip Hop dancers is a narrative of how an initial raw enthusiasm for dancing slowly evolved into an understanding and appreciation of dance as something that required attention, dedication, and commitment, both to maintain a critical level of physical stamina and to improve as a dancer. Along with this came an understanding of one's dance crew as a form of extended family. Within this, the older dancers serve as role models for younger dancers. That is to say, through their exhibited commitment to Hip Hop dance over a number of years and their disciplined approach to the teaching and learning of dance, they symbolize the importance of understanding that fully taking up dance involves a significant level of personal transformation, whereby dancing stops being merely a pleasurable leisure activity and becomes, in effect, a way of life.

BODY

The emergence of body studies in sociological and cultural theory is a relatively recent development (see, e.g., Shilling 2007, 2012). Earlier work in these fields tended to locate the body purely as a reflection of the underlying structural processes that were said to shape and dominate its actions. Such an interpretation of the body also permeated the study of youth culture, style, and music to a fair degree. For example, Hebdige (1979) depicted punk style as a "cut and paste" display of the whole history of post–Second World War youth style on the surface of the body. For Hebdige, the stylistic chaos of the punk image mirrored the socioeconomic crisis created by deindustrialization. Similarly, Willis (1978) flagged the importance of youth cultural bodies as the mediums through which a predetermined relationship, or to use Willis's terminology, a "homology" between class background and a collective response to style and music (in the case of youth) is manifested. According to Willis (1978), homology represents "the continuous play between the group and a particular item which produces specific styles, meanings, contents and forms of consciousness" (191). As the examples of Hebdige and Willis thus serve to illustrate, in much of the early work on youth culture, the body was regarded as merely a vessel that absorbed and re-articulated, in a largely unreflexive fashion, a mass consciousness shaped by the circumstances of one's socioeconomic existence.

In the wake of the cultural turn (Chaney 1994), however, new theories based on the concept of reflexivity began to redraw the sociocultural landscape, not as something rigidly determined by the social structure but rather the product of an ongoing and dynamic struggle between structure and agency. Within this new conceptual discourse, the body was no longer regarded merely as an empty vessel to be filled with a predetermined false consciousness. Rather, the body came to be seen as a dynamic, shifting, and evolving entity, a means through which the individual was free to engage in choice and decision, guided by their own active agency. The work of Shilling is highly instructive in terms of advancing the thinking about the body in sociological and cultural theory, positioning it as central to the coproduction of individual and collective identities in an age of what Giddens (1991) refers to as "reflexive modernity." Thus, observes Shilling (2012),

> the growth of cosmopolitan cities, the spread of global media such as the Internet and satellite television, and the increased internationalization of consumer culture that valorizes the body as a bearer of symbolic value, have encouraged people to become increasingly reflexive about their embodied identities. (4)

More recent studies of youth culture have embraced these key tenets of reflexive modernity in their interpretation of youth cultural bodies as incorporating a reflexive awareness of their circumstances and their actions in relation to this. For example, in his important work on patterns of body modification among youth, Sweetman (2004) considers how making an individual choice to get a tattoo is based both on an understanding of what this means in terms of how it will alter the appearance of the body. Such action then informs a premeditated desire to achieve a particular effect, such as individual distinctiveness or a display of a deeply felt sense of commitment to an alternative scene or lifestyle (or both). Similarly, in another study that attempts to rethink the body as a more reflexive aspect of youth cultural practice, Driver (2011) revisits Willis (1978) work on homology (discussed above). According to Driver, though the concept of homology may be of use in examining the acquired stylistic competencies of youth within the context of a particular assemblage of structural circumstances, its implication that youth therefore maintain only a "half-known" awareness of the meaning of style in their everyday lives is unworkable. Thus, Driver argues, through recasting youth cultural experience as an embodied experience, it becomes possible to perceive the body as a medium for affect and emotion, key qualities in the expression of individual agency as it (re)negotiates the circumstances of its everyday surroundings.

In a more recent study, Driver and Bennett (2015) have sought to extend this understanding of the body as reflexively engaged in the production and articulation of youth cultural practice through considering how, in moving through space, the body continues to articulate the learned practices and cultural competencies acquired through scene membership. In assuming this position, Driver and Bennett are attempting to both better position the body's presence and currency in the production and reproduction of scenes and scene identities, while at the same time considering sceneness as something not merely restricted to certain spaces and places but as something exhibiting an omnipresence through its manifestation in bodies. In making this point, Driver and Bennett cite Kahn-Harris (2007) observation that the "concept of everyday life draws attention to the ways in which individuals, who may spend their lives moving within a plurality of contexts, may nonetheless experience these contexts as part of a seamless flow" (55).

Although Driver and Bennett, and, indeed, Kahn-Harris, are here suggesting frameworks that can be applied across a range of different music scenes, their related arguments have, perhaps, a distinctive resonance with Hip Hop dance given the significance of the body as a medium for this practice. This is highly evident in the work of Fogarty (2012a, 2012b), where the scenario described is one of a deep, often lifelong immersion in dance and where the dancers literally communicate their sceneness between themselves and to others through their bodies. Within this, the practice of dance is important on a number of levels. Most fundamentally, it is a core focus of the scene and the primary reason for its existence. Moreover, even when dancers are not directly engaged in dance, their sense of bonding and community is articulated around a shared understanding of the commitment to dance, this, informing to a large extent whom they choose to socialize with, the spaces and places they choose to socialize in, and the kinds of activity they pursue, in addition to dancing, in those spaces and places.

Conclusion

The purpose of this chapter has been to discuss a range of social and cultural concepts and theories relevant to the study of Hip Hop dance. Four key conceptual themes have been examined—namely, space and place, scenes, identity, and the body. The fact that Hip Hop dance began as a cultural practice located in the street embeds within it a form of spontaneity that other forms of dance do not share in quite the same way. Thus, while other forms of dance may depend on more institutionalized spaces and places—clubs, ballrooms, dancehalls, and so on—to be fully legitimized, Hip Hop dance has a currency that allows it to transcend such spatial notions of performative legitimacy. Similarly, Hip Hop dance is not shackled by the temporal limitations of many other forms of dance, which are often thought to be restricted, or largely restricted, to the sphere of evening leisure and entertainment. On the contrary, Hip Hop dance is regarded as organically interwoven into the continuous flow of everyday happenstance in urban neighborhoods and communities. Within this, notions of space and place, scene, identity, and the body become the primary means through which the local and vernacular and the translocal and global qualities of Hip Hop dance are played and replayed over time and through the ongoing participation and commitment of successive generations of dancers in a worldwide context.

Note

1. For Benjamin, the critical element here rests in the fact that the aura of the object, is carried over from the original artefact to its mass-produced equivalent and is thus accessible to a mass audience. Benjamin's notion of the aura has been most widely discussed in relation to its application in cinema film (see, e.g., Hansen 2008), although it has also been applied in relation to other fields of mass cultural production, notably popular music (see Middleton 1990; Bennett 2009).

References

Alexander, J. (2008). "Iconic Consciousness: The Material Feeling of Meaning." *Environment and Planning D: Society and Space* 26: 782–794.

Bakhtin, M. M. (1984). *Rabelais and His World*. Translated by H. Isowolsky. Cambridge. MA: MIT Press.

Banes, S. (1985) "Breaking." In *Fresh: Hip Hop Don't Stop*, edited by N. George, S. Banes, S. Flinker, and P. Romanowski, 79–111. New York: Random House.

Beaulac, J., Olavarria, M., and Kristjansson, E. (2010). "A Community-Based Dance Hip-Hop Program for Youth in a Disadvantaged Community in Ottawa: Implementation Findings." *Health Promotion Practice* 11 (3): 61–69.

Benjamin, W. (1973). *Illuminations / Walter Benjamin*. Edited with an introduction by H. Arendt. Translated by H. Zohn. London: Fontana.

Bennett, A. (1999). "Rappin' on the Tyne: White Hip Hop Culture in Northeast England—an Ethnographic Study." *Sociological Review* 47 (1): 1–24.

Bennett, A. (2000). *Popular Music and Youth Culture: Music, Identity and Place*. London: Macmillan.

Bennett, A. (2001). *Cultures of Popular Music*. Buckingham, UK: Open University Press.

Bennett, A. (2005). "In Defence of Neo-Tribes: A Response to Blackman and Hesmondhalgh." *Journal of Youth Studies* 8 (2): 255–259.

Bennett, A. (2009). ' "Heritage Rock': Rock Music, Re-presentation and Heritage Discourse." *Poetics* 37 (54–6): 474–489.

Bennett, A. (2011). "The Post-Subcultural Turn: Some Reflections Ten Years On." *Journal of Youth Studies* 14 (5): 493–506.

Bennett, A. (2013). *Music, Style and Aging: Growing Old Disgracefully?* Philadelphia: Temple University Press.

Bennett, A., Stratton, J., and Peterson, R. A. (2008). "The Scenes Perspective and the Australian Context." *Continuum: Journal of Media & Cultural Studies* 22 (5): 593–699.

Bird, S. (2014). "Flash Mobs and Zombie Shuffles: Play in the Augmented City." In *Mediated Youth Cultures: The Internet, Belonging and New Cultural Configurations*, edited by A. Bennett and B. Robards, 213–231. Basingstoke: Palgrave.

Bjurström, E. (1997). "The Struggle for Ethnicity: Swedish Youth Styles and the Construction of Ethnic Identities." *Young: Nordic Journal of Youth Research* 5 (3): 44–58.

Blackman, S. (2005). "Youth Subcultural Theory: A Critical Engagement with the Concept, Its Origins and Politics, from the Chicago School to Postmodernism." *Journal of Youth Studies* 8 (1): 1–20.

Bodden, M. (2005). "Rap in Indonesian Youth Music of the 1990." *Asian Music* 36 (2): 1–26.

Borden, I. (2000). *Skateboarding, Space and the City: Architecture and the Body*. Oxford: Berg.

Chambers, I. (1985). *Urban Rhythms: Pop Music and Popular Culture*. London: Macmillan.

Chaney, D. (1994). *The Cultural Turn: Scene Setting Essays on Contemporary Cultural History*. London: Routledge.

Clarke, J., Hall, S, Jefferson, T. and Roberts, B. (1976). "Subcultures, Cultures and Class: A Theoretical Overview." In *Resistance Through Rituals: Youth Subcultures in Post-War Britain*, edited by S. Hall and T. Jefferson, 9–74. London: Hutchinson.

Cohen, P. (1972). "Subcultural Conflict and Working Class Community." *Working Papers in Cultural Studies, vol. 2*. Birmingham: University of Birmingham.

Cohen, S. (1987). *Folk Devils and Moral Panics: The Creation of the Mods and Rockers*. 3rd ed. Oxford: Basil Blackwell.

Dodds, S. (2011). *Dancing on the Canon: Embodiments in the Value of Popular Dance*. Basingstoke, UK: Palgrave.

Driver, C. (2011). "Embodying Hardcore: Rethinking 'Subcultural' Authenticities." *Journal of Youth Studies* 14 (8): 795–990.

Driver, C., and Bennett, A. (2015). "Music Scenes, Space and the Body." *Cultural Sociology* 9 (1): 99–115.

Epstein, J. S., ed. (1998). *Youth Culture: Identity in a Postmodern World*. Oxford: Blackwell.

Fogarty, M. (2012a). "'Each One Teach One': B-Boying and Ageing." In *Ageing and Youth Cultures: Music, Style and Identity*, edited by A. Bennett and P. Hodkinson, 53–65. London: Berg.

Fogarty, M. (2012b). "Breaking Expectations: Imagined Affinities in Mediated Youth Cultures." *Mediated Youth Cultures*. Special edition. *Continuum: Journal of Media & Cultural Studies* 26 (3): 449–462.

Giddens, A. (1991). *Modernity and Self-Identity: Self and Society in the Late Modern Age.* Cambridge: Polity.

Haenfler, R. (2006). *Straight Edge: Clean-Living Youth, Hardcore Punk, and Social Change.* Piscataway, NJ: Rutgers University Press.

Hall, S., and Jefferson, T., eds. (1976). *Resistance Through Rituals: Youth Subcultures in Post-War Britain.* London: Hutchinson.

Hansen, M. B. (2008). "Benjamin's Aura." *Critical Enquiry* 34: 336–375.

Hazzard-Donald, K. (2004). "Dance in Hip Hop Culture." In *That's The Joint: The Hip-Hop Studies Reader,* edited by M. Forman and M. A. Neal, 584–597. London: Routledge.

Hebdige, D. (1979). *Subculture: The Meaning of Style.* London: Routledge.

Hodkinson, P. (2002). *Goth: Identity, Style and Subculture.* Oxford: Berg.

Huntington, C. S. (2007). *Hip Hop Dance: Meanings and Messages.* Jefferson, NC: McFarland.

Huq, R. (1999). "Living in France: The Parallel Universe of Hexagonal Pop." In *Living Through Pop,* edited by A. Blake, 131–145. London: Routledge.

Janssen, S., Verboord, M., and Kuipers, G. (2011). "Comparing Cultural Classification: High and Popular Arts in European and U.S. Elite Newspapers." *KZfSS: Kölner Zeitschrift für Soziologie und Sozialpsychologie* 63 (special issue 51): 139–168.

Jefferson, T. (1976). "Cultural Responses of the Teds: The Defence of Space and Status." In *Resistance Through Rituals: Youth Subcultures in Post-War Britain,* edited by S. Hall and T. Jefferson, 81–86. London: Hutchinson.

Kahn-Harris, K. (2007). *Extreme Metal: Music and Culture on the Edge.* Oxford: Berg.

LaBoskey, S. (2001). "Getting Off: Portrayals of Masculinity of Hip Hop Dance in Film." *Dance Research Journal* 33 (2): 112–120.

Laing, D. (1985). *One Chord Wonders: Power and Meaning in Punk Rock.* Milton Keynes, UK: Open University Press.

Lipsitz, G. (1994). *Dangerous Crossroads: Popular Music, Postmodernism and the Poetics of Place.* London: Verso.

MacDonald, N. (2001). *The Graffiti Subculture: Youth, Masculinity and Identity in London and New York.* Basingstoke: Palgrave.

Massey, D. (1993). "Power-Geometry and a Progressive Sense of Place." In *Mapping the Futures: Local Cultures, Global Change,* edited by J. Bird, B. Curtis, T. Putnam, G. Robertson, and L. Tickner, 59–69. London: Routledge.

Middleton, R. (1990). *Studying Popular Music.* Milton Keynes, UK: Open University Press.

Miles, S. (2000). *Youth Lifestyles in a Changing World.* Buckingham: Open University Press.

Mitchell, T. (1996). *Popular Music and Local Identity: Rock, Pop and Rap in Europe and Oceania.* London: Leicester University Press.

Muggleton, D. (2000). *Inside Subculture: The Postmodern Meaning of Style.* Oxford: Berg.

Ntarangwi, M. (2009). *East African Hip Hop: Youth Culture and Globalization.* Chicago: University of Illinois Press.

Ojofeitimi, S., Bronner, S., and Woo, H. (2010). "Injury Incidence in Hip Hop Dance." *Scandinavian Journal of Medicine and Science in Sports* 22 (3): 347–355.

Pabon, J. (2006). "Physical Graffiti: The History of Hip Hop Dance." In *Total Chaos: The Art and Aesthetics of Hip-Hop,* edited by J. Chang, 18–25. New York: Basic Books.

Peterson, R. A., and Bennett, A. (2004). "Introducing Music Scenes." In *Music Scenes: Local, Translocal and Virtual,* edited by A. Bennett and R. A. Peterson, 1–15. Nashville, TN: Vanderbilt University Press.

Rajakumar, M. (2010). *Hip Hop Dance.* Santa Barbara, CA: Greenwood Press.

Ritzer, G., and Jurgenson, N. (2010). "Production, Consumption, Prosumption: The Nature of Capitalism in the Age of the Digital 'Prosumer.'" *Journal of Consumer Culture* 10 (1): 13–35.

Rose, T. (1994). *Black Noise: Rap Music and Black Culture in Contemporary America*. London: Wesleyan University Press.

Shildrick, T., and MacDonald, R. (2006). "In Defence of Subculture: Young People, Leisure and Social Divisions." *Journal of Youth Studies* 9 (2): 125–140.

Shilling C. (2007). *Embodying Sociology: Retrospect, Progress and Prospects*. Oxford: Blackwell.

Shilling, C. (2012). *The Body and Social Theory*. London: Sage.

Stahl, G. (2004). "'It's like Canada Reduced': Setting the Scene in Montreal." In *After Subculture: Critical Studies in Contemporary Youth Culture*, edited by A. Bennett and K. Kahn-Harris, 51–64. Basingstoke: Palgrave.

Straw, W. (1991). "Systems of Articulation, Logics of Change: Communities and Scenes in Popular Music." *Cultural Studies* 5 (3): 368–388.

Sweetman. P. (2004). "Tourists and Travellers? 'Subcultures,' Reflexive Identities and Neo-Tribal Sociality." In *After Subculture: Critical Studies in Contemporary Youth Culture*, edited by A. Bennett and K. Kahn-Harris, 79–93. Basingstoke: Palgrave.

Tarassi, S. (2012). "Independent to What? An Analysis of the Live Music Scene in Milan." Unpublished PhD thesis. Catholic University of Milan.

Thresher, F. (1927). *The Gang: A Study of 1313 Gangs in Chicago*. Chicago: Chicago University Press.

Warren, A., and Evitt, R. (2010). "Indigenous Hip-Hop: Overcoming Marginality, Encountering Constraints." *Australian Geographer* 41 (1): 141–158.

Waters, C. (1981). "Badges of Half-Formed, Inarticulate Radicalism: A Critique of Recent Trends in the Study of Working Class Youth Culture." *International Labor and Working Class History* 19: 23–37.

Weinstein, D. (1991). *Heavy Metal: A Cultural Sociology*. New York: Lexington.

Willis, P. (1978). *Profane Culture*. London: Routledge and Kegan Paul.

Films

Beat Street. (1984). Dir. Stan Lathan. USA: Orion Pictures.

Flashdance. (1983), Dir. Adrian Lyne. USA: Paramount Pictures.

....

CHAPTER 10

THROUGH SOUND AND SPACE

Notes on Education from the Edge of the Cypher

....

EMERY PETCHAUER

INTRODUCTION

....

BECOMING a b-boy or b-girl is an educational process. For most of hip hop culture and hip hop dance history, this process has happened through relationships among dancers of various levels of expertise and in the same relative age range. It has happened less in dance studios and more in the kinds of spaces that b-boys and b-girls have made work for them: gymnasiums, parks, rec rooms, garages, and off-the-grid spots. This education has happened and continues to happen through the relationships and spaces that we often call "the scene."

I've seen and experienced this process of education up close in five different scenes. Around 1998, I started b-boying at a practice session at The Point community center on 55th Street and Lakeshore Drive in Chicago. A mysterious tape that showed footage of people breaking and rocking initially made me search out this space. That same year, after months of prompting from the girl who lived next door to me, I finally met her boyfriend: Ron AKA DJ Groove, a Chicago party DJ by way of Montego Bay, Jamaica. As my neighbor had predicted, Ron and I quickly became friends, and I started helping carry his records and equipment to the incredibly live house parties he would DJ around Chicago. (Little did I know, my apprenticeship had just begun.) In not too much time, I would manage to get my own turntables, become his understudy, and eventually work my way up to playing those parties with him, once I had mastered the foundations of hip hop DJing he was teaching me, directly and indirectly. Then I started moving around.

My professional journey as an educator and scholar has taken me to San Diego, Virginia Beach, Philadelphia, and now the Detroit metro area. My first point of entry to each of these locations has been the places where people create hip hop, especially breaking practice spots and events. The progression usually goes from b-boying at local practice spots, to becoming a go-to DJ for local events, to starting my own breaking-oriented nights or events.[1] This pattern in different parts of the country has mean that—as DJ Ill Literate—I have enjoyed a proper view from the edges of the cypher since, roughly, the turn of the century. In part, I mean this literally because the DJ setup at most jams, competitions, or events is at the edge of the cypher. I've played at the edge of hundreds of cyphers locally and, occasionally, abroad. But I also mean this figuratively, wherein the cypher is a metaphor for the entire scene where people connect through dance and culture. Because of my relocations, I've navigated the edges of community cyphers in four different regions of the United States.

Over and over in these scenes, I've seen the educative process whereby people become b-boys and b-girls—entering scenes as beginners, going through the process of earning stripes, and eventually becoming recognized b-boys and b-girls. A number of changes happen along this journey. They learn foundational movements of the dance and start using them as creative building blocks. They stop imitating moves from other dancers and start developing their own style with unique move variations. They start dressing fresh instead of wearing grubby sneakers, both in and out of the cypher. Seasoned b-boys and b-girls start interacting with them differently, too. Instead of being largely ignored by these core members, they get called out to battle or battled into a crew, a sure sign that one is recognized as a b-boy or b-girl. People also go through meaningful identity changes along this journey. They begin thinking about themselves differently, investing emotionally in their new b-boy or b-girl self and the principles and values associated with it.

Music is woven throughout this educative process of becoming a b-boy or b-girl in these spaces (Fogarty 2012b). A great deal of this education concerns how to relate to the music and aesthetic forms—like flow, layering, and ruptures—that are common across hip hop elements (Rose 1994). People learn to dance in, around, and in relation to the music, responding to what they hear and feel: how to break on the break. This education also concerns how to present oneself in the midst of this music, and with respect to its sonic qualities. Breaking certainly involves learning to do things with the body and learning about the historical context of the dance. But the relationship between the dance (moves, steps, etc.) and the music is integral to what it means to be a b-boy or b-girl.

I will focus on this process of becoming a b-boy or b-girl as it relates to sound and space. Specifically, I focus on the sonic qualities of music that are woven into the process of becoming a b-boy or b-girl and the spaces where this takes place. Breaking scenes and the spaces that make them up are not stable. They change over time as people and resources move in and out of them, altering the opportunities that people have to become b-boys and b-girls. My focus is mostly on the postmillennial era of breaking thus far, though I conclude with some thoughts about what the emerging changes in sound and space might mean for the future of learning in breaking scenes and becoming b-boys and b-girls.

The Sound of Learning

Music is an essential resource in the process of becoming a b-boy or b-girl. Here, I don't mean that b-boys and b-girls need music to dance to, though that's obviously true. I mean that developing a type of relationship with music—and the ways that DJs like me play this music at jams and battles—is necessary to becoming a b-boy or b-girl. This need is wrapped up in an early lesson that novice b-boys and b-girls often learn—that is, what the "b" in b-boy and b-girl represents. In *The Freshest Kids*, DJ Kool Herc, regarded to be the person who introduced the term, explains that the letter *b* comes from 1970s street terminology around the word *break*: reaching the breaking point, doing something extreme, or "going off." In the context of the dance, this points to a kind of reaction dancers might have—or perhaps should have—to a specific segment of the music, the break. Because of this relationship, dancers in scenes also historicize the letter to represent the break of the record or the break beats to which people dance and respond (Schloss 2009).[2]

The role of music is also evident in one of the most important concepts in breaking: *foundation*. Joseph Schloss, in interviews with b-boys and b-girls in New York City, discusses foundation as both the knowledge that dancers acquire through other members of a scene (particularly elders) and the process of obtaining that knowledge. Foundation is not only the moves and steps of the dance, but also the meanings, styles, cultural context, tradition, and lineage of the dance. YNOT speaks to this concept in a 2008 minidocumentary that focused on him and DJ Skeme Richards. YNOT expounds:

> Foundation is not just moves. Foundation *has* moves. You got swipes, you got fuckin' backspins. You got sweeps. You got chair freezes. You got top rock. You got footwork. Like, yeah, that's foundation. You know what I'm saying? But, foundation really ultimately is having that, and understanding what the dance is. That's another part of foundation. If you don't understand the movement, or if you don't give what the music is giving you—you know what I'm saying?—then you're not doing foundation. Just because I can do a chair freeze doesn't mean I know about foundation. It's the *way* I do my mufuckin' chair freeze. It's *when* I do it. You know what I'm saying? That's what makes it foundation . . . . Now it's just like, "Ok, well I'm throwing CC's and I've got Pro-Keds on. I'm a b-boy." No. That's not the end all say all of what a b-boy is [original emphases].[3]

At the core of YNOT's excerpt is an argument that the essence of being a b-boy or b-girl is much more than moves, movements, and even certain clothing items. Foundation involves having a broader, more comprehensive understanding of the dance, a particular set of listening practices, and demonstrated musical competence (Fogarty 2010). "If you don't give what the music is giving you" calls upon listening as an embodied experience (Fogarty 2012b). The statement sets forth a conditional if-then proposition about the personal, affective relationship between a dancer and sonic elements. "It's *when* I do it" is a claim to aural kinesthetics: the temporal relationship between movements and the sonic elements of music (Johnson, 2012). Moves are evidence that one has gotten their foundation only when a dancer executes them with respect to music.

"The music" in these instances is what is in a DJ's crate, actual or digital. Footage and oral histories from premillennial scenes attest to the ways dancers' musical tastes (and what DJs played) varied by geographical location across the scenes (Fogarty 2010). In the current postmillennial era of breaking, music echoes a bit differently across scenes. There is greater access to music because of the Internet, digital platforms for sharing, and DJs who travel internationally through scenes. A track is played in the finals of a battle, and in not too much time, the comments section of its YouTube video will almost certainly have questions and answers about the track's name. This greater access means there is more musical continuity across global breaking scenes compared to past eras. B-boys and b-girls in different geographical locations are getting down to a similar body of music, even though this body is much larger compared to eras past. I was reminded of this point a few years ago while in Mexico City for no hip hop reasons whatsoever. I was on a bus that was about to start off to its destination when I heard the psych rock guitar and driving organ of the Spencer Davis Group's version of "I'm a Man" (1967) blasting from around the corner. As the bus pulled away and I craned to see around the corner, my suspicions were confirmed: a small group of b-boys were setting up speakers and getting ready to practice.

In addition to greater musical continuity across the global scene, the music that circulates through global scenes has expanded beyond "breaks" based on the strict drum-based definition of the term. The maxim *It's not what the break is but what the break can be* helps articulate this modern approach that many DJs take. Without a doubt, breaking-oriented DJs still search for breaks that sit in funk, rock, and other records—those fat, dark rings that shine off the vinyl. But DJs also tune their listening practices to other sonic elements in the records that will move the dancers—bring them to the *breaking* point, so to speak—even if these elements are not in a break. These sonic elements may derive from a horn, guitar, organ, or any other instrument overtop driving drums that, if looped up in the right way, functions like a break. These records often contain sections that approximate a break as well: a boiled-down, rawer version of what is heard in the rest of the song but not quite a pure drum-only break. With production methods becoming easier though digital technologies, more DJs are trying to create these qualities in their own tracks to play out at events. This expanded notion of what a break can be means that b-boys and b-girls today are presented with more varied layers of sound when they enter the cypher.

From behind the turntables, it is easy to see (and hear) how this spectrum of sound plays out in the relationships dancers create with the music and how they rely on the DJ to make that spectrum of sound. The language dancers use to describe the kind of music they want is a focal point. Dancers use terms like *hype* to describe fast music to match the quick footwork or power moves they prefer. Others use terms like *hard* for songs that are primarily drums. Still others use a term like *funky* to represent music with instruments, horn stabs, and interesting arrangements and drum patterns that give them opportunities to adapt to music that other dancers might not know. Each of these terms reflect a different relationship with music and dance, as well as the different listening practices dancers have developed, often through their relationships with mentors and other dancers in their scene (Fogarty 2010). A good DJ knows how to play music that is within the range of particular dancers, so the dancers will stretch to demonstrate this important relationship. In an organized competition, dancers will often look over to the DJ right before a battle begins and give a look that universally says, "Gimme what I need!" When DJs drop these key tracks at the right points in battles, people around the cypher and the dancers during mid-round often show their appreciation. More subtly, if a dancer feels a track has gone on too long or doesn't have the sonic qualities they want, they will try signaling to the DJ to change the track. When a DJ doesn't change the track, or isn't in tune with the musical aesthetics of breaking, dancers are *still* faced with the task of demonstrating a relationship to this music, even if the relationship is contrived.

Dancers hunt down and catalogue thousands of MP3s and DJ mixes for practice sessions. But jams, battles, and other events always have a live DJ. This is not something to overlook. In part, the DJ as a fixture at breaking events is simply hip hop tradition and reflects how breaking scenes often hold onto facets of early hip hop years, including items of clothing, even though today they are not always ideal. For instance, it would be cheaper and altogether more streamlined for promoters *not* to have DJs at events and to simply play recorded music for battles. Many b-boys and b-girls have much of the music that DJs play at events on their hard drives. They do not *need* a DJ to hear the music, which is much different from needing to attend a Kool Herc party to hear certain music and to hear it through a powerful sound system. But an event without a DJ is not an event at all. It's a practice session. Having a DJ at an event forces dancers to react spontaneously to the music that the DJ plays. By meeting this challenge, dancers demonstrate their musical competency and grasp of foundation.

In the context of breaking scenes, it is not only vital to think about music and the range of sonic qualities dancers respond to. It is also important to think about *how* DJs like me play these songs for b-boys and b-girls live at events and the opportunities and challenges live DJing presents to dancers. The method of DJing that is most common across scenes today centers on backspinning and rocking doubles of drum-based segments of records. We call these "breaks" even if these segments do not fit the strict definition of the term. Broadly, we trace this method to DJ Kool Herc and other pioneering DJs, who at parties played the parts of records that seemed to get people dancing the most—what Herc called the "merry-go-round." Most specifically, Grandmaster Flash's perfected *quick mix theory* and the live performances of the 1970s and 1980s more closely represent how this style of DJing looks in breaking scenes. Like much of hip hop, this method begins with the break as a key unit of creative potential. DJs manually loop and extend these breaks from one turntable to another—over and over again—and use different cutting techniques to transition from one record to another. In my view, these are essential practices that distinguish hip hop DJing from the methods of DJing in other scenes. Traditionally in live hip hop settings, the product that comes from using this approach to DJing is what emcees rhyme over and what dancers get down to. In scenes from *Wild Style* (1983), we see Chief Rocker Busy Bee and other MCs controlling the party and dancers getting down over breaks backspun by Grand Wizard Theodore.

Flash's quick mix theory, however, entails more subtle and profound techniques that are relevant to breaking scenes than simply looping breaks of records together in a seamless way, with some scratches and cuts to boot. Flash also isolated parts of the break that were musically different from one another, looped these in different combinations during live performance, and created an evolving sonic tapestry that MCs had to navigate in front of an audience. Loren Kajikawa (2015) illustrates this process and product by analyzing the audio recording of Grandmaster Flash and the Four MCs on December 23, 1978, at the Audubon Ballroom in Harlem. Kajikawa focuses on how Flash uses the break from Brooklyn Dreams's "Music, Harmony, and Rhythm" (1977). Like many breaks, this segment consists of more than drums. Against a backbeat, a wandering bassline pushes the segment forward during the first eight measures before dramatic piano keys take over at the ninth measure. In Flash's live performance, after dropping the break and cueing up the second copy, he loops only the first two measures of the break for roughly one minute. By looping *only* the first two measures, he keeps the bassline steady, preventing the record from playing into where the bassist's fingers walk up and down the neck of the instrument. More to the point, looping the break in this way prevents the dramatic piano section on the record from playing. When Flash finally lets these keys drop, we feel a forceful change of mood in the song. Further, when Flash returns to the opening measures of the break and loops them again, we *anticipate* this dramatic piano section and hold on until he gives it to us. Letting these keys play in a live performance serves a practical function for his MCs as well. The group uses the new segment to coincide with passing the microphone to Melle Mel and Kid Creole. The piano section then functions as a kind of interlude, where the MCs can improvise while passing the mic and getting back into the groove.

This application of quick mix theory guides how seasoned DJs in breaking scenes play for b-boys and b-girls in this post-millennial era. Like Flash, DJs identify and isolate segments that they hear *as* breaks by manually looping them. This practice builds anticipation for the actual raw break sections of the records or sections with a prominent instrument that dancers will feel and respond to. The opening measures of Perez Prado's "Circle" (1973) illustrate this clearly. Broken into the scene by Skeme Richards, the track opens with four measures muscled forward mostly by bass. At the fifth measure, a high-pitched plucking from the top of a guitar neck comes in at each eighth note of the next four measures. The guitar plucking sounds like a percussive tapping. Then at the ninth measure, the horns blast in and take it from there. Heard through quick mix theory, the track has three different break segments to loop in different sequences, and that is exactly how Skeme and other DJs play the track. (I don't play this track because I consider it one of Skeme's signature records—and I'm no biter). Each of these segments features an additional sonic element, with different affordances for dancers, particularly, the second segment with distinct guitar plucks hitting on each eighth note. While being funky enough in its own right, each looped segment builds anticipation for the next.

The cuts that DJs impose on these segments create other elements of this evolving sonic tapestry. DJs often signal they are about to restart the break or drop a new song by cutting overtop of the track toward the end of a measure. The cutting is a signal to dancers to be ready for the change, but it also builds anticipation for the restarted break or new track. This effect is most pronounced when DJs bring the fader completely over to the channel of the new track, cutting off all the music except for the final cuts before dropping the track. Dancers often respond to these cuts not by somehow dancing along with the unpredictable rhythm of the cuts but by coordinating a move with the first beat of the restarted break that they sense coming. Other DJ techniques also offer dancers opportunities to show their spontaneous relationship with the music. When restarting a break, DJs will occasionally let the first few beats of the "old" break's subsequent measure play overtop first few beats of the "new" break's segment. In effect, this layering technique moves sonic elements from the "old" break's next measure to the first few beats of the "new" break's measure. Skilled dancers who pay attention to this technique respond to it in different ways, such as coordinating a move with the relocation of this sound. There are instances as well, when DJs allow certain tracks to play for more extended periods of time rather than backspin break segments. Typically, these are songs where the progressions between song parts give dancers opportunities to show their relationship with and knowledge of the music. (Boris Gardner's "Ghetto Funk" [1973] is one such song that has gotten this treatment.) This practice is more evident in top rock battles, cyphers, and--a bit differently-- rocking battles or Apache lines, where DJs let entire songs play.

These techniques from quick mix theory and the sonic tapestry they create demonstrate aesthetics that are common across hip hop and Afro-diasporic expressions. Tricia Rose (1994) inaugurates scholarly attention to these aesthetics, noting how flow, layering, and ruptures exist in graffiti lettering, emcee's rhymes, hip hop dance forms, and DJing. YNOT provides a rich illustration of aesthetic continuity across hip hop elements in his short film "Make the Letters Dance."[4] The film features Popmaster Fabel showing how he creates the flow and ruptures of urban stylized lettering through dance (popping, specifically). Backspinning and looping sections of records together—keeping them on time for dancers—creates flow. Layers of sounds derived from the wide spectrum of records DJs now play at events exist within this flow. Rearranging the break segments of records through different techniques and changing songs at relatively predictable points puts ruptures upon this flow. B-boys and b-girls must respond in creative ways to flow, laying, and ruptures. They must dance within this flow and to these sonic layers while navigating, anticipating, and using ruptures to their creative benefit. Dancers also anticipate certain songs that are signature tracks of DJs who are playing, and they might only get the opportunity to dance to these tracks if they get into the deeper rounds of an organized competition. Dancers must also adapt to new tracks that DJs introduce to scenes, whether or not these tracks are well-received by the scene, or tracks played by an inexperienced DJ that might not fit b-boy and b-girl aesthetics. For tracks that are considered classics, dancers have the opportunity to demonstrate deep, embodied knowledge of them.

How intricately these challenges and opportunities are woven into the cypher always becomes apparent to me when I show people who are not acquainted with breaking some footage from a battle. The first question they usually ask, in amazement, is if the dancers plan ahead of time which song they are going to battle to. Or they ask if the dancers give the DJ the song to play. They assume that for a dancer to have such a pronounced relationship with intricate aspects of the music, they not only must have chosen the song but also rehearsed their set in advance. My internal reaction, naturally, is "Of course not!" These questions are understandable because the kinds of dance performances most familiar to the popular public are planned and choreographed. But in breaking, selecting the songs or knowing beforehand which songs a DJ is going play would eliminate what is at the core of foundation: adapting to and having a relationship with the flow, layers, and ruptures that DJs create.

THE SPACE OF LEARNING

People develop a relationship with music and become b-boys and b-girls through the learning that happens in particular spaces. Here, I am referring to something a bit different from a dance class or workshop that a person may take at a studio. As I noted at the start of the chapter, institutional settings like these are newer inventions in the history of hip hop and different from the settings where most of the learning in hip hop has taken place. Learning in hip hop, and in breaking specifically, most often takes place in the spaces that people create when they engage with one another around hip hop.

Regarding space, b-boys and b-girls are typically concerned with whether there is enough of it, the shape of it, and whether the surface is conducive to dancing (Schloss 2009). Yet the ways that b-boys and b-girls populate flat surfaces—the ways that they create these spaces—entail rich opportunities for learning. Murray Forman (2001) calls these kinds of hip hop spaces "material spaces of 'the real'": physical spaces that come with sensory and tactile details, where people encounter practices and one another (22–25). With respect to breaking, Imani Kai Johnson (2012) notes sound's role in producing social space and situated physical movements. Informing both of these spatial perspectives is Henri Lefebvre's (1991) argument that space is not only a plane that people walk, stand, and dance on but a social product—something that people (and sounds) produce. Hip hop creators produce material spaces of the real by *using* space. That is, by using space, they attach subjective meanings to it and relate to one another in ways that are unique to those spaces.

The differences between practice sessions and cyphers illustrate what Lefebvre, Forman, and Johnson mean by "space." At practice sessions in gymnasiums and similar locations, you can find people spread around the room in loose clusters or sometimes alone, working on specific moves or steps they are trying to master or sharpening what they already know. They might do drills connected to certain moves or try out new ideas and innovations. Dancers will be interacting as well, giving each other tips and advice, especially when they are friends or in the same crew. They may share a laugh with one another when failing at a move or crashing. A great deal of learning happens in these kinds of spaces.

How people interact and carry themselves *in these same locations* might change if a cypher starts or, even more, if a battle happens in the cypher. In this same location, a different kind of space is created. Accordingly, people start drawing from their arsenal of moves rather than pushing to try something new or attempting something that is at the threshold of their abilities. Their signature moves or steps they mastered long ago become weapons to deploy. They project a more confident self and pay more attention to the music, coordinating their moves with grooves and sounds to embody musical competence. Instead of laughing when they fail or crash, they cover up the mistake by integrating it into their next step or move. If a battle happens in this cypher, the relationship among the dancers who are battling and the people on the outside of cypher changes as well. People on the outside may show their support for a dancer by standing behind them at the edge of the cypher, notably, if they are all in the same crew. These people model surprise and excitement at their crewmate's moves, even though they have seen their crewmate perform these moves dozens, even hundreds, of times. Even observers on the outside of the cypher with no crew affiliation take on different roles in this different kind of space. They become the informal judges of who is winning the battle, providing a type of ongoing evaluation with oohs, ahs, and other reactions.

These changes happen because the cypher is a spatial creation different from a practice session, even when they occur in the same location. Each type of space facilitates a different set of relational dynamics among dancers and the particular ways in which dancers project themselves. Abstract principles about what is good and valued in breaking guide how dancers participate in the cypher, what they attempt to embody in their dance, and how they make meaning of participation. Joseph Schloss (2009) unpacks many of these principles: controlled aggression; knowledge of and a relationship with primarily funk-based music; possessing a diverse arsenal of moves suitable for different opponents, battle situations, and physical dance spaces; unique variations and innovations of foundational moves that are, ideally, distinct to self; and ability to respond to one's opponent *in* the battle instead of dancing a fully premeditated round. Dancers demonstrate they possess these values by developing specific ways to embody them so that they are recognizable to other dancers in the cypher. In other words, dancers must not only hold these values but also develop ways to show and prove they have them in tested situations.

The cypher teaches other important parameters for participation as well. One of these is the absolute nature of participation: a dancer is either *in* the cypher or *out* of the cypher. Being in the cypher is a binary either/or status. Additionally, being in the cypher is an individual occupation of space: only one person is in at a time. This absolute use of space is not a function of available room either. Even when the cypher is large enough for more than once dancer, more than one person in at the same time would be absurd by the norms of the dance, dangerous, or disrespectful.

What is important about these norms and the physical spaces they create is how they help b-boys and b-girls to learn the ways of participating in the dance and presenting themselves. The parameters I have described lead dancers to enter the cypher deliberately and unambiguously, signaling to other dancers that one is beginning a round—and doing so confidently. Sometimes participation hinges on entering in such a way. In my first few months of living in Philadelphia, before I had made any local connections, a good friend living in Virginia, Meen 187, stayed with me for a night on his way to New York. The night he arrived, we stopped by a small, sweaty jam on Lancaster Ave in West Philly, just in time to catch the last part of the jam when people were cyphering. The first time either Meen or I tried to enter the cypher, a Philly dancer quickly cut us off, beating us to the center point and starting her round before either of us could. Then it happened again with a different dancer. And then again. This was not an accident, of course. Upon our arrival, the dancers picked up the rhythm and speed by which they traded rounds in *their* cypher. For us to enter it—to become part of the conversation, so to speak—we each had to claim the space as ours more immediately and forcefully than anyone else around the cypher, which we eventually did. This feat was also an individual one. We could not enter the cypher together, though we could (and did) help transition each other into the cypher using a commando to trade off the space between us so that another dancer couldn't cut us off.[5] The other dancers around the cypher, many of whom are my friends today, were not mean-spirited.[6] Like swinging Double Dutch ropes at a higher velocity, there actions outlined a certain manner required for us to enter the space and participate: unambiguous, deliberate, and forceful. Efforts to participate in any other way would have failed.

Also related to space are VHS tapes, DVDs, and Internet-based clips—all of which I will simply call "videos," given my analog orientation. Here, we can think about a loose collection of genres that parallel the documentation-from-within of other scenes such as skating or punk. Videos of major events like Freestyle Session, Mighty 4, B-Boy Summit, and others contain not only the main battles of the judged competition but, oftentimes, footage from cyphers, interviews, and performances. Many individual dancers or crews have released videos that have functioned as a mixtape of highlights, personal footage, travel experiences, and instruction. Mary Fogarty (2012a) has illustrated how these circulated media, particularly in the 1990s, produce imagined affinities among the dancers who create and view them. Similarly, these videos are also representations of breaking spaces. As artifacts of breaking and of hip hop culture more broadly, they create a window into these spaces for people who were not or cannot be there. Providing a window into these spaces does not ensure that people will accurately understand the norms of the space or the meanings that people infuse into them. Videos and footage are simply an entry point. Because videos from events are also documentations of what happened there, they also create shared knowledge and experience. For example, I can write, "Do you remember when K-Mel pulled El Niño out of a duffel bag at Lords of the Floor?" If you don't, you can go watch it on YouTube because at some point someone uploaded the clip from the LOTF 2002 DVD.[7] Or, I can make a vague reference to a certain Radiotron battle, and you can go online and in not much time find out and watch the important battle I am referencing.

It is notable that what initially made me search for where b-boys and b-girls practice in Chicago was a grainy VHS tape that had been dubbed way too many times. An acquaintance of mine named Micah had a tape full of spliced together clips of b-boying, rocking, popping, and other hip hop dances. He got it from someone who lived in Pittsburgh. That's all we knew about it. Some of the clips were from television dance shows, and others seemed to be footage from clubs or battles around the country. We were mesmerized by the scene of a whole floor of rockers jerking in unison, despite having no idea at the time what we were seeing, hearing, and feeling. Micah was not a friend of mine before the tape; we became friends *because* of the tape and by spending a good amount of time rolling around on cardboard and hardwood floors trying to imitate what we saw. The tape was the first connection to these spaces and communities, and it prompted me to eventually find The Point on 55th and Lakeshore Drive, one of the material spaces of the real. This nexus of relationships, circulated media, and material spaces plays prominently across some hip hop dance experiences (Fogarty 2012a).

The relationships breaking spaces facilitate among dancers are also instructive. Foremost, people learn a great deal from the dancers with whom they have a close relationship, like crewmembers. Crewmembers offer feedback, evaluation, and information. This information can deal with moves, b-boy philosophy, or overall hip hop historical knowledge. Relationships with dancers who are not in one's crew but still populate breaking spaces also teach important lessons, although indirectly so, about what it means to be a b-boy or b-girl. More indirectly, dancers learn a great deal about how they should be through the violations that people call out against one another during battles. This learning happens most frequently when dancers do not embody a principle or value central to breaking in the judgment of their opponent. B-boys and b-girls call out these violations through subtle gestures that have common meaning across scenes and are targeted to a specific value that an opponent should be (but is not) embodying. Fitting with the overall aesthetic of the dance, many of these gestures, though subtle, are also exaggerated (Schloss 2009). The biting symbol is perhaps the most common one (arms extended, elbows bent, forearms parallel on top of each other, opening and closing—to represent teeth and jaws biting). Also common are slapping the floor after an opponent crashes to signal that he or she lacks the necessary controlled aggression, counting on one's fingers to point out that a dancer has repeated a move or step, and pointing at one's ear while an opponent is dancing to signal that the he or she is not listening to the music or lacks the necessary relationship with the music. Dancers often make up gestures like these on the spot that are appropriate for the given context.

All of these gestures are educative. They teach dancers and observers about the embodied principles connected to the sonic tapestry DJs create. Each one points to an embodied principle in a scene that is considered valuable and good. Of course, this teaching is indirect. B-boys and b-girls make these gestures while an *opponent* is dancing, but the gestures are primarily for everyone else around the cypher or judging the battle. In other words, the purpose of the gestures is not to convince an opponent that he is wack, but to convince everyone else who is watching. These gestures also can be a battle tactic to point out an opponent's mistakes or to take attention off of them, but many are given at times when an opponent can't notice the gesture, such as when he or she is performing a combination of power moves that have no relationship to the music. The gestures indirectly instruct people on the outside of a cypher, particularly novices, about the kind of relationship a dancer should have with the sonic elements of music.

THE FUTURE OF SPACE AND SOUND

I noted at the start of this chapter that sounds and spaces are not stable in breaking scenes. Although my treatment of sound and space has focused on postmillennial trends in breaking, the spaces in which people learn to become b-boys and b-girls and the music that fills these spaces will continue to change. In the early twenty-first century, many of these changes are related to digital platforms that provide different ways of creating and accessing space. Other changes come from new markets and economic resources injected into scenes via corporate sponsors such as Red Bull, nonprofits like the UDEF/Pro Breaking Tour, and, most recently, the Youth Olympic Games. These resources have meant bigger stages, brighter lights, and more eyes watching—often from afar on screens instead of up close around a cypher. New markets and economic inputs will continue altering the spaces in which people become b-boys and b-girls.

As I noted previously, videos, DVD, and Internet-hosted clips have all made breaking spaces visible to a broader spectrum of people. What people once could only learn by finding the material spaces where people congregated to break, they can now start learning by watching videos of what happened in these spaces or instructional videos. Digital and Internet-based technologies will continue to evolve breaking spaces as scenes progress into the twenty-first century. One example of this evolution is the launch of the B-Boy & B-Girl Dojo platform by Focus and AT of Flow Mo.[8] The site expands on previous instructional formats where people simply purchased an instructional tape or DVD and learned by watching demonstrations and practicing drills; B-Boy & B-Girl Dojo, at the time of writing, is a monthly digital subscription platform providing instruction and drills in multiple languages and four skill levels. What is most notable about this format with regard to space is that subscribers battle Focus and AT in a battle simulator at the end of each skill level.[9] To my knowledge, this is the first such feature in any breaking instructional format.[10] Instead of simply drilling and practicing what Focus and AT teach, a dancer has to respond to the rounds that Focus or AT throw at them in this simulation. Of course, some aspects of a cypher battle cannot be replicated in this format, such as interactions with and reactions from people on the outside of the cypher or having one's opponent (i.e., Focus or AT) dance in response to the learner's rounds. Regardless, this feature of B-Boy & B-Girl Dojo is an attempt to replicate breaking spaces and the important lessons that people learn in them. We should consider how digital platforms, technologies, and opportunities for monetization will shape the learning and interactions in breaking spaces further into the twenty-first century.

The sounds that b-boys and b-girls dance to will also undergo changes into the twenty-first century. As noted, some of these changes are already in motion through the resources Red Bull and UDEF/Pro Breaking Tour are putting into scenes. In addition to creating more events around the world, the largest events connected to these organizations are streamed live on YouTube and other Internet platforms. This streaming creates incredible access to the global scene. It is also why many people like me stay up into the late hours of the night to watch the finals of an event happening in a time zone far away. This access, however, in most cases prevents DJs from playing music that is copyrighted, unless the promoter pays for these tracks to be played. Thus, this broad access eliminates most of the music that b-boys and b-girls have danced to over the course of breaking history. Playing a copyrighted track on a YouTube live stream runs the risk of killing the link. Consequently, the songs played for battles at these streamed events are increasingly made by the DJs who are spinning.

This change with regard to the music in breaking spaces presents some potential trade-offs. Since skilled breaking-oriented DJs are familiar with the musical tastes of the scene, it follows that the music they produce will be more tailored toward the aesthetics they perceive b-boys and b-girls to enjoy and perhaps DJs' own practice of backspinning doubles.[11] However, at least in the early stages of this era, few DJs have the refined production skills to create this music.[12] Much of it sounds like simple copy-and-pastes from stock sound kits and without the richness to play over big sound systems.. Predictable horn stabs at the end of musical measures abound. More importantly, DJs creating music specifically *for* b-boys and b-girls reverses what has been the typical relationship among musicians, DJs, and dancers. For most of breaking history, b-boys and b-girls have gotten down to music that has not been made with them in mind as the sole audience.[13] Certainly, many musicians who created songs that are played in breaking spaces had no knowledge of breaking at the time they wrote them. Yet doing their job, DJs have found certain sonic qualities in these songs, put them through a creative process on turntables to emphasize those qualities, and made dancers experience the songs as "b-boy tracks." Many of the most important musical segments in the breaking cannon— like the extended horn solo in "It's Just Begun" (1972) and the descending guitar of "The Mexican" (1972)—have sonic qualities that dancers must stretch themselves and adapt to in order to demonstrate a relationship with the music. They must stretch and adapt because the music was not made as a direct response to their aesthetic priorities. A similar point applies to lyrics and phrases in the canonical breaking songs, none of which were made about breaking. One learns to "dance to the drummer's beat," "get involved!," and "feel the groove"—all sacred lessons and direct instructions about how to become a b-boy or b-girl (Fogarty 2012b).

As music made specifically for breaking scenes becomes more prevalent, the affordances that music provides dancers to demonstrate their grasp of foundation and, in essence, become b-boys and b-girls will continue to evolve. Or, perhaps the change is less one of evolution and more one of different available criteria (and much disagreement) for what it means to become a b-boy or b-girl. A similar change has already taken place in the rap battle scene, such as Smack/Ultimate Rap League. There, battles now take place acapella and with hardly any improvised or freestyled lyrics. In fact, competitors are expected to do meticulous research about their opponent, battle history and personal life included, and to craft memorized verses around this content. Changes such as these would have been unthinkable decades ago since they violate the long-held principle of freestyling and related standards of authenticity. All of this aside, it turns out that this acapella, prescripted product is more marketable, widely entertaining, and financially lucrative for promoters and participants. Especially given breaking's recent entrance into the Youth Olympic Games, it is possible the sounds related to one's musical competency will racially change (Myers 2019).

FINAL WORDS

The educative process of becoming a b-girl or b-boy takes place in sound and space. These sounds and spaces evolve over time, changing the process that people must go through, or what is required of them, to become and be recognized as b-girls and b-boys. As such, paying attention to the evolving nature of the music and how DJs play it will lead to a richer understanding of the dance as it evolves. Similarly, attending to new kinds of spaces and shifting spatial arrangements will yield important insights about the dance and how people embody it. Whether it is the kind of space created from old, disposed-of linoleum flooring sitting outside an apartment building in the Bronx, or by an elevated stage under bright lights at Red Bull BC One, these spaces are always connected in some way to markets and economic influences. Ultimately, sound and space—in fact, sound *in* and *of* space—make it possible to understand how and why we jam on the groove.

NOTES

1. The regular events I either started or supported include The Breakroom in Norfolk, VA (weekly); The Gathering in Philadelphia (monthly); Lovers' Rock (mostly annually); and Yaktown Sounds in Pontiac, MI (beatmaking, weekly).
2. *The Freshest Kids* (2002), Israel (Dir.), documentary video, DVD, USA: Image Entertainment. In the video Mr. Freeze, Mr. Wiggles, and Crazy Legs in separate interviews define the *b* as referring to the break of the record or break beats on that part of the record. It's also worth noting how Ken Swift and Popmaster Fabel sought to clarify the term in the July–August 1993 issue of *The Source*: "The term B-boy was introduced by the inventor of hip hop culture, Kool DJ Herc, who was referring to the brothers who anticipated the

'break' part of a song . . . . The B-Boys' response to these rhythms is a sudden outburst of specific dance styles." Their clarification encompasses "the break" as both a part of a song and the dancer's response by "going off."

3. "DJ Skeme and Bboy Ynot, Rock Steady Crew's Dynamic Duo," YouTube, https://www.youtube.com/watch?v = pMmn67eJ9MQ.

4. YNOT (2016), "Make the Letters Dance," episode 1 featuring Popmaster Fabel." https://vimeo.com/167284096.

5. A *commando* is a strategy for a dancer in a cypher to fluidly transition a dancer outside the cypher (often a crewmate) into the cypher; effectively they change positions. A commando is a way to control the energy and attention of the cypher, keeping it among crewmates or allies and away from opponents.

6. These good folks were B-girl Macca and some other members of 360 Flava, a crew who always reps hard for Philly.

7. Floor Brats vs. Head Hunters, *Lords of the Floor 2002.* This clip can be viewed on YouTube. https://www.youtube.com/watch?v = j3nCA7SafLo.

8. B-Boy & B-Girl Dojo. http://www.bboydojo.com.

9. This feature exists at the time of writing and, of course, may be eliminated at some point.

10. This is not the first such feature in any hip hop instructional format, however. In some of DJ Q-Bert's early scratch instruction videos, you could battle against Q-Bert (dressed up in silly, outlandish costumes) in a question-and-answer–call-and-response battle format. Each of the characters played by Q-Bert battled at different skill levels.

11. An interesting parallel here is when scratch DJs began pressing their own records that tied practical features to their aesthetic priorities, for example, certain sounds, infinity loops, and "skip-proof" records, due to parallel sound arrangement in grooves.

12. Yes, this statement is kind of a dis.

13. Some labels, such as Breakin' Bread in the UK, have for some time now released music with an ear to breaking aesthetics. Many of these tracks have been played in breaking scenes, for good reason. In my view, these releases have never been directed *solely* to breaking scenes, though. They have sat equally, for example, in the funk and soul scene.

REFERENCES

Fogarty, M. (2010). "Dance to the Drummer's Beat: Competing Tastes in International B-Boy/B-Girl Culture." PhD diss., University of Edinburgh.

Fogarty, M. (2012a). "Breaking Expectations: Imagined Affinities in Mediated Youth Cultures." *Continuum: Journal of Media & Cultural Studies* 26 (3): 449–462.

Fogarty, M. (2012b). "Each One Teach One: B-Boying and Aging." In *Ageing and Youth Cultures: Music, Style and Identity*, edited by A. Bennett and P. Hodkinson, 53–65. Oxford Berg Press.

Forman, M. (2001). *The 'Hood Comes First: Race, Space, and Place in Rap and Hip Hop.* Middletown, CT: Wesleyan University Press.

Johnson, I. K. (2012). "Music Meant to Make You Move: Considering the Aural Kinesthetic." Sounding Out! https://soundstudiesblog.com/tag/imani-k-johnson/.

Kajikawa, L. (2015). *Sounding Race in Rap Songs.* Oakland: University of California Press.

Lefebvre, H. (1991). *The Production of Space.* Oxford: Wiley-Blackwell.

Meyers, D. (2019). "If the Olympics Wants Breaking to Succeed, They Have to Get the Music Right." *Deadspin*. https://deadspin.com/if-the-olympics-want-breaking-to-succeed-they-have-to-1833104488.

Rose, T. (1994). *Black Noise: Rap Music and Black Culture in Contemporary America*. Middletown, CT: Wesleyan University Press.

Schloss, J. (2009). *Foundation: B-Boys, B-Girls, and Hip Hop in New York City*. New York: Oxford University Press.

CHAPTER 11

THE VAULT

Collecting and Archiving Streetdance Footage

MARC "SCRAMBLELOCK" SAKALAUSKAS

INTRODUCTION

IT may be strange to start a chapter about collecting streetdance footage with a comparison to Prince, but his influence on artists is far-reaching and even extends to my own archiving practices. One intriguing thing about Prince was his ability to produce music at an incredibly rapid rate, faster than his music was actually released to the public. Most of his work never saw the light of day, and instead was stored in The Vault, a highly secured room at Prince's Paisley Park complex in Chanhassen, Minnesota (Nilsen 2004). Like Prince, I have built a collection, not of music but of streetdance footage, and I respectfully refer to it as "the Vault" in homage to the Purple One. The collection is focused on the various forms of streetdance styles—such as b-boying, locking, and popping—and their musical and cultural influences. It is as old as my personal dance career (twenty-two years at the time of this writing). Unlike Prince's vault, my footage archive was not created to protect it from exposure. My goal was the opposite—to showcase the historic value of these dance forms, and to make this history accessible to students and others interested in researching the dances.

Archiving Hip Hop has been common practice among pioneers, practitioners, and fans of the culture since its inception in the mid-1970s. In recent years, academic institutions have started to build archives that incorporate the private collections of well-known MCs, DJs, graffiti artists, photographers, and documentarians (Diaz 2013). The Cornell Hip Hop Collection, founded in 1999 by Johen Kugelberg at Cornell University, is one of the most famous Hip Hop archives to date, and includes contributions by Joe Conzo Jr., Charlie Ahearn, Ernie Paniccioli, Jorge "Popmaster Fabel" Pabon, Richie "Seen" Mirando, Bill Adler, Richie "Crazy Legs" Colon and DJ Afrika Bambaataa, to name a few (Diaz 2013). Included in this archive are photos, videos, magazines, black books, clothing, and even entire record collections. Yet, as vast as the academic archives may be, there appears to be a real lack of attention on streetdance footage (Fogarty 2012a). And with the exception of the more famous Hollywood films like *Breakin'* (1984) and *Body Rock* (1984), there is even less focus on the dance styles of locking and popping, which originated in California during the early 1970s (Guzman-Sanchez 2012).

Outside the academic world, practitioners and fans of streetdance have also been collecting videos for years. Some of the well-known collectors include the late Frosty Freeze (USA), Jorge "Popmaster Fabel" Pabon (USA), Beto "Mooncricket" Lopez (USA), Tuf Tim Twist (UK), Shell Toe Mel (UK), Kevin "DJ Renegade" Gopie (UK), Fabrice "Gemini" Aragones (France), Niels "Storm" Robitzky (Germany), Karl "Dyzee" Alba (Canada), Frank "Frank Boogie" Luisi (Canada) and David "DKC Freeze" Dundas (Canada). Many of these archives are on VHS cassettes, Hi8, MiniDV, and DVD, and there is a growing concern over the decomposition of materials as they age over time (Straw 2009). What makes collecting streetdance footage even more difficult is that most early footage is either nonexistent or lost, since these dances originated at a time when recording technology was not widely available to the public (Fogarty 2010; Schloss 2009).

This chapter discusses my personal journey in developing this ever-growing streetdance footage library— how the collection was built, archived, and disseminated— with a special focus on the challenges of building a locking video library. Since locking predates b-boying by close to a decade, early footage is extremely hard to come by, and makes for one of the biggest challenges for historic preservation. Streetdance is a visual art, and to understand where these dance styles come from and how they evolved, archived footage is critical.

ORIGINS

The growth of my video collection has complemented and influenced my development as a dancer in both b-boying and locking, so it is worth describing that journey along-side this discussion. Music videos were my first means of witnessing breaking, back in 1986 when I was just four years old. My uncle showed me videos of Michael Jackson and other recording artists that had breaking in them. Even though I did not fully under-stand what I was seeing, I did attempt to mimic what I saw later that year at my uncle's wedding. My father recorded the event on tape. As far back as I can remember, my father was always a technology enthusiast. He always had a video camera at family occasions, from birthdays to vacations. He would record the footage to VHS and label and organize the tapes by date, building a mini library of our family. My brother and I used to watch these tapes on rainy days or on days when we were bored. The memory of dancing at my uncle's wedding remained with me for the next eleven years, not only as an anecdote of my past, but as an actual tape I could reference.

When I turned fifteen and entered high school in 1997, I was reintroduced to breaking. Academically, I was an above-average student, but I wasn't always accepted by my peers. I vividly recall the moment at a school dance, soon after the start of 9th grade, in September 1997, when I heard "Triumph" (1997) by the Wu-Tang Clan and saw a group of students form a circle on the dark gymnasium floor. I ran over to see what was happening. Some students were breaking, and one of them was a close friend from elementary school who had begun to bully me when we entered high school. It was a shock to see this estranged friend spin around on his hands, and do all these complex steps on the ground. The next week, after seeing all the attention he received for learning how to dance, it inspired me to learn to break, if only just to be able to do it better than him one day!

Though I was determined to learn how to break, there were not very many options available for a fifteen-year-old to learn at the time. There were no formal streetdance studios, and the only way you could learn was if you knew someone who danced in your community or if you went to an event or battle. My parents were not keen on letting me go to many events because they started late at night and sometimes took place in night clubs. The first place I looked to was MuchMusic, the Canadian equivalent to MTV. Every night, *Rap City* (a 30-minute segment featuring only Hip Hop music videos) would air, and I would stay up to catch a glimpse of breaking in any music video, with the VCR on standby. This was the same time as the release of Jason Nevins's remake of Run DMC's "It's Like That" (1997). The video for this song featured a crew of b-boys battling a crew of b-girls. This video was the gold standard for me at the time because the length of time the dancers were shown executing their sets made for a perfect study tool. Like many dancers of my generation, being able to record the video to a VHS tape allowed me to watch and re-watch the video as many times as I needed in order to understand the moves being performed (Simard 2014).

My father not only introduced me to film and video but also taught me about computers at an early age. During the time I started to learn to break (1997–1998), the Internet was just in its early stages of public availability, and we were fortunate to have access to it at home. Some of the early searches on "breakdance" led me to Bboy.com, a website that featured written, step-by-step instructions on some of the basic moves of breaking, including the six-step, backspins, windmills, floats, and head spins. This website had two other important features. The first was a message forum that allowed users to interact, ask questions, and communicate with other online users. Some users were more experienced and willing to share advice and knowledge in all areas of streetdance. The second feature was a series of links to other Hip Hop–related sites, including ones that listed names of various b-boy videotapes and contact information for shops worldwide that sold them. Streaming videos online was not yet possible, so thus began my search for b-boy videotapes.

Although my parents did not initially support my desire to learn breaking, they were influential in several key moments of my journey. One moment in particular was the time my father bought me my first two b-boy videotapes: *B-Boy Summit 2* (1995) and *Ken Swift Volume 2: The Epitome* (1997). My father acquired these videos by contacting the video distributor directly and arranging orders by mail. While Ken Swift's tape focused more on footwork and the overall finesse of his movements with attention to style, the B-Boy Summit tape included more dynamic and powerful moves along with various footwork styles. This was a key moment where collecting footage became important to me, because I learned that each tape features different dancers with various approaches to breaking techniques.

In time, I met other dancers in my city and learned that they had breaking tapes and were interested in trading. After an incident where I lent a friend a tape and never got it back, however, I decided it was better to invite my friends over to watch the videos, or to make copies instead to avoid the risk of losing the tapes. This strategy allowed my collection to grow as crew and solo videos, international, and local event footage were shared among the network of collectors I had built. This was effective at first, but a lot of other recordings of events in the United States and Europe also existed, copies of which were limited and often expensive. Moreover, many people refused to share footage in order to fiercely guard their trade secrets (Fogarty 2012b).

TRANSITION INTO THE DIGITAL ERA

In the early 2000s, the Internet quickly became a powerful resource for collectors. Online communities for collecting and trading breaking videos were initially set up using programs like mIRC, an Internet Relay Chat (IRC) client, and later SoulSeek, a peer-to-peer file-sharing program. Collectors could post their lists of videos, and other users could then contact one another and agree upon which videos they would trade. Trading was done by digitally copying (ripping) videos into .avi, .mov or .dat file formats, which could then be played on video applications like Windows Media Player or VLC Media Player. These "VHS rip" files, normally 500–800MB in size, could be transferred online through a secure sharing connection. It would take several hours to download, depending on the connection speed. In most cases I would exceed my bandwidth limit, running up extra charges on my parents' Internet bill, much to their displeasure. As transfer speeds and bandwidth limits increased, it made for easier transfers. Despite the growing accessibility of VHS rips, the quality of the files was not as high as that of DVDs, and there was a risk that the sound was not in sync or that the tracking was off during recording. The main issue with the VIDEO_TS folders of DVDs that could be copied was that the files were much larger (4GB), thus taking longer to download and consuming more bandwidth. High-speed cable connections remedied this issue.

My video collection also grew as I started traveling to events across the United States and Canada in the mid-2000s. Vendors who sold breaking DVDs were normally present in large numbers at these events, which made it possible to purchase videos that were not as readily available in my city. Online b-boy shops were not well established at this time either, so events like Freestyle Session and B-Boy Summit were prime locations to purchase these videos.

My collection had its greatest period of growth from 2004 to 2009, primarily because of the online alliances I made by sharing files on Soulseek. I connected with one user from Europe and another from Asia, and we agreed to purchase DVDs on our respective continents and share them with one another via online transfers. This period was also the period when the streetdance video scene reached its peak. The advent of YouTube in 2005 (and other digital video platforms such as Facebook, Vimeo, Dailymotion, etc.) made it significantly easier to access breaking and other streetdance videos, which eventually led to a decline in the production of DVDs. By 2010, most online videos were short trailers of an event, crew, or dancer, or playlists of separate individual battles or performances from a specific event. VHS and DVD Rips were also uploaded to these video hosting sites. This made it possible to access both older and more recent dance footage since users began posting their collections online. However, searching for these videos remained complicated because users could upload videos across various platforms without a standard naming convention or the proper use of keywords. With a video downloader, such as YTD Downloader, video downloading websites, such FBDown, or basic browser programming knowledge, it was easy to save videos to a computer's hard drive, as a safeguard in case a user removed a video from their account.

CURRENT DIRECTIONS

In more recent years, the collection began to diversify beyond just streetdance. Since dances like b-boying and locking were based on jazz, funk, Hip Hop, and soul music (Vincent 1996), the collection of concerts, live performances, interviews, and documentaries of artists in these genres became an area of interest for further understanding and the preservation of the culture as a whole. There are separate communities from the streetdance network that continue to collect and trade videos in these specific areas of interest. For example, I have been able to get full episodes and highlight videos of *Soul Train*, *The Arsenio Hall Show*, *Yo! MTV Raps*, *Solid Gold*, *Showtime at the Apollo*, and other television shows from the late 1960s to the 2000s. Similarly, concert footage of James Brown, the Parliament-Funkadelic family, Prince, Sly and the Family Stone, Michael Jackson, and numerous others have also been added to the collection. A personal visit to New Orleans sparked my interest in learning more about the music and dance cultures that evolved from the Southern United States, with particular interest in early jazz, second line parades, buck jumping, and the Mardi Gras Indian traditions and their close connection to footwork movements found within Hip Hop and funk style dances. Documentaries like *All on a Mardi Gras Day* (2008), *Faubourg Tremé* (2008), and *Bury the Hatchet* (2011) detail these traditions and are included in my collection.

ORGANIZATION METHODS

On occasion, other video collectors have contacted me because they want to have the footage on tapes that they have collected over the years digitized. I have always agreed to do this for the collectors, as long as I could make a copy to add to my archive. This method of collecting has helped in the organization of local footage primarily from events, shows, and practices in Toronto and Montreal in the mid-1990s to the 2000s.

Dancers who wish to know more about Hip Hop history or specific genres like breaking, popping, and locking often visit and access videos from the archive using spreadsheet catalogues that I designed. The archive is organized and catalogued first by lists organized alphabetically and numerically, and then, in some cases, by episodes. All official streetdance videos are listed alphabetically in one document by title, and identified as DVD, VHS, or VHS Rip. These videos are also added to a spreadsheet including all videos containing official and unofficial titles. As videos are added to the spreadsheet, a number is labeled on the disc that matches the name and unique numeric ID of that particular video found in the spreadsheet. For example, Disc 16 is a DVD of *War is War 5*, a b-boy event in Montreal in the early 2000s. Disc 46 contains two VHS Rips: *Dance Town Jack* and the *Jr. Boogaloo* solo video. Discs in this part of the collection currently number over a thousand, and range from events, solo videos, practice sessions, documentaries, interviews, concerts, and TV clips.

There is a separate list for *Soul Train* episodes, which is organized by episode number, and includes the airdate and the names of artists and songs performed on that date. A label "ST-xx" is given to each disc where "xx" represents the number of the disc as it is added to the collection. For example, Zapp and Roger performed on *Soul Train* episode 500, which aired April 12, 1986. The label of the disc where the episode can be found is ST-73. Similar lists were designed for *The Arsenio Hall Show* performances, *Yo! MTV Raps*, *Solid Gold*, *Showtime at the Apollo*, and Prince footage.

COMPLETE DIGITIZATION
AND RECATALOGING

From March to September 2020, because of the COVID-19 pandemic lockdown, I had time to do a complete digitization and re-cataloging of the collection. All the VHS tapes were digitized using a VCR and a 2012 MacBook Pro (containing 16GB RAM). The VCR was connected to the laptop using an Elgato Video Capture adapter cable and related software. Each tape could be played in its entirety in the VCR, and the software was able to convert the analog audio and video to .mp4 video files. A VHS tape containing six hours of footage could result in files of up to 2GB in size. When the plastic erasure protection tabs for the tapes were missing, a piece of masking tape was placed over the tab area to prevent any quality degradation while the tape is being played. Some VCRs varied in tracking adjustment ability, and so several backup VCRs were available to make sure the best quality video was captured. Once the digitization was completed, the tape would not be rewound so as to reduce any additional wear and tear to the VCR, since many of these analog devices are now harder to find and replace. If a tape contained multiple videos, events or shows, the main file could be spliced via QuickTime Player and saved in its appropriate folder (see the section "Digital Archive Organization").

Digitizing DVDs required a slightly different approach. A DVD's VIDEO_TS folder contained .vob files that were converted to mp4 format using either a 2012 MacBook Pro (16GB RAM) or a 2015 iMac (32GB RAM), the iMac being able to digitize discs at a faster rate. Handbrake, an open-source video transcoder software, was used to scan each disc for .vob files and convert each one individually to the .mp4 format. Because many DVD files contain chapters, it is not always possible to convert a full DVD to a single mp4 file automatically. A final concatenation step using FFMPEG, an open-source program, was used to combine converted chapter files into a single .mp4 file. Any additional bonus features on a disc would be individually converted and saved to a separate "Bonus Features" subfolder for that disc. A disc conversion could take between fifteen minutes and an hour to complete, depending on the size and processing power of the computer being used. Files could range in size from 100MB to 4GB, depending on the length of video on a disc.

At the time of writing, the entire archive is a little under 8TB in size. The original discs, tapes, and spreadsheets now serve as a master for the files that have been digitally transferred to an external 10TB hard drive. Each file was duplicated to a secondary 10TB hard drive for backup purposes. The archive remains a dynamic work in progress, but in the future the archive may be moved to a cloud server and database for the purpose of developing an online version of the archive that would allow users to access and stream videos by either browsing the complete archive or searching for files based on keywords. There are many challenges associated with this next phase, including design, scalability, search performance optimization, storage and bandwidth costs, session management, permissions, and security to name only a few.

Digital Archive Organization

Currently, the digital archive is organized into four main folders: Dance, Music, TV, and Movies. Videos in the Dance folder are sorted as follows:

> Dance Style → Continent → Country → Province (if applicable) → City (if applicable) → Decade → Event Name (if multiyear event)

Files are named in one of two ways: Official videos are labeled "Event Name (Year). mp4." Unofficial footage is named "YYYY-MM-DD – Event or Video Name – Venue, City, State or Province (if applicable), Country.mp4."

As an example, one could find "Freestyle Session 3 (1998).mp4" in the "Breaking → North America → USA → 90s → Freestyle Session" folder. However, raw locking footage from Funk Fo Yo Feet 2007 may be found in the "Locking → North America → Canada → Ontario → Toronto → 2000s" folder and would have the name "2007-07-16 – Funk Fo Yo Feet Locking – Trinity St. Paul's Church, Toronto, Ontario, Canada.mp4."

Videos in the Music folder are sorted by Genre → Artist Name and named in a similar fashion to unofficial dance footage. So if you were looking for a 1979 Parliament Funkadelic concert, you would find the file "1979-02-01 – Parliament Funkadelic – Capital Center, Landover, MD, USA.mp4" in the "Funk → Parliament Funkadelic" folder.

Files in the TV folder are placed in *Show Name* and *Season* (if applicable) subfolders. For *Soul Train*, episodes are named according to series episode number, air date, and featured artists. Episode 500 is named as follows: *500 – 1986-04-12 – Zapp, Lisa Lisa, Meli'sa Morgan.mp4*.

Finally, files in the Movies folder are arranged in alphabetical order by title, and named "Movie Name (Year).mp4." If a movie has bonus features, then a "Movie Name (Year)" folder would be created and contain the "Movie Name (Year).mp4" file and a "Bonus Features" subfolder.

LOCKING: THE CHALLENGE OF ESTABLISHING A COMPREHENSIVE ARCHIVE

It's worth elaborating on the funk-style videos in my collection, especially those showcasing locking, as this topic highlights interesting challenges that pertain to the historical preservation and video collection of this dance style. As mentioned earlier, locking footage is extremely difficult to find, and there is no single, complete collection of footage to date.

The "Campbellock" aka "Locking" is an improvisational performance dance based on the expression of the individual, with "The Lock" as its base, which everything flows from (Don Campbellock Campbell Official Website, 2019). It was created in Watts, Los Angeles, in the early 1970s by Don "Campbellock" Campbell, initially as an attempt to perform some of the local party dances of the time (Guzman-Sanchez 2012). The dance became popular in the South Central Los Angeles club scene, and many others started to add to Campbell's dance style, helping to create moves that are now considered the foundational steps of locking. Like many of the early streetdances, locking developed in nightclubs before video cameras were accessible, let alone affordable. *Soul Train* was one of the main exceptions—it provided a glimpse into the early era (1971–1973) of locking. Originators like Don Campbell (RIP), Jimmy "Scoo B Doo" Williams, Greg "Campbellock Jr." Pope (RIP), Damita Jo Freeman, Bill "Slim the Robot" Williams, Leo "Fluky Luke" Williamson, Fred "Penguin" Berry (RIP), Tony "Go Go" Lombard, and Aldolpho "Shabba Doo" Quinones (RIP) were dancers on the show. Viewers could see the dance during brief segments of the show that featured the Soul Train Gang dancing to a song, or dancing in pairs down the Soul Train Line. In fact, Don Cornelius, the show's host, interviewed Don Campbell in episode 26 (aired March 25, 1972), and this is where he first referred to the dance as "the Campbellock." Episode 50 (aired February 17, 1973) included a dance contest in which Scoo B Doo and Damita Jo Freeman performed locking in their set, and went on to win the contest.

Soon some of the top dancers from the club circuit, and those featured on *Soul Train*, formed a group called The Lockers. With their manager Toni Basil, The Lockers began to perform on various TV specials and even toured across the United States with Frank Sinatra. The Lockers appeared on *Soul Train* as featured guests for the first time on episode 189 (aired September 18, 1976).

By 1977, the group had broken up and some members began solo careers. Fred Berry had a leading role as the character Rerun on the comedy series *What's Happening*; and Shabba Doo was featured on the TV variety special *The Big Show* before starring in the movie *Breakin'* (1984), released during the Hip Hop explosion of the 1980s. During this period, locking became associated with Hip Hop largely because of the media's inability to differentiate between dance styles, and a tendency to label everything "breakdancing" (Simard 2014). A great deal of historical information on locking was lost in the years after the 1980s explosion because many of the dance's originators became less active and did not always pass their knowledge directly down to newer generations of dancers. But by the mid- to late 1990s, there was a renewed interest in locking, largely due to the popularity of breaking events like B-Boy Summit and Freestyle Session. At these events, dancers from both the current and past generations interacted and exchanged knowledge of the dance. Locking has continued to grow in popularity in many countries worldwide since. Thus, the forefather of breaking and popping has now established itself as a crucial element within streetdance.

OBTAINING LOCKING FOOTAGE

Collecting locking footage for historical purposes has proven to be a difficult task, even more so than the collection of breaking footage. Most students are left with only the stories, accounts, and occasional photos from that original generation to determine how the dance originated and who its key individuals were. This has made learning and understanding locking very challenging.

For example, most of the *Soul Train* footage was difficult to find in North America. Reruns were not aired until 2006, after the syndicated show had been canceled (George 2014). However, one key link to obtaining *Soul Train* episodes was Japan (George 2014). In the 1990s, *Soul Train* reruns were aired on Japanese television, which some viewers recorded. These tapes soon began circulating through underground trading networks. In more recent years, these episodes, transferred to DVD, have been traded by collectors online. Many of these episodes feature some of the earliest moments in the history of locking. Despite the fact that the dancers were performing in front of a camera, and not in an actual club setting, this footage provides insight to at least some of the social interaction that the dance is based on.

When The Lockers group was formed and began performing on national television, locking became even more popular, and the result was a growing number of recordings featuring the dance. From 1974 to 1977, The Lockers performed on a wide variety of shows, including *The Carol Burnett Show, ABC in Concert, Saturday Night Live, The Tonight Show, 90 Minutes Live with Peter Gzowski, The Dick Van Dyke Show,* as well as at the Grammy Awards and other award ceremonies. The Lockers even filmed a pilot for a Saturday morning children's special. For years, this footage was extremely hard to find. Major TV stations owned most of the footage, and obtaining it from the company's archives was expensive. The documentary *Underground Dance Masters,* initially released in 1996 and rereleased in 2013, featured extensive footage of The Lockers, some of which was purchased from the TV stations. This was the first video that featured an interview with Don Campbell where he told his story. I received a tape from one of the original Lockers, Greg "Campbellock Jr." Pope, in 2002, which featured a lot of the aforementioned performances and is now a highlight of my collection.

As locking developed in the 1980s, it continued to be present in TV shows, news reports, and specials, as well as in home videos. Eventually, the Hollywood films *Breakin'* (1984) and *Body Rock* (1984) brought locking to a bigger audience, though it was mixed in with other dance styles like b-boying and popping. Except for the major "studio" films, most of the recordings of these performances were not easily obtained, unless you knew the people who had recorded them or had a copy on tape. Eventually, the B-Boy Summit and other events in California in the mid-1990s helped bring a lot of lost footage to light. Old school lockers active in Los Angeles during the 1980s, such as Richard "Richie Rich" Lenchner and Manuel "Loose Caboose" Tristan, came to these events. They helped increase awareness of locking through their showcases and discussions, and were responsible for inviting lockers from the original generations (the OG's) to attend.

Dancers from other countries came to these Los Angeles streetdance events to learn about locking, myself included. One very influential dancer who attended these events was Fabrice "Gemini" Aragones, a practitioner from France who was intent on learning locking as thoroughly as possible. From roughly 2000 to 2004 Gemini spent a lot of time in Los Angeles, meeting and learning from as many lockers as possible. During this time, many of the old school lockers provided him with footage of the dance from the seventies, eighties, and nineties, which he began to organize into a footage library. The library consists of over fifty labeled VHS tapes of locking shows, battles, performances, documentaries, and instructional videos from the United States, France, the United Kingdom, and Japan. Gemini went on to become one of the most successful and important figures in the locking scene. Over the years, he's won numerous international locking dance contests including Juste Debout (France) and the B-Boy Summit (USA). He also released the independent film *Obsessive Funk* (2005), which pays homage to the pioneers of locking. As founder of the Locking4Life movement, Gemini teaches worldwide, continues to unite lockers, and helps the dance form to grow. I received a large number of tapes from Gemini's collection in 2008. In return for digitizing some of his videos, Gemini generously donated the original tapes to my collection because he wished to contribute to this growing video library of locking.

There is still a great deal of locking footage to be unearthed. Many performances of The Lockers—and of subsequent pioneering groups such as the Ghetto Dancers, Wild and Peaceful, or 33RPM—have never been publicly released, and may still be in the archives of the TV networks that aired their performances. Toni Basil is a key link to building a more complete collection of historical locking footage. She has many old tapes of rehearsals and practices from her time with The Lockers. Some of these tapes are on delicate, deteriorating media, and transferring this footage may prove challenging. But it is of utmost importance that this footage be made public for the sole purposes of education and preservation of this dance form for future generations.

Locking is a difficult dance to fully understand, and there may never be a complete collection of footage. Many of the existing early videos are of television and stage performances. We may never truly understand how locking was performed in clubs during that time. Students of the dance today have to piece together what they can from the past by remaining in contact with the surviving pioneers. It is crucial to hear and whenever feasible record as many accounts as possible, and to view everyone's oral history as a contribution to the growth and evolution of this dynamic dance form.

It is a goal of mine to someday have as complete a collection of locking footage as possible. This may seem overly ambitious, because locking is now being taught and performed worldwide, and each country has its own unique history. New videos of locking battles or showcases appear online daily. We may never see all the practice sessions or footage from parties and clubs. Event organizers have even recently restricted cameras at some events to give participants a truly unique experience that can only be passed down by word-of-mouth. The goal of collecting is not to recreate history completely, but it serves as a method of consulting the legacy of the past generations, and allow for transmission of knowledge to younger dancers who wish to pursue locking more deeply in their dance careers. Learning about what came before may help guide current-generation lockers to forge a path that will allow the dance to thrive in the future as trends in music, fashion, and styles evolve. As DJ Renegade explains, "Collecting videos helps to preserve the feel of the particular era . . . whether through fashion, attitude, music or other clues." There is much to be learned from building such a collection. As with the growth of Hip Hop in its formative years (Fricke and Ahearn 2002), it is clear that streetdances like breaking and locking do not have a single definitive history. Rather, there is an accumulation of personal histories, as varied as the perspectives and cultural backgrounds of the dancers who were present during each period. Nonetheless, there are some facts that do appear consistent within the various stories told by the originators, and these consistencies help to build a more solid understanding of the dance's roots. Moreover, these dance styles have evolved in close relation to the musical and cultural evolutions of the time. This is especially evident in funk music, a genre fundamental to locking, popping, and breaking (Vincent 1996). Despite the fluctuating popularity of these dances, it is of paramount importance to give credit, not only to the originators, but also to those in subsequent generations who have carried their legacy and contributed to streetdance's gradual evolution.

FINAL REMARKS

By taking the time to reflect on my experience of building the video collection, I began to see more clearly *why* I collected. Initially, I started because breaking and locking were new and exciting to me. I wanted to learn as much as I could about these dances, and there was a thrill in seeing new moves and trying to learn them. There was also a thrill in finding a tape to add to the collection. Whether it was purchased, traded, or given to me, in a way it felt like finding hidden treasure. With the transition into the YouTube era of video collecting, new videos were posted daily, and it was easy to find footage. That same thrill I got from digging to find a rare tape wasn't as prevalent, until I found new communities of collectors of music, concerts, and television shows. I believe collecting became a bit of an obsession for me, as I hunted down footage to get that feeling of new discovery. Perhaps it was a trait passed on from my father and his passion for technology. Regardless, the amount of time I invested in searching for footage, building databases, and diversifying in areas beyond streetdance was well beyond what most streetdance practitioners cared to undertake.

As I gained experience as both a dancer and archivist over the years, the act of collecting became a personal means of giving back to a culture that has provided me with many blessings and opportunities. I have been fortunate enough to learn from some of the elders of locking, who have instilled in me the importance of passing the torch. As many of the originators approach the end of their lives or have since passed away, collecting and archiving video footage serves to preserve their legacy and to highlight their roles in a powerful cultural movement.

REFERENCES

Diaz, M. (2013). "Restoring Hip Hop's Legacy Through Artifacts, Preservation and Education." In *The Center of the Movement: Collecting Hip Hop Memorabilia*, edited by K. el-Hakim and D. Jenkins, Detroit, MI: Moore Black Press.

Don Campbellock Campbell Official Website. (2019, July 19). *Don "Campbellock" Campbell - Creator of the Campbellock*. https://campbellock.dance.

Fogarty, M. (2010). "Dance to the Drummer's Beat: Competing Tastes in International B-Boy/B-Girl Culture." PhD diss., University of Edinburgh.

Fogarty, M. (2012a). "Breaking Expectations: Imagined Affinities in Mediated Youth Culture." *Continuum: Journal of Media & Cultural Studies* 26(3): 449–462.

Fogarty, M. (2012b). "Each One Teach One: B-Boying and Ageing." In *Ageing and Youth Cultures: Music, Style and Identity*, edited by A. Bennett and P. Hodkinson, 53–65. London: Berg.

Fricke, J., and Ahearn, C. (2002). *Yes Yes Y'all: The Music Experience Project Oral History of Hip-Hop's First Decade*. Cambridge: De Capo Press.

George, N. (2014). *The Hippest Trip in America: Soul Train and the Evolution of Culture and Style*. New York: Harper Collins.

Guzman-Sanchez, T. (2012). *Underground Dance Masters: Final History of a Forgotten Era*. Santa Barbara: Praeger.

Nilsen, P. (2004) *The Vault: The Definitive Guide to the Musical World of Prince*. Linghem, Sweden: Uptown.

Schloss, J. G. (2009). *Foundation: B-Boys, B-Girls and Hip-Hop Culture in New York*. New York: Oxford University Press.

Simard, H. (2014). "Breaking Down the Differences Between Breakdancing and B-Boying: A Grounded Theory Approach." Unpublished MA thesis, Université du Québec à Montréal.

Straw, W. (2009). "In Memoriam: The Music CD and Its Ends." *Design and Culture* 1 (1): 79–92.

Vincent, R. (1996). *Funk: The Music, the People, and the Rhythm of The One*. New York: St. Martin's Griffin.

CHAPTER 12

....

CRITICAL HIPHOPOGRAPHY IN STREETDANCE COMMUNITIES (HARD LOVE PART 2)

....

IMANI KAI JOHNSON

INTRODUCTION

....

As the field of Hip Hop studies develops, inevitable questions about and interests in
Hip Hop-centered research methods become more crucial and warrant greater attention. This chapter explores the contours of what some call hiphopography, an ethnographic research method that is grounded in Hip Hop culture's distinct sensibilities,
and is aligned with multiple critical methodological practices. This chapter explores
hiphopography as part of a growing inquiry into Hip Hop as a method or a praxis
(Chang 2006; Lindsey 2014; Dimitriadis 2014). Ethnography in particular has become
a subject of inquiry in film (Dattareyan 2018), music (Appert 2017), education (Petchaur
2009; Love 2017; Marsh 2012), Hip Hop feminist studies (Durham, Cooper, and
Morris, 2013; Love 2017), cross-disciplinary conference panels (University of Southern
California 2014), and so on. As an approach, hiphopography demands an ethic that is
attuned to cultural imperatives and thus cognizant of and responsive to histories of exploitation and misrepresentation.

   When I began researching breaking cyphers and Hip Hop culture in 2005, I sought
to engage the numerous women ethnographers that I came across. This chapter
accompanies "Hard Love Part 1: Corporealities of Women Ethnographers of Hip Hop
Dances" (chapter 8, this volume) which focuses on the corporealities (or corporeal
realities) of women ethnographers, particularly as they navigate the gender politics of
a given site and the embodied experiences of field work. Through a continued focus on
women ethnographers, most of whom are also scholar-practitioners, my attention shifts

to examining the challenges of researching in community and strategies for proceeding in a critically engaged way.

For this chapter, I conducted over nine-and-a-half hours of in-depth Skype interviews with seven women ethnographers and started a private Facebook group for them; after which I spent countless hours listening to their recordings and studying the transcripts. The group has approximately a dozen participants. Nearly all the participants, in both the full interviews and the Facebook group, are scholar-practitioners with dance practices that also inform their research approaches. Those interviewed include trans and cis women of multiple ages, differing professional positions, and various races and ethnicities who research a wide array of movement practices that fall under the umbrella of Hip Hop streetdances.[1] I have opted to anonymize my informants out of respect for the candid nature of some of the interviews, their differential professional standings, and their ongoing relationships to the communities they research. And though the experiences of each interviewee are distinct, where they converge and diverge constitutes the content of this work.

Toward a Critical Hiphopography

One might infer from the term *hiphopography* that it is simply a combination of Hip Hop and ethnography. Its full definition, though, is more nuanced. Historian and journalist James G. Spady coined the term, and he and linguistic anthropologist H. Samy Alim have subsequently expounded on its meaningfulness (Eure and Spady 1991; Spady, Dupres, and Lee 1995; Spady, Lee, and Alim 1999; Alim 2006a; Alim 2006b; Spady, Alim, and Meghelli 2006; Spady 2013; Meghelli 2013).

> Hiphopography can be described as an approach to the study of Hip Hop culture that combines the methods of ethnography, biography, and social and oral history. Importantly, hiphopography is not traditional ethnography. Hierarchical divisions between the "researcher" and the "researched" are purposely kept to a minimum, even as they are interrogated. This requires the hiphopographer to engage the community on its own terms. Knowledge of the aesthetics, values, and history as well as the use of the language, culture, and means and modes of interaction . . . are essential to the study of Hip Hop culture. (Alim 2006b, 969–970)

Hiphopography both samples from traditional disciplinary fields and actively seeks to dismantle the logics of academic hierarchies. In doing so, it takes elements from various approaches as long as they serve foundational cultural values such as engaging the community "on its own terms." Alim names strategies for researching both with integrity and as a way to critique and subvert academic practices that can reproduce violence. Hiphopography's intervention, then, is not that it is positing brand-new ideas—it clearly borrows from Black feminist, critical, and decolonial ethnographic practices—but that it centers community interests over academic ones as a foundational premise.

Hiphopography has various influences, including those evident in D. Soyini Madison's (2005) explanation of critical ethnography, which "begins with an ethical responsibility to address processes of unfairness or injustice within a particular *lived* [original emphasis] experience" (5). Critical ethnography politicizes and personalizes the importance of a self-reflexive ethnographic approach, endorsing transparency around the power dynamics between the researcher and the researched as a "moral obligation" to contribute to the researched's "greater freedom and equity" (5). Critical ethnography also overlaps with decolonial methodological practices. Linda Tuhiwai Smith (1999) argues that decolonial methodologies emphasize the importance of indigenous epistemologies that have been violently suppressed or invisibilized. She proposes instead that decolonial methods stay attuned to communities who maintain "a collective memory of imperialism" and resist reproducing the Other through academic research practices that have been historically intertwined with colonial endeavors (2). Alim's definition of hiphopography clearly builds on this intervention, situating Hip Hop where "indigenous" would be. Madison and Smith challenge researchers to vigilantly disrupt the colonial project embedded in Western academic approaches by embracing community-driven ways of knowing and doing that are rooted in an ethics of freedom and equity.

Hiphopography also overlaps with Patricia Hill Collins's (1990) pivotal work *Black Feminist Thought*, wherein she focuses on Black feminist epistemologies. Several of its key features resonate with hiphopography. She names the following: concrete or "lived experience as a criterion of meaning" (208–209); the "use of dialogue in assessing knowledge claims," which she ties to collective engagement and call-and-response practices (212–215); an "ethic of caring" (215–217); and an "ethic of personal responsibility," wherein the knowledge claims we assess also allow for evaluations of a researcher's character (217–219). Hiphopography, too, values lived experiences and centers the voices of the people themselves as credible authorities and theorists of their own work. One distinction might be that Collins overtly addresses issues of care and personal responsibility, which are only implied in Alim's (2006b, 11) analysis. Although Collins's focus is on theorizing, it is clear that she and Alim share a political commitment to legitimizing other forms of knowledge that extend from lived experiences and the practice of everyday life.[2]

The term *hiphopography* alone does not necessarily invoke all that is encapsulated in Black feminist or critical or decolonial approaches, yet its stated agenda to subvert academic tenets and engage Hip Hop on its own terms moves in their direction, both conceptually and politically. My exploration of these concepts is not to suggest that hiphopography, critical and decolonial ethnography, and Black feminist thought are the same. Instead, my use of the term "critical hiphopography" is an attempt to bridge these connections.

Those who agreed to participate in this study did not describe their methodological approaches in these terms. Yet women ethnographers of Hip Hop dances bring to life much of what hiphopography aspires to be. As well, they expound on their methods in ways that seem expansive to the concept. For example, when asked about the role of or responsibilities that Hip Hop dance researchers can or should possess, one scholar-artist offered the following:

The very first obligation that you have [as a researcher] is to make sure that the inferences that you make are supported by the evidence that you gather . . . The second obligation is fairness. One of my aims as a person, and as a spiritual person, is harm reduction. Nothing that I do should harm the subjects that I write about. Even if I have a difference of agreement, *and I do* . . . And if there's a third [obligation], I would say to qualify, . . . anticipating the fact that what I say is going to be contested from get-go and qualifying that—especially in this level, in this line of inquiry. So instead of roles I would say those three obligations. Back up inferences with evidence, be fair, and qualify are really part of the obligation of a researcher. Especially within a network of dance traditions that come from oppressed people, where the notion of oppression is omnipresent within the movement forms instead of being, you know, not a part of it.

Rather than "role" as a position one steps into (and can thus step out of), she shifted my language to "obligations," capturing a sense of duty that one cannot simply shirk off. This is not a checklist of tasks but a commitment to a set of values that should resonate in any research project. Most of the above also speaks to the writing-up stage, the stage when the researcher's power to impact those they have researched is most pronounced. The obligations she names underlie this chapter, setting a tone for thinking about critical hiphopography as a set of political and ethical demands, from the data-gathering stage through publication.

Researching Hip Hop streetdances demands taking risks, whether in the form of stepping into a cypher, contesting academic ways of doing research, or negotiating institutional power while trying to meet community demands. Researchers have to put their work out to the community and let them be the judge. Risk is about potential loss and potential benefit. The women who participated in this study took risks by talking to me, sometimes very candidly, about the corporealities of being women ethnographers of Hip Hop dances. Their anonymity here is part of my effort to make taking that risk worthwhile. For those I interviewed, considerations of approach and the ethical care for the community are at the heart of their successful ethnographic projects. Their comments reveal and explore the challenges of researching Hip Hop streetdances and how they have attempted to work through those challenges. Moreover, since the ethnographers featured here are predominately scholar-practitioners, I would argue that some of them learned these critical methods as dancers. Thus, Hip Hop streetdances may not only encourage a hiphopography approach, but also socialize dancers into it.

THEMATIC ANALYSIS

Three key themes emerge in this chapter: (a) the impact of the "show and prove" ethos in Hip Hop; (b) the challenges of researching community and family; and (c) critical hiphopography research strategies and concerns in the context of one's institutional power. These themes speak to the particularities of long-term involvement in Hip Hop dance spaces, including the competing values of Hip Hop and academia, the constant negotiation of relationships, shifting dynamics of power, and the challenges and rewards of community.

Show and Prove

The resistance ethnographers encounter when first entering the field is, in a way, an extension of a "show and prove" attitude, an ethos that privileges action over words or demonstrating skills over merely talking about them. In fact, show and prove can also be an indirect critique of academics, who, in reductive terms, write on the actions of others. Show and prove also entails qualities such as community accountability, the importance of an ongoing practice, and the value placed on demonstrating one's commitments. Ultimately, show and prove reminds you that respect is earned by doing, and for researchers in streetdance spaces, the first hurdle is earning that respect.

Questions abound in these early experiences: Who are you? Why are you here? Why should we care about and support your work? Is it reciprocal? While most of my interviewees noted the challenges of entering their Hip Hop dance scenes as researchers, two actually outright named it "hazing." For one practitioner-ethnographer, "The worst hazing could've just been, I'm just going to ignore you. You just keep showing up and then, once you are sort of that familiar face in the crowd, then people start to open up." Another researcher-artist said that she was, "hazed for three years straight." She goes on to state that "within the underground dance community it's very, very old school . . . 'What are you doing? I'm gonna sue you. Fuck you.' A whole bunch of shit, because I had a camera." Perhaps because of "a sense of proprietary-ness," as another informant calls it, what she recounts is not just dismissal but clear distrust. And with a camera in her hand, her experiences also reflected some of the burden she shouldered because of previous photographers who might have exploited dancers or left some feeling as if they had been exploited. One could say that these women entered the field through modes of initiation that demanded a thick skin, long-term demonstrations of commitment, and a deep appreciation for other dancers. A dance scholar concluded, "It's like anything in Hip Hop. Everything is a challenge, you know? Everything is a challenge. Okay, well, now you've got the floor. *What you gonna do?*" The only appropriate response to the rhetorical question and implied challenge is to show and prove.

Despite their hazings, proving themselves came in multiple forms. A practitioner-researcher recalled, "In the early 2000s, mid-, and late nineties people became very wary of cameras. So, it was a matter of explaining myself. And also, a big thing was learning to dance. I wanted to learn to dance, 'cause I was like, 'Oh my god, this is incredible. I wanna do this, too!' But I feel like the biggest thing that has helped me, my biggest asset, is my ability to dance." In a grammatical shift from the past tense to the present tense, she emphasizes that her dancing ability helped in the past and continues to benefit her today. Dancing was and is an "asset," an investment in the time and effort it took to encode the movement and cultural sensibility into her body, and undertaken out of an appreciation for the practice and a desire to learn. It is also an ongoing project, not confined to a particular research period.

Though practitioners can show and prove in cyphers and in their research, non-streetdancers are also given room to communicate through other movement expressions. For one informant, her general dance background worked in her favor:

> The youth who were doing either popping, mostly popping and breaking, they loved what I did as an older female researcher. They would always nod the head and do the hand, and I would get acknowledged. That gave me more credibility to actually embody what I did within the Hip Hop cypher, dance cypher. So, having been a performer before becoming an academic really helped. That's, I think, my main point: having been a performer and dancer, and feeling comfortable with my body, and dancing from an Africanist aesthetic perspective—that really helped me in terms of my fieldwork.

Their respect for someone older may have played a part, but it is clear that dancing made the difference. It acknowledged a degree of cultural awareness and embodied knowledge that such communities are trained to assess. That she already had a movement background gave her credibility; that she offered this movement in a cypher earned their respect.

Though I have always been a social dancer, I do not have a particular practice. I took the occasional class (e.g., breaking, rocking) for the sake of getting a beginning sense of the movement in my body, but I often stayed one step behind the other students. My sluggish body did not pick up the movement as quickly as the young students surrounding me. While it didn't seem to matter to practitioners if I had a sustained practice or could do well in a class, it mattered that I had rhythm, and on multiple occasions I was tested to see if I at least could dance. It felt like it mattered, especially because I am Black.

All of these instances are variations on the demand to show and prove. And perhaps this demand establishes the conditions for a "hard love," a term one informant used to describe how it felt to enter a new scene as a practitioner just beginning to conduct research:

> I found it really hard to win over their trust. It wasn't the kind of scene you could go in and say, "Hey, I want to interview you." They were really opposed to anyone: "Who are you? Who do you think you are? What do you know about this?"
>
> I made this documentary work about my own experiences and how hard it was to navigate a scene where b-girls weren't really welcomed . . . They would say, "Girls don't do this." Or they would say, oh, they had tried to help girls before, but they just always quit. They were always already *not* willing to help, but clearly paying me some kind of attention. I think that was the hard love of that time period, if that makes sense . . . It was a kind of hard love where you had to prove yourself, but they were paying attention to let you know that you had to prove yourself.

It was that hard line that just reminds me now of the '90s. I don't get that anymore. I don't see that kind of behavior they exhibited. I could be out of touch, but I don't see it so much.

After reiterating the kind of clarifying questions that come when one is beginning Hip Hop dance fieldwork, she goes on to discuss the resistance she encountered as a woman researcher, which mirrored her reception as a practitioner. The other dancers' behavior was dismissive. Their sexism evident, and though dated, it was no less disconcerting. These details provide context, but her story emphasized the more poignant irony of the situation: being both ignored yet on their radar enough to know that they were watching and waiting for her to prove herself. Hard love was evident both in her persistence and in her recognition of the lesson in their faux inattention. Dancing did not guarantee acceptance, but it opened that door.

Earning trust requires ample time. Thus it becomes all the more important to develop creative research strategies that provide different kinds of access. One practitioner-scholar spoke enthusiastically about the untapped resource of the nondancers in the scene, particularly dancers' romantic partners who had little interest or stake in hazing her. She stated, "I started to really make a point of getting to know girlfriends, which is something I did anyway . . . Girlfriends don't have the same investment in the scene. They're willing to give you insights and tell you things that maybe other people would keep from you, and they have a different perspective, . . . different kinds of insights into the culture that became really stimulating."

For another informant, interviewing existing friends meant that trust was already built into their dynamic. They knew her and so did not have the same concerns about being misrepresented or exploited that they might have with someone new. As she stated plainly, they "know who I am and what my intentions are." Understanding the trials of a researcher, though, did not prevent her from hazing someone else. At one point while dancing, this scholar-practitioner recounted hurling similar such questions at another researcher, likening her own actions to that of a parent determining the intentions of someone courting her daughter, because the dance floor "was such a sacred space."

Similarly, I took the path of least resistance. In my own experience while researching my dissertation, though some members of the scene eventually welcomed the opportunity to share their insights, others continued to ignore me. I learned to focus my efforts on those who already seemed receptive. Still, getting the interview was just the beginning. One pioneering b-boy agreed to an interview but would not agree to be recorded until after he had a sense of my character, and how I understood and would eventually represent his insights. Once I could show and prove, then he would risk letting me record him. It seemed only fair. In this case, the expectation was that I would interpret his words and write-up my analysis *before* I recorded an interview, which is the opposite of an academic approach. His insistence on this has shaped my priorities.

While the completed dissertation and eventual book were years away, at the time in 2006 I decided to start blogging edited versions of my field notes on my MySpace page (which I opened solely to reach out to dancers). My blogs were attempts at transparency, and they allowed me to rehearse my analyses. It felt risky. Though never negative, the comments section opened me up in a very public way for the first time. The second person I attempted to interview agreed to talk to me briefly, would not allow me to record, and then hesitated when I started to take notes. After a brief pause, he said, "Yeah, you can take notes," drawing attention to the fact that I had already started scribbling in my notepad without having first gotten consent. (Lesson learned.) While a recording might have allowed for more precise replication of the exact words, the "test" was in my valuing the opportunity to get those interviews at all and using them responsibly, even without a recording. These examples also illustrate the tension between Hip Hop imperatives and academic demands; prioritizing one can undermine the other.

The women ethnographers I interviewed understood that gaining trust was worth the effort, but also that there are sacrifices involved in researching, especially for scholar-practitioners who might be treated like virtual outsiders. Once practitioners take on formal research, they become subject to questions about shifting loyalties, and risk losing their established relationships and accumulated cultural capital as a result. For one scholar-practitioner, research offered a way to continue her participation after an injury left her barely able to walk for a year: "I wanted to stay a part of the culture even though I was injured ... [Ethnography was] a way to still belong to this thing that I immersed my whole identity in, and my identity would be lost without it. But at the same time, I fundamentally understood that me writing about it would not be cool." Researching and writing about breaking offered a path to stay connected to community and thus her identity; at the same time, she was concerned about occupying the role of the "bad academic," who had no place in community: "That my limited cultural capital would be immediately ejected by being this nerdy white, like, this bad image of the academic ... I thought writing about it and not dancing was probably 'game over' for inclusion." For her, research offered a medium for continued participation after an injury, but scholar-practitioners who already have relationships with a scene might still have to reestablish their commitments and rebuild community trust after an extended absence. That is what comes into question, whether one's commitments have changed to fit the institutional demands outside their subjects' cultural context.[3]

Moreover, gaining entry is only one of many potential minefields, as one scholar-practitioner noted:

It's also really hard to be so closely, so intimately a part of a scene, and then also to be a researcher of that because, I feel in some ways, a very high degree of respect for the folks that I research and for the culture. On the other hand, as a scholar, I have to think critically about it, and sometimes that means making arguments that aren't necessarily going to be easy to make, you know? That might be critical of certain ways that the scene is, or relationships. Who gets what kind of opportunities?, for example. Those kinds of things. So, [to] really look at the scene with a critical eye, which sometimes is not always celebratory, basically, that is a difficult thing because I have to negotiate that, always, in terms of thinking about who are the communities that I'm a part of. And how do I engage in a conversation that is going to be productive and that's not just going to create boundaries and separation, but that's going to get folks to also think critically themselves, but in helpful ways that help us to kind of rethink our practices in fruitful ways.

As a scholar who is a member of several communities with vested interests in her research, the precarity of her positionality is informed by the fact she is not merely telling celebratory stories. She wants to offer arguments that contribute to the community's growth. At the heart of this, though, are her concerns about her reception by the people she risks slighting. It matters how the research and the scholarship it produces get done, and the spirit in which one offered back to the culture. This also might be part of the "hard love" in the chapter title—saying the hard thing out of a love for the culture.

She went on to state that one should "be able to continually exercise an attitude of self-reflection, and also, again, to really understand why you're engaging the community you are. Why do you want to do this work? What are your motivations? To be really honest and to have a lot of integrity around that." In other words, the kinds of questions community members aggressively hurl at researchers are precisely the kinds of questions they should ask themselves. Clarifying one's self-interests helps in establishing a relationship to a chosen community: "This is because you are often working with communities where power differences are real. And histories of violence or histories of difference, histories of oppression, are real, and they still continue into the present. And so, you have to be prepared to face those kinds of histories and treat folks with respect. The most important way to do that is to understand who you are." Perhaps this is another obligation of a hiphopographer.

For one informant, sharing who she is on the dance floor allowed for her relationships to shift more quickly, and added dimension to her research:

> You will pay dues one way or another. If you feel physically inclined, it might help you to learn a couple of steps, or at least have a sense of rhythm. It's also a way of bonding with people and learning about dancers. I've learned a lot about dancers and been able to break down and analyze the way they move and the way they anticipate music by dancing with them, and break down a lot of the kind of social "who the fuck are you?" barriers.

She made clear that dancing is a dimension of her research, providing her both insight about a dancer that might otherwise go unrecognized and another means of breaking down barriers in the field. Simply put, showing and proving on the dance floor offered another mode of study. Dancing with people is a study in how they move in relationship to her and the music, which is perhaps why even having "a sense of rhythm" can go a long way in building bridges.

On the other side of paying dues is earning the respect of those who had previously been suspicious of you. Yet one practitioner-researcher recounts that she still had a lot of anxiety about showcasing her research project because of the hazing she had received. But a practitioner friend reminded her: "You've earned your stripes. You've been through it. You've been through the battle. You've had to prove who you are. You've been in the game, so you, if anybody, deserves to be able to go and put your work out there and represent our community." In the end, though, navigating community acceptance is challenging. To truly show and prove, one has to put themselves and their work out there for judgment. That is ultimately the call of the cypher.

Researching Community and Family

Anyone doing this work can forge profound connections to the people they spend time with and learn about. The scholar-practitioners especially spoke regularly about the challenges and benefits of working within their own communities and among people they already consider family. Over time, even I forged friendships that continue to matter to me. In all the interviews, women ethnographers expressed concerns about how to navigate and protect the meaningful personal relationships that were important to them beyond the project, even if they were formative of the project.

One informant felt a clear distinction between commuinty members and "fam-fam" (true family)—those "that are going to be there for you no matter what"—which, in her case, were not necessarily those she met in the dance scene. Keeping these groups separate in fact increased her ability to navigate relationships and intimacies in her research sites.[4] For some researchers it is easier to work with new people because, as another scholar-practitioner explained: "You don't have, sort of, all the other background information going on. You just go with what's happening in the moment. And that will naturally lead you to ask, 'Oh, well what about this?' or 'Can you tell me something else about this moment?' As opposed to trying to impose, 'Well are you going to get to this part yet?'" Put simply, the pleasure of discovery in the moment of exchange with a new contact can make for rich interviews, an approach that used to be held above others as it was once considered more "objective."

Being a practitioner gave one dancer-researcher access to private archives and new teaching networks. Being down for the culture had led her to her research interests, so much so that she credited her dance community for teaching her how to be an ethnographer: "One of the other things [streetdance] got me to [do], as well, is learning how to be an ethnographer. [It] was one of the values that came out of it . . . But I think the scene would feel that way—they basically raised me. They taught [me]; they gave me a lot of experiences. You could say that they trained me in ethnography." The use of the word "raised" captures how the scene helped her develop during her formative years as a streetdancer and as an ethnographer, as well as her growth over time. She referred to the community's training in ethnography as "values," suggesting that these lessons were both ethical and practical.

What does it mean, then, to research in one's home dance scene? One scholar-practitioner clarified the responsibilities that come with actually being part of a community or choosing to move in that direction: "It's hard to put yourself in a role but, do you just wanna be a scholar? Alright, then there's a certain way you move through the world.

Do you want to actually be a part of the community? And if so, is it just purely, 'Oh, I'll see you at the club,' or is it on a social level?" She then unpacked what she meant by "social level":

> I babysit people's kids. I go to Thanksgiving dinners with them. I know their mothers. I see them in the grocery store and it's like, "Hi Mrs. X. Do you need help with your bags?" I realize now that that was a choice I made and I'm glad I made the choice. But it's just, I guess, being aware of the different ways you can be connected to, or not connected to, the community. And what works best for you and your project?

The care she offered to a friend's mother is an endearing example of showing up for people. Her choice, though perhaps a subconscious one, gave her a presence in community that I have not experienced. Perhaps because I opted for a multi-sited approach, and subsequently moved back and forth across the country multiple times, I remained peripheral to various dance communities (e.g., New York City, Los Angeles), and thus relatively less connected (no grocery store run-ins). This practitioner-researcher's deep involvement in people's lives carried responsibilities and reciprocity. Citing the care and attention she received when she tore a ligament, she goes on to acknowledge her appreciation for the people who stayed with her, who made sure she stretched before dancing, and then continued to check in on her two to three years later. "So, seeing that sense of community and the fact that people actually care, and I wasn't just another . . . whatever, kind of made an impression on me." The community can return any support given.

I share feelings of responsibility. In my case it often manifests in using my PhD on behalf of others and in whatever ways it can have influence. I have written letters to parole boards and parole officers, and recommended people for employment, vouching less for their dance skills, historical knowledge, and teaching than for their ability to speak well and teach (predominately white) college students. Once I was even asked to simply be the PhD in the room, validating someone's efforts to secure a venue for an event (though I don't think they really needed me).

There are challenges that arise when a researcher is deeply intertwined in the personal lives of an extended dance family and community. The personal nature of the research can necessitate performing those friendships differently for on camera interviews: "Trying to negotiate our relationship as researcher and interviewee versus 'just girls'—because we were mediated by this recording device or two recording devices—that was a little bit like, alright, how do you just keep it relaxed?" The question posed challenges for her in the field when one close friend refused to talk on camera. Close relationships do not guarantee what will be on the official record, prompting another set of concerns: "I sometimes didn't get the information that I thought I was going to get. And I was like, Oh crap, now what is this? What is this research? How much of it do I just have to go [with] from the information that I collected on tape? Do I bring in this other side? Do I actively ask her to address x, y, z?" In another example, she had to check in with her interviewee off the record in order to move forward:

So, for example, I stopped the tape, and I stopped the interview, and we had a conversation. And I was like, "You're talking about this person, right?" And she's like, "Yeah, but I don't want to acknowledge that person ever existed in my life." And it's like, "This is a big part of who you are and your personal experience." And she's like, "I never thought about it that way." So, I think when we turn the mics back on, she started naming that person.

Her positionality as a streetdancer and as a friend cultivated an emic perspective, yet the wealth of information that comes as a result was not directly usable. A preexisting personal relationship meant that, in that interview, she and her informant had to find a new way of communicating because the researcher-researched divide began to breach the modes of communication they had already established as friends. At the same time, she knew how to intervene in those conversations because they were friends.

In one case the politics of taking advantage of personal relationships actually produced a distrust that had direct bearing on how a scholar-practitioner wrote up her findings. She described the pressure to keep quiet about her familial ties in the community: "Many members of the community where I'd interview, they did not want me to trade on my associations in order to get my work out there. They didn't. That was a major thing. So, for many years I did not tell anybody. I didn't include it in my papers . . . I didn't include the fact that the people who I interviewed were members of my family." The hint of concern in her statement captures the difficulty of being in a position of prioritizing community concerns—keeping quiet about family ties—but recognizing how that may compromise the integrity of the work by academic standards, because readers only get part of the story. The written work lacked details that mattered to the dynamics in a given interview, details that might have impacted how someone interpreted her findings.

The disjuncture between the demands of the community and the academy were pronounced in that moment. One can recognize the maneuvering that goes into getting information on the record, thus making it available as the evidence that grounds academic study. Such efforts also gesture toward the performative nature of the evidence, that it acts as proof only when it is spoken on the recording. In the previous example, she has to facilitate the conditions in which her interviewees' knowledge could become evidence in her research.

Another ethnographer offers a different kind of emic perspective, suggesting that there was never a division between her research and her life because they were one and the same:

All of my writing—as an ethnographic journalist, as a creative writer—it comes from my relationships with the people and the issues that are percolating within my life. And, now this is why I don't use the word "personal" in the way that other people use it . . . When people use the word "personal," they're really, for me, they're talking about "private." And when something is private, nobody knows about it. [*Scoffs*] . . . But "personal" can never, in my view, be divorced from the lives that we lead.

The personal nature of her research is precisely what makes it political, echoing the Black feminist mantra. "Private," in contrast, captures an underlying privilege to

determine and maintain a distinction between public and private life, which is not available to everyone. Her personal life was very much a part of the public discourses that
shaped her research, and was not hidden from debate, judgment, or critique. Her distinction between private and personal implicates academic practices as well, those built
around maintaining a distance between the researcher and the researched (which reeks
of a kind of academic elitism that Hip Hop communities are wary of to begin with). Such
a distance fortifies notions of "objectivity," and positions insider perspectives as biased.
That she scoffed at "private" suggests how foreign the idea of demarcating a distinction
between her everyday life and her research actually is.

Always with an eye to the ethics of method, she clarified how one can do sound research without collapsing into outmoded notions of objectivity, which hold that the personal nature of the work between the researcher and the researched somehow nullifies
the scholarly rigor and value of her labor. She added, "What we do to manage the personal is we subject it to fairness, we subject it to the system that works for competitive,
multivocal views to understand it, that really weighs the evidence for us with scrupu-
lousness." Again, professional integrity is at the core along with a deep understanding of
why it matters.

She offered a specific critique of objectivity to explain why competitive views matter.
I quote at length because, in wonderfully accessible detail, her comments get at my own
discomfort with objectivity:

> Competitive plausibility. Understanding that absolute truth within a real circum-
> spect world are very, very rare. And you have to really . . . work for fairness, to weigh
> competing views in order to get at this thing that you will present as the truth, truth
> of the meaning . . . It [objectivity] is often a conservative weapon used to undermine
> and to write about marginalized lives. "Oh, you're too close to it!," you know? "Oh,
> you're not being objective!," you know? "Only the people who are not a part of the
> world, who are not feminine, who are not *Black*, who are not whatever can write
> about it. You're too close to it. You'll be biased." And quickly, as soon as you write, to
> try in your work to redirect meaning and redirect stereotypes and to get at emic (as
> they say in anthropology)—the insider's or the actual people's views and not just the
> stereotypical or etic views that are said about them—when you try to get at that kind
> of knowledge, they'll turn it around. The naysayers, some of them being conserva-
> tive, they'll turn it around and say, "Oh you're being biased." And your entire goal
> and point is to work against the bias by really flushing out the loopholes and the gaps
> of knowledge by getting at ways of life that don't have [a] dominant, prided place
> in the world. And someone who comes from these low-income worlds that I came
> from, and [I] came from a world where I literally didn't have the resources in terms of
> parents and support and money, and all that. It wasn't just something I was interested
> in as an academic inquiry. It was *my life*!

As she ventriloquized the predictable responses of critics, she also cataloged the various discourses used as weapons to undermine the authority of "native" ethnographers,
whose tactics are meant to empower their distinct positionalities (Jacobs-Huey 2002).
In doing so, she also told the story of how her labor got dismissed or is misread.
Borrowing from historian Martin Bernal's (1987) concept of "competitive plausibility,"

a heavily debated "method of reconstructing the distant past" (Bernal 2001, 217) meant to challenge conventional wisdom and attend to the absences and erasures—her approach speaks to her efforts to get at the deeper truths residing in the "loopholes and gaps of knowledge." In contrast, the critiques of this approach appear more invested in maintaining the very structures of power and oppression that then classify emic interventions as "too close" to be objective. As "*my life!*," her exclamation makes clear the absurdity of being told that a lifetime's worth of experiences disqualified her perspective. To research *in* community, then, is to recognize how aspects of everyday life are precisely the terms for political intervention.

Building on this critique, one scholar-practitioner also talked about how her clearly stated political leanings often connected her to people in ways that fostered trust.

> I'm very clear from the beginning what my politics are. People know that I'm very interested in the Black political project; that I'm very interested in thinking about issues of blackness and [the] racialization of the Black community specifically, within streetdance . . . But I think it also means that the people that I work with, to a certain extent, trust me to be concerned ethically about who they are and their history.

For a non-Black woman, vocalizing a "Black political project" with potential informants is bold thing to do, potentially turning off some while enlivening others. As an ongoing practice, though, she implies that this type of political clarity, on her behalf and for others' consideration, cleared the way for engaged political discussions in her project. She was also clear about the ethical care necessary in handling their words, especially at the writing stage, when academic demands become more pronounced. At that point, our research obligations become all the more important.

Critical Hiphopography and Institutional Power

When one considers that formal degrees and institutional backing allow one to claim a position of authority over the streetdancers whose labor is the basis of our research, subverting academic hierarchies becomes all the more crucial. One way to accomplish this is by challenging academic language to better represent the labor of streetdancers, signaling an authority that comes with labels like "scholar" versus "informal researcher." This scholar-practitioner argued, "It's important to be able to think differently about the idea of knowledge transmission when we look at these kind of forms." Here she recounted one way this transmission took place among streetdancers:

> I really argue in my work that streetdancers are scholars. Of course, I'm not trying to say that what we do as academic scholars is the same as what we do as practitioners of streetdance. But I think it's very important to understand that the structures of the dance styles themselves offer opportunities to study, and that what we are doing, for example, when we enter a dance cypher is studying movement. It is a form of study that does not take place within the institutional walls of the academic classroom or

the dance studio . . . But a lot of practitioners who really have devoted a huge amount of their time to studying, documenting, theorizing in different ways . . . That kind of embodied archive of knowledge that these folks carry with them is really valuable.

Echoing another informant's stance about knowledge gained from dancing with someone, she took it further by representing cyphers as distinctly Hip Hop sites of deep study. The degree of analysis captured at any given moment by closely reading the varied ways that dancers produce and exchange knowledge in a cypher is essentially a scholarly endeavor. Institutional definitions do not hold for her, and the knowledge embodied by practitioners warrants respect. Advocating for it becomes part of her work as a scholar. Even in this chapter, "ethnographer" is defined broadly, beyond the terms of academic disciplines, negating ivory tower exclusivity in favor of approaches adopted within communities based on their values and sensibilities.

If researching in Hip Hop dance scenes can teach someone how to be in community, it is also true that being in community teaches lessons about how to research. Those insights, when taken seriously, can profoundly impact fieldwork. In the words of one informant,

It's an unruly field experience. And, uh, the street, *the* street is a—it's streetdance for a reason now. It's street. It's streetdance because the street—you're moving, you know? You're having a certain animation, your certain texture of life that's different than if you're going to do your interview with a ballet dancer in between rehearsals. And so, the very nature of the fieldwork is going to be different . . . You have to be there. You don't know when someone is not—you don't know when *they will not be there*! You don't know when next week they get the chills, and they've got pneumonia; they're gonna be, you know, they're suffering from the advanced stages of AIDS, and they're gone. You don't know. Violence from the street, illness. Oh, incarceration is another thing. You know, "So and so 'went away.'" "Where did they go?" Then you get a call from them collect: "Send me $25 so I can get my commissary" . . . or "Visit me. Apply to visit me. Get on my list."

It is clear in her examples that the larger structural issues—prison, violence, healthcare—in the context of everyday living shape how fieldwork should or perhaps *needs* to happen. She invoked research concepts like "being there" and the "unruly field" to clarify how streetdance modifies standard academic expectations. For example, "being there" in this instance is not simply about being physically present at live performances to experience their ephemeral elements (e.g., a performer's energy, the smell of the space etc.), such as dance studies might write about. It was about an being active presence in the lives of those who come from communities that are especially vulnerable to "premature death," a phrasing I borrow from Ruth Gilmore's powerful definition of racism.[5] "Being there" is a lived, daily reality. In the 1990s, HIV/AIDS was the pandemic of concern; today, it is COVID-19. In each of their historical specificities, the urgency of *now* persists and "being there" also meant showing up before circumstances extract someone from community. Rather than wait for more comfortable accommodations, she conducted interviews in, for example, a marijuana-smoke-filled bus station bathroom or sitting on a sidewalk outside a club while her informant took a smoking break. The urgency of this approach was once made palpable when she found out that someone she had just interviewed under such conditions had been murdered less than a week later. I wish I'd had her insight prior to my own research. On at least two separate occasions, I put off interviewing someone I was initially too intimidated to approach, only to learn soon after that they had died. Ultimately, if one's research on Hip Hop streetdance actually extends beyond the studio to the streets, then one's methods have to be adapted to the conditions and contexts at hand.

Language, again, is another area where scholars work to both assuage concerns about academic elitism and share an understanding. One scholar-practitioner articulated a strategy for talking about gender and sexuality in interviews: "For me, always rooting questions to actions and artifacts and practices became really, really important. I never began—I never would just ask a general question about race, gender, sexuality, et cetera. I would sort of spell out what the word 'sexuality' for example meant, or 'gender' meant . . . I didn't rely on [theoretical terminology] in the interview process." Opting to avoid academic jargon during interviews, her advice includes the simple practicality of defining taken-for-granted terms to put informants on the same page.

The women I interviewed for this chapter readily recognized issues of power and their capacity to exacerbate the vulnerabilities of research subjects. For example, one researcher shared that her decision to use pseudonyms for her informants was more impactful than she had realized: "One person, Eric (a pseudonym that I used), you know, he was like, 'You know, thank God you used that because, you know, I'm on parole' . . . And that's a reality. And it's a significant thing, the gathering of the data." In consideration of the power we wield, others actively work to "level the playing field" at the outset of their research. A scholar-practitioner grappling with her own strategies stated, "I think that the assumptions around what a researcher does and the ways in which researchers have been—basically go into a community, take, and then leave— was a big assumption, was an operating assumption, which is real." She dealt with it by "right away" addressing consent and making sure that its material evidence (the institutional review board form) was signed so that the person interviewed felt protected. And because Hip Hop dance practitioners have anxieties about choreographic theft, dispelling that fear is important. In contrast, my challenge was when dancers (particularly older generation practitioners) felt ambivalent about signing a form. To some participants, signing a form beforehand is suspect, feeling more like a signing away rights than protection. In my experience, the "oral informed consent form" was less cumbersome.

About her efforts to dispel informants' anxieties, this same scholar-practitioner suggested that taking streetdances classes alongside younger students, learning with and from them "made me more vulnerable because that's not my form so I'm struggling. I think that I was willing to be vulnerable in that space with them might have done something. I'm not quite sure what. In terms of relating, if you're with someone who's willing to be vulnerable then it makes it more okay for you to be vulnerable." By putting her novice skills on display, she put herself in the position of a learner, someone who could learn from their expertise.

Despite their discernible privilege in society, those with academic credentials have to navigate complicated cultural expectations in Hip Hop sites, which invariably also shapes our interpersonal and professional relationships. Because academics are still often regarded with suspicion, many of us have adopted habits like deferring to the authority of practitioners as a gesture of respect. On the flip side is the reality that respect might not be mutual, regardless of our efforts. One dancer-scholar discussed a realization:

> People see me as powerful now . . . You know how I'm framing power? Like I'm an academic. That's clearly coded as bad. Then, on top of that, the relationships are more difficult to navigate because of that, because people want—you need to treat them like they're the authorities. There's not a space for me to be an authority . . . The only thing I can do is be a collaborator who just appreciates what other people do and bring.

Although she was a practitioner, that background had less bearing on her relationship to the community. That she lacked "authority," deferring to practitioners because she is a scholar, and as a consequence invisibilizing her own knowledge as someone who has put in years of practice. Moreover, in academic spaces, her authority might get undermined because she is a woman, further confusing her analysis of situation. She elaborated: "That's got to be gendered? Maybe not. Actually, maybe not in Hip Hop . . . I don't know how to describe that. It's been a new experience . . . It might not always be the case, and it hasn't always been the case, but it's possible that getting older has that effect, right?" Her questions lingered: Is it Hip Hop? Is it gender? Is it, perhaps, age? Or all of the above? The lack of clear answers masks deeper concerns about whether students and practitioners respect her and her labor on their behalf.

If being an academic seemed to mask the source of certain biases, it also heightened her awareness of how race and her whiteness functioned in her scenes. She recounted that her efforts to encourage her students' awareness of whiteness was undermined by white practitioners' appeals to the oft-repeated refrain, "It's about skills."[6] Her training in how to deal with such issues with her students felt limited and unclear: "I feel like I didn't necessarily get that training. In my MA, I read some things about whiteness, and I contextualized it, and I knew it was something that I felt uncomfortable with, and I didn't know how to talk about." Though she did not always feel equipped to confront race and whiteness, academia had nonetheless solidified the necessity of at least acknowledging issues of power and positionality in direct ways that are not necessarily demanded of practitioners. At the same time, Hip Hop platitudes spouted by white practitioners became tools they used to skirt their responsibility to also attend to power and positionality in their practice of an African diasporic form. I quote the following at length to for context:

Now I've got a bunch of students that are white . . . They say things like, "Hip Hop is based on skill," [or] "it's where you're at, not where you come from." There are all of these things that don't make us challenge our position and our privilege and *understand* it. I know, for me, I really made a big deal about not coming from anything because, I feel like I struggled in a variety of ways in my life . . . I put in so much work, right? It doesn't feel like, it's not like—because when you hear the narratives about white privilege, it seems like someone's just like, "Oh, here you go"—but that's not actually how we experience it; but it still is that. But then I experience it, like, I worked so hard. Nobody else worked. I sacrificed fitting in. I feel like there are all these things that, I feel like, "I did that. I deserve . . . " Maybe, I don't know how to frame that advice, but it's just like, to be aware that even though the scholarship that doesn't sound like it relates to your experiences, the stuff that the scholars are saying might actually be things that you need to question and think about . . .

I don't think we even have the frameworks . . . I feel like, I don't know what to recommend to my students to read to start to actually take that apart, take apart the fact that they love breaking *and* they want to study . . . We start to try to tear apart race, racism, ethnicity, and there's not a text to bring to them. And it's not like that's the solution! That's a very academic response to have, like, "We just need an article that we can recommend that will fix this problem." [*Laughter*] To just be, not just aware of it, but actually ask the hard questions earlier on, maybe. If you're not being asked to ask the hard questions, then that's a sign that they're the real questions, right? But, if they're not being asked, that's a sign of a kind of privilege . . .

Though she did not yet possess a clear strategy for pushing her students beyond the mantras and defensiveness, she draws attention to the disjuncture between being privileged and feeling privileged. The gap between the two may account for some people's defensiveness—and hints at her own at one time—but key here is that this gap can become a chasm for those unwilling to hear critiques around race and whiteness. Ultimately, recognizing larger power structures means operating beyond one's individual life experiences, recognizing our complicity with institutions that are not of our making, and taking on responsibilities (or duties) that come with adopting a culture rooted in the very communities those structures exploit and oppress. Her positionality also shifts, from privileged to not, from academic who interrogates dance to embodied practitioner who loves it. Each voice reveals a dimension of her experiences as a streetdancer and a scholar, and the ongoing effort to bridge the two. Her incomplete efforts to work through discussions of white privilege with her students and their avoidance of the topic reveal an area where scholars can and should intervene in dance because "skills" alone cannot cover it.

White privilege haunts other areas of her research experiences. Later in the interview she revealed a growing ambivalence about her professional success, evident in the increasing number of students, the majority white, that she continues to teach and help to get employment. This is not a concern about white people per se, but a concern about the invisibilized workings of white privilege that position her to perpetuate it even as she and tries to counteract it. She had a tone of near disillusionment on how to sub-stantively move forward, yet her conclusion was relatively settled: "I don't know how to give them [students] advice on this, but I feel like we need, white people doing research need to check themselves." This echoes the aforementioned point, that as a *critical* hiphopography our job is not simply celebratory but speaks to the necessity of engaging structures of power in our research.

Other Hip Hop dance ethnographers have also struggled to engage with discussions of whiteness and with being positioned as the problem as a result. One scholar-dancer of African descent recalled a group discussion she facilitated with streetdancers:

> It was specifically around issues of race, and it was a mixed group. It was clear that the young white men were not talking about race at all. Not only were they not talking about it, they didn't want to talk about it. Their discomfort was displaced on me—so I was the problem, that I was raising this. That was really hard. That was a really hard moment, to actually feel that put on my body as not only a woman but as a woman of color. That, that was displaced onto me.

Again, whiteness and ideas of authenticity intersect. As someone learning the streetdances she was researching, she did not carry the same authority in the eyes of white practitioners who chose to avoid talking about race altogether, and instead dis-counted her as the problem academic. When I asked how she handled it, she could not fully recall: "Let me think back. I think that the way I addressed it, it would be the way I would address it in a classroom." Her response suggested that what struck her more was how it felt to be made a "problem" rather than how she handled it. Having taught for years, she elaborated that she, "allow[ed] them to talk but also push[ed] back a little bit on whatever their discomfort was." Her capacity to deal with it in the discussion was a result of her experience as an academic who attends to race in her classes already. With an emphasis on the white b-boys in the room, who "were really interested in dealing with the surface"—meaning the technique and acrobatics of the dance—their resistance to engaging discussions of race in any depth meant refusing to consider how this might impact their practice. As a result, she began to consider "the limits for white bodies to really engage fully in what I think Hip Hop culture and dance is really all about, which is not only technique." Quite literally, to even begin grappling with the complexities of race, the sheer act of getting certain practitioners to move past a "surface" level discus-sion can be a challenge.

Academic training can but does not guarantee one's ability to address these issues. Yet that same training can too easily position women ethnographers as the problem rather than a resource, someone to help but not lead. In the previous two examples, pro-fessional standing was used against several informants to undermine uncomfortable conversations. With that said, women ethnographers of Hip Hop streetdances also re-mind us that even awkward exchanges present opportunities to push for the kinds of critical conversations that the community needs to move forward.

Conclusion

"My role simply is to illuminate the cultures that I'm interested in, and try to share those as honestly as I can."

—scholar-practitioner

Moving people beyond a surface understanding of Hip Hop streetdance is the project. To do so *honestly* then entails a critical lens that both advocates for and challenges Hip Hop streetdance communities to move and grow in critical ways. As one streetdance scholar-practitioner put it,

> I hope that the work that I do as a scholar helps streetdancers re-value their practices and helps them think differently about why they do what they do in ways that will really kind of change, on a larger level, change the kind of structures that govern who we are, how we relate in society. I really feel that what I'm trying to do is to put a different lens or a different outlook on what streetdance is.

The "outlook" includes how streetdance is recognized and valued, both in the broader dance world and by streetdancers themselves:

> I'm trying to draw out threads of meaning within streetdance culture that are already there but that sometimes aren't focused on. You know? Ideas about collectivity, about coming together and being collective rather than always thinking about, say, the pioneers or the forefathers or the godfathers or the inventors or the authors of these styles . . . What is the cypher about? Why is it important to have a kind of collective grouping of folks coming together? . . . There's no appearance fee to appear in the cypher . . . , but that's probably one of the places that we most appreciate, and we most value . . . And that's where we determine value. Before you can even do that world tour or go teach in Japan or whatever, or judge at Juste Deboute, you better be able to cypher.[7]

Moving beyond the surface opens up spaces to better understand the culture, whether that be unearthing the taken-for-granted values embedded in rituals like cyphering or the outright overlooked sensibilities evident in collectivities rather than individuals. By extension, her hope was to help empower practitioners, and enliven understandings of streetdance collectivities in ways that can challenge dominant social structures.

In the dance world and in society, a viable critical hiphopography can and should advocate for a dismantling of the hierarchies that position people and practices as *less than*, less worthy of study, less intellectually rigorous. As one dancer-scholar put it, "To me, I consider this still cutting-edge research . . . How one positions Hip Hop research as a scholarly endeavor is, I think, still an important question to consider, an important issue to consider. To me there's no question that it is a scholarly endeavor." Hip Hop as an area of research offers nothing short of new forms of knowledge, which can take us in all kinds of unexpected directions. At a panel discussion titled "Hip Hop as Method," held at the University of Southern California in 2014, photographer and filmmaker Brian "B+" Cross offered the following: "Hip Hop actually produces knowledge. And in a whole other series of ways than Western thought allows us to think about . . . Hip Hop produces a kind of knowledge, a kind of diasporic knowledge, I think; a knowledge that has to do with improvisation; a knowledge that has to do with thinking history in different ways. And it does all that while having a good time" (University of Southern California 2014). Though Cross names history as a field that Hip Hop reconfigures, Hip Hop dancing and the lessons it teaches in hiphopography activate this same sentiment.

Hip Hop dance studies is primed to amplify the deep study of embodied knowledges and strengthen Hip Hop studies as a whole. To move more purposefully in this direction, one practitioner-researcher had a vision of evolving critical hiphopography into a more collaborative approach: "I know scholarship isn't a solo enterprise, but I'm thinking more of like discussion group or a reading group, that sort of thing." She went on to suggest that collaboration acts as a more reliable means of fact-checking, and even offers opportunities to check-in with one another as a way of combating the isolating tendencies of research and of academia. Moreover, collaborative reading and discussion on a community level can happen in fundamentally different ways and outside of exclusive institutional walls.[8] Collaboration here also strengthens future research: "There's about ten people on the planet I can call to fact-check. That's it. Mind you, there's a million people that do Hip Hop dance." The contrast she draws between doing the dance and knowing reliable sources to go to for information is stark. So, the call for working together more can mean, for example, structuring our scholarly labor in a manner not unlike a cypher—collectively engaged even in the context of competing ideas. Her comments are a gentle reminder that, as much as the field is growing, so too is our capacity to determine and create practices that are not beholden to the academic status quo. Instead she favored strategies that helped to foster the most accurate possible work on and for the culture, from an emic perspective.

Though my advocacy for Hip Hop dance studies and ethnography is a bit self-serving, the value of this work still holds. Hip Hop dance ethnographers provide insight about critical research strategies for centering community, being attentive to issues of power, and challenging academic discourses that are structured to dismiss especially vulnerable groups altogether. Women hiphopographers may risk relationships, but by showing and proving through our respective mediums (articles, photography, books, conferences etc.), we are showing that critical hiphopography beckons those who heed the call to deepen our understanding of the knowledges streetdances produce, to challenge disciplinary constraints, and to foreground cultural sensibilies. To end with the fitting words of one practitioner-scholar, "To do this work is a gift and an honor. Just treat it like that."

NOTES

1. The Hip Hop dance genres researched by the women I interviewed for this chapter include locking, popping, waacking, breaking, voguing, Hip Hop party and social dances, house, and turfing. These are distinct genres, each with its own history and aesthetic elements. *Hip Hop*, a term with roots in mid-1970s New York City (particularly, the Bronx), does not adequately represent all of the dances discussed in this chapter. In practice though, at practitioner-oriented dance events, including battles, *Hip Hop* is also treated as an umbrella term for all of these genres. Although some people prefer the term *streetdance*, I also employ Hip Hop in part because it captures both the shared histories of post–Civil Rights era, working-class, urban environments across the United States alongside roots in Black vernacular expressive cultural forms. Thus, the terms *Hip Hop dances* and *Hip Hop streetdances* capture a body of originating dances from an era fundamentally informed by African diasporic aesthetic traditions, as they manifest in the United States along with other genres subsequently born out of Hip Hop culture.

2. Their insights are in direct conversation with literary scholar Barbara Christian (1987), whose "The Race for Theory" eschews theory as an academic product in favor of the theorizing practices—dynamic narrative forms such as proverbs, riddles, and storytelling— of people of color.

3. One scholar-practitioner shared this concern over one's standing as both a community member and a researcher, stating that it's "'cuz of people, white people who have mistreated members of the community or traded off of them! You know? or who have sort of parachuted in[to] the community to do their work, and parachuted out . . . So the suspicion is warranted. But when the suspicion is turned on someone like me, who came from different circumstances, and who has a different—and did not come in as a researcher." In this case as well, she has to carry the burden of past "bad academics" and researchers' missteps and exploits. It can be a jarring and disheartening experience because, ultimately, one is reminded that acting in community with others does not guarantee unconditional acceptance, and that you could still be misread. (See Johnson, chapter 8, this volume).

4. Johnson, chapter 8, this volume, for more on navigating intimacies in the field.

5. I am drawing on Ruth Wilson Gilmore's (2007) definition of racism. In her book, *Golden Gulag: Prisons, Surplus, Crisis, and Opposition in Globalizing California*, she writes, "Racism, specifically, is the state-sanctioned or extralegal production and exploitation of group-differentiated vulnerability to premature death" (28).

6. Streetdancers often invoke the mantra "It's about skills" to refer to the capacity of movement to level the playing field across all kinds of difference—age, race, gender, nationality, class— such that only one's skills matter in a cypher, for example. It is a kind of colloquial explanation for why Hip Hop dance spaces are diverse, modeling the many ways to be different yet in community, in contrast to acts of violent exclusion that we see in the world. "It's about skills" makes embodied practices more significant in cross-cultural exchanges, but it does not actually work through the inevitable frictions and tensions that arise in hierarchical societies.

7. Juste Debout is an international Hip Hop dance event in Paris, started in 2002 .

8. For example, in the mid-2000s, b-girl Rokafella hosted a series of "sit-down" talks at breaking events across the United States to create a space to talk about gender in the breaking community. This is an example of the community having a collective exchange wherein challenging and sensitive conversations take place. It models a way of thinking outside the academia box in support of a larger commitment to the culture (Pabón-Colón 2017).

REFERENCES

Alim, H. S. (2006a). *Roc the Mic Right: The Language of Hip Hop Culture.* New York: Routledge.

Alim, H. S. (2006b). "'The Natti Ain't No Punk City': Emic Views of Hip Hop Cultures." *Callaloo* 29 (3): 969–990.

Appert, C. M. (2017). "Engendering Musical Ethnography." *Ethnomusicology* 61 (3): 446–467.

Bernal, M. (1987). *Black Athena: The Afroasiatic Roots of Classical Civilization.* New Brunswick, NJ: Rutgers University Press.

Bernal, M. (2001). *Black Athena Writes Back: Martin Bernal Responds to His Critics.* Edited by D. C. Moore. Durham, NC: Duke University Press.

Chang, J., ed. (2006). *Total Chaos: The Art and Aesthetics of Hip-Hop.* New York: BasicCivitas Books.

Christian, B. (1987). "The Race for Theory." *Cultural Critique* 6 (Spring): 51–63.

Collins, P. H. (1990). *Black Feminist Thought: Knowledge, Consciousness, and the Politics of Empowerment.* New York: Routledge.

Dattareyan, E. G. (2018). "Critical Hip-Hop Cinema: Racial Logics and Ethnographic Ciphas in Delhi." *Wide Screen* 7 (1–24).

Dimitriadis, G. (2014). "Framing Hip Hop: New Methodologies for New Times." *Urban Education* 50 (1): 31–51.

Durham, A., Cooper, B. C., and Morris, S. M. (2013). "The Stage Hip-Hop Feminism Built: A New Directions Essay." *Signs Journal of Women in Culture and Society* 38 (3): 721–737.

Eure, J. D., and Spady, J. G., eds. (1991). *Nation Conscious Rap: The Hip-Hop Vision.* New York: PC International Press.

Gilmore, R. W. (2007). *Golden Gulag: Prisons, Surplus, Crisis, and Opposition in Globalizing California.* Berkeley: University of California Press.

Jacobs-Huey, L. (2002). "The Natives Are Gazing and Talking Back: Reviewing the Problematics of Positionality, Voice, and Accountability among 'Native' Anthropologists." *American Anthropologist* 104 (3): 791–804.

Lindsey, T. B. (2014). "Let Me Blow Your Mind: Hip Hop Feminist Futures in Theory and Praxis." *Urban Education* 50 (1): 52–77.

Love, B. (2017). "A Ratchet Lens: Black Queer Youth, Agency, Hip Hop, and the Black Ratchet Imagination." *Educational Researcher* 46 (9): 539–547.

Madison, D. S. (2005). *Critical Ethnography: Methods, Ethics, and Performance.* Thousand Oaks, CA: SAGE.

Marsh, C. (2012). "Research Overview Hip Hop as Methodology: Ways of Knowing." *Canadian Journal of Communication* 37 (1): 193–203.

Meghelli, S. (2013). "Remixing the Historical Record: Revolutions in Hip Hop Historiography." *Western Journal of Black Studies* 37 (2): 94–102.

Pabón-Colón, J. N. (2017 Autumn). "Writin', Breakin', Beatboxin': Strategically Performing 'Women' in Hip-Hop." *Signs: Journal of Women in Culture and Society* 43 (1): 175–200.

Petchaur, E. (2009). "Framing and Reviewing Hip-Hop Education Research." *Review of Educational Research* 79 (2): 946–978.

Spady, J. G. (2013). "Mapping and Re-membering Hip Hop History, Hiphopography and African Diasporic History." *Western Journal of Black Studies* 37 (2): 126–157.

Spady, J. G., Dupres, S., and Lee, C. G. (1995). *Twisted Tales in the Hip Hop Streets of Philly.* Philadelphia: Black History Museum and Loh Publishers.

Spady, J. G., Lee, C. G., and Alim, H. S., eds. (1999). *Street Conscious Rap*. Philadelphia: Black History Museum and Loh Publishers.

Spady, J. G., Alim, H. S., and Meghelli, S. (2006). *The Global Cipha: Hip Hop Culture and Consciousness*. Philadelphia: Black History Museum.

Tuhiwai S., L. (1999). *Decolonizing Methodologies: Research and Indigenous Peoples*. London: Zed Books.

University of Southern California. (2014). "Check the Technique: Hip Hop as Methodology." Panel discussion. Annenberg School of Journalism and Communication, December 10. YouTube. https://www.youtube.com/watch?v=GFI9iWc2mno.

PART III

OVERSTANDING IDENTITIES IN HIP HOP STREETDANCE PRACTICES

CHAPTER 13

....

BREAKING IN MY HOUSE

Popular Dance, Gender Identities,
and Postracial Empathies

....

THOMAS F. DEFRANTZ

INTRODUCTION

....

DOES breaking belong within the forms of dance recognized as "house"? How did Hip Hop and house emerge as separate sorts of dance cultures among African Americans, Latinx folx, Asians, Native, and others, and how have they reconciled in contemporary global circumstances? What are some of the ways that gender and racial identities still function in considerations of Hip Hop and house dance? What are some of the important interstices of Hip Hop and house in academic discourses? What are some implications of race in the articulations of popular dance cultures and their circulations? Constructed as a listing of themes elaborated to performative effect, this chapter wonders at the possibilities to write into Black social dance as a rhythmic playing through words; words that might represent thinking-through-dancing as the source of a communal activity.

HOUSE FIRST

....

Dancing beyond spirit, outside of time, in the place of personal invention and rediscovery. To dance *house* is to cycle flow; it is to shore up rhythm in a run-on sentence of impulse and insight. **"In the beginning there was . . . House."** House as a groove and an attitude, an approach, a technique for dancing strong, dancing the self, dancing as communion. Deliverance.

House, a form of dance built from improvisation pulled from the spaces of minoritarian claiming of subjectivity in public dance. See, Black social dance has a complex history in relation to rhetorics of public and private, commodity and ex-pressivity. Our social dances were born in the slave quarters as public/private demonstrations of agency and group-individual formation. We can always note a con-nection to certain "tribal" dances from the continent, of course; movement patterns and approaches to creativity get mapped during infancy, and the "will to move" as a "will to power" never lets up, in terms of dance development. So Black social dances born in the USA bear family resemblances to certain dances of the continent now and so long ago, and as infants we are always in the presence of expressive rhythmic motion that constitutes dance. Yes, dance is learned body to body; and it is also learned toddler to child, adolescent to young adult. Black social dance practices persevere across genera-tions **because we believe in them** as having crucial capacity for expression, and for the renewal of possible social identities. As embodied practices, the dances remind us what we need to know about what came before.

Black social dance, though, is already public in its very naming; it arrives as some-thing Black by way of comparison to some other [white] norm (see DeFrantz 2019). To consider Black social dance, we travel through the eyes of the outsiders who experience it, not from infancy, and not from familial practice. These are the dances that led to the cakewalk and the eccentric dances of the 1920s; the burnished versions of steps and rhythmic patterns that always seem "fun" and "approachable," exciting and dynamic, available (see DeFrantz 2010a). Black social dance materializes as a public commodity, available to any who witness it regardless of the ethnic identity or race of the viewer. This has always been a problem in the study of Black social dance and, in particular for our purposes, house dancing. It seems private and illegible in some ways, but it is also fizzy, entertaining, and entirely of the public moment. What makes it Black? The people who used to dance it? Whose house is this really, anyway? Can we all just dance and get along, without noticing the coercion implicit in the public commodity that marks the calling forth of Black social dance?

House dance as a practice within Black social dance threads spiritual searching with of-the-body excitation and sharing through the group. As we consider its historical moment, we might understand that house grew up as a question for embodied crea-tive sharing. It asks, and answers: what sort of dance practice could gather durational responses to music, and work in the crucible of spirit and group? How could people throw down together, sweat, commune, shout, and share through physical gesture? What could it be to share joy and a turn toward happiness through dancing?

House didn't set out to be a "battle" form—all of that happened later, in response to a world that made so little room for dance as a valued, intergenerational social practice. House emerged back in the 1970s, as its own gathering pool for dancers alongside Hip Hop, and in response to the horrid backlash to civil rights legislations and seeming-gains for People of Color in the United States. And it did, indeed, grow up in the USA amid the difficult afterlives of slavery, among the economic regressions that led to pri-vatization and continued miseries for those not already plugged into systems of wealth and middle-class aspiration.

When house began to become itself, it responded to its surroundings of Hip Hop and its predecessors of disco and funk.

DISCO NEVER SUCKED,

... but its economic aspirational characteristics confused many dancers of the diaspora. When disco came onto the scene, after civil rights movement machinations had given rise to Black power dances, it offered a crucial site of interracial correspondence (see DeFrantz 2010(b). Disco allowed for large white, Asian, Native, and Latinx presence in its rendering of Black style available to the masses. Disco glides and bounces, and even when it throbs and thrusts it means no harm to the imaginary smooth politics of social integration. Studio 54 as a beacon of partying communal hope—for those who could get past the doormen. Disco dances of the good life, outside racialized differentiation; disco predicts Black dance as a premeditated availability, compliant in its movement politic rather than resistant, and reliant on costume to differentiate gender more than actual movement vocabularies. Disco dancing could be narrated as the bleached version of house, making room for men and women to move as one in coupled alignment or simple line dances that identified, and consolidated—however briefly—the group.

House dancing, like the eccentric dances of the 1920s, emerged as a solo form. Yes, it comes alongside and from disco, but to be practiced as dance done one near the next. No more couples, no more groups in unison. House came forward as a claiming of rampant individuality.

Disco wondered what it would be like if Black social dance was shared across races and classes; if it could arrive available for rich and poor: middle-class, luxury-laden, working-class, or impoverished. Disco tried to be the bridge form of Black popular music that would allow itself to be hybrid and available to white and ultra-commodified input from its first reckonings. Leaning into its ersatz sensibility, it gathered a gliding-across-the-floor hi-hat backbeat as its foundational rhythmic concept. Carefully orchestrated symphonic strings bled harmonies of triumph atop grooving bass lines, with horn ensembles offering accents that open out toward a promise of wondrous future prosperities. Disco songs tended to tell stories of complicated work lives that could be set aside on the dance floor. "Good Times," "I Will Survive," "Everybody Dance." Work might have been a backdrop container for everyone's desire to release through music and dance, and disco answered with a possibility for gay and straight Black, white, Asian, Latinx, and Native recovery through shared sweaty fun that really didn't need to be more than its own emergence and dispersal. Hollywood movies featured disco prominently—*Car Wash*, *Thank God It's Friday*, and, most famously, *Saturday Night Fever*—and the cinematic promise of a sensual social dance available to all enjoyed its shiny moment on a world stage.

But this was music and dance born of the sound studio and the dance studio more than from the call-and-response among local musicians and dancers in the Black neighborhoods that typically produce Black dances. The backlash to disco came from many sides. Whites who resisted the possibility of an interracial, sexually open mode of fundamentally Black expression began campaigns to disavow the form. Black artists who wanted to keep Black music Black moved away from the strange assemblies of disco music that minimized spontaneity or recourse to Spirit as a technology of performance. Disco explored a smoothness of affect within its rhythmic play that seemed simplistic to some artists, and its desire to connect people across vectors of identity failed to reinforce the centrality of Black expression that inspired its sounds and moves. Disco emerged in a sort of mixed-race aspirational space that aspired to connect people through hybrid assemblies, but that aspiration didn't last, and we are hard-pressed to identify other genres of Black social dance that allowed this significant multi-identity presence. The aspiration to work among each other across race in an imaginary post-race, in order to create Black music and dance, surely didn't last.

Before Disco We Found the Funk

Funk not only cures, it abcures.[1] Meaning: funk played its politics out in the world where we could all see them. Funk became one of the first forms of Black social dance that arrived with an explicitly resistant physical politic, one that said, "Resolve to resist, make some physical noise, and recognize your enlivened beauty as an agent of social change in motion" (see DeFrantz 2012).

Funk emerged from the soulful harmonic gestures of R & B but explored the raucous possibilities of bass-heavy rhythmic propulsion as its guiding method. Funk tended toward an unapologetic intensity of Blackness as a nodule of intertwined political and aesthetic imperatives of motion to its musicians and dancers. Funk was serious, intentional, and decidedly nonassimilationist. Where disco assumed that its dancers would be a mixed-race crowd gathering to imagine a shared future of some sort of luxury, funk sought Black life as we know it **now** as its raison d'etre. Funk took seriously its ability to structure Black social dances that could inspire hybrid political identities, but identities steeped in all manner of Black social life. Funk artists worked in Afrofuturist assembly *avant la lettre*; staging extraterrestrial meetings of Black Native American cyborgs; arriving in spaceships to sing songs about funk's capacities and requirements. Dancing to funk, people understood a politicized group identity laid bare by the outrageousness of the music and its affect. In return, funk dancing arrived as vigorous, sweaty, get-down motions that were hard to characterize, name, or classify. Funk dancers didn't produce a large swath of named dances—although neither disco nor house would manage this either in their first arrivals—and, rather, tended to elaborate on the rhythmic implications of the live funk band.[2] And funk music was best experienced live. While mass popularity may have been available to funk musicians as they appeared on television, funk's musical integrity was surely bound up in its defiant Blackness, one "proud" and "loud" enough to exceed prerecorded television appearances. While disco was rarely played live in a manner that sounded like its records—its combination of string musicians with horn musicians and a rhythm section preempted its liveness in most settings—funk bands could be small, medium sized, or large and still *make it funky.*

Funk recordings from the 1960s and 1970s help us understand the energetic capaciousness of the idiom. Inevitably, recordings sound raw and include musical "mistakes;" often crowds of responding listeners are included cheering the musicians forward. Funk recordings resist the stringent radio requirements for three-minute songs that could be played in rotation, focusing instead on seven- or twelve- or fifteen-minute elaborations of rhythm and harmony that could inspire dancing out of time. Funk established itself as a pointed alternative to the assimilation-minded efforts of both disco and Black pop music. Directed explicitly to Black audiences, funk offered a muscular genre of playful, expressive resistance.

Twinned, disco and funk provided the platforms for house and Hip Hop. Funk arrived before disco, drawing on R & B that seemed fairly happy with its gendered norms of boys singing about girls they liked and women singing about men they longed for, or who had done them wrong. But funk pushed outward the normative narratives of heterosexual courtship with its aliens and monsters; gender-ambiguous presenting Black hipster figures who were usually more concerned with their own eccentricities and the dancing of the group than with encounters of intimacy. (Of course, an important tradition of funk ballads stress intimate heterosexualized encounters among men and women in counterpoint to the prevalent dance grooves). Disco conceived sexuality as a movable target, aligning itself with the sexual liberation of an earlier generation. Disco offered welcome attendance to gay presence and a smiling nod to bisexuality as a feature of the abundant, future-forward "good life."

In this rendering of gender and sexualized identities mapped onto musical/dance genres, we can understand how the polyamorous sensibilities of disco might lead more gracefully toward house, while the masculinist brashness of funk tilted toward the achievements of Hip Hop. These tiltings are speculative interventions, borne of my own grand reductions of myriad creative practices and achievements. Still, the characterizations can help us understand how assumptions of gendered identities can envelop the ways that people understand music/dance genres to operate, and how people make choices to move inside these different sorts of sounds according to their moods, desires, and needs. House arrived as a space of open sexualities, to be danced forward in joyful diversity; Hip Hop arrived to answer the need for palpable masculinities—male, female, and in-between—that would demonstrate Black identities in urgent, forceful, take-no-prisoners performances.

Black Popular Culture Opens
to the World

It produces structures of group affinity and possibility that endure. Black popular culture leads global interests in expressive cultures: jazz, Hip Hop, Black style and swagger, Black feminist resistance, and the articulation of **sass**, as in, *Talk to the Hand. I woke up* *like this.* These playful modes of expression contain the roots of human survival in unabashedly creative responses to the savagery of life pressurized by capitalism.

Black popular culture is hugely important to the world. This is why we continue to crave the documentaries about the lives of Hip Hop pioneers: **Mr. Wave** and **All the Ladies Say!** among many other dance artists who deserve the focused attention of documentary excavation (Wesley and Bullock 2015; Garcia 2010). The stories of the lives of these professional artists of color: their trials and achievements, their ruminations and self-discoveries, and, especially, their prescriptions for our general betterment all speak to our intuitive sense that Black culture will save us all, as it routinely manages to save its best practitioners from lives otherwise far too ordinary. And it isn't only the Hip Hop pioneers we want to hear from in this regard; biographical narratives of early jazz musicians, of many internationally renowned athletes, of ministers in the Black church and self-help gurus, and a smattering of politicians following in the footsteps of Booker T. Washington offer the "up by the bootstraps" narratives that represent Black survival, a survival most unlikely given the rage enacted against Black presence in the world. Young people of any ethnic location are drawn to stories of impossible Black accomplishment exactly because it seems unimaginable and in direct relationship to a degenerate, attendant assumption of Black death. Young people think, "If Mr. Wave had a moment of success, against all odds and every expectation of his demise like that of Mike Brown or Trayvon Martin, well, if Mr. Wave can do something, then surely I can too." This patronizing logic replenishes itself again and again. And, yet, these really are our stories of resistance, of brief triumph over the machine that would have our young men, women, and trans children dead and buried before they reach adulthood.

So, we need a house. A house of safety, a place where most anything goes, a place to be ourselves as fully as possible and without social censure. Our house can't be our father's house, with its rules and its anxieties about failures of the past; so Booker T. Washington doesn't really have a place here. And it can't be our mother's house, with its expectations and constant disappointments, tied to the birth canals that set us flowin' but unsure if our queer desires are god-fearing enough to be celebrated. We need to build our own house, a place that stands outside of the birth familial, to represent the chosen familiars. My play brothers and sisters who are more than family to me. My play mother who allows me to be as nelly and queer as I need to this day and tomorrow; my play father who reminds me to reach higher and trust in a welcoming spiritual transcendence. This is the **house that jack built**, a house of open opportunities, physical explorations, and moves upon moves that test boundaries of identity, gender, sexuality, or faith. We built this house as a refuge and a place of triage. We go into the deep house, where we can explore **what it might be to be free**.

Like every invention of Black popular culture, our house opens out to the world. It welcomes all, even those who don't understand its particularities or its ambitions. It welcomes those who cannot fathom the disavowal at its root. It makes space for queers of every stripe, for wealthy legacy folx alongside street kids hustling a bed to sleep in two weeks at a time. House presumes that all of us are invited inside as celebrants; the space is open for us to engage. House asks only for our belief in its possibility and its physical truth: dancing outside of our body toward the communal transcendence of spirit.

In this, house reveals its composite assembly of aspects of disco and funk. Like disco, house makes space for sexual disidentifications; for polyamorous pursuit of soulful expression unbound by gender. Like funk, house demands a full-bodied dancing that reaches beyond normative shapes or predetermined dance steps. House stirs between the genres to imagine even more openness: mixing beyond measure, dancing toward the spirit house. But what about Hip Hop?

"The Gangs Gave Way to Hip Hop"

We let it be said again and again: the gangs produced the art form. This recurrent narrative sets Hip Hop up as a sort of social project, a creative response to ridiculous social circumstances constantly meted onto the lives of people of color. Of course, there's a problem with this narrative that assumes "new art" might be invented without relationship to previous idioms of Black creativity and craft. The gangs didn't come from nowhere, and Hip Hop is entangled with Black creative desires. Is Hip Hop only to be narrated in terms of a constantly criminalized childhood lack?[3] In this telling, Hip Hop is conceived as a hypermasculine stand-in for the presumably inevitable posturing, fighting, and death that are to "naturally" accompany young Black and Brown life in the ghetto. This narration is very popular; Afro-pessimists rejoice. Black artists make something from nothing. In this common telling of Hip Hop, the violence of the streets—naturalized here as part of living without access to resources—gives way to the arts of the streets: style, writing, rapping, and dancing (yes, b-boying is dancing); musical creativity. The story that the original b-boys/b-girls and rappers are always already former gang members adds to the sense of Hip Hop belonging to the streets, outside of the house. Hip Hop belongs to the harsh hypermasculine spaces of urban exposure, asserting brash political resistance as a physical stance. Hip Hop dance forms cycle aggressive propulsive energy, physical dynamism that must be visible and palpable in execution. Stand and prove; go hard or go home. We know we need this genre, because everyone isn't comfortable in the intimate spaces of a house. Some of us do want to be *outside* where emotional logics can capitulate to survivalist action. The streets force us to compete. In the house we might express. On the streets, we proclaim.

But maybe it is because Hip Hop thrives in the refinement of gesture, as in the fillips of exactitude that produce b-girling or aerosol art, that we're so willing to put gang rhetoric above artistic impulse. It gives us a way to think *differently* about Hip Hop and its emergence, as if it arrives **special**. Black culture has always produced incredible artistry; the story of Hip Hop exceptionalism—as if Black culture had suddenly stopped needing art practice to recognize itself in the age of Reagan—well, this is a story that allows us to pay props to the founders. Hip Hop founders arrived unlike the heroes and heroines of, say, ragtime music, who figured out how Black settings of marches and waltzes could be the new dance music for the generation. Those musicians were able to move into lives as artists, without constant reference to their childhoods of social lack and disenfranchisement. Of course, at that time, all Black lives were essentially bounded by racist disavowal. But what sorts of future trajectories were available to the Black and Brown kids of the Bronx who founded Hip Hop style? Was it possible for them to become artists? No, they had to be confined to the lives of the streets. Hip Hop emerged in its largest international popularity tied to Reaganomics; it is the first form of Black popular culture entirely in lockstep with neoliberal capitalism. So Hip Hop needs a narrative that places it outside of previous forms of Black artistry; this becomes its brand. It's not as though our children don't always produce awesome, phat, chill forms of performance; it's that this particular generation of young artists aligned itself with the expectations of the 1980s marketplaces. Time to get paid. The branding of the streets as teachers—as opposed to the Motown acknowledgment of middle-school music programs and musical education as the basis for that company's musical innovations—allows Hip Hop to stay raw, fresh, divergent, outlaw.[4] The outlaw brand costs. Motown produced Diana Ross and Michael Jackson, celebrities who understood their profession to be entertainment. Hip Hop produced Biggy and Tupac; both dead, murdered young and in public. Outlaws as entertainers. Queen Latifah transformed; she left some of the youthful pugnaciousness aside. She hosted a talk show for a time. Is she hip hop? Of the street? What do we do with her, or with Ice-T as an actor on the television show *Law and Order*? Wait, he plays a sort of outlaw cop, his credentials somewhat intact. But Latifah? The Cover Girl? Second generation, not one of the originals. The mythology repeats: the originals were all gang members; all grew up in the street. Outside the house.

This narrative restricts access; it polices the boundaries of early Hip Hop. Only the outlaw boyz or the ride-or-die-b*tches are to be considered the originals, and their lack of access to resources confirms their status of the streets. This narrative *masculinizes* Hip Hop and its mythical pasts; it scrubs away the queer creativities at the heart of all artistic innovation. Check it: artists *have* to think beyond normative arrangements of race, gender, sexuality, class, and the like; the best artists move way beyond white supremacy and recitations of heteronormativity to fashion the new beats and moves that can inspire a generation. The original Hip Hop artists developed their *mad skillz* by drawing on their creative intuitions and resisting the paradoxes of Black and Brown life. They practiced resistance through their creative actions. Which were permeated by assessments of taste, value, affect, and felicity. So while Hip Hop arrived **hard** it also arrived within the creative corridors of imagination; of hearing and moving beyond what already had been toward an unknowable future sound. The artists of Hip Hop had relationships to the gangs, but the gangs didn't produce Hip Hop. Artistic innovation can take credit where that credit is surely due. Let me try to say it another way. Young people who discovered their capacities as artists for the people created Hip Hop among and for each other. Not only or mostly among and for "the gangs." But for the promise of a future emboldened by creativity.

WHITE HOUSE

It just doesn't sound right. It sounds just too hard.

White Hip Hop, we know. "Jump Around!" "Hey, Ladies!" "Hi! My name is . . . ." We might love it or abhor it, but it keeps coming, and by now, it is a thing. Aesop Rock, Lady Sovereign, Macklemore, Machine Gun Kelly, and on and on and on.

But white house? Sigh. How did house make its turn toward variegation, from a Black mode of dancing toward deliverance to the ridiculous subcategories and genres that mark the pleasure zones of white fanboy delimitations? Acid house, deep house, tribal house, happy house, diva house, funky house, old schoolhouse. . . A dizzying array of possibilities, each deciding what can and can't belong within its assembly. These divisions of house came amid the opening outward of house toward white DJs and producers, to musicians who felt the call of house but didn't have access to the deep sexual cut that produced Black peals of pain and New World dance musics (Moten 2003). Parceling house into tiny bits of beats-per-minute assessment, or assemblages that didn't need to reference Black life in any particular manner allowed house to drift toward techno, or rave, or punk musics. As with trap music in the 2020s, which has at least two distinct soundings—one Black and one white—house has endured distension that allows for a bleaching of its soul.

House had emerged as a pansexual, open spirit, multiracial Black gathering space. The Black part of its foundation comes from Black church practice. House builds on Black ministries of word, song, and dance, ecstatic performances that operate outside of normative concerns of time or appropriateness of gesture. Speaking in tongues and dancing in unexpected flow, house emphatically secularizes the performative addresses of Black church practices. Like Black church procedures, house is spiritually grounded and available to any who seek its practices and teachings. And it emerges in relationship to the specialness of Black American living and loving, improvising in the tempo of emergency that underscores Black gesture.

Breaking is similarly available to all, but its historical narratives have contested racialized imperatives that make it continue to feel Black and Brown first, and others come later. Who can be Hip Hop? We like to say, "One love, live it, and you are it." But, well, you know. "Hi, my name is . . ."—well, not so much anymore. Hip hop scholarship tends to call colored folks to the front of the historical line, for a change. Dancers might claim some sort of "freedom from race" as they practice, but, well, you know. #Black Lives Matter.

We consistently undervalue Latinx contributions to the foundation of Hip Hop's physicalities, even as we wanted the Hip Hop nation to emerge free of racial identifications. This freedom from race that Hip Hop wanted in the world didn't really happen, though, because Hip Hop isn't actually the world, but it is in the world, and the world is very hung up on race. Race is still The National Thing that, by 2022, has become the world thing. It's hard to talk about race. Let's talk about sex.

LET'S TALK ABOUT SEX

Let's go back to the need for form and genre, and the need to create community. Hip Hop and house each turn toward sex and sexuality as expressive subjects foundational to their existence. This matters, especially, since Black communities don't much like to talk about sex or sexuality. We're okay with the open secrets of the gay church choirs and gay pastors, lesbian celebrity talk show hosts and newscasters, closeted civil rights leaders and organizers. But what's ever been gained by talking about Black Sex in the publics of the United States? Yet and still, Hip Hop gave us ways to mainstream those conversations, and house gave us spaces to explore moving through myriad sexualities in danced commons.

But let's take it back yet again. The rhetorics of Hip Hop performance can be easily aligned with African American creative practices that stretch from blues and jazz traditions of the early twentieth-century (DeFrantz, 2006). The importance of bragging as a trope of performance crosses from the emcee's art to the movements of the dancer. Surprising the gathered witnesses with an improbable and tasty rhyme or gesture supports the ability of the artist to work successfully in this idiom. The ability of the performer to signify on someone else's effort operates as both an honoring and a challenge to excel. If you can bite someone else's style, then maybe their style wasn't strong enough to be distinctive in the first place. Hip Hop and breaking's gathered witnesses celebrate the unexpected twists that amaze the group with brashness and wit.

Bragging about sex offers a fairly direct route to notoriety, so we can't be surprised that so many rappers focus on sexual prowess in their performances. And because most emcees and b-girls are young people, they also might be more concerned with sex as an end in and of itself than older artists. But Hip Hop created the shift that allowed public circulation of explicit, intensely sexualized lyrics in mainstream media. In its battle formations, breaking turned first toward sexual innuendo as a physical rhetorical stance. As technologies of mass distribution advanced through ubiquitous digital files, rhyming and dancing that might have been contained within closed Black spaces in previous generations became fodder for global markets. We note with wry attention that the rampant sexualization of Black and Brown bodies that Hip Hop heralded also fit into white supremacist thinking about Black degeneracy. Hip Hop couldn't have it both ways: it wasn't able to operate as an expressive opening to important public conversations about sex while resisting a further collapse of sexual stereotypes for Black and Brown people. Hip Hop seemed to confirm that people of color explored sex with a too-voracious appetite. In this modeling, yet again, Black expressive cultures were characterized by outsiders as patently immoral and lascivious, without other redeeming artistic consequence.

In terms of physical embodiment, this meant the mass media revelation of easily-sexualized movements came forward via breaking. Early b-boys and b-girls might have resisted this tendency, to focus on demonstrations of strength and creativity more akin to mixed martial arts. But their battles tended toward the easy gestures of erotic innuendo, and films like *Beat Street* (1984) and *Flashdance* (1983) made breaking somewhat "sexy" for an inexperienced audience (DeFrantz 2014). House dancing always made more room for the danced portrayal of sexual and gender diversity, but note that both Hip Hop and house rely on mainstream portrayals of "femme" to punctuate movement sequences, whether as deprecation or affirmation. A femme flounce lives in both forms, to be called upon in moments of rhetorical crisis that need representational heat.

Dancing is not sex, and any dancer understands that being engaged in the process of crafting a sequence as a b-girl or expressing through a series of house movements is seldom like an intimate encounter with a lover. Yet, as we still invest in the Puritanical values surrounding sexual practices, and as we are still in the presence of rampant misogyny as young men learn to subjugate young women at every turn, the sex-positive aspect of Hip Hop continues to be a titillating liability to its presence in the world.

The Neoliberal Turn Impacts Us All

So let's dig into the problem again: the problem of neoliberal agency, assumptions of freedom, and the double bind of needing commerce but wanting to hold back cultural treasures so that they might best work for cultural insiders.

Monetizing Black creativity has been an ongoing site of exploitation, raising any number of questions and concerns of appropriation and appropriateness. Are the creative expressions of Black and Brown youth always considered to be fair game for any number of white dancers? What do we make of Asian interests in Black dance and Black style? Does breaking follow the Cakewalk, the Charleston, and the Lindy Hop as a trending form of expression that should be made available to any dancer under any circumstance who seeks to enjoy its practicing? Does house dancing also require a mixed-race audience and participation base? Why do white people tend to feel "free" when they work inside Black expressive idioms, including breaking and house?

Black modes of expressive culture have been recurrently called upon to generate a danced rhetoric of freedom in terms of an easy, appealing musicality-in-motion that is apparently endemic to the conditions of Black life (DeFrantz 2012). The challenges of this sort of creative exchange are many. Freedom inside Black modes of dance arrives surrounded by Black fugitivity, Black death, and the impossibilities of Black stability in the mainstream American social world. The elusiveness of Black freedom generates a sort of taboo impossibility that attracts dancers and musicians eager to these forms of expression. In some ways, monetizing access to Black expressive cultures creates a demand for the continuations of Black disavowal. For too many, Hip Hop seems to have been generated by lack, abjection, and disavowal.

While Black dance and music are easily spreadable, a competent understanding of the historical actions that have produced Black identity are almost entirely absent from global discourses of creativity. Meaning that most people who engage breaking or house—who would be people who claim identities that are not Black or Latinx—have little understanding of Black life in the context of the United States that produced these forms of expression. This lack of awareness creates an all-consuming awkwardness that separates Black participation in these forms from the dancing of others. For most Black and Latinx people of the United States, Hip Hop emerged as a youthful refusal of old-men white hegemonies and patriarchies that intended to constrain and restrict Black possibility (Rose, 1994). House emerged as a pansexual space of danced deliverance with reference to the Spirit houses of New World religious practices. These conceptual roots were easily displaced as the forms gained their fizzy attractiveness for global audiences.

As these forms became monetized, the ability to profit on poverty, lack, and rampantly sexualized presentations was not lost on cultural outsiders who saw breaking and house only as mediated television events. Mass distribution of aspects of Black life—in music videos or recordings of house music—encouraged a detached, pleasure-forward sensibility that effectively undermined how outsiders understood the need for social supports for Black people. Too many Hip Hop headz and house dancers come to appreciate only the fun, freeing possibilities of these crucial forms of expression, without understanding the complex contexts for Black expressive culture.

This dissonance of encounter with Black life leads to the awkward encounters that place whites at odds with Black people engaged in these forms of Black expression. Too often, uninitiated dancers think little of how Hip Hop or house attend to the vagaries of Black indeterminacy. It isn't that these forms are not available to any who seek their possibilities. Rather, it's that too many people understand only a tiny bit of these possibilities, and focus on the opportunity to be crass and seemingly "free" of the binds of everyday lives.

But Black people tend to be underresourced and underpaid by the markets that trade our creative expressions. The neoliberal impulse to privatize property and services creeps into the space of music and dance, encouraging artists to claim unique iterations of what are essential communal sounds and moves. Maybe this is part of how we have so many of our dance elders in Hip Hop claiming their versions of dance as the originary moment, as though dance could actually be something like real estate: owned, disciplined, bordered, exclusionary. To me, this seems like trying to claim a patent on joy. And this is the trouble: Black artists create structures of joy but have little access to the market share in any realm related to that creativity. Black joy is always bound up in Black disavowal, so the freedoms that it produces are tempered by their temporariness and impossibilities. What are we to do? Go hard or go home?

Go home. Go to the house. In the house we can maybe *be* momentarily? We can maybe resist the harsh insistence on *capital* and *value* as the mode of understanding achievement? House dancing, in and of itself, means to confirm an outside to market subjugation. While breaking takes on the marketplace with its physically resistant stance. But of course, it's never so simple as that. We dance in relationship to a politic already in motion; in terms of Black creativity, those relationships are ever-shifting, never fair, and grossly asymmetrical.

It makes me wanna shake all over.

NERVOUS SYSTEMS

In the beginning. The nervous system of house is all flow and continuity; pauses amid circles and eddies of movement that emerge in response to an imagining outward toward spirit. Releasing energy through a song of the body, a gasping breath outward toward curving lines and their intersections and interruptions. Spin, turn, dip, and connect the dots as part of continual motions of exhalation. No holding back; a cycling through and around toward deliverance. The nervous system is encouraged to continue through gestures, watery systems of flow and tiny sparklings that speak to an eternal tide of energy in motion. The nervous system of breaking is all stops and starts: holding and clenching, controlling and exploding. Dancing in a variety of Hip Hop modes, we explode outward, fists clenched when locking and waacking; bodies taut when popping and uprocking. In the six-step, even as energy is deployed powerfully, it is the attack and velocity of gesture that matter most. A strong six-step moves dancers into the power moves and spins that define the form. Hitting hard and holding a freeze at the end of a sequence, we contain energy to affirm our ability to hold space, to control time, to grab on to the *right now*. Dancing, these forms call for nearly opposite emotional approaches. The show of strength versus the exploration of spirit. Of course, these forms of physical address do not exclude each other, and spirit calls on strength just as strength might revel in spiritual support. But breaking and house call on divergent addresses of energy and execution. To break: have a plan; practice regularly; demonstrate strength and ability. Stand and prove; go hard or go home; show out. To dance house: question and explore; cycle through emotion and change; hesitate and pause, switch up the beat; feel a possibility and dance through toward tomorrow. Extend time; revel in the fluids of sweat and its circulations.

Imagining these speculative nervous systems for dancing, we can appreciate how the forms have been cast into gendered roles in the popular imaginaries. Masculine breaking: all aggressive and showing strength, strong and vital with angular, hard-edged energy. Feminine house: mostly as a matter of distinction from Hip Hop; powerful and mysterious with curvaceous, shape-shifting pluralities of energy. In this binary, the feminine might be much more interesting, unusual, adaptable, and surprising. But then, the many valences of femme from softness through strength might often seem more vibrant than the opacities of masculinity that seldom admit care.

Indeed, breaking quickly transformed from its expressive roots to emerge as a form of stylized combat. Like other forms of Black music/dance, the earliest inventions in breaking were surely designed to demonstrate physical capacity in response to the emerging DJ-mixing sounds. But breaking almost immediately took on a competitive aspect in New York, and a demonstration aspect in Los Angeles; each mode concerned with spectatorship and the ways that dancers were viewed by others. House dancing grew up without a sense of "needing to be seen." Its collection of movements expressed toward the end of group communion rather than demonstration or competitive triumphs.

This history of distinctive beginnings makes the twenty-first-century house dance battles all the more interesting and unusual in their execution. While Hip Hop and house each began as physical expression without an inherent necessity for battling, breaking moved quickly toward the possibilities of danced combat, familiar in histories of tap dance and cakewalking. Breaking seemed to be ideally suited to offer strategic gestures of resistance to the uncaring, disinterested worlds that surrounded young people of color. Its fast repurposing as a form of danced group combat made sense, given the circumstances that encouraged dancing for young people of color in the 1970s, and under the continued economic disavowals of the 1980s.

House dancing, though, might have no natural purpose as a battle form. The twenty-first-century predilection for dance as demonstration and competition aligns with the commerce-controlled media-saturated environments of today. House grew up as a cycling of energy outward and through; its terms of performance in sites of assembly for queer people of color resisted its weaponization and the implications that some might be better than others in a dance off. House went for decades without any particular demonstration or competitive mode. The craving for Black dance as a spectacle and as a commodity that can be evaluated, taught, and redistributed has forced house dancing into a mirror of itself. House emerged to provide sanctuary for queers of color as an embodied musicality that resisted the governing eyes of the heteronormative state. Its redefinition as a form of dance taught in studios and engaged in battles forces it into a very different landscape, one more aligned with the bullying cultures of the twenty-first century and the assumption that there are always winners and losers.

But maybe house dancing didn't necessarily want that. Maybe it didn't emerge in order to be witnessed by immobile dancers, scrutinizing its contents. The infusion of Hip Hop's imperatives as a masculinist competitive form have transformed house. By 2022, house dancing might easily seem to be breaking without floorwork, six-steps, or power moves, but with all of the flash and finish of any competitive dance form designed to be watched and admired from afar.

Hip Hop Dance Scholarship

Black dancing seldom emerges as a solo practice. The best dancers—who would be the people most invested in the varied possibilities of dancing—bring others along with them as they dance. Dancing with cousin Myrtle, Uncle Andre, an old boyfriend, my girl Shirley. The memories of their gestures made manifest, now, through my body, or maybe in the way they make me feel, now, thinking and moving in reflection on them. To "bring the noise" is to honor the ancestors, yes, to reference the sounds from before and their ensemble, vetted now through this performance and this dance. We bring the noize and bring the people with us as we dance, whether they are there in physical body or not.

So, Black dancing is not a solo practice but an invitation to share physical expression *among*. Among others in the room, yes, but also among those in the memories. We dance to remember, and also to forget. We work in these divergent directions simultaneously.

So, yes, the dance makes reference to the movements of the last generations. Funk and disco are referenced in house dancing, and they become foundational approaches to breaking. But the new elaborations of older forms also intend to help us imagine forward; to leave behind the traumas and impossibilities of our Black pasts. We dance to create new potentials for future.

This line of truism puts Hip Hop dance scholarship into a funny bind. On one hand, scholarship intends to stabilize the field, to bring focused attention to its practices and methods, techniques and innovations. To do this, and to honor the politics of citation that surround scholarship as a practice, researchers connect the dances to historical events and eras, to older dances and social events that produce context for gestural expression. Some scholars connect Hip Hop dance to forms practiced in the Caribbean or South America, and, yes, floorwork is surely related to capoeira in some ways.

But dance is also a creative embodied reckoning with futurity, and a physical demonstration of moving *beyond*. Moving beyond language and outside linguistic rhetorics through places of intuition and emotion not bound by responsibilities to sensical discourse. Dance *is*, of and for itself and its emergence; it doesn't have to answer to histories or disavowals. But it probably does. It doesn't have to resist normative gestures or repeating stereotypical assumptions. But it often does. It doesn't have to push a person beyond their own sense of themselves, into motions that surprise and delight them in their very production. But it usually does.

Dance usually opens unexpected, intuitive spaces of creative invention. It arrives fizzy and unlikely. Scholarship that stabilizes this sort of arrival also reduces it; flattens it, captures it and tames it. In writing the dance down, and tethering it to all manner of literary flourish, we might depreciate its potentials. Dancing operates outside the logics of literary discourse. Scholarship is not so lucky and tends to need its grounding devices to be found in the citations of ideas from others.

What's a dance researcher to do? Writing performatively, we might approach the essences of how dance practice feels; the capaciousness of house, relocated into run-on sentences with made-up words that glow with the promise of spiritual deliverance. We can write **hard** toward breaking's powerful dynamisms; structuring phrases with authoritarian, take-no-prisoners slay-fullness. Ultimately, though, the writing pales in relation to the body in motion.

But this probably shouldn't discourage us from producing scholarship and literary writing about house and breaking. Maybe we can write toward the tiny adjustments of energy and encounter that produce recognizable differences, and think outward from those noticings toward speculative assessments of moving and its implications. We can begin to account for house dancing and its divergence from Hip Hop gestures in motivation and effect, and characterize different possibilities made manifest in these danced forms of expression and address. We can tell stories about how we danced, when and where, and what our shared recalling of those gestures means to us now that we aren't dancing.

Maybe what we needn't do, though, is try to fix these dances by overdefining them, policing them, or restricting them. Black dancing tends to emerge not as a collection of steps, but rather as approaches to moving. We can surely characterize the approach, the kinds of relationships between sound and gesture that coalesce in music and dance forms, emerging amid each other to satisfy the needs of their participants. The dancing will not be denied.

There are far fewer scholarly explications of house dancing as a practice; fewer ethnographic studies than those that arrive consistently for breaking or Hip Hop musicality. House seems to thrive in its somewhat-obscurity as an academic object. House seems to know that it doesn't need scholarly explication to continue its effort to provide solace and motion to those who need it. When Hip Hop movements appear inside of house dancing, it reminds us of a world bound by strengths and dissent, resistance and fashioning toward the group. Hip Hop places house back in the world.

So breaking belongs in my house, so long as it helps me express in the moment. So long as it expands my creative gesture toward something else, so long as it adds to my tactics of enlivening the motions among us. Hip Hop might push house toward its prevalent competition idioms: by 2022 we see all manner of house dance competitions staged by government arts programs and corporations all over the world.[5] But house wants to remind us, somehow, that movement and sound can combine to explore an open mesh of possibilities, moving outward from sexuality, gender presentation, and racial identity, at least, to wonder at the world in continuous motion toward a shared communion of danced deliverance.

I *feel* for you, House. Gratitude. Honor, made manifest through gesture, and a possibility of Black Joy. To House!

NOTES

1. George Duke's "Reach for It," on the album *Reach For It*, Epic Records, 1977.
2. Mass-produced fad dances like "The Funky Chicken" of "The Funky Penguin" stabilized an accessible patterning of motion and allowed some Black artists a moment of celebrity and compensation. These sorts of dances continued to circulate as gathering notions for dancers curious about funk. Of course, these sorts of dances were engineered to satisfy a vaguely stable construction of musicality, rather than to allow Black people to express in unexpected physical manner, as at the heart of funk dancing.
3. See Aprahamian (2019) for an alternative version of this critical rendering toward how Hip Hop is traditionally narrated.
4. See Early (1995) for elaborations on the importance of the public school education system on the developments of Motown.
5. As example, Summer Dance Forever is a festival in Amsterdam that promises an international dance battle where the best of the international dancers want to participate, and it takes place every year. This "Mother of all Forever battles" attracts hundreds

of dancers each year from the Netherlands and abroad. See https://www.summerdance forever.com. Red Bull produces an annual streetdance competition event that includes house. See Red Bull Dance Your Style USA, https://www.redbull.com/us-en/events/red-bull-dance-your-style-usa.

References

Aprahamian, S. (2019). "Hip-Hop, Gangs, and the Criminalization of African American Culture: A Critical Appraisal of 'Yes Y'All.'" *Journal of Black Studies* 50 (3): 298–315.

DeFrantz, T. F. (2006). "Hip Hop Sexualities." In *Handbook of the New Sexuality Studies*, edited by S. Seidman, C. Meeks, and N. Fischer, 303–308. New York: Routledge.

DeFrantz, T. F. (2010a) "Popular Dances of the 1920s and Early '30s: From Animal Dance Crazes to the Lindy Hop." In *Ain't Nothing Like the Real Thing: How the Apollo Theater Shaped American Entertainment*, edited by R. Carlin and K. Holman Conwill, 66–70 and 182–186. Washington, DC: Smithsonian Books.

DeFrantz, T. F. (2010b). "Popular African American Dance of the 1950s and '60s." In *Ain't Nothing Like the Real Thing: How the Apollo Theater Shaped American Entertainment*, edited by R. Carlin and K. Holman Conwill, 182–186. Washington, DC: Smithsonian Books.

DeFrantz, T. F. (2012). "Unchecked Popularity: Neoliberal Circulations of Black Social Dance." In *Neoliberalism and Global Theatres: Performance Permutations*, edited by L. Nielson and P. Ybarra, 128–140. London: Palgrave Macmillan.

DeFrantz, T. F. (2014). "Hip Hop in Hollywood: Encounter, Community, Resistance." In *The Oxford Handbook of Dance and the Popular Screen*, edited by M. Blanco-Borelli, 113–131. New York: Oxford University Press.

DeFrantz, T. F. (2019) "What Is Black Dance? What Can It Do?" In *Thinking Through Theatre and Performance*, edited by M. Bleeker, A. Kear, J. Kelleher, and H. Roms, 87–99. London: Methuen Drama.

Early, G. (1995). *One Nation under a Groove: Motown and American Culture*. Hopewell, NJ: Ecco Press.

Garcia, A., dir. (2010). *All the Ladies Say*. New York: Full Circle Productions.

Moten, F. (2003). *In the Break: The Aesthetics of the Black Radical Tradition*. Minneapolis: University of Minnesota Press.

Rose, T. (1994). *Black Noise: Rap Music and Black Culture in Contemporary America*. Hanover, NH: University Press of New England.

Wesley, T., and Bullock, B., dirs. (2015). *Wave: A True Story in Hip Hop*. Upper Marlboro, MD: Bundy Films.

....

CHAPTER 14

GLOBALIZATION AND THE HIP HOP DANCE CIPHER

....

HALIFU OSUMARE AND
TERRY BRIGHT KWEKU OFOSU

INTRODUCTION
....

HIP Hop dance was the *first* element of the culture adopted when it proliferated globally in the early 1980s. Rap necessitated English language skills and the DJ's turntables and mixers were far too expensive for many youth around the globe to immediately purchase. Therefore, the body was the direct universal instrument for young people to mimic the moves and styles they saw in early Hollywood films such as *Flashdance* (1983), *Breakin'* (1983), *Beat Street* (1984), *Breakin' 2: Electric Boogaloo* (1984), and *Krush Groove* (1985). Even early rap music videos used b-boying (breakdancing), popping, and locking to sell the Hip Hop recordings of such artists as Kool Moe Dee, Big Daddy Kane, Kurtis Blow, and Grandmaster Flash. In the early days of Hip Hop's commercialization, the elements were still intact, representing the holistic culture. However, increasing corporate influence in the United States disconnected Hip Hop's elements from each other, proclaiming rap as its signature expressive practice. Although rap is the most financially lucrative component of Hip Hop, the culture's dance has never died. It continues to develop from neighborhood and club ciphers to well-publicized international competitions, with crews competing from all over the world.

The authors view Hip Hop dance as bodily *text*, which becomes even more complex and verbose in the international sphere. We investigate the internationalization of the dance element of Hip Hop as a clear example of movement that, in the words of dance scholar Jane Desmond (1997), is "primary, not secondary social text" (31). As Randy Martin (1997) also notes, dance itself is "an embodied practice that makes manifest how movement comes to be by momentarily concentrating and elaborating in one place forces drawn from beyond a given performance setting" (5). If so, the dancer is creating visual sociopolitical, cultural, and historical discursive statements that obviously draw from the dancer's and choreographer's own place within these vital forces, wherever they take place on the globe. This will become clear in our case studies.

As a collaborative essay, this chapter draws upon Osumare's Hip Hop globalization texts—*The Africanist Aesthetic in Global Hip Hop* (2007) and *The Hiplife in Ghana* (2012)—and Ofosu's Ghanaian popular dance essays and integral participation in Ghana's Hip Hop dance scene. Osumare is a former dancer-choreographer turned academic who has written extensively about Hip Hop culture. As a former "freestyle" dancer in Ghana, Ofosu has become a noted thinker on Ghanaian popular culture and dance. His 2009 MFA thesis, "Popular and Scholarly Choreography in Ghana: A Synthesis of Dance Aesthetics and Current Trends," and subsequent published essays (Ofosu 2013/2014, 2014, 2015), examines the concept of Hip Hop as a "foreign popular dance" that invaded Ghana and informed young Ghanaian dancers and their approach to the contemporary dance cipher. From these two backgrounds, we dissect the improvisational freestyle "cipher" within the Africanist Hip Hop aesthetics as a site of the construction of nonverbal text that can simultaneously uphold and subvert tradition. We then interrogate that "text" as a manifestation of the paradigm of performance and performativity. The theory is explored through examples of the Hip Hop global dance cipher in Hawai'i in the 1990s and Ghana in the 2000s. Investigating Hip Hop dance over such a wide scope of time in two international sites allows this chapter to question how generations of dancers within the Hip Hop dance cipher potentially figure into the global-local problematic.

THE DANCE CIPHER: REINFORCING AND
SUBVERTING THE SOCIAL ORDER

Although the music industry has encouraged solo artists in the rap game rather than promoting the many early groups that first proliferated Hip Hop culture from the street corners of the 'hood (e.g., Wu Tang Clan, NWA, Tribe Called Quest), dance always needs a collective in order to produce the energy that this artistic element engenders.[1] Collectivity links the individual soloist to a community, as she or he represents the communal values established by the group. However, the adept dance artist takes the collective values to a new level by inserting a disruption of difference. This is what James Snead (1981) calls "repetition with critical difference" (148), and what Hip Hop scholar Tricia Rose (1994) calls an aesthetics of "flow, layering, and rupture" (67–74).

Dance cultures like Hip Hop, just as culture in general, must replicate themselves generation after generation to survive, yet innovate to progress. The dancer who enters the center of a dance cipher,[2] or circle, must reinforce the group dynamic; yet the best dancers always extend the accepted traditions and thereby build new traditions with their critically inserted difference. The process of extending cultural tradition necessitates the soloist's relationship to the group. This is essentially the purpose of the cipher, defined by Hip Hop scholar Imani Perry (2004) as "a conceptual space in which heightened consciousness exists . . . [and that] is a privileged outlaw space" (107). If all things are aligned, the danced text in the conceptual space provided by the group can create a heightened consciousness for the entire collective. This is the goal of a dance cipher, from a b-boy circle in the South Bronx at the Rock Steady Crew Headquarters, or a street-corner cipher in the Osu district of Accra, Ghana, or even a Séné-Gambian village *bantaba* circle with traditional drummers.

The cipher, then, is a sacrosanct site where the group's values are reinforced, made manifest again, and extended in new, articulate challenges. Perry (2004) notes the spiritual aspects of this kind of collectivity: "Those inside the cipher are central, so it claims an insider rather than outsider consciousness, [and it can indicate] a mystical and transcendent yet human state, [and] creates a vibe amid a community, as well as a spirit of artistic production or intellectual/spiritual discursive movements" (107). Within the production of both intellectual and spiritual discourses through the body, challenging new movement statements by knowledgeable dancers are created, allowing subversion of the old, expected order by these artists. In this tradition-innovation paradigm new dance traditions are proposed. During the mid-1980s, a time of Hip Hop *groups* that established the culture in the United States, one of the most prolific rap crews was A Tribe Called Quest. Along with De La Soul, they were a part of a larger Hip Hop collective known as the Native Tongues. In one of A Tribe Called Quest's tracks, titled "Youthful Expression" (1990), they spoke to the importance of collectivity while riffing on their own group name and intimating the cipher's metaphysical dimensions: With rhythmic instinction to be able to travel beyond existing forces of life / Basically, that's tribal / And if you want to get the rhythm, then you have to join a tribe

In Africanist cultures, from which Hip Hop extends, change occurs within the continuity and endurance of tradition.

Continuity and change conjures up Hip Hop's connection to African culture and performance ritual. Osumare has written extensively about this at various stages of her scholarship. In her 1993 essay, "Aesthetic of the Cool Revisited: The Ancestral Dance Link in the African Diaspora," she relied on the Africanist anthropologist Margaret Drewal who has written prolifically on African performance and ritual. Drewal (1991) had this to say about the layered nature of African performance and, by extension, the Hip Hop cipher:

> In Africa, performance is a primary site for the production of knowledge, where philosophy is enacted, and where multiple and often simultaneous discourses are employed . . . performance is a means by which people reflect on their current conditions, define, and/or re-invent themselves and their social world, and either reenforce, resist, or subvert prevailing social orders. Indeed, both subversion and legitimization can merge in the same utterance or act. (8)

Besides Hip Hop's connection to the very nature of African performance practices, the key point here is the "simultaneous discourses" that are active in the cipher. The idea that several concomitant movement statements can be made in a dance solo within the dance cipher is crucial to comprehending how legitimization of tradition and subversion of it can "merge in the same utterance or act." This concurrence of complicity and resistance within the same dance solo, for example, must be grasped to truly "get" the Hip Hop dance cipher. In Ghana, for example, Ofosu (2009) notes the importance of recognizing "syncretic genre of movements" resulting from the blend of American Hip Hop dance and locally created popular dance with some traditional dance moves. In this way, global US Hip Hop dance influences are subverted by local Ghanaian dancers through engaging indigenous Ghanaian phrasings recognized by local cipher participants.

Of course, this kind of African diaspora performance research relies heavily on the groundbreaking research that Robert Farris Thompson 1974, 1983, 1996) conducted in African performance, African diaspora connections, and Hip Hop in the Bronx, respectively. His concept of the "aesthetic of the cool" was crucial to understanding the cultural links between Africa and the African diaspora.

> The re-occurrence of this vital notion in tropical Africa and in the Black Americas, I have come to term the attitude "an aesthetic of the cool" in the sense of a deeply and complex motivated consciously artistic interweaving of elements serious and pleasurable, or responsibility and of play. (Thompson 1974, 41)

The possibility that seriousness and pleasure and "responsibility and play" can occur in the same performance moment is key in comprehending the Africanist dance cipher. Binaries that don't account for seemingly contradictory motivations do not "compute" in the Africanist dance cipher; simultaneity of competing discourses is the order that allows for the dance cipher to accomplish its larger role of transforming the moment intellectually and spiritually. These "rules" of Africanist performance link Hip Hop to its African cultural source, which, in turn, gets localized over time and space as the subculture travels internationally.

PERFORMANCE AND PERFORMATIVITY: HAWAI'I AND GHANA AS CASE STUDIES

Given the Africanist aesthetics underpinning Hip Hop dance globally, our two case studies, Hawai'i and Ghana, become quintessential examples of tradition and innovation in Hip Hop sites thousands of miles apart. In Hawai'i, the complexity of Hip Hop culture and dance is due to the islands' multicultural influences as a Pacific Ocean crossroads. For example, Hawaiian b-boys and b-girls can have direct contact with Crazy Legs of New York City's Rock Steady Crew, who occasionally comes to Hawai'i and has created a Rock Steady Crew chapter in Honolulu. Those same dancers can easily travel to Japan to compete in international breaking competitions, as well. Hawai`i Hip Hop dance also occurs in clubs in Honolulu that cater to Hip Hop, as well as neighborhood community centers, and even churches that lure young people to their congregation through Hip Hop culture's incorporation into their worship service. Hence, Hawaiian b-boys and b-girls are acutely aware of the multiple languages of Hip Hop bodily expression—Native Hawaiian, Filipino, Chinese, Japanese, Caucasian as local *haole* (whites born in Hawai`i), and mixtures of all of them.

In Ghana there are ethnic divides as well, but class becomes an even more salient social aspect that influences Hip Hop culture and its localized dance. Ironically, the Ghanaian class divide played right into the snare of American pop cultural hegemony. Antonio Gramsci ([1971] 2010), as a Neo-Marxist theorist, defined hegemony thusly: "The 'spontaneous' consent given by the great masses of the population to the general direction imposed on social life by the dominant fundamental group; this consent is 'historically' cased by the prestige (and consequent confidence) which the dominant group enjoys because of its position and function in the world of production" (12). Indeed, classism in Ghana is often based on British-imposed cultural values during colonialism that continue to foster a "spontaneous consent" of anything American or Western, and was apparent in the early near-wholesale imitation of early Hip Hop dance in Accra.

According to anthropologist and hiplife scholar Jesse Shipley (2009), early Hip Hop collectives like Reggie Rockstone's Gravity Rockers and the Sakura Boys, who came from the upscale Cantonment district of Accra, the capital, were concerned with replicating the Hip Hop movements they watched in American films and videos verbatim (646). This early imitative phase of Hip Hop in Ghana was almost exclusively about the "performance" of global Hip Hop, representing the cultural hegemony of American pop culture. The early reification of American culture, without little attention to local "performativity," preceded what Osumare (2012) calls the adaptation and ultimately indigenization phases to which Ghanaian Hip Hop culture would eventually progress (15). Today's Ghanaian hiplife dance and music has found its own maturity due to an acquired balance between performance—globalized MTV-projected Hip Hop dance—and performativity—indigenized hiplife culture that celebrates local references and meanings.

The authors' use of the terms *performance* and *performativity* is a cultural adaptation of feminist scholar Judith Butler's gender theorizations, which Osumare (2007) has used previously:

> Butler's theories of performativity can be directly applied to physical enactments as performed text or bodily speech acts. She interrogates performativity from the perspective of Pierre Bourdieu's concept of *habitus*, the accumulation of cultural and individual learned patterns that are unconsciously enacted as a part of everyday personal behavior. (55)

Butler's use of *habitus*, taken from Bourdieu's social theory, can encompass a particular people's bodily proclivities, or unconscious body language. Habitus, then, factors into the indigenization process as culturally learned patterns within Hip Hop dance. As the dance cipher unfolds a "def" constructed Hip Hop solo must contain locally learned movement behaviors to "speak" to the cipher participants. Hawai'i b-girls, for example, must know the multi-lingual bodily nuances of multicultural Hawai'i, and Ghanaian b-boys must embody the contemporary class dynamics of the dance cypher in which they engage, as well as many commonly known traditional Ghanaian moves discussed below.

In global Hip Hop dance the local habitus must, however, comingle with received Hip Hop styles from the culture's origin, along with its dominant media image narratives (i.e., gangsta, pimp-playa, backpacker, video 'ho) that have, in fact, helped proliferate the global youth subculture. These narratives becomes a part of what Bourdieu calls "the field"---or the various social domains in which the individual hip-hoper outside the US has to interact. However, the most important domain is the economic marketplace that influences the habitus. When Osumare (2007) did her Hip Hop research in Hawai'i in the 1990s, she found that

> Hawai'i's local styles of bodily posturing and practices, as an example of habitus de-
> veloped out of almost 200 years of Polynesian and Asian social and biological mixing
> on Hawai'i's sugar cane and pineapple plantations. [But] these indigenous embodied
> practices are affected by movements that are generic to innumerable MTV and BET
> music videos, featuring breaking, pop-locking, rap dance, and general posturing by
> rappers. (55)

Therefore, the received Hip Hop dance style from "the field," or codified "performance," interacts with the local habitus, or "performativity," creating the global-local dynamic within the Hip Hop dance cipher.

However, to complicate this two-pronged bodily text, localized social identities are already embedded within codified Hip Hop performance exported to the marketplace field. As DeFrantz (2014, 227) assesses, "If breaking and b-girling had been conceived to speak physical truth to oppressive forces that would deny the presence of young people of color, by the 1990s these forms stood largely as referents to resistance coopted by a nimble marketplace eager to commodify the cool." Hence, physicalized Africanist aesthetics, reinvented in the diaspora through specific sociopolitical circumstances, exist implicitly in performed global Hip Hop dance ciphers. The danced social identities inherited by the field are, therefore, mapped onto the local identities, body languages, and indigenous symbolism of the receiving habitus.

Osumare's chart, "Hip Hop's Two-Pronged Bodily Text," demonstrates the interdependence of performance and performativity in Figure 14.1, resulting in what she calls the "Intercultural Body." These two powerful forces in the global-local problematic are facilitated by the Africanist aesthetic mandate of improvisation, or "freestyling," in Hip Hop culture. It is difficult to fake either performance or performativity in the moment-by-moment improvisational dance cipher. One must represent the soul force implicit in individual dance improvisation as one "reps" one's hood.

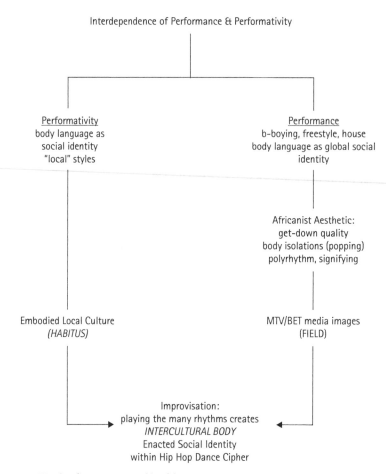

FIGURE 14.1. Hip hop's two-pronged bodily text.

Local dancers in Hip Hop's diaspora are not mindless consumers of US pop culture but, in fact, are proactive participants in this global transfer by re-inscribing new meanings onto received Hip Hop dance styles, and in the process form the Intercultural Body. Ofosu acknowledges that, in Ghana, imported Hip Hop dances are indigenized in various ways. For example, Hip Hop social dances like the running man and genres like popping, locking, sliding, and tutting are "syncretized" with locally created popular social dances like *gbeohe*, *korgon*, and *kpe*, as well as traditional military movement traditions and even sacred ritual dances (Ofosu 2009). These global-local dance mergers can happen in one dance solo within the cipher, and within developed Hip Hop choreography performed by Hip Hop dance groups in Accra. Therefore, Hip Hop dance freestyling within the cipher integrates both the received global US Hip Hop dance styles that have been passed down over the last forty years through the field, as well as the imperatives of local styles that in many cases have been developed over hundreds of years. Therefore, Bourdieu's "field" becomes a big part of globalized and corporatized Hip Hop received by local sites throughout the globe.

We acknowledge that *corporate* Hip Hop proliferated through the media can emanate "negative" commercial aspects of the subculture, such as materialism, gangsterism and misogyny. However, we also recognize that these perceived deleterious aspects of imported Hip Hop can match similar forces in the local sphere. Hip Hop performance from the field brings the codified dances like breaking and popping that have established the culture, defining global Hip Hop dance culture while creating the linkages that allow scholars to establish the construct of the Global Hip Hop Nation (GHHN). However, the hybridity created by the intermingling with performativity of local styles is crucial in establishing the vitality of discrete global Hip Hop dance ciphers in each site. Local members of recognized dance crews must also be adept in these local embodied styles containing indigenous popular and traditional dances, as well as their own myths, folklore, and iconic symbols that distinguish each global site within the GHHN.

The Global Hip Hop Nation: The Case of Honolulu, Hawai'i

By virtue of Hawai'i's (colonial) history with the US mainland and its unique geographic position as a crossroad between East and West, America's fiftieth state offers a particularly complex example of the globalization of Hip Hop culture. Hawai`i floats geographically and culturally in the North Pacific, connecting Asia, Polynesia, Micronesia, and the Americas in historical and contemporary ways. Particularly as gateway to the Pacific Rim—the mid-way point between the Continental United States and Asia—Hawai`i is an interesting composite of Native Hawaiian, American, and Asian cultural factors, which complicates the global-local problematic in relation to the exportation of Continental US Hip Hop popular culture to the islands.

Osumare lived in Hawai'i for seven years (1994–2000) and did extensive fieldwork on Hip Hop in Honolulu and the Hilo-Pahoa district of the Big Island. One of her cultural bearers in the Honolulu Hip Hop club scene in the late nineties was TeN (Justin Alladin), a Hawai'i-born Japanese and African American b-boy, who participated in weekend club ciphers, as well as international b-boy competitions in Japan. The following is an extensive quote from an interview with him that captures international encoded protocols that the Hip Hop dance cipher has become. He reveals the necessary Hip Hop performance codes that travel globally, creating the possibility of the GHHN:

> When I was last in Japan, there were two kids battling. One kid came in and cut the other off before he was finished, and so they walked around in a circle looking at each other. And all of a sudden they jumped like this, boom, together, at the same time, knowing exactly what they were doing. It was the "Brooklyn rock." Do you know what a "Brooklyn rock"[3] is? No, I can barely do it. These two kids—one from Japan, one from Hawai'i—had never met each other before, got to the park not even an hour

before, and just started dancing, and cannot communicate [verbally] with each other. They walked in the circle, jumped at the right time together and landed at the same time together, and started Brooklyn rocking together. That is international communication. That is people of the same culture. (personal interview, March 28, 1999)

Even when they can't speak the same verbal language, TeN argues for the cohesiveness of the GHHN, where participants know the codes of what is perceived as "real" lived b-boy culture and its protocols, with the priorities of the dance cipher facilitating this global cohesion.

TeN also distinguishes between commercial Hip Hop and the grounded Hip Hop culture in which he participates:

That is the difference between someone really from hip hop and someone from commercialized hip hop. A person in commercialized hip hop cannot do that, does not know what that is, don't know anything about it, and could not do it to save their life. That's just [the difference in authenticity] on the dancing level. The same difference exists on the emcee level, on the deejay level, on the [aerosol] art level. That part about them knowing what to do is what you [I, the interviewer] are talking about: how traditions are passed on. Who passed it on? They didn't go to school. They lived it, you know. That's their life, so they know it. They have the same values. That kid knows that he cut the other kid off, and he should not have done that. That's why they jumped into the Brooklyn rock. They knew and they were ready for it. They knew what a [hip hop] battle was. (Alladin interview)

Participants in the GHHN see themselves as a global culture distinct from corporate Hip Hop promulgated by the international MTV subsidiaries and the global music distributing industry. One can also surmise from TeN's assessment that one of the primary differences between the GHHN and corporate-generated Hip Hop is that all the elements of the former are still intact, as opposed to the perceived divide-and-conquer strategy of commercial Hip Hop—the field.

The GHHN takes pride in the inherited "performance" of Hip Hop that preserves the decades-old Hip Hop dance traditions and cipher protocols, but also recognizes the "performativity" of their various cultural styles as different languages of Hip Hop. In October 1998 Osumare observed TeN in a now defunct Honolulu nightclub near the University of Hawai'i, and recorded this observation of his unique cultural influences in his b-boy solos, while following the age-old cipher conventions:

TeN moves in to fill the center of the circle as if selected by some invisible spirit. He obviously has studied the Brazilian martial art, capoeira, for his martial art style, mixed with deft rhythmic dance moves, sets him apart as he spins into a final "freeze" pose before he exits. Each exit is someone else's entrance—the energy must be ever more intense—while the crowd, encircles mesmerized, attentive to every nuance of the displayed body language, like an articulated communal text. This is community. This is creative individualism being supported by the collective. This is hip hop culture (2007, 121–122).

Often, TeN would also use the Okinawan martial arts weapon, the nunchuks (danger stick) in his dance solos, revealing Asian influences in the habitus of Hawai'i's Hip Hop dance style. Performance and performativity live in proximity within the global Hip Hop dance cipher, developing out of the dancers' lived local and virtual global experiences.

The following month at the Wave Waikiki nightclub in Honolulu a Hip Hop dance event took place called "Urban Movement." By midnight, there was enough of a critical mass of people that the show got underway. The club patrons numbered about two hundred people, who consisted of Black, white, Asian, Hawaiian, military service men, and civilians mostly in their late twenties—a typical ethnic mix for Hawai'i with its strong US military presence. "Urban Movement" linked several styles of contemporary Hip Hop dance, while the whole event demonstrated what Hip Hop scholar Tricia Rose (1994) calls the "reimagination and symbolic appropriation of urban space through sampling, attitude, dance, style, and sound effects" (22). The mix of East, West, and Polynesia makes Hawai'i an important site of Hip Hop's transnationalism, a literal crossroads between nations that traffic through the island on a daily basis. With 85 percent of the state's multiethnic population living on the island of Oahu, along with several US military bases and the big tourist "machine" of Waikiki Beach, the cultural dynamics of any performance in Honolulu potentially becomes a multilayered, multicultural, and transnational event.

Three dance acts during Urban Movement demonstrate the various styles and approaches that are often lodged under the umbrella of Hip Hop dance in Hawai'i. The first dance group to perform was the Evolution Dancers, a six-member "street dance" girl group predominantly of Asian descent. They were clad in baggy black-and-red sweat clothes and were accompanied by an Asian drag queen in a blue satin nightgown, platinum wig, and athletic shoes and socks. The girls strutted with panache and rhythmically isolated their torsos, à la Janet Jackson, in perfect sync to the fast-thumping techno music. The drag queen vamped in front of the changing first line of dancers, taunting the audience with his vogueing, rhythmic dance posing that originated in Black male gay clubs in New York in the 1970s.

The Evolution Dancers' show represented an intriguing juxtaposition indicative of Hip Hop's tenet of flipping the script. The dancers performed a commercialized Hip Hop style more typically exhibited on MTV and BET behind current-day rappers, while the drag queen's style, using Madison Moore, offered a juxtaposition of "bricolage and 'talking back' to dominant culture." Moore (2018) proposes that challenging styles, like the one the drag queen's costume represented, is actually a form of "authenticity," meaning "showing off that sense of creative strangeness, [as a kind of] fabulousness linked more to imagination than the marketplace" (81).

The discipline of queer studies, just emerging in academia around the time of the Urban Movement showcase, allows for an understanding of "embodied queer aesthetic that appears in everyday and everynight life" as it did in the Evolution Dancers performance. Madison explains: "In theory circles the word *queer* is typically thought of as a resistance to the 'the norm' as well as to 'regimes of the normal'" (quoted in Moore 2018, 6).[4] Hence, while the female Evolution Dancers' routine represented what Katrina

Hazzard-Donald (1996) calls commercial "rap dance" (227–228), their drag queen partner simultaneously flipped the script by transgressing that expected embodied parlance and style associated with the marketplace.

The next two dance performances took place in a more traditional cipher circle format. Josiah, a slight and nimble "local" guy of primarily Caucasian descent (*local haole*), cut loose with his freestyle "house" dance.[5] Josiah combined an eclectic array of highly individualized moves of breaking floor work mixed with popping and locking, reinterpreted into "Josiah-speak." Performance and performativity comingled seamlessly in his solo in the middle of a ringed cipher on the dance floor. After Josiah's solo, Skill-Roy and Strategy, two members of the Hawai'i chapter of the Rock Steady Crew, followed with traditional b-boying. Their breaking style represented the late '90s, the then "new school" that included a strong juxtaposition of the six-step, or low rocking, with the athleticism of power moves.

Skill-Roy and Strategy's "new school" b-boy style, which indicated a shifting generational style, complicated the global-local problematic. Both their solos contained the repeated juxtaposition of six-stepping (feet and hands working together while crouched close to the floor) and athletic power moves (improvised acrobatics containing a myriad of spins and flips) that marked the emerging "new school" of the day. Strategy's focus on inserting creative six-stepping with his power moves display rendered a more rhythmically complex dance that complemented the music. This aesthetic difference was also emphasized in Osumare's interviews, and in the late 1990s was becoming increasingly important in Hawai'i.

This aesthetic change occurring in the execution of b-boying was in fact the performative manifestation of a potential philosophical expansion underlying what is *valued* in the b-boy cypher. Over time, according to Hip Hop dance theorist Imani Kai Johnson (2011), this aesthetic shift "encouraged a power-versus-style debate[; while] ideas around authenticity, tradition, progressive change, and cultural evolution all come into play." She goes on to say, " 'Old' and 'New' Schools are more far-reaching than the style/power debate. They are symbolic terms that refer to particular ways of understanding b-boying's esthetically rich core philosophies, on the one hand, and performative principles that privilege innovation and change, on the other" (180). Additionally, Skill-Roy's and Strategy's solos were examples of a point that the Japanese Hip Hop scholar Ian Condry (2006) makes as he rethinks the global-local problematic in Hip Hop: "A history of breakdancing around the world deserves its own book, but at least we can note that distinctions between generations are appearing in the global scene. This suggests that the key dynamic may not be a rivalry between foreign and local Hip Hop but between factions and generations across international lines" (67). As the culture matures, these are some of the philosophical implications emerging out of the globalization of Hip Hop dance.

Like any good Hip Hop dance cipher, as opposed to choreographed routines or even structured group battles, both Joisah's dance solos and those of the dancers of the Rock Steady Crew necessitated improvisation, in which moment-by-moment choices are made that allow performativity and performance to co-mingle. Spontaneous performance decisions within an improvised solo represent the dancer's personal agency that dictates a mediation of performativity with global Hip Hop performance styles. In tandem, all three dance performances in "Urban Movement" represented variations of today's global Hip Hop dance culture, including choreographed rap dance that is taught in aerobic studios in the West, and when performed often include kitsch characterizations, like the drag queen, that capture audience attention. While having its own set of globalized codified movements, Josiah's house improvisations was highly individualized, showcasing his unique and singular personality. Traditional b-boy/b-girl collectives that frequent clubs usually start the dance cipher at the behest of the hired club deejay. In this way Hawai'i represents the variety of Hip Hop dances that had evolved by the late 1990s and have only multiplied over the twenty-one years of the twenty-first century.

The Global Hip Hop Nation: The Case of Accra, Ghana

Osumare (2012) built on Robert Farris Thompson's foundational African diasporic connections in her concept of "the arc of mutual inspiration" articulated extensively in *The Hiplife in Ghana: West African Indigenization of* Hip Hop: "The circle of musical and dance influences from Africa to its diaspora and back again, represented by these rhythmic musical genres from regions of the African continent, is what I call an arc of mutual inspiration that has existed since the Atlantic slave trade" (1). For example, Ofosu (2013/2014) compares the La Kpa music and dance types to that of Hip Hop of the diaspora by pointing out some striking semblances in dance structure and rap style, a reverberation of African traits in American arts (43). The arc is the sweep of time and space in the reinvention of African rhythmic sensibility that is manifested corporeally, orally, and aurally in the Americas; then migrated back to the continent itself through technology; young Africans hearing and seeing these connections are attracted to these diasporan reinventions like Hip Hop, which in turn sparks them to reinvent their own new variations. This Black Atlantic process is not only crucial to understanding Hip Hop's particular resonance in Africa, but also its international vitality all over the world.

Ghana, as one of the primary Anglophone countries of West Africa, clearly represents a part of the world we today refer to as the Global South. Ofosu notes that Ghana has been considered an underdeveloped nation, but in recent years has been growing its middle-class with a significant increase in technological infrastructure and engagement with the global socioeconomic landscape (e-mail comm., February 15, 2015). African American cultural influence has been a part of this sociotechnological shift. Historically, "The British colony of the Gold Coast becoming independent Ghana was the sign of African empowerment and the emblematic end of a long history of direct European colonial exploitation, and Ghana's interest in and involvement with Africans Americans began with [Kwame] Nkrumah, [Ghana's first Prime Minister]" (Osumare 2012, 6). African American and Caribbean expatriates, such as George Padmore, Bill

Sutherland, W.E.B., and Shirley DuBois, among others, worked in the early government of Nkrumah. One can say that African American and Caribbean influences, which Hip Hop represents, have been interacting with Ghana over the decades since independence. In a 2015 CNN interview, Reggie Rockstone referred to his experience of this long-standing interaction with the diaspora as the "three Bs"—that is, Brooklyn (where many Afro-Caribbean immigrants live in New York), Brixton (a suburb in London where Jamaicans reside), and Bukom (a suburb in Accra, the capital of Ghana, where the Gas live as the major ethnic group of Accra). This cultural triad of one of the most influential hiplife artists demonstrates the interaction with of Ghana, in particular, with its diaspora.

Ghana, a country of about 25 million, has always had a fascination with African American vernacular dance, with its similarities to Ghanaian dance styles. Ghanaian fascination with Black American exported social dance did not start with Hip Hop, but was generated by previously adopted American pop music genres of R & B, soul, and funk. Today's Hip Hop music in Ghana is called *hiplife* as a conjunction between West African *highlife* pop music and imported Hip Hop music. But before indigenous hiplife became a recognized musical genre, an imitative US Hip Hop culture led by dance represented the inchoate beginnings of Ghanaian Hip Hop culture.

In the early 1980s, there were formal dance contests at local highlife dances under the auspices of the Ghana Arts Council in Accra. Ofosu (1993) notes that "these dances included the robot, break, body pop, and electric dances. Competitions in these dances are now organized under a common heading called 'freestyle'" (23). This early Ghanaian freestyle dancing can be categorized under popping and locking, as opposed to breaking. Ghanaian freestyle dancing, though stylistically similar to movements in Ghanaian social and traditional dances, was considered "foreign dancing" and generated tensions with the older generation from its first appearance in the '1980s. But even with this social opposition, there were nationally organized "Embassy Double-Do" competitions, where the winning dancers began making some money, while the Hip Hop rappers at the time remained at the street-sold mixed-tapes level.

In examining Hip Hop as an imported youth culture, as mentioned earlier, one must also examine Ghana as a former British colony in which issues of class, economics, and education are prominent status markers. The imported styles of Hip Hop dance were positioned within these Ghanaian class divisions and could be read as such. During this early period of Hip Hop dance, most of the participants in the freestyle dances and competitions were from the poorer areas of Accra, whereas the affluent upper-middle-class boys usually performed breakdance. Reggie Rockstone (Reginald Ossei), the purported founder of hiplife music, started as a b-boy and performed the middle-class b-boy style. The class divide within Ghanaian Hip Hop dance was centered around education and its secondary and tertiary institutions. Not only were more-educated youth able to develop a facile use of American rap because of their fluent knowledge of English, but they also had the funds to rent music videos and see Hollywood breakdance films, and some had the ability to travel to the United Kingdom and the United States.

Ofosu notes that high schools, which are not free in Ghana, were sites in which dance collectives formed and performed during school programs and battled, in and around the school grounds. These were the youths who also had access to global technology, such as video, and Internet access that was provided by school institutions. Poorer youths, who could not afford to continue their schooling beyond primary school, had fewer facilities in which to practice or rehearse; nor did they have access to technology to access the globalized video imagery and references that would have allowed them to become facile. Contrary to the stereotype of US Black ghetto youths needing "street cred" to be taken seriously in Hip Hop, in Ghana the more educated youths with the envied higher education became the revered rappers and b-boys, and thus Ghana represents a case study where, in the early days, access to Hip Hop had everything to do with one's class status.

This issue of class in global Hip Hop dance deserves elaboration from the point of view of Bourdieu's theory of habitus and the field. Firstly, education in the Ghanaian case study makes the all-important difference in the ability to receive Hip Hop culture from hegemonic glocal field. Bourdieu (1984) articulates this reality in relation to the typical class usage of "Culture" with a capital C.

> Whereas the ideology of charisma regards taste in legitimate culture as a gift of nature, scientific observation shows that cultural needs are the product of upbringing and education: surveys establish that all cultural practice . . . and preferences in literature, painting or music, are closely linked to education level . . . and secondarily to social origin. (1)

Although not exclusively, the majority of the early hiplife artists in Accra and beyond were from families who could afford high school, which is not free in Ghana, and were college attendees, giving them access to the inner codes of globalized field of American pop culture.

In his *Distinction: A Social Critique of the Judgement of Taste*, Bourdieu (1984) positions class itself in the context of habitus.

> Life-styles are thus the systemic products of habitus, which perceived in their mutual relations through the schemes of the habitus, become sign systems that are socially qualified (as "distinguished," "vulgar" etc.). The dialectic of conditions and habitus is the basis of an alchemy which transforms the distribution of capital, the balance-sheet of a power relation into a system of perceived differences, distinctive properties, that is, a distribution of symbolic capital, legitimate capital, whose objective truth is misrecognized. (172)

Indeed, the power of the new sign systems created by Accra-based b-boys and emcees, using the habitus of Ghanaian cultural nuances, did create a new level of "distribution of symbolic capital," which was initially "misrecognized" by the older highlife generation. In this way, both class, developed from British colonialism, and the precolonial indigenous traditions of Ghana comingled in the developing Ghanaian Hip Hop dance cipher.

The indigenization phase that turned Ghanaian Hip Hop into hiplife manifested in both the music and the dance. In the music it meant the use of indigenous languages of Twi, Ewe, Ga, and Hausa, underlying highlife melodic phrasing and musical structure, and local sociocultural references with the use of traditional proverbs in rap verses. In the dance, indigenization became evident in the habitus referencing of Ghanaian popular and traditional dances that are commonplace among all the youths battling in Ghanaian dance ciphers and among choreographers in Accra dance crews. For example, Ofosu and Dei (2015) have documented the Ghanaian popular dances used in the Accra dance ciphers, including *gbeohe*, which means "open your thighs"; *korgon*, which refers to miming climbing a hill; and *kpe*, which simulates holding a gun.

Ofosu also notes that long-term traditional dances from both the secular and sacred aspects of the culture influenced the performativity side of Ghanaian Hip Hop dance. For example, militaristic acrobatic movements from the *Asafo* marching dances can easily intertwine with inherited b-boy moves. The Asafo is the traditional warrior class within the Fante ethnic group from Ghana's coastal Central Region, who were the first to interact with European explorers, from as early as the 1470s. Asafo fighting battalions grew out of the encounter between Fante traditions and European military pomp and ceremony. Therefore, local dances such as *kpe*, with its weaponry references woven into the Ghanaian Hip Hop dance cipher, could either have Asafo or American Hip Hop gangsta sources.

Additionally, the traditional Asafo battalion always uses a solo flag bearer who had both virility and spiritual connotations in his movement. As Ghanaian dance theorist Joseph Knox (2010) explains, "Through European influences, the flag was integrated into Fante warrior or 'military dance' culture culminating in this Flag dancer." He then associates this Asafo figure with Hip Hop: "The Fante Asafo flag dancer of the Fante region is prototypical b-boy for all intents and purposes. He advocates for his gang, or crew, by displaying his acrobatic and rhythmic prowess against all enemies" (2010). Given these common cultural values, protocols, and actual movement styles, as performance and performativity comingle, discerning *exact* sources for Ghanaian Hip Hop dance moves within the cipher can be difficult.

Two traditional sacred dances that have influenced Ghanaian Hip Hop dance ciphers, according to Ofosu, are *Adzogbo* and *Kundum*. Adzogbo is a cult war dance from the Ewe people of the Volta Region of Ghana, and has to do with Adzo, the Ewe war god, whose dances involve vigorous virtuosic theatrical movements inherited from a ritual dance of the Fon people of Benin. The present-day dance essentially "is used to display mental, physical and spiritual power and still carries some of its original cult and war dance characteristics" (Badu 2015, 1). Traditional cult war dances, such as Adzogbo, can easily be syncretized with aggressive b-boying power moves in the Ghanaian Hip Hop dance cipher, again making sourcing sometimes difficult as knowledgeable local dancers improvise from both codified Hip Hop performance and performativity's local habitus. Another traditional Ghanaian dance that b-boys utilize within the cipher is Kundum, a ritual dance of the *Ahanta* people of the Western Region of the country, which is associated with spiritual cleansing and the harvest and, like Adzogbo, assumes a strong acrobatic dance style.

Because of the strength and agility of inherited b-boying performance (power moves) from the globalized *field*, the uses of indigenous dance repertoire can establish parallel strong moves, such as war and ritual dances that represent both physical and spiritual intensity and potency. Newell and Okome (2014), using Hecht and Simone (1994), offer a view of Africans' everyday lived experiences that can illuminate these dynamics of the Ghanaian Hip Hop dance cipher:

> David Hecht and Maliqalim Simone (8) argue that what gets ignored in main-stream economic analyses of Africa, where the emphasis is on poverty, political corruption and suffering, are "the means by which Africans have learned to compensate for the impossibility of their everyday lives." At the heart of their study is the desire "to locate complex and fundamentally ambivalent African social conditions," and to reach into the epistemological vortex that this complexity produces. To do so, they suggest, one must insert oneself into "the anamorphic matrices of conflicting knowledges and desires" produced for Africa and sometimes by Africans about themselves. (14)

The Hip Hop dance cipher potently exposes "complex and fundamentally ambivalent African social conditions," as participants (de)cipher these complexities through their bodies. Negotiating the global-local problematic through the dancing body is an everyday practical way of working out seemingly "conflicting knowledges" in the Ghanaian Hip Hop cipher.

Today, besides b-boy ciphers in schools, spontaneous ciphers on the Atlantic shoreline beaches, and in Accra neighborhood squares, there are also organized and funded corporate competitions. The biggest of these corporate-sponsored dance competition events is the Malta Guinness Street Dance Competition, which is national in scope with a substantial financial prize. The Ghana competition is actually a part of the continent-wide Malta Guinness Street Dance Africa, which has held competitions in major cities across the African continent since 2008. The nonalcoholic energy-malt-drink corporation joins other multinationals, particularly telecom companies, in sponsoring Hip Hop culture throughout the African continent. Alliances between multinationals and African Hip Hop pose new quandaries in these late-capitalist times where corporations and popular culture collaborate to capture the attention of youth populations globally. As an adjudicator of the 2010 Malta Guinness Street Dance finals, Ofosu recounts how almost all the participating groups showed up on stage with their flags, a practice that became increasingly quotidian, just like the local Asafo groups.

In a poor country like Ghana new sources of revenue for unemployed youths in exchange for their honed artistic skills are definitely welcomed. However, as Ghana joins larger global economic networks through dance, it must be noted that there are dual forces at work. Osumare (2012) analyzes that a "dual hiplife allegiance is centered in the indigenization of Hip Hop, creating both the exigencies of participating in 'economic transnational circuits' [through corporate sponsorship] while personally creating an enjoyable link with Ghanaian musical [and dance] traditions in aesthetic dialogue with the diaspora" (123). One must always be vigilant about corporate usurpation of street culture globally, taking a lesson from US Hip Hop that was transformed from a self-empowered neighborhood street culture to a multi-billion-dollar industrial complex of corporate manipulated music, dance, and style. Africa, because of its history of blatant exploitation, can easily succumb to what Osumare calls a form of "corporate recolonization."

CONCLUSION

The global Hip Hop dance cipher is a microcosm of larger international forces at work as US popular culture is exported around the world and local sites grapple with imitation and adaptation to create their own a frameworks and meanings. Hip Hop dance is movement *text* that speaks to these global and local forces in the context of the ancient Africanist circle that we call the cipher. Today, the global Hip Hop dance cipher is a spiritual "outlaw space," where dominant narratives are simultaneously reinforced and subverted. Adept Hip Hop dancers—breakers, poppers, lockers, freestyle, house dancers— take their turns in the center reinforcing received traditions and offering critical differences that often challenge and innovate the established traditions. As such, the Hip Hop dance cipher creates both flow and rupture, as it should.

This chapter has sought to explicate the dance cipher through the theoretical paradigms of globalization. Performance and performativity represent one model that allows us to understand globally exported Hip Hop dance cultures that have created an international tradition, which has, in turn, facilitated a Global Hip Hop Nation (GHHN) that links youth dance collectives across the globe. At the same time, local cultural imperatives disrupt received codified Hip Hop performance through local performativity's body language and indigenous dances. Pierre Bourdieu's (1984) concept of field and habitus, as discussed by Judith Butler (1996), articulates how the global and the local necessarily wrangle for primacy, creating a dialogue particularly suited for dance because of its spontaneous ephemerality. This theoretical model yields what Osumare calls "Hip Hop's two-pronged bodily text." However, theorists are rethinking our relationship to the global, for example, communications scholar Fabienne Darling-Wolf (2015), who writes:

> "The global," in other words, is a space that is envisioned and imagined rather than directly experienced . . . The most critical question to ask, in other words, is not whether hybridity exists or even matters (we know it does), but *how* it matters. How do individuals "imagine the global" as cultural products and social relations are lifted out from local contexts to be restructured 'across indefinite spans of time.'" (1–2)

Two considerations of performance and performativity through the lens of the field and habitus—those of Hawai'i and Ghana or, more specifically, Honolulu and Accra—might help us think through how the imagined global is actually enacted through the dance cipher. Hawai'i presents a multicultural case that links the United States, Asia, and the

Pacific islands, negotiating all those dance identities into a "local" style that shows that the Hip Hop dance cipher can be flexible and open-ended, engaging the habitus of various cultures. Yet it remains filtered through the protocols of inherited Hip Hop performance of the GHHN. Ghana, in contrast, seems to offer a more culturally homogenous habitus. But on closer examination, the Ghanaian habitus actually incorporates the historical dance styles of many different ethnicities that have far-reaching connections in West Africa, often encompassing several centuries of encoded text. These traditional dance references become syncretized with similar contemporary characteristics, from inherited Hip Hop styles televised from the technological field.

The global Hip Hop dance cipher is an arena that is quite potent with multiple dimensions of cultural innovations, societal norms, economic incentives, and technological priorities, belying the often-simplistic interpretations of popular dance. The theoretical concepts and practical examples that have been explored should give pause to contemplate how complex Hip Hop dance text actually is, as a confluence of the past and the present converging in the twenty-first-century global Hip Hop dance cipher.

Notes

1. For an exploration of the role of "posses" as a counterhegemonic force in rap music production see work by Murray Forman, especially, the chapter "Homeboys and Production Posses" in Forman (2002, 176–183). Also see Sujatha Fernandes (2011, 14–16) for her argument about the record industry's creation of "corporate rap" that is outside the community-oriented origins of rap music and Hip Hop culture.

2. We use the spelling "cipher" versus "cypher," following Hip Hop scholars such as Imani Perry. Both spellings are acceptable.

3. The term "Brooklyn Rock" is an older terminology, often used in the 1990s when Osumare was doing her Hawaii fieldwork. Today it is simply known as "rocking." Mary Fogarty, the coeditor of this handbook says, "Most of the misconception in terminology and context—like those TeN describes—curiously came from people learning the style through videos and the Internet, although perhaps some travelling practitioners were using this terminology too?"

4. Moore uses Michael Warner (1993, xxvi).

5. House dancing is performed to house music, a derivative of techno music that originated in Europe and became popular at rave events in the United States. House music is driven by a strong, thumping bass beat, and does not necessarily lend itself to the acrobatic breakdance style; instead, it utilizes some b-boy moves with a more upright dance style.

References

Badu, Z. C. M. (2015). Abstract of "Ewe Culture as Expressed in Ghana West Africa through Adzogbo Dance Ceremony." McGill Library and Collections. http://digitool.library.mcgill.ca/R/?func=dbin-jump-full&object_id=82826&local_base=GEN01-MCG02. Accessed February 10, 2015.

Bourdieu, P. (1984). *Distinction: A Social Critique of the Judgement of Taste*. Translated by R. Nice. Cambridge, MA: Harvard University Press.

Butler, J. (1996). "Performativity's Social Magic." In *The Social and Political Body*, edited by T. R. Schatzki and W. Natter, 29–48. New York: Guilford Press.

Condry, I. (2006). *Hip Hop Japan*. Durham, NC: Duke University Press.

Darling-Wolf, F. (2015). *Imagining the Global: Transnational Media and Popular Culture beyond East and West*. Ann Arbor: University of Michigan Press.

DeFrantz, T. F. (2014). "Hip Hop Habitus v.2.0." In *Black Performance Theory*, edited by T. F. DeFrantz and A. Gonzalez, 223–242. Durham, NC: Duke University Press.

Desmond, J. (1997). *Meaning in Motion: New Cultural Studies of Dance*. Durham, NC: Duke University Press.

Drewal, M. (1991). "The State of Research on Performance in Africa." *African Studies Review* 34(3): 1–64.

Fernandes, S. (2011). *Close to the Edge: In Search of the Global Hip Hop Generation*. London: Verso.

Forman, M. (2002). *The 'Hood Comes First: Race, Space, and Place in Rap and Hip Hop*. Middletown, CT: Wesleyan University Press.

Gramsci, A. ([1971] 2010). *Selections from the Prison Notebooks*. Translated by Q. Hoare and G. Nowell-Smith. New York: International Publishers.

Hazzard-Donald, K. (1996). "Dance in Hip Hop Culture." In *Droppin Science: Critical Essays on Rap Music and Hip Hop Culture*, edited by W. E. Perkins, 211–219. Philadelphia: Temple University Press.

Hecht, D., and Simone, M. (1994). *Invisible Governance: The Art of African Micropolitics*. Brooklyn, NY: Autonomedia.

Johnson, I. K. (2011). "B-Boying and Battling in a Global Context: The Discursive Life of Difference in Hip Hop Dance." *Alif: Journal of Comparative Poetics* 31: 173–181.

Knox, J. (2010). "What Starts in Africa Returns to Africa: B-Boy Culture as Embodied Knowledge of the Diaspora: One B-Boy's Journey of African Re-assimilation." Unpublished Article.

Martin, R. (1997). *Critical Moves: Dance Studies in Theory & Politics*. Durham: Duke University Press.

Moore, M. (2018). *Fabulous: The Rise of the Beautiful Eccentric*. New Haven: Yale University Press.

Newell, S., and Okome, O. (2014). "Introduction: Popular Culture in Africa: The Episteme of the Everyday." In *Popular Culture in Africa: The Episteme of the Everyday*, edited by S. Newell and O. Okome. New York: Routledge.

Ofosu, T. B. (1993). "Dance Contests in Ghana." MA thesis. University of Ghana, Legon.

Ofosu, T. (2009). "Popular and Scholarly Choreographies in Ghana: A Synthesis of Dance Aesthetics and Current Trends." MFA thesis, University of Ghana, Legon.

Ofosu, T. B. K. (2014). "Rap Culture and its Parallels: The 'La Kpa' and Akan Praise Singing in Perspective." *Journal of Performing Arts* 4: 41–44.

Ofosu, T. B. K. (2013/2014). "Conceptualisation of Mental Breaking Grounds with Popular Dance Technique: Findings on Azonto Dance." University of Ghana Research Report. Accra, Ghana: Sub-Sub-Saharan Publishers.

Ofosu, T., and Dei, T. (2015). "The Azonto Dance, a Ghanaian New Creation: Exploring New Boundaries of Popular Dance Forms." *African Performance Review* 1(1).

Osumare, H. (2002). "Global Breakdancing and the Intercultural Body." *Dance Research Journal* 34(2).

Osumare, H. (2007). *The Africanist Aesthetic in Global Hip Hop: Power Moves*. New York: Palgrave Macmillan.

Osumare, H. (2012). *The Hiplife in Ghana: West African Indigenization of Hip Hop*. New York: Palgrave Macmillan.

Perry, I. (2004). *Prophets of the Hood: Politics and Poetics in Hip Hop*. Durham, NC: Duke University Press.

Rose, T. (1994). *Black Noise: Rap Music and Black Culture in Contemporary America*. Middletown, CT: Wesleyan University Press.

Snead, J. A. (1981). "On Repetition in Black Culture." *Black American Literature Forum* 1 (4): 146–54.

Shipley, J. W. (2009). "Aesthetic of the Entrepreneur: Afro-Cosmopolitan Rap and Moral Circulation in Accra, Ghana." *Anthropological Quarterly* 82 (3): 633–678.

Thompson, R. F. (1974). *African Arts in Motion*. Berkeley: University of California Press.

Thompson, R. F. (1983). *Flash of the Spirit: African and Afro-American Art and Philosophy*. New York: Vintage Books.

Thompson, R. F. (1993). *Face of the Gods: Art and Altars of Africa and the African Americas*. New York: Museum of African Art.

Thompson, R. F. (1996). "Hip Hop 101." In *Droppin' Science: Critical Essays on Rap Music and Hip Hop Culture*, edited by W. E. Perkins, 211–219. Philadelphia: Temple University Press.

Warner, M. (1993). *Fear of a Queer Planet: Queer Politics and Social Theory*. Minneapolis: University of Minnesota Press.

"Reggie Rockstone talks about Hiplife On CNN's Inside Africa-GhCampus.com," YouTube Video. Accessed August 6, 2015. https://www.youtube.com/results?search_query=Reggie+Rockston+CNN

CHAPTER 15

....

ASIAN AMERICAN
LIMINALITY

Racial Triangulation in Hip Hop Dance

....

GRACE SHINHAE JUN

INTRODUCTION

....

FUSION, according to its website, is one of the longest running and most "highly anticipated" hip hop dance competitions in Southern California. Since its inception, in 1999, FUSION has been an expansive platform for many of today's most popular crews, such as the Jabbawockeez and Kaba Modern. Hosted by the Multi-Asian Student Association (MASA) at the University of California, San Diego (UCSD), "FUSION isn't just a hip-hop dance competition. It's an amalgam of talent, dedication, and culture that also seeks to educate its viewers, day of and after, about the Asian American presence in the hip-hop community. It is a unique competition in the sense that it also has a focus on the cultural aspect of the community, bringing Asian American talent into the lime-light" (see http://www.fusionhhdc.org/about/). My interest piqued, I decided to attend FUSION in 2014 and became curious about its history and its centering of the presence of Asian Americans in Hip Hop dance. What was going on in this unique space with FUSION marketing itself as an Asian American space? And where did this eruption of Asian American dancers come from? Given how different my own experience both in high school and as an undergraduate at UCSD was, I was honestly puzzled by the tremendous growth of Asian American participation in Hip Hop dance, in particular by Asian American men. What was their attraction to the style? Why were these coming-of-age Asian Americans building community and finding their identities through the performance of Hip Hop culture? At FUSION, performances to Hip Hop music featured unison choreography that hinted of Hip Hop dance movement, but the choreography was markedly different from the party dances or b-boying that I associated with Hip Hop dance. What were these bodies saying, or, in dance scholar Thomas DeFrantz's (2005) term, what was the "corporeal orature" of Asian American Hip Hop dance?[1]

I will examine Asian Americans in Hip Hop and on dance teams, and argue that the practitioners perform racial liminality by simultaneously challenging their own racial marginalization and evading the racialized roots of the form. What I saw at FUSION was Asian American youth contesting their own erasure and subjugation by building an expressive community, with a palpable absence of the African American cultural, political, and historical context that had birthed Hip Hop. The dancers were, to borrow Claire Kim's (2000) formulation, "triangulated" racially in a liminal space that permitted their desire to be seen, without their losing ground in terms of social status and life opportunities. FUSION as a cultural phenomenon raises important questions about race and representation at a critical historical moment, when racism persists unabated in every area of American life.

There are only a few published studies about Asian American Hip Hop dance. I draw from my own experience as an Asian American woman who has been teaching Hip Hop movement classes at UCSD and other nearby colleges and universities for over twenty years. I frame this analysis by engaging Hip Hop scholarship, scholarship in American studies and ethnic studies, and related scholarship on Asian Americans in Hip Hop. Although Hip Hop originated in the Black and Brown neighborhoods of New York City, Hip Hop culture has been celebrated, consumed, and represented by youth of various cultures around the world. Oliver Wang (2006), points out: "Journalists and scholars alike have focused on hip-hop's massive appeal among youth globally, drawing attention to how, as an expressive form, hip-hop finds deep resonance with a wide array of communities spanning racial, gender, class, and other social lines" (147). Despite the mass commercialization of Hip Hop, the culture continues to serve as a means of expression. Ethnomusicologist and hip hop scholar Joseph Schloss (2009) also argues that this expression through Hip Hop creates agency: "What I am suggesting is that hip-hop culture gives its participants the power to redefine themselves and their history, not by omission or selective emphasis, but by embracing all of their previous experience as material for self-expression in the present moment" (45). Vietnamese spoken-word artist Thien-Bao Thuc Phi (2008) adds that Hip Hop performance also gives the "opportunity to communicate and convey signifiers and ideologies through art. It contains the opportunity to represent ourselves, our stories, and our people. In Hip Hop is the power and sensibility to educate and uplift our communities" (303).

Yet despite the acceptance of Hip Hop as multicultural, some critical voices challenge its appropriation. African American writer and activist Kenyon Farrow (2004) asks, "What is it about Black people (and especially Black masculinity in the case of hip-hop), and what they represent to others, that is so attractive to other people, including non-white people of color?" FUSION and the Asian American dance teams call into question how we define marginalization, how we think about multiculturalism and the powerful appeal of Hip Hop, and what happens when Hip Hop is performed in places of privilege with an overwhelming absence of Black people or connections to Black communities. Situated in the changing demographics of American higher education and the changing context of the transmission and circulation of Hip Hop dance, these Asian American dancers struggle between visibility and invisibility and between fitting in and finding their identity, engaging in cultural contestation without knowing the history of what they are performing, and why that matters.

ASIAN AMERICANS ON CAMPUS

The University of California, San Diego's Institutional Research website reports that, between the years 2001 and 2016 (Table 15.1), the proportion of enrolled students who identify as Asian or Asian American increased from 32% to 48.5%; the Caucasian percentage decreased by nearly half; and African Americans remained a tiny proportion despite more than doubling in number. The table categorizes Filipino as distinct from Asian, though most if not all Flipinx students identify as Asian American. It is also important to note the increase in the number of international students on the UCSD campus, many of whom come from Asian countries, which affects the overall look and feel of the campus.

This growth in the number of Asians and Asian Americans as part of the student body is reflected in their representation in theater and dance courses, and specifically, in my Hip Hop movement classes. Although my classes do include some non–Asian Americans, often in a class of forty-five students, around 75 percent are Asian or Asian American. The significance of this demographic shift has affected my own reflections on Hip Hop culture and the manner in which I approach teaching and our class discussions, as well as what I require in their reflection papers. In every Hip Hop movement course I teach, I highlight the history of the culture and initiate class discussions about the appropriation of Hip Hop culture. In our first meeting, I ask them to define Hip Hop and to give the reason they signed up for the class. Some students situate Hip Hop culture in the African American community; others describe it as a specific music and dance style. Many of them describe Hip Hop as a form of expression and see the course as extracurricular. Most of them write about wanting to learn how to dance and do something fun outside their major courses. Many of these students in the past have come in with little or no dance skill or knowledge of Hip Hop movement vernacular; however, I have experienced a shift in the growing numbers of skilled dance-team members who have enrolled post 2010. In students' written definitions of Hip Hop, what was apparent was the consistency in how narrow the definitions of Hip Hop were.

In our discussion of the appropriation of Hip Hop, we focus primarily on the appropriation of Hip Hop as a Black cultural practice on a campus with a disproportionately low number of African American students. The lectures lay out some of the historical examples of appropriation to the present day. Prior to these class lectures and discussions, many of the Asian American students do not necessarily consider their participation in Hip Hop as a form of appropriation, as they write in their reflection papers. Although in theory, the idea of appropriation is not new to many of them, the idea that they might be contributors is often jarring and unsettling. The students that are already knowledgeable about the discourse of appropriation are vocal in

TABLE 15.1 Undergraduate Enrolment by Ethnicity

2001	2006
Total = 17,505	Total = 21,369
32% Asian (5,554)	39% Asian (8,287)
5% Filipino (896)	5% Filipino (1,058)
1% African American (211)	1% African American (276)
8% Mexican American (1,322)	9% Mexican American (1,844)
2% Latino (375)	3% Latino (567)
<1% Native American (81)	<1% Native American (99)
38% Caucasian (6,652)	31% Caucasian (6,557)
14% Other/Undeclared (2,414)	13% Other/Undeclared
2% International (353)	3% International (640)
6,450 Asian and Filipino combined	9,345 Asian and Filipino combined

2011	2016
Total = 23,046	Total = 28,127
44% Asian (10,142)	45.8% Asian (12,891)
4% Filipino (1,009)	5.3% Filipino (1,501)
2% African American (442)	2.5% African American (691)
12% Mexican American (2,787)	13% Mexican American (3,787)
3% Latino (792)	3% Latino (984)
<1% Native American (111)	<1% Native American (121)
24% Caucasian (5,584)	19.9% Caucasian (5,609)
9.5% Other/undeclared (2,179)	9% Other/Undeclared (2,543)
6.6% International (1,511)	19.4% International (5,445)
11,151 Asian and Filipino combined	14,392 Asian and Filipino combined

Source: Institutional Research: Undergraduate Statistics. University of California, San Diego
Institutional Research. http://studentresearch.ucsd.edu/about/index. html.

articulating cultural appropriation and the ways in which it is problematic. And then
I sometimes have students who, in reflecting on their own participation, struggle with
how and where to locate themselves within a culture they have little knowledge of and
do not claim. They think their participation in this form of popular culture is harmless
but fail to see the consequences. It is precisely because of the general lack of knowledge of Hip Hop culture, and the overwhelming and dominating presence of Asian
Americans who profess a love for Hip Hop in these classes, that I emphasize its history
and current practices. The combination of the changing demographics in my classes
and on the campus in general, the rising number of dance teams on campus, and the
influx of dance team members into my classes has made me feel that these discussions
are more urgent than ever.

DANCE TEAMS

A microcosm of UCSD's demographics, the dance teams reflect the high percentage of Asian Americans on campus. Since the introduction of dance teams in California's colleges and universities in the 1990s, UCSD has participated in the growth of this trend. For example, between the years 2008 and 2016, approximately ten new teams were formed. Each had approximately forty members, predominantly Filipinx, Chinese, and Korean, with a roughly even balance of women and men. The focus of the teams varied, based on how they categorized themselves. Some teams participated on the competitive circuit; others primarily performed as exhibition teams. A few teams advertised themselves as noncompetitive and inclusive, regardless of skill, and one team was open to women only. More recently, project teams and concept videos have emerged. Project teams are made up of dancers from different teams who work together to perform at specific events, while concept videos are consequent on dancers coming together specifically to create for film.

Many of these earlier teams, across Southern California college campuses from the 1990s, grew out of ethnic-specific cultural groups that incorporated dances to be performed as part of their cultural night. Dancers would perform "modern" or current dances alongside their traditional dances. These "modern" dancers began to splinter off to create dance groups that focused solely on creating and performing current dances. One of the well-known dance teams, Kaba Modern, founded in 1992, grew out of the Pilipino American student organization, Kababayan, at the University of California, Irvine. PAC (Pilipino American Coalition) Modern was established at California State University, Long Beach; and shortly after that NSU (Nikkei Student Union) Modern was established at the University of California, Los Angeles. These groups renamed themselves, keeping part or the initials of the traditional group's name to signify their cultural heritage, but adding "modern" to situate themselves within the broader and current American culture.

These first-generation collegiate teams came together in the midst of the 1980s Hip Hop party dances and New Jack Swing Era, when producer Teddy Riley began to mix R & B and soul with Hip Hop beats. Prior to New Jack music, films such as *Beat Street* (1984), *Breakin'* (1984), and the clip of the Rock Steady Crew in *Flashdance* (1983) had laid the groundwork by bringing b-boying to a wider audience. Hip Hop dance was becoming more accessible, and as party dances like the Wop and the Running Man took shape, dancers performed them as choreographed routines for high school talent shows and house parties. High school dance teams began to sprout all over California, and eventually competitions between the high school dance teams followed. Channel Islands High School had one of the first all-male teams, and many of these dancers enrolled in CSU Long Beach (Nefalar 2017 interview). Similarly, dance team members at Mira Mesa High School enrolled at UCSD and filtered into the team 220 (Second to None). These dancers became the first generation of the dance team phenomenon.

The dancers who followed this first generation continued to have greater exposure to Hip Hop movement and culture, albeit through more commercial avenues. In addition to dance films in which Hip Hop was a central component (*Save the Last Dance* [2001], *Honey* [2003], *You Got Served* [2004], *Step Up* [2006]), videos (thanks to the invention of YouTube [2005]); competitive shows like *So You Think You Can Dance* (2005) and *America's Best Dance Crew* (2008); and studio classes and instruction made Hip Hop dance even more accessible. Dancers increasingly learned the movements, not by being connected to the Black community, but through video and the Internet. And as the collegiate dance teams began to expand outside the campus cultural groups, they started renaming their movement style, calling it "modern choreography" at the end of the 2000s, and eventually using the terms *urban dance* and *urban choreography* (Nefalar 2017 interview). What differentiated these dance groups' style from Hip Hop dance was an emphasis on precise, in-unison choreography, as opposed to the freestyling done in cyphers and at house parties.

Although there have been shifts in the past couple of years, the dances or performances of these teams, for the most part, follow a predictable formula. They include a high-energy section, a woman-only section, a man-only section, a couples section, and an emotional section, all accompanied by different songs to match the choreography. Many of the teams incorporate a hypersexualized section, performed by either only the women or couples. The dance's movements are performed in strict unison, but the dance will also juxtapose two groups performing two different choreographies, or sometimes will highlight a soloist performing a different choreography from the rest of the group. Duets are commonly performed between a man and woman. Women-only sections are more sexual, with curvy and circular movement and the use of the head and hair. Men-only sections involve more angles, shapes, and precision, and there is less use of curves and the pelvis. Typically, these dances fall into heteronormative representations of gender; however, teams will sometimes flip the presentation, with the men dancing the sexier movement, and the women dancing the more aggressive section. Since "crowd appeal" is one of the scored competition categories, this reversal of gender performance is done to get a response from the audience and from the judges, a moment of surprise to provoke a reaction.

In general, the movement and choreography connect to the lyrics of the songs, or are choreographed to specific beats and sounds within the song to showcase the intricacies and the choreographers' ability to hear beyond the basic rhythm. Faces or facials are incorporated into the choreography, and the dances are mostly forward facing, performed in a proscenium fashion. As one of the crucial parts in the judging in their performance, the teams focus on spatial patterns or blocking to manage the forty-plus dancers, from everyone on stage to smaller groups to half the team, and so on. Unless a certain dancer is highlighted, for the most part no dancer is isolated, as uniformity is valued and precision is scored highly. These sets or performances are approximately five to six minutes long, comprise several songs, and do not necessarily uphold continuity in theme or message. In asking the dancers I interviewed how songs are chosen, some of them responded with whatever the choreographer is interested in, or what song the choreographer finds that suits their aesthetic. Songs are also chosen to best display the team's various skills, and more recent trends include teams' choosing one song or a medley of songs by one artist.

By continuing my observations of various competitions, performances, and online videos of different dance team groups, it became clear why the dancers began renaming their dance style as distinct from Hip Hop. Hip Hop dance practitioner and scholar, E. Moncell Durden (2018) writes that Hip Hop "includes a myriad of dance forms and styles such as locking, popping, krumping, b-boying, waacking, waving, and tutting. However, of all the dance forms associated with hip-hop, only two are in fact hip-hop dances: b-boying and hip-hop party dancing" (76). Although some of these associated Hip Hop dance forms appear in the choreography of the teams, the lack of freestyle, heavy emphasis of gestures, loss of individuality and musical selections all reflect a divergence from Hip Hop. What, then, is *urban dance*, or *urban choreography*? STEEZY, an Asian American–founded online blog popular in the urban dance community, whose mission is to "share the dance experience by making it accessible to everyone," centers urban dance on choreography (http://blog.steezy.co/about-us/). Jessie Ma, one of the blog's founders and a contributor states that urban dance choreography "is a style of dance, community, and lifestyle revolving around choreographed pieces and performances by a dancer or groups of dancers. Choreography is influenced by several different dance styles, but is ultimately based on the choreographer's own interpretation of the music. A big part of the modern Urban Dance culture stemmed from collegiate dance teams and competitions" (Ma 2017). She prefaces this definition of urban dance by clarifying that it is separate from Hip Hop and streetdance. And in various conversations I have had with colleagues and students, they consistently differentiate the movement crafted and performed by the dance teams from what is understood as Hip Hop dance. At the same time, members of the urban dance community acknowledge the dance's roots in Hip Hop. This process of renaming reflects an uncertainty and confusion that has always characterized Asian American racialization, a liminal place within the US racial order.

Triangulating Asian American "Urban Dance" Identity

In *Bitter Fruit: The Politics of Black-Korean Conflict in New York City*, political science scholar Claire Kim (2000) uses her study of the Red Apple boycott in New York City to situate Asians and Asian Americans in the American racial order: "Asian immigrants and their descendants have been 'triangulated' insofar as they have been racialized both as inferior to whites and superior to Blacks (in between Black and white) and as permanently foreign and unassimilable (apart from Black and white)" (16). Using the image of the triangle (Figure 15.1), Kim (2000) places whites at the highest point and

Blacks at the lowest point, directly below whites. The third point of the triangle is designated for Asians, and is located to the right, in-between the two other points. This third point indicates that Asians are higher on the scale of superior–inferior in comparison to Blacks, but they are also to the right of both Blacks and whites on the scale of insider–foreigner. Permanently regarded as foreign, yet lauded as hardworking, Asians become the "model minority."

In applying Kim's triangulation theory to Asian American participation in Hip Hop, I argue that Asian Americans begin by moving toward the lowest point of the triangle. This movement toward Blacks, more specifically, Black culture, is a way to push back against the foreign, to be seen as American by assimilating an American cultural art form. For the Asian American dancers on these teams, participating in Hip Hop is intended as a movement *toward* the domestic axis, not *down* the superior–inferior axis; it is not an identification with Blackness or becoming Black, but a desire to be "American." However, this move to appropriate Black culture comes with cost. As American Studies scholar George Lipsitz (1994) writes:

> Popular culture routinely provides opportunities for escaping the parochialisms and prejudices of our personal worlds, for expanding our experience and understanding by seeing the world through the eyes of others. But it can also trap us in its own mystifications and misrepresentations, building our investment and engagement in fictions that misrepresent the lives of others and hide the conditions of their own production—the contexts of power, hate, hurt, and fear in which we live. Popular culture often reduces the lived experiences of gender, ethnicity, class, and race that contain and constrain people to exotic stereotypes that serve to build dramatic tension and texture, but which elide history. (160)

In attempting to erase Asians and Asian American stereotypes through Hip Hop dance, dancers perform selected interpretations of Blackness. However, the

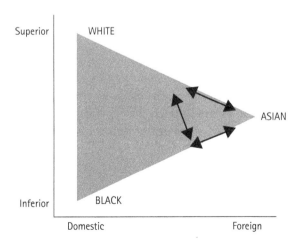

FIGURE 15.1

appropriation is often difficult to perceive because, in the process of becoming com-mercialized and easily accessible, Hip Hop presumably has come to represent a mul-ticultural youth voice. This multicultural voice, while powerful, often conflates youth experiences at the expense of neglecting a specific African American experience.

As noted earlier, some of these dancers come to the form without thinking about race or Hip Hop's roots. This goes back to my students' responses, how seeing themselves as appropriators felt confusing and unsettling. Cultural theorist Tricia Rose (2008) states, "Researchers have also shown that white fans of Hip Hop take up a color-blind approach to the consumption of Hip Hop's black coded images, stories, and style as a means by which to retain associations with progressive coolness afforded by black cul-ture through Hip Hop and simultaneously avoid direct confrontation with their own racial privilege" (230). Different from white consumption of Black culture and Hip Hop culture, Asian American consumption of Hip Hop is an attempt to gain legitimacy, thus it appears to be a movement toward white or whiteness, but, in fact, is a circling up-ward away from Black or Blackness, as Figure 15.1 shows. Not recognizing the privilege of their triangulated status, Asian American dancers fail to see that being labeled racially superior allows them to take part in a multicultural and "colorblind" Hip Hop, without having to face anti-Black oppression.

The community-building aspect of the teams moves the Asian American dancers back toward a definable Asian American shared identity (Figure 15.1). They do not try to become "white;" their self-identification as Asian American is what binds them. As one dancer shared,

> I definitely don't think that Asian Americans come to this style of dance for the same reasons as the Black community did, because even though Asian Americans are a minority, they are the most privileged minorities in the whole US so I don't think it's a form escape from oppression but it might be in that we see a lot of things because this community is predominantly Asian American not just at UCSD but in So Cal. But not to escape oppression but to feel more inclusion to be surrounded more like you who share the same origins as you but do it through dance. (personal interview with a group of dancers, September 21, 2017)

Another dancer added, "We want to be with the people that look like us because it gives us a sense of community and these people know what it's like to be an outsider. We are all Asians and proud. It's not everyone hates us so we need to come together" (Group interview). This sentiment carries through the experiences of most if not all of these dancers, who are drawn together because of cultural similarities.

Their own cultural pride and celebration of parallel Asian cultural practices remain central to their connections. These dance team spaces provide an alternative community for Asian Americans and a place of respite amid the stressful structures of academic life. This desire for community is strong and often dictates their campus social life. It is the reason these young people seek out dance teams, and spend countless late-night hours in marginal, less-than-ideal physical spaces. Because they have only minimal access to recreational dance studio spaces, many of the rehearsals and workshops offered by the dance groups take place in campus parking garages or outside buildings that provide a "mirror" through the reflection of the windows. Several of the dancers calculated that they spend at minimum of twenty hours a week choreographing and rehearsing, on top of attending classes, doing their schoolwork, and working at jobs or internships. However, because these teams provide a sense of belonging among peers with similar life prospects, they keep returning year after year.

The circular movement toward the Asian, Black, and white points in the triangle represents Asian American liminality, a seemingly perpetual struggle to locate themselves. The movement also opens opportunities to challenge prevailing stereotypes, such as the quiet, demure Asian female and the emasculated Asian male. There is a freedom in learning and performing Hip Hop or urban dance that momentarily allows them to exist beyond the limiting stereotypes and tropes assigned to their bodies. In one experience, it became known to my students that I was going to be judging an all-styles, all-female battle hosted by the all-female team on campus. Several of the students told me to look out for one particular dancer I will call Donna, describing her only as "small and Asian," saying that I would be surprised. When I watched Donna's performance at the battle, I understood what my students had meant. Not only did Donna's thin and petite frame make her look more like a middle schooler than a college student, but her face, demeanor, and voice only heightened the confusion. Her performance was in opposition to her bodily presence. Her whole body moved in a confrontational, in-your-face, and aggressive style toward her battle opponent. No longer did I see a modest and timid Asian woman. Donna had powerfully challenged that gender and racial stereotyping and the consigned invisibility of her body. Performing in these team settings creates for dancers a space to be heard, to be visible, and to be seen as expressive.

Despite the momentary visibility, the liminal space perpetuates a crisis of grounding that is evident in the dance teams' use of the term *urban*. I argue that their renaming of Hip Hop dance as urban dance or urban choreography reflects the Asian American dancers' struggle around their own identity, and thus continues the spiraling motion of the circle and an abandoning of the roots and connection to Black culture. The urban dance style is, according to Jessie Ma (2018), an "act," or choreography, and that choreography is "more or less completely up to the individual choreographer. They draw from whatever style(s) they were trained in or influenced by, or come up with random moves with no stylistic origin—to interpret the music in their own way." This erasure of the authentic point of origin exemplifies what dance scholar Brenda Dixon Gottschild (2003) critiques. She writes, "In every instance, the cultural riches are diluted by segregation from the cultural source, resulting in an artistic vacuum and an aesthetic loss" (140). In this sense, the expression of "urban" is anti-Black. The roots of the culture and Blackness of Hip Hop is erased. All that remains is a space where non-Black dancers, in this case Asian American dancers, can explore, express, and "find" their own voice. Thus "urban" signals a problematic disengagement that misses the potential liberatory direct engagement with Black culture and Black people.

CONCLUSION

As today's college dancers get further away from the first generation of Asian American team dancers, their connection to the foundations of Hip Hop weakens. I have seen efforts made to bring the instruction of foundational Hip Hop styles to their groups; however, the focus of these dancers continues to center on stylistic choreography by individual team leaders and to follow commercial trends in choreography. Asian Americans may enter the liminal space from different points and move in different directions, but in the complexity of their participation I see Asian American dancers struggling to find their identity, aesthetics, and cultural values. This process of racial triangulation means that Asian American dancing bodies communicate a discomfort with their otherness and a desire to be seen as more American, as more than an ostracized other. Their bodies challenge the constraints of a racial system, while simultaneously avoiding a more serious encounter with the grim consequences of that system. It is a hobby that is most often left behind when they graduate and move onto their nondance career paths, never having had to directly face the effects of their complicity in sustaining the individual and group advantages that anti-Black racism denies to Black people. It is for these reasons that I insist on engaging my students in discussions around appropriation and the erasure of Blackness, and ask them to critically analyze their own participation. In class, we can recognize the connective marginalities (Osumare 2005, 267), acknowledge that people of color in the United States do not always come to the table with the same perspective, and then take it a step or a few steps further. As cultural theorist Miles White (2001) puts it, "The deeper implications and challenges for youth who appropriate, admire, consume, and transform African American cultural expressions is to move beyond such fetishizing representations of Blackness and masculinities to embrace the transformational possibilities of racial transgression" (130). It is my hope that, with knowledge and deep reflection, these massive groups of Asian American dancers can, as theater and performance scholar Harry J. Elam (2005) says, "produce progressive politics or promote avenues for social change and black liberation" (386), instead of picking up only the "attractive" and "cool" aspects of the culture without acknowledging the whole. In their process of creating, rehearsing, and performing, dance teams should help Asian Americans to dismantle the notions of racial triangulation, and work toward a more equitable society that reveres Black culture and Black lives, and fashions new possibilities for new solidarities.

NOTE

1. An earlier version of this article titled "Corporeal Transmission of Asian Americans in Hip Hop Dance" was presented in October 2017 at the inaugural Dance Studies Association Conference "Transmissions and Traces: Rendering Dance" in Columbus, Ohio.

References

Chung, B. (2016). "Started in the Streets . . . : Criminalizing Blackness and the Performance of Asian American Entrepreneurship on America's Best Dance Crew, Season 1." In *Contemporary Directions in Asian American Dance*, edited by Yutian Wong, 117–142. Madison: University of Wisconsin Press.

DeFrantz, T. F. (2005). "The Black Beat Made Visible: Hip Hop Dance and Body Power." In *Of the Presence of the Body: Essays on Dance and Performance Theory*, edited by A. Lepecki, 64–81. Middletown, CT: Wesleyan University Press.

Durden, E. M. (2018). *Beginning Hip-Hop Dance*. Champaign, IL: Human Kinetics.

Elam, H. J. (2005). "Change Clothes and Go: A Postscript to Postblackness." In *Black Cultural Traffic: Crossroads in Global Performance and Popular Culture*, edited by H. J. Elam Jr. and K. Jackson, 379–388. Ann Arbor: University of Michigan Press.

Farrow, K. (2004). "We Real Cool? On Hip-Hop, Asian-Americans, Black Folks, and Appropriation." Kenyon Farrow (website). http://www.kenyonfarrow.com/ selected-writing/. Accessed August 2018.

Gottschild, B. D. (2003). *The Black Dancing Body: A Geography from Coon to Cool*. New York: Palgrave Macmillan.

Kim, C. J. (2000). *Bitter Fruit: The Politics of Black-Korean Conflict in New York City*. New Haven, CT: Yale University Press.

Lipsitz, G. (1994). *Dangerous Crossroads: Popular Music, Postmodernism and The Poetics of Place*. London: Verso.

Ma, J. (2017). "What Is Urban Dance?" *SteezyBlog*. September 27. http://blog.steezy.co/what-is-urban-dance/. Accessed January 2018.

Ma, J. (2018). "Why You Shouldn't Call Urban Dance 'Hip Hop.'" *SteezyBlog*. January 15. http://blog.steezy.co/urban-dance-and-hip-hop/. Accessed June 2018.

Nefalar, B. (2017). Personal interview. San Diego. September 12.

Osumare, H. (2005). "Global Hip-Hop and the Africa Diaspora." In *Black Cultural Traffic: Crossroads in Global Performance and Popular Culture*, edited by. H. J. Elam Jr. and K. Jackson, 266–288. Ann Arbor: University of Michigan Press.

Phi, T.-B. T. (2008). "Yellow Lines: Asian Americans and Hip Hop." In *Afro Asia: Revolutionary Political and Cultural Connections between African Americans and Asian Americans*. edited by F. Ho and B. V. Mullen, 295–317. Durham, NC: Duke University Press.

Rose, T. (2008). *Hip Hop Wars: What We Talk about When We Talk about Hip Hop; and Why It Matters*. New York: Basic Books.

Schloss, J. G. (2009). *Foundation: B-Boys, B-Girls, and Hip-Hop Culture in New York*. Oxford: Oxford University Press.

Villegas, M. (2017). "Kaba Modern, AZN Pride, and Reconsidering Cultural Arrival." Paper presented at the Association for Asian American Studies. Portland, OR, April.

Wang, O. (2006). "These Are the Breaks: Hip-Hop and AfroAsian Cultural (Dis)Connections." In *AfroAsian Encounters: Culture, History, Politics*, edited by H. Raphael-Hernandez and S. Steen, 146–164. New York: New York University Press.

White, M. (2001). *From Jim Crow to Jay-Z: Race, Rap, and the Performance of Masculinity*. Champaign: University of Illinois Press.

CHAPTER 16

BREAKIN' DOWN THE BLOC

Hip Hop Dance in Armenia

SEROUJ "MIDUS" APRAHAMIAN

INTRODUCTION

IN the summer of 2005, I traveled to my native Armenia to spend two months volunteering and touring the country. A few weeks into the trip, I was having lunch at a café near the fourth-century cathedral Etchmiadzin, when our group's local guide, a university student studying Armenian history, asked us what kind of music we listened to. She said she liked rappers like Eminem, 2Pac, and 50 Cent. I responded that I break and listen to rap too, just a bit more of an underground variety. Curious and excited by our conversation, she told me that she loved breaking and had friends in the city who do the dance. I almost fell out of my seat.

I had tried to find breakers in Armenia since I first traveled there in 2003, but I was convinced there were none. In a society that cherishes its traditional culture and was only slowly opening up to the world following the collapse of the Soviet Union, finding young people involved in a dance born in the Bronx, New York, was hard to imagine. At the time, even in the United States, breaking was a largely community-based practice existing outside of the bounds of the dominant culture (Osumare 2002). It was one thing to hear our tour guide say she listened to rap, quite another to learn that she knew breakers in the city. I turned to her and insisted that she introduce me.

Two days later, we arranged to meet in downtown Yerevan, the capital of the country. I got there fifteen minutes early and saw her approaching with two girls at her side. They stood out like sore thumbs, wearing baggy pants, bandanas, loud colors, and sneakers. Rarely did you see a woman back then in Armenia wearing anything but high heels, dark colors, and traditional "ladylike" garb. The Soviet legacy of suppressing individuality, mixed with traditional gender roles, resulted in a blanket standard of femininity that did not allow much room for an "unkept" look. To be dressed how they were was not only an expression of diversity; it was a statement of defiance that screamed independence and disregard for social constrictions. As they approached me, I could not help but notice the bewildered stares they were getting from onlookers. These two b-girls personified what dance scholar Imani Kai Johnson (2014) has aptly termed "badass femininity": a rejection of traditional norms of passive womanhood in favor of explicit expressions of female strength and irreverence.

The girls' names were Marina and Ani, and it turned out that, not only did they dance, but they were also aspiring rappers. They called themselves Seize Crew. It was surreal. The last thing I had expected was to meet a crew of female breakers who rap! Even back in Los Angeles, it was rare to encounter Armenians who were involved directly in Hip Hop.[1] Especially young women, who are often encouraged to refrain from activities deemed *odar* (foreign)[2] or male-centered. To my delight, these two b-girls were breaking down those patriarchal norms and, with it, my skepticism about the existence of Hip Hop in the country.

They agreed to take me to practice with them in a neighborhood on the outskirts of the city. There, in a ramshackle studio, I met three other dancers who were trying out intermediate moves like windmills, backspins, and swipes. After about an hour of practicing, I asked if they knew any other breakers. They told me about a group called Mad Force Crew (MFC) but explained that they were not on the best of terms with them. I was in the company of a rebellious bunch, who preferred to dance independently from the more established group.

However, after some persuading, they agreed to introduce me. We ran into two members of MFC as we walked to the practice venue, a former Soviet cultural center called "Kanaz" in a suburb of Yerevan. I introduced myself, and upon hearing my name and where I was from, one of the dancers realized he had seen me in an online trailer for a popular breaking video called *Detours* (2002). He could not contain his excitement, knowing that a fellow Armenian, with a recognized name in the breaking community,[3] was in his city giving him a Hip Hop hug (a handshake with the right hand and a one-armed embrace with the other).

Within twenty-four hours, I was in touch with the entire Hip Hop dance scene in Armenia. At the time, there were only three crews and a total of about fifty dancers in the country—all of them confined to the capital. The scene was extremely small and consisted almost exclusively of weekly practice sessions. Rarely were there any organized competitions or direct interactions with dancers abroad.

Today, a decade and a half later, there are at least fifteen active breaking crews and over five hundred dancers throughout Armenia. You can find a weekly class that teaches breaking in every neighborhood in Yerevan, as well as in outlying areas such as Abovyan and Charentsavan, which are about twenty- and forty-minutes northeast of the capital, respectively. Competitions take place on a regular basis, with guests and judges traveling from as far away as Russia, Ukraine, Georgia, Iran, France, Finland, and the United States. A handful of dancers even make a living off breaking, doing commercials, theatrical shows, and teaching classes.

How did breaking get introduced and grow so rapidly in a developing, post-Soviet country like Armenia? What impact did it have on society, and vice-versa? What relation does the dance have with the highly connected, globalized world we live in today? How were its aesthetics adapted to local conditions? What lessons can be drawn from Armenia's experience for the development of Hip Hop dance in other parts of the world? These are the questions that immediately come to mind when we think about the remarkable spread of breaking to a region so distant from its birthplace.

From 2013 to 2015, I lived in Armenia and actively participated in the breaking community there, judging competitions, giving workshops, organizing events, documenting developments, and closely interacting with the scene's main practitioners. Through field research, historical analysis, and direct personal observation, I hope to shed light on those questions. In the winter of 2014, I conducted open-ended interviews with five of the leading dancers in the country to gain a deeper understanding of their backgrounds, motivations, and views regarding the dance. What follows is a narrativization of the evolution of Armenia's post-Soviet breaking history, rooted in both my ethnographic research and personal experiences. I aim to show that Hip Hop dance in Armenia has served as an important conduit for breaking down social constrictions and forging new identities at a time of immense socioeconomic transformation.

GODFATHER FLASH

During the Soviet era, contact with the West was nearly impossible for Armenians. Nevertheless, certain films and magazines clandestinely made their way into the country, giving people a glimpse into Hip Hop culture. By getting their hands on movies like *Flashdance* (1983), *Breakin'* (1984) and *Beat Street* (1984), a small segment of local dancers began trying out the moves they were seeing for the first time on the screen. Breaking can be said to have emerged in Armenia during this mid-1980s period, but it did not take hold. Most people treated it as a fad, just something fun to try out. More crucially, the country's isolation behind the Soviet Iron Curtain, and a series of tumultuous shocks in the late 1980s to mid-1990s, prevented Hip Hop from fully taking root in Armenia as it had in other parts of the world.

In 1988, the country was rocked by a devastating 6.8 magnitude earthquake, which left 25,000 people dead and about 500,000 people homeless. In that same year, a movement began to liberate Nagorno-Karabakh—an ethnically Armenian enclave that was placed under Azerbaijani jurisdiction by Soviet authorities—resulting in a bloody conflict that would take the lives of nearly 30,000 people and produce an estimated one million refugees (Chorbajian 2001). Both Azerbaijan and its ally Turkey imposed blockades on Armenia as a result of the war, exacerbating the harsh economic strain the country was already facing. The dissolution of the Soviet Union in 1991 also severed Armenia's ties to its main markets for goods, triggering a sharp financial collapse. The GDP fell by 53% in 1992 and dropped another 15% the following year. By 1995, nearly a million citizens had left the republic in search of work and better opportunities abroad (Welt and Bremmer 1997; Dudwick 2003). Under these ravaged conditions, putting food on the table and having enough heat to survive the winter far outweighed any desire to pursue interests such as breaking. Although Hip Hop culture is often theorized as a response to rupture and survival in the midst of dislocation (Rose 1994), young people in Armenia generally did not have the psychic energy or resources necessary to pursue artistic practice during these "dark years."[4] Not until after the 1994 ceasefire in the Nagorno-Karabakh War did conditions slowly begin to stabilize.

It was during this period of stabilization that Sargis "B-Boy Flash" Andreasyan would begin planting the seeds of Hip Hop in Armenia. After coming back from his two-year mandatory army service in 1999, Andreasyan—a twenty-year-old resident of Yerevan— was trying to figure out which direction to take in his life. Like other post-Soviet countries at the time, Armenia was undergoing a radical transition to free-market capitalism; many state-owned enterprises were being privatized, and public spaces were being commercialized, and a small handful of well-connected elites were growing rich. Andreasyan was lucky enough to find work as a security guard at a lamp factory but felt a sense of alienation and disillusionment in his new surroundings. "I started working but felt something boiling up inside of me," he recalls. "I knew that I had to do something more than just be a security guard or policeman. That life wasn't for me" (interview with the author, December 2014).

One day, Andreasyan saw a Russian television program called *Fresh* that featured the breaking crews Jam Style and Da Boogie. The program not only had dancing but also interviews with the crew members about where they were from, why they danced, and what competitions they had been in, as well as brief tutorials on how to do basic moves. Andreasyan was mesmerized. He waited for a rerun of the clip and successfully recorded it. He would also catch other clips from movies and music videos, always ready to record any glimpse of the dance. With no classes or teachers to learn from, he began trying the moves on his own. He was encouraged by the fact that he could actually pull them off.

Full of energy and a new sense of purpose, he went out to gather others who were interested in the dance, starting with his cousins and friends in the neighborhood. They would soon recruit other *dursi tgherk* (street kids) and practice wherever they could: living rooms, courtyards, and subway stations. The most talented and dedicated of this group eventually formed the Hai Jumping Crew[5] in 2001, the first full-fledged breaking crew in Armenia.

From the start, the group had the spirit of Hip Hop in their movement. B-Boy Flash's younger brother tried his hand at aerosol art, and other members started DJing and rapping. In addition to practicing, they would perform at talent shows and film their own video clips. But the crew would be short-lived. By 2002, most of its members had either stopped dancing, emigrated out of the country, or were focused on other pursuits.

Flash, however, never lost his passion for the dance. He began recruiting other young adherents and, about a year later, formed a new group called Mad Force Crew (MFC). Soon after, he encountered a dancer at a gymnastics studio in Yerevan who had remarkable proficiency in breaking. His name was Garik Aleksanyan and, unbeknownst to Flash and his crew, he had been dabbling in the dance for as long as they had. They began hanging out, exchanging videos, practicing together, and developing a new sense of community. "In those days, it was like finding an oasis in the desert," says Aleksanyan about meeting the MFC members. "Finding each other gave us a huge boost" (interview with the author, December 2014).

Determined not to let the fate of Hai Jumping Crew befall that of MFC, Andreasyan continued to actively recruit young b-boys and b-girls, personally mentoring them, bestowing identities on them through nicknames, organizing practices, and cultivating an environment where the dance, and the culture overall, was able to develop beyond being a mere hobby or pastime. He adopted the "each one, teach one" pedagogical tradition of Hip Hop (Fogarty 2012) and became a pillar of the burgeoning breaking scene. Virtually every accomplished b-boy or b-girl in the country attributed their development, in one way or another, to Andreasyan. By the time I met him in 2005, he had gone from being known as B-Boy Flash to "Godfather Flash," a term of endearment bestowed by others who recognized his role in fostering the development of Hip Hop in the country.

"HEADS ARE FOR THINKING, NOT SPINNING"

When I met Flash at the Mad Force Crew practice in the summer of 2005, he had about twenty-five apprentices under him. In turn, he introduced me to Aleksanyan, who with his younger brother had recently begun putting together his own crew, which they called "Alekstyle" (in homage to their family name). However, despite the formation of these various crews and the relative stabilization of the economy, the breaking scene was still small and relegated to practices in cultural centers, dance studios, and gymnasiums. It was a very underground phenomenon, still stigmatized in the wider society.

"When I started, the country was closed off from the rest of the world," explains Flash, adding that many people erroneously assumed that breaking was associated with drug use. They would ask him why he was throwing his body on the floor and say things like, "Heads are made for thinking, not for spinning" (Andreasyan interview). Breaking's hallmark of doing prolonged dance moves on the ground was a radical concept for people in Armenia. It was considered crazy to spin on every conceivable part of your body or circle around on your hands and feet in a seemingly frenzied fashion. Traditional Armenian dances consisted mostly of upright movements conveying elegance and form, rarely done individually or spontaneously. Viewed through this narrow cultural prism, breaking was simply incomprehensible. Some even assumed one had to be intoxicated or mentally unbalanced to do it.

That early generation had to withstand such negative reactions from not only their parents and the older generations but also from their peers. When they danced in public, they would often get into fights with youth who would criticize or poke fun at what they were doing. But influenced by their own pride and Hip Hop imagery in 1980s movies, such as *Beat Street*—which were still their main visual and cultural references— they refused to be disrespected. They stood up for themselves and responded in kind. "If you think that we are lesser because we dance on the floor," Flash recalls saying to people back in those days, "I could get up from this floor and it will be very bad news for you" (Andreasyan interview).

The disdain breakers encountered on the streets eventually led them to confine their dance to mostly indoor spaces, and once they secured such practice spaces, they were no longer interested in breaking outside. Even in 2005, the b-girls and b-boys I met were ambivalent about street performing, despite the opportunity to make money in a developing economy with a large influx of summer tourists (mostly from Armenia's large ethnic diaspora communities). The threat of conflicts with local passersby far outweighed the benefit of earning money from foreign visitors. Given that most of the breakers I met were either unemployed or from working-class backgrounds, this refusal to street perform exemplified the truly intolerant attitude society had toward the dance. That they pursued the dance at all in the face of such opposition spoke to their passion for breaking and their determination to grow the local scene.

In addition to not knowing much about Hip Hop, most Armenian citizens looked at breaking negatively as a foreign influence. Throughout the twentieth century, Armenians were subjected to genocide, Sovietization, and countless attempts to erase their culture (Hovannisian 1997). As such, they are wary of anything that is "not their own" and take special pride in their ancient history and culture. Breaking was viewed, by many, as a diversion from this national agenda. The dancers themselves are cognizant of this and quick to affirm their pride in their heritage. Aleksanyan, for instance, explains, "I tell my students to this day that there is no dance you can disregard . . . especially Armenian dance, because you're Armenian" (Aleksanyan interview). Thus, instead of taking them away from their national identity, they found that breaking brought them closer to it.

Hip Hop's encouragement to be proud of who you are and to add your cultural influences to the dance was an important element of this appeal in Armenia. As dance scholar Halifu Osumare (2002) has noted, the Africanist aesthetics within breaking—including the traditions of signifying, improvisation, originality, and so on—have allowed for the mixing of cultures globally, resulting in what she calls the "intercultural body" of local movement subjectivities combined with African American vocabulary imported from the United States. This ability to incorporate your own identity into breaking is central to its proliferation, she argues, adding that it may also offer a vision for transcending narrow constructions of borders and divisions around the world. For practitioners in Armenia, breaking has certainly allowed them to identify with the roots of the dance in New York, while also allowing them to celebrate (not suppress) their own cultural heritage and contributions.

By the late 2000s, adversarial public attitudes were also beginning to shift. The years of dedication put in by Flash, Aleksanyan, and others began to be appreciated and respected. The gradual transition to a free-market system, despite creating inequality and alienation, also brought new access to information and companies eager to appeal to young people using neoliberal discourses of freedom and individuality (DeFrantz 2012). Many dancers started getting booked for photo shoots, films, and television commercials, and companies like Coca-Cola and local Internet operators used breaking to personify a new, energetic, individualistic youth culture—in contrast to the rigid identities of the Soviet era. In turn, these advertising campaigns helped the dance gain wider appeal, associating it in the eyes of the public with contemporary culture.

Adaptations of foreign television programs also gave breakers greater exposure; Aleksanyan, for example, participated in Armenia's version of *So You Think You Can Dance* in 2010. Gaining recognition through these platforms led to further media coverage and commercial offers. In 2012, Armenia's public television channel, H1, even invited Godfather Flash to do special live commentary during the broadcasting of the Red Bull BC One World Final. In this way, the growth of breaking in Armenia paralleled the opening of the country to the outside world through economic liberalization and mass entertainment. The more consumer culture entered the local market, the more breaking began to be utilized and accepted as a vibrant new dance form.

But it was not that these commercial forces *established* breaking in the country. Indeed, the dance initially developed as a counterculture practice, at a time when most people derided it. Its early adherents were attracted to its radical aesthetics, as well as to its values and principles, which they gleaned from underground films and public television programs. As the post-Soviet market opened and cross-border flows increased, the existing grassroots network of breakers took advantage of the changes to gain a wider audience. Thus, the rapid growth of breaking in Armenia was, in many ways, closely intertwined with wider shifts the country experienced in its post-Soviet transition.

The Internet Generation

As part of the neoliberal reforms Armenia underwent following independence, the country's telecommunications industry was handed over to the Greek-owned Hellenic Telecommunications Organization in 1998. In exchange for promises to invest in Armenia's telephone and IT sector, the company was granted a fifteen-year monopoly. Yet, instead of bringing Armenia's network up to international standards, the company utilized its exclusive position to hike up prices and prolong poor service (Mitra, Andrew, and Gyulumyan 2007). There were social protests around this issue, as oppositional parties, business groups, and nongovernmental organizations called for an end to the monopoly (Tchilingirian 1999). In 2004, the government took action and eventually ended the company's monopoly, and new companies quickly stepped in to fill the void. Diversification brought immediate improvements in communications and a growing IT sector that affected everything from social fashions to political movements in the country (Vardanyan 2013). Indeed, by the time I visited in 2005, Internet cafes had sprouted all over Yerevan, frequented regularly by young people.

Prior to that, b-girls and b-boys had to keep a close eye on their TV sets to record rare snippets from music videos and TV shows. They would hunt through stores to find material related to Hip Hop, hoping to catch a glimpse of the dance. If they saw titles like

"Born to Breakdance" or "Breaking it Down" on imported VHS tapes, they would buy them immediately and watch them with their friends until the tape wore out. Relatives from abroad would also send DVDs of international competitions like Battle of the Year and the UK B-Boy Championships. Cultural sociologist Mary Fogarty (2006) has written about the global proliferation of breaking via this "transnational network" of independently produced underground videos and events, and its impact was certainly felt among practitioners in Armenia, as well. For instance, it was through underground videos that local dancers were exposed to groups like Jam Style & Da Boogie from Russia, Flying Steps from Germany, and Suicidal Lifestyle from Hungary, who were all revered for their visually appealing spins and acrobatic movements commonly referred to in breaking as "power moves."

Thus, along this mediated spectrum of influence and information, dancers in Armenia spent most of their time trying to emulate the dynamic combinations they saw in breaking videos, rather than the more traditional footwork vocabulary, upright dance steps, and creative floor transitions of breaking. As Johnson (2011) points out, this pattern of initially gravitating toward breaking's more dynamic movements is commonly witnessed throughout the world. Gravity-defying twists and difficult physical contortions are often adopted as the centerpiece of the dance, gaining the practitioners who can do them the most local respect. In a context of limited information, such visually appealing moves stood out, and learning the more technical aspects of the dance was somewhat challenging for breakers in Armenia. Many would frequent gymnastics studios, where they learned how to do flares[6] and balance on their hands but struggled with more traditional floor movements like footwork.

However, when the Internet became more readily available in the mid- to late 2000s, greater access to information both increased the number of adherents to the dance and altered their approach toward it. B-girls and b-boys tell stories of going to Internet cafes in the wee hours of the night (when access fees were cheaper), searching on terms like "break dance," "b-boying," or "breaking," and downloading as many clips as possible onto their USBs. They discovered a plethora of new styles and moves, began learning the names of other well-known practitioners, and started having contact with the outside world.

By 2010, Wi-Fi access and faster connection speeds led to the closure of many of the Internet cafes that had once dotted the city. With affordable Internet at home and on their phones, breakers not only followed leading websites that featured dance clips, but they also began getting in touch directly with dancers abroad, enhancing their sense of belonging to a transnational community. Practitioners such as Marina and Ani of Seize Crew found inspiration in leading female figures around the world, motivating them to equally excel in Hip Hop's artistic expressions. They also realized how far behind the rest of the world they were but were determined to catch up.

These changes in attitudes, aesthetics, and appearances in the country were not only confined to the breaking scene. Armenian society in general was becoming more receptive to diversity. A strong segment of young people could be seen distancing themselves from the customs of the Soviet times during this period and gravitating more toward the styles of dress, music, art, and individuality associated with cultural movements such as Hip Hop. Whereas Marina and Ani elicited stares in 2005 for their deviation from the standards of female fashion, the variation in styles seen on the streets of Yerevan only five years later had them fitting in seamlessly. In other words, increased interaction with the outside world was helping to break the homogeneity of the past and fostering greater encouragement for expressions of uniqueness. Vanush "B-Boy Booble" Shahinyan attributes the bulk of these changes directly to the Internet, suggesting that it has expanded people's worldview and led to more open-minded thinking. "Whether we are talking about dancing, fashion, or even hairstyles," he says, "the Internet has had a big effect. If you use it the right way, it is a very powerful tool" (interview with the author, January 2015).

Thus, once the privatized telecommunications monopoly was broken, what remained of the Iron Curtain separating Armenia from the outside world began to break down. By the late 2000s, broadband access seemed to be everywhere and structural changes in the IT sector were making an impact in all avenues of life, including the breaking scene. By 2011, Flash's classes had tripled in size, to the point that many of his former students branched out and began opening their own classes in different areas. New crews also began to form, and b-girls and b-boys were learning in a month what took their teachers years to pick up. In addition, they were engaging the dance with broadened horizons and a new attitude that sought to further disintegrate the regimented approaches of the past.

The Way of the B-Boy

One of the most interesting aspects of breaking in Armenia is the athletic and martial arts background of virtually all its lead practitioners. Flash did tae kwon do up until he started breaking. Aleksanyan trained in boxing from the ages of five to sixteen. Both attribute their physical abilities and discipline to their early experience in organized sports and martial arts. Other dancers who have played a significant role in the scene have similar histories in karate, capoeira, judo, and gymnastics. When questioned about this phenomenon, many reply that it was a widespread trend in the late 1990s and early 2000s for Armenian parents to put their male children in some sort of self-defense or sporting activity.

Given this background, it was only natural that many Armenian dancers were drawn to the physical aspect of the dance as opposed to the more rhythmic and expressive elements. They were amazed by the spins and power moves and wanted to be able to do what seemed like superhuman feats. They knew breaking was not a sport yet they were attracted to its athletic characteristics. At the same time, they identified with what is perhaps the biggest difference between breaking and other disciplines: individuality. "It was about freedom," says Aleksanyan when recalling what drew him away from boxing toward breaking. "Whatever I want, I can create . . . In other disciplines, the rules are much more" (Aleksanyan interview).

Just as boys were taught martial arts, young girls in Armenia were often put in formal dance classes. The current head of the Firestyle Dance Crew, Lia Hovakimyan, a prominent b-girl who became involved in Hip Hop in the late 2000s, was trained in classical dance as a youth. Like Flash and Aleksanyan, she insists that what attracted her to breaking was its emphasis on creativity:

> In other dance forms, you have to be like everyone else. You're not supposed to deviate much. Meanwhile, in breaking, you can use your differences to your advantage. Being short might help you do power moves better, having long arms might help you thread easier, being flexible can be a hallmark of your style. Where something is a *defect* in another dance, it is in *effect* in ours. (interview with the author, December 2014)

Other studies on breaking have similarly acknowledged that the dance's embrace of diversity is one of its most notable qualities (Fogarty 2012). In the post-Soviet context of Armenia, this had a profoundly liberating effect on young people; breaking's encouragement to be yourself and utilize your talents provided a unique space for participants of all ages to find confidence in themselves and not simply conform to the rules and norms of society.

Nevertheless, the background of practitioners in traditional movement disciplines also impacted how breaking developed in Armenia, differentiating it in many ways from other Hip Hop dance scenes around the world. For example, many of the classes that teach breaking operate in a fashion reminiscent of martial arts dojos and classical dance schools, where students serve as pupils under a trainer. In turn, most crews in the country emerge from these classes and maintain their top-down character. In contrast, the concept of a breaking crew in other parts of the world is usually based on friendship among peers and voluntary association. In my experience, these relationships are not beholden to a single trainer or choreographer.

The martial arts background of practitioners has also informed how they have sought to organize the rapid growth of the breaking scene. In 2010, Aleksanyan founded the Armenian Breakdance Association and officially registered it as a nonprofit organization with the government. He openly acknowledged that he had modeled the organization on the Armenian Karate Federation and other sports groups active in the country. He had researched their bylaws and modes of operation and applied their approaches to Hip Hop dance, with the goal of organizing competitions and harnessing interest in the dance. Flash founded a similar organization soon after, naming it Hip Hop Congress Armenia.

The athletic background of practitioners also affected the performative context of breaking; the dance, for example, is rarely done in a social or party atmosphere. This latter point is crucial because it further incentivized the physical qualities of the dance as opposed to the musicality and creative improvisation that are central to it. When breaking emerged in the Bronx in the early 1970s, its main showground consisted of the impromptu dance circles that would form in response to a specific canon of percussion-based songs (known as "breakbeats") played at parties (Schloss 2006). Such dance circles (commonly referred to today as "cyphers") are recognized not only for their historical significance but also for their unique ability to foster rhythm, free expression, and spontaneity (Johnson 2009). Thus, cyphers are a core component of the dance, upheld to this day, and most breaking events around the world make it a point to allow time for them before, during, or after the main competitions. Until very recently, however, this custom was almost nonexistent in Armenia, resulting in an aesthetic that was far more skewed toward the acrobatic elements of breaking.

Thus, the athletic and martial arts backdrop of the scene had both positive and negative effects. Systemized classes and competitions gave practitioners a place to go where they could easily learn the dance—something that the first generation did not have—and facilitated a familial environment where students were closely mentored and supported by their trainers and fellow classmates. On the other hand, the vertical nature of these schools and their emphasis on competition often incentivized technical perfection in executing the steps and techniques over free expression, experimentation, and originality. In an inversion of earlier values, the same factors of regimentation that drew many dancers away from martial arts seeped, in varying degrees, back into the local breaking scene.

Yet, these approaches have also shown signs of withering over the years. A new crop of young people, most of whom began dancing in the Internet era of the late 2000s, are being influenced by interaction with breaking scenes around the world, both directly and through their computer screens. "I would watch breaking clips of events abroad and then look at my own dancing," explains twenty-year-old B-Boy Booble, one of the most recognized dancers of the newer generation. "Now I understand that what we were lacking was the true b-boy style and flavor" (interview with the author, January 2015), by which he means dancing in tune with the music, executing fundamental footwork steps, and innovating unique signature moves. Once again, increased openness to the outside world was resulting in challenges to the local standards of the past. As the older dancers themselves admit, younger breakers are even more interested than they were in expressing themselves without limits. Aleksanyan points out, "For young people today, everything is more free, more light . . . They can see things around the world with just one click" (Aleksanyan interview). This propensity for change not only has to do with the aesthetics of the dance but also with the way breakers associate together. Like the Seize Crew members I met in 2005, more and more young dancers in Armenia today are straying away from traditional structures.

One such faction is the Funky Monsters Crew, which formed in 2013 by a handful of students at Flash's and Aleksanyan's schools. They decided to pool their resources to rent their own practice space and develop their dancing independently. B-Boy Azo, one of the members of Funky Monsters, explains their decision to start their own crew:

> Yeah, I understand that there are teachers everywhere, that it's good to have someone explain the moves, but there are also crews where all of the members in the group are just friends, they are equals. I don't believe in just learning under one person because

you will just take on that person's style. You'll be a carbon copy." (interview with the author, December 2014)

The dancers who have broken away from the school system tend to have a greater interest in the style, rhythm, and expressive aspects of breaking. While they also practice power moves and spins, they pride themselves on having their own individual character. "Breaking is a dance that is supposed to be free," insists Azo, "where you choose your own path, have your own style" (Azo interview).

These changes in the aesthetics and structure of breaking are indicative of broader trends in Armenian society, as well, as many young people are challenging the prevailing sociopolitical relations of the past (Ishkanian et al. 2013; Matosian 2012). Conflict, financial collapse, natural disasters, and poorly managed reforms served as major obstacles to such development in the country's first decade of independence. But stability and greater openness in recent years have set the stage for significant transformations. Indeed, the dramatic 2018 "Velvet Revolution" in Armenia—which overthrew the authoritarian ruling regime in a series of nonviolent civil disobedience actions—was led largely by young people. These activists have been praised the world over for harnessing the "winds of hope" and demonstrating "the potential of youth to use their voice to advance democracy" ("UN Chief Hails Armenia" 2018). Not coincidentally, Ani from Seize Crew whom I met in 2005 is one of the young activists at the forefront of such social change today. And she is not content with the mere removal of the previous authoritarian regime. Even after the "Velvet Revolution," she continues to struggle as a prominent voice of the local environmental movement, challenging the mining companies' exploitation of the country (Khachatryan 2018). It is my contention that her early outspokenness as a female involved in Hip Hop is related to her later outspokenness on the critical issues facing the country. Although Armenian society has by no means completely broken the fetters of the past, the new attitudes and tendencies among young people like Ani are noteworthy—and breaking has been both an exemplar and conduit for these broader social changes.

Breaking Down the Bloc

Although breaking was born in the Bronx in the 1970s, and popularized globally through media exposure in the 1980s, its development did not take hold in Armenia until the 2000s. The turbulent geopolitical and socioeconomic changes occurring in the country as it broke away from the Soviet Union prevented the dance from fully developing. In fact, only very recently has it begun maturing in all its aspects. In this way, the history of breaking in Armenia can be mapped along the path of structural and socioeconomic changes in the country itself. The impact of the Internet's spread on breaking's development is one of many examples of how external factors have affected Hip Hop dance. Such processes as stabilization and liberalization increased the exposure of breaking to practitioners locally and gave them greater opportunities to spread the dance and engage with others involved in it.

Although it may appear that neoliberal forces helped import the dance from the United States, it should be noted that the establishment of breaking in Armenia, as in other parts of the world, has not been a product of commercial endeavors but, rather, of the transnational network of grassroots events, people-to-people contacts, and local groupings that keep the dance rooted and alive. Both in Armenia and the United States, the dance experienced a period of considerable social opposition and disdain—and it was in this very period that the groundwork for it was cultivated by the likes of Flash, Aleksanyan, and others. Only later did media exposure come in to amplify and capitalize on their activities. To this day, when participants are drawn to breaking through television or movies, they are still integrated into its embodied practices through community-based workshops, competitions, and local associations.

More importantly, the question of *why*, not just how, breaking was adopted in Armenia—a country so far removed and seemingly distinct from the dance's birthplace—is crucial in understanding its significance. The fact that breaking developed in the face of widespread local opposition and a lack of institutional support only further speaks to its remarkable resilience and appeal. Yes, the dance is visually appealing and dynamic, but there seems to be something more to its practitioners' continued dedication to it. Scholars who have explored this question in other regions have concluded that breaking provides young people with an opportunity to forge new identities and resist their subordination within mainstream society (Kopytko 1986; Deyhle 1998; Bode Bakker and Nuijten, 2018). Most notably, Osumare (2007) argues that the proliferation of a global Hip Hop underground is due to the "connective marginalities" of young people from different countries who find an affinity with the counterhegemonic values and aesthetics of African American culture.

My research and experience in Armenia strongly support these findings. In a traditional society with a wide range of social constrictions, where most practitioners come from a background of regimented extracurricular activities, and a post-Soviet context of inequality and disillusionment, breaking has given participants an important conduit to expressing their individuality and forging meaningful new identities. The transition from Soviet authoritarianism to neoliberal democracy has been as much social and psychic as it has been political and economic. During this trying period, breaking has had an empowering effect on young people seeking to find new meaning and to embody values that were promised to them in independence but never delivered. Indeed, the most common thread throughout the stories of almost every dancer I encountered was the liberating impact the dance has had on their personal growth. They point to the way Hip Hop has helped them channel their energy in a positive direction, think independently, express their creativity, establish a sense of community, and enact values beyond passive material consumption.

These benefits of breaking, so evident in the case of Armenia, are notably similar to the qualities many of early practitioners point to when reflecting on their own experiences with the dance in New York City. For example, Ken Swift, an iconic b-boy who helped popularize the form in the early 1980s, explains the impact of dance on his life growing up on the Upper West Side of Manhattan:

When I walked up the block, everything had rules. At home, things had to be done a certain way. At school . . . you know you had all these pressures. With hip hop, there's an outlet. Somewhere you can go . . . I just think that it's for the communities. I think that what it gave me was essential for me in my life. What it truly gave me. (quoted in Silver 2005)

It should be remembered that New York in the late 1970s and early 1980s was also undergoing socioeconomic transformation, and the African American and Latino communities were especially hard hit by social-services cuts and demonization in public discourse (Phillips-Fein 2017). Breaking was not only a new and exciting dance in these communities; it was also an empowering discipline that imparted values of camaraderie, community, self-expression, and peer admiration. And these values have proven to be vital even for those who do not live in such urban conditions. Indeed, I believe this trajectory of breaking helps explain its remarkable longevity and adoption in so many corners across the globe.

At the same time, it is also important to keep in mind the way economic and political forces have affected the dance's trajectory. The values and aesthetics of breaking are not static or disembodied from broader society. As the case of Armenia shows, *how* and *why* the dance is being performed has fluctuated from the early 1980s until today. And the same is true of breaking in the Bronx and other parts of the world. The various temporal, cultural, structural, and economic contexts within which Hip Hop dance is practiced must be closely examined in order to understand the deeper meaning and form it is taking on. As the breaking community continues to expand internationally—in places many people never expected it to take hold[7]—further comparative studies into the diverse local histories and dynamics of each scene, and how they relate to their broader social and institutional factors, are needed if we want to truly understand the global impact and potential latent within it.

NOTES

1. I use the term *Hip Hop* in accordance with its initial reference to the interlinked artistic expressions of *breaking* (dance), *DJing* (music), *MCing* (poetry), and, more tangentially, *style writing* (aerosol art). I use the term to discuss this broader cultural movement that emerged in the Bronx, New York, in the early 1970s, and has subsequently spread throughout the world. I do not employ the term *Hip Hop* simply as a euphemism for rap music, as is often the case in contemporary writings. For a discussion of how commercial forces have affected this discursive shift of "Hip Hop" away from community-based practices to the private consumption of commodities, see Dimitriadis (1999).
2. As a people that have been subject to genocide and persecution, many immigrant Armenian families discourage serious association with anything *odar* (meaning "non-Armenian") as a strategy for maintaining their heritage. For an analysis of how this plays out among Armenian American women, see Manoogian, Walker, and Richards (2007).
3. I have been involved in breaking since 1997, gaining notoriety, under the moniker "Midus," for my unique approach to the dance. Over the years, I have been featured in prominent

VHS tapes, DVDs, and online breaking videos and have taken part in competitions and taught classes throughout the United States, Europe, and Asia. I remain active in both the Armenian and international breaking scene and am a member of the Style Elements Crew, a group widely credited for contributing a new vocabulary to breaking in the 1990s.

4. Due to the shortages of electricity, fuel, and necessities following the collapse of the Soviet Union, the early 1990s in Armenia are referred to, both figuratively and literally, as the "dark years" (Miller and Miller, 2003, 97–137).

5. The native term for someone of Armenian descent is *Hai* (pronounced like the English word "high"). It derives from the historic name of Armenia, which is Haiastan. Thus, the crew's name represented both Armenian ethnicity and "jumping/flying high."

6. Flares were created by gymnast Kurt Thomas for the pummel horse and were incorporated into breaking in the early 1980s. They consist of alternating between the left hand and right hand while one's legs are spread apart, elevated off of the ground, and swinging in a circular rotation around the body.

7. For a recent look at the impact of breaking in developing countries such as Colombia, Cambodia, Uganda, and Yemen, see the documentary *Shake the Dust* (Sjöberg 2014).

REFERENCES

Bode Bakker, M., and Nuijten, M. (2018). "'When Breaking You Make Your Soul Dance': Utopian Aspirations and Subjective Transformation in Breakdance." *Identities: Global Studies in Culture and Power* 25 (2): 210–227.

Chorbajian, L. (2001). *The Making of Nagorno-Karabagh: From Secession to Republic.* New York: Palgrave.

DeFrantz, T. (2012). "Unchecked Popularity: Neoliberal Circulations of Black Social Dance." In *Neoliberalism and Global Theatres: Studies in International Performance,* edited by L. D. Nielsen and P. Ybarra, 128–140. London: Palgrave Macmillan.

Deyhle, D. (1998). "From Break Dancing to Heavy Metal: Navajo Youth, Resistance, and Identity." *Youth & Society* 30 (1): 3–31.

Dimitriadis, G. (1999). "Hip-Hop to Rap: Some Implications of an Historically Situated Approach to Performance." *Text and Performance Quarterly* 19: 355–369.

Dudwick, N. (2003). "When the Lights Went Out: Poverty in Armenia." In *When Things Fall Apart: Qualitative Studies of Poverty in the Former Soviet Union,* edited by N. Dudwick, E. Gomart, and A. Marc, 117–154. Washington, DC: World Bank.

Fogarty, M. (2006). "'Whatever Happened to Breakdancing?' Transnational Boy/Bgirl Networks, Underground Video Magazines and Imagined Affinities." Unpublished master's thesis. Brock University.

Fogarty, M. (2012). "'Each One Teach One': B-boying and Ageing." *Ageing and Youth Cultures: Music, Style and Identity,* edited by A. Bennett and P. Hodkinson, 53–65. London: Bloomsbury.

Hovannisian, R. G., ed. (1997). *The Armenian People from Ancient to Modern Times.* Vol. 2: *Foreign Domination to Statehood: The Fifteenth Century to the Twentieth Century.* New York: St. Martin's Press.

Ishkanian, A., Gyulkhandanyan, E., Manusyan, S., and Manusyan, A. (2013). *Civil Society, Development and Environmental Activism in Armenia.* Report. London School of Economics and Political Science. http://eprints.lse.ac.uk/54755/.

Johnson, I. K. (2009). "Dark Matter in B-boying Cyphers: Race and Global Connection in Hip Hop." PhD diss., University of Southern California.

Johnson, I. K. (2011). "B-boying and Battling in a Global Context: The Discursive Life of Difference in Hip Hop Dance." *Alif: Journal of Comparative Poetics* 31: 173–195.

Johnson, I. K. (2014). "From Blues Women to B-girls: Performing Badass Femininity." *Women & Performance: A Journal of Feminist Theory* 24 (1): 15–28.

Khachatryan, N. (2018). "Environmental Activists Halt Construction at Armenian Gold Mine." *Bellingcat*, August 20. https://www.bellingcat.com/news/rest-of-world/2018/08/20/environmental-activists-halt-construction-armenian-gold-mine/.

Kopytko, T. (1986). "Breakdance as an Identity Marker." *Yearbook for Traditional Music* 18: 21–28.

Manoogian, M., Walker, A., and Richards, L. (2007). "Gender, Genocide, and Ethnicity: The Legacies of Older Armenian American Mothers." *Journal of Family Issues* 28 (4): 567–589.

Matosian, M. (2012). "The Development of Grassroots Activism in Yerevan and the Role of Political Parties." *Hetq*, March 29. http://hetq.am/eng/news/12533/the-development-of-grassroots-activism-in-yerevan-and-the-role-of-political-parties.html.

Miller, D. E., and Miller, L. T. (2003). *Armenia: Portraits of Survival*. Los Angeles: University of California Press.

Mitra, S., Andrew, D., and Gyulumyan, G. (2007). *The Caucasian Tiger: Sustaining Economic Growth in Armenia*. Washington, DC: World Bank.

Osumare, H. (2002). "Global Breakdancing and the Intercultural Body." *Dance Research Journal* 34 (2): 30–45.

Osumare, H. (2007). *The Africanist Aesthetic in Global Hip Hop: Power Moves*. New York: Palgrave.

Phillips-Fein, K. (2017). *Fear City: New York's Fiscal Crisis and the Rise of Austerity Politics*. New York: Henry Holt.

Rose, T. (1994). *Black Noise: Rap Music and Black Culture in Contemporary America*. Middletown, CT: Wesleyan University Press.

Schloss, J. (2006). "'Like Old Folk Songs Handed Down from Generation to Generation': History, Canon, and Community in B-Boy Culture." *Ethnomusicology* 50 (3): 411–432.

Silver, T., dir. (2005). *Style Wars*. DVD. USA: Plexifilm.

Sjöberg, A., dir. (2014). *Shake the Dust*. DVD. USA: BOND360.

Tchilingirian, H. (1999). "Nobody's Listening: Armenia's Telecom System." *Armenian International Magazine* 10 (2): 18–19.

"UN Chief Hails Armenia during General Assembly Remarks." (2018). *Asbarez*, September 25. http://asbarez.com/175231/un-chief-hails-armenia-during-general-assembly-remarks/.

Vardanyan, G. (2013). "Elections, Social Movements and Internet Penetration in Armenia." *Caucasus Analytical Digest* 53–54 (July): 19–22. http://www.css.ethz.ch/publications/pdfs/CAD-53-54-19-22.pdf.

Welt, C. and Bremmer, I. (1997). "Armenia's New Autocrats." *Journal of Democracy* 8 (3): 77–91.

CHAPTER 17

···

TWERKING AND P-POPPING IN THE CONTEXT OF THE NEW ORLEANS LOCAL HIP HOP SCENE

···

MATT MILLER

As a search on Google Trends reveals, interest in the word "twerking" surged dramatically in August 2013, after Miley Cyrus performed the dance at the MTV Video Music Awards ceremony. Cyrus's performance drew attention—including widespread scorn, criticism, and parody—not only because it entailed the latest step in the transformation of a virginal teen starlet into a much more sexualized and transgressive young adult "bad girl," but also because of the challenge that twerking itself posed to mainstream ideas of appropriateness and respectability. To some observers, the dance seemed nothing short of pornographic, and represented the encroachment into popular culture of an exploitative approach to sexuality nurtured in strip clubs. Other commentators criticized Cyrus for appropriating a dance with clear African American origins. While she was not without her defenders, the celebration of Cyrus's performance was muted; however, judging by the estimated $79 million worth of free television exposure it gave her, Cyrus's performance was a masterpiece in the marketing of sexuality and controversy (Della Cava and Ryan 2013).

Twerking undoubtedly has its place in the repertoire of exotic dancers; however, its origins are much more complicated—and more interesting—than is commonly assumed. Before exploding into mass consciousness in 2013, the dance had existed for at least a quarter of a century within the local New Orleans rap scene. Its emergence in New Orleans was enabled by that city's rich history of African American music, dance, and expressive culture. Twerking and other aspects of New Orleans musical culture are best understood in the context of an African cultural grammar that historically has been an organizing principle for popular culture in the city. The dance's reception on a national level, as mediated through Miley Cyrus and others, demonstrates the power of these locally generated expressive cultural forms, as well as the ways in which their sudden de- and recontextualization can alter dramatically the ways that they are perceived and evaluated.

I explore the recent history of twerking in the context of New Orleans' African American communities, its roots in that city's vernacular music culture, and its exposure to national audiences. New Orleans has been a focal point for the development and evolution of African American social dance since the late eighteenth and early nineteenth centuries. Throughout the twentieth century, the city has been at the center of the emergence of several important dance music genres, including jazz, R & B, and funk. Since the late 1990s, as Hip Hop and rap have become the dominant frame of musical reference among African American youth, the city has continued to be an influential presence in the national scene, its musical and dance concepts drawn from New Orleans's grassroots "bounce" genre gaining national exposure at the hands of artists from inside and outside the city. Among the many dance styles to emerge within the local Hip Hop scene, "twerking" or "p-popping"—dances involving the isolation and rapid agitation of the hips and buttocks—attained a central importance within the block party and club scene in which the local rap style was incubated. Referenced in song lyrics and in journal articles, these highly popular dances were sometimes the focus of controversy in New Orleans. When national audiences were exposed to twerking by Beyoncé, Miley Cyrus, Big Freedia, and other artists, the popular and critical response was characterized by ridicule and scandal. Despite its highly erotic reputation, however, twerking or p-popping is not a product of strip clubs or the adult-entertainment industry but, rather, a dance with deep roots in the vernacular African American music culture of New Orleans.

The origins of the word "twerk" are murky. Writer Nik Cohn speculated that it is a combination of the "twitch" and "work" (Floyd 2003), whereas New Orleans rapper Cheeky Blakk (who released the first song to use "twerk" in its title) asserted that she created the word "because it used to be F-something . . . It was way too explicit for me to do kids parties yelling about F-something" (MacCash 2014). As a dance, twerking has been characterized in a variety of ways. Jonathan Dee (2010), writing about the local New Orleans scene for the *New York Times Magazine*, described it as dancing "in the most sexualized way imaginable," with dancers "bent over sharply at the waist, and bouncing their hips up and down as fast as humanly possible, if not slightly faster" (24). Dee adds that "others assumed more of a push-up position, with their hands on the floor, in a signature dance whose name is sometimes helpfully shortened to 'p-popping.'" In an article titled "Explaining Twerking to Your Parents," Teddy Wayne (2013) describes a "dance move typically associated with lower-income African-American women that involves the rapid gyration of the hips in a fashion that prominently exhibits the elasticity of the gluteal musculature." New Orleans rapper Big Freedia noted that "you have to use your body in the upright position, you can use your knees for support" while twerking (Carucci 2013). As the dance has moved into the mainstream, understanding of twerking as "sexually suggestive" has become commonplace, although this conclusion says more about the observer's cultural perspective than it does about twerking itself.

TWERKING IN NEW ORLEANS AND BEYOND

The emergence of the word "twerk" in the New Orleans rap and Hip Hop scene can be traced to the early 1990s, when a local style called "bounce," characterized by an emphasis on dance, audience participation, and the cultivation and referencing of a sense of local distinctiveness, took the city by storm. As I showed in my book *Bounce: Rap Music and Local Identity in New Orleans* (Miller 2012), the local style defined and expressed a New Orleans aesthetic in a multiplicity of ways. In combination with particular samples and backing beats, bounce employed catchy, call-and-response-based lyrics laden with locally significant references. Nationally marketed rap music from places like New York and California found a receptive audience in New Orleans, but the city also supported its own vibrant and dynamic rap music scene. In the early 1990s, this scene was at a peak of its grassroots creativity, and would fuel the growth of several important local independent record labels in the decade that followed.

The "twerking" dance—which was also commonly referred to as "p-popping" (i.e., "pussy popping")—originated within, and was thoroughly embedded in, the New Orleans scene of the late '80s and early '90s, which unfolded against the backdrop of nightclubs and neighborhood "block parties" held in the street or in the courtyards of housing projects. The dance was also referenced with the phrase "catch the wall," describing the position of the dancer, whose hands were placed against a wall or other stable surface (including the floor or ground) to anchor them while dancing. "Twerking" was one of many words used to describe the shaking dances of 1990s New Orleans. As rapper Big Freedia observed, "We shake, wiggle, wobble, work, bend over and bust it open. We've been twerking for years, but that's just one of the words in the vocabulary of bounce" (quoted in Fensterstock 2013).

Prior to the first explicit mention of "twerking" or "p-popping," New Orleans rap artists referenced similar concepts. In 1991, rapper Bust Down released the song "Pop That Thang" on the Miami-based Effect Records, in which he described a club scene with women "dancing, bouncing [their] butt . . . working it, jerking it and touching the floor." The lyrical imagery of dance resembling twerking appears in two songs from 1992 that are credited with establishing the conventions of bounce as a genre: "Where Dey At" by MC T. Tucker and DJ Irv and "Where They At" by DJ Jimi. The songs included lyrics such as "shake that ass like a saltshaker," and "put a hump in your back and lift your rump," which would serve as apt descriptions of twerking. Though the twerking dance had doubtless existed in some form prior to 1993, it was in that year that recordings containing references to it were released in New Orleans. DJ Jubilee included an exhortation to "twerk baby, twerk" in his 1993 song "Stop, Pause (Do the Jubilee All)," which can be characterized as a near-encyclopedic list of locally popular dances (which also included the beanee weenee, the Eddie Bauer, and the bus stop). The video produced for the song showed the rapper and his backup dancers twerking. The 1993 song "Hey P-Poppers" by Devious (featuring Jisaidie and child rapper Lil Trap) stands out in its singular engagement with the p-popping or twerking concept, using the two words interchangeably (see below).

The extensive history of references in sound recordings to twerking or p-popping chronicles the development and proliferation of the dance in the New Orleans grassroots rap scene of the late 1980s and 1990s. The dance's popularity and familiarity to local audiences were reinforced by two popular twerk-themed songs by rapper Cheeky Blakk, who released "Terk Something" in 1994 and "Twerk Something, Part 2" the next year, titles which in their divergent spellings of the word reveal the emergent state of the twerking concept at the time. The basic idea of Cheeky Blakk's songs—the chanting of the phrase "twerk something"—was more or less reiterated in the 1996 song by local duo Big Al & Lil Tee, "Twerk something, Aggin [i.e., Nigga]!" and, to a lesser extent, in the 1999 song "Twerk Some'm" by Moby Dick, a producer and recording artist associated with Master P's No Limit Records label. Many other songs in the local New Orleans market described similar dance styles without mentioning twerking by name. Some of these, such as Juvenile's 1999 hit "Back That Azz Up" and Mystikal's 2000 song "Shake Ya Ass," caught the ear of national audiences.

The bounce scene underwent an important shift in the first decade of the twenty-first century, but twerking remained an important component of the local scene. In these years, the scene was energized by the emergence of a cohort of rappers, often referred to (by themselves and others) as "sissy rappers" who, in various ways, contested the heteronormative conventions of rap music. These artists performed music that was highly oriented to local preferences and renewed the emphasis on dancing, which had always been a core value of bounce. Songs with titles and hooks using words such as "shake," "wiggle," "pop," "bop," and "work" proliferated, as the general tempo of the music slowly crept upward to support ever more frenetic movement.

Since the early 1990s, twerking has framed several distinct areas of tension within the local African American youth culture. The lyrics of Devious's song "Hey P-Poppers" exemplify the multiplicity of meanings and attitudes encompassed by twerking. The song is, in many ways, a tribute to local "p-poppers"—it begins with the rapper complaining, "I'm looking at TV, and all that I ever see / Is some girls from Miami trying to pop they p," asserting the superiority of New Orleans women in the area of dancing and implicitly referencing the geopolitics of the rap scene at the time. Miami was one of the only cities in the South to have developed a nationally recognized music scene and industry in the early 1990s, and (among other out-of-towners) Miami's Luther Campbell was mining the local New Orleans scene for recording talent and song ideas. The song lays out some of the central sexual politics of twerking, involving a male spectator for whom women are performing in a sexually titillating fashion. However, the lyrics also denigrate p-poppers with the classic misogynistic trope of the unscrupulous "ho" who uses her sexuality to extract money from or otherwise exploit men.

As the lyrics of "Hey P-Poppers" indicate, the dance was understood in highly gendered terms in the New Orleans scene: twerking and p-popping (the latter explicitly inscribing an anatomically defined female gender) were generally understood as dances to be performed only by women or feminized men. However, the lines were often blurred; some early bounce rappers performed with women backup dancers, but other performers, such as DJ Jubilee, employed men in this capacity, whose performance repertoire included a variety of shaking dances, including twerking. With the rise to prominence of several "sissy rappers" beginning in 2000, the negative association of "shaking" with a feminized or nonmasculine identity was reinforced. As Pernell Russell (Crawford and Russell, 2009) noted, "My mom and my family support me, but not my dad. He doesn't like it. He thinks that's for gay people. And my friends who I grew up around, they are, like, "you dancing, you shaking—that's for girls. That's for fags" (121). Interviewed in 2009, Javae Turner, another male dancer from New Orleans, made a gender-based distinction with regard to the centrality of shaking for female dancers: "When boys dance there's more to it. When girls dance, they're just shaking" (quoted in Crawford and Russell 2009, 121). These comments show how twerking often operates within a structure of stereotypes and expectations in terms of gender roles and sexuality; when dance does not conform to prevailing conventions, it becomes problematic on a social or moral level.

While straight-identified men are not likely to take center stage in the public performance of twerking, this does not necessarily mean that they are always the primary intended audience for the dance. Several articles about local New Orleans rap events point to the phenomenon of women "taking over" the dance floor: as Jonathan Dee (2010), writing in *The New York Times Magazine*, observed, "The crowd . . . instantly segregated itself: the men were propelled as if by a centrifuge toward the room's perimeters, and the dance floor . . . was taken over entirely by women surrounding Freedia." Dee's image illustrates the ways in which twerking resists simple characterization as a sexual performance by women for a literal or implied heterosexual male gaze (Mulvey 1975). In other instances, women have denied this reductive understanding of the dance—as rapper Mia X insisted in 1998, "It's not sexual; dancing to bounce is about freedom." Mia X framed her perspective on twerking within a grassroots idealization of African cultural values: "It's like African women dancing for themselves. You can pull any 14-year-old aside who is dancing to bounce and ask her if she's dancing for the boys and she'll tell you, 'No, I'm dancing for me'" (Dvorak 1998). Similarly, a journalist summed up the views of Jamilah Y. Peters-Muhammad, a great-grandmother from New Orleans' Central City neighborhood, on twerking "as an expression of freedom and joy" rather than a sexual come-on (Reckdahl 2014).

Twerking or p-popping in New Orleans has been thoroughly embedded in a multigenerational, grassroots culture. Like other popular dances in African American communities, twerking has been taught to youngsters by siblings, peers, and parents, often at outdoor block parties or other events that are open to people of all ages. At such events, children younger than two years old can be seen anchoring themselves on a curb and performing the dance, and prepubescent girls are often socialized within a competitive, peer-driven milieu in which they perfect their ability to articulate their buttocks in time to the music. This behavior was often accepted by parents and others, as exemplified by New Orleans resident Sylvia VanBuren's comment as she watched her preteen granddaughters warm up for a world record attempt at twerking: "All they do is twerk" (quoted in Reckdahl 2014). In the grassroots New Orleans context, the performance of twerking, p-popping, and similar dances spans a wide continuum, ranging from explicitly sexual performances by women for an audience of eager male observers, to those among groups of children, seemingly devoid of adult sexual intent or design. Parents may forbid their children to perform the dance because of its sexual connotations, but it often encompasses multiple divergent meanings or associations. These facts not only speak to the ways in which the dance has been learned and propagated in New Orleans but also call into question the understanding of twerking or p-popping as an inherently sexual performance.

Twerking's ability to bring into focus certain notions of sexual identity as they relate to dance and public space connects to related issues of propriety and respectability. The tension around p-popping or twerking in the Black working-class communities where bounce emerged and grew was the subject of a 1998 article in the *Times-Picayune* by Petula Dvorak. Interviews with residents of housing projects and with local rappers presented divergent perspectives on twerking. Opposition to the dance was based on the ways in which its perceived sexual nature was considered improper and lacking in respectability, especially for young people. Although some opposed p-popping entirely, others saw a problem only in its consumption by the wider public. Interviewed in 1998, Yolanda Marrero, a resident council president at a large public housing complex, remarked, "I don't let my kids do that dance outside . . . Only inside" (Dvorak 1998). Twerking or p-popping was defended on the grounds of its African cultural background and the empowering effects of girls and women being able to express themselves through dance without moral censure.

As twerking continued as a local phenomenon in New Orleans, the dance was spreading to other locales during the 1990s. The hinterlands of New Orleans included large swathes of Louisiana, Alabama, and Mississippi, and extended to Memphis and East Texas, places which doubtlessly became aware of twerking or p-popping along with other aspects of bounce in the early 1990s. To a large extent, this organic process was undocumented, with a few important exceptions. One of these came in the form of an article by Greg Baker (1991) about the 1991 single by 2 Live Crew, "Pop that Pu__y," which the Miami-based music journalist described as "another groin-oriented dance song" like the group's earlier single, "Trow the Dick." Baker noted that "Pop that Pu__y" was "inspired during a trip to New Orleans, where a dance by that name is already making the club rounds." 2 Live Crew had a longstanding relationship with the New Orleans scene, as evidenced by the signing of New Orleans–based rapper Bust Down to Effect Records, a label owned by group leader Luther "Luke Skyywalker" Campbell. The cover of the twelve-inch single for "Pop That Pu__y" depicted members of the group chest-deep in a pool, spraying water upon several women wearing bathing suits and posing in a classic p-popping/twerking posture (bent at the waist in a semi-squat with hands braced on knees or thighs, looking back at viewer over the shoulder). 2 Live Crew's appropriation of p-popping was an important early step in the establishment of the longstanding association between twerking and strip club culture.

Awareness of twerking among rap music listeners grew throughout the 1990s, as several of the major cities of the South—including Atlanta, Miami, New Orleans, Memphis, and Houston—emerged as centers of a new southern turn in Hip Hop music. Independent labels in the region, including So So Def and LaFace Records in Atlanta, Select-O-Hits in Memphis, Luke Records in Miami, and Rap-a-Lot Records in Houston, had been steadily expanding within the regional rap scene. By the mid-1990s, southern independent labels were claiming an unprecedented portion of national and international markets, bringing with them ideas and conventions drawn from the grassroots southern rap scenes. While several other southern cities preceded New Orleans in gaining the national spotlight, by the late 1990s, the two most successful independent rap music labels in the United States were both located in New Orleans and drew heavily from the talent in the city. No Limit Records, founded by Percy "Master P" Miller, recorded New Orleans–based artists like Magnolia Slim (later Soulja Slim), Skull Dugrey, and Mystikal. Cash Money Records, run by brothers Bryan ("Baby") and Ronald ("Slim") Williams, signed local favorites including Lil Slim, Ms. Tee, Juvenile, and Lil Wayne, whose rise to international stardom kept the company profitable long after No Limit and other New Orleans–based labels from the 1990s had folded (Miller 2008).

Other southern cities proved to be fertile ground for twerking, and as the South, and New Orleans in particular, rose to new levels of prominence among rap and Hip Hop audiences, awareness of the dance expanded. The Atlanta-based group Ying Yang Twins referenced the dance in their 2000 song "Whistle While You Twurk," a bawdy tribute to strip-club culture. Journalists were also tuning in to twerking: a 2001 article by Tony Green in the *Village Voice* devoted to southern rap was titled "Twerk to Do." The dance was spreading beyond the genre boundaries of rap and Hip Hop, into allied genres like R & B, where artists, including Beyoncé, incorporated twerking into their stage shows and music-video performances.

Roots of Twerking

New Orleans is widely understood as one of the "most Africanized" cultures in the United States. "Because of its origins and development," explains historian Michael Gomez (1998), "African-derived culture in Louisiana is unique" (58). Louisiana's cultural distinctiveness began early in its history. During the colonial period, many of the slaves imported into the colony in its early decades were from the Senegal River basin, and as Johnson (1991) notes, they "brought with them an already formed and highly cohesive shared Bambara culture" (126). According to Gomez, "The substantial number of Fon-Ewe-Yoruba, their early presence and steady replenishment over the years, their notoriety in New Orleans, and their resonance with both Bambara and Congolese perspectives help explain their apparent and eventual cultural preeminence" (153). Further, contrary to common assumptions, "There is no hard evidence to support the popular notion that newly arrived Africans of the same ethnicity or area of origin were separated. Rather, there is every reason to believe that they were kept together" (173). This cultural integrity was enhanced when, after the initial round of slave importations, the introduction of enslaved Africans to Louisiana was halted around 1731 and did not resume for decades, allowing for the establishment of a "creolized" culture. All of these factors combined to make New Orleans home to an unusually cohesive and persistent African-derived identity.

The musical life of New Orleans, and its subsequent impact on the national music culture in the United States, has been shaped by its location at the northern rim of an Afro-Caribbean cultural zone. In the nineteenth century, the population of New Orleans experienced demographic infusions from Haiti and other parts of the Afro-Caribbean, as well as continual immigration of Blacks from the city's hinterlands in the Mississippi River basin. The dynamic nexus of African-derived culture that existed in New Orleans became visible to outsiders at public markets like the celebrated Place Congo or Congo Square, which served as a gathering place and location of musical and dance performance in the late eighteenth and early nineteenth centuries. The political and civil rights of the city's Black people were increasingly restricted after the American takeover in 1803. African Americans in places like Faubourg Tremé, the oldest Black neighborhood in the United States, resisted these changes through political and cultural means. Members of the city's educated Black middle class played important roles in organized challenges to white supremacy and Jim Crow (as in the *Plessy v. Ferguson* decision, in which the US Supreme Court affirmed the legality of segregation in response to a suit brought by Homer Plessy, a light-skinned New Orleans creole); but support for music, dance, and public performance drawing heavily on West African cultural values was most prominent in working-class and poor neighborhoods, popularized and perpetuated in the streets and saloons of the city. New Orleans maintained its status as a reservoir of African-derived cultural perspectives and practices throughout the nineteenth and twentieth centuries. This fact is central to the city's influential role in the emergence and elaboration of innovative genres of popular music, including jazz, rhythm and blues, soul, funk, and rap.

What aspects of twerking, then, can be viewed through a West African cultural lens? As many scholars have shown, New Orleans has been a center of Africanized culture in the United States for centuries. These distinctly African roots have enabled New Orleans's musical culture to contribute a number of innovative—and, in their time, controversial—concepts into the wider national popular music culture of the United States. Like twerking, many of these expressive cultural forms were criticized for their presumed sexual nature and were debated in a context in which expressive culture and ideas of race, class, gender, sexuality, and respectability were deeply intertwined. Music and dance have often been viewed through the lens of race, a perspective that colored both negative and positive receptions of particular trends. Jazz, an art form that grew out of working-class African American culture in New Orleans and is now recognized as one of the United States' most important cultural contributions, was denigrated because of its association with African Americans (and their reputedly loose sexual mores); at the same time, some of the enthusiasm for jazz among whites was tied to its transgressive status as a "Black" cultural form (Monson 1995, 402–406), representing a way for whites to step outside their own cultural boundaries. (Hersch 2007, 9). Similarly, controversy swirled around rhythm and blues and the rock and roll genres (both with significant connections to New Orleans)—as Bertrand (2007) writes, "Many news columns and columnists denounced rock 'n' roll and all of its practitioners, black and white, as immoral, degrading, and a contributing factor in the rise of juvenile delinquency" (79). These prejudices were fueled by perceptions of the racial identity of the music and dance forms—in this sense, the evolution of twerking from a subcultural practice within African American communities to a more broadly exposed phenomenon follows familiar historical patterns, in which decontextualization and long-standing associations between culture, race, and sexuality are highly influential.

Expressive cultural forms are highly mobile and cannot be carbon-dated or tested for DNA—still, several aspects of twerking speak to an African cultural grammar that underlies the dance. To begin with, twerking can be contextualized within a long history of what Chadwick Hansen (1967) calls "erotic shaking dances" in African American culture. Hansen concludes that it is "very probable that such dances were brought here in the seventeenth century by the first Negroes to arrive and have been continuous within the Negro community ever since" (562). The awareness of these practices on the part of members of the wider (white) American culture was negligible until the twentieth century, "where they have spread beyond the confines of the Negro community and become a part of American popular culture" (558). The perception of various shaking dances (whether associated with jazz, rhythm and blues, or rock and roll) as transitory, controversy-causing fads is based on an incomplete understanding of the centrality and persistence of these dances within the Black community: "We must keep in mind that from one point of view it is quite wrong to speak of shaking dances coming back. They have clearly been continuous within the Negro community" (561).

Brenda Gottschild's (2003) observations support the understanding of twerking as informed by African-derived cultural practices and values. Gottschild, a trained ballet dancer, notes that the buttocks and their use in dance go to the heart of long-standing divergences in cultural values between African- and European-descended peoples. "The prominence of the buttocks is a positive cultural and aesthetic value indicator in Africa and African diasporan communities, [where] daily postures and dance aesthetics emphasizing the buttocks have been practiced for centuries" (140). Whites often read this divergence from the "Europeanist" ideas about the body within a "savage-versus-civilized dialectic" in which "buttocks symbolize the historical dichotomy between Africanist and Europeanist aesthetic principle" (147). This aesthetic divide is mapped onto ideas about Blacks' hypersexual nature: "By Europeanist standards, the Africanist dancing body—articulating the trunk that houses primary and secondary sexual characteristics—is vulgar, lewd" (148). Gottschild notes that "[the rhythmic articulations of] the breast, belly, and buttocks . . . were essential movements in 1920s African American fad dances such as the Shimmy, Shake, Quiver, Grind, and Mess Around" (159). These values gave rise to a succession of similar dances, from the black bottom of the 1920s to the bump and "da butt" of the 1970s and 1980s, respectively (166). Contextualized in this way, the emergence of twerking, as well as its cultural background and its reception by the wider public, should come as no surprise.

The prominence of the buttocks in twerking can thus be understood as part of its African cultural orientation. Certain contemporary African dances, such as the Mapouka (a dance from the Ivory Coast, which Alex Fredkin (2013) identifies as representing "twerking's earliest origins") or Bakoko, certainly resemble twerking in their basic form, although it would be unwise to draw a direct link between them. Similarly, African-influenced folk and popular dances of the Caribbean also share aesthetic features with twerking: "Much Caribbean movement is centered around the pelvis, particularly in dances revealing more African retentions" (Carty 1988, 88). The isolation of body parts involved in twerking resemble those associated with Jamaican folk dance "in which the body parts will work alone: the shoulders, pelvis, feet, hands will often move independently of the accompanying body parts to complete the movement" (88). The ways in which body parts are isolated in twerking also speak to its Africanist cultural values: the buttocks work within "a democratic equality of body parts," reflecting the aesthetic prioritization of the "articulation of the separate units of the torso (pelvis, chest, rib cage, buttocks)" (Gottschild 2003, 15). In the Europeanist aesthetic, such practices are in erotic to the point of vulgarity, a perception that dovetails with stereotypes about Black hypersexuality.

In her study of the rise to popularity of the shimmy in the 1910s and 1920s, Rebecca Bryant (2002) identifies several elements that are germane to the study of twerking and, again, point to the cyclical pattern of the emergence of social dances—and their relation to gender, race, and sexuality—in America. Bryant notes that the shimmy "developed from African American roots" (168) and "was not really a dance in the sense of having specific steps. Instead," she continues, "it was defined by a rapid horizontal shaking of the upper body, especially the shoulders. Movements sometimes also included shaking of the torso and hips" (168). Bryant describes the African American dance that gave rise to the shimmy, the shim-me-sha-wabble, as "a dance step that involves hobbling, shaking, and bouncing" (170). Several things are relevant here: the shimmy was part of the continual development and elaboration of what Hansen called "Negro shaking dances" in the United States, relying on isolation and polyrhythmic movement for its effectiveness. Secondly, the shimmy as it eventually became known to the wider public experienced a significant amount of formalization or rationalization. In its journey from African American folk origins to a mass-marketed concept, the shimmy lost a great deal of its ambiguity or nuance and was performed according to a much more concrete and specific conceptualization.

For white Americans, both the appeal of the shimmy and the reason to oppose it rested in the dance's association with sexuality, a connection that came through both its shaking movements and through its African American origins. The shimmy also had important gendered aspects that correlate to twerking: "Although the shimmy was usually performed by women, male musicians in jazz bands were sometimes found shaking their shoulders" (Bryant 2002, 172–173). Bryant makes an important distinction in her observation in that "the shimmy wasn't associated just with women—it was associated with female sexuality" (174). Further, Bryant argues that the popularity of the shimmy among amateur dancers in the United States "[signaled] socially important shifts in American views of female sexual autonomy" (168), a possibility that should certainly be considered with regard to the rise of twerking. The way the shimmy was popularized—"largely due to [white] female entertainers such as Mae West, Gilda Gray, and Bee Palmer" (175)—is strikingly similar to what happened with twerking. The opposition to the shimmy is also eerily familiar: opponents "saw the flagrant motion and sexualized movements of the female body as contributing to women's debasing of themselves" (181). Like the recent efforts to prohibit twerking and other dancing considered lewd at school dances and other events, the shimmy was widely banned, branded by the National Association of Dancing Teachers as the "'most vulgar and dangerous' of all American dances in 1919" (180).

THE SPREAD OF TWERKING

Since the early 1990s, p-popping or twerking has retained its status as a local tradition in New Orleans, ever present if subject to periodic ebbs and surges in popularity. It percolated through the regional rap network, and was easily integrated into the influential Miami Bass scene, where artists like 2 Live Crew and the Dogs linked rap music and strip clubs in their lyrics, imagery, and artistic personae. Since the late 1990s, ideas drawn from bounce, including dance styles, have increasingly been appropriated or referenced by artists working at the national level. Songs by Beyoncé, such as "Get Me Bodied" (2007) and "Single Ladies (Put a Ring on It)" (2008), along with songs like Soulja Boy's 2007 "Crank That (Soulja Boy)" showed how musical and performance ideas drawn from or influenced by New Orleans bounce could be used to reach a national audience.

Another important venue for exposing twerking to a national audience has been the rise to wider popularity of "sissy rapper" Big Freedia (Freddie Ross), one of the most prominent New Orleanians in the national rap or Hip Hop scene since 2011. Big Freedia maintains a steady schedule of local performances, but has frequently performed outside New Orleans, often appearing on bills alongside white artists from the rock and pop genres. Freedia and, to a lesser extent, other "sissy rappers" from New Orleans have enjoyed a large amount of exposure to different audiences (with this difference encompassing aspects of region, race, social class, musical genre, and sexuality). Freedia, along with her crew of backup dancers, has facilitated this cultural crossover by offering audiences preconcert instruction on twerking and other dances associated with New Orleans bounce. The rapper has also appeared on national television, such as on the late-night talk shows hosted by Jimmy Kimmel and Conan O'Brien, as well as the reality show *Big Freedia: Queen of Bounce*, which premiered on the Fuse TV network in 2013 and is in its fourth season at the time of writing.

The emergence in New Orleans of a cohort of so-called "sissy rappers" (this name, which is sometimes used by the rappers themselves, employs a pejorative term for gay men that has a long history in the expressive culture of New Orleans) beginning around 2000 was an important moment of transition in bounce, one that entailed a return to an ultralocal perspective in terms of the musical and cultural values guiding its production. Katey Red (Kenyon Carter) was the first "sissy rapper" to release an album in the bounce genre. The 1999 multi-artist album *Melpomene Block Party* served as Katey Red's recorded debut and was quickly followed by the 2000 release *Y2Katey: The Millennium Sissy*. Several other "sissy rappers" released singles and albums between 2000 and 2005, including Vockah Redu, Chev off the Ave, Sissy Nobby, and others. Big Freedia's debut recording, the 2003 double CD *Queen Diva*, featured locally popular songs including "Gin in My System" and "A'han, Oh Yeah." In addition to emphasizing the core musical values of bounce—handclaps, tempi around 105 or 110 beats-per-minute, and samples from the 1986 song "Drag Rap" by the New York–based group The Showboys—the music produced by the sissy rappers, as well as their stage shows and performances, were intensely focused on dance, and prominently featured twerking or p-popping. While these rappers' contestation of rap's deeply inscribed conventions of heteronormativity may have turned off some New Orleans listeners, they developed a strong following (especially among female audience members), and their local orientation helped make their music central to the bounce scene after the year 2000.

SHAKING UP THE MAINSTREAM

Until 2013, twerking was still a subcultural phenomenon, one of many regional forms of expressive culture that circulated among music fans and critics but was unfamiliar to the vast majority of Americans. Several events that year, however, vastly increased the exposure of twerking and, in the process, crystalized the tensions produced by the rapid decontextualization that the dance experienced. The first was a mildly controversial series of concerts in which Big Freedia opened for the Postal Service, a white pop band popular in the Seattle area. As Andrew Matson (2013) reported on a *Seattle Times* blog, the Postal Service audience did not share the band's enthusiasm for "sissy bounce" and the dance performance that went along with it. Matson noted that the "incongruous, provocative pairing was deliberate," conceived by Postal Service frontman Ben Gibbard, who was "excited to see how people [would] react" to his choice of opening act. Matson wrote that "audience members were irritated, seemed to be uncomfortable with Freedia's brand of sexual expression and questioned whether the performance was 'real music.'" In addition to challenging audience members' musical preferences, the performance also caused tension in the area of sexual identification: "Men in the stands conspicuously proclaimed their own heterosexuality, and in general the response was uneasy."

Katie Ryder (2013) wrote about the negative reaction of Postal Service fans to Big Freedia's performance on Salon.com, in an article provocatively titled "White Music

Fans Are Afraid of Difference." Ryder's article can be contextualized within a racialized debate around "Indie rock" that began in 2007 with an article in *The New Yorker* by Sasha Frere-Jones, entitled "A Paler Shade of White: How Indie Rock Lost Its Soul," in which the author claimed that the "Indie" genre represented "a racial re-sorting" of rock music in the 1990s, in which "many white rock bands [retreated] from the ecstatic singing and intense, voice-like guitar tones of the blues, the heavy African downbeat, and the elaborate showmanship that characterized black music of the mid-twentieth century." In her Salon.com article, Ryder chastised the audience for their failure to appreciate Big Freedia's performance and suggested that racism was at the root of the chilly reception. The numerous comments posted in response to the article ranged from agreement with to complete rejection of Ryder's conclusions about the prejudices of white "hipster" audiences. Some commenters, presenting themselves as fans of Big Freedia, nonetheless argued that the audience had been justified in responding negatively to the near-total lack of stylistic similarity between the two musical acts. On the other hand, a writer named "Truthseeker" argued that audiences should not be "subjected to a 'performer' who objectifies women's bodies in his songs and uses the female dancer(s) as pornographic illustrations of those lyrics." This commenter likely summed up many people's view of twerking, describing it as "pornography" rather than "a dance move [or] a musical style."

More nuanced comments were posted by people who identified themselves as New Orleans natives. One named Victor Pizarro wrote, "I think the author of the article is SPOT ON and completely on to something," whereas another New Orleanian, posting as Robert1969, countered: "A white person who isn't racist should reject this gay-black-drag queen minstrel show." Robert1969 argued that Big Freedia's performance appeals to "hipster white liberals" not in spite of but because of its conformity to historical stereotypes of African Americans. As they relate to twerking in particular, the article and comments demonstrate how notions of sexuality, race, class, and respectability are thoroughly entangled when it comes to the reception of a performance like that of Big Freedia and her dancers.

Undaunted by mixed reviews from crossover (mostly white) audiences, and no doubt buoyed by the resultant controversy, Big Freedia continued to bring the idiosyncratic New Orleans bounce style to ever-wider audiences. Twerking—performed on stage, taught to audiences in preshow workshops, and referenced in song lyrics—remained at the center of this presentation. While Big Freedia insisted during a 2014 interview at the New Orleans Jazz and Heritage Festival that she was "over talking about Miley and the whole twerking situation," the dance and the controversy that swirled around it continued to be a prominent part of the New Orleans rapper's efforts at publicity and promotion (Fensterstock 2014). Freedia set two world records for group twerking; the first, held in Herald Square in Manhattan in September 2013, featured 358 participants. The second, held in New Orleans at the Central City Festival, broke that record when approximately 500 people performed the dance (Reckdahl 2014).

While reports of Freedia's opening performances at shows by The Postal Service caused a minor stir within the circles of "indie" music fans and those with an academic interest in the racial and sexual politics of popular music, twerking did not become a household word the United States until the infamous Miley Cyrus performance at the MTV Awards. Cyrus, the daughter of the country star Billy Ray Cyrus, had been engaged in a radical transformation of her public image for the several years preceding that appearance. Cyrus had broken through to national fame in the Disney television show *Hannah Montana* as the fictional Miley Stewart, a wholesome girl country singer. The Hannah Montana franchise, which also included several feature films, produced an impressive amount of income for Cyrus. But as she entered adulthood, she had been communicating a departure from the confines of the Hannah Montana character in a variety of ways—through an embrace of an overt sexuality (including revealing outfits and coquettish sexual posing), the use of illegal drugs (most prominently marijuana), and, perhaps most importantly, a stylistic transformation in her music and performance. To an important extent, this entailed an embrace of conventions associated with African Americans.

Cyrus's association with twerking began in 2013 when she released the album *Bangerz*. The music video for the song "We Can't Stop" featured a images of sexuality and youthful partying, including an image of a spoonful of alphabet soup letters spelling the word "twerk." Cyrus then performs the dance, encouraged by three African American women. Twerking is just one of several references to contemporary African American culture in the video; another is the ending shot, where Cyrus flashes "peace" hand signs while showing her pop-in gold teeth. "We Can't Stop" was written by African American songwriters Timothy Thomas and Theron Thomas and produced by Mike WiLL Made It; according to Timothy Thomas, the song was pitched to Cyrus after she insisted, "I want urban, I just want something that feels Black" for her new album (quoted in Platon 2013).

Among the other notable aspects of the MTV performance was its subversion of images associated with childhood—Cyrus emerged from a giant teddy bear, wearing a leotard emblazoned with an image of a cartoon mouse sticking its tongue out. The medley of songs began with Cyrus's "We Can't Stop," and showed the singer and her backup dancers (some of them wearing oversize teddy bears as backpacks) twerking. She was joined on stage by Robin Thicke, with whom she provocatively performed in a twerking posture, bent over at the waist, and backed up against the male singer's crotch as he performed his songs "Blurred Lines" and "Give it 2 U."

The controversy and curiosity produced by Cyrus's performance at the Video Music Awards brought twerking suddenly into mainstream consciousness. Discussion of Cyrus's performance also included speculation about how the pop star became acquainted with twerking. Journalist Alison Fensterstock (2013) wrote, "Miley Cyrus's interest in twerking may have, in fact, come directly from the Crescent City. In late 2010 and early 2011, she was indeed here, filming the action-comedy 'So Undercover.'" Fensterstock's conclusion is supported by an interview with Travis Laurendine, the promoter who organized a DJ Jubilee concert that Cyrus had attended: "She was up in the top section watching everything that was going on . . . as far as I can tell, she got introduced to twerking straight from the source."

Cyrus's performance was criticized from a variety of perspectives. The majority of negative reactions had to do with the perception that twerking is obscene or at least in poor taste, due to its purportedly erotic character. A more nuanced perspective was voiced by Big Freedia: Cyrus's performance was an inadequate rendering of the dance. "She really didn't twerk, you know. She attempted to twerk, but she didn't really twerk properly and so people were confused and a little baffled about the dance moves that she did do" (Carucci 2013). New Orleans–based DJ Rusty Lazer, who has toured with Freedia, decried the performance as "loaded with mockery and ineptitude," ultimately "insulting" to the culture from which it was appropriated (Fensterstock 2013). In a similar vein, Teddy Wayne (2013) called Cyrus out for "a brazenly cynical act of cultural appropriation being passed off as a rebellious reclamation of her sexuality after a childhood in the Disneyfied spotlight." Annie Lennox, the Scottish singer who fronted the band The Eurythmics in the late 1980s, warned, "Twerking is not feminism. . . . It's not liberating. It's not empowering. It's a sexual thing that you're doing on a stage. It doesn't empower you" (Morning Edition 2014). For Lennox, the use of twerking and similar dances in the repertoire of female pop artists like Cyrus, Beyoncé, or Rihanna represented and perpetuated a blurring of the line between legitimate entertainment and "highly styled pornography with musical accompaniment."

While the defense of Cyrus was less strident than the criticism, it was nonetheless effective in pointing out some of the limitations of the condemnations. Writing in *The Atlantic*, Steve Berlatsky (2014) questioned whether Annie Lennox was "just approaching sexuality from a slightly different cultural place—a place that has, maybe, something to do with whiteness?" He suggested that Lennox's exploitation of her own sexuality was merely a matter of stylistic rather than categorical difference in comparison with the work of the female entertainers she criticized. Berlatsky calls attention to Lennox's privilege, with her "body of a petite white woman," in being able to define her own, acceptable form of sexual performance: "Black women have to negotiate a different set of expectations and stereotypes." Like Lennox, Cyrus exploits her white privilege, which allows her to choose her own sexualized image rather than have one imposed on her. Still, her efforts were viewed through a tolerant lens by New Orleans rapper Cheeky Blakk, an important figure in the early dissemination of twerking, who counseled acceptance and understanding: "I think she's all right, and I'm glad she's putting it out there" (Fensterstock 2013).

Conclusion

Despite its veneer of novelty and hype, and its imbrication within a culture of female erotic performance for the male gaze, the movements associated with twerking can be understood within a long history of similar dances that have existed in the United States for centuries. Like those earlier dances, twerking evokes a variety of social issues. Dances like the shimmy and the twist became controversial when they crossed social boundaries related to gender, race, class, sexuality, and place. The style and concept of twerking are strongly influenced by its African American origins, which also contribute to the ways in which it has been received—as an image of uncontrolled sexuality, liberating or dangerous according to one's perspective—within the wider cultural mainstream in the United States and Europe. The racial identity of the performer has a strong influence on both the level of prior exposure to this and similar dances, and the interpretation of their meaning.

In addition to her superstar status (and in important ways, related to it), Miley Cyrus's location within a category of white womanhood is a central reason why her use of the dance generated significantly more controversy than the performances of artists who preceded her like Rihanna, Big Freedia, and Beyoncé. Like the shimmy and other earlier dances, twerking has become an avenue for sexual self-expression for young women, related to changing attitudes about female sexuality and respectability more broadly. In these respects, the story of twerking and its passage from a subcultural, local practice to a mainstream media talking point and symbol of moral wantonness and corruption conforms to a historically repetitive pattern: as dance historian Barbara Glass (2007) observes, "Typically, new dances with the ancient [African] characteristics were joyfully embraced by dancers, hotly condemned by moral authority, and enthusiastically written about by the press" (246).

The symbolic aspects of twerking were never completely absent from its earlier life as a local New Orleans phenomenon; however, as the dance has been decontextualized and attracted wider and more diverse audiences, perceptions of it have also changed significantly. Twerking was never universally accepted or celebrated in New Orleans, but it was recognized as a grassroots cultural phenomenon. With its passage into a more mainstream context, the connections between twerking and historical New Orleans popular culture—connections which ultimately trace back to West African cultural roots—have been overshadowed by the sensationalistic media coverage of the dance as a scandalous flashpoint over the representation of young women's sexuality. In this way, twerking is a prime example of how expressive cultural forms can bring wider social issues and tensions into focus and, in the process of mass popularization, often lose some of their cultural specificity and nuance.

References

Books and Articles

Baker, G. (1991). "Crew You, Too." *Miami New Times*, July 31.

Berlatsky, N. (2014). "Annie Lennox, Let Twerkers Twerk." *The Atlantic* online, October 24. www.theatlantic.com.

Bertrand, M. T. (2007). "Elvis and the Politics of Popular Memory." *Southern Cultures* 13 (3): 62–86.

Bryant, R. A. (2002). "Shaking Things Up: Popularizing the Shimmy in America." *American Music* 20 (2): 168–187.

Carty, H. S. (1988). *Folk Dances of Jamaica: An Insight*. London: Dance Books.

Carucci, J. (2013). "Rapper Big Freedia Brings Bounce to TV Audience." Associated Press State Wire Louisiana, October 22.

Crawford, D., and Russell, P. (2009). *Beyond the Bricks*. New Orleans: Neighborhood Story Project.

Dee, J. (2010). "Neither Straight nor Outta Compton." *New York Times Magazine*, July 25, 22–29.

Della Cava, M., and Ryan, P. (2013). "Miley's Showbiz Plan—Twerk It." *USA Today*, October 4, 1a.

Dvorak, P. (1998). "Bounce: Rap Music Meant for Dancing Fuels the Phenomenon of New Orleans Block Parties, Where the Action Is Sometimes Provocative, Always Passionate." *Times-Picayune*, October 25, E1.

Fensterstock, A. (2013). "We Can Twerk It Out." *Times-Picayune*, August 30.

Fensterstock, A. (2014). "Big Freedia Puts the Azz in Jazz." *Times-Picayune*, April 27.

Floyd, C. (2003). "Mista Triksta." *Guardian*, Weekend Pages, December 6, 32.

Fredkin, A. (2013). "A History of Twerking: No Miley Cyrus Included." *State Times* (State University of New York at Oneonta), October 30.

Frere-Jones, S. (2007). "A Paler Shade of White: How Indie Rock Lost Its Soul." *New Yorker*, October 22.

Glass, B. (2007). *African American Dance: An Illustrated History*. Jefferson, NC: McFarland.

Gomez, M. A. (1998). *Exchanging Our Country Marks: The Transformation of African Identities in the Colonial and Antebellum South*. Chapel Hill: University of North Carolina Press.

Gottschild, B. D. (2003). *The Black Dancing Body: A Geography from Coon to Cool*. New York: Palgrave Macmillan.

Green, T. (2001). "Twerk to Do." *Village Voice*, October 23, 149.

Hansen, C. (1967). "Jenny's Toe: Negro Shaking Dances in America." *American Quarterly* 19 (3): 554–563.

Hersch, C. (2007). *Subversive Sounds: Race and the Birth of Jazz in New Orleans*. Chicago: University of Chicago Press.

Johnson, J. (1991), "New Orleans's Congo Square: An Urban Setting for Early Afro-American Culture Formation." *Louisiana History* 32 (2): 117–157.

MacCash, D. (2014). "Is It Worth It? Let Miley Twerk It." *Times-Picayune*, March 21.

Matson, A. (2013). "Big Freedia Opens for the Postal Service, Bewilders the Crowd at Key Arena." *Seattle Times* blogs (Soundposts), July 19. http://blogs.seattletimes.com/soundposts/2013/07/19.

Miller, M. (2008). "Dirty Decade: Rap Music and the U.S. South, 1997–2007." Southern Spaces. http://www.southernspaces.org/2008/dirty-decade-rap-music-and-us-south-1997-2007.

Miller, M. (2012). *Bounce: Rap Music and Local Identity in New Orleans*. Amherst: University of Massachusetts Press.

Monson, I. (1995). "The Problem with White Hipness: Race, Gender, and Cultural Conceptions in Jazz Historical Discourse." *Journal of the American Musicological Society* 48 (3): 396–422.

Morning Edition. (2014). "You Cannot Go Back: Annie Lennox on 'Nostalgia.'" NPR Radio Show, October 21.

Mulvey, L. (1975). "Visual Pleasure and Narrative Cinema." *Screen* 16 (3): 6–18.

Platon, A. (2013). "Miley Cyrus Asked for a 'Black' Sound for Single, Says Songwriters Rock City." *Vibe*, June 12. http://www.vibe.com/article/miley-cyrus-asked-black-sound-single-says-songwriters-rock-city.

Reckdahl, K. (2014). "Twerk Team Triumph: Queen of Bounce Breaking Backs, World Record with Dance." *New Orleans Advocate*, November 16.
Ryder, K. (2013). "White Music Fans Are Afraid of Difference." Salon.com, August 1. http://www.salon.com/2013/08/01/white_music_fans_are_afraid_of_difference/.
Wayne, T.(2013). "Explaining Twerking to Your Parents." *New York Times*, September 1, SR2.

Sound Recordings

2 Live Crew. 1991. "Pop That Pu__y."
Beyoncé. 2007. "Get Me Bodied."
Beyoncé. 2008. "Single Ladies (Put a Ring on It)."
Big Al & Lil Tee. 1996. "Twerk Something Aggin."
Big Freedia. 2003. "A'han, Oh Yeah."
Big Freedia. 2003. "Gin in My System."
Bust Down. 1991. "Pop That Thang."
Cheeky Blakk. 1994. "Terk Something."
Cheeky Blakk. 1995. "Twerk Something, Part 2." Devious. 1993. "Hey P-Poppers."
D.J. Jimi. 1992. "(The Original) Where They At."
D.J. Jubilee. 1993. "Stop, Pause (Do the Jubilee All)."
Juvenile. 1999. "Back that Azz Up."
Katey Red. 1999. "Melpomene Block Party."
Katey Red. 2000. *Y2Katey: The Millennium Sissy*.
M.C. T. Tucker & D.J. Irv. 1992. "Where Dey At."
Miley Cyrus. 2013. "We Can't Stop."
Miley Cyrus. 2013. *Bangerz*.
Moby Dick. 1999. "Twerk Some'm."
Mystikal. 2000. "Shake Ya Ass."
Robin Thicke. 2013. "Blurred Lines."
Robin Thicke. 2013. "Give It 2 U."
The Showboys. 1986. "Drag Rap."
Soulja Boy. 2007. "Crank That (Soulja Boy)."
Ying Yang Twins. 2000. "Whistle While you Twurk."

CHAPTER 18

....

IS SHE B-BOYING OR B-GIRLING? UNDERSTANDING HOW B-GIRLS NEGOTIATE GENDER AND BELONGING

HELEN SIMARD

INTRODUCTION

....

ALTHOUGH members of the general public often use the terms *breakdancing, breaking,* and *b-boying* interchangeably to refer to the original solo improvisational dance of Hip Hop culture, many Hip Hop pioneers have rejected the term "breakdancing" (Schloss 2009). These dancers, known as "b-boys" (break-boys) or "b-girls" (break-girls), claim that "breakdancing" represents the commercial exploitation of their dance during the 1980s, and insist that its proper name is *breaking* or "b-boying" (Fogarty 2006; Israel 2002; Schloss 2009). The fact that the term "b-boying" is explicitly masculine is no coincidence: since the emergence of Hip Hop culture in the 1970s, its associated arts (deejaying, graffiti, emceeing, and b-boying) have overwhelmingly been characterized as expressions of youthful male bravado and masculinity (Banes 2004; Hazzard-Donald 2004; Ogaz 2006). Created by young African American and Puerto Rican men and women living in the economically depressed Bronx, New York, the raw, aggressive aesthetic of b-boying and the explosive physicality required to perform it are rarely associated with Western, heteronormative, mainstream perceptions of women as "naturally" peaceful, nurturing, and submissive (Ogaz 2006). Indeed, although women were present, and most probably dancing at the social gatherings that gave birth to Hip Hop culture, early accounts of this dance form by journalists and commentators suggest that breaking was primarily performed by young men (Banes 2004; Holman 1984).

And yet, today, women of different races, ages, and socioeconomic backgrounds from around the world practice breaking and participate in its associated lifestyle community

(Cooper and Kramer 2005; Huntington 2007; Johnson 2014; Rivera 2003; Washington 2007). So, if "b-boying" is a normative name for this dance form but a female breaker is a "b-girl," is a woman "b-boying" or "b-girling" when she dances? If she is b-boying, does this mean that she is, in a way, performing the implicit masculinity of the dance form? Or is she automatically b-girling simply because she is a woman? Are b-boying and b-girling two different dances created by the biological sex of the dancer performing them? Or do they differ structurally and stylistically in ways that suggest they are different expressions of gender?[1]

This chapter considers the practices of b-boying and b-girling through the lens of gender, by examining the discourses surrounding the dance practices of female breakers, and some of the ways these discourses impact on women's social interactions within their dance community. Drawing from West and Zimmerman's (1987) conception of gender as not a fixed identity or possession, but "a complex of socially guided perceptual, interactional, and micropolitical activities that cast particular pursuits as expressions of masculine and feminine 'natures'" (126), I discuss some of the ways in which gender is "accomplished" by female breakers, at the discursive, embodied, and interactional levels. In doing so, I highlight both the struggles women may face when participating in this implicitly masculine lifestyle community, and the ways in which their presence and participation can contribute to challenging hegemonic definitions of masculinity and femininity.[2]

GENDER, LABELING, AND IDENTITY

To talk about how female breakers negotiate questions of gender through their dance practices, I need to start by discussing what I mean by "gender." The Oxford Dictionary defines the word *gender* in two different ways: first, as "each of the classes (typically masculine, feminine, common, neuter) of nouns and pronouns distinguished by the different inflections which they have and which they require in words syntactically associated with them" and second, as "the state of being male or female (typically used with reference to social and cultural differences rather than biological ones"; http://www.oxforddictionaries.com/definition/english/gender).

I have adopted West and Zimmerman's (1987) sociologically informed understanding of gender, which defines gender not as a core essence or identity, or something that a person "is" but, rather, as something that a person "does," or a fluid series of social actions, interactions, and strategies that exist, in part, to create "difference" between men and women. The authors argue that gender is accomplished through social interaction and is thus not only an individual activity but also a social act that is always performed "*at the risk of ... assessment* [original emphasis]" (136). Put differently, individuals consciously or subconsciously "do" gender in relation to the norms, roles, stereotypes, and values of their community, which might differ or vary depending on the context. As such, gender is "an outcome of and a rationale of various social arrangements, and as a means of legitimating one of the most fundamental divisions of society" (126).

One of the ways that individuals express gender is through the words they use to identify the various social roles or identities they occupy during social interactions. Indeed, the words that one uses to label oneself and one's social practices—or the labels that one is assigned by one's community—are central to the process by which identity is constructed and performed in social contexts (McConnell-Ginet 2011). In modern English there are three linguistic genders—masculine, feminine, and neuter—which are organized through what is referred to as a "natural" gender system, where inanimate objects are neuter, and masculine and feminine genders are applied to words that refer to male and female animals or humans holding similar, paired positions (prince/princess, lion/lioness etc.; Curzan 2003).[3] As such, female breakers are faced with the choice of labeling their dancing with the gender-neutral term "breaking," a masculine term such as "b-boying," or the feminine term "b-girling," which marks them as being different from their male counterparts because it "implies that the activity [dancing] is different simply by virtue of the gender of the person performing it" (Schloss 2009, 64).

Of course, some critics might argue that *b-boying* and *b-girling* are "just words." Yet gender labeling is one of the first ways in which social identities are constructed: when a baby is born, "it" remains, in a way, an inhuman, inanimate thing until the moment it stops being an "it" and is pronounced a "boy" or a "girl" (Butler 1993; Eckert and McConnell-Ginet 2013). Moreover, and far from insignificantly, this labeling of babies as "boys" and "girls" will go on to influence how their respective bodies will be allowed to train and develop, in regard to the kinds of activity considered "appropriate" for men and women by their given culture (Fausto-Sterling 2005; West and Zimmerman 1987). Physiological factors such as bone density (Fausto-Sterling 2005), muscular strength (Fausto-Sterling 2000), and even hormone levels and brain-activity patterns (Eckert and McConnell-Ginet 2013) are influenced and transformed by the kinds of activities individuals are permitted to engage in, in a given time and place, which in turn influences the kinds of activities they will be able or be encouraged to engage in, in the future. Thus, in asking whether female breakers are b-boying or b-girling when they dance, I am asking about more than these gender-specific words they might use to label themselves; rather, I am asking how social labeling practices might influence or inform the ways that female breakers negotiate, accomplish, and express gender through their dance practice.

RESEARCH DESIGN

I have employed a methodological approach known as discourse analysis.[4] Discourse analysis is not simply an examination of language but, rather, the examination of "language use relative to social, political and cultural formations . . . language reflecting social order but also language shaping social order, and shaping individuals' interactions with society" (Jaworski and Coupland 2014, 3).[5] I am examining how individuals and discourses interact to produce and assess gender, and how "the pressure of broad social or institutional norms is brought to bear on the identities and classifications of individuals" (Jaworski and Coupland, cited in Clarke 2005, 158). In examining the discourses that surround female breakers and their dance practices, this chapter "aspires to dissect, disrupt and render the familiar strange" (Graham 2005, 4) in order to reveal how discourses operate to "create and manage personal, social, and cultural meanings and identities" (Kendall and Tannen 2001, 548).

I collected data from multiple sources, including a review of popular and academic literature available on female breakers; a collection of visual and media artifacts, including print, video, and online interviews with pioneering b-boys and b-girls; video archives of battles shared on websites such as YouTube and Vimeo; online discussions on message boards and social media websites; and promotional materials for breaking competitions. I also drew on transcriptions of qualitative interviews conducted with female breakers in Montreal, Canada, from an empirical study that took place between 2011 and 2013 on the choreological, social, and symbolic differences between "b-boying" and "breakdancing" (Simard 2014). Although these interviews covered issues other than gender, they yielded a number of statements about how female breakers experienced and negotiated this male-dominated environment. This kind of cross-referencing of data sources was not simply done to address issues of validity or credibility through triangulation but also to connect "media representations to people, discourses to our daily practices of subject making (including the resistant)" (Clarke 2005, 152).

Data was analyzed through thematic comparison. I began by identifying statements on how female breakers do, or should, label their dance practices, then moved to looking for broader statements on how these labels informed, impeded, or enabled performances of gender in different discourses or social interactions in the breaking community. My reading of data revealed multiple perspectives on gender that were at times contrasting or even paradoxical; as such, in considering how female breakers construct or accomplish gender through their dance practices, I have presented multiple perspectives, looked for contingencies rather than causes, and have avoided coming to overgeneralized conclusions in order to highlight the complexity of the phenomenon at hand.

RESULTS AND DISCUSSION

Being "One of the Guys"

Scholars and dancers alike have struggled with the question of how to label the dance practices of female breakers. For example, Guevara (1996), Gunn (2012), Smith Lefebvre (2011), and Schloss (2009) have suggested that b-boying can be used as an unmarked, blanket term to describe the dance practices of both male and female participants.

Indeed, pioneer Asian American B-Girl Asia One of the Mighty Zulu Kweenz insists that she is "representing the official cultural dance of Hip Hop, which is b-boying. I don't call it b-girling . . . I feel like we do the style of dance that's called b-boying" (Antics 2010). Similarly, Hanifa "Hanifa Queen" McQueen,[6] a British b-girl of Jamaican descent, considered by many to have been one of the first b-girls in the United Kingdom, states on her website that she "started B-Boying in 1982 at the age of 12" (Art Breaker, n.d.), referring to her "b-boying days" and "b-boying culture" when she talks about her history as a dancer (TruFamTV 2013). Another pioneer, Karima of Actuel Force from France, does not go so far as to call her dancing b-boying but has stated, "for me, the title B-girl means nothing. I've never been called a B-girl, it's almost ridiculous" (Haire 2014, para. 2).[7] Karima refers to herself and her crewmates as "brothers of the Floor" (Kramer 2015, para 8), suggesting that she does not see herself as different from the b-boys she dances with. The way these b-girls see it, since they do the same moves (top rock, footwork, freezes, spins, and power moves, among others) as their male counterparts, and adhere to the same aesthetic codes, their dance practice should not be seen or labeled differently.[8]

Some women might be attracted to b-boying specifically because it provides a performative space that allows them to construct and perform what Halberstam (1998) has referred to as a kind of "heroic masculinity" that "inevitably conjures up notions of power and legitimacy and privilege" (2). Indeed, Langnes and Fasting (2014) observed that some female breakers want to be seen as "one of the guys" (11) and will dress in a "masculine" fashion (baggy shirts/pants, ball caps, no makeup) in order to mask their bodies and "present themselves as detached from femininity" (11) so they can embody the masculine aesthetics and character of breaking. Ogaz (2006) proposed that, through their dancing, female breakers create a "third space of play, resistance and creative achievement" (180), where they can experiment with masculine social identities that transcend stereotypical expectations of gender. Similarly, Monteyne (2013) has suggested that this performing of masculinity through their dancing allows female breakers to "parody or usurp male power and identity through the stylings of hip-hop culture" (170). Moreover, the physically demanding nature of breaking, and the hours of training that a woman (or man, for that matter) must invest to master the dance form, allows female breakers to develop a level of physical strength, full body awareness, orientation in space, and freedom of motion that, according to Young (1980), is not generally associated with feminine modes of bodily comportment in white, middle-class, Western culture. Thus, through their dancing, female breakers may experience a dual pleasure of challenging and critiquing the stereotypes and gender roles associated to femininity, all while experiencing the strength, power, authority, privilege, and bodily freedom associated to hegemonic masculinity.

But while some female breakers may agree that traditionally "masculine" movement qualities such as strength, speed, aggression, and explosiveness are considered to be more aesthetically pleasing by the community, this does not mean that they are necessarily interested in performing or critiquing gender with their dancing. If we remember the earlier discussion of Asia One's use of the term *b-boying* to label her dance practice, her reasoning for using the masculine term did not come from a desire to be a "man" or "masculine." Indeed, Asia One has explicitly stated elsewhere, "When I do it [breaking], I don't try and act like a man, or do my moves like a man. I do 'em how I do 'em" (Raimist 1999). As such, her use of the masculine terminology appears to stem more from a desire to show respect for a conceptualization of proper history and form of the dance, than from an interest in performing gender.

Indeed, one must consider that in choosing to label their dancing as b-boying or dance in a conventionally "masculine" way, female breakers might simply be interested in performing the dance "correctly." For example, Beebish, a Franco-Algerian b-girl from France who gained international recognition in the early 2000s, has stated:

> When I started there were very few of them [b-girls] around the world. And I'll admit that when I came to the United States [to battle], I wanted to be equal to men, not just women. I wanted to be equal to men, but not just equal, I wanted to be better than them. This meant showing that even though physically we [men and women] didn't have the same assets, or the same physical predispositions, this was a handicap that I was able to overcome by working at it. But at the beginning, this was very difficult. I wanted to show that it was just a technique, and that at a certain point . . . maybe I could be as strong and talented as they [b-boys] were. And I succeeded, and I'm very happy about that, I'm proud of it, because at the beginning girls contented themselves with doing simple movements. [They] didn't go to the end of their physical potential. They really limited themselves in that way. Whereas I did not give myself any limits, it was like, Beebish, just arrive, and dance like they [b-boys] do. That's it. That's what the dance is? They [b-boys] can do it? Well, me too, I'll be able to do it as well. (Groupe Nice-Matin 2011)[9]

Similarly, B-girl Roxy from the United Kingdom encourages b-girls to:

> Stop making excuses that you're a girl. That's what a lot of b-girls do. It doesn't make any difference. Don't look up to other girls because they're a girl. I look up to [b-boy] Hong10[10] because he's AMAZING . . . If you're going to be like, 'I want to be like that person,' do it for the best people, not just the best girl. (TooMuchFlavour, 2011)

On the one hand, for Beebish and Roxy, idolizing and wanting to dance like b-boys does not appear to be a matter of wanting to be masculine. Rather, they perceived that, since the best dancers in the international breaking community happened to be male, they would have to strive to dance not only like them but to be better than they were to succeed. Indeed, judging from their appearances, it would be difficult to label Beebish or Roxy as "masculine" or a "tomboys": despite their aggressive attitudes and explosive movement qualities, their traditional feminine markers such as makeup, long hair, and form-fitting clothes give them a distinct air of "womanliness" (Adams, Schmitke, and Franklin 2005). On the other hand, it is interesting to note that these female breakers do not want to be perceived as "feminine" either, seeing their female bodies as a "handicap," or a troublesome or annoying obstacle they had to "stop making excuses" for. Beebish and Roxy do not want to be considered good "for girls" or even "as girls." They want spectators to look past their gender, and to evaluate their dancing based on their skill as dancers and ability to execute the moves properly. However, it is important to note that what they recognize as the "proper" form of the dance is associated with Western standards of masculinity.

Dancing "Like a Girl"

Some female breakers, however, do not want to be "one of the guys" and prefer to distinguish themselves from the male norm. They see the distinction between b-boying and b-girling as positive, and as a chance to celebrate women's accomplishments. For example, during my fieldwork in Montreal, an Asian b-girl in her early thirties told me, "It's kind of cool to say b-girling, because I'm a girl that does this crazy male-dominated, masculine dance form" (interview with the author, March 2011). To this informant, labeling her dance as "b-girling" was a way to bring awareness to the fact that they are women succeeding in a historically male-dominated dance, and allowed her to shed light on alternative modes of feminine expression.

Similarly, Los Angeles–based Asian American b-girl Peipei "Peppa" Yuan has explained:

> It's important for b-girls to understand that you are a woman, you are a female. So yes, we learned a lot of these moves from b-boys, and some of the first dancers breaking were men, but it's really important to know that you can still dance feminine, you can still be strong and fierce and powerful. Because otherwise, if you want to break like a b-boy, and just only look like a b-boy, dress like a b-boy, move like a b-boy, that's b-boying. It's not b-girling. It's a difference. (Antics 2010)

Of course, Peppa's comments go beyond a question of labeling, and suggest that she feels that her dancing differs from the dancing of her male counterparts because she is female. Developing a dance style that reflects this difference, at both the discursive and embodied levels, allows her not only to express herself as an individual, but also to redefine herself as a strong and powerful woman.

Other authors have echoed this statement, suggesting that female breakers view their dancing as a unique expression of their femininity. For example, Gunn and Scannell (2013) have proposed that breaking allows women to escape the implicitly masculine "hip-hop habitus" and "transcend the superficial concepts of feminine identity," creating a unique corporeal "power of becoming" (59). Johnson (2014) has argued that female breakers challenge hegemonic definitions of femininity by performing a "badass femininity," or an alternative femininity that "eschews notions of appropriateness, respectability, and passivity demanded of ladylike behavior in favor of confrontational, aggressive, and even outright offensive, crass, or explicit expressions of a woman's strength" (6). According to Johnson, although confrontation and aggression might be more aligned with hegemonic masculinity, badass femininity should not be understood as an example of "female masculinity" or "tomboyism," but as a manner of "re-signifying femininity is a distinctively Hip Hop way" through "strong, fierce, powerful feminine performances" (11). Pioneering Afro–Puerto Rican b-girl Rokafella of Full Circle Crew says that she strives to "balance the femininity with the hardcore aggression that it takes . . . to be a master breaker" (SaborLatinoGlobal, 2013). Some b-girls find this balance by adopting a softer, slower, more fluid, more "feminine" style in the dance (Guevara 1996; Rose 1994; Washington 2007). Others might balance the "hardcore aggression" of breaking by emphasizing their physical appearance, adopting the more "feminine" style of dress by wearing the traditional feminine markers (form-fitting clothing, loose hair, jewelry, and makeup; Gunn and Scannell 2013). When asked about the way she dressed, one b-girl in Montreal told me, "I to want to be funky but still be feminine . . . I don't want people to think I'm a guy" (interview with the author, March 2011).

Examining this statement, however, one can note that while this b-girl begins by acknowledging a personal desire to dress in a manner that expresses her femininity, she also reveals that part of her motivation to do so is rooted in a concern that others might interpret or judge her as being masculine. This example is a reminder that gender is not simply an individual expression, but rather an ongoing social act, which is informed by and evaluated in relation to the dominant gender norms, roles, and stereotypes in a given social context that set guidelines for "appropriate" or "deviant" behaviors and appearances for men and women (Schur 1984 West and Zimmerman 1987). While the participant was able to express a "badass femininity" through her dancing—thus challenging dominant discourses that associate femininity to passivity, weakness, fragility, and submission—she felt a need to compensate for her violation of one set of gender norms (behavior) by emphasizing her compliance to another (appearance).

Another strategy that some female breakers historically employed to avoid being labeled masculine was to develop slower, smoother, jazzier dancing styles, emphasizing flow and musicality over spectacular, acrobatic movements and aggressive attitudes (Guevara 1996; Rose 1994; Washington 2007). As Puerto Rican American b-girl Baby Love, member of the Rock Steady Crew and one of the first b-girls to receive media attention in the 1980s, has explained: "We [b-girls] do a more feminine style [of breaking] than the guys just to show that we're not girls trying to look like guys" (quoted in Guevara 1996, 59). Here, too, one can note that Baby Love's motivation for asserting her femininity in her dancing was, at least in part, to "show" others that she is not a man. As such, while Washington (2007) has argued that expressing their femininity through their breaking can be empowering for some female breakers, because it allows them to "assert themselves, differentiate their style, and distance it from b-boying" (83), it can also lower expectations about the skill level they will be able to achieve in the dance form. As such, some b-girls might find the insistence that they need to express femininity through their dancing restrictive, and may only cultivate a feminine appearance or bodily comportment as a strategy to avoid being labeled "deviant" or "masculine."

No Easy Props

Whether they prefer to refer to their dancing as b-boying or b-girling, and whether they present themselves and dance in a more stereotypically masculine or feminine manner, it is worth noting that female breakers are scrutinized and evaluated based on their gender and appearance in a way that their male counterparts are not. Indeed, during my fieldwork in Montreal (Simard 2014), several female breakers expressed annoyance because they felt they were often evaluated as females first and breakers second when they danced. One participant told me, "As a conscious decision I call it [the dance] 'breaking,' because I don't like 'b-boying' or 'b-girling.' It's too gender specific and it shouldn't be" (interview with the author, March 2011). For her, being a woman should not have any impact on how her dancing is received: she wanted her dancing to be assessed on the basis of her skills: "I just want to be dope for being dope, and not being dope *for being a girl* [emphasis added]."

This frustration with not wanting to be considered good "for a girl" is a reoccurring theme among female breakers, who do not want to be recognized or applauded simply for being "brave enough" to participate in the b-boy community, but rather for their capacities as breakers (Washington 2007). Unfortunately, some dancers have suggested that, since it is assumed that female breakers are not as good as their male counterparts, women automatically receive more praise than men would for performing the same movements (Blagojević 2009; Gunn 2012; Rajakumar 2012; Washington 2007). This phenomenon has been referred to as getting "girl props" or "easy props." Veteran Latina American b-girl Honey Rockwell of the Rock Steady Crew described her experiences of getting easy props:

> When I would go in the circle when there weren't any women doing it [breaking], I would get a lot of cheers. I wouldn't even do a move and they'd start clapping. I'd walk into the circle [makes noise of excited crowd], and people would wonder what I was going to do? I would get down. I would literally get busy like the boys. Everything they were doing, I was doing. Windmills, backspins, flipping, and head spins . . . It didn't matter what I did back then. I could have done a ballerina twirl. (Maniaci 2006, question 15)

When asked about the specific struggles she faced as a woman in a male-dominated dance form, B-Girl Cleopatra from Montreal said she found it difficult to know

> if you're really good, cause you always get easy props . . . a lot of times girls get easy props, like from the general public. When they see a girl break, it's like "oooooh!" Anything she would do, everyone claps. So, you don't know if you're really good. (Bboy North 2014)

One can sense Honey Rockwell's and Cleopatra's frustration that they might receive praise for performing almost any movement, whether it was part of the breaking vocabulary or not, and whether or not they performed it well. Although one could think that being judged less severely than their male counterparts might put female breakers at an advantage of sorts, it has been shown that low expectations of women's physical capacities can, in fact, inhibit their level of performance in sports (Chalabaev et al. 2013), and can discourage women from wanting to participate in male-dominated environments.

To improve as dancers, many female breakers feel a need to push themselves to challenge these lower expectations. For example, Asia One created the all-female crew No Easy Props "to create a space for women to support each other in advancing skills but also as a space where they challenged each other to exceed the standards set for women in breaking and Hip Hop" (quoted in Washington 2007, 86). According to the No Easy Props website, the crew's mission is "to inspire greatness in Hip Hop, where merits were awarded based on authenticity, hard work, and skills!" (No Easy Props, n.d.). Although No Easy Props is an all-female crew, Asia One has stressed that she is not interested in pitting herself against or segregating herself from the b-boy community: "We're not trying to compete against men, we're just trying to build our own, you know? It's not about 'us versus them,' it's about us [b-girls] helping ourselves, because we shouldn't expect them [b-boys] to do our shit for us" (Raimist 1999).

It is worth noting in Honey Rockwell and Cleopatra's statements, however, that often, it was not b-boys who were holding female breakers to a lower standard and giving them unwanted and undeserved praise, but rather nondancing spectators from the general public. Indeed, b-girls might not want to think about their dancing through the lens of gender, but those watching them certainly might. During my fieldwork, one b-girl recounted an incident that made her consider how gender stereotypes dictating what was an appropriate way for women to move might lead people to evaluate the way that female breakers dance. She explained:

> When I do toprock I try to do toprock period. I don't try to do a "girl" toprock or a "guy" toprock. I try to make my shapes traditional, classic shapes [of the dance form]. I don't think of them as "man" shapes or "girl" shapes, I just think of them as shapes. I'm trying to do a character; I hunch my back and I put some angles in my arms and I get low. To me, I just consider it funky. But I could see how an outside observer would see it as a man's dance and male movement. Like, a friend of mine invited her friend to come see a battle. And at the end she said to me, "Oh you dance just like a guy." And I was taken aback . . . I was like is that how you see it? She was expecting when the girl came out to dance that the girl would dance differently. (Interview with the author, March 2011)

These comments make it clear that, though the participant had not herself perceived her actions as being gendered, "insofar as inclusion in a sex category is used as a fundamental criterion for differentiation, doing gender is unavoidable" (West and Zimmerman 2002, 21). While this female breaker had felt she was simply recognizing and respecting the aesthetics of her dance form, others had read her dancing body through the lens of gender. This suggests that, whether they liked it or not, female breakers' dance performances are assessed in relation to the strict, societal, heteronormative conceptions of what constitutes appropriate appearance and behavior for men and women, and notions of how female bodies "should" express themselves through movement in a given social context.

B-Girl Battles or B-Boy Battles?

One place where female breakers might be held particularly accountable for the way they "should" dance is in competitions, or "battles" as they are called in the breaking community. According to Schloss (2009), "Battling is foundational to all forms of Hip Hop, and the articulation of strategy—'battle tactics'—is the backbone of its philosophy of aesthetics" (10). Yet, considering the importance placed on battling in the breaking community, there are still very few women who compete in battles that are open to both men and women. In 2014, there were only two b-girls (Roxy from the United Kingdom and Ayumi from Japan) in the top sixteen dancers at the prestigious R16 Korea international competition, and no female participants made it into the top sixteen at any of the other international one-on-one Undisputed World B-Boy Series events, such as the Chelles Battles Pro, Battle of the Year, Notorious IBE, Outbreak Europe, or Red Bull BC One (Undisputed BBoy 2014). Breaking battles are still dominated by men.

Gupta-Carlson (2010) and Washington (2007) have suggested that it can be intimidating for female breakers to participate in or even attend battles or breaking events where the majority of participants are men. Indeed, Baby Love has stated that, in the 1980s, she did not often get to battle with Rock Steady Crew "because the other groups don't have a girl for me to battle, and it's kind of weird a girl battling guys" (quoted in Guevara 1996, 59). Similarly, Lady Jules, a white American b-girl who is well known for her performances with her crew Beat Freaks on the television show *America's Best Dance Crew* and for playing the lead role in the movie *B-Girl* (2009) has addressed how difficult it can be for female breakers to participate in mixed competitions:

> When I first started, there was not that many [b-girls] . . . it was really intimidating, because it's just like . . . so much testosterone. And you're coming in the circle and it's like "ahhhh" [pretends to be scared]. And all eyes are always on you, because you're the only girl. And I think that a lot of girls in today's day and age, that's what's intimidating is that we're such a minority that it's exciting for everyone to watch us, they're like "whoa, a female!" You know? So I know that that's one thing that b-girls have to get passed, just the fact that there's such a spotlight on them all the time. (TooMuchFlavour 2009)

Jules brings up two ways in which female breakers might feel intimidated to enter battles: first, in that they are competing against men; and second, because of the additional attention paid to them by spectators because they are women. Moreover, she hints at the fact that because they are a minority, female breakers have few women around them to look up to or emulate, which might make it harder for women to become involved in the breaking community.

To encourage more female breakers to participate in battles, Washington (2007) suggests that women create "safe," or all-female, spaces in Hip Hop, where they can develop their artistic skills, consciousness, and sense of self through their relationships and interactions with other women. She proposes that by creating events or battles specifically for female breakers, these dancers will be able to build "confidence and courage to participate freely and without fear" (82) within the greater b-boy community. Since the early 2000s, there has been a growing number of b-girl battles and events taking place around the world: from the B-Supreme festival in the United Kingdom, to the We BGirlz battles hosted around the world, to the Queen Sweet 16 battles in the United States, and the Keep Rocking You B-girl Movement events in Canada. Moreover, larger international competitions, such as Battle of the Year or Notorious IBE, often feature a separate b-girl or "Bonnie and Clyde" (two-on-two battles featuring mixed male/female teams) categories to encourage female breakers to enter battles, and the Red Bull BC One event added a one-on-one b-girl competition to their world finals in 2018. These events and organizations do not merely create spaces for women, but also often have mandates to inspire and empower dancers and spectators alike: for example, the We B*Girlz website states that the organization's mandate is to "present strong, smart, independent B-Girlz and other Hip Hop females as role models for upcoming generations to show everyone that there is a significant place for women in this worldwide culture" (We B*Girlz, n.d.).

The idea of creating separate battles or events for b-girls parallels the predominant approach used in sports, where male and female competitors are generally segregated and do not generally compete against each other (Chalabaev et al. 2013). Often, the idea is that creating a "womanspace within sport," or spaces and services specifically for women, brings increased visibility to female athletes, which will in turn help challenge gender stereotypes and roles, and hopefully increase interest and participation in women's sports (Stevens and Adams 2012, 659). In some instances, these efforts have been highly successful. For example, community efforts and resources put into developing women's hockey leagues in Canada and the United States have not only resulted in a dramatic increase in the number of women participating in the sport, but also an improvement in the quality of women's hockey (Pelak 2002).

Some female breakers prefer competing against other women in b-girl battles, as Lady Jules explains:

> Honestly . . . I like battling girls more than guys. And a lot of girls will say, "Oh that's so ridiculous, you should battle guys!" But I like battling girls, because we have a different way of approaching the dance than guys do. And, yes, we can do what the guys are doing, but there will always be a difference, because men are just naturally stronger. Don't hate me for saying that. We can be just as good as they can, but it's a different, difficult thing. So, I like to go against the girls; we have a camaraderie, I think. It's a little bit . . . I don't want to say it's sweeter, because we can be just as crazy. But it's just a different vibe. (quoted in TooMuchFlavour 2009)

Lady Jules's statement highlights a number of points: for one, she could be seen to be making the "excuses" alluded to earlier in Roxy's statement by limiting herself by seeing women as being "naturally" weaker than men. However, Jules also suggests that this physical imbalance allows female breakers to develop a different, unique approach to breaking, which she feels deserves to be showcased and developed in a competitive, woman centered environment. Moreover, she feels that competing together and against each other in this way, female breakers can develop a sense of connection and camaraderie that is different from the experience of battling against b-boys.

It is interesting to note, however, that even though Lady Jules prefers battling against other women, she is aware that others would tell her that she "should" want to compete against men. This discourse—female breakers "should" measure their performances with those of their male counterparts—is very present in the breaking community. Several prominent b-boys and b-girls have argued that since b-boys are the ones who set the standards in competition, b-girls, if they want to be seen as equals, need to compete against men. For example, Ken Swift has stated:

> It shouldn't segregate or separate, boy or girl. Everybody is a dancer, it doesn't matter. If you're a boy you can't dance with the girls, or the girls can't dance with the boys. We shouldn't separate and . . . start making b-boys feel that like girls are not involved, or girls be like, boys are not involved. Because I see that happening now, where it's like "b-girl events." We never said, "boy events," and girls are not invited. So I mean, to me, it's kind of stupid. But that's my opinion. I think it's more, I don't know, I don't know what the underlying theme is. That's not the way to do it. We need to be together everybody. So, b-girls, practice every move you see from the guys. And if somebody comes after you, tries to battle you, just go for it. It's always a win, there's no failure. (bjhiphopcollective 2009)

On the one hand, Ken Swift is calling for unity between b-boys and b-girls, encouraging female breakers to see themselves as equal to b-boys and to feel confident participating in the breaking community at large. On the other hand, saying that female breakers need to practice every move they see "from the guys" could be understood as implying that men's performances are inherently superior to women's, and that men set the standards against which all dancers will be judged. As such, much as in traditionally "masculine" sports where there is a perception that women's events are "inferior to and not as noteworthy as men's sport" (Knight and Giuliano 2001, 218), b-boy battles are framed here as the unmarked or "real" manifestation of the dance, while b-girl battles are viewed as inferior. Indeed, during my fieldwork in Montreal, I remember one participant telling me that battles organized specifically for b-girls could feel like "pony shows," and that they were not usually taken seriously by the community as "regular" (meaning b-boy) battles.

Entering "b-boy" battles, however, is not without its problems for female breakers. Over the course of my fieldwork, several of the b-girls I interviewed told me they had, at different times, been discouraged from entering a particular battle because it had been advertised as a b-boy battle, and was thus, implicitly, only open to male competitors. I vividly remember my own first experience with this problem: in 2002, I traveled with my all-female crew, DysFunkShn, to an event called the B-Boy Masters Pro-Am in Miami, Florida. We had decided to enter the b-boy crew battle. When our turn came and the emcee called our name, we took our spot on the side of the dance floor. Quickly, a male bouncer came up to us to tell us we would have to move out of the way because we were standing where "the crew" was going to stand. Because my crew had entered a *b-boy* battle, this male bouncer had assumed that "the crew" would be male. Luckily, he did not intend any malice, and after he realized his mistake, we were made to feel welcome. As one b-girl in her early thirties noted, "I don't think they [b-boys] do mean to exclude women, but that's the way it comes out. I think there's more of a conscious effort now; when I see flyers [for events] these days, I'll see 'b-boy/b-girl battles,' or 'b-boy/b-girl event' " (interview with the author, April 2011). Of course, simply putting the words "b-boy" and "b-girl" together on a flyer will not automatically increase the number of female breakers entering battles, but it could help foster an unsegregated, gender-inclusive community that more female breakers will feel motivated to participate in.

CONCLUSION

Whether they refer to their dancing as "b-boying" or "b-girling," whether they enter "b-boy" battles or "b-girl" battles, and whether they even mean to or not, female breakers challenge societal perceptions of women every time they step into the cypher and dance. In their own way, these women are redefining dominant Western gender roles and stereotypes, and transforming "our understandings of what gender is and what gender does" (Moloney and Fenstermaker 2002, 189). At the same time, female breakers' dance performances are constantly assessed in relation to complex social norms that have historically dictated how women are permitted to act and appear. To compete—and succeed—in the highly competitive breaking community, female breakers may, at times, find themselves caught somewhere between pushing for change and maintaining the status quo, feeling pulled by contrasting discourses of masculinity and femininity and views on how they "should" participate in the breaking community. And as more and more women choose to participate in this traditionally male-dominated environment, we will have to consider how women of different ages, races, and nationalities might develop different strategies as they struggle to earn and maintain both their rightful place on the dance floor and the privilege of being recognized as breakers first and women second. By understanding the multiple—at times contradictory—ways female breakers negotiate, accomplish, and express gender through their dance practices, we can perhaps discover new ways in which embodied practices such as dance can help promote more fluid understandings of gender in contemporary society.

Notes

1. I first came across the "b-boying" versus "breakdancing" debate through my firsthand experiences as a b-girl and my participation in the b-boy/b-girl community in Montreal, Canada, since 1998. As such, the questioning of how to label or orient oneself as a woman in this male-dominated masculine environment originates from a questioning of my own identity as a dancer. For an in-depth discussion of my "insider/outsider" position as a practitioner-slash-researcher, see Simard (2014).

2. I recognize that this chapter addresses gender in a binary manner, not only because of the binary nature of the gendered labels that are discussed, but also because all of the b-girls quoted are cisgender women. Although the question of how trans, nonbinary, or gender-queer individuals would choose to label their dance practice when faced with the binary terms "b-boying" and "b-girling" is of great interest to me, this question is, for now, beyond the scope of my research. For readers interested in knowing more about trans, genderqueer, and nonbinary genders, see Richards, Bouman, and Barker (2017).

3. Some inanimate objects are referred to as *he* or *she* in English, at least in conversational, vernacular language. For further discussion on the reasons for these deviations, see Curzan (2003, 13–27).

4. Discourse analysis is a broad research method that can "range from the description and interpretation of meaning making and meaning understanding in specific situations through to the critical analysis of ideology and access to meaning-making systems and discourse networks" (Clarke 2005, 154). Although the term "discourse" can be used to describe the formal organization of speech and conversation, I use it here in a broader sense, as "both the an overall term to refer to all statements, the rules whereby those statements are formed and the processes whereby those statements are circulated and other statements are excluded" (Mills 2009, 62). Discourses are not simply constructed, or products of social interaction, but are in fact constructive because "they do not simply describe the social world, but are the mode through which the world of 'reality" emerges" (Macleod 2002, 18).

5. Clarke (2005) has highlighted that "discourse is not limited to language but also includes visual images . . . symbols . . . nonhuman things/material cultural objects . . . and other modes of communication (e.g., nonverbal movements, signals, sounds, music, dance)" (148).

6. Hanifa Queen previously went by the name B-Girl Bubbles.

7. In French: "Pour moi, le titre de B-Girl ne veut rien dire, je n'ai jamais été appelée une B-Girl, c'est presque ridicule." Translated by the author.

8. Interestingly, the same labeling issue exists for cowgirls, or "female cowboys," as they sometimes refer to themselves. For example, pioneer American rancher Anna Lindsey Perry-Fiske has said: "I never called myself a cowgirl. I'm a cowboy—doing a man's work on the ranch, riding and lassoing and doing all the things a man does" (quoted in Ford 2009, 94).

9. In French:

Moi, quand je suis arrivée, il y en avait très peu [de b-girls] dans le monde. Et j'avoue quand même que, quand je suis arrivée aux États-Unis [pour faire des *battles*], j'ai voulu égaler l'homme et pas forcément que la femme. Je voulais égaler l'homme, mais non pas que l'égaler, mais le dépasser. Ça veut dire montrer que, même si physiquement on n'avait pas les mêmes atouts, les mêmes prédispositions physiques forcément, moi, c'est un handicap que j'ai pu maîtriser en travaillant. Mais, au départ, ça a été très difficile. J'ai voulu prouver que c'était justement de la technique et qu'à un moment donné . . . Peut-être que je pouvais être aussi forte et douée qu'eux. Donc, j'ai réussi et j'en suis contente, j'en suis fière, parce que les filles au départ se sont contentées de simples mouvements. [Elles] n'allaient pas au bout de leur potentiel physique. Elles se limitaient vraiment à ce niveau-là. Alors que moi, je ne me suis mise aucune limite. Ça a été: Beebiche, tu arrives, tu danses comme eux [les b-boys]. Voilà. C'est ça la danse? Ils sont capables de le faire? Bien moi aussi, je serai capable de le faire. (Translated by the author)

10. Hong10 is an internationally recognized South Korean b-boy, who won the RedBull BC B-boy World Final in 2006 and 2013 (Smith 2013).

REFERENCES

Adams, N., Schmitke, A., and Franklin, A. (2005). "Tomboys, Dykes, and Girly Girls: Interrogating the Subjectivities of Adolescent Female Athletes." *Women's Studies Quarterly* 33 (1–2): 17–34.

Banes, S. (2004). "Breaking." In *That's the Joint: The Hip-Hop Studies Reader*, edited by M. Forman and M. A. Neal, 13–20. New York: Routledge.

Blagojević, G. (2009). "Belgrade Breakdance Girl: Breaking Gender-Specific Stereotypes with Dance." *Glasnik Etnografskog Instituta* 57 (2): 19–24.

Butler, J. (1993). *Bodies That Matter*. Routledge: New York.

Chalabaev, A., Sarrazin, P., Fontayne, P., Boiché, J., and Clément-Guillotin, C. (2013). "The Influence of Sex Stereotypes and Gender Roles on Participation and Performance in Sport and Exercise: Review and Future Directions." *Psychology of Sport and Exercise* 14 (2): 136–144.

Clarke, A. (2005). *Situational Analysis: Grounded Theory after the Postmodern Turn*. Thousand Oaks, CA: SAGE.

Cooper, M., and Kramer, N. (2005). *We B* Girlz*. New York: powerHouse Books.

Curzan, A. (2003). *Gender Shifts in the History of English*. Cambridge: University of Cambridge Press.

Eckert, P., and McConnell-Ginet, S. (2013). *Language and Gender*. Cambridge: Cambridge University Press.

Fausto-Sterling, A. (2000). *Sexing the Body: Gender Politics and the Construction of Sexuality*. New York: Basic Books.

Fausto-Sterling, A. (2005). "The Bare Bones of Sex: Part 1—Sex and Gender." *Signs: Journal of Women in Culture and Society* 30 (2): 1491–1527.

Fogarty, M. (2006). "'Whatever Happened to Breakdancing?' Transnational B-Boy/B-Girl Networks, Underground Video Magazines and Imagined Affinities." Unpublished MA thesis, Brock University.

Ford, E. B. (2009). "Race, Gender, and Cultural Identity in the American Rodeo." Unpublished PhD diss., Arizona State University.

Graham, L. (2005). "Discourse Analysis and the Critical Use of Foucault." Paper presented at the Australian Association for Research in Education, November. Sydney, Australia.

Guevara, N. (1996). "Women Writin' Rappin' Breakin'." In *Droppin' Science: Critical Essays on Rap Music and Hip Hop Culture*, edited by W. E. Perkins, 49–62. Philadelphia: Temple University Press.

Gunn, R. (2012). "Re-articulating Gender Norms through Breakdancing." Unpublished graduate essay, Macquarie University.

Gunn, R., and Scannell, J. (2013). "Overcoming the Hip-Hop Habitus." Paper presented at the International Association for the Study of Popular Music Australia-New Zealand Conference, Hobart.

Gupta-Carlson, H. (2010). "Planet B-Girl: Community Building and Feminism in Hip-Hop." *New Political Science* 32 (4): 515–529. doi:10.1080/07393148.2010.520438.

Haire, O. (2014). "B-Girls (France Ô): Le hip-hop n'est pas reserve qu'aux garcons!" Téléloisirs online, October 17. Accessed January 19, 2015. http://www.programme-tv.net/news/tv/58258-b-girls-hip-hop-pas-reserve-aux-garcons/

Halberstam, J. (1998). *Female Masculinity*. Durham, NC: Duke University Press.

Hazzard-Donald, K. (2004). "Dance in Hip Hop Culture. In *That's the Joint: The Hip-Hop Studies Reader*, edited by M. Forman and M. A. Neal, 505–516. New York: Routledge.

Holman, M. (1984). *Breaking and the New York City Breakers*. New York: Freundlich Books

Huntington, C. S. (2007). *Hip Hop Dance: Meanings and Messages*. Jefferson, NC: McFarland.

Jaworski, A., and Coupland, N., eds. (2014). *The Discourse Reader*. 3rd ed. New York: Routledge.

Johnson, I. K. (2014). "From Blues Women to B-Girls: Performing Badass Femininity." *Women & Performance: A Journal of Feminist Theory* 24 (1): 15–28.

Kendall, S., and Tannen, D. (2001). "Discourse and Gender." In *The Handbook of Discourse Analysis*, edited by D. Schiffrin, D. Tannen, and H. E. Hamilton, 548–567. Oxford: Blackwell.

Knight, J. L., and Giuliano, T. A. (2001). "He's a Laker; She's a 'Looker': The Consequences of Gender-Stereotypical Portrayals of Male and Female Athletes by the Print Media." *Sex Roles* 45 (3–4): 217–229.

Kramer, N. (2015). "Karima: France's Queen B-girl." Red Bull BC One, January 27. http://www.redbullbcone.com/en/blog/karima-frances-queen-b-girl//

Langnes, T. F., and Fasting, K. (2014). "Identity Constructions among Breakdancers." *International Review for the Sociology of Sport* 51 (3): 349–364.

Macleod, C. (2002). "Deconstructive Discourse Analysis: Extending the Methodological Conversation." *South African Journal of Psychology* 32 (1): 17–25.

Maniaci, P. (2006, August 28). "Honey Rockwell." In *Career Cookbook: Inspiring Career Paths*. Accessed January 30, 2015. http://thecareercookbook.com/article.php?article_id=28

McConnell-Ginet, S. (2011). *Gender, Sexuality, and Meaning: Linguistic Practice and Politics*. New York: Oxford University Press.

Mills, S. (2009). *Michel Foucault*. New York: Routledge.

Moloney, M., and Fenstermaker, S. (2002). "Performance and Accomplishment: Reconciling Feminist Conceptions of Gender." In *Doing Gender, Doing Difference: Inequality, Power and Institutional Change*, edited by S. Fenstermaker and C. West, 189–204. New York: Routledge.

Monteyne, K. (2013). *Hip Hop on Film: Performance Culture, Urban Space, and Genre Transformation in the 1980s*. Jackson: University Press of Mississippi.

Ogaz, C. (2006). "Learning from B-Girls. In *Feminism in Popular Culture*, edited by J. Hollows and R. Moseley, 161–182. New York: Berg.

No Easy Props. (n.d.). "Our Mission." "No Easy Props: Creativity in Dance, Art, and Music." Accessed January 29, 2015. http://noeasyprops.tv/?page_id=38

Pelak, C. F. (2002). "'Women's Collective Identity Formation in Sports': A Case Study from Women's Ice Hockey." *Gender & Society* 16 (1): 93–114.

Rajakumar, M. (2012). *Hip Hop Dance*. Santa Barbara, CA: ABC-CLIO.

Richards, C., Bouman, W. P., and Barker, M.-J., eds. (2017). *Genderqueer and Non-binary Genders*. London: Palgrave Macmillan.

Rivera, R. Z. (2003). *New York Ricans from the Hip Hop Zone*. New York: Palgrave Macmillan.

Rose, T. (1994). *Black Noise: Rap Music and Black Culture in Contemporary America*. Middletown, CT: Wesleyan University Press.

Schloss, J. G. (2009). *Foundation: B-Boys, B-Girls and Hip-Hop Culture in New York*. New York: Oxford University Press.

Schur, E. (1984). *Labeling Women Deviant: Gender, Stigma, and Social Control*. Philadelphia: Temple University Press.

Simard, H. (2014). "Breaking Down the Differences between Breakdancing and B-Boying: A Grounded Theory Approach." Unpublished MA thesis. University of Quebec at Montreal.

Smith, M. (2013). "Video: Watch Amazing Korean Breakdancer Win Head-Spinning World Championship." *Mirror*, December 1. Accessed January 30, 2015. http://www.mirror.co.uk/news/world-news/red-bull-bc-one-world-2871734

Smith Lefebvre, H. (2011). "B-Boy (Dance) Cipher: An Innovative Knowledge Community's Shared Activity." Unpublished MA thesis, McGill University.

Stevens, J., and Adams, C. (2012). "Together We Can Make It Better": Collective Action and Governance in a Girls' Ice Hockey Association." *International Review for the Sociology of Sport* 48 (6): 658–672.

Undisputed World Bboy. (2014). "The 2014 Ranking." Accessed January 27, 2015. http://worldbboy.org/ranking/

Washington, A. D. (2007). "Not the Average Girl from the Videos: B-Girls Defining Their Space in Hip-Hop Culture." In *Home Girls Make Some Noise: Hip-Hop Feminism Anthology*, edited by G. Pough, E. Richardson, A. Durham, and R. Raimist, 80–89. Mira Loma, CA: Parker Publishing.

We B*Girlz. (n.d.). "Philosophy." We B*Girlz website. http://www.bgirlz.com/. Accessed January 21, 2015.

West, C., and Zimmerman, D. H. (1987). "Doing Gender." *Gender and Society* 1 (2): 125–151.

West, C., and Zimmerman, D. H. (2002). "Doing Gender." In *Doing Gender, Doing Difference: Inequality, Power and Institutional Change*, edited by S. Fenstermaker and C. West, 3–23. New York: Routledge.

Young, I. M. (1980). "Throwing like a Girl: A Phenomenology of Feminine Body Comportment Motility and Spatiality." *Human Studies* 3 (1): 137–156.

Video

Antics. (2010). "What Is a BGirl?" Video file, December 16. http://www.youtube.com/watch?v=SGVWBQNeubU Accessed January 15, 2015.

Art Breaker. (n.d.). "Who Is Hafina Queen?" Video file. http://bboyart.com/about-hanifa-mcqueen-hudson/. Accessed January 26, 2015.

Bboy North. (2014). "BBN Interviews Present: BGirl Cleopatra EP 3—How She Started & Challenges of a BGirl." Video file, June 13. Accessed January 14, 2015. https://www.youtube.com/watch?v=lKVkgPTS_mY

bjhiphopcollective. (2009). "Ken Swift on Bgirls." Video file, February 22. Accessed January 23, 2015. https://www.youtube.com/watch?v=D2LhGxgoLmk

Groupe Nice-Matin. (2011). "Parcours de Beebish: Du hip hop à la reinsertion en prio." Video file, March 2. Accessed January 22, 2015. https://www.youtube.com/watch?v=mjL-LH-A6wo

SaborLatinoGlobal. (2013). *Sabor Latino Global: Interview with BGirl Rockafella—Old School Hip Hop*. Video file, April 8. Accessed January 24, 2015. https://www.youtube.com/watch?v=2aExYv_yEwU

TooMuchFlavour. (2009). *B-Girl the Movie: Lady Jules (Beat Freaks) on Being a B-Girl and Smoking B-Boys*. Video file, October 11. Accessed January 19, 2015. https://www.youtube.com/watch?v=BpJvBqTNvnI

TooMuchFlavour. (2011). "Bboy News/BGirl News: B-Girl Roxy on B-Girls Entering Regional Conflict/Bboy Championships Battles." Video file, July 8. Accessed January 18, 2015. https://www.youtube.com/watch?v=Q-ElQCD0Z2A

TruFamTV. (2013). "Hanifa McQueen-Hudson: Exclusive Interview—22nd Oct 2013." Video file, October 22. Accessed January 16, 2015. https://www.youtube.com/watch?v=07tEvqJETNc

Film

Israel, dir. (2002). *The Freshest Kids*. Motion Picture. USA: QD3 Entertainment.

Raimist, R., dir. (1999). *Nobody Knows My Name*. Documentary film. USA: Women Make Movies.

PART IV

BREAKING WITH CONVENTION

CHAPTER 19

STREETDANCE AND BLACK AESTHETICS

NAOMI MACALALAD BRAGIN

INTRODUCTION

CONTEMPORARY dance studios have become centers for the distribution and exchange of Hip Hop dance as part of global commercial industry. A site where casual, amateur, and professional dancers intermix, the studio also manages discourses of diversity and inclusion, asking: Who has access to studio dance? Who teaches in the studio? What do they teach and how? These questions are consequential for the ways embodied knowledge of Hip Hop circulates, especially considering the general modes of economic and political exclusion with which Hip Hop culture's innovators contend. Dance teachers (amateur and professional) play a key role in shaping embodied cultural knowledge, not only as carriers and transmitters but as importantly, *translators* of cultural history. At the same time, Hip Hop dances continue to thrive and transform beyond the studio's boundaries. Dancers who teach styles not created as studiocentric techniques must nonetheless negotiate the studio's defining terms, specifically as those terms have been historically drawn and upheld by Western Eurocentric ideals of proper technique. How does contemporary Hip Hop dance adapt or conform to studio norms, and how do teacher-practitioners critique and disrupt studio-fication of Hip Hop dance through their own creative pedagogies?

In this chapter I study black aesthetics that drive innovation within Hip Hop dance cultures and their role in shaping Western paradigms of the studio as an ideological construction of space that structures relations between practitioners, students, teachers, performers, and audiences. How do black aesthetics circulate in studio classes, where a gap between lived experience and what counts as "technique" is magnified and modulated by the studio's cultural-social-symbolic expectations? I attend to little pedagogical moments that arise in the studio and activate black aesthetics, putting pressure on quick consumption of black culture. In these moments, black aesthetics hold the capacity to critique the studio's Eurocentric investments, which cannot perfectly translate cultural knowledge. In revealing the constraints that necessarily produce black aesthetics, these moments also offer an ethical critique of the global production, circulation, and transmission of Hip Hop dance.

Brenda Dixon Gottschild's (1996) "Premises of an Africanist Aesthetic" expands Toni Morrison's study of Africanisms in American literary history to craft a revisionist history of American dance, detailing features of African Diaspora cultural practices that adapt, persist, recycle, and innovate, against attempted historical erasure. Within an Africanist framework, Gottschild identifies a key principle of process: "The movement of the action—is as important as getting it done, the static fact of the result or product" (11). Black vernacular style cites the aesthetic of the dancer's motion: *poppers'* muscles contract and explode; *lockers'* arms click into place at the joints, *waackers'* arms strike out, cut through, stir up air. Dance scholar Anna Scott's (1998) theory of "tenaxis" challenges the reduction of blackness to a static cultural identity, weighing dancers' transcultural labor of tenaciously forming communities of practice that are interconnected through a material sense of place. Tenaxis differentiates dance as a consumable product from dancing practices (9).

"Swing: From Verb to Noun" (1999) Amiri Baraka's similarly describes black aesthetics as an active process, posing the notion of appropriation in terms of a calculated strategy of whiteness to overlook black social activity by consuming and exchanging culture as object. This performative "noun-ification" of black culture extracts form from context (black culture lived as verb) to invest it with market value, erasing cultural diversity even as the play is justified, not ironically, by an ethic of inclusion (everyone can love black culture so long as black social life is assumed to be immanently *ex*clusionary and valueless). Differently said, noun-ification is underwritten by official colorblindness, a discourse of "free" use that exploits culture to negate possibilities of black agency and reify the permanent exclusion of blackness from the political realm.

Nathaniel Mackey's (1992) "Other: Movement from Noun to Verb" questions the ends of such depoliticizing discourses in an aesthetic theory of *black artistic othering* that plays on Baraka's critical phrasing by flipping it. Mackey reminds us that "*other* [original emphasis] is something people do, more importantly a verb than an adjective or a noun" (51). Othering locates black aesthetic performativity in the choices of black artists "to impact upon and to influence the course of the medium, to *move* [original emphasis] the medium" (68). Black artistic othering animates black aesthetics, not as mere features inherent to black culture, but generative of struggle and a provocation to action. The insistent, imaginative work of black artistic othering creates experimental points of departure from which to generate critical dance practices.

In the Western dance studio, casual, amateur, and professional students eager to learn "urban" or "street" styles can easily misapprehend dances as nouns, hastened by the studio's market drive and its failure to translate cultural context (style as verb and everyday activity of doing) into "steps and "moves" (style as noun). Hip Hop artist-educator Buddha Stretch distinguishes "the ones who take it seriously and school themselves" when he says, "Don't just do the steps, learn the energy, the feeling behind the steps."[1] Stretch uses the black vernacular practice of making nouns behave like verbs—'school' meaning a dancer's own effort to actively participate in their learning process beyond institutionally-established spaces of study. Getting schooled requires moving beyond studio culture to build less easily translatable embodied knowledge of a dance's "energy and feeling." If Stretch's commentary suggests that the school for Hip Hop dance expands beyond the scope of studiocentric learning or acquiring steps, then practitioners' pedagogies may likewise activate black aesthetics within the studio, shaping and transforming studio practices.

In a similar vein, Marya McQuirter (2002) theorizes Malcolm X's autobiographical recounting "of moving from awkwardness to ballroom accomplishment," in order to flag a dearth of attention to how people learn to dance outside of formal or professional contexts, an overlooking that denies the cultural labor of learning processes created by and among practitioners of vernacular forms (91). Acknowledging the role of acculturation in Hip Hop dance communities is a step toward articulating what happens when vernacular dance cultures transition into studio styles.

The stakes of transition from culture to style are heightened in studio-based learning that has historically relied on Western Eurocentric assumptions about "proper" technique—not only as a set of principles for embodiment but also as a pedagogical model which, Paolo Freire (2006) has argued, positions teachers as possessors of cultural knowledge they deliver in a hierarchical unidirectional flow to students as passive consumers. Acts of cultural translation in the studio are performed through the widespread use of choreography as a primary mode of studio-based learning and professionalization. Yet Western notions of choreography are also tied to cultural ideas about proper technique as a practice trained in studios separate and elevated from everyday lived experience.

McQuirter (2002) emphasizes that learning to dance happens through processes of acculturation, arguing for "a fuller and more complex understanding of the role of dance in community and cultural formation" (91). In shaping black vernacular dance styles, artists carefully study and improvise off what Diana Taylor (2003) has termed the *repertoire*—the ways embodied memory is stored and transmitted performatively as a people's archive of living cultural traditions (see grimes 2008c). Style is a verb, activated through the choreographic repertoire of lived experience. The repertoire links aesthetics, culture, memory, and embodiment, asserting a politics of transfer inherent in who teaches and learns a dance style.

Black vernacular dance calls on practitioners to sustain intimate, meaningful conversations that stay relevant to active and changing community traditions, values, and expectations. Improvisation is a key way to sustain the choreographic repertoire. Dance scholar Cleis Abeni, who formerly wrote as Jonathan David Jackson (2001),[2] shows how a conceptual divide between choreography and improvisation falls apart in black vernacular dancing, which calls for improvised performances that include choreographic concepts. Improvisation challenges binary understandings of innovation/tradition and individual/collective expression as well (46). Yet for students learning in the studio, aesthetic principles of improvisation and collectivity do not necessarily surface as inherent to the dance. Incorporated into the scheduled time and place of studio classes, vernacular dances can move from verb to noun when quickly consumed as styles freed from the historical complexities of black culture and social life.

James "OG Skeeter Rabbit" Higgins explains that young artists innovating dance styles in the 1970s used the term *streetdance* to "differen[tiate] between what was taught in the studios and what was taught in the streets. At first, we weren't welcome in the studios, until we became of value."[3] Streetdancers were not seen as legitimate dancers, nor were streetdances protected as proper forms of dance to be housed within authorized art institutions. Contemporary streetdancers must contend with this history of structural positioning. While practitioners still use terms like "street" and "urban" to reference this cultural dance umbrella, potentially validating euphemisms for pathologizing blackness, *the street* holds, nonetheless, a critique of institutional power through its alignment with the unsettled language of the vernacular.

In defining "streetdance," dance artist-scholar d. Sabela grimes (2008a) articulates stakes inherent in a transition to studio study:

> [A] dance studio, for example, provides an architectural confine wherein professional, amateur, and recreational dancers (everyday people as well) follow and help maintain a different hierarchical structure than that of these everyday folk in everyday spaces . . . this architectural construction is an environment where the structured hierarchical ideologies are cemented into its foundation and the ghosts of these thought forms linger between the walls. The studio environment is perceived to be space to implement previously learned movement material that rarely, if ever, provide fertile ground for the type of cultural production that develops in the *Streets*.

The consequences of streetdance study in the studio vary, depending on practices of acquiring movement vocabularies, who's teaching steps, and how their pedagogy speaks to cultural histories and lived experiences of everyday struggle and survival—the "previously learned movement material" that is abstracted in the aesthetics of style.

I recycle the term *streetdance* to underscore the labor of dancers who continue to maintain an ethics of connection to cultural histories and lived experiences of streetdance communities. Streetdance affirms the informal, unprofessional study of dancing that remains unaccountable to linear methods of acquiring technique prevalent in a model of scheduled, level-based studio learning. My aim is not to reproduce false divides between street/studio/stage, but to consider how streetdance interanimates these paradigmatic spaces, creating a metacritique of the hierarchical division of space, the racial-gender assumptions that undergird it, and ideologies of value that maintain it. Streetdance is that "dislocating tilt of artistic othering" that maintains a critically unstable relationship to institutions of cultural production, especially in connection with ideas of privacy, ownership, individualism, and property (Mackey 1992, 68).

Stretch reflects, "Anybody can do choreography. Find someone who's passionate about what they're doing."[4] The statement indirectly references tensions that inhere in the increased transit of Hip Hop dance through the professional dance world, indexed by world dance competitions and dance reality shows that center Hip Hop dance choreography as opposed to improvisation. In citing passion in contrast to a reductive understanding of choreographic practice, Stretch invokes the figure of the amateur, the "one who loves" as "distinguished from *one who prosecutes it professionally*; hence, sometimes used disparagingly."[5]

A neoliberal discourse of professionalism—the idea that building careers in dance can be a way of coaching productive, disciplined citizenship—is attached to the increasing global popularity of contemporary dance. In his analysis of African American and Asian relations on the TV dance reality show *America's Best Dance Crew*, Brian Chung (2016) gives a thoughtful response to the antiblackness on which this discourse relies:

> On *ABDC*, the public memory of hip-hop dance is entrenched within
> normative discourses of neoliberal citizenship. Stripped of any reference to
> black intellectual and political discourse of black social dance, the conditions
> of possibility for hip-hop dance's blackness on *ABDC* are structured
> by a neoliberal narrative where African Americans become productive citizens
> by turning leisure into a billion-dollar entertainment industry. (121)

Not only is Hip Hop's social value determined by its capacity for commodification, but Hip Hop dance that's studied at leisure (read as black social life, not for capital gain) holds no value. It's often the Hip Hop dance happening in informal everyday social contexts, outside the studio and offstage, that is reimagined as aimless leisure, a lack of discipline or true technical ability—markers not easily extricated from the ways black people are racialized.

Meanwhile, Hip Hop dance in the studio can be coded black in gesture, posture, glances, affect, to access blackness without committing to engage with or care for black life. This "everything-but-the-burden" phenomenon is buttressed by attendant ideas of inclusion and diversity that exclude blackness in order to shape and discipline the figure of the neoliberal dance professional with technical breadth and fluidity for the market (wanted: modern/ballet/contemporary dancer, familiar with Hip Hop; Tate 2003). The transformation of cultural styles into techniques acquired by industry professionals must be weighed alongside the marginalization of black aesthetic traditions and the artists who adhere to them. When choreography becomes the primary mode of learning streetdance, absent accompanying modes of black artistic othering, the dance form becomes a noun—steps to be passively consumed and replicated. How teacher-practitioners address this gap is important, as they teach form *and* translate culture into form, making creative choices about how to represent the complexity of lived experience.

POPIN' PETE: "THE GROOVEMEANT"

Teaching a master class in popping style, funk dance innovator Popin' Pete points to a common misapprehension of popping. He offers a sideways note to students who focus exclusively on the visual appearance of popping movements, over and against their social connection to popping's groove: "Some of you are doing the movement before the groovemeant. That means you have to mean to do the groove."[6] Pete's wordplay puts emphasis on the value of popping as a meaning-making process which, rather than comprised of isolated movements, is fundamentally bound to "do the groove."

Grooving is the vernacular basis of improvisation in streetdance, cultivating sensory knowledge including the practitioner's "sense of repetitive ongoingness" and "sensing [of] the rhythmic inseparability of music and dance" (Jackson, 2001, 47). The principle of grooving troubles standard divisions of sense perception in Western culture (sight, hearing, touch, taste, smell) by encompassing synesthesia (the way senses blend in expressive action) and accentuating kinesthesia (the sense of motion). Grooving blurs boundaries of sight, hearing and moving, troubling the categorical separation of music and dance. As Abeni offers, this blurred sensory-somatic capacity of the groove is fundamentally rhythmic. Groovers generate rhythm in the simultaneous expressive act of listening-moving-seeing. Grooving could be described as expressing the dancer's kinesthetic seeing of sound and hearing of movement.

Imani Kai Johnson (2012) offers an analysis of aural kinesthesia that opens a way into theorizing the link between sense perception and social relations. She describes aural kinesthesia as "a frame for analyzing the simultaneity of social dance and music (and sound broadly)," asking for closer attention to instances when the "sound and feel of dance experiences are often overridden by the spectacle of dancing." Kai Johnson gives the example of a battle dance video that splices together stunning displays of skill, cutting out the more nuanced social dynamics of exchange between the dancers. I would add that a racialized economy of visual spectacle is tied to historical relations of objectification, extraction, and commodification—of peoples and cultures—which downplay and devalue the aural kinesthetic within a Western cultural sensorium. In the case of highly competitive TV dance reality competitions, which often demand shows of extreme physicality to win, audiences develop a passive ocularcentric relation to dance, building an acute focus on dance's visual effects that minimizes their aural-kinesthetic attention. Yet social relations in home spaces may configure different modes of aural-kinesthesia, where the culture of viewing values people actively moving together in kinship with each other and with the music. In other words, viewing is also a synesthetic act that builds different types of sensory-social connection, depending how sociality is configured through cultural values.

Pete rejects the assumption that performing movement equates to doing the dance of popping. He de-emphasizes popping as a sight-centered practice of doing steps and moves, in order to begin with groovemeant—an aural-kinesthetic attunement to the production of social meaning. His pedagogy calls poppers to reorder their practice, learning how to groove first and allowing movement to follow from that intention. In challenging the privileging of sight in the Western cultural sensorium, grooving builds culturally specific modes of sense perception and meaning-making that function to organize social interactions and relational systems of value in dance communities. The groove's aural-kinesthetic process of "repetitive ongoingness" builds perception less reliant on visual spectacle but more dependent on the dancer's awareness of how they relate to the culturally specific dance of popping and the social connections that adhere therein (Jackson 2001).

Echoing Pete's description of groovemeant as a precursor to steps, master teacher Moncell Durden first teaches the *bounce*—a type of groove which undergirds and grounds all Hip Hop movement—before demonstrating how to "add some movement to it." The bounce trains a "slumped over" posture, bent knees, and the relaxed, repetitive, up-down-backward-forward motion of interconnected limbs and joints, especially head, arms, torso, hips, and knees.[7] Bounce aesthetics train a culturally specific responsiveness to Hip Hop rhythms, and while this training may include visual imitation, Moncell shows that exact replication of physical form is less important than building rhythmic feeling for bounce motion.

Artist-practitioner Caleaf Sellers describes how seeking social connection through the groove is enabled through a relational process of self-seeking:

> When you find your own groove, whatever that is, then you're able to connect. It's easier for you to pick up other movements when you know what your groove is. Becoming more in touch with yourself . . . will open you up to receive the other information that's out there and find out how it works in your body.[8]

Caleaf suggests the intimacy of "becoming in touch" with one's groove initiates with a social process of learning a new dance style through deep study of one's lived experience of embodiment—always already social and historical. To "have your own groove" negates the taking of culture as a relation of property and ownership. Instead, studying self-in-relation entails accountability and defining one's relationship to others, as well as different culturally specific aesthetics. Grooving is not an isolated process of self-discovery, but rather brings the practitioner into relation with the dance by seeking their unique fit with the rhythm.

Abeni similarly defines an aesthetic of *individuation* in black vernacular dancing: "The dancer moves to establish a unique identity according to [their] own physical capabilities, personal style, and capacity for invention . . . [and, simultaneously] according to the aesthetics that inform the dancing" (Jackson 2001, 45). The circulatory feedback loop of individuation heightens a practitioner's accountability in relation to community expectations. Grooving puts responsibility on the dancer to deepen a process of self-seeking which, rather than copying someone else's movement, facilitates social connection.

D. Sabela grimes:
"Don't Replicate, Circulate"

d. Sabela grimes (2008b) identifies a streetdancer's aim to make meaningful conversation in the process of performing embodied cultural knowledge, distinct from those who "use the body language/vocabulary [but] have no idea what they're saying, and, flippantly don't care." Teaching Funkamentals, a movement system that he has created "focuse[d] on the methodical dance training and community building elements evident in black vernacular and Street dance forms,"[9] he tells students, "Don't replicate, circulate."[10] The term "replication" points to the ways streetdance styles become vulnerable to consumption under unidirectional models of transmission that allow students to copy steps and moves at a distance, without entering into intimate relationships of reciprocity that are a core principle of streetdance culture.

Replication is qualitatively different from the ways streetdancers access personal style through their relationships with specific aesthetic communities, a dialogic process suggested by Abeni's definition of individuation. Abeni further explains that aesthetics always integrate "common principles of black vernacular dance" with adaptations of these principles that "reflect the aesthetics of specific black communities" (Jackson 2001, 45). While imitating steps may be part of streetdancers' training process, imitation is not an end in and of itself but a springboard for accessing personal style, offered to the community in the spirit of mutual improvisatory exchange. Steps integrated with improvised expression are tools that build a streetdancer's capacity to participate in ways that build community ties and support innovation.

When dancers go no deeper with learning than replicating steps, they reproduce static modes of exchange that are antirelational in the sense that Jodi Melamed, citing Ruth Wilson Gilmore, describes the driving dialectic of racial capitalism: "a technology for reducing collective life [. . .] in which forms of humanity are separated (made "distinct") so that they may be "interconnected" in terms that feed capital" (Melamed 2015, 78). The move of separation is double, extracting the dance step from its danced context and also, separating the student's sense of how they're connecting to the step. Circulation calls dancers to do the work of studying themselves as a way of entering with clarity, risk and vulnerability, into a conversation with the dance.

I remember well the moment Hip Hop dancer Tweetie frustratedly stopped a choreography class with the sharp reprimand, "You're not *getting* it."[11] She elaborated, showing the step. Hands tucked to armpits, her bent-up elbows burst out flapping rhythmically like a flustered city bird. Black and yellow hi-top Jordans glued together to form a single appendage, she pops upward in a tightly controlled jump. Firmly driving the transformed foot-limb floorward, she delivers the final, triumphant downbeat. "*This* means something. But you're not saying anything. This comes from somewhere. But you're not getting it."

In one way, the teacherly reprimand is an expected part of the dance studio drill—we come to learn moves, we simply need to perform better. The deeper implication I am attending to here, is that learning steps does not translate into understanding their cultural context—the somewhere, the place embedded in the dance (and the dancer). Whether in the informal sense of understanding or the formal sense of gaining possession, "you're *not* getting it" acts, I am saying, as a refusal of ownership that performatively decenters our potential assumption, as paying students, of a privileged place in the political economy of Hip Hop dance. Dance steps are not words without grammar, without structure. They point to a bigger conversation, with a place, with people embedded in that place. Listen to how they're talking and why.

We face the studio's mirrored wall, which catches and reflects our diligent expressions back at us. Tweetie's extended pause puts all of us, momentarily, in a position to see ourselves more deeply reflected in the dance. "Who are you? Where are you from? Why are you here?"[12] How do you contribute? What do you have to say? The pedagogical moment pauses our motion, calling us to more careful attention and undoing the quickness with which we might attempt to acquire this dance.

Sabela's replication/circulation distinction critiques acts of acquisition, suggesting that different approaches to learning influence the quality of students' relationships to streetdance. grimes asserts that streetdancers co-participate in the production of knowledge of streetdance style. Attention to how one moves within this figurative circle of conversation is key. As co-participants dancers are continuously receiving information and self-reflecting on how they translate, transmit and transform movement in the conversational flow.

Dance scholar Raquel L. Monroe recounts her experience of transmitting Hip Hop vernacular practice into competition choreography in the studio:

> I could Snake, Prep, Wop, Reebok, Smurf, and Guess with the best of them. My expertise with the popular dance styles served me well at my dance studios. My teachers would ask me to teach the dances to them and my peers, so they could "clean up" the steps and insert them into our two-minute competition choreography. (Monroe 2011, 39)

Monroe highlights one way that transmission happens between studio and "street"— here understood as informal social dancing in non-professional contexts and also a learning process of acculturation, as McQuirter's work has shown. Importantly, Monroe's teachers not only teach but also *learn and acquire* her embodied technical knowledge, which she has honed over time, outside the dance studio. It's worth emphasizing she has cultivated expert knowledge, regardless of the nonstudio basis of practices she has previously learned. Simultaneously, the process of studio transmission and reproduction is partially erasing the repertoire that Monroe has incorporated in the specific, everyday-lived cultural contexts of the dance styles.

A key phase of this aesthetic shift happens after the teachers learn the dances, wherein, as Monroe (2011) describes, they "clean" and "insert" the steps into a quick stage choreography (39). The "two-minute" time count reveals another important tension between the temporality of street and studio, as the practice and performance of everyday social dancing does not necessarily conform to the more linear, scheduled timeframes of studio and dance competition culture. The discourse of cleaning is significant in the studio transmission of streetdance styles—in this case the party dances of Hip Hop's 1980s and 1990s golden era. On TV reality shows, the judges' critiques often focus on how visually "clean" the steps look, assigning value to the competitors' ability to exactly replicate form and timing across the corps. The clean aesthetic promoted in the commercial production of choreographed streetdance is closely tied to the production of visual spectacle for the camera. Clean choreography parallels a general tendency in choreo-centered group dancing to assemble a corps of dancers of similar body size and shape. In TV reality show dancing as well, sameness of physical appearance is underscored by a preference (sometimes a rule) for binary, cisgender presentation, reducing the range of body types more commonly embraced in everyday Hip Hop and streetdance cultures.[13]

Thomas DeFrantz takes up the symbiotic relationship between studio Hip Hop dance classes and the line of films that have featured streetdance styles since the early 1980s:

> Throughout the 1990s, a rise in hip-hop dance classes and studio-based training practices led to the codification of hip-hop as a form with a pyramidal structure—something that could be learned from a teacher, rather than developed by the artists involved, as had been the standard of transmission until that time. This shift in teaching and transmission restabilized hip-hop as a form that could be controlled by the marketplace; a form suitable for film production that could be organized and overseen by a hired choreographer or dance director. Hip-hop dance moves continued to trade in the individual innovation of its practitioners, but over time, young artists contributed fewer and fewer movements to the choreographic soup that became screen versions of hip-hop dance. (DeFrantz 2014, 129)

Considering the political economy of training practices, studio and film dance cannot fully account for less hierarchical ways that black aesthetics are learned and transmitted among practitioners.

Burgeoning in popularity over the last decade, contemporary studio-derived styles like Hip Hop choreo or lyrical Hip Hop (a fusion of Hip Hop and jazz-inspired movement) have become a prominent feature of group routines in competition and entertainment industry dance that turn up the volume on spectacle.[14] Often performed in large groups with proscenium stage orientation, competition styles task the corps with executing rigorously high-paced choreographies, delivering sharply accented steps interspersed with perfectly timed acrobatic moves.

Competition dancers achieve a highly clean choreography through dedicated practice and often use specific techniques of structuring time and space, not only with unidirectional facings but also by numbering steps on an eight-count timeline. The performance of eight-count linear counting in the 2018 Hollywood dance film sequel *Honey: Rise Up and Dance* reflects this key aesthetic shift as streetdance enters the studio. *Honey's* narrative positions the studio as a prime point of access to the professional world of dance and posits a muted ideological divide between "formally trained" dancers and the "raw, edgy talent" of (non-studio-trained) streetdancers.[15] Five minutes into the film, studio owner and artistic director Miss J (Charmin Lee) sets the scene of choreographic practice, facing her dancers in front of the mirror and firmly pronouncing: "Alright ladies, now make it sexy . . . here we go. Startin' on the left. Five, six, seven, go."[16]

Linear counting is only one language through which streetdancers interpret the rhythmic flow of a choreographed sequence, for example shifting into the alternative communicative mode of non-verbal rhythmic vocalization: shoop, wop, *uhm DTAH!* Yet linear counting fixes movement to a unidirectional timeline, diverting the dancers' attention away from the nuanced polyrhythmic and syncopated capacities of the beat.[17] Operating under the logics of the commercial entertainment industry in relation to which these dance practices have evolved, linear counting aids dancers to organize a work of choreography into sequenced and numbered steps and moves that can be treated as distinct parts of the choreographic arrangement. While numbering facilitates the organizing of steps it can also distance the dancer from the rhythmic complexities of movements embedded in the streetdance repertoire. If a dancer does not have access to or actively cultivate awareness of the repertoire, the steps become stripped of a deeper connection to cultural meaning. In the process, streetdance becomes vulnerable to objectification and consumption, such that specific aesthetic traditions can be transmitted and reinterpreted as non-culturally-specific movement. Extracting steps from cultural context, and interrelated processes of cleaning and counting, override a principle of meaning-making that is core to black aesthetics.

This is not to say streetdancers trained in improvisation cannot successfully deliver a Hip Hop choreo or that dancers who use eight-counts cannot dance with rhythmic flow; yet choreocentric dancing does not train and may inhibit improvisatory skill. I hesitate to conclude that studio and competition dance completely negate black aesthetic practices of circulation, even in highly commercialized forms reliant on frontal-facing choreography, training in the mirror, and linear eight-counting. That being said, these choreocentric practices do circulate in a viral political economy of cultural extraction, with the potential of reproducing exploitative social relations configured by global racial capital. In this respect, it's necessary to articulate the ways in which black aesthetics maintain ties to everyday lived practices that are qualitatively different from studio-centered techniques and professionalizing institutions.[18]

NUBIAN NÉNÉ: "FIGURE OUT YOUR WAY"

Threaded through principles of circulation and grooving, streetdance is intimately concerned with how streetdancers form relationships to community. I'm attending a toprocking class taught by streetdance artist Nubian Néné at the 2017 Ladies of Hip Hop Festival in Toronto.[19] Students are moving in lines across the floor, following Néné's demonstration of a basic toprock. As I follow, repeating the sequence, I notice a slight shift in her rhythm that instantly makes my regular stress of the step on the music's downbeat seem clunky and flat. Before stepping out on the one, she's adding a twisting, tapping rhythm, an off-the-beat syncopation that creates an electric flow from toe to hip. The flair is subtle but introduces a dynamic rhythmic complexity and stylistic bounce to her toprock. I stop, asking for clarification.

"You're doing something specific with your footwork that's different from how we're doing it. Can you break that down?"

"No." She answers me pointedly. "You have to figure out your way, this is my style. You have to find yours."[20]

By teaching the step but refusing to "break down" the uniqueness of her stylistic approach, Néné's also teaching a different kind of lesson that's basic to Hip Hop philosophy, marking the complexity of how streetdancers negotiate teaching in the studio. Echoing Tweetie's reprimand, Néné's response implies that copying moves doesn't equate to learning style. In this brief exchange, streetdance enters the studio by challenging my assumption of having immediate access to the dance as a paying student. Our interaction flips the idea of privilege, for in fact, it is Néné who articulates a refusal to allow me access to her privileged knowledge of toprocking. She offers a Hip Hop worldview that rarely gets delivered in the fast-paced exchange of commercial studio classes. While I can learn steps, "paying for class doesn't mean you can get all these other things," another teaching artist Toyin Sogunro explains, expressing her frustration when students ask for her playlists after class. "But see, I did the work to get these [tracks], why don't you do the work?"[21]

These types of lessons are common in dance festivals like Ladies of Hip Hop that bring teachers who live and work in streetdance culture and have earned the support of streetdance communities over time, through the rigorous labor of training, battling, judging, teaching and performing. Yet teachers must also confront the commercialization and commodification of streetdance, a flattening process that promotes Hip Hop as a style that's "fun" to do, unlike the always already presumed labor and painstaking refinement of technique that produce a trained ballet dancer. A principle of innovative flair within improvisation, transferred through Néné's critical pedagogy, shifts the easy replication of steps and locates streetdance style in the work of negotiating community values.

TOGETHER-DANCING

"Be in time, not in sync. I don't care if you're in unison."[22] Shabba Doo is drilling a short routine for his Locking 2.0 class at the Performing Arts Center located at the end of an inconspicuous street of office buildings, in back of the 405 Freeway running through the San Fernando Valley city of Van Nuys. Our small group appears markedly different from the masses of bodies that typically pack Hip Hop choreography classes at industry dance studios like Studio City's Millennium Dance Complex franchise. Stressing the words in rhythm to the music, Shab calls out the order of steps: lock / *step* / Scoo B Doo / doublelock / *hop* / Skeeter Rabbit *two times*! Scoo Bot / hop *kick*. It's instructive that Shabba Doo does not count the routine but calls steps, vocalizing the principle of meaningful communication core to streetdance. The rhythmic calls also reconnect us to locking's repertoire—not simply static steps in the archive but embedded life experiences of dancers and the ways they move—in this instance, first-generation lockers James "Skeeter Rabbit" Higgins and original *Soul Train* dancer Jimmy "Scoo B Doo" Foster.[23] The calls rhythmically organize the choreography into repeated sets of steps, yet the instruction to dance "in time, not in sync" flags an important shift in Shabba Doo's pedagogy—his subtle critique of the emphasized uniformity typical of choreocentric group routines in global competition and Hollywood industry dance.

Shabba Doo's distinction between dancing "in time" and "in sync"/ "in unison" foregrounds practices of participatory rhythm-making that don't require universal rhythmic interpretation and unchanging replication of the choreography. To "be in time," for Shabba Doo, aligns with what Abeni calls precision-work—"not mean[ing] dancing with the exact same dynamic quality [but] rhythmic interplay and the finely tuned sense of connection among the group" (Jackson 2001, 48). Abeni goes further to describe precision-work as "a matter of sensual connectivity" and "an instruction in . . . *improvised inexactness* of hands and arms" (48, emphasis added).

Dancing "in sync" is most noticeably heralded by the familiar utterance "five-six-seven-eight" preceding the start of the routine. Putting Abeni's work in conversation with Shabba Doo's studio pedagogy, dancing "in sync" tasks the group with synchronizing time to produce a consistent univocal "dynamic quality" that resists the impulse for change the group might otherwise perform and which would allow for the unpredictability of individual dancers' unique interpretations of a movement sequence. Instead, the group focuses on accurate replication of visual form, flattening the appearance of difference. Differently said, the aim is to reduce the possibility of finding multiple and changing meanings in the choreography, in order to produce an unambiguous expressive effect.

Shabba Doo's "in time" dancing calls for "sensual connectivity" of the group—a heightened relational sensibility of the ensemble. In seeking rhythmic cohesion (which accounts for temporal shifts and different interpretive acts) the dancers move in rhythm together, less concerned with looking exactly alike than including the possibility of performances with nuanced stylistic flair. I describe these practices as *together-dancing* to emphasize the ways dancers move in relation, generating a synesthetic sensory-somatic capacity that circulates among the group of participants in the moment of performance. The adaptable rhythmic connectivity of precision-work and dancing in-time builds shared sensory experiences of together-dancing.

While movement-in-relation offers an understanding of embodiment not limited to the boundaries of an individual self, together-dancing does not default to an idealized achievement of unity. Kyra Gaunt's (2002) expansion of ethnomusicologist Charles Keil's theory of participatory discrepancy is critical here. Gaunt stresses the aesthetic politics of dissonance in group rhythm-making, always already "informed first by practices, discourse, and values that take shape long before the music starts" (121). Gaunt's ethnographic work attunes to the participatory aesthetics of events in which "black folks can feel 'out of sync' with musical experience and discourse in primarily white academic settings especially when Western classical music is no longer the subject" (121). This careful intervention into the universalizing tendencies of theories and institutional spaces that manage and control difference must guide any understanding of movement-in-relation with, as Gaunt emphasizes, an articulation of "lived incongruities of difference" and structural power (128).

OPEN ENDINGS

I've attempted to disarticulate structural logics of the dance studio as a historically protected site of knowledge production that magnifies and modulates hierarchies of culture and power. Studying black aesthetics through the discursive lens of streetdance practitioners' studio-based pedagogies, I address the consequences of studio-fication of vernacular forms. Here the work of pedagogy includes not only transmission of cultural knowledge, but also its interpretation and translation. Black aesthetics activated through streetdance study can prompt a critique of social relations in the studio, with concern for the correspondence of movement technique *and* the movement of lived experience.

Boogie McClarin, a Chicago native, dance artist, street historian and underground philosopher, underscores the politics of translation from culture to style, operative in Chicago house vernacular:

NAOMI: What is jacking? How do you define jacking?
BOOGIE: It depends what you're asking and the context. In the context of this
    interview, I will presume it is talking about the movement that is often done with
    the music that has been now labeled house. But my gut wanted to just answer
    and say jacking is when you go up to somebody and you steal somethin'. And you
    punch 'em in the face. From it being the '80s snatch-your-gold-chain culture to
    stealing your ability to define yourself by yourself. I think that those places lay at
    the core of the movement itself. If you don't really feel that, if you've never felt that,
    if you never felt like something could get taken from you, you wouldn't be drawn to
    that music or move in that way. You wouldn't reach for your gut. You wouldn't bend
    at the hip flexor. You wouldn't crouch before rising.[24]

Boogie attends to the politics of lexicons and the vernacular's escape from attempts at extraction which would presume to classify and interpret dance as a static object of knowledge. Within the context of the interview, which already positions us in hierarchical roles of scholar and cultural practitioner, it bears emphasis that Boogie grounds lexicons of house style in her own longstanding commitments to study.[25]

Students may learn the jack as a foundation movement of house style, yet Boogie contends that jacking is not reducible to dance technique stripped of lived experience. Layers of definition are abstracted in house style aesthetics which travel beyond the social-political contexts of house culture's creation, such that "social values of the original practitioners thus remain encoded in the dance" (Schloss 2009, 57). The sensory-somatic meanings of these contexts resurface in Boogie's response—a "reach for your gut . . . bend at the hip flexor . . . crouch before rising" feeling. Boogie articulates the ways house calls on its students not simply to incorporate jacking movement but more carefully to dwell with what *reaching-bending-crouching-rising* means, given the history of jack's creation.

The group of streetdance practitioners I am bringing into conversation here center dancers' attentions, intentions, accountability, and commitments to the circula- tion of social meanings within and beyond streetdance communities. Resisting ex- tractive practices of replication, they describe and perform principles of circulation, groovemeant, becoming-in-touch, in-time, individuation, and precision-work that point to the emphasis streetdance study places on locating one's sense of embodiment socially and historically. These principles also restore value to the aural kinesthetic, rejecting the hierarchical separation and elevation of visuality linked to an extractive so- cial relation of objectification and consumption. This is not to say sight is unimportant to streetdance practices, but that overemphasizing sight in the transmission of cultural knowledge and values distorts aesthetic principles of streetdance realized in imbricated sensory activity (especially devaluing sensory registers of sound and movement, as well as smell and touch).[26]

I am interested in how lowered registers of black aesthetics operate through artist- practitioner pedagogies in dance studios, challenging passive modes of cultural con- sumption and social exchange. Practitioners negotiating the studio's terms create pedagogies that activate black aesthetics, putting pressure on noun-ification and re- vealing the failure of the studio to perfectly translate the unsettled improvisatory life of the street. Black aesthetics ask different investments of dance practitioners to actively challenge global commodification of black culture.

This is neither to say streetdance has no place in studios or industry competitions, nor to limit the authentic performance of streetdance to improvisation alone. Instead, a critical study of black aesthetics can begin to dismantle racial-gendered hierarchies of representation and value that attempt to erase vernacular dance practices and the labor of the people who work to innovate them.

This essay is dedicated to Adolfo Shabba Doo Quiñones (1955-2020) a spirited teacher and storyteller, who lived and breathed streetdance.

Notes

1. Throughout, I have chosen to use the names by which practitioners self-identify in streetdance culture, rather than using legal surnames as is a practice of conventional ac- ademic scholarship. Where dancers have published written work, I refer to their chosen name for publication. Emilio Austin Jr., quoted in Wisner (2006, 76).

2. See http://cleisabeni.com/index.html and https://treeturtle.com/index.html.
3. James Higgins, text message to author, May 4, 2018. The term *streetdance* was used both by entertainment-industry producers and dancers, yet as both OG Skeeter Rabbit's and d. Sabela grimes's statements suggest, streetdancers use the term to celebrate their living cultural forms rather than to reinforce a hierarchy of value. I spell *streetdance* as one word throughout to distinguish this specific history of African American vernacular dancing from any general dancing done in the streets.
4. Emilio Austin Jr., quoted in Wisner (2006, 76).
5. My emphasis. *OED Online*, s.v. "amateur." http://www.oed.com/view/Entry/6041?redirec tedFrom = amateur#eid, accessed September 3, 2018.
6. Timothy "Popin Pete" Earl Solomon, teaching at "Street Style Lab," New York City, New York, August 2013. Popin Pete is an original member of dance crew the *Electric Boogaloos* of Fresno, California.
7. Moncell Durden teaching "Basic Movements Hip-Hop: Basic Bounce," published by DanceProject, June 9, 2011. https://www.youtube.com/watch?v = F_xK9F9AP48 (accessed July 9, 2019).
8. Caleaf Sellers, telephone interview with author, August 19, 2015. Caleaf Sellers is a key innovator of hip hop and house, coming out of the 1980s New York dance scene, and a core member of the groups Moptop Unit and Dance Fusion.
9. Faculty website for USC Glorya Kaufman School of Dance at the University of Southern California. https://kaufman.usc.edu/faculty/d-sabela-grimes/.
10. d. Sabela grimes, teaching Funkamentals technique at the Illadelph Legends Festival, Oakland, California, June 26, 2015.
11. Lenaya "Tweetie" Straker, teaching at the Ladies of Hip Hop Festival, Toronto, Canada, November 10, 2017.
12. Traci Bartlow, teaching for my introduction to hip hop dance class, University of California, Berkeley, June 26, 2013. https://www.youtube.com/watch?v=89bmWfKfvhE.
13. Vogue Evolution was the first self-identified gay group to perform on Fox reality show *America's Best Dance Crew*, Season 4 (2009) and faced transphobic comments from the judges' table. See "Started in the Streets" (Chung 2016, 136–137).
14. Hip hop choreo and lyrical hip hop are also popular among college campus dance clubs and linked to industry dance. For example, Kaba Modern originated from a group of dancers in the Filipino cultural club Kababayan at UC Irvine. They made the top-three finals for the Fox TV reality dance show *America's Best Dance Crew*. Dancer/choreographers Arnel Cavalario and Mike Song now travel and teach internationally.
15. "Honey: Rise Up and Dance—Trailer," published by YouTube Movies, April 2, 2018 https://www.youtube.com/watch?v = oiIaKQiFpWE (accessed May 4, 2018). Also see Melissa Blanco-Borelli's (2014) in-depth examination of mulatta narratives engaged by Jessica Alba's performance of the mulatta body in the original 2003 film.
16. Despite *Honey*'s inability to fully hold dancers in the studio scenes within binary gender categories, the casual language of "ladies . . . fellas . . . guys" reproduces the binary sorting of the dancers' bodies.
17. For example, in African diasporic dance classes that incorporate live drumming, teachers often perform nonverbal vocalization of rhythmic patterns as a basic training practice for developing rhythmic sensibility.
18. Laura Robinson's (2014) study of hip hop dance on TV reality dance shows theorizes the appearance of Africanist aesthetics in competition dancing, showing that transnational

adaptations of black vernacular aesthetics are necessarily complex (and variously theorized as black, Africanist, and hip hop). Robinson argues that these performances "can be better understood through Halifu Osumare's concept of the 'transnational body': hip hop aesthetics exported globally through commercialization and subcultural networks and subsequently recontextualized and adapted with localized articulation" (308).

19. Nubian Néné is a self-described "urban dancer," performer, choreographer, and teacher, born and raised in Montreal and currently based in New York. Toprock is the upright footwork used in breaking to establish a dancer's style and rhythmic foundation, before they go down to the floor.

20. Nubian Néné, teaching at the Ladies of Hip Hop Festival, Toronto, Canada, November 10, 2017.

21. Toyin Sogunro, teaching at Ladies of Hip Hop Festival, Toronto, Canada, November 10, 2017. Sogunro is artistic director of Urban Artistry, a non-profit dance organization "dedicated to the performance and preservation of art forms inspired by the urban experience." She is a multiple winner of top international dance competitions Juste Debout and House Dance Forever. Urban Artistry, "Mission," http://urbanartistry.org/home/, accessed September 4, 2018.

22. Adolfo "Shabba Doo" Quiñones, teaching class at Performing Arts Center, Van Nuys, California, April 2014. Shabba Doo passed December 29, 2020. He is a founding member of the Original Lockers, an original *Soul Train* dancer, and star of the first mass-distributed 1984 hip hop dance films *Breakin'* and *Breakin' 2: Electric Boogaloo*. *Wild Style* (1983) is the first hip hop motion picture. Hip hop documentary *Breakin' and Enterin'* was released in 1983 and featured several of the same artists to eventually appear in *Breakin'*.

23. At the same time, the absence of women's names in the dance's lexicon reveals the gendered tensions of naming and history. Some key women lockers are Damita Jo Freeman, Arnetta "Netta Bug" Johnson, Freddie Maxie, Lorna Dune, Shelly Cepeda, and Toni Basil.

24. Boogie McClarin, telephone interview with author, August 19, 2015.

25. Codification of dance style is a critical way that practitioners create lexicons to circulate knowledge about their aesthetic practices, encoding complex cultural histories of these dances. In conversations circulating online, practitioners have also noted ambivalence within their communities toward the politics of naming and cataloguing steps, even as the codification process involves dancers in community-engaged research, including sustaining relationships with early innovators to support the cultural legacies of black vernacular traditions.

26. Synesthesia extends to the sense of smell in funk vernacular, communicating a preference for stinky over clean.

References

Borelli, M. B. (2014). "A Taste of Honey: Choreographing Mulatta in the Hollywood Dance Film." In *The Oxford Handbook of Dance and the Popular Screen*, edited by M. B. Borelli, 225–239. Oxford: Oxford University Press.

Chung, B. S.-J. (2016). "'Started in the Streets . . .': Criminalizing Blackness and the Performance of Asian American Entrepreneurship on *America's Best Dance Crew*, Season 1." In *Contemporary Directions in Asian American Dance*, edited by Y. Wong, 117–142. Madison: University of Wisconsin Press.

DeFrantz, T. (2014). "Hip-Hop in Hollywood: Encounter, Community, Resistance." In *The Oxford Handbook of Dance and the Popular Screen*, edited by M. Blanco Borelli, 113–131. Oxford: Oxford University Press.

Gottschild, B. D. (1996). *Digging the Africanist Presence in American Performance: Dance and Other Contexts*. Westport, CT: Greenwood Press.

Freire, P. (2006). "The Banking Model of Education." In *Critical Issues in Education: An Anthology of Readings*, edited by E. F. Provenzo, 105–117. Thousand Oaks, CA: SAGE Publications. (Original work published in 1970).

Gaunt, K. (2002). "Got Rhythm? Difficult Encounters in Theory and Practice and Other Participatory Discrepancies in Music." *City and Society* 14 (1): 119–140.

grimes, d. S. (2008a). "STREETdance." *Social*Dance*Media: Old Shuffles in a New Paradigm* (blog). http://socialdancemedia.blogspot.com/2008/08/streetdance.html.

grimes, d. S. (2008b). "STREETdance[R]." *Social*Dance*Media: Old Shuffles in a New Paradigm* (blog). http://socialdancemedia.blogspot.co.uk/2008/08/streetdancer.html.

grimes, d. S. (2008c). "The People's Archive." *Social*Dance*Media: Old Shuffles in a New Paradigm* (blog). http://socialdancemedia.blogspot.com/2008/08/peoples-archive.html.

Jackson, J. D. (2001). "Improvisation in African-American Vernacular Dancing." *Dance Research Journal* 33 (2): 40–53.

Johnson, I. K. (2012). "Music Meant to Make You Move: Considering the Aural Kinesthetic." *Sounding Out!* (blog), June 18. http://soundstudiesblog.com/2012/06/18/music-meant-to-make-you-move-considering-the-aural-kinesthetic/.

Jones, L. (1999). *Blues People: Negro Music in White America*. New York: William Morrow. (Original work published in 1963).

Mackey, N. (1992). "Other: From Noun to Verb." *Representations* 39: 51–70.

McQuirter, M. A. (2002). "Awkward Moves: Dance Lessons from the 1940s." In *Dancing Many Drums: Excavations in African American Dance*, edited by T. F. DeFrantz, 81–103. Madison: University of Wisconsin Press.

Melamed, J. (2015). "Racial Capitalism." *Critical Ethnic Studies* 1 (1): 76–85.

Monroe, R. L. (2011). "'I Don't Want to Do African . . . What about My Technique?' Transforming Dancing Places into Spaces in the Academy." *Journal of Pan African Studies* 4 (6): 38–55.

Robinson, L. (2014). "The Dance Factor: Hip-Hop, Spectacle, and Reality Television." In *The Oxford Handbook of Dance and the Popular Screen*, edited by M. B. Borelli, 304–319. Oxford: Oxford University Press.

Schloss, J. (2009). *Foundation: B-Boys, B-Girls, and Hip-Hop Culture in New York*. New York: Oxford University Press.

Scott, A. (1998). "It's All in the Timing: The Latest Moves, James Brown's Grooves, and the Seventies Race-Consciousness Movement in Salvador, Bahia-Brazil." In *Soul: Black Power, Politics, and Pleasure*, edited by M. Guillory and R. C. Green, 9–22. New York: New York University Press.

Tate, G. (2003). *Everything but the Burden: What White People Are Taking from Black Culture*. New York: Broadway Books.

Taylor, D. (2003). *The Archive and the Repertoire: Performing Cultural Memory in the Americas*. Durham, NC: Duke University Press.

Wisner, H. (2006). "From Street to Studio: Hip Hop Comes Inside." *Dance Magazine* 80 (9): 74–76.

CHAPTER 20

LIVING IN THE TENSION

The Aesthetics and Logics of Popping

ROSEMARIE A. ROBERTS

INTRODUCTION

SOCIAL justice practices are typically defined by descriptors or, as we learned in grade school, "action words," such as *envisioning*, *speaking*, *participating*, *creating*, and *transforming*. In the popular imagination, social justice enactments can conjure an image of unrestrained performing bodies—walking, running, arms up in the air—moving in the streets and other public spaces. Alternatively, contained voices and bodies are antithetical to the movement-defining actions that people involved in social justice movements enact to achieve their aims. However, the oppression that social justice practices seek to end is never singular. Rather, there are "myriad ways oppression can alternatively seduce our minds and hearts or inspire us to further learning and activism" (Bell 2007, 2). Thus, social justice enactments and practices require an array of strategies for achieving equitable social conditions (Apfelbaum 1999; Scott 1990). Secondly, because power is never conceded, liberation is an incomplete ongoing process. In a ground-breaking paper written in 1979, social psychologist Erika Apfelbaum wrote about power dynamics, seeking to "deconstruct the historical and cultural performances of power" (Fine et al. 2004). Among the interventions Apfelbaum posed to social psychology's appraisal of power as based in interpersonal conflicts, she analyzed "structures and concerns of power as relational, embedded and circular dynamics within domination" (Fine et al. 2004). Apfelbaum asserts that everyday enactments of resistance powerfully reveal mechanisms of dominant social power that are untold in recorded history. In a similar vein, anthropologist and political scientist James Scott (1990) argues that power is relational. In his analysis, Scott concludes that acts of resistance to power come in many guises—guise that in the presence of the powerful are likely to appear as acquiescence or compliance. Drawing on Apfelbaum and Scott, I argue that the most effective social justice practices are defined by a set of on-the-ground, fluid enactments because they are responding to a constant intertwining stream of oppressive tactics.

I will consider containment as a physical expression that is constructed and enacted by bodies at the nexus of domination and resistance in Hip Hop dance. I argue that containment in Popping involves a set of movements that structure and order the body and simultaneously articulate and reveal social injustices. Secondly, I will argue that embodied containments double as embodiments of social justice in the context of a world that is teeming with oppression and resistance to oppression by disenfranchised, marginalized, underrepresented peoples. To understand how containments reveal social injustices and push back against them, I examine the ways in which the aesthetics and logics of Popping produce and perform subjugated/subversive knowledges. I focus on the weight, in fact, hanging around in it in order to conjure a critical social analysis that reveals the fissures, the problematics with analyses that rely too heavily or exclusively on language and signs (Martin 1990; Jackson 1998; Roberts 2013a). To be sure, Mr. Wiggles's utterances are important. However, I resist an overreliance on utterances. I join Randy Martin and John L. Jackson (see Roberts 2013a) in a critique of semiotics and systems of signification as the basis for theorizing bodies because of the ways in which "phonological accumulations that amount to the utterance 'body'" (Jackson 1998, 188) conceal sociohistoric and political meanings. Moreover, narrowly focusing on semiotics renders the body invisible. Using an interdisciplinary methodology, I will focus on what active bodies are *saying* and *doing* and how they intervene in the interplay between subject/object and individual/structure. In other words, beyond showing how history and subjectivities shape one another in social interactions and settings, as if either social structures or people enactments are determinative, I aim to consider embodied enactments and utterances to understand "how the histories and the performances that persons live are shaped by forces that exist behind their backs" (Marx, quoted in Denzin 2003, xi), and how people shape the forces that exist behind their backs.

Taking the "performance turn" (Denzin 2003) in the direction of knowledge production, the broader question this chapter addresses is, What does a critical interrogation of the micro-level physical performances of dancing bodies reveal about the individual body's capacity to carry and bare the weight of collective histories, experiences and sensibilities? By contrasting these micro-embodiments with macro-level structural social injustices, I propose that the physical/bodily expression of containments, pops, and tensions make legible enactments of social justice in ways that speak truth to power, when that speaking is done through the body. Moreover, I argue that reading Popping logics and aesthetics as epistemic articulations, foregrounds the ways in which the dancing body's performance of the historic, concrete, and accumulated affects of power discontents transforms individual bodies into a collective body, acting to transform the weight of social injustices.

In 2009, I launched a study of the relationship between performance and knowledge production. As a research fellow of the 2009 Cultural Traditions: Hip Hop Continuum Program at The School at Jacob's Pillow, I examined corporeal and discursive practices of the pioneering Hip Hop artists Rennie Harris, Stephan "Mr. Wiggles" Clemente, Marjory Smarth, Moncell Durden, and Anthony "YNOT" DeNaro during the two-week program of dance and exploration of the historical roots of Hip Hop. Hip Hop has been conceptualized as a multifaceted intellectual, cultural, social (Forman 2004), and global movement (Alim 2006; Mitchell 2002; Osumare 2007; Spady Meghelli; and Alim 2006). Hip Hop has been defined as pedagogy (Akom 2009; Pulido 2009), curriculum (Hall 2009; Baszile 2009), a means through which young people construct identities (Flores 2004; Dimitriadis 2009; Ogbar 2007) and articulate and critique oppressive conditions of racism and other forms of social injustices (Duncan-Andrade and Morrell 2008; Fisher 2007; Fine et al. 2004; McCormick 2004; Roberts, Bell, and Murphy 2008; Weiss and Herndon 2001). With few exceptions (see Bragin 2015; DeFrantz 2004; MacCarren 2013; Osumare 2007) Hip Hop research findings and analyses have been grounded in the lyrics, music, and texts produced and performed, and not in the dance or the postures, movements, and gestures enacted by Hip Hop dancing bodies. Beyond acknowledging or nodding at the body and embodiment, I aim to locate and account for the body in Hip Hop.

I draw on traditional Afro-Caribbean dance, the form I am trained in, where in-motion Black and Brown dancing bodies have long been saying and doing things that cannot be otherwise said or revealed—something that may otherwise remain concealed. Dance (bodily) practices tend to be read as ephemeral and fleeting; but Hip Hop dance is the culmination of centuries of movement, especially movement flowing from the African diaspora, which are passed on and circulate globally (Randy Martin, interview with the author, November 2011). This danced history is practiced in and through Black and Brown bodies. Black and Brown embodiments circulate history, culture, and lived experience—beyond words that are said—through action and produced in motion, creating the possibilities for critical insights (Browning 1995; Martin 1990; Jackson 1998; DeFrantz 2004). Here I focus on the pedagogy of an accomplished teacher of Popping, Stephan "Mr. Wiggles" Clemente. I argue that the history and lived experience contained in his teachings reveal the ways in which Mr. Wiggles's dance practice seeks to re-script ideas and perceptions of Black and Brown Hip Hop dancing bodies, who are accountable to the weight of oppressive historical conditions and what constitutes knowledge.

AESTHETICS OF POPPING IN HIP HOP

In his historical analysis of dance on the streets of California and of the Bronx, New York, from 1965 to the 1970s, Guzman-Sanchez (2012) locates Popping together with "Funk Boogaloo, Robot, Zig-Zag, Locking, Crossover Locking . . . Punking, Jacking, Rocking, and B-Boying" (1). Though Popping circulated way beyond the borders of California, Maranan (2005) states that it developed in California in the 1970s. Bragin (2015) asserts, "Popping (and poplocking) are common umbrella terms used in reference to a group of illusionary styles that often combine in performance" (46). For many Popping practitioners, Popping is its own dance style, in part because it is often done to funk music instead of Hip Hop music; nevertheless, it "is part of the hip hop and funk dance family of styles" (Fogarty 2011, 23). According to dance scholar Katrina Hazzard-Donald (2004), the dance is "both a way of handling the body and a movement quality in which a jerking and freezing of movement takes place" (509). In Popping, "the quality of isolation is high-lighted by small, very precise, isolated muscular explosions like popcorn pop-ping" (Engel 2001, 363). In his interview of Jerry Rentie, a member of the Funk Boogaloo generation in Oakland, California, Guzman-Sanchez (2012) writes, "A key movement within Funk Boogaloo was the Freeze . . . an abrupt movement stop or hesitation during a broad movement . . . [which] was the precursor movement to what would many years later be referred to as Popping or Hitting" (15). The stop, hit, freeze, or hesitation is initiated by the muscles and emphasizes the beat. Bragin (2015) puts it this way, "Popping trains rapid and continuous muscular relaxation to achieve the concentrated muscular contraction signified by the "pop" and effect the most dynamic hit of the beat" (47). Since it is my purpose here to discuss the aesthetics of Popping and unpack the knowledges that are contained by the physical, I relate Popping to other Afro-diasporic social dances that predate street dance and Hip Hop, as well. For instance, Hazzard-Donald (2004) identifies the roots of Popping in Afro-diasporic dance:

> The pop-and-lock[1] technique could also be observed in the snakehips, as that dance was performed by the Cotton Club's Earl "Snakehips" Tucker in the 1920's. Going farther back, a dance called the snakehips was popular in the Georgia Sea Islands and throughout the antebellum plantation South, and I have no reason to doubt that it resembled the version I learned in a 1950's Midwestern African American community (509).

When I look at Popping, I see a physical containment and tension—a holding back of the flow of energy—which is also found in Afro-diasporic dance forms. Rumba and Samba are not only the national dances of Cuba and Brazil, respectively, they embody the sensibilities, identities, histories, and knowing of a people (Daniel 2005; Hazzard-Donald 2004). Heeding Kyra Gaunt's (2006) call for a "somatic historiography of black music and dance" (186), I am interested not only in "the stories that the body can tell" (186); I am also examining social meanings associated with and contained by the Hip Hop dancing body as they are made legible in their performance. There is a long tradition of Black and Latinx performance theater "as a weapon for fighting racism and white privilege" (Denzin 2003, 5). Postcolonial critic Homi K. Bhabha uses the term "performative" to talk about the practice and action "that incessantly insinuates, interrupts, interrogates, antagonizes, and decenters powerful master discourses, which [Bhabha] dubbed 'pedagogical'" (quoted in Conquergood and Johnson 2013, 27). In Afro-diasporic dance, there is an equally rich tradition that understands Black and Brown dancing bodies as taking in-motion revelatory action (Browning 1995; Gottschild 1996, 2003; Osumare 2007; Roberts 2005). It's the something more than meets the eye. I refer to this something more as the *excess*. I examine the ways in which the dancing body animates and deploys this excess, or accumulated knowledges that are constitutive of fragmented histories and experiences of domination and resistance to oppressive forces, through a set of moves in which the physical containment of energy is achieved in alternating muscle tension and relaxation.

In a broader sense, I join DeFrantz (2004), Fogarty (2011), Johnson (2011), MacCarren (2013), Osumare (2007), and Schloss (2009) in claiming the legitimacy of Hip Hop dance practices as aesthetics, culture, politics, and, I would add, knowledge. This examination necessitates sensing into the micro-level Black and Brown physical performances of culture to ask what they reveal about macrolevel social injustices. Put another way, what knowledge has accumulated in these acts of containment, and when it is released, what is revealed? And what of the macro (social systems of injustice) is contained in the micro (bodily movement practices)?

As I've written elsewhere,

> Scholarly treatment of the Black body, for instance, by W. E. B. DuBois, Dorothy Roberts, and Robin D. G. Kelley, provide evidence of how racist constructions of Black men and women, which originate in slavery, continue to be deployed to control their bodies and influence policy, law and everyday social inter-group interactions. Methodologically, these and other scholars use historical text, social science research, and popular images to document the practices that reduce Black bodies to problematic, pathological objects. An embodied analysis of dance, unlike textual or text-based analyses, harness and expose the micro level movements, postures and gestures (MPG), what they reveal about macro-structural racial inequalities and the acts of resistance to that oppression. (Roberts 2013a, 8).

Intersecting micro and macro realities that seem *more than* or *excessive* to the dance, insofar as dance is defined as entertainment rather than as a critical site of meaning-making (Dunham 2005) and cultural production (Chatterjea 2004) and of theorizing about its relationship to aesthetics, politics, and knowledge (Bragin 2015; Daniel 2005; DeFrantz 2004; Fogarty 2011; Johnson 2016; Schloss 2009). Within dance studies, divisions between Western concert dance (read White forms) and social, traditional, street, urban, popular (read Black and Brown forms) together with the assumption that Black and Brown "cultural expression as non-technical" (Bragin 2015, 12) extends the devaluation and delegitimization of Black and Brown dancing bodies. I join with scholars whose work is in social and popular dance (see DeFrantz 2004; Fogarty 2011, 2012; Johnson 2011, 2012; Valis-Hill 2010) in order to reconstitute dance epistemology and center the contributions of Black and Brown peoples to the production of knowledge. From the standpoint of social justice, language and movement can work together to interrupt what Lee Anne Bell (2010) has identified as the numbing affects of the multileveled and multidimensional levels of social power, privilege, and oppression.

Focusing on the physicality of meaning making (Dunham 2005; Foster 1996) as corporeal events and practice, I trace the physical movements, gestures, and postures in

Popping, as well as the sensations that are generated in me based on what is made legible in the dance. As I have documented elsewhere (Roberts 2013a; 2021), I filmed and later viewed and analyzed videotapes of the teaching and dancing practices of the Hip Hop Continuum faculty. Using case-study methodology involving fieldwork, participant observation, in-depth interviews, and archival research, I examined the physical shapes and postures assumed by the performative Hip Hop dancing body and discourses of Hip Hop dance, culture, aesthetics, and the body.

It is beyond the scope of my study and analysis to examine the extent to which the perceptions of this multiracial, ethnic, and gendered group of students were changed by the experience. Rather, I will analyze the ways in which Mr. Wiggles, and thus the Hip Hop dancing body, gestures to speech and, by extension, to language as a call to action to produce both historical and subversive knowledges. In the language of social justice, I will analyze the ways in which Mr. Wiggles connects an individual narrative of oppression and resistance to oppressive forces to a collective narratives of injustice (Bell and Roberts 2010).

Drawing upon Gilligan et al.'s (2006) *Listening Guide* to analyze the video-taped data that I collected during the Hip Hop Continuum, I engage in sequential viewings, "designed to bring the researcher into relationship with a person's distinct and multi-layered voice by tuning in or listening to distinct aspects of a person's expression of their experience within a particular relational context" (255). Instead of relating to voice, I position myself as a knowing body (dancer, choreographer, social scientist) to document and interrogate the physical sensations observing Hip Hop dancing bodies provokes in my body.[2] These analyses of videotaped data are further analyzed alongside interviews and thick detail physical, perceptual, and emotional experimentations and interpretations of observations during my experience in the field. These field notes together with videotaped dance workshops provide data of corporeal practices. Here I consider a one-hour segment of a workshop in which he is teaching Popping. I ask, What is Mr. Wiggles conveying through his body? What do micro-level gestures, postures, and movements convey about the structural realities within which they were produced? Through these analyses of Mr. Wiggles's embodied pedagogy (Roberts 2011), I account for Hip Hop dance epistemology by asking about what the dancing body is containing and what is tension in Popping containing? Moreover, I ask how the boundaries between individual and collective bodies slip and slide in and through Hip Hop dance.

The Power in Holding Back

On this hot July day in the Berkshires, Mr. Wiggles announces to a racially and ethnically mixed group of young people that he is teaching Popping. Like the entire Hip Hop Continuum faculty, Mr. Wiggles is very accomplished. He is a choreographer, actor, dance pedagogue, music producer, and graffiti artist. Schloss (2009) notes that, along with "b-boy elders Ken Swift, PopMaster Fabel, [and] Crazy Legs," Mr. Wiggles "published a sort of manifesto in *Source* magazine in 1993," in which they wrote, "As B-Boy and Boogie-boy pioneers of this culture we feel obligated to preserve and maintain true historic understanding of terms and facts connected with hip-hop" (63). These pioneers have since earned titles such as scholar and historian of hip hop culture, and especially b-boy culture (63), because "they have focused their efforts on documenting and critically evaluating claims about the origins of moves and styles (126). Mr. Wiggles is also a member of Rock Steady Crew, Electric Boogaloos, Tribal Click, and the Zulu Nation. As Mary Fogarty (2011) has documented, in the 1980s Mr. Wiggles was featured in the work created by Marie DeAngelos, the founding director of a ballet company in Mexico. This ballet was the first to include Hip Hop dance. Fogarty (2012) also documented that he was the first to offer Hip Hop dance classes at the Broadway Dance Center in New York City. Together with "well-known dancers from New York with the b-boy/b-girl scene such as Ken Swift, Honey Rockwell . . . and Flo Master" (455), Mr. Wiggles also danced with GhettOriginal Dance Company. Interested in recording the scene and dancer histories from their travels, Mr. Wiggles and Ken Swift interviewed "local dancers about the history of the local scenes" (455) and dancer genealogy. Ultimately, Wiggles and Ken Swift created videos to share "their travel experiences [which they called] 'underground travel video magazines'" (456–457). I raise Mr. Wiggles's pedigree because, tucked between the layers of the stereotypes about Hip Hop dancers, and the corporate and popular culture cooptation and extraction of style for consumption, lies an artistic philosophical approach to Hip Hop and to Popping that he developed over years of being involved in and innovating much of what we call Hip Hop culture. You'll hear it when Mr. Wiggles talks about "the conditions that led to particular artistic decisions being made . . . [and] the community's abstract understanding of—and approach to—those conditions" (70).

Mr. Wiggles begins his class by talking about Popping. He explains, "It's all about control, relaxing the shoulders, shoulders down, tension is isolated in wrists and knees," continuing, "tapping to the bass of the music. Make it compact—one single tap." Situated in front of the mirror and the students, Mr. Wiggles demonstrates the dance sequence: arms raised shoulder height; wrist and knees flexing and straightening in quick, coordinated movements, while his upper body and lower body move in two different directions. Arms are crossed in front of the body, legs wide apart in a warrior stance. The left legs straightens; the back leg bends as the straightened leg slides away from the body; the right arm extends away from the body. Head and chin drop downward. The neck disappears into the shoulders and the face is partially hidden by extended arms, which move back behind the body as the legs lift into space away from the body. Mr. Wiggles bends his left arm at the elbow toward his face and straightens the right bent knee in front of his body. His lower body twists and swirls downward and then spirals back up. His wrist, chest, and knees flex and straighten again in quick movements on top of sliding, lifting, skipping legs and feet. Each limb and body part moves in short, small, staccato progressions. Mr. Wiggles repeats this sequence several times, each time urging students through demonstration followed by speech to linger in the sharp, angular, the slow and rocking. "Don't throw it away," Mr. Wiggles says. "Hold back. Live in the tension."

I've seen, indeed have sensed, this juxtaposing of contrasting forces—sharp and short staccato movements layered on undulating, round, swirling movements—before in Afro-diasporic dance. Whether it's the tumbao in the Afro-Cuban rumba, the quick flitting of the skirt or hands in Afro-Puerto Rican Bomba, the undulating, writhing spine in Haitian Yanvalou, all of these dances, not unlike Popping, require an isolation and control of body centers, a gathering of and then quick and measured meting out and drawing in of energy, together with "an inner release between each muscle contraction" (Bragin 2015, 53). To execute, the dancer isolates, holds back and contains a contraction, leading to a weight-bearing movement and hit on the beat.

Talking through each movement as he demonstrates, Mr. Wiggles continues, "Both wrists and one knee at a time. "I want you fully relaxed." "Tap the knee that's our power. Put your weight on it and tap." Some versions of the phrases "put your weight on it and tap" and "relax your shoulders" are repeated countless times throughout the hour-long class. At one point during the demonstration, Mr. Wiggles stops dancing; he walks away from the mirror and to the corner of the room, where he pauses. He returns to his spot in front of the students and demonstrates the difference between lifting a shoulder up toward the ears and contracting the wrist and forearm simultaneously and releasing them. I observe the students, who are throwing their arms forward with little to no isolation, contraction, or containment.

To achieve the containment of energy, followed by a short, deliberate release or extension, the dancer is required to alternately relax and tense. Kinesthetically, this tension creates increased physical power when opposing movements, postures, and/or gestures are danced at the same time. Just before he says, "Don't throw it away. Hold back," I feel the tension heave in his wrists and in one knee, followed by the other knee. With lightning speed, a short burst of energy is released. Mr. Wiggles adds, "If you're going to make it in the streets, you have to move fast, from zero to 100 and back to zero." This is the first social reference he has made to a sensibility and a lived experience that infuse and are contained in Mr. Wiggles pops.

Suddenly, Mr. Wiggles goes from executing the movements in half time to doing them in double time. Strikingly, the quickened pace does not affect the sharp punctuation and articulation of each pop. Because he is able to relax and contract his muscles at lightning speed, he can achieve a more intense and discernible pop. Then turning and moving diagonally toward the corner of the room, he finishes the sequence in a deep knee bend, a quick swirl in the hips, arms bent at the elbows, hands facing up in a warrior stance. He stands up and claps as he walks away. The students struggle to keep up. The students clap, too, looking puzzled and laughing nervously as most of them follow Mr. Wiggles to the far end of the studio. There is an air of uncertainty and suspense in the room, as if something has been left unresolved. A young Black woman stays in front of the mirror, practicing the basic wrist and knee flex/straightening action as the other students walk away. Another Black woman quickly turns around and joins her. Soon a Black man and White woman join her. A handful of the students follow Mr. Wiggles to the back of the room and the others take a break, getting water or leaving the studio to use the bathroom.

While he's changing the music in the back of the room, Mr. Wiggles tells the class that he wants them to lock down the hips in a synchronized way and add that move to the basic wrist- and knee-popping movements they have already learned. As soon as he starts talking, the students who have been practicing in front of the mirror turn around to listen. Mr. Wiggles walks back to the front of the studio. Positioning himself in front of the mirror, Mr. Wiggles stands with his legs hip-width apart, knees bent, while popping his wrist in front of his body and around his head. He adds his hips and chest in a funky, undulating movement, while shifting his feet slightly and popping his knees. Mr. Wiggles explains, "This is the key to Popping: We're always on zero. This is where we live. The pop is only a fraction of the beat. We go from zero to 100 and back to zero on every beat. Knees, wrists—no shoulders. Zero to 100, zero to 100, but we live on zero."

With the students close behind him, hanging on his every move, Mr. Wiggles shifts back. The students to do the same. "We're going back to the basics." he tells them. Standing in place, Mr. Wiggles extends one arm forward and the other back, the hip and leg weight shifting back as the knees alternatively pop. He says, "We know now what we call the Fresno. The fundamentals of Popping are right here. Without this step you cannot do Popping. What I'm going to teach you is to walk, while you synchronize all the pops in one beat." For the next twenty minutes, Mr. Wiggles proceeds to break down the sequence, from head to foot. He repeats the Fresno, adds the Lurch,[3] a movement where the head is compressed into the shoulders and the chin slides forward as the arm extends and wrists pop. At the same time, the opposite straightened leg slides forward. Then as he places his sliding foot down on an angle, his knee pops in tandem with his wrists. Mr. Wiggles travels across the space by angling his body toward the right and left diagonals of the studio. Facing front, he ends the phrase. The entire sequence in repeated half time for two counts and then double time for two counts. When the pace quickens, the students loose precision and the capacity to contain tension. Mr. Wiggles says, "Do not throw your arm forward. Don't throw your hit away. Over the music, he shouts, "Don't throw your hit away! I mean . . . ," and then he demonstrates by extending the front leg and punctuating the slide with a pop in the knee and wrists. He stands in front of the students and admonishes, "I want to see control!" He looks around to make sure that they have taken his correction. The music changes and so does Mr. Wiggles. Instead of continuing with the sequences, snapping he fingers to the beat, he smoothly transitions into a slow groove. His body appears to melt down into the ground, as his hips rock from side to side. After about four counts, Mr. Wiggles returns to the sequence. This time, a more contained movement, his groove is a visibly prominent feature in the sequence. The groove gives way to an "inner space of release" among this mixed-race, -ethnic, and -gender group.

During the preceding class, Mr. Wiggles had explained that his "native dance" is Rocking:

> Rocking came before breaking. Rocking is the father of many dances; you see Rocking dance, you see Rocking from Salsa, from the Boogaloo, from Breaking, from Tapping, from the Wobble. [Rocking] is the missing tip from the styles that were coming out of New York, and this particular dance is really about soul; plain, simple, soul.

Now, as I watch his students struggling to translate Mr. Wiggles's movements in their bodies, I wonder if they remember this critical teaching about soul. In rocking and in soul, the body is held tightly, and the movements are small and contained. Much as in the tumbao that I described earlier, control, isolation, and a holding back are all essential features. Soul is not only a groove that is expressed physically in dance; it is also a powerful sensibility and marker of Blackness. In a series of interviews for *The Black Dancing Body: A Geography from Coon to Cool*, Brenda Dixon Gottschild (2003) asked prominent White, Black, and Brown choreographers about soul/spirit. Doug Elkins says, "In African and Latino . . . cultures . . . the body is a dialogue and the body is allowed to represent the individual and that person's cultural community." (231). Soul, according to Sean Curran, is "a connectedness to . . . spirit. About not just how African American people move, but the African American experience, and survivors, and a musicality and a profound understanding of the complex rhythms" (231). For Gottschild herself, "Soul is a capacity to render the universality of pain and suffering . . . specific through the particular life experience of black Americans" (220). In Hip Hop dance as in other Afro-diasporic forms, soul is a sensibility, embodying a fusion of political, philosophical, and theoretical practices and a history that has accumulated and is expressed in and through movement. A complete release, or what Mr. Wiggles calls "throwing away," cuts loose that accumulated knowledge. And an inability to get down and rock foregoes the possibility of creating and getting into an inner space of release.

I wish to also make a distinction here between the body as container and the space that is created within the body when it is put through the paces of muscular contraction and release or contained. Bragin's (2015) theorizing of that inner in-between space as one of Black and Brown ontological possibility, of what she calls a kinesthetic politics of Blackness, is useful here. Bragin asserts, "The pop opens up a zero space of un-seeing/un-knowing . . . As a theory of cultural resistance, the break builds a capacity of lingering inside the beat to open up the infinite—a paraontological space of expansive possibility" (53). I imagine that space as being partially made up of that accumulated knowledge. Through his body pedagogy, Mr. Wiggles labors to create the conditions that will allow students to explore the limits and possibilities of sensing into a space that is contained and structured by accumulated knowledge.

Documenting the flurry of physical sensations, I experience a sense of heaviness as I watch Mr. Wiggles bearing down on his knees to create a pop. But what if one does not have that lived experience to lean into, to "tap" into? What if the students have not lived what Bill T. Jones calls a "bittersweet, paradoxical human condition" (see Gottschild 2003, 232)? I suggest that this is precisely why Mr. Wiggles presses his students to have a physical experience of holding back in the dance and to live in the tension before tapping on the accumulations, physicalized as a sense of weight. Rennie Harris says that getting into the pocket, into that space which is filled with accumulations, whether musical or physical, gets the dancer in touch with the "grit and grizzle" and is a necessary condition for dancing Hip Hop (interview with the author, July 2009). As he grooves and moves between zero and a hundred and back to zero again, Mr. Wiggles is also laboring to create a moment of sharing accumulated knowledges.

With Mr. Wiggles leading, the students move across the floor, line by line, repeating the dance sequence. I observe that the rock, sharp articulations in the technique, and weightedness are still absent, indeed illegible, in the students' movements, gestures, and postures. After the last line completes the sequence, Mr. Wiggles offers in gesture and speech the following corrective, "Put your weight on it and tap." From behind the camera, I sense a weight again as I watch Mr. Wiggles flex, bear down, tap, shift side to side, and release. The tap and shift bring forth with force and speed a moment of production (Eng and Kazanjian 2003). It's fast—but there is a slight, discernible break, like one in a music phrase that is punctuated by an "and" before the "1" beat or between "1-2" beats. It's in that break that Mr. Wiggles's body moves from 0 to 100 mph, stops and pops in the center of the speed range, and then returns to zero. Even though I/we cannot access Mr. Wiggles's lived experience or the experience of African Americans, it is through the physical cues of Popping and Rocking, where they can connect with the beat and verbal cues of "control," "hold back," "go from zero to 100 and back to zero," "don't throw your hit away," Mr. Wiggles is creating the conditions for us to sense into the structural realities that he describes as weight. He creates a space for getting into the pocket where structural inequalities that inform the movement and are compressed in the disappearing neck, rocking hips, and popping wrists and knees, as well as the grounded, low-to-the-ground and warrior stances are animation and become legible. The quick tapping gesture is an exertion of physical energy that gives the popping motion power, and the physical bearing down releases the accumulated knowledge.

Dancing Accumulated Knowledge

In the social justice context, what is contained in an act of containment? In other words, what is the power of containment? Despite problematic stereotypic constructions that suggest that racialized bodies acquire rhythm "naturally," Mr. Wiggles was not born knowing how to dance. His capacity to compress knowledge through bodily practices, create corporeal spaces contained by knowledge, and knowing when to alternate between containment and release was gained from a life lived in the birthplace of Hip Hop, the South Bronx, which was also a site of creative innovation and community. By teaching the aesthetics and physical aspects of Popping, Mr. Wiggles is doing important social justice work by creating the conditions for animating and rendering alive a set of structural realities and putting into motion strategies for putting the dancing body to the service of revealing those realities. I interviewed Mr. Wiggles about his experience growing up in the South Bronx during the 1970s and 1980s and how those experiences shaped his dance and critical consciousness. He narrated these days when youth danced on the rubble of burned-out buildings to bring attention to "how we were particularly oppressed during that mothafuckin' time and how it made us feel" (interview with the author, July 2009). According to Mr. Wiggles, the movements, postures, and gestures that became codified into Hip Hop dances, gestured toward the ways in which Oscar

Lewis's, Daniel Patrick Moynihan's, and Charles Murray's ideas about the "culture of poverty" were swiftly taken up by local and national business people and politicians, to explain/manufacture and conceal the war zone that was just behind the beautified façade of burned-out buildings (Wiggles interview).

In the seventies and eighties when Mr. Wiggles was growing up, Hip Hop was still being defined on the streets, in living rooms, and at local community centers rather than in books.[4] For the African American, Puerto Rican, and Caribbean descendants living in the South Bronx then, life was as hard as the concrete on which he learned to dance. The hard-edged, sharply angular shapes and postures are an embodiment of those days in the South Bronx, where windows, curtains, and flowerpots painted on the face of buildings, concealed the wreckage and ruin of property and lives from the public. At that time, landlords were paying to burn down buildings so that they could make a return on the money they invested—so that they could run away from the blight that made the South Bronx infamous (Chang, 2005). According to Mr. Wiggles, the more showy, acrobatic, head spinning moves of b-boys were techniques performed to bring attention to the harsh social and economic realities experienced by South Bronx residents (interview with the author, July 2009). What read as entertainment to the world, was a strategic move to reveal what is concealed behind painted windows, curtains, and flowerpots. Each pop of the wrist and knees, Mr. Wiggles releases the weighty, aching disenfranchising and oppressive practices, such as "redlining and planned shrinkage"—that is, retreating material resources and social services (Banks 2011)—borne by Black and Brown South Bronx residents. They are more likely to live on the margins and to know more about the circuits of power and privilege than those who live at the centers of power. Moreover, viewed within the frame of Afro-diasporic dance, Hip Hop dance "coheres around a tradition of confronting the racial politics of domination, resistance, authentication, invisibilization, appropriation, and inclusion" (Amin 2011, quoted in Bragin 2015, 14). I read this historical reality and Mr. Wiggles and the b-boys to which he refers as strategic and, in his retelling, as a way to give legitimacy to his and their creative innovation, not as a story about how the boys from the 'hood make it against all odds. Neither is it an embodied story of victimhood that is somehow lodged in the body. These narratives are now documented and historicized (Chang 2005; Banks 2011), but at the time, the weight contained by in-motion Black and Brown bodies was the evidence of structural injustice and lives struggling for justice.

Notably, the performance of Hip Hop dancing bodies cannot be understood as knowledge production unless their knowledge of and resistance to structures of oppression and domination and the critical place of dance forms rooted in community and "counterpublic spaces of spiritual communion and collective creation" (Bragin 2015, 14) are foregrounded. The apparent appetite for the tricks and showier acrobatic moves that, according to the faculty, is taught in dance studios, suggests that the weight, groove, and soul are in excess of executing the movements. Rather, this excess is a powerful mix of racialization of Black and Brown bodies, the South Bronx's history of social injustice, Black and Brown histories and experiences of oppression as well as the cultural knowledge of improvisation and experimentation (Bragin 2015) which is excessed from the historical record (Roberts 2013b), that Mr. Wiggles and the Hip Hop Continuum faculty aim to teach. Mr. Wiggles is working to teach the participants a Popping aesthetic—how to physically relate to the history of inequality and marginalization contained in the weightedness, the soul, and rock. Mr. Wiggles and the faculty are intentionally producing a social experience through dance—one meant to be conveyed in and through the bodies in performance.

Creating a Collective Body to Perform

In her study of the samba and Orixa dance, Barbara Browning (1995) wrote that "dance is a complex dialogue in which various parts of the body talk at the same time, and in seemingly different languages . . . That is to say [the complex dialogue] spins itself out over time, increasing in meaning as it recounts its origins; and yet it compresses its significance in a momentary image" (2). Though Browning is describing samba, a similar argument can be made about Popping. Mr. Wiggles is laboring to resuscitate a space of "spiritual communion and collective creation" by having everyone in the groove and in the tension created by juxtaposed knees and wrists beating out small, fast movements while the torso and hips spin smoothly and fluidly. To be clear, these accumulations don't exist in an essentialist kind of way. They have accumulated and been preserved through and by the dancing body over time. Mr. Wiggles is reliving, or bringing into the present, those moments when Black and Brown bodies performed to bring awareness to a reality that was not at the time being televised, to dance for the sake of a collective, rather than for self. Indeed, individual bodies are dual in their possibility of also being and producing collective bodies (Haug 1987) in a process of connecting with historical knowledge. Each time Mr. Wiggles repeats the sequence, he reminds his students to hold back and contain. Mr. Wiggles urgings are embodied in "don't throw it away." "Hold back. Live in the tension" is a call to lean into the weight and to engage kinesthetic power so that "the past is brought to bear witness in the present—as a flash of emergence, an instance of emergency, and a moment of production" (Eng and Kazanjian 2003, 5) of fragments of historical knowledge or the accumulated excess that compose the weight. Mr. Wiggles's movements convey the accumulated excess that he is beating out with his body. In performance, accumulated excess becomes a trigger point of knowledge production. In this public space, he is animating the accumulated knowledge toward circulation beyond words—that is, "said" in action and produced in motion—creating possibilities for critical insights (Martin 1990; Jackson 1998; DeFrantz 2004). With every pop, roll, and rock, Mr. Wiggles presses the dancers to sense and to embody the weight. Within the context of racialized power relations, his Brown body is not supposed to blur and bend the lines between the individual and the collective, the personal and the political, the micro and the macro. But this is what the moving, dancing body can do in the performance of accumulated knowledge.

Living in the Tension

A proposal that historical and experiential knowledges of oppression accumulate and are contained in the movement is not an assertion that these knowledges can take hold on bodies with no such experiences. Rather, I am suggesting that the space created by Mr. Wiggles and a program dedicated to teaching the historical and aesthetic principles of dance give students a very different experience from what they would get in a studio, where the focus is on mechanics, and Hip Hop dance tends to be taught in a decontextualized way. This aim is not without its problems.

Mr. Wiggles and the Hip Hop Continuum faculty are negotiating a tension, which is deepened by teaching a group that is ethnically and racially mixed. Hip Hop is subject to intense commodification and purveyed or trafficked as a way to embody cool Blackness, without any of the "problems" of Blackness.[5] Some students appear to resist taking on the weight, approaching the popping movements, postures, and gestures mechanically, moving their bodies like rag dolls, releasing completely at the point of energy exertion. During the teaching breaks, some of the students who identify as b-boys go into head spins and the big showy, acrobatic moves about which Mr. Wiggles speaks, without tension and containment in the body.

Hip Hop dance is much more than a response to or an outcome of racial or socioeconomic marginality. As Bragin (2015) noted, to claim such a narrow response would "naturalize aesthetics as organic artifact and raw material detritus of decaying urban environment" (9). Rather, I aim to highlight the ways in which Popping, specifically, and Hip Hop dance, generally, are kinesthetic sites of engagement and artistic expression, rendering "abstract statements about things that are important" to the dance practitioner (156). Mr. Wiggles is rousing a tension between past and present and individual and collective in this moment of knowledge production. To be sure "oppressed" is more than an individual feeling and experience. In this setting, it is, therefore, important to read the performance of individual bodies as a collective body that the Jacob's Pillow Continuum faculty and Mr. Wiggles is composing. Mr. Wiggles is telegraphing a collective reality rather than an individual experience. He is teaching dancers not only to see with their eyes but also to sense with their bodies, moving past what is seen and said and toward a full-bodied, sensorial, kinesthetic experience. He is choreographing a racial, ethnic, and gendered mix of bodies for the purpose of creating a collective encounter between dancers and, during the weekly performance, between the dances and the audience such that the performance of Popping becomes a condition that allows the accumulated knowledge contained by the dancing body to move and flow. "Hold back" and "put your weight on it and tap" are not only verbal utterances; they are also spoken through the body in the way that Barbara Browning (1995) talks about samba. "The skilled Sambista is able, and obliged to *dizer no pe*'—speak with feet. No other language is required; song is redundant, words are superfluous . . . The feet keep up a rapid patter, while the hips beat out a heavy staccato and the shoulders roll a slow drawl. It is all funky with message" (2). The weight Mr. Wiggles carries and bears down on to produce a pop rolls across the boundaries between the individual weight of lived experience and collective realities and actions.

I propose that no matter what social, political, and economic resources are put in the service of obscuring and forgetting disenfranchising and oppressive practices, the weight of that history is laid bare and contained in movements, postures, and gestures that bring it back into existence, thereby creating a collective body. Mr. Wiggles's physical enactments and verbal utterances work together strategically against the social forces of oppression, which have physical, sentient features that affect individual and collective bodies. From the standpoint of the knowing body, it is characterized by a contained, heavy, *stifling*—that is, in this case, transformed by a sudden break, followed by the relaxation of the wrist and knee and the fluid, conscious release of a contracted torso. To the extent to which Mr. Wiggles cannot completely and thoroughly pass along his individual lived experience, this transformation, which has brought about a sense of aching contained in and by the weight of lived experience, is also limited. Nor can any (one) body stand in for all bodies. Through this toggling between muscle tension and relaxation, Mr. Wiggles can pass along a way into the historical and cultural knowledge that has accumulated in the movements, gestures, and postures. A recent public popular-culture example is Beyoncé's performance of "Formation" at the 2016 Super Bowl. Beyoncé's nod to the Black Panthers formation rehearses a gathering of a powerful, cool, composed, and contained collective Black body in the face of trying, oppressive, even dangerous social conditions. Through this embodied pedagogy, the aesthetics and logics of Popping put into action a project larger than self, where the power of critically conscious bodily practice is, in the hopes of provoking participants to stay in it, to shake up the torpid weight and bridge the distance between acrobatics and dance performance as knowledge production. Thus, when physical expressions of containment as an enactment of social justice come together in performance, the boundaries between the conceptual containment and the conceptual social justice become intimately related and suffused in collective relations of power.

In this performance setting, a public space is created in which Popping triggers a process of knowledge construction for the conceiver, performers, and consumers of dance (Martin 1990). All those drawn into the encounter become involved in some taking-in or processing of the encounter. In a broader sense, the choreographer of the event, Mr. Wiggles, creates an aesthetic experience for the audience and a sentient/embodied experience for the dancers.

Focusing on Mr. Wiggles's micro-level Black and Brown embodiments reveals the macro-level structural injustices that are at stake. Shifting between units of analysis further reveals Mr. Wiggles's experience of the social world and the interaction between collective and individual knowing. A sentient grasp of the space that containment creates in the body and in the performance of Popping is choreographed in order to lead to a deeper understanding of the ways in which the quest for social justice is ever shifting in important and powerful ways. It is not only about what we can learn from containments, but what can we learn from Popping as an enactment, of speaking truth to power, when speaking is done through the aesthetics and logics of Popping and in a broader sense through the dancing body.

NOTES

1. The term "pop-and-lock" is a conflation of two distinct Hip Hop dance styles. While both Popping and Locking can be observed in Earl "Snakehips" Tucker, they are grounded in different histories and contexts.
2. In "How Do We Quote Black and Brown Bodies? Critical Reflections on Theorizing and Analyzing Embodiments" (Roberts 2013b), I detail my analytic process of reaching toward texture and sentience when my visual sense is blurred by hegemonic notions of Black and Brown youth. I discuss how I disrupt problematic, flat, and one-dimensional renditions of Hip Hop dancing youth that my visual perception seems to be fixed upon.
3. The Lurch was a dance made popular in the sixties on *The Addams Family*, a television show whose giant doorman, Lurch, was a prominent character.
4. Since the publication of Tricia Rose's (1994) groundbreaking book *Black Noise*, much has been written about hip hop culture.
5. Bragin (2015) extends this argument:

   If the global cultural forms, including the ways "blackness" is codified and performed by non-black bodies, happens at the expense of critical attention to black radical politics, how do practitioners ethically participate and reflect on their cultural practices? The power to embody the codes of "blackness" seems quite easily to create the belief that participation makes one more accepting, tolerant and appreciative of black culture and black people and in fact, that acceptance, tolerance and appreciation of black culture and black people are reasonable enough social justice aims. This dissertation has taken the view that participation and enjoyment, empowerment and pleasure may encourage appreciation of black culture without encouraging awareness, if not actively encouraging ignorance of antiblackness. (109)

REFERENCES

Akom, A. A. (2009). "Critical Hip-Hop Pedagogy as a Form of Liberatory Praxis." *Equity & Excellence in Education* 42 (1): 52–66.

Alim, H. S. (2006). *Roc the Mic Right: The Language of Hip Hop Culture*. New York: Routledge.

Amin, T. N. (2011). "A Terminology of Difference: Making the Case for Black Dance in the 21st Century and Beyond." *Journal of Pan African Studies* 4 (6): 7–15.

Apfelbaum, E. (1999). "Relations of Domination and Movements for Liberation: An Analysis of Power Between Groups" (Abridged). *Feminism & Psychology* 9: 267–272.

Banks, D. (2011). *Say Word! Voices from Hip Hop Theater*. Ann Arbor: University of Michigan Press.

Baszile, D. M. T. (2009). "Deal with It We Must: Education, Social Justice, and the Curriculum of Hip Hop Culture." *Equity & Excellence in Education* 42 (1): 6–19.

Bell, L. A. (2007). "Theoretical Foundations for Social Justice Education." In *Teaching for Diversity and Social Justice*, edited by M. Adams, L. A. Bell, and P. Griffin, 1–14. New York: Routledge.

Bell, L. A, and Roberts, R. A. (2010). "The Storytelling Project Model: A Theoretical Framework for Critical Examination of Racism through the Arts." *Teachers College Record* 112 (9): 2295–2319.

Bragin, N. (2015). "Black Power of Hip Hop Dance: On Kinesthetic Politics." PhD diss., University of California, Berkeley.

Browning, B. (1995). *Samba: Resistance in Motion.* Bloomington: Indiana University Press.

Chang, J. (2005). *Can't Stop Won't Stop: A History of the Hip-Hop Generation.* New York: Picador.

Chatterjea, A. (2004). *Butting Out: Reading Resistive Choreographies through Works by Jawole Willa Jo Zollar and Chandralekha.* Middletown, CT: Wesleyan University Press.

Conquergood, D., and Johnson, E. P. (2013). *Cultural Struggles: Performance, Ethnography, Praxis.* Ann Arbor: University of Michigan Press.

Daniel, Y. (2005). *Dancing Wisdom: Embodied Knowledge in Haitian Vodou, Cuban Yoruba, and Bahian Candomblé.* Chicago: University of Illinois Press.

DeFrantz, T. F. (2004). "The Black Beat Made Visible: Hip Hop Dance and Body Power." In *Of the Presence of the Body,* edited by A. Lepecki, 64–81. Middletown, CT: Wesleyan University Press.

Denzin, N. K. (2003). *Performance Ethnography: Critical Pedagogy and the Politics of Culture.* New York: SAGE.

Dimitriadis, G. (2009). *Performing Identity/Performing Culture.* New York: Peter Lang.

Duncan-Andrade, J., and Morrell, E. (2008). *The Art of Critical Pedagogy.* New York: Peter Lang.

Dunham, K. (2005). "Form and Function in Primitive Dance." In *Kaiso! Writings by and about Katherine Dunham,* edited by V. A. Clark and S. E. Johnson, 502–507. Madison: University of Wisconsin Press. (Original Dunham essay published in 1942).

Eng, D. L., and Kazanjian, D. (2003). "Introduction: Mourning Remains." In *Loss,* edited by D. L. Eng and D. Kazanjian, 1–25. Berkeley: University of California Press.

Engel, L. (2001). "Body Poetics of Hip Hop Dance Styles in Copenhagen." *Dance Chronicle* 24 (3): 351–372.

Fine, M., Roberts, R. A., Torre, M. E., Bloom, J., Burns, A., Chajet, L., Guishard, M., and Payne, Y. A. (2004). *Echoes of Brown: Youth Documenting and Performing the Legacy of Brown v. Board of Education.* New York: Teachers College Press.

Fisher, M. T. (2007). *Writing in Rhythm: Spoken Word Poetry in Urban Classrooms.* New York: Teachers College Press.

Flores, J. (2004). "Puerto Rocks: Rap, Roots and Amnesia." In *That's the Joint! The Hip-Hop Studies Reader,* edited by M. Forman and M. A. Neal, 69–86. New York: Routledge.

Fogarty, M. (2011). "Dance to the Drummer's Beat: Competing Tastes in International B-Boy/B-Girl Culture." PhD diss., University of Edinburgh. https://www.era.lib.ed.ac.uk/bitstr eam/handle/1842/5889/Fogarty2011.pdf

Fogarty, M. (2012). "Breaking Expectations: Imagined Affinities in Mediated Youth Cultures. *Continuum: Journal of Media & Cultural Studies* 26 (3): 449–462.

Forman, M. (2004). "Introduction." In *That's the Joint! The Hip-Hop Studies Reader,* edited by M. Forman and M. A. Neal, 1–8. New York: Routledge.

Foster, S. L., ed. (1996). *Corporealities: Dancing, Knowledge, Culture and Power.* London: Routledge.

Gaunt, K. (2006). *The Games Black Girls Play: Learning the Ropes from Double-Dutch to Hip-Hop.* New York: New York University Press.

Gilligan, C., Spencer, R., Weinberg, M. K., and Bertsch, T. (2006). "On the *Listening Guide*: A Voice-Centered Relational Method." In *Emergent Methods in Social Research,* edited by S. N. Hess-Biber and P. Leavy, 253–272. Thousand Oaks, CA: SAGE.

Gottschild, B. D. (1996). *Digging the Africanist Presence in American Performance: Dance and Other Contexts*. Westport, CT: Greenwood.

Gottschild, B. D. (2003). *The Black Dancing Body: A Geography from Coon to Cool*. New York: Palgrave MacMillan.

Guzman-Sanchez, T. (2012). *Underground Dance Masters: Final History of the Forgotten Era*. Santa Barbara, CA: Praeger.

Hall, M. R. (2009). Hip-Hop Education Resources. *Equity & Excellence in Education* 42 (1): 86–94.

Haug, F. et al. (1987). *Female Sexualization: A Collective Work of Memory*. Translated by E. Carter. New York: Verso Classics.

Hazzard-Donald, K. (2004). "Dance in Hip-Hop Culture." In *That's the Joint! The Hip-Hop Studies Reader*, edited by M. Forman and M. A. Neal, 584–597. New York: Routledge.

Jackson, J. L., Jr. (1998). "Ethnophysicality, or an Ethnography of Some Body." In *Soul, Black Power, Politics, And Pleasure*, edited by M. Guillory and R. Green, 172–190. New York: New York University Press.

Johnson, I. K. (2011). "B-Boying and Battling in a Global Context: The Discursive Life of Difference in Hip Hop Dance." *Alif: Journal of Comparative Poetics* 31: 173–195.

Johnson, I. K. (2012). "Music Meant to Make You Move: Considering the Aural Kinesthetic." *Sounding Out!* (blog), June 18. https://soundstudiesblog.com/2012/06/18/music-meant-to-make-you-move-considering-the-aural-kinesthetic/

MacCarren, F. (2013). *French Moves: The Cultural Politics of le Hip Hop*. New York: Oxford University Press.

Maranan, D. S. (2005). "Dance Illusioning the Cyborg: Technological Themes in the Movement Practices and Audience Perception of Three Urban Dance Styles." Unpublished MA thesis, Simon Fraser University. summit.sfu.ca/system/files/iritems1/12499/etd7483_DMaranan.pdf

Martin, R. (1990). *Performance as Political Act: The Embodied Self*. New York: Bergin & Garvey.

McCormick, J. (2004). *Writing in the Asylum: Student Poets in the City Schools*. New York: Teachers College Press.

Mitchell, T. (2002). *Global Noise: Rap and Hip Hop Outside the USA*. Middletown, CT: Wesleyan University Press.

Ogbar, J. O. G. (2007). *Hip-Hop Revolution: The Culture and Politics of Rap*. Lawrence: University of Kansas Press.

Osumare, H. (2007). *The Africanist Aesthetic in Global Hip-Hop: Power Moves*. New York: Palgrave Macmillan.

Pulido, I. (2009). "Music Fit for Us Minorities": Latinas/os' Use of Hip Hop as Pedagogy and Interpretive Framework to Negotiate and Challenge Racism." *Equity & Excellence in Education* 42 (1): 57–85.

Roberts, R. A. (2005). "Radical Movements: Katherine Dunham and Ronald K. Brown Teaching toward a Critical Consciousness." PhD diss., City University of New York Graduate Center.

Roberts, R. A. (2011). "Facing and Transforming Hauntings of Race through the Arts." *Equity & Excellence in Education* 44 (3): 330–347.

Roberts, R. A. (2013a). "Dancing with Social Ghosts: Performing Embodiments, Analyzing Critically." *Transforming Anthropology* 21 (1): 1–14.

Roberts, R. A. (2013b). "How Do We Quote Black and Brown Bodies? Critical Reflections on Theorizing and Analyzing Embodiments." *Qualitative Inquiry* 19 (4): 280–287.

Roberts, R. A., Bell, L. A., and Murphy, B. (2008). "Flipping the Script: Analysis of Youth Talk about Race and Racism." *Anthropology and Education Quarterly* 39 (3): 334–354.

Roberts, R.A. (2021). *Baring Unbearable Sensualities: Hip Hop Dance, Bodies, Race, and Power.* Middletown, CT: Wesleyan University Press.

Rose, T. (1994). *Black Noise.* Middletown, CT: Wesleyan University Press.

Schloss, J. G. (2009). *Foundation: B-boys, B-girls and Hip Hop Culture in New York.* New York: Oxford University Press.

Scott, J. C. (1990). *Domination and the Arts of Resistance: Hidden Transcripts.* New Haven, CT: Yale University Press.

Spady, J. G., Meghelli, S., and Alim, H. S. (2006). *Tha Global Cipha: Hip Hop Culture and Consciousness.* Philadelphia: Black History Museum Umum/Loh Publishers.

Valis-Hill, C. (2010). *Tap Dancing America, A Cultural History.* New York: Oxford University Press.

Weiss, J. and Herndon, S. (2001). *Brave New Voices: The Youth Speaks Guide to Teaching Spoken Word Poetry.* Portsmouth, NH: Heinemann.

CHAPTER 21

STAGING HIP HOP DANCE: FLY GIRLS IN THE HOUSE

LEAH "MCFLY" MCKESEY, DIANA "FLY LADY DI" REYES, AND MARY "MJ" FOGARTY

INTRODUCTION

IN a chapter titled, "Not the Average Girl from the Videos: B-Girls Defining Their Space in Hip-Hop Culture," Alesha Dominek Washington (2017) discusses the contributions to Hip Hop culture made by the influential B-Girls Baby Love, Honey Rockwell, and Asia One. Washington argues that the underground Hip Hop spaces, especially those created by women, provide an alternative to how the "bodies of Black women and other women of color are being commodified and sold through the entertainment industry for economic gain" (81). We want to discuss this from the other way around, considering the agency of performers—namely, Black women and other women of color—*within* the entertainment industries, and to argue for their place in Hip Hop histories as well. Women move through spaces both underground and highly-commercialized, as this chapter will demonstrate. In doing so, we want to encourage future research into the "average girl from the videos", insisting that their stories as dancers be foregrounded in future work.[1]

In the spring of 1990, the sketch-comedy television show *In Living Color* served as an influential portrait of Hip Hop culture, presenting the music, comedy, fashion, and, particularly, the dances of its time. Filmed and based in New York City, the show featured an all-(cis)woman dance troupe named the Fly Girls, who performed multiple dance routines at the top of each episode. Weekly, the Fly Girls were introduced by name by the show's creator, Keenan Ivory Wayans. For a dancer to be recognized by name on live television was out of the ordinary at this time, when dancers were usually nameless, as they continue to be in music videos (see Woehrel 2019; Fogarty 2020). Although other variety shows at the time featured dancers, none gave them the celebrity status that this fresh format brought. *In Living Color* gave dancers not only a platform to present Hip Hop routines on a nationally syndicated television show, but also the opportunity to become known as artists in their own right, performing routines that were mostly choreographed by the actor and Brooklyn native Rosie Perez.

Rosie Perez was already a household name before she began choreographing for the Fly Girls. She had already done choreographic work for artists such as Heavy D and the Boyz, LL Cool J, and Diana Ross. Perez's (2014) autobiography describes her early experiences with dance in the family, as well as coping with childhood struggles (and loving the Beatles, among other things that her peers gave her a hard time about). She also talks about issues with entertainment-industry contracts, why she left *Soul Train*, and how she began doing choreography for popular music acts. What becomes clear in her stories is the way that women have to navigate power structures and fight for their right to get paid adequately and to be treated with respect in the culture industries.

Rosie Perez also famously danced for the entire opening sequence of the film *Do the Right Thing* (1989), directed by Spike Lee, which featured crosscuts of her in different outfits including boxing gloves, since the Public Enemy song commissioned for the film, "Fight the Power," provided the soundtrack. According to Lee (1989), by the late 1970s there had been shifts in the experiences of women in society: "Even women in Brooklyn were different. They were more independent than the women I had known, financially, sexually, and emotionally" (15). Lee goes on to write in his journal for the film on April 9, 1988, about considering Rosie Perez for the role, "The thing about Rosie is her intelligence. She is from the street and knows the street" (77). Rosie Perez herself has explained how important this role was to her, and at what personal cost. After filming *Do the Right Thing*, she was recruited by Keenan Ivory Wayans to work on *In Living Color*.

There is no doubt that Perez captured many hearts along the path of her career. What many have noticed about her was her confidence, spunk, courage, and raw street vibe. If anyone in the Hip Hop scene wanted authentic vibes, it is right to say that she would be the perfect fit to understand the true energy needed to accomplish the goal at hand. Perez (2014) herself explains:

> Hip-hop moved me in a way like never before. I never was a "street" kid, but I was part of the post-Vietnam generation who grew up with the residue of inflation, parents' broken dreams, poverty, and heroin-cluttered streets; who had something new and more innovative to offer than the prejudiced world around us predicted for us. Hip-hop was so incredible—mostly poor, West Indian, African American, and Puerto Rican kids from the Bronx created it, but white people and other various racial, social, and economic backgrounds throughout the city also contributed. (It always bothers me when people in the industry state that it was solely a black thing.). (222)

She also describes working with the Fly Girls and her responsibilities, which included selecting the music, editing the tracks, sorting out the music licensing for the songs, creating the choreography, and running the rehearsals.

Taking its inspiration from sketch-comedy institutions like *Saturday Night Live, In Living Color* featured a predominantly African American cast, and presented fresh comedy and culture. The Fly Girls' routines added extra spice and punctuation to the format, providing bumpers between the sketches and commercial breaks, and for the first few seasons appearing at the start of the program. The opening dance sequence was hugely popular with television audiences growing up in the early nineties. Rosie Perez acknowledges how important the dancers were in teaching her about dance. Jossie Harris has said that she didn't have formal dance training, but the other Fly Girls did, so they would teach each other what they knew.

Even in analyses of Hip Hop dance, particular styles and performances are downplayed as mere entertainment, as opposed to serious, lived culture. (See Perillo 2012 for an example of how entertainment is set up as a derogatory category.[2]) Whereas *Soul Train* was respected, many in the African American middle-class community felt that *In Living Color* presented Black social life as cliché street culture and, along with other television shows that arrived at this time, created an unflattering vision of Black culture as "street" culture.

Thomas DeFrantz (2002) has identified how even earlier historical accounts, such as the work of jazz scholars Marshall and Jean Stearns, set up "jazz dance" as a "vernacular" form. In so doing, the Stearns would include white performers' accounts in their categorizations and thereby "overshadow the professional achievements of the artists they interview" (13). As DeFrantz asserts, "Surely, many of the artists included here, such as Aida Overton Walker and the Nicholas Brothers, achieved transcendent mastery in their transformations of 'vernacular' social dance structures of the stage" (13), thereby escaping such derogatory categorizations. For the Fly Girls, their prominent professionalization also excluded them from accounts of Hip Hop dance histories because they didn't fit in neatly. Historians don't place their choreography on the same level as that of artists such as the Nicholas Brothers, excluding them entirely from lineages of serious artists representing Black cultural forms and innovations. And yet, most Hip Hop dance competitions today consist of organized choreography, and the formations are greatly informed by the ideas that the Fly Girls championed.[3]

The Fly Girls have, at best, been a footnote in Hip Hop dance histories. Yet they offer up some rich perspectives about the dances of Hip Hop, which also tend to be excluded from music-focused histories. The majority of the Fly Girls were classically trained in ballet, jazz, tap, and modern dance, presumably because, at the time, Hip Hop dance had yet to be recognized as a legitimate dance form to be taught in a formal setting by esteemed instructors. Since Hip Hop dance took place in streets, parks, community centers, and clubs (see Gaunt 2006), to come in with a formal dance background might have diminished the Girls' validity as authentic Hip Hop dancers in the eyes of some. Dance classes were often seen as sites of inauthenticity, and they still are in some Hip Hop circles, yet taking dance classes is a typical experience for most young girls. In other words, this value judgment, which appears to be a "street versus institution" assignment, might be more accurately reorganized as describing male versus female childhood experiences, especially for aspiring dancers, who take what they can get where they can get it. But by the same token, being a Fly Girl gave these dancers credibility because they had been given a mainstream platform on which to perform Hip Hop dance, where their dance training helped with the technical aspects and in dealing with the pressures of performing on television.

Another reason the Fly Girls might not have been recognized in Hip Hop historical accounts is that they mainly performed choreography, as opposed to the spectacular and vibrantly improvised Black creative expression that was seen on television shows like *Soul Train*. Hip Hop, particularly as a dance form, is rooted in innovation, improvisation, and social dance, so that performing choreography could easily be seen as a form of glorified puppetry, appropriating Hip Hop flavor and fashions in choreographed routines done by beautiful, young, able-bodied women. In their defense, one can easily argue that it was the choreography in and of itself that made their performances accessible, packaged in a way that was presentable, polished, and professional. A hybrid dance form that wasn't ordinarily shown on television was, then, given space and refinement. Routines have always been a part of Hip Hop culture (Gaunt 2006; Morgan 2009), going back to the earliest days of Kool Herc's parties, when the Legendary Twins would plan out routines in advance (Fogarty 2019). Although the B-Boys and poppers who featured in the movies of the 1980s would later become legends in the scene, the same fate did not await the Fly Girls.

Lastly, and unfortunately, the fact that the Fly Girls were women also contributed to their seeming lack of credibility and ultimate erasure. Although several B-Girls (females who "break") represented on street level and even in feature films, the Hip Hop dance world was, and remains, male dominated (Gunn 2021). Although countless women represent Hip Hop internationally, the Fly Girls existed at a time when the only exposure given to women in Hip Hop was either as scantily clad "rump-shakers" or clothed from the neck down with an emphasis on their intellect. We need all types of Hip Hop feminism (Morgan 1999; Grey 2012). Yet, for the Fly Girls to be viewed as respectable women with their sexuality still intact was an anomaly in Hip Hop. These are reasons why they deserve the recognition for what they achieved—to be attractive and skilled and intelligent women, performing in a professional arena, familiar to the masses, representing a culture that often demeaned, objectified, and marginalized women of color.

The aim of this chapter is to ask what it means to see Hip Hop dances in an Afro-diasporic continuum (Fogarty 2020; Durden, this volume) that celebrates women, and thus to challenge some of the exclusions faced by women entering into professionalized roles. Following the work of Tricia Rose (1994), Hip Hop feminist Joan Morgan (1999), Kyra Gaunt (2006), and the Crunk Feminist Collection (Cooper, Morris, and Boylorn 2017), this chapter seeks to consider what Black Hip Hop feminist perspectives offer to the dialogues about Hip Hop dance, from rap fandom to professional Hip Hop dance practices. It needs to be acknowledged that the circulation of Black popular culture is also not without its erasures of the queer corporeal experience (DeFrantz 2012, 2016). We recognize that the styles we talk about are deeply indebted to queer Black men, including our love of *Soul Train* and the space that show takes up in our accounts.[4] We have all had successful careers in our own right, but Leah "McFly" McKesey and Diana "Fly Lady Di" Reyes have viewed the Fly Girls specifically as formative role models to guide their paths. Both were born and raised in metropolitan Canadian cities (Montreal and Toronto respectively) that in the early 1990s lacked viable, local resources for Hip Hop, such as professional mentors.

THE IMPACT OF THE FLY GIRLS

What does it mean for students to engage with Hip Hop dances, and to aspire to be professional dancers who are also versed in choreography and multiple dance styles and techniques? How can they negotiate with streetdance cultures and competitions, while also being professional dancers in various entertainment industries and art worlds? When authenticity is in the eye of the beholder, how can women negotiate building their professionalism (at times positioned as the antithesis of street politics) while still showing their seriousness about Hip Hop, Funk, and Disco techniques?

The Fly Girls dance sequences were shot on the *In Living Color* set, which, in the first two seasons, was constructed to resemble a New York City rooftop. The Girls would do their routines on the roof's flat surface, occasionally taking to the ledges as the camera moved from place to place. Their DJ (DJ SW-1, Shawn Wayans, for the first three seasons and DJ Twist for the final two) would perform atop what was constructed to resemble a fire-escape landing that ascended from the roof. The use of multicolored lighting, spotlights, silhouettes, and smoke machines added extra effects to the already exciting dance routines and fast editing. The dancers were filmed from multiple camera angles in shots that ranged from wide to close-up to pan to in-out zoom to hand-held, making it almost impossible not to want to watch their dance sets to their conclusions. The sequences themselves were only thirty to sixty seconds long, but there was a multitude of them, averaging three spots per episode.

The routines, usually a verse and the beginning of the chorus long (approximately six counts of eight), were generally happy, light, and, one might say, "bubbly," and viewers might catch a close-up of a dancer with a big smile, predominantly in the first two seasons. Thereafter, the dancers took on an occasionally serious tone, their moves increasingly "street" in feel, as opposed to the airy, jazzy vibe in the previous seasons. Their postures also became more hunched in a groove shape as the seasons progressed, giving a more authentic representation of Hip Hop dance in the early 1990s. The Girls had a very "New York" essence—after all, the city was the birthplace of Hip Hop and, at the time, the center of the culture. One probably couldn't find a more legitimate portrayal of Hip Hop dance on a program that aired so widely across North America.

What also made the Girls' inclusion authentic was the music that was used for their routines. Although Hip Hop music was already well out in the world and gaining greater popularity, particularly with the help of other programs such as *The Fresh Prince of Bel-Air* - which began airing the same year as *In Living Color* - it wasn't as ubiquitous as it is today. One could argue that the songs chosen for the Fly Girls' routines were relatively obscure, as most of them weren't exactly singles being played on the radio. Some were known as "b-sides," or songs released in albums but not necessarily recognized in the charts. For example, Queen Latifah's "Mama Gave Birth to the Soul Children," or EPMD's "I'm Mad" were used for routines, and these were songs that may have been heard in an underground club or at a house party, but not so much on the radio, let alone on television. The Fly Girls' performances provided exposure for this music, carefully curated to reflect the authenticity of the voices it represented.

The Role of Routines

The Fly Girls performed onstage in routines that offered a professional and organized way of showcasing Hip Hop dance. Aiming to entertain the audience by always remaining unpredictable, the Girls would constantly be creating new formations and material. As an example, a demonstration onstage might include a group of six dancers posing, while the seventh one hops onstage, busting into a dance and wowing the crowd, followed by an eighth dancer, who flips onstage, going into freestyle, and then the seventh and eighth dancers get into a duo choreography or perhaps a combo dance together; then the rest of the group will come together, and they all get into choreography for a while, which continues easily by bringing on props, or by getting into another variation called the *domino*: this means forming a line, and in a sequence of their two, four, six counts, one person will do a move that will flow along the line, and each dancer does the same, one after another, creating the domino effect (or canon). Another component of a routine would be splitting the group into two or more parts, where each part would do a routine expressing a certain beat of the song: a group of moves on the beat, another on the words, and another group on the snare. This helps the audience to "see" the music with their own eyes. This component would definitely bring the musical form to light by highlighting the different parts of the music. The DJ was usually in a booth overhead - and a man - sometimes with a couple of women dancing beside the turntables.

Fashion Inspiration

Females in Hip Hop were often used as eye-candy, on the periphery in music videos and stage performances. This show was one of the first occasions that female dancers were in the spotlight, sex appeal intact, but with a factor of approachability that we didn't see prior to their reign. With women in Hip Hop often either objectified (e.g., by 2 Live Crew) or seen as intellectuals and covered from the neck down (e.g., Queen Latifah), the Fly Girls' costumes were body conscious with a street edge, with pieces one might find at a high-end department store. What set them apart was their individuality. Each dancer dressed in her own unique way, though together they formed a cohesive look. Their costumes were a testament to Rosie Perez, who wanted to present these women in a tasteful, respectful way, in pieces that were simultaneously aspirational and authentically street. Their costumes were a chance for young girls to see dancers in a light that was creative, fun, and rife with *flava*.

Their fashions also told the story of the song they were presenting, as their outfits were adapted to suit each vibe. For example, when performing to the song "Rump Shaker" by Wreckz-n-Effect, they wore body-conscious yet tasteful, classy outfits to reflect its overtly sexual lyrics and energy. For another performance, they wore oversized plaid button-downs and bandanas. In their dance pieces, their street jazz style was always the base, on top of which they threw in other styles, such as locking, house, and breaking, and vogue/waacking-style-like poses. House is a footwork-centric club dance with Afro-Latin influences ranging from West African dance, salsa, samba, Hip-Hop, and Capoeira, practiced with connection to house music. Waacking/whacking is an African American, queer-founded dance style suggesting "to strike with force," using powerful and dynamic arm gestures to imitate classical Hollywood ingenues, and embody underground Disco music.

These stylishly dressed women entering the stage, wearing clothes expressing different themes, made many people crazy over the fashion. It was really inspirational to see how they would go from wearing prints, to shapes, neon, or spandex, highlighting the creativity that was presented onstage. It was such an amazing experience as a viewer to watch, and imagine what it would be like to be on that stage. The freshness of their style dictated fashion not only to aspiring female dancers, but to everyone watching. Their outfits influenced fashion trends, and viewers would make shopping decisions based on what they saw in each episode—helping revolutionize what was considered Hip Hop fashion.

Firsthand Accounts

The following sections are firsthand accounts by each of us about how the presentation, empowerment, and recognition the Fly Girls received, through the platform of television, had a direct influence on our careers, in terms of both the fashion and the choreographed routines. We introduce ourselves to you as individuals, and tell the story of the Fly Girls through our own perspectives, in order to situate histories of these women through our memories of the impact they had on our lives as professional dancers.

Leah McFly

I'm a passionate artist of many facets, known internationally as Waackeisha for my dancing (Figure 21.1). I teach various dance styles like Hip Hop, waacking, and reggae/dancehall worldwide. I'm also a creative director, stylist, and event planner, mentoring

FIGURE 21.1. Leah "McFly Waackeisha" McKesey. Photograph (c) Julie Soto.

and sharing knowledge of Hip Hop culture in locations from daycares to universities. I've been mentored by Tyrone Proctor (original *Soul Train* dancer), MOPTOP (NYC), Dazl, Blak Kat, and Shauna Roberts (Montreal), and I've formed a deep-rooted base here in Montreal. My background is rooted in Barbados (mother) and Belize (father).

My mother is a body builder and now a caregiver for the mentally challenged, and my father was a dental technician, model, bodybuilder, jeweler, and dancer. My father, who did popping and locking (different dance styles, for those unfamiliar), understood the desire my siblings and I had for entertainment, and he nurtured our interests. For me, my two older brothers, Lincoln and Lance, and my younger sister named Lydia, dancing was a big part of our family life.

Growing up in the 1990s, TV played a big role in our lives and helped us to keep up to date. We would rush home from school to catch certain shows on TV or look through *Jet* magazine or the TV guide to find out when our favorite shows would come on. I loved tuning into *Soul Train* on Saturdays while we did our chores. My brothers and I would make sure our chores ended up in the basement by one o'clock, so we could watch the show. We would put on decent clothes and act like we were dancing live on the show with all the dancers. The problem was that some shows wouldn't be on until past our bedtime, like *Saturday Night Live* (*SNL*) or *In Living Color*. The latter was a more culturally diverse version of *SNL*, but they both entailed funny skits. *In Living Color* was a more street version, with more stories I could relate to, but what I really watched on the show was the Fly Girls.

These women gave inspiration not only to young girls like me, but also to grown men like my dad. Everyone looked forward to watching these girls come out, dancing to the opening theme song in funky, stylish outfits, and doing creative and versatile routines. They consisted of about six, ethnically diverse girls with versatile backgrounds in dance forms such as jazz, breaking, House, and Hip Hop. They were energetic and confident. I remember them as powerful, strong women who were respected by the cast. It was essential that the Fly Girls were given the spotlight and introduced by their names. Though some of the members changed along the way, their names were: Carl French, Deidre Lang, Lisa Marie Todd, Michelle Morrison, Jossie Harris, Carie Ann Inaba, and Jennifer Lopez. This show was iconic. It launched the careers of many of the dancers who were a part of the show.

My father always let me watch the Fly Girls open the show at midnight, and he would then promise to record the rest of the show for me to watch the next day. Having a father who was heavily into music and dance made it easier for me to fully enjoy my journey in Hip Hop through my life growing up. I had wished and wondered what it would be like to be in their position; waiting for my dad's recordings was like waiting for Christmas—I was so excited to see the new vibes displayed on each new show.

After school I would rush home to pop in the videotape and get ready to dissect every vibe, move, and style of the Fly Girls. I would watch *In Living Color* all dressed up in my outfit, ready to rewind the tape to get the routine down. Sometimes my brother would join me, or even my dad would get involved, rewinding the tape for us so we could focus on the moves. Once learned, we would then showcase our moves, and sometimes drop some combos on kids in the park or basketball court, or even show our cousins. But we would also create and remix some of the choreo after, because we felt that if we tried to invent moves, and not just copy them, we could be creative enough one day to choreograph or be entertainers ourselves. This is proof that the Fly Girls also inspired males like my brother, and we all learned something each and every episode.

The Fly Girls would hype up the live studio crowd as they hit the stage. The stage scene had that natural rawness from the New York City streets, brought to life on the set, which really taught the general public how to receive Hip Hop openly in its truest form. Based on the choreographic vision of Rosie Perez, the character of the dancers throughout each performance would match how they were dressed. Their spandex look, for example, was reminiscent of a scene in *The Fresh Prince of Bel Air* when Vivian went to a dance class.

I recall my brothers and I making a shopping list of things we wanted to buy on our family trip to New York. Watching *In Living Color*, music videos, dance shows like *Soul Train*, or sitcoms like he *Fresh Prince of Bel Air* definitely inspired our list, as we were excited to get our hands on the latest Hip Hop streetwear, which we couldn't easily access in Montreal, which was still behind on trends. After watching the Fly Girls in a few episodes, I wanted to get a multicolored blazer and matching jeans suits to have for my talent show. What excited us most about our New York trips was coming back home and flaunting our new outfits to our friends at school, at parties, or at social gatherings. Waiting for people to ask where we got it from, with the feeling of looking fly like the television opening sequences we admired, and them wanting to be in our shoes, did quite a number for our confidence. This is what encouraged my love not only for dance but for fashion, and, as I grew older within the dance community, style was a big part of my representation. Many people would call me "Fresh Princess," but the name didn't stick with me. So, being known for my love of fashion and being fly, wanting to be a Fly Girl and my last name being McKesey, not to mention loving the movie *Back to the Future* and admiring the character Marty McFly, it was right to then say I birthed my official Hip Hop name, "Leah McFly."

Fly Lady Di

I'm a multidisciplinary artist with a focus on dance performance and DJing (Figure 21.2). I've also been a known educator in Hip Hop, House Dance, and Waacking in my hometown of Toronto, having learned from the pioneers of those styles, such as Elite Force, MOPTOP and Dance Fusion (RIP Marjory Smarth), in New York City, where I also lived for four years.

Years before the television debut of the Fly Girls, I had become fixated on Janet Jackson's "Rhythm Nation" music video. Watching that video at age seven had sealed my fate as a professional dancer. But then, here were these gorgeous girls—a multi-racial cast of them—donning their brightly colored, body-con costumes, offering up multiple routines per episode on a weekly basis. Not to mention that Rosie Perez choreographed these routines, someone I had fawned over in movies as a raw, authentic New York

FIGURE 21.2. Fly Lady Di DJing and dancing at Chocolate Jungle, Montreal, 2019. Photograph (c) Julie Soto.

woman, whose accent I would imitate in the schoolyard to many laughs. The Fly Girls were introduced by name by the show's creator, Keenan Ivory Wayans, in every episode. It was a chance for people to identify each individual dancer and recognize them for their work. Every single episode.

Their debut had happened before I learned how to record live television with a VCR, so it was only after 1994 that I was able to record the Fly Girls' routines. When *In Living Color* was syndicated on BET in 1998, I was able to record the routines on a daily basis. This was aptly timed, as I had become increasingly familiar with one par- ticular dancer named Jossie Harris (now Jossie Harris Thacker). Jossie was a fixture in all of the televised and recorded dance performances that I was obsessed with: Janet Jackson's "You Want This, That's the Way Love Goes" and "If"; Mary J. Blige's "Real Love"; Michael Jackson's "Remember the Time," and so on. I studied Jossie on a daily basis, and knew all her facial expressions, her hard hits, her grooves. It was the era of *In Living Color* with Jossie Harris, Lisa Thompson, Deidre Lang, and Jennifer Lopez. I felt closely connected to the music of the time, and to their vibes and their costumes. The four of them also had a cohesiveness that wasn't as apparent in eras before or after them. Additionally, Jossie and Jennifer were from Uptown and the Bronx, a place I al- ways somehow had a connection to, and knowing they were from there drew me to them even more.

I don't know where I found it, but I had cut a photo of the four of them out of a mag- azine and pasted it onto my diary in 1994 (when I was twelve years old and entering grade 7). I had just started taking dance class for the first time, and had become obsessed with graffiti and Hip Hop culture, in general, from all the cassettes and magazine clippings my cousin Jon the Barber sent me from Florida. These were exclusive, because that era (pre-Internet) forced tangible items to be sent via snail mail, and many things containing Hip Hop culture were simply unavailable at the time in Canada. Through my cousin, I came to know style, slang, and music I had never heard of. I also realized that I needed a graffiti name; something I could identify myself with in the culture - like an alter ego of sorts. I had always admired the females in the graffiti scene, like Lady Pink. My family had nicknamed me Lady Di, since my mother named me after Princess Diana the Princess of Wales. Princess Diana was expecting Prince Harry the same time I was born. And I was knowingly obsessed with the Fly Girls. Lady Di. Fly Girls. Fly Lady. Fly Lady Di! I had a name. I wrote it down everywhere. Fly Lady Di wuz here.

My mother had only been able to afford one year of dance classes for me at a pro- fessional dance studio, and so I was left to my own devices after that. I was inspired to apply to a high school dance program at a school adjacent to where I lived. We had an opportunity at the audition to perform a two-minute solo dance routine to a song and style of our choosing. I chose to do a Hip Hop routine to R. Kelly's "Be Happy," featuring the Notorious B.I.G. The judging panel was mortified. They had never seen or heard of Hip Hop, and they sure as hell wouldn't accept my non-ballet-trained self. It was the first time I got a sense of reality. I was going to have to fight my way through to get to my dream. At the time, Hip Hop was not as widely accepted as it is today.

By the time I entered grade 9, I had become an outcast because of a party that had happened prior to the start of the school year. I was with my best friend at the time, Kristine, and we were getting very hype off the music. We had celebrated our first ever Caribana [Festival] that summer as well, so we were particularly fond of each other and our willingness to dance at any given point. I had danced hard through the whole party, and at one point my dancing became a little too racy. Nothing too obscene happened; I just became particularly open—grinding on dudes and doing the splits. The result of this was that at the start of the school year no one really talked to me. I also wasn't a staple of any particular group of friends. I became kind of a loner, someone who ate lunch either alone or with one other person, or I did some sort of school activity to mask the lack of social engagement. I remember learning about the spring talent show and thinking I could maybe do a solo since I had done one over the summer in the mall to much success. I had worked really hard on my routine; every day after school, I would practice either in front of the TV or in my room for, at least, an hour and a half to two hours. I would often watch and rewind Fly Girl routines to assist in my "choreo" creation. The time had come, May 1997. I was going to show the school what I was really about. As soon as I hit the stage, people got on their feet and screamed. Everyone grooved along. Numerous people, students and teachers alike, came up to me the next day to congratulate me; even if they hadn't seen my performance, they had heard about it. It was nonstop. Everyone wanted to be my friend. I had gained my superpower.

FIGURE 21.3. Diana Reyes, age 14. Markville Mall Hip-Hop dance solo, 1996. Photograph (c) Weldon Reyes.

"Mary-Jane" Fogarty

I started off as a B-Girl (Figure 21.4), got badly injured, went to graduate school, and eventually became a professor of dance. My grandparents immigrated from the UK to Canada after World War II—my last name is an Irish one, but we also have British and Scottish in the family—and my parents grew up in Southern Ontario. I was born in Calgary, Alberta, and raised in Brandon, Manitoba and then Thunder Bay, Ontario. I grew up making music, dancing, playing sports, and trying to keep up with my older brother, who read encyclopedias for fun and by grade 6, carried a briefcase to school for his papers. I didn't watch much television, and we didn't have cable except for one summer.

I was the first B-Girl in London, Ontario, to start representing in battles. I had an all B-Girl crew in the early 2000s and for a short-lived time a crew called the Organic Mechanics. Between those crews, I organized a big event called Operation B-Droid with over 500 people in attendance to watch breaking events and the name was given out of my frustrations over the gendered language in breaking. After I got my PhD, I joined the Flyin' Jalapeno crew, who I had performed with already at Edinburgh Festival Theatre, and became the lead facilitator/lecturer for KeepRockinYou arts collective that runs the Toronto B-Girl Movement and was founded by Judi Lopez. Both Judi and Soupy

FIGURE 21.4. Mary Fogarty aka Bgirl Mary-Jane, judging LUNAR BUGout Jam with Dana Schnitzer aka Bgirl Radio (*immediate left*) and Jennifer Casimir aka Bgirl Bounce. Montreal, Canada, December 2014. Photograph © Emmanuelle LePhan aka Bgirl Cleopatra, Tentacle Tribe.

Souphommanychanh of KeepRockinYou were Hip Hop dancers doing routines long before they became B-Girls.

On visits to Toronto, when I was only a few years into breaking, I had performed at Honey Jam events (organized by and featuring women of color) and Nathan Philip Square (with Nylda "Lady Noyz" Gallardo and Miranda "Tangerine," the only out B-Girl at the time locally), and we tried to incorporate a bit of a routine for the "show" aspect of these sorts of performances. I don't love doing choreographed routines, because freestyling is how I practiced and felt most comfortable, even for public performances, since I was a young dancer. Lady Noyz was more familiar with routines and grew up inspired by the Fly Girls.

I am open to all experiences being counted, especially thinking about how women can navigate their identities with confidence as authentic and meaningful, whether they have formal dance training or not. A lot of girls' parents enroll them in dance programs growing up, so it's often part of what it is to be female. Treating girls' childhoods as inauthentic is a strategy of misogyny in the hip hop circles where this occurs (see Roberts 2011, 2013a, 2013b, and this volume, for scholarship on racial tensions and bids for authenticity in dance spaces and studio culture). One of my memories from an early Back 2 Da Underground event, hosted by B-Boy Dyzee, involved a group of mostly women of color performing a Hip Hop dance routine inbetween breaking battles. At the time, I was always a bit cross when b-girl battles were treated like intermissions etc. These women were doing a hip hop routine, and I can remember some novice B-boys, new to the scene, on the side making fun of their movements. Benzo from Bag of Trix got on the microphone and shut them down, though. He said that the women performing were more Hip Hop than these b-boys making fun of them. He is an influential dancer, so people took note, and this also clarified for me what Hip Hop is and who it's for.

Leah McFly

The inspiration I had gotten from the Fly Girls led me to create my own Fly Girl path within my waacking crew that was formed in 2008, internationally known as IHOW, the Imperial House of Waacking, now called "The Chapter Canada." Montreal was the birthplace of the first chapter of this house, which has now spread to many countries with the mentorship of pioneer Tyrone Proctor (an original *Soul Train* dancer) and Aus Ninja, his young protégé. Tyrone coached our Mother of the House, Nedge "Blak Kat" Valme, and Princess Samantha "Shayla" Hinds, who was also the first chosen one initiated into the crew. She was followed by me, Essence, Duchess, Foxy Lou, Deyva, Cherry, Mean Jean, Dominique, and our recently recruited member Haze. Our group today consists of eleven members who all come from different dance backgrounds, but many of us do a minimum of three styles. To present unique choreography, we often mix waacking with another dance style, such as waacking/house, waacking/locking, or even waacking/Hip Hop. When we decided to start with Hip Hop, I had the idea to make the

Fly Girls our reference point. Like rapper Biggie Smalls would say, "Well if you don't know, now you know." I let the girls "know who didn't know" about this TV show, and the meaning and value of the show for Hip Hop. I gave the dancers some homework to watch the Fly Girls compilation videos on YouTube, and study what they were wearing and their character and vibes, and told them if they couldn't match up with the package, they wouldn't be able to perform.

They all took on the challenge, embraced it, and admitted learning a lot from the process. Even watching the clips for the first time, they were very drawn in and intrigued by the Fly Girls. We were all entering a battle in New York, and decided to ask the event organizers if we could perform our Fly Girls homage there. We took a theme we saw on the show using primary colors and items of black sequins. We did another one wearing black-and-white polka dots and stripes with a pop of color, and we've done a neon one with bathing suit tops and spandex. We performed the neon style at a big dance event called Juste Debout, which originates in Paris, France, but had a qualification battle in our city, Montreal.

We opened with a song of the '90s R & B group Black Street "Baby Be Mine" acapella remix. I remember we had a standing ovation after performing this. Dancing to New Jack Swing was difficult because of the high tempo, and the inclusion of many moves and jumps. Also, using all elements of the body at the same time meant we needed a lot of cardio training to execute this, while looking like you're not about to drop dead onstage. Performing with character really comes in to save the day. This helps to hide the fatigue, and you can dim and vibe your moves while expressing different things with your face. Waacking is performed with Disco and a diva vibe, adding Hip Hop, such as the "running man." We also added waack arms, which can be a double workout, but is very interesting to watch. We would take little combos from the show as reference points, and then add our own shapes to showcase our creativity with a fusion of dance styles.

My commitment to the dance led me to travel, teach, choreograph, battle, and perform worldwide. I loved traveling to New York, where I would often go to festivals throughout the summer. Seven or eight years into my travels, I was in New York City taking part in the Ladies of Hip Hop Festival, which at the time was probably my third or fourth time attending. I judged a battle that day and Fly Lady Di was one of the contestants. The organizer Michelle told me there was a Fly Girl somewhere in the room. I got so excited! I looked behind me, and there I saw the Original Fly Girl herself, Jossie Harris!

Keeping my cool, but still very overjoyed, I expressed how much I loved watching her dance and seeing her appear in almost all my favorite music videos, like Michael Jackson's "Remember the Time," Mary J Blige's "Real Love," Bobby Brown's "Humping Around," and Janet Jackson's "That's the Way Love Goes," to name a few. Through speaking to her, I got to learn about the things she's doing now, like with her BeFLYCreate company (www.beflycreate.com), which provides acting coaching, mentorship, and teaching about the industry to youth. Michelle gave me a very nice introduction, which helped lead our conversation. Going from hearing my pioneer dance friends Voodoo

FIGURE 21.5. IHOW, now The Chapter Canada. Photo taken in Montreal for Juste Debout qualifiers, January 29, 2012. IHOW performed a special Fly Girls tribute performance and got a standing ovation. This old-school dance style takes a lot of energy, and they had fun doing it. *From the left*: Leah "McFly Waackeisha" McKesey, Martine "Cherry" Bruneau, Erich "Mean Jean" Etienne, Sabrina "Duchess" Del Duca, Valerie "Deyva" Chartier, and Nadine "Essence" Sylvestre.

Ray, Buddha Stretch, Link, Suga Pop, and others relate the events and stories from their day to seeing them interact together in the same room with me was very refreshing, and validated my success at living my own Fly Girl dream. With Michelle the organizer and two other friends of mine, we made sure to take a '90s-style Fly Girls picture using their iconic jazz poses to conclude our first meeting. As she hung around and jammed with us during the event, I was very happy to be able to call one of the Fly Girls my friend.

The next day, Fly Lady Di and I performed for the Ladies of Hip Hop Showcase at Alvin Ailey. We performed a sexy duo number together. We practiced online, and at our friend Voodoo Ray's house once in NYC. We wore gold dresses and gold heels; we were there to represent for the ladies. Later, after the show, Jossie came up to us outside to tell us how much we killed it, and that she loved our looks and energy onstage. I remember Lady Di and I looked at each other in excitement, responding to her, "Thank you sooooo much, we're so glad you got to see us perform!" It meant a lot to have that exchange with her after having watched her growing up, and now seeing our inspiration give us props, and to see the performers we've become; it was truly a rewarding moment. Once again,

FIGURE 21.6. Leah "McFly Waackeisha" McKesey was a guest judge at the All Ladies Battle at Ladies of Hip Hop, July 19, 2015. *From left*: Leah "McFly Waackesiha" McKesey, Michele Byrd McPhee (creator of Ladies of Hip Hop), Jossie Harris Thacker (original Fly Girl), Melissa "Melly Mel" Flerangile, and Nadine "Essence" Sylvestre. Photograph by Melika Dez.

we concluded by taking selfie pictures with her, to have a warm memory of us being true fans and now newfound friends.

Fly Lady Di

In May 2004, I made the bold move of moving to New York City to follow my dance dreams. Out alone one night, at a party thrown by my dance friends the Amount Boyz, at the end of the night, sitting at the opposite end of a banquette, a curious face emerged, staring at me. "What are you?" He blatantly asked about my ethnicity, as did many people I met in New York. I couldn't help but laugh. That face belonged to none other than the legendary dancer and party promoter Raymond "Voodoo Ray" Ultarte, who almost instantly after meeting him became my best friend for over a decade.

Sitting on his couch one day, and watching countless VHS tapes of his dance work in the '90s, I mentioned my obsession with Jossie Harris, and I sat in disbelief when he told me they had dated for four years. They were known to the dance world as the hottest dance couple, booking all the gigs, as evidenced by their high visibility in music videos, tours, and award shows they were invited to in their prime. He mentioned that she was also a Capricorn, which made me feel even closer to her. I was one degree away from Jossie now, and I felt that much more fulfilled.

FIGURE 21.7. Chocolate Jungle Fly Girls Edition performance at Chocolate Jungle, Montreal, 2019. *Left to right*: Lynn "DJ Bles-sed" Corcuera, Leah "McFly" McKesey, and Diana "Fly Lady Di" Reyes. Photograph (c) Julie Soto.

Meeting Jossie Harris (Fly Lady Di)

Summer of 2015, Leah and I met up in New York to perform a routine she and I had created through FaceTime for the Ladies of Hip Hop showcase at Alvin Ailey, but before that was the annual battle which she judged for waacking, and which I competed in (made it as far as Top 8 in House). Then Jossie appeared in all her splendor, as if floating on a cloud beside Ray at that very moment. I stood there in awe. "Oh my God, that's Jossie." I said to him, hiding behind him as a shy little girl would with her mother's skirt. "I'll introduce you," he said. Which he did. She was so kind and bubbly, her dimples so distinct as she smiled. I was literally speechless in her presence.

The following evening, after Leah and I performed, Jossie was there, congratulating us on our performance, "You ladies killed it up there," she said. I couldn't believe it. Was this really happening? Did Jossie Harris, the one source of inspiration that I've had up to that moment, really just compliment me on my performance? She did. She actually just did.

Jossie had taught an acting workshop the next day which Ray attended. I met up with them in midtown, after I had crashed an audition to tour with Azealia Banks and got cut after the second round. After the class, she was filming snippets for her website at the time, JustJossie.com, and she filmed an interview with Ray and also myself, saying, "The next time we interview you, you'll be on tour." Encouraging words from my idol. Flabbergasted.

We kept in touch, and a few years later, in October 2017, Ray's untimely passing hit us both incredibly hard. I felt closer to her, knowing that she was very close to him and loved him as much as I did. He was a big reason for my success as a dancer, and if it hadn't been for him and his encouragement (I later learned), Jossie would have never pursued a career in dance. He planted seeds in both of us, and his uplifting support for our gifts were in large part what helped us grow. Would I be as close to Jossie without Ray's connection? I'll never know. But it is a fact that Ray connected me to my idol, someone who has had, and forever will have, an enormous impact on me as a dance artist.

Leah McFly

Since our meeting with Jossie in 2015 at the Ladies of Hip Hop festival, Jossie and I have kept in touch on social media, with various likes and comments for her throwback posts of her back-in-the-day music videos and her times as a Fly Girl. Still exploring my love and passion for the Fly Girls, I'm now talking in schools about my life as a female dancer of color in Hip Hop culture, and I wanted to get a deeper, clearer understanding of some personal details she could retell from her past, from being on the show and the impact she felt they have made thus far. Knowing this would help reassure me about the things I've been doing right in my career, and to closely look at elements of her experience that I can take from, learn, and apply from this point on. It would be nice to look back and see the components of our lives that we do have in common.

I connected with Jossie to ask her some more questions about her experience as a dancer in the industry. Jossie described her dancing practices as follows:

> The dances I do now are mostly Hip Hop, but I also love African dance and salsa; those have always been my styles, and obviously dancing to house music, where it all started for me. With my family, being that I'm mixed, I'm half Puerto Rican half African American, on my Spanish side I listen to a lot of Latin music; on my father's side I listen to African American music.

When asked about Hip Hop culture, Jossie explained:

> [Hip Hop] is an expression that comes from the music relationship with the type of beats and an urban influence Hip Hop comes from the streets, I originally, . . . I grew up in Harlem so it's very much a part of me. Hip Hop is me. I have a very close relationship with Hip Hop the music, the style, the attitude even that we were going to make it no matter what.

Here Hip Hop is seen as deeply connected to the music, to where she is from, and to an attitude of survival. This is the aesthetic blueprint of the dance. Her influences, though, were not always Hip Hop based, and speak to a larger tradition of African American dance lineages and celebrities:

It was the Nicholas Brothers who paved the way for us before Debbie Allen; the whole *Fame* movement was a big influence for me as well. Watching it really opened me to a lot of things I wasn't really exposed to at first, so dance became that: watching them. In terms of back in the day, the guys who were doing the popping and locking was an influence for me, like the *Soul Train* dancers, the Electric Boogaloos, dancers like Fluky Luke, Greg Campbell Junior, Pope, Bill Slim the Robot Williams, Shabbadoo. Tony Basil would later dance with them.

As we noted above, choreography and fashion choices worked together to highlight the Fly Girls' Hip Hop style; as Jossie put it:

I think we brought more of the choreography. I think the Fly Girls represented that embodied Hip Hop. We weren't about freestyling, so we institutionalized it and gave it a little more structure, because it was all about the choreography with us, and so I think we brought to the forefront more, I guess, that part of our contribution. We stepped it up in the style of clothing; we made it sexier, with our choice of clothing, whereas Hip Hop was a little more tomboyish with sweatpants, sweatshirts, sneakers, and we sophisticated it more and made it sexier as the Fly Girls.

Style or fashion was a big inspiration for us when I look back at it, how we rocked our clothing, and also what was going on in the world at the time. Rosie Perez was the choreographer, and what was going on then were the riots, the Tupac and Biggie rivalry, and that the whole East Coast / West Coast thing. I think what was happening in the world was a huge inspiration in terms of the songs we danced to.

Besides the Fly Girls performances, Jossie has continued to be versatile in her dance styles, and has continued in her practice:

I'm still doing the same dances. I was mostly a house head and was doing Hip Hop. I was doing it all actually, can't say I'm only doing one particular dance. In terms of moves, we would vogue. Voguing was . . . it was really hot back then, and we did moves like the Roger Rabbit, Cabbage Patch, and the Running Man, which they did a lot of that. Kid-n-Play was very influential. Biz Markie was hot, and the new jack swing was a big deal then.

Going from watching the Fly Girls on TV to emulating them bedroom dancing or in my talent shows to then traveling, meeting new people, and also talking and connecting to a Fly Girl is surreal. It has proved to me every day that, in search of your own soul, you connect with other souls, who then inspire you to continue your journey. Jossie and the other Fly Girls paved the way for many women in Hip Hop, and deserve all the credit for their hard work in representing where they are from, and how it was done.

Final Thoughts (Fly Lady Di)

To this day, I reference the Fly Girls routines. No matter how much more complex and intricate dance routines have become today, there is something so satisfying

FIGURE 21.8. Chocolate Jungle Fly Girls Edition performance at Chocolate Jungle, Montreal, 2019. *Left to Right*: Samantha "Sam I Am Montolla" Hinds, Leah "McFly" McKesey, Diana "Fly Lady Di" Reyes, Lynn "DJ Bles-sed" Corcuera 2019. Photograph (c) Julie Soto

about watching routines, fashion, and music that were made in the '90s. In a way, the Fly Girls entity was ahead of its time. There is a reason people still mention and pay homage to them. Since then, there hasn't been a nationally televised show that took as much care with the cohesion, presentation, authenticity, and impact that an all-female, in-house dance troupe could have. The attention to detail, the individual stytes, the visually intense editing, and the different moods that were created have yet to be matched on a consistent and forthcoming basis. It's easy to take for granted the amount of time, energy, and effort that it took to create such ground-breaking work—they made it look so easy and fun. It remains a breath of fresh air for me to watch their routines, and I am endlessly inspired by them and the creativity of Rosie Perez.

I can't even begin to explain why having positive female mentors and/or role models in dance is so important. I'm not even sure if the creators of the Fly Girl entity were aware of their eventual impact on young aspiring dancers for multiple generations, across ethnicities and socio-economic backgrounds. They gave Hip Hop dancers not only a sense of attainable cool, but a huge power to be seen as often and as fiercely as they were, on a polished and professional platform for the general public to take in. I would only wish that something as unique, innovative, and visionary would be created for this generation; or maybe it's now up to us to create it.

FIGURE 21.9. Jossie Harris Thacker, Diana Reyes, and Leah McKesey pose for a pic after the Ladies of Hip Hop showcase festival weekend, at which Leah and Diana performed, July 21, 2015. New York City.

ACKNOWLEDGMENTS

Thank you to Tommy DeFrantz, Naomi Bragin, Michele Byrd McPhee, and Moncell Durden for feedback on the chapter as it developed.

NOTES

1. This is continuing the work of one of Fogarty's first academic inspirations, filmmaker and author Rachel Raimist (2007), who argues that we need to complicate "good girl/bad girl dichotomous frames" in which "heterosexist society divides us" (3).
2. See Katrina Hazzard-Gordon's (1990) *Jookin': The Rise of Social Dance Formations in African American Culture* for a longer history of Black social dance as entertainment, especially in live settings.
3. The accounts that follow, especially McKesey's of her childhood experience of watching *In Living Color* and then creating her own dances, demonstrate how choreography and

improvisation inform each other, blending into less dichotomous understandings, as true for theatrical traditions and club settings and living-room performances.

4. Nelson George traces this television dance lineage back to *American Bandstand* in his interview in the PBS show *Everybody Dance Now*, in the episode that first aired October 2, 1991. Tricia Rose (1994) points out how this documentary demonstrates early Hip Hop dance's influence on developments like the Fly Girls "illustrating the centrality of Hip Hop dance style in contemporary popular entertainment" (51).

References

Cooper, B. C., Morris, S. M., and Boylorn, R. M. (2017). *The Crunk Feminist Collection.* New York: Feminist Press.

DeFrantz, T. F. (2002). "African American Dance: An Unchecked History." In *Dancing Many Drums: Excavations in African American Dance*, edited by T. F. DeFrantz, 3–35. Madison: University of Wisconsin Press.

DeFrantz, T. F. (2012). "Unchecked Popularity: Neoliberal Circulations of Black Social Dance." In *Neoliberalism and Global Theatres: Performance Permutations*, edited by L. Nielsen and P. Ybarra, 128–140. Basingstoke, UK: Palgrave MacMillan.

DeFrantz, T. F. (2016) "Bone-Breaking, Black Social Dance, and Queer Corporeal Orature." *Black Scholar* 46 (1): 66–74.

Fogarty, M. (2019). "Why Are Breaking Battles Judged? The Rise of International Competitions." In *The Oxford Handbook of Dance and Competition*, edited by Sherril Dodds, 409–428. New York: Oxford University Press.

Fogarty, M. (2020). "Following the Thread: Toronto's Place in Hip Hop Dance Histories." In *We Still Here: Hip Hop North of the 49th Parallel*, edited by C. Marsh and M. V. Campbell, 97–115. Montreal: McGill-Queen's University Press.

Gaunt, K. D. (2006). *The Games Black Girls Play: Learning the Ropes from Double-Dutch to Hip Hop.* New York: New York University Press.

Grey, L. (2012). "True Fuckin' Playas: Queering Hip-Hop through Drag Performance." In *Hip-Hop(e): The Cultural Practice and Critical Pedagogy of International Hip Hop*, edited by B. J. Porfilio and M. J. Viola, 79–94. New York: Peter Lang.

Gunn, R. (2021). "Where the# bgirls at? Politics of (in) visibility in breaking culture." *Feminist Media Studies*, 1–16.

Hazzard-Gordon, K. (1990). *Jookin': The Rise of Social Dance Formations in African American Culture.* Philadelphia: Temple University Press.

Lipsitz, G. (1994). *Dangerous Crossroads: Popular Music, Postmodernism and the Poetics of Place.* London: Verso.

Morgan, J. (1999). *When Chickenheads Come Home to Roost: A Hip Hop Feminist Breaks It Down.* New York: Simon & Shuster.

Perez, R. (2014). *Handbook for an Unpredictable Life: How I Survived Sister Renata and My Crazy Mother, and Still Came out Smiling (with Great Hair).* New York: Three Rivers Press.

Perillo, J. L. (2012). "An Empire State of Mind: Hip-Hop Dance in the Philippines." In *Hip-Hop(e): The Cultural Practice and Critical Pedagogy of International Hip Hop*, edited by B. J. Porfilio and M. J. Viola, 42–64. New York: Peter Lang.

Raimist, R. (2007). "B-Girls, Femcees, Graf Girls and Lady Deejays: Women Artists in Hip Hop." In *Home Girls Make Some Noise: Hip Hop Feminism Anthology*, edited by G. D. Pough, E. Richardson, A. Durham, and R. Raimist, 1–3. Mira Loma, CA: Parker Publishing.

Roberts, R. A. (2011). "Facing and Transforming Hauntings of Race Through the Arts." *Equity & Excellence in Education* 44 (3): 330–347.

Roberts, R. A. (2013a). "Dancing with Social Ghosts: Performing Embodiments, Analyzing Critically." *Transforming Anthropology* 21 (1): 4–14.

Roberts, R. A. (2013b). "How Do We Quote Black and Brown Bodies? Critical Reflections on Theorizing and Analyzing Embodiments." *Qualitative Inquiry* 19 (4): 280–287.

Robinson, C. (1983). *Black Marxism: The Making of the Black Radical Tradition.* London: University of North Carolina Press.

Robinson, D. (2020). *Hungry Listening: Resonant Theory for Indigenous Sound Studies.* Minneapolis: University of Minnesota Press.

Rose, T. (1994). *Black Noise: Rap Music and Black Culture in Contemporary America.* Middletown, CT: Wesleyan University Press.

Washington, A. D. (2007). "Not the Average Girl from the Videos: B-Girls Defining Their Space in Hip-Hop Culture." In *Home Girls Make Some Noise: Hip Hop Feminism Anthology*, edited by G. D. Pough, E. Richardson, A. Durham, and R. Raimist, 80–91. Mira Loma, CA: Parker Publishing.

Woehrel, M. F. (2019). "On Popular Dance Aesthetics: Why Backup Dancers Matter to Hip Hop Dance Histories." *Performance Matters* 5 (1): 116–131.

CHAPTER 22

BATTLES AND BALLETS

Hip Hop Dance in France

ROBERTA SHAPIRO

TRANSLATION BY DAVID LAVIN[†], ROBERTA
SHAPIRO, AND IMANI KAI JOHNSON

In France today, nearly forty years after making its first appearance, Hip Hop dance retains an element of equivocacy. Critics celebrate it as a buoyant and original artistic form, an exciting "trend in contemporary dance" (Bédarida 1997). At the same time, in the collective imagination it is associated with the underclass: frightening young men who come from alleged "bad" neighborhoods. What does this mean? To understand the emergence of Hip Hop dance as an art form we must take into account two logically distinct but historically intertwined processes: the constitution both as *dance* and as *art* of something that, when it first appeared, was seen as fun and games for working-class children. It had neither meaning nor standing outside that very small circle of practitioners.

IN THE BEGINNING WAS SMURF: A MEETING OF OPPORTUNITIES

The prime event of the Hip Hop movement's expansion from the United States to France was the New York Rap City Tour in November 1982, organized by a major radio station, Europe 1. The New York–based Rock Steady Crew (RSC) performed on stage in Paris on November 21 and 27 at the Bataclan theater and at the Hippodrome de Pantin.[1]

According to reports, audiences were sparse, bewildered, and hardly grasped what was going on. Some people, however, were "electrified." Most interestingly, after the show, members of RSC went to the Trocadero esplanade, opposite the Eiffel Tower, where they taught their moves to a few eager teenagers. From then on, "Troca" was a hotspot for doing those outlandish dancing motions and the practice slowly began to spread.

Nevertheless, the main conduit of breakdancing's diffusion was the media. Its popularity was boosted by films like *Wild Style* (1982) and *Flashdance* (1983). The turning point came in 1984, when television channel TF1, France's most-watched channel, decided to commission a show on Hip Hop. Patrick Duteil, aka Sidney, the first Black anchorman to appear on French television, presented a TV series called *H.I.P.-H.O.P.* It was to become a legend. One of the most popular parts of the program was "the Lesson," during which Sidney and his associates taught the basic moves of "breaking" and "smurf"[2] to flocks of assiduous children, and encouraged them to show off their skills in rudimentary cyphers. The show rapidly became popular, especially among youngsters from working-class Arab, African, and West Indian families. These youth would wait impatiently for their favorite program every Sunday. Indeed, archive television footage of enthusiastic youths, almost exclusively male, "undulating frenetically" (Wais 1987) outside the tower blocks of council estates backs up the claims of contemporary witnesses regarding the show. Today, dozens of older Hip Hop dancers still recall the awe and thrill they experienced when they first saw smurf on television at the age of eight or ten, and how Sidney and his partners galvanized them into learning how to do it themselves. The program stopped airing in December 1984, coming as a shock to the young viewers who were bitterly disappointed and aggrieved (interviews).

At the time, most observers considered smurf to be no more than a flash in the pan, "a derisory entertainment for adolescent TV viewers" (Bachman and Basier 1985). It was thought to be a form of entertainment destined to disappear without a trace. However, smurf corresponded perfectly with a thirst for expression, action, and recognition among youngsters from working-class *banlieues*, who, in the 1980s, literally threw themselves into this unconventional activity. Released in 2002, the documentary *We Aren't Cheap Brands* (*On n'est pas des marques de vélo*) captures something of the intensity of the commitment of the boys, now men, who over three decades after the event, are still deeply moved by the memory of Sidney's TV show. "For us it was the only important thing in life!" explains Bruno Lopès, aka Kool Shen, now a celebrated rap star and cofounder of the group NTM (Thorn 2002).[3] This TV show was aired in the era of the *Marche des Beurs*—the March for Equality and against Racism, which took place from October to December in 1983—and the beginning of mass unemployment and structural precariousness, whose devastating effects on the working classes, in particular, on young people from immigrant families, were beginning to be felt. "They razed the football ground, they took away the gardens," explained another young man in the documentary. "This hip hop show, we grabbed the opportunity, we hung on to it!" (Thorn 2002).

Recognizing themselves in Hip Hop, young people transformed it into a social project. They found in the movement "a way of freeing themselves from the categories assigned to them" (Milliot 2006). As anthropologist Virginie Milliot (2006) has shown, they viewed Hip Hop as a godsend, a vehicle for agency, expression, and representation. But "smurfers" were not the only ones concerned with the movement. Many other people were (and are) engaged in Hip Hop in a variety of ways: dancers, social workers, choreographers, theater directors, administrators, politicians etc., and from their interdependent, interweaving actions and intentions a gradual process of institutionalization slowly developed (Elias 2000, 347). The trajectory of four historic Hip Hop dance groups founded in the 1980s serves as an illustration of this process. They emerged in the greater urban areas of Paris, Lyon, and Lille-Roubaix, where they thrived for decades and remain active to this day.

In 1983 in Vénissieux, near Lyon, Marcel Notargiacomo, director of the town's Youth and Culture Center, founded the dance company Traction Avant. Meanwhile, in Saint-Quentin-en-Yvelines, a suburb to the west of Paris, Jean Djemad founded the troupe Black Blanc Beur—"officially, in 1984, in a car park" (Site officiel 2011). Community workers had always played an important role as mediators, but their approach became truly influential in the early 1990s with the government's introduction of Urban Policy (*La politique de la ville*), which paved the way for partnerships with local politicians and administrators. They also invited partnerships with contemporary dancers and choreographers who saw in breakdancing "an aesthetic and technical revolution" (Ministry of Culture official, interview with the author, 2001) to renew their repertoire at a time when subsidies were increasingly hard to come by and some commentators were complaining about a lack of creativity in the world of established contemporary dance (Izrine 2002, 104, 118). A similar path was followed by Frédéric Tribalat, a militant grade-school teacher in Roubaix, an industrial city near Lille in northern France. From 1984 to 1986, he helped local boys found the group Dans la Rue la Danse (In the Street, the Dance) and, thanks to support from local and national government agencies, secured impressive benefits for the troupe, remaining in charge for years thereafter[4]. Aktuel Force is the fourth example of a perdurable dance company. It started as a group of four friends in 1983 in the banlieue of Dugny, north of Paris, and is still active today under the aegis of breakdancer Gabin Nuissier. All these groups come from working-class neighborhoods. Aktuel differs from the three others in that its inception did not depend on a professional adult organizer but, rather, was rooted in teenage club culture. Interestingly, though, this group also benefited from outside support in its first year, and from an unlikely source—the fashion designer Paco Rabanne (Thorn 1996). Later, it also received public subsidies.

Lastly, the victory of the Left coalition in the 1981 general elections created a favorable context for such activities and, under the culture minister Jack Lang, "youth culture was . . . 'admitted into national belonging'" (T. Edensor, quoted in Looseley 2003, 25). The "shift took the form of support for popular arts . . . *chanson* and rock music, comic strips, fashion, the circus and so on. Backed by a doubling of the Ministry's budget in 1982 and successive increases there-after, this official legitimation was a genuine transformation" (Looseley 2011). In the mainstream newspaper *Le Monde*, the Socialist president François Mitterand was fancifully caricaturized in the daily cartoon as a ghettoblaster-toting b-boy.

La Danse Hip Hop, Made in France

What is the world of Hip Hop dance like today? Schematically, the Hip Hop dance scene in France is made up of two major forms: ballet and battle. Each one constitutes a particular social space, a form of expression, a set of aesthetics, and a type of organization. Hip Hop ballet[5] is a concert dance form, and battle is competitive dance.

The originality of the French situation should be underlined. From 1982 on, Hip Hop dance in France experienced precocious, widespread, and practically uninterrupted growth. Indeed, it arguably had more success in France than in any other country. Links with the aesthetics and modes of organization of classical and contemporary dance performed on the stage were developed early on. In France, instead of battles, as in other countries, it was ballets and Hip Hop dance companies that spearheaded the enthusiasm for and, gradually, the institutionalization of this dance form. Battles developed later. Furthermore, the working-class popular-education movement called *éducation populaire* left a deep mark on Hip Hop dance. The community workers who promoted the dance influenced the way in which it was organized, the development of its aesthetic, and its worldview, which was based on an ethos of egalitarianism, social progress, and intraclass cooperation (Tétard 2002). Moreover, what distinguished French Hip Hop was the recognition and aid provided to practitioners by public institutions. There has been a public policy of support from local authorities for Hip Hop since the mid-1980s, and from the national government, since around 1990. Despite minor fluctuations, this policy has been pursued consistently by governments of both the Left and the Right. Loïc Lafargue (2008) gives specific examples of this consistency for the cities of Marseille and Bordeaux.

In France, these characteristics came together to create a specific choreographic genre called "Hip Hop dance," with its own repertoire and specialist dancers.[6] This was the material basis for the process of artification. Lastly, this configuration, which crystallized the actions and interests of a broad range of actors, has proved to be sustainable. However, it should be borne in mind that it is marked at once by the effects of the employment crisis among the working classes and by postcolonial domination.

These characteristics are particularly evident when compared, for example, to what occurred in the United States. In New York City, most of the pioneering breakdancers stopped dancing in or around 1986, about thirteen years after the style was said to have first developed, the lucky ones finding low-paying jobs and others experiencing great distress. Interviews reveal young people living in dire circumstances, isolated and powerless in their dealings with agents and the owners of discotheques, who exploited the talent of a handful of dancers for a short period of time and then dispensed with their services. Some of these pioneers did not survive the shock, descending into a world of drugs and delinquency (Chang 2005, 110, 205; Israel 2002). Nearly fifteen years went by before breakdancing experienced a renaissance in the United States between 1998 and 2000. The chronology of the expansion, disappearance, and renaissance of the genre was similar in the United Kingdom and Canada (Fogarty 2006).

In France, although dancers did spend a certain amount of time in the wilderness, their Calvary was much shorter and its consequences considerably less severe. After Sidney's TV show was axed, there was a drought of four or five years.[7] However, dancers were soon to find sources of support. Those who had stopped began dancing again with their friends and forming groups. In a few years, the groups became troupes. Thus the 1990s were a good time for the genre.

WHAT *ARE* THEY DOING? DESIGNATING THE PRACTICE

In the early years of the French Hip Hop movement, the idea of using the term "dance" to define these strange gestures was far from universally accepted. Some time passed before the notion became self-evident and everyone accepted the new phenomenon as a dance form in the established sense. From the feeble beginnings of smurf in 1982 to when the process of institutionalization started gaining momentum—that is, with the founding of the first Hip Hop dance companies in 1983 and 1984, the introduction of Hip Hop in contemporary dance festivals in 1991 (at the Pompidou Center in Paris, and in Montpellier), and then the organization of specific Hip Hop dance festivals starting in 1992 (in Villefranche-sur Saône, near Lyon)—the question of the definition and designation of the practice remained open. This is confirmed by an examination of the comments of those who were directly involved and an analysis of the vocabulary they used.

When they think back to the beginning, the pioneers of what is now known as Hip Hop dance remember how difficult it was to describe what they did in terms of anything that had existed before; anything, that is, other than play. After all, they were either children or pre-teenagers at the time; the age of the TV fans ranged from ten to fifteen.[8] These early practitioners had no sure conception of what they were doing. "When we started, we just did it to have fun," explains Gabin Nuissier, of Aktuel Force (pers. comm., 2006). Born in 1973, Mourad Merzouki of the group Käfig, similarly recalls, "The word 'dancer' never crossed our minds. We were passionate about movement, about energy. We really had no idea that what we were doing had anything to do with dance with a capital 'D'" (quoted in Louchart 2008). Interviewed when he was twenty-eight years old, a well-known dancer from Nantes also said, "Personally, I discovered dance later on . . . In 1984, I didn't know what dance was! What we did was performance and all that . . . we were having fun!" (quoted in Shapiro, Kauffmann, and McCarren 2002). Farid Berki, choreographer of the Melting Spot troupe from Roubaix, tells a similar story: "When I began, I didn't know that dance existed" (Rabaté 2003).

Neither should we underestimate the importance of the transition from smurf to Hip Hop dance. This terminological shift is not just nominal but reflects at once a socialization and an artification of the practice. An examination of the archives of the French

National Audio-Visual Institute (INA) reveals that smurf is indeed a 1980s neologism directly linked to Sidney's TV program on TF1. However, the term had practically died out by 1998.[9] It was replaced by the term *la danse hip hop*, initially used on TV in 1996, just as the Rencontres nationales des danses urbaines (National Urban Dance Meetings) first opened at the Grande Halle de la Villette and the newspaper *Le Monde* began to take a serious interest in this new dance form, liberally referring to canonical ideas of artistic criticism in its reports and articles. The following year, danse Hip Hop eclipsed both smurf and *danse rap* (rap dance), consolidating its status as the official term for the new form (Shapiro 2003). These changes in the nomenclature focus our attention on the role of institutions such as the press, television and major cultural venues in the diffusion and stabilization of the relevant vocabulary: they converge and succeed one another in naming, publicizing, and valorizing the new practice as a form of dance.

Smurf is a whimsical but absurd neologism that had no referent, no history, and no institutional links in the French language, and it gave way to a more complex phrase. While the term *smurf* was, from a social perspective, little more than a word,[10] the term *Hip Hop dance* is open to a more diverse analysis. Taking as its model the kind of terms used to describe known genres of dance, it is an interesting hybrid that applies the signifier of old institutions and solidly anchored social representations to a recent and still largely unknown popular movement. With *danse hip hop*—a phrase analogous to *danse classique*—we have an expression that, although apparently simple, has considerable descriptive, cognitive, and prescriptive power. It is a programmatic phrase that traces for the activity it designates a perspective at once institutional, professional, and aesthetic. "Institutional" in that it places, in no uncertain terms, the activity within the world of established classical and contemporary dance, with all their codes and practices, and, at the same time, links it to the Hip Hop movement. Thanks to the way in which it is constructed, the term links these two cultural and social spheres. "Professional" in that, in so doing, it highlights a serious aspect: Hip Hop dance is not a game but an activity that demands commitment; it is a discipline in all senses of the term. And, lastly, "aesthetic" in that the analogy makes Hip Hop dance an *artistic genre* in its own right, on the same level as contemporary and classical dance. These were the two dominant genres in France. Alongside jazz dance, they were recognized and regulated by the French Ministry of Culture by means of the State Diploma in Dance, introduced in 1989.

Finally, the term *danse hip hop* not only links the social worlds of, on the one hand, contemporary and classical dance, and, on the other, Hip Hop as a popular cultural movement but also creates an internal unification of different styles of dance within Hip Hop. Indeed, if in other countries these styles may have a distinct identity—for example, in the United States it is debated whether it is legitimate to call boogaloo, locking, and b-boying Hip Hop (Guzman-Sanchez 2012, 3, 141)—in France the invention of Hip Hop ballets and the possibility for dancers to have a career, however precarious, encouraged the stylistic polyvalence and stabilization of a unified designation. Convention rationalized the vocabulary by subsuming the profusion of styles into two subgenres: "upright dance" (*la danse debout*)[11] and "breakdancing" (*la danse au sol*, literally, "ground dance"). Hip Hop dance is an umbrella idiom that has structure; it is a rigorously arranged lexical and gestural ensemble (Shapiro and Kauffmann 2006).

All these semantic operations contributed to constituting Hip Hop dance as an artistic *genre* that has been stabilized by over thirty years of an ongoing process of institutionalization. We will now examine the main stages of this process: displacement and distantiation vis-à-vis the Hip Hop movement, organization, professionalization, singularization, and, lastly, intellectualization. These are some of the constituent processes of the overarching process of artification.[12] We will describe the process and broach some of the movements that counter its development.

DISPLACEMENT

The expression "from the street to the stage" was commonly used as a shorthand description of the metamorphosis of Hip Hop. It is a hackneyed phrase, but we can take it *à la lettre* for tearing the new practice away from the "street" (a signifier of day-to-day working-class life) and bringing it to the "stage" (the site of its transfiguration) as one of the preconditions of artistic elaboration. In other words, you really do have to take to the stage if you want to be taken seriously as an artist. This process of extraction and decontextualization or displacement, both physical and semantic, gave rise to new descriptions previously applied exclusively to the world of established dance.

The expression is also valid in that it is a metaphor for a distancing of the dancers from the world of Hip Hop, a process that started in the earliest years of the movement in France. In this case, the word *street* becomes a signifier of both origin and authenticity. Based on a certain degree of stability in terms of practice, skills were developed and specializations elaborated. The various disciplines of Hip Hop (rap, graff, dance, DJing) grew apart, even though the ideal of interdependence between the movement's component parts persisted. With the formation, in 1983, of the first companies, Hip Hop dance began to become autonomous. The actors themselves confirm this development, as when Sidney (Patrick Duteil) explained: "Dancers are a separate thing within hip hop . . . they put on a show . . . they don't need rappers to do that" (Bazin 1995, 156).

The type of music chosen for dance productions is an index of this process of detachment from Hip Hop in its earlier forms. In 1990, the group Black Blanc Beur performed to music by Bach and Chopin. In 1998, Farid Berki produced *Petrouschka*, with music by Igor Stravinsky and James Brown. The whole of *Solo d'Ernesto* by Ernesto Cortès (2000) was performed to the strains of Franz Schubert's *Death and the Maiden*. In 2001, Anthony Egéa's *Culture Choc* included extracts from Beethoven. And scores of Hip Hop shows used jazz, rock, flamenco, Bharata Natyam (classical Tamil music), African, and Arab music, as well as original scores.

ORGANIZATION

Starting in the early 1980s, social workers and educators began to see in Hip Hop both an original form of expression and a resource for social action. According to one of them (Marcel Notargiacomo, mentioned earlier), "Artistic practice could become a necessary catalyst for a fresh approach to social issues in the banlieues."[13] This is why they helped teenagers to persevere with their passion, on the one hand, by founding dance troupes, and, on the other, by encouraging them to adopt the kind of approaches used in dance performed on stage and having them work with contemporary choreographers. Stage-based work led dancers to take on new challenges, to abandon the logic of competition and to make the transition from individual performances to a collective dramaturgy, and from improvisation to objectification. For anthropologist Virginie Milliot (2006), these changes were part of a transition from an oral to a written—choreographic—form of dance (188). All of this presupposes a form of coordination based on forecasting and the division of labor, as well as on the adoption of ordinary theatrical conventions: costumes, make-up, stagecraft, lighting, ticketing, scheduling, etc.

It should be noted that, initially, it was the *ballet* form that was proposed rather than, for example, variety-style sketch numbers. The young dancers were engaged not only in mastering the minutiae of stagecraft but also in learning about dramatic construction, duration, and structure. They linked their form not only to the art world but to an approach focused on an aesthetic of ensembles, togetherness and collective organization. The durable and collective character of the approach was one of the traits of the process of artification of Hip Hop dance *à la française*. It was reflected in the wide alliance of actors who facilitated the development of government subsidized organizations (associations, ballets, companies, festivals, etc.) characterized by a concern for sustainability and solidarity, underpinned by a philosophy inspired by the popular education movement. The trend toward individual career trajectories was to emerge much later.

In 1991, a policy of urban social development was introduced with the aim of promoting "integration through culture." The policy was designed to address the problem of the representation of young French people from an immigrant background living in working-class banlieues by providing them with access to what Milliot (2006) calls "scenes of recognition." A large number of associations were founded, and Hip Hop dance was institutionalized within the framework of popular education, acquiring a legal status and legitimacy vis-à-vis the local authorities that agreed to subsidize them. Groups became stable, obtaining funding and joining a network of associations and municipalities. Their members learned about bureaucracy and politics: how to reserve a venue, take out an insurance policy, elaborate requests for subsidies, talk to local politicians, and so on.

The links between the association network and dance companies were, therefore, very close. Initially founded and organised for social work, the associations gradually transformed into incubators of artistic content and values. Community organizers acted as mediators, serving as a bridge to the world of established dance as practiced in the theater. Some of those organizers—such as Notargiacomo and Djemad mentioned earlier—went on to become the directors of the first Hip Hop dance troupes. This associative structure supported and consolidated the work of dancers and choreographers, providing a collective framework, while at the same time transmitting both the love of art and a worldview typifying the popular education movement. At the same time, it furnished a form of rationalization in terms of organization that sometimes led to entrepreneurial initiatives. The very existence of French dance companies that specialized in Hip Hop impressed observers by their sheer numbers; there were dozens of them all over the country. Of the 520 companies receiving subsidies and enjoying "a certain notoriety," according to the French National Dance Center in 2009, fifty-four (or 11%) focused on Hip Hop dance (Répertoire des compagnies chorégraphiques françaises 2009).[14] Lately, both the number and proportion have grown, as over 13 percent (70 out of 531) of the companies in the center's data base defined themselves as Hip Hop in November 2015.

Lastly, festivals have played a central role in artifying Hip Hop dance and in structuring the milieu. Festivals are formidable machines for fabricating and legitimizing art and have played a major role over the years in transforming performance, performers, and audiences. An interesting comparison can be made with museums: the role of festivals for performance can be compared to that of museums for artefacts. In his recent study on the "aesthetic turn" taken by many ethnographic museums, Benoît de l'Estoile (2007) has shown how the multiple decisions staff take daily and the tasks they do to keep their museums functioning (making acquisitions, organizing, exhibiting, advertising etc.) can be summarized as three main processes: staging, formatting, and putting things in orderly form on the basis of aesthetic criteria (18). Similar processes are at work at festivals that participate in the ongoing artification of Hip Hop dance.

Hip Hop dance was seen in festivals for the first time in 1991: first in Paris at a week-long dance-fest at the Pompidou Center in May, then in July, with greater media coverage at Montpellier Danse, a well-known annual festival, where the American choreographer Doug Elkins presented a breakdancing workshop organized with local youths. But the first sizeable event entirely dedicated to the discipline took place in 1992 in the shape of the Rencontres de danses urbaines (Urban Dance Meetings) in Villefranche-sur-Saône, which were supported by the Ministry of Culture.[15] In the following years, a substantial number of festivals were to see the light of day. Two stood out for the influence they exerted on the world of Hip Hop dance and on dance in general. These "motivational" festivals, as they were called by the Ministry of Culture, were the Rencontres de la Villette and Suresnes Cités Danse.

Les Rencontres de la Villette was founded in 1996 and lasted until 2009. Subsidized by the French Ministry of Culture and other public bodies and held at the Grande Halle de la Villette in Paris, the event emanated directly from the socio-educational and artistic efforts of the previous years. It made news on the Paris scene and, with its multiple stages, sprawling premises, and numerous opportunities for socialization and debate, the Rencontres presented a vast arena for having fun, circulating information, and experimenting. As a place of internal exchange, theorization, and education, the festival served for fourteen years as a theater, arena, and place of learning for young people from the working-class neighborhoods of eastern and northern Paris and the adjacent suburbs; at once a conservatory and a platform for Hip Hop dance within the framework of a multidisciplinary event. During the year preceding an upcoming festival, organizers traveled all over the country in search of dance troupes worthy of selection. Some worked as part of a support mission organized by the Fondation de France, which provided subsidies and support for new productions.[16] At the time, the Rencontres de la Villette was the biggest Hip Hop festival in France, with an attendance rate from 10,000 to 15,000 per year. It was to have a major influence on scheduling in the country as a whole.

The smaller Suresnes Cités Danse festival had a completely different orientation. Founded in 1993 by the director of the local municipal theater, the project was initially supported by the town council alone. However, in 1997, local and national government bodies also started to contribute. In contrast to La Villette, the event did not have any educational objectives. The director, the son of a banker, who unabashedly describes himself as "bourgeois," supported Hip Hop because "it's beautiful and strong," and defended the principle of art as a socially neutral form. A particularity of the festival was that it put Hip Hop dancers in contact with contemporary choreographers, from whom original works were commissioned. The aim was to discover new talent and promote an original style of dance, while at the same time providing a framework guaranteeing "quality." For this reason, some observers described the festival as a positive initiative "that marked the history of dance," while others considered it as a peremptory imposition of tutelage on Hip Hop dancers. In fact, the selection process for dancers, based on the model of individual auditions for ballet and contemporary dancers, was gradually professionalized, and new dance productions were characterized by a mixture of the vocabulary of Hip Hop and a contemporary aesthetic. Over the years, the festival has become more prominent, especially after the opening of a training center for Hip Hop dancers in the Suresnes theater in 2007 (and the demise of its sister and rival festival, La Villette, in 2009).

PROFESSIONALIZATION

These organizational innovations recall the earliest approaches to professionalizing the careers of dancers, approaches with which they were contemporary. In the early 1990s, Christian Tamet, at that time director of the Théâtre Contemporain de la Dance (Contemporary Dance Theater),[17] demanded that the Ministry of Culture recognize Hip Hop dancers as professionals and their art "as an aesthetic enterprise" worthy of being performed "in prestigious venues" as "a current of contemporary dance" (Ménard and Rossini 1995; Tamet and Galloni D'Istria 1996, 31–36).

Tamet's relatively aggressive approach to getting support for dancers culminated in the production of the first high-visibility professional Hip Hop production, with dancers receiving contracts, payments, touring, and the status of intermittent workers in the entertainment industry, making them eligible for unemployment benefits. *Sobedo* was first performed in 1994 at the Casino de Paris; the run lasted for four months. Tamet was the first person to claim and then demonstrate that the professionalization of Hip Hop dancers was a precondition of the artistic elaboration of the dance according to current conventions. Tamet also organized the first Rencontres des danses urbaines at la Villette in 1996.

Festivals were to play an important role in terms of professionalization. For the dancers who performed at the Rencontres and at most festivals, professionalization was, first and foremost, a collective adventure associated with the success of the Hip Hop dance company to which they belonged and which they had helped to set up. On the other hand, Suresnes Cités Danse was based on individual recruitment and promoted individual professional careers. Dancers signed employment contracts with contemporary dance companies, who auditioned them prior to hiring them. This important distinction between collective and individual trajectories of professionalization brings us to the next topic.

Singularization

The two festivals used very different evaluation approaches. At the Rencontres, collective organization was emphasized, while at Suresnes the skills of individual dancers were foregrounded. But both festivals, thanks to their remarkable longevity (the Rencontres lasted for fourteen years, Suresnes celebrated its thirtieth anniversary in 2022 and is still going), combined with the sustainability of the dance companies, favored the constitution of a veritable repertoire of works. The publicly funded establishment of La Villette lists them in a database of several hundred works. This is taken as proof of the existence of a recognized repertoire. Indeed, some works have attained a quasi-classical status. A good example is Käfig company's *Récital*, called the "founding spectacle of Hip Hop culture in France" by Yacine Amblard, a well-known organizer of Hip Hop dance events (Lettre d'information 2008). The piece was performed all over the country in 2008 to mark its tenth anniversary. Originally for six dancers, it is now performed in various formats worldwide as a classical workshop piece: *Récital* for forty dancers, twelve dancers etc. (CCN 2016). The authorship of the piece is sometimes credited to the Käfig company, or sometimes to the group's director Mourad Merzouki.

With the process of professionalization, the figure of the auteur gradually emerged and, alongside it, the value not only of individuality but also of singularity. According to sociologist Nathalie Heinich (1997), singularity is one of the prime values that define modern art and the modern artist. To understand the development of this value it is necessary to distinguish, in the history of French Hip Hop dance companies, four ideal-typical situations in the way choreography is created. Between 1980 and 1990, groups often spent their early years with a community worker who acted at once as organizer, social worker, and choreographer. Then came a period of time spent with a professional choreographer, learning the conventions of concert dance. A substantial majority of dance troupes then went through a third period wherein all members participated in creating choreography as a collective activity. Lastly, this phase was followed by a split, after which Hip Hop choreographers, both independent artists and auteurs, came to the fore and, providing they had sufficient resources, formed their own companies. In press releases, Hip Hop began to be described as "a dance created by *auteurs.*"

This is the kind of career trajectory experienced by Mourad Merzouki, now head of the group Käfig, and Kader Attou, now head of the group Accrorap. The two had started out dancing together in the same group, Traction Avant, as youngsters, and later parted ways. These two Hip Hop choreographers, both from immigrant working-class families near Lyon, have since reached the highest levels in terms of recognition and responsibility within established institutions. Attou was appointed director at the National Dance Center (CCN) of La Rochelle in 2008; Merzouki became director of the CCN of Créteil in 2009.[18]

During a public debate about Hip Hop choreography I attended in 2013, two male dancers confirmed these trends. One group leader said it was risky to try to maintain collective choreography, because in the long run, the process was unpredictable and uncontrollable. Another leader had this to say:

> All hip hop groups will tell you the same story, its banal; we all start writing up the choreography together and then, after a while, two or three of us do it; and then a year later I was doing it, and for three years now I'm the one who does it.[19]

INTELLECTUALIZATION

Lastly, as in other disciplines, the emergence of a learned discourse is part of a process of intellectualization that is an integral part of the artifying process. Intellectualization can be considered as an internal process (from the point of view of the practitioners) and as an external process (from the point of view of the observers), as well as from other perspectives. Of this manifold process I will mention only two factors here—namely, the deployment of a discourse of support and the life of organizations developing that discourse.

Festivals provide a good example of the intellectualization process. They are a place where participants (organizers, dancers, specialized and lay audiences) simultaneously produce a discourse of celebration, through the programs and flyers they distribute, and a reflexive critique,[20] by means of the many public debates they organize, which are followed with passionate interest by fans and available on the Internet. At the same time, the notion of "transmission" took on a life of its own, to the point that the institutions were unable to keep up with the increasing national demand for Hip Hop dance courses, traineeships, and training workshops. The general trend of organizing debates and discussions contributed to an intellectualization of the discipline and rendered festivals and workshops lively arenas of education and theoretical reflection. Both technical and abstract notions about Hip Hop were debated widely in these arenas.

During the 1990s, a structured critical discourse emerged in the press, both generalist (*Le Monde, Libération*) and specialist (dance journals, Hip Hop magazines). As previously mentioned, after smurf hit its high point in 1984, media coverage ground to a halt. With the development of festivals came renewed press interest, but the discourse had changed radically: journalists stopped focusing on the sociodemographic characteristics of the dancers and began to engage in artistic critiques. The "aesthetic turn," beginning in 1992, was very clear, and by 1996 it had become standard practice. The perspective is still applied today (Shapiro 2003). Journalists no longer wrote about "youths" but about "artists," "stellar dancers," "interpretations," and "works," analyzed according to categories normally applied to art history. Around 2000 television also changed its approach, with channels regarded as serious (France 2, France 3, Arte) broadcasting programs and documentary films on Hip Hop ballet and festivals. Previously, in the mid-1990s, social science researchers had also begun to take an interest in Hip Hop, which spread throughout the discipline, and contributed, in turn, to the elaboration of a reflexive discourse.

This process of intellectualization was also the result of the actions of what political theorist Antonio Gramsci called "organic intellectuals." The last twenty years have witnessed the emergence of a generation of young entrepreneurs, often equipped with university degrees,[21] who project a Hip Hop identity and hold management positions. Hip Hop dancers, choreographers, journalists, and policy officers establish and develop festivals, direct associations, organize dance courses, and manage venues. They theorize their reflections, write and publish books and articles, and appear in the media. They are the new entrepreneurs, the new spokesmen and spokeswomen of Hip Hop. Lastly, the intensity of their reflections is evident in the content of Hip Hop ballets, in the titles of their works, their narrative structures, their mises-en-scène, as well as, among other things, in their costumes and dance techniques.

One of the consequences of the development of this discursive activity considered as a whole (spokespeople, schedules, newspaper articles, public debates, training, university research, dramaturgy) was the production, starting at a particular time—probably around 1998, when the Rencontres de La Villette's database was set up, and when the "aesthetic turn" of media critiques became effective—of a shared perception of Hip Hop ballets, not only as discrete entities but as forming a distinctive ensemble defined, both by a *repertoire* and, by a specific artistic *genre* called Hip Hop dance. Genre and repertoire: these are two powerful agents of the artification of this innovative gestural practice.

BACK TO THE ROOTS?

In the past fifteen or twenty years, things have changed. Whereas during the 1990s, Hip Hop dance developed and was popularized largely via its theatrical format, the next decade saw the massive development of a new form—new for France, that is. The rapid upsurge of Hip Hop dance *battles* started around the year 2002 and can be seen as a resistance movement vis-à-vis the artifying process, which it doubtless was, especially in its early days. But, contrary to appearances, this new stance is also an integral part of the artification movement, albeit in a paradoxical, ambiguous manner.

Small-scale challenges, called *défis*, between persons or crews who know each other have been practiced since the 1980s; they are the equivalent of what English-speakers call *cyphers*. They are organized informally in public spaces, such as shopping malls, parks, and near housing projects. But twenty years later, a new form started to develop, inspired by competitions organized in Germany and the United States. They resemble major sport events championships; they typically have substantial budgets, are held in venues the organizers have reserved in advance, and welcome numerous anonymous spectators, all of whom pay for the privilege. Such events are publicized, require prior registration, and have paid juries who in some cases apply marking systems. Many are held annually (the Battle of Saint-Denis in the Paris Area, Hip Opsession in Nantes, Juste Debout in Paris, the Battle Pro, etc.). Generally speaking, the initiatives that tended to institutionalize ballets were taken by people outside the Hip Hop movement; however, the initiatives to institutionalize battles were taken by the dancers themselves, who had benefited from the experience of the previous generation in regard, notably, to negotiation, funding, and organization.

The world of battles is at once in tension with and closely related to Hip Hop ballet. At first sight, they are different in every way—one, a competitive space occupied by young amateurs; the other, a professional artistic space, open to different kinds of people of different age groups.[22] One consisting of brief performances (sixty seconds); the other presenting a dramatic composition (thirty to sixty minutes). Battles encourage stylistic specialization, since opponents challenge one another in a single style (breakdancing or popping, for example), while ballets encourage polyvalence in terms of genres, dancers being competent in several styles which, together, make up the Hip Hop dance genre.

Nonetheless, it is clear that there are not only numerous links but also a balanced dynamic between these two scenes. On the one hand, the increasing popularity of battles reflects the desire of a new generation of Hip Hop dancers to regain control in terms of both organization and the definition of the expressive codes of dance (Shapiro 2004, 327–328). Some of the dancers dispute the eirenic perspective held by members of the popular education movement and feel strongly about reinstating the concept of the challenge as a fundamental mode of expression and representation,[23] while also renewing links with the whole of the Hip Hop movement. On the other hand, dancers work to build bridges between the world of battles and that of ballet. One explanation for this is that, as dancers grow older and experience the tolls of competition, the only prospect available for those who want to continue their career in the Hip Hop dance world is to target the less strenuous and more financially secure positions in ballet, education, or administration. Those responsible for organizing the Battle of the Year (BOTY), a major international battle, forcefully explain this situation on their website.[24] But, on a deeper level, art is a value in which everyone believes and dance, in all its forms, is an expression of that belief. In a documentary film about the Juste Debout battle, held yearly in Paris, one well-known dancer and judge insists: "Even if we battle, this is an art, not a competition" (Rabah Mahfoufi, quoted in Matos and Quiroz 2011).

Now, Hip Hop battles are both a port of entry to the concert-dance labor market and creative laboratories for the stage. This phenomenon is illustrated by the careers of groups such as Vagabond Crew, Wanted Posse, and Pockémon Crew who, after winning competitions at the highest level, started second careers producing ballets. To do this, they changed their names from "crew" to "company," found new allies, adopted theatrical conventions, obtained subsidies from the Ministry of Culture, and changed their work schedule. Recently, it seems that a new phase in the development of Hip Hop dance has commenced; individual dancers have been able to carve out careers for themselves in entertainment, without being members of a dance troupe as was necessary to succeed in a previous stage. Some leading dancers have had roles in film, theater (musical comedies), and on television shows. In effect, their trajectories represent what Pierre Bourdieu called conversions of capital. The symbolic capital (reputation) they have accumulated in Hip Hop battles is converted into material capital (remuneration) on theater stages and film sets.

Reciprocally, Hip Hop ballets influence the aesthetics and organization of the competitions; the musicality, creativity, and quality of choreography are part of the criteria used by Hip Hop battle juries. The very format of battles is undergoing a process of spectacularization (Kauffmann 2004, 398).

Lastly, the concert dance establishment[25] now integrates excerpts of battles or mock battles and occasionally promotes this form of dance as being of aesthetic value. For example, in September 2004, the contemporary dance festival La Biennale de Lyon hosted a mock choreographed battle, which was attended by the French minister of culture, who, for the first time, publicly praised breakdancing as part of France's cultural heritage (Boisseau 2004). Even the director of Suresnes Cités Danse—a festival dedicated to Hip Hop dance—who had previously kept the hardcore version at a distance by commissioning hybrid pieces in which Hip Hoppers were under the sole authority of contemporary dance choreographers—started organizing a "choreographic competition" in 2009, later referred to as a "battle." The winner was given a slot in the festival proper and was asked to put on his or her own show the following year. A few years later, the procedure was discontinued.

Conclusion

As we have seen, smurf has undergone many transformations since it first arrived in France, in 1982, in aesthetical, temporal, and organizational terms, and in the manner in which bodies are put in motion. These changes have led to the emergence of a new artistic genre—namely, *la danse hip hop*. Among other reasons, this innovative genre of dance emerged thanks to collective forms of organization (ballets, troupes, associations), a new combination of styles and vocabulary (smurf and breakdance), and the use of theatrical conventions derived from established art forms. Elements of popular culture, such as battles and sportswear, have, in turn, influenced modes of representation and aesthetic forms that are designated as art.

It is important to grasp the distinctive socioeconomics of Hip Hop in France. For the first twenty-five or thirty years of the dance's development, French Hip Hoppers were almost completely insulated from the marketplace. Unlike their American counterparts, French street dancers did not work in commercial settings but in the not-for-profit sector. A great number of dancers developed via voluntary associations that were subsidized by public authorities.[26] That local and central governments supported Hip Hop as a tool to implement social and cultural policy cannot be emphasized enough and helps account for the fact that the dance is organized in durable troupes and inclines toward artistry. Only in recent years has Hip Hop dance started to be seriously supported by private capital as well (radio, television, the Internet, transportation, fashion, sports etc.). Thus, a whole new arena of employment for Hip Hop dancers has appeared that hardly existed before.

This recent development has created a shift in the kind of controversy that dancers may entertain. In the previous decade, there was tension between those who experienced Hip Hop predominantly as battle and those who gave most of their time to the stage. But as older competitors leave the big battle circuit for Hip Hop theater production, administration, and teaching, today's younger dancers move seamlessly from battles to concert dance and back again, as professionals. What used to be in contradistinction is slowly becoming a unified scene.

Interestingly, this integration of competitors and concert dancers is now clearly upheld by the main regulating authority of the dance establishment, the Ministry of Culture. Indeed, starting in 2019, the minister nominated not a sole choreographer, as is the usual practice, but a Hip Hop collective to direct the National Choreographical Center of Rennes, in Brittany. This new directorate consists of two administrators and six artists; the latter are all experienced battle-circuit competitors, concert dancers, and choreographers.[27] It will be interesting to see how they will use their unique experience to act upon and within a French dance establishment they are now part of.

As the polarity between battles and concert dance is gradually declining, a new sector is emerging: commercial Hip Hop dance. This may be an old story for Americans but not in France, and it takes on a special twist. The debate between authenticity and the sellout revolves around commonality and art. The sellout points toward individualism, while authenticity is related to "coming together" and art as a foundation of community building. In this respect, the public-service ethos based on social cohesion that was upheld by the community workers and civil servants who have supported Hip Hop since the 1980s is compatible with Hip Hop's motto of "peace, love, unity and having fun." This contrasts with an ethos of commercialism expressed as brash individualism, merciless competition, and thirst for big money. The divergence has to do with values and aesthetics but also with work schedules in the different spheres, because the two do not always click. Whether Hip Hop dancers will integrate this, or, rather, which dancers will do so and how, remains to be seen.

Finally, and importantly, the extraordinary success of Hip Hop dance over the past decades has rested on significant expansion in the number of practitioners and increased diversity among this population compared to its initial sociodemographic composition. While informal observation suggests that Hip Hop dancers number in the many thousands, there are hardly any statistics to be had. Working as a Hip Hop dancer, teacher, or organizer (the three often being entwined) afforded a trajectory of upward social mobility for many persons from working-class families. But it is also the case that dancers remain in particularly precarious, badly paid occupations (Rannou and Roharik 2009).

Artification is not the only process at work here. Hip Hop dance evolves at the crossroads between a number of spheres (art, sports, commerce, entertainment, popular education) whose practices and values may clash (Shapiro 2004). But for everyone involved, art remains a point of reference and a value to be upheld. Historically, art was one of the primary institutional justifications for Hip Hop in that it provided a platform from which community-service workers could lobby for and obtain government subsidies, even though funding for such activities had not originally been factored into the culture budget. This link to the concept of "art" retains its prestige for another reason. In fact, it legitimizes the idea of pursuing a career as a dancer. It is possible to make a living as a Hip Hop dancer, as a production administrator, or as a dance teacher; but it is not possible to make a living as a competitor in the long run. Someone who organizes battles is called an "artistic director"; he (or occasionally she) is not called a "tour manager" or an "agent." It is claimed that art is an intrinsic part of Hip Hop in whatever form it takes, even when that form is outside the purview of what is traditionally defined as art by the cultural establishment. Thus, major competitions such as the Battle of the Year in Braunschweig, Germany, or Juste Debout in Paris are presented by their organizers as places of creativity, and the battle is defined as "an artistic confrontation" (Rencontre-débat 2006). However, in spite of the accumulation of signs of recognition associated with the status of art and what they are supposed to provide in terms of marks of noblesse, the cultural and class stigma attached to Hip Hop persists. Backed up by the popular-education movement, French Hip Hop demonstrates the degree to which the artification of dance is linked to long-lasting organizations and a militant practice of social cooperation consolidated by the engagement of the Welfare State. It is based on a wide alliance of highly committed actors who seem to agree on the status of art as a righter of wrongs and payer of debts engendered by socioeconomic exploitation and colonization (Rémy 2006). If it was possible to artify Hip Hop dance, it is, perhaps, because in France there is a belief in art as a value capable, to a certain degree, of paying these debts, or at least subsuming them.

NOTES

1. The Tour visited other cities in France and then London. There was dancing, rap, DJing, graffiti, and double dutch, performed by RSC, Phase 2, Futura 2000, Dondi, Afrika Bambaataa, GrandMixer D.ST, Rammellzee, and the Fantastic Four. See Meghelli (2004);

and Wikipédia, "New York City Rap." https://fr.wikipedia.org/wiki/New_York_City_Rap, accessed April 2, 2017.

2. The emergence and acceptance of a stabilized terminology is a long process, and how to designate Hip Hop dancing and its various subgenres was not determined for many years. In the 1980s and 1990s, *smurf* was used in France as an umbrella term for breakdancing in general, and then as a way to refer to all upright dances. It is still used occasionally for popping. For a discussion on terminology in the French context, see Shapiro and Kauffmann (2006). For a discussion in the American context see Schloss (2009, 58–66).

3. Like most French pioneer rap singers, Kool Shen discovered Hip Hop via breakdancing.

4. I am grateful to historian and dancer Janoé Vulbeau for communicating an unpublished article from which I obtained this information. Vulbeau, J. (2016). "Une histoire de la danse Hip Hop à Roubaix (1983–1997)."

5. To my knowledge, it was Philippe Mourrat who coined the expression "Hip Hop ballet," around 2000, when he was in charge of the Encounters of La Villette. Mourrat has been a major figure in the institutionalization and dissemination of Hip Hop dance in France.

6. In 2003 there were about 750 professional Hip Hop dancers registered as *intermittents du spectacle* (in the state subsidized insurance scheme for the performing arts), out of a total in France of about 5,000 dancers of all genres. This is my estimate based on statistical data from Rannou and Roharik (2009, 122–123). Obviously, this does not account for dancers who are not registered. In addition, there are probably a few thousand dancers who give courses and training in Hip Hop dancing. In the estimate of a researcher studying more recent data (October, 2016) from the insurance scheme, the number of dancers in France today has had an increase of approximately 20% since 2003 (pers. comm.).

7. According to Philippe Mourrat, the "barren spell" lasted from 1988 to 1991. According to Patrick "Sidney" Duteil, it lasted from 1985 to 1989. These two Hip Hop experts differ on the dates but agree about facts and duration: the hard times for French breakdancers lasted about four years. In the United States the "dark ages" lasted about fifteen years.

8. The television viewers who wrote to Sidney's show *H.I.P.-H.O.P* were age fourteen on average, according to the magazine *Danser* n° 11, 1984, p. 20. Most of the dancers we interviewed had started dancing between the ages of eight and twelve.

9. For example, the keyword *smurf* extracted eighteen television programs from the database Archives de l'INA/TV in 1984, when the system did not yet recognize the keyword *danse hip hop*. Fourteen years later, smurf has all but disappeared, yielding only four programs from another television database called Dépôt Légal, while the keyword *danse hip hop* extracts fourteen programs (1998).

10. *Smurf* is an English word used to designate the little blue people invented by Belgian cartoonist Pierre Culliford, aka Peyo. As used in Hip Hop (and in no other locus in the French language), the term is said to come from the way of California, where early dancers used to dress in a comical homage to the popular cartoon characters: in striped suits, funny caps, and white gloves.

11. The international battle Juste Debout that takes place in Paris every year in March takes its name, in part, from this stylistic designation.

12. For more on artification, see Shapiro and Heinich (2012) and Shapiro (2019).

13. Interview conducted by Marie-Christine Bureau in 1998 in Vénissieux, a working-class suburb of Lyon. Quoted in: Bureau, Leymarie, et al. (1999), page unkown.

14. The paper edition, published annually, was discontinued after 2010. Subsequently, information on French dance companies has been available online (https://www.cnd.fr) and at the offices of the Centre national de la danse in Pantin, near Paris, rue Victor-Hugo.

15. Actually, the regional offices of the Ministry: Direction régionale des affaires culturelles du ministère de la Culture (DRAC).

16. This agency still exists. It is now called Initiatives d'action en danses urbaines (IADU).

17. The TCD was a private association subsidized almost exclusively by the Ministry of Culture, established in Paris in 1984. Its missions were transferred to the Centre national de la danse (CND), a public agency founded in 1998, now established in Pantin, in the Greater Paris area.

18. There are nineteen CCNs disseminated throughout France. They are public agencies whose directors are appointed by the Minister of Culture. Among past and present directors are the dancers Carolyn Carlson, Jean-Claude Gallotta, Angelin Prejlocaj, Maguy Marin, and Joseph Nadj.

19. Excerpt from my notes at a roundtable discussion that took place on April 19, 2013 at the Parc de La Villette in Paris, called "Ecritures chorégraphiques en danse hip-hop" (Writing Choreography for Hip Hop Dance) during the Festival Hautes Tensions.

20. In her classic work on the market for paintings, sociologist Raymonde Moulin (1992, 206) distinguishes between a critique of celebration and a reflexive critique.

21. According to a study conducted in five French *départements*, 34 percent of all persons teaching Hip Hop dance classes in 2007 had a college degree (Apprill and Djakouane 2008, 397–416).

22. Amateurs and professionals are defined here according to their legal status in relation to work. Amateurs are persons who dance without pay. They usually bear the costs of participating in battles and shows (registration, travel etc.) themselves and may have no statutory protection against accidents or injuries. Professionals, by contrast, have work contracts and the attendant social and legal rights, such as health insurance, holidays etc.

23. According to Virginie Milliot (2006), challenge (*le défi*) functions on the premise of a "mutual recognition of equality," and this "relational logic is engrained in a way of being that is . . . particular to the youths from French working-class neighbourhoods" (169).

24. This was true when I accessed the URL http://www.battleoftheyear.de/about/change-of-direction.html, April 15, 2010. At that date, BOTY organizers Dirk Corell, Thomas Hergenröther, Mode 2, and Niels "Storm" Robitzky wrote that "breakdance is an artistic expression" and "the BOTY wants to take more responsibility for the skills & future of the b-boys/girls, showing them more/new opportunities, eg. professional performances in the fields of theater and contemporary dance." But as I wind up this article in 2021, these concerns are no longer advocated on the BOTY website. Perhaps because of the growing presence of sport adepts among b-boys and their followers.

25. I define the *dance establishment* as a long-standing network of persons, often in the mid- to high occupational and economic strata, who control the resources they use to promote classical and contemporary dance forms. Hip Hop dancers and persons in a lesser strata are newcomers and outsiders, who are only starting to have access to similar resources that they can channel into Hip Hop practice (Elias and Scotson 2008).

26. This is understandable in a country where the whole theatrical field is split between two sectors: private theater, almost exclusively in Paris, and public subsidized theater, a complex series of structures throughout the country (Proust 2019).

27. With this nomination, three of the nineteen prestigious CCNs are now under a Hip Hop artistic leadership. The members of the Rennes collective called FAIR[E] are the artists Bouside Aït-Atmane, Iffra Dia, Johanna Faye, Linda Hayford, Saïdo Lehlouh and Ousmane Sy (died December 28, 2020, age 40, of heart failure), and the administrators are

Céline Gallet and Marion Poupinet. See http://accn.fr/les-ccn/cartographie/5_Centre-cho
regraphique-national-de-Rennes-et-de-Bretagne-Musee-de-la-Danse.

References

Apprill, C., and Djakouane, A. (2008/9). "La transmission à l'épreuve de l'enseignement : le cas
de la danse hip-hop." In *Figures contemporaines de la transmission*, edited by N. Burnay and
A. Klein, 397–416. Namur: Presses universitaires de Namur.

Bachman, C., and Basier, L. (1985). "Junior s'entraîne très fort ou le smurf comme mobilisation
symbolique." *Langage et Société* 34: 57–68.

Bazin, H. (1995). *La culture hip-hop*. Paris: Desclée de Brouwer.

Bédarida, C. (1997). "Toutes les cultures urbaines bivouaquent à La Villette." *Le Monde*,
October 10.

Boisseau, R. (2004). "Les débuts en fanfare et en hip hop de la Biennale de la danse de Lyon." *Le
Monde*, September 16, 31.

Bureau, M.-C., Leymarie C., Mbia E., and Shapiro R. (1999). *Activités artistiques et métissages
: dynamique de création, professionnalisation et inscription urbaine*. Document de travail.
Paris: Plan urbain, Centre d'études de l'emploi.

CCN Créteil et Val-de-Marne / Compagnie Käfig (2016, posted May 13), "Récital, Spreading
Hip-Hop Repertoire Throughout the World", accessed October 5, 2016. https://www.yout
ube.com/watch?v=HskrI4O7ulY.

Chang, J. (2005). *Can't Stop Won't Stop: A History of the Hip Hop Generation*. New York: Saint
Martin's Press.

de l'Estoile, B. (2007). *Le goût des autres: de l'Exposition coloniale aux arts premiers*.
Paris: Flammarion.

Elias, N. (2000). *On the Process of Civilization*. Rev. ed. Dublin: University College Dublin
Press. (Original work published in 1939).

Elias, N., and Scotson, J. L. (2008). *The Established and the Outsiders*. Rev. ed. Dublin: University
College Dublin Press. (Original work published in 1965).

Fogarty, M. (2006). "'Whatever Happened to Breakdancing?' Transnational B-Boy/B-Girl
Networks, Underground Video Magazines and Imagined Affinities." Unpublished MA
thesis, Brock University.

Guzman-Sanchez, T. (2012). *Underground Dance Masters: Final History of a Forgotten Era*.
Santa Barbara, CA: Praeger.

Heinich, N. (1997). *The Glory of Van Gogh: An Anthropology of Admiration*. Princeton,
NJ: Princeton University Press.

Israel, dir. (2002). *The Freshest Kids*. Motion Picture. USA: QD3 Entertainment.

Izrine, A. (2002). *La danse dans tous ses états*. Paris: L'Arche.

Kauffmann, I. (2004). "Génération du hip-hop. Danser au défi des assignations." Thèse de
sociologie, Université de Nantes.

Lafargue de Grangeneuve, L. (2008). *Politique du hip-hop. Action publique et cultures urbaines*.
Toulouse: Presses universitaires du Mirail.

Lettre d'information. (2008, October). *Interview de Yacine Amblard*. Pantin: Centre national de
la danse.

Looseley, D. (2003). *Popular Music in Contemporary France: Authenticity, Politics, Debate*.
Oxford: Berg.

Looseley, D. (2011). "Notions of Popular Culture in Cultural Policy: A Comparative History of France and Britain." *International Journal of Cultural Policy* 17 (4): 365–379.

Louchart A. (2008). "Identité en mutation. Une danse, un style: le hip-hop." http://www.evene. fr/theatre/actualite/danse-hip hop-break-chaillot-joey-starr-1649.php.

Meghelli, S. (2004). "Returning to The Source, en Diaspora: Hip Hop in France." *ProudFlesh: New Afrikan Journal of Culture, Politics and Consciousness* 3. https://www.afr icaknowledgeproject.org/index.php/proudflesh/article/view/212

Matos, J., and Quiroz, C. (2011). *Juste Debout, le doc.* Documentary film. France: CanalStreet. TV

Ménard, F., and Rossini, N. (1995). "Les défis de la danse: une expérience de formation de danseurs de Hip Hop." *Recherche Sociale* 133: 34–71.

Milliot, V. (2006). "The French Touch: le hip-hop au filtre de l'universel républicain." *Anthropologie et Sociétés* 30 (2): 175–197.

Moulin, R. (1992). *L'artiste, l'institution et le marché.* Paris: Flammarion.

Proust, S. (2019). "Portrait of the Theater Director as an Artist." *Cultural Sociology* 13 (3): 338–353.

Rabaté, J. (2003). *Rencontre du chorégraphe Farid Berki avec les élèves de l'école d'Evreux sur le thème du spectacle "Petrouchka"* CLC, film 30 min.

Rannou, J., and Roharik, I. (2009). "Vivre et survivre sur le marché de la danse." In *L'artiste pluriel. Démultiplier l'activité pour vivre de son art,* edited by M.-C. Bureau, M. Perrenoud, and R. Shapiro, 109–125. Lille: Septentrion.

Rémy, J. (2006.) "La dette en trop: face à la domination postcoloniale." *Revue du Mauss* 2 (28): 257–272.

Rencontre-débat. (2006). "Le battle en question(s)." *5e Rencontres internationales de danses urbaines en Essonne,* December 12. Adiam 91. Accessed March 3, 2007. http://www.artel91. org/docs/BATTLE.pdf.

Répertoire des compagnies chorégraphiques françaises (2009). Pantin: Centre national de la danse.

Schloss, J. G. (2009). *Foundation: B-Boys, B-Girls and Hip Hop Culture in New York.* New York: Oxford University Press.

Shapiro, R. (2003). "L'émergence d'une critique artistique: la danse hip hop." *Sociologie de l'art* OPuS 3: 15–48.

Shapiro, R. (2004). "The Aesthetics of Institutionalization: Breakdancing in France." *Journal of Arts Management, Law and Society* 33 (4): 316–335.

Shapiro, R. (2019). *Cultural Sociology.* "Special Issue: Cultural Sociology and Artification" SAGE Publications. Volume 13, Issue 3, September.

Shapiro, R., and Heinich, N. (2012). "When Is Artification?", *Contemporary Aesthetics* Special Volume 4 <http://www.contempaesthetics.org/newvolume/pages/article.php?articl eID=639>

Shapiro, R., and Kauffmann, I. (2006). "Dire la danse: le vocabulaire de la danse hip-hop." In *A la recherche du mot: De la langue au discours,* edited by C. Gruaz. Limoges: Lambert-Lucas: 175–190.

Shapiro, R., Kauffmann, I., and McCarren, F. (2002). *Apprentissage, socialisation, transmission: la danse hip hop.* Rapport pour la Mission du patrimoine ethnologique. Nantes, Paris: LAUA, ministère de la Culture.

"Site officiel de la compagnie de danse Hip-Hop Black Blanc Beur. 1ère EPOQUE." Accessed April 4, 2011. http://www.blackblancbeur.fr/spip.php?rubrique124.

Tamet, C., and Galloni D'Istria, I. (1996, hiver). "Chronique d'une ouverture." *Rue des Usines,* (32– 33): 31–36.

Tétard, F. (2002). "De l'affaire Dreyfus à la guerre d'Algérie, un siècle d'éducation populaire." *Esprit* 283 (3–4): 39–59.

Thorn, J.-P. (1996). *Faire kiffer les anges*, 88 min., Agat Films & Cie / Arte 6.

Thorn, J.-P. (2002). *On n'est pas des marques de vélo*. Mat Films, Arte, CRRAV.

Wais, A. (1987). "Mantronix au Rex-Club." *Le Monde*, February 17.

CHAPTER 23

NEGOTIATING THE METASPACE

Hip Hop Dance Artists in the Space of UK Dance Theater

PAUL SADOT

INTRODUCTION

THE term *hip hop theater* arose in the 1990s and early 2000s and referred to dance and theater artists whose work had its roots in Hip Hop culture (Davis 2006). Since that time there has been a growing body of written work about Hip Hop theater and the micro-expression of particular forms that emerge from it.[1] Yet little attention has focused on the uniquely British form of Hip Hop dance theater (HHDT), and no research to date has examined the United Kingdom's institutional framework in which this particular form has evolved. Some articles on HHDT focus on a celebration of its institutional legitimization (Prickett 2013); others briefly touch on it in wider debates about Hip Hop theater and Hip Hop (Fogarty 2011; Hoch 2006; Uno 2006).

The institutional negotiation with HHDT in the UK bears some similarities to the institutional negotiation with breaking in France (Shapiro 2004), where the government's will to "rehabilitate popular art forms" (317) led to a process of "artification." However, HHDT has grown primarily within a mono-institutional framework, and rather than being seen as the object of "artification," it is best understood as an institutionally supervised and legitimized form/brand that, through interrelated sociocultural, economic, and political structures, is in danger of being authored by the state.

Adding to these concerns and the wider debate about HHDT are the UK media reviews that present homogenous eulogizations that are generally superficial in tone and lacking in what writer and critic Lyn Gardner (2011) describes as "restraint, consideration, contextualization and enough space to write meaningfully and thoughtfully about a show."[2] And, while eulogizations may be deserved, I suggest that it is time to examine HHDT in a way that interrogates, and explicitly politicizes, the complex negotiations that are being enacted in the space of UK dance theater.

With patronage from powerful mainstream institutions, HHDT today is under the influence of cultural industry conditions, thereby becoming a commodity that is, in its ascendancy, part of the UK's creative economy (McRobbie 2016). This process is linked to debates regarding the industrialization of UK arts that stemmed from New Labour's (1997–2010) cultural policies, regarding which Jen Harvie (2005) argues that cultural commodification risks "limit[ing] the right to artistic expression to those who can make it economically productive" (23). Adding to the complex discourse surrounding cultural commodification, performance scholar André Lepecki (2016) draws on McKenzie (2001) to contend that the institutions and corporations that drive neoliberal societies are necessarily fusing cultural performance with organizational performance to both "plunder and foster the performance of creativity" (8). Furthermore, the hegemonic supervision of artists working in HHDT ensures that long-established notions of "what dance is" are perpetuated via interconnected elements, including mentorships, funding strategies, and the state-led commodification of arts and culture. These processes have an impact on the agency and (im)mobility of artists working in the HHDT mold and are connected to the wider processes of gentrification and "culturfication" (a neologism for the manufacture of culture) that presently permeate London's sociocultural, political, and artistic landscape.[3]

In the chapter I make a clear distinction between *hip hop theater* as a generic term used to capture the work of Hip Hop artists making theater around the globe and the term *hip hop dance theater*.[4] HHDT is a "terminological change" (Shapiro and Heinich 2012, 6) instigated and adopted by the Sadler's Wells Theatre, London, in 2003, at the suggestion of Jonzi D, who chose the name to differentiate the work from Hip Hop theater "because there's a focus on dance" as the primary element in the creation of theater (Jonzi D, interview with the author, December 14, 2014). Therefore, I use the term HHDT to denote a particular form/brand that has emerged in the UK under the supervision of Sadler's Wells Theatre's Breakin' Convention project.[5]

My aim is to widen the critical debate surrounding HHDT in the UK by questioning the nature of its institutionally supervised production through a concept I have called *metaspatial knowledge*. *Metaspatial knowledge* denotes critical thinking about the wider space (*metaspace*) in which HHDT circulates; this is a multidimensional space that brings multiple sociocultural and historico-political spaces into critical juxtaposition.

Often referred to as the "fifth element" of Hip Hop, knowledge is not a new ideal or novel concept in Hip Hop culture. Yet, in the British context at least, I argue, after having interviewed and worked with many UK artists, that the broadly held conceptualization of "Hip Hop knowledge" centers on the *micro* sociocultural, historical, and temporal space of Hip Hop rather than on the *meta* sociocultural, historical, temporal, and political space that frames it. This micro lens is part of a canon that is subject to Hip Hop's hegemony, particularly notions of the four founding elements of b-boying (breaking), MCing (rapping), graffiti (writing), and DJing. The micro lens recognizes that possessing Hip Hop–specific knowledge endows dancer-artists with subcultural capital (Thornton 1996, 163) which focuses specifically on Hip Hop legacies, such as the role of founding figures and practitioners, the evolution of movements, and the development of terminology.

This chapter develops the idea of the metaspace as a construct that comprises the wider sociocultural, historical, economic, and political space in which HHDT artists move. I propose that the conceptualization of a complex and politicized metaspace challenges the normative processual and performative modes that currently dominate HHDT and, in doing so, brings to the field a new way of thinking about making work with Hip Hop dance artists in the space of UK dance theater. I develop the discussion about movement, freedom, and spatial politics by considering national artistic practices, arguing that HHDT artists are confined by the metaspace of UK dance theater. It is the acknowledgment of, and sometimes the reaction against, these forces that I call for. So, with this in mind, I examine the nexus between HHDT and the UK's institutional framework to consider how this relationship informs the agency and (im)mobility of the artists and the form itself. I discuss HHDT artist supervision by looking at ideas of choreopolicing, whose purpose is to is to "de-mobilize political action by means of implementing a certain kind of movement that prevents any formation and expression of the political" (Lepecki 2013, 20).[6] In doing so I consider institutional strategies regarding artistic governance in the UK in relation to HHDT. The discussion weaves together multiple components and entities of governance as I perceive them in order to unpick, describe, and contextualize the supervision of HHDT artists in a UK institutional setting. I investigate interconnected supervisory structures, including Sadler's Wells' project Breakin' Convention, National Portfolio Organisations' (NPO) funding models, the imperatives of cultural and creative industries, the prerogatives of Arts Council England (ACE), and artistic mentorships.

I draw on my own voice and on interviews with artists that I conducted between 2014 and 2016.[7] Three of these artists were pioneers in the early exploration of UK Hip Hop theater: Benji Reid, Jonzi D, and the lesser-documented Robert Hylton. Additionally, I use interviews with two emerging young artists, Botis Seva (Far From the Norm) and Lee Griffiths (The Company and Artists4Artists) who are, at the time of writing, branded by the creative industries as HHDT, though not without some resistance from the artists themselves.

UK Pioneers

It would be difficult to consider the arguments I propose in relation to HHDT without first acknowledging the genesis of Hip Hop theater in the UK. The subject matter that inspired the work of the UK Hip Hop theater innovators was informed and shaped by issues of exclusion, displacement, discrimination, and marginalization. These pioneering artists entered the space of UK dance with maverick intentions to proclaim the arrival of a new form that was to leave a lasting and continuing legacy.

Jonzi D has been actively involved in British Hip Hop culture, rapping, and b-boying since the early '80s and his performance background is eclectic and innovative. His early training at the London School of Contemporary Dance was fused with an immersion in the UK Hip Hop scene. He was a founding member of Bedlam Dance Company and an associate artist at The Place contemporary dance center in London. His exploration of "choreo-poetry" (lyrically motivated movement) led to the creation of *Aeroplane Man* and *Silence the Bitchin'* in 1995. These and other pieces were subsequently developed for *Lyrikal Fearta* in 1996, the success of which led to invitations to perform in Europe, North America, and the UK. During this period *Aeroplane Man* was developed into a full-length show, with Benji Reid as codirector, and toured the UK in 1999 and 2000. Jonzi D was approached in 2003 by Alistair Spalding, the incoming artistic director of Sadler's Wells Theatre, London, to become an associate artist, and in 2004, Breakin' Convention was launched as a Sadler's Wells Theatre project with Jonzi D as the artistic director.

A former collaborator of Jonzi D, Benji Reid, was a member of the legendary Broken Glass Crew from Manchester, a European body-popping champion, and a world-ranked dance champion. He went on to study at the Northern School of Contemporary Dance, toured as a dancer with British soul group Soul II Soul, and worked as a performer with celebrated UK physical theater companies, including the David Glass Ensemble, Trestle Theatre, and Black Mime Theatre.

Reid's career is prolific; his early touring solo shows included *15 Seconds of Fame* and *Paper Jackets* and he founded the Manchester-based Hip Hop theater company Breaking Cycles. This innovative work—combining music and the language of breaking and body popping with the theatricality of text and movement theater—won wide critical acclaim, and *The Pugilist*, *The Holiday*, *Style 4 Free*, *13 Mics*, and *B Like Water* toured the world to sell-out audiences, including at the Sydney Opera House and the London Royal Opera House. As a performer and director, Reid has left a lasting imprint on the UK ecology of Hip Hop dance, Hip Hop theater, and physical theater. Today, his theater and photographic work continues to be innovative, and it challenges the boundaries of performance and its dissemination through the exploration of multimedia platforms. His approach is interstitial, and he deliberately pushes against the constraints of creative industry-led categorizations. Within the context of his current work, he describes himself as a "choreo-photolist" whose photographic images contain a constant dialogue between the choreographer, the director, and the photographer.

Finally, among the pioneers is the often-overlooked figure of Robert Hylton. Hailing from the North East, he is a dancer who is immersed in the UK Hip Hop scene and active in the UK jazz dance scene. Hylton trained at the Northern School of Contemporary Dance, was an apprentice with Phoenix Dance Company, and, like Jonzi D, went on to become an associate artist at The Place, in London. His work is daring and innovative and draws on a fusion of styles to create challenging pieces that are often as confusing as they are exciting: notably a solo, *A Step into Urban Classicism*, danced to the recorded lyrics of Amiri Baraka in 1999. Like Reid, Hylton is an interstitial artist, interested in hybridity and moving away from the constraints of commodified forms. He is also an emerging scholar who regularly contributes to the discourse surrounding Hip Hop dance in the UK.

These key figures evolved through a DIY ethic and brought their own ideology, politics, and audiences into the space of UK theater. They notably defined the form rather than the form defining them, as, arguably, HHDT now does for many artists. As Reid notes, the situation is considerably more difficult now, "because artists are coming in, and this happens to be a form that they don't necessarily fit into, or want to be part of, but yet it's been legitimized, and now everybody is viewing them through this canon" (interview with the author, June 25, 2015).

UK INSTITUTIONAL FRAMEWORK

There are presently two dominant expressions of the HHDT form, both of which maintain the fourth-wall end-on staging paradigm that has long defined the institutions of British dance and theater.[8] The first of these uses staging aesthetics "structured around a series of set pieces or visual punch lines, flourishes of physical bravado that require a vocal response" (Logan 2014). And here it is possible to draw comparisons to aspects of nineteenth-century melodramas, pantomimes, spectacle plays, and story ballets: they employ narratives that illustrate a simplified moral universe via stock characters and present them in a series of short declamatory scenes. The second expression of the form navigates a different route, assimilating the staging aesthetics and, quite often, the movement of a European-derived aesthetic tradition of modern and postmodern contemporary dance.

It is possible to argue that HHDT has inherited these traditional production values under the supervision of Sadler's Wells, which, dating back to the eighteenth century, is London's second oldest theater.[9] Alistair Spalding joined the theater's administrative team in 2000 as the director of programming and was appointed as the new artistic director in 2004. In 2005 Spalding announced: "You've got the National Theatre for drama, English National Opera for opera and I want Sadler's Wells to perform the same function for contemporary dance" (Higgins, 2005). These words, invoking concepts of monolithic national and artistic values in the UK high-arts continuum, were to herald the rise of Sadler's Wells Theatre to a position as one of the UK's prominent cultural and artistic gatekeepers.

Breakin' Convention is a registered trademark of Sadler's Wells Trust Limited; the project is funded by Arts Council England through an award given to Sadler's Wells Theatre: "[The] money is ring-fenced, so Sadler's Wells can only spend that money on Breakin' Convention stuff, but ultimately, it's given to Sadler's Wells" (Jonzi D interview).[10] Breakin' Convention's annual International Festival of Hip Hop Dance Theatre showcases, among other things, poppers, lockers, house dancers, breakers, lindy hoppers, flexing, dancehall, and krump, and features an exclusive risqué burlesque cabaret night called WorX.[11] The project has been recognized by the national press and through major funding initiatives as the key developer of HHDT, and with a program that includes artist mentorship, national and international tours, platforms for sharing work in progress, and school-based courses, Breakin' Convention's influence extends far beyond the yearly festival. The project is regarded as an Arts Council National Portfolio Organisation (NPO) situated within Sadler's Wells administrative framework, meaning that its funding is reviewed quadrennially. We might also note that the Arts Council's government partners include the Department of Digital, Culture, Media and Sport and the Department of Education and that it openly shares priorities and formal working arrangements with the BBC and the British Council (Arts Council England 2013, 15).[12] The endogamous nature of these relationships and their collective political and economic agenda is problematic for the arts, as was recently highlighted when the right-wing media mogul Rupert Murdoch's daughter was appointed to the National Arts Council.[13] Moreover, these relationships highlight that the UK arts discourse is imbricated with complex dialogues of constraint and liberation, and HHDT cannot be excluded from these concerns.

The discourse of the arts in London is increasingly focusing on cultural tourism. For example, the document *Take a Closer Look: A Cultural Tourism Vision for London 2015–2017* sets out a strategy to develop an intimate dialogue between art and culture, and dance and theater are clearly highlighted, along with museums, exhibitions, and other attractions, for their potential to offer authentic "brag-able" experiences for cultural tourists (Mayor of London 2015, 28).[14] Operating within this climate, Sadler's Wells' promotion of HHDT is layered with agendas that are guided by ideas about socioeconomic governance. For example, funding structures, such as the NPO strategy (discussed in detail later in the chapter), are closely linked to the apparatus of the state and are a part of an ensemble of forces that have an impact on institutionalized forms; these forces are summarized in Foucault's (1980) term the *dispositif* (194).[15]

The Arts Council's channeling of support through a Sadler's Wells Theatre NPO project sets the stage for Breakin' Convention to be heavily driven institutionally instead of running itself as an autonomous organization. Consequently, Breakin' Convention and HHDT are involved in the workings of this institution, which can impact their artistic expression in particular ways. Here, important questions arise as to what artistic, political, and cultural compromises are demanded and made in order to remain in a funding cycle that is dictated by the financial machinations of the metropolis. The NPO strategy is highly contentious and has been extended across the UK with the aim of centralizing the governance of the arts around major national organizations: its aim is "increasing investment to organizations that produce and present art of international significance, and that also contribute to tourism and the local economy" (Hill 2014). This appraisal of artistic work based on economically driven outcomes bears out Harvie's (2005) suggestion that the industrialization of the arts compromises "democratic expression" (9). This policy essentially means that "[artistic] work now is seen as a product, and you have to have something that sells. And it has to be packaged and marketed within a box that an audience recognizes" (Reid interview). We might conclude, then, that the NPO strategy jeopardizes free artistic expression in the UK by explicitly tying public money to governmental concerns and proposing a meritocracy based on national economic growth rather than the artistic voice.

This strategic funding framework has an explicit impact on artists and NPOs, including Breakin' Convention, enforcing artistic compromises to match the criteria of national strategic arts funding. Furthermore, quadrennial funding reviews and cuts discipline projects that stray from the contractual demands imposed by the Arts Council's investment. It might be presumed that sitting within the embrace of one of the dominant national artistic institutions greatly strengthens the chances of longevity for the Breakin' Convention project. But, as Jonzi D points out, the project's position at Sadler's Wells is not secured and is subject to "continual negotiation" (Jonzi D interview). I suggest that this "continual negotiation" encompasses a continual compromise imposed by the HHDT brand and its financial and cultural capital values (Bourdieu, 2010).

METASPATIAL KNOWLEDGE

It is important to avoid adopting a binary view—artists versus institutions—and I am not suggesting a binary wherein artists must choose between the independent unfunded route to making work or the funded constraints of institutional supervision. A hardened stance, as Danielle Goldman (2010) wrote, "is the result of a reification of freedom as freedom is the necessity of not taking a hardened stance" (4). Furthermore, improvisation arises from these very circumstances and in reaction to "various kinds of constraint" or "tight spaces" (3).[16] Similarly, Foucault (1991) suggested that practices of freedom are only afforded because of the existence of power relations and that power is productive and embedded in all human interactions; it is an inescapable truth where "one is always 'inside' power" (95). In this sense, the seemingly oppositional notions of coercion and liberation propose a symbiotic relationship that informs an improvised "practice of freedom" where power inevitably produces resistance.

To support the development of choreographic strategies that resist dominant processual structures in HHDT, it is necessary first to understand the full complexity of the constraints within which HHDT moves. The production of HHDT is linked to current governmental and ACE prerogatives aimed at strategies of cultural consumerism, and the apparatus maintaining this supervisory structure is built on a network of complex negotiations. *Metaspatial knowledge* engages with the governing apparatus and is, essentially, *knowledge* of the wider sociocultural, historical, economic, and political space in which HHDT artists move, and it leads us to a clearer understanding of how the environment of UK dance shapes their performance, including the consideration of how imposed and inherited preconceptions of what dance should be circulate in this arena. Therefore, I urge the development of *metaspatial knowledge* so that Hip Hop dance artists might fully explore new ways of negotiating the territory of UK dance theater and, in doing so, develop choreographic strategies that resist dominant processual structures in HHDT.

HHDT is supervised through the spaces that define its circulation, and therefore in this context, mobilization might be seen as the act of moving away from the institutionally driven commodification of the form/brand. In these circumstances, Reid notes, "one is forced to start thinking about [one's] box" (Reid interview), and here I suggest that HHDT is the box that we should think about. By identifying their *metaspace*, Hip Hop dance artists can mobilize new ways of thinking and doing that challenge the structure presently imposed by HHDT. In this way, a clearer understanding of agency and (im)mobility can lead toward the consideration of alternative routes that resist "states of domination" (Foucault 1997, 283).

To illustrate how *metaspatial knowledge* can inform a broader reading of artists' agency and (im)mobility, let us examine the connection between London's "East Bank" cultural district and HHDT.[17] In 2015 Sadler's Wells' influence on HHDT was further acknowledged and consolidated with the announcement of a second Sadler's Wells Theatre location, to be built on the site of the 2012 Olympic Stadium as part of the new East Bank cultural district.[18] The building will sit alongside outposts of Washington DC's Smithsonian museum, the V&A (Victoria and Albert Museum), the BBC, University College London, and London College of Fashion. Referred to as Sadler's Wells East, the new building will house a choreographic school providing spaces with facilities for dance research and the development and production of new work, and will notably include the UK's first Hip Hop academy. However, given that the academy will rely on the patrimony of both the state and Sadler's Wells, multiple anxieties present themselves, not least of which is that "when art is blessed with public funding it is simultaneously cursed by the state's imperium" (Beech 2015, 17). Here, once again, the funding does not grant artistic autonomy but instead includes it as part of a strategically linked governmental program aimed wholly at the capitalization of the arts.

For many people, the inclusion of a Hip Hop academy in the £1.3 billion project is seen as a positive step toward recognizing the talent and potential of HHDT, a cause for celebration as the state continues to legitimize Hip Hop through a dialogue of cultural inclusion and funding, even though it is still under the supervision of a gatekeeping institution. I suggest that, rather than being a benign force, the sudden momentum toward promoting HHDT in the UK might be aimed at ticking "of-color" and "young" boxes in order to secure funding and build social and cultural capital for the institutions involved (Bourdieu 2010). These associations also raise questions about who gets to perform how, what kinds of identities are being made, and the extent of what Harvie (2005) calls the "profound and inescapable influence of government policy and practice in manufacturing these associations: in a continual rebranding of Britain and particularly London, as a multi-cultural metropolis" (16). In such a corporate-driven environment, it might be argued, the commercialization of culture is contributing to a collapsing of race and culture.

This notion of rebranding appears implicit when we consider that the Olympic Games have been widely linked to gentrification, "evict[ing] more than two million people in the past twenty years, [making it] one of the top causes of displacement and real-estate inflation in the world" (Kumar 2012).[19] Furthermore, the data elicits more suspicion when we see that the London borough of Newham, one of the most ethnically diverse boroughs in the UK, suffered mass evictions to make way for the Olympic Village.[20] The East Bank vision systematically capitalizes on these events by "expanding the terrain of profitable activity" (2012), compounding the assumption that the aim of this large-scale project is to globalize rather than revitalize, the "primary beneficiaries [being] cultural tourists, major property holders, and the egos of public officials" (Cocotas 2016, 6).[21] Moreover, the promised inclusion of affordable housing in East Bank has not materialized, causing many people, including architects and artists, to voice fears about issues of gentrification, social cleansing, and London's rapidly changing cultural landscape.[22]

These worries are partially directed at the national arts institutions that will supervise the cultural district, and some have suggested that East Bank is displacing artists through a consumer-led gentrification of London where "the consumption of culture is driving the production of culture out of the city" (Heathcote 2015). This argument means that the national artistic institutions that will dominate the East Bank cultural district might be viewed as artistic gatekeepers that are sustained by strategic policies of tourism and consumer-led artistic curation. The evolving discourse surrounding gentrification leads me to return to consider the Hip Hop academy that will be housed, governed, and supervised by Sadler's Wells, a major player in the East Bank development, and to question HHDT's role in the ACE strategic vision for commodified dance.[23]

Drawing on these perspectives, I posit that the significance of this discourse extends beyond the movement of artists on stage to their movement in the city of London. In the near future, many HHDT artists may not be able to subsist in London owing to the high costs of living, which are incompatible with freelance dancers' wages, or because they become immobilized or displaced by the forces of rapid gentrification and commoditization. From my experience of working with these artists, I know that many are facing a rapidly escalating struggle for economic survival in the capital. In this regard, the inclusion of a Hip Hop academy in an area that was cleared of lower-income families and independent artists for the 2012 Olympic Games and was subsequently developed into a new cultural district becomes problematic.[24] Considering the tightly controlled funding strategies, the apparent openness of the mainstream arts establishment to the cultural differences and new identities represented through HHDT appears questionable. I suggest that developing the East Bank in London is less a process aimed at protecting cultural differences than one of assimilation, which serves the mainstream arts establishment's imperial purposes, or "the cultivation of a self-promoting and self-interested narrative of the metropolis as benignly tolerant of difference" (Harvie 2005, 16). This notion seems prescient in relation to arguments raised about access, supervision, and displacement regarding the East Bank development. Furthermore, current developments indicate that the cultural district itself, purported by the architects to "intensify the urban grain and make the stadium and park feel more special" (Bevan 2016), will remain an exclusive landmark of London's elite, including its elite artistic institutions.

In the context of the East Bank development, political and economic immobilization might therefore be said to have an impact on the physical (im)mobility of Hip Hop dance artists in several ways. For example, the supervision by Sadler's Wells of the Hip Hop academy raises questions about dancers' artistic agency, while rising travel and living costs will limit their access to the area and, consequently, to the artistic and developmental opportunities within it. This is a type of artistic and fiscal disciplining that can be considered to contribute to dominant systems of coercion that seek to maintain the subordination of particular groups and particular modes of cultural production.

I am not proposing that institutional collaborations represent a wholly negative force; rather, that they call for close scrutiny by the artists moving within those frameworks. When I asked Jonzi D about the dangers of HHDT's institutional supervision, he expressed the dichotomy of a situation born out of necessity: "Personally for me, I say bring it on, mate, and basically, OK, if they don't do that, then what you gonna do?" (Jonzi D interview). Here Jonzi D raises an important question in the current climate of UK arts. HHDT as a successful UK arts brand has notions of currency running through it on many levels, meaning that though many young dancers are drawn to it, others experience it as a constrictive box. One such artist, Botis Seva—an increasingly celebrated young theater artist who uses Hip Hop dance as a creative element—struggled to define HHDT, saying, "People told me, 'This is the way you're doing theater now.' I didn't know what it was. Is it Hip Hop in a theater?" (interview with the author, June 6, 2015).[25] Seva sees the form/brand as artistically constrictive, and this is felt by other artists I have spoken to, who also feel boxed in by the institutional need to label, claim, and commodify them as HHDT.

Another emerging voice, Lee Griffiths, has encountered similar problems of marketing forces placing her work in the HHDT box. She feels "constrained by the funding system" (interview with the author, June 19, 2015), a system that awards very short periods of supervised support that is often linked to celebrity choreographers or commercially focused outcomes. Seva's case illustrates this: contemporary dance icon Hofesh Schechter has been tied to him via mentorship-linked funding. I suggest that this can be seen as canonical policing, a legitimizing process that makes economic and aesthetic links to the European postmodern contemporary dance canon to justify the negotiation between the UK high-art continuum and HHDT. Griffiths, along with others, calls instead for helping Hip Hop dance artists who are exploring theater by giving them "longer periods of funded time" (Griffiths interview) and the space to create work unfettered by such supervision.

However, the concept of unsupervised artistic space is unlikely to materialize in the present corporate-driven economic climate of UK dance, and here I offer an educational analogy. Since 1981 successive governments have imposed a "business school conception" on UK universities, reforming them so that they now resemble public limited companies rather than "research intensive institutions." Nowadays, the majority of university students are encouraged to study vocational or professional subjects and to strive toward economically rather than artistically driven futures (Collini 2012). And we can surmise that the same strategy is being applied to the economization of UK dance. Unsurprisingly, HHDT is no exception and is being constructed in deference to this model, which does not encourage free artistic movement:

You don't necessarily get the freedom to make work that is your true essence and then find the language to sell it. It almost works in the reverse. It lies about the art. It lies about the artist. And it lies about our times, because theaters are getting more and more scared that they are investing in work that they don't think that they can sell and they are forcing you to be something that you're not. (Reid interview)

This model, then, places tight restrictions on artists who want to explore new points of departure.[26] Moreover, I would add to these constraints the economic pressure of everyday survival in a rapidly gentrifying London, which is a coercive force that maneuvers many young artists into taking whatever support they can get. And, within my analogy, this can be equated to the anxieties imposed by the student-loan system, which often leaves young people immobilized and coerced by a lifetime of financial struggle and debt.

These power relations can be seen to immobilize artists, imposing disciplining techniques (Foucault 1991) via economic constraints. Furthermore, this knowledge, gleaned from scrutinizing the wider space in which HHDT circulates, leads us to now consider how these forces guide Hip Hop artists in the space of UK dance theater toward brand conformity.

Supervision, Surveillance, and Kettling

The position of HHDT in the strategic agenda of UK arts is determined not only by its multidimensional capital but also by its deference to the modern and postmodern contemporary dance canon that Sadler's Wells curates. In this respect, and in the wider spatial context I have discussed, the supervision of Hip Hop dance artists constitutes a type of "choreopolicing" (Lepecki 2013), the purpose of which is to enforce "a prechoreographed pattern of circulation, corporeality, and belonging" (20). Through the concept of choreopolicing, it is possible to bind together ideas of *movement, freedom*, and the *political* (15) to argue that the institutional supervision of HHDT equates to the idea of surveillance. Consider the wider context of societal policing, where surveillance cameras, cell phones, loyalty cards, credit cards, computer-linked location-tracking systems, and other devices track our movements: "This condition, where no one is left alone for long, reveals how an apparent 'freedom of movement' is under strict control thanks to constant surveillance" (15). By following this line of thought, it is not difficult to identify choreopolicing in HHDT, where surveillance, represented by the watchful eye of funders, mentors, press reviewers, and artistic curators, defines "pathways for circulation that are introjected as the only ones imaginable, the only ones deemed appropriate" (15).

I propose to expand the lexicon of choreopolicing by adding 'kettling' to the list of surveillance methods. Kettling is a complex spatial strategy, a twenty-first-century tactic whereby police control the protesters' space, confining their movements and how they enter and leave an area, which is usually through a signified spot:

To get closer to an understanding of kettling we need to unpick its political logic in relation to neoliberalism . . . kettling aims to achieve two seemingly relational results: to control and incite the crowd in order to produce 'good' social effects by agents of neoliberal governance, and displace dissent and resistance in order to defuse the fear of revolution (Taşkale 2012).

Using kettling as a metaphor, where Sadler's Wells (or another major institution) becomes the signified spot through which HHDT must pass, and where funding, mentorships, and other supervisory apparatus define/confine the movements of the artists, it is possible to see choreopolicing at work. All too often, artists perceive the strategic funding of HHDT as the granting of artistic freedom, only to later realize that there is a marked difference between freedom and liberation. In this context, liberation can be seen as HHDT artists being given access to venues such as Sadler's Wells, the Barbican, and The Place, but only under strict supervisory conditions that operate via dominant institutional structures. Here, freedom can be seen as the daily practice of ethical self-governance that resists conditions of domination so that new power relations can be negotiated: this involves working toward the determination of individual and collective consciences. To contextualize this idea, we might view HHDT artists entering mainstream bastions of high art as a momentary act of liberation while recognizing that their "practice of freedom" is compromised by institutional demands (Foucault 1997, 284).

The direct choreopolicing of movement and artistic aesthetics in HHDT is consistently enacted through assigned mentorships, where artists who define the UK legacy of postmodern contemporary dance transmit established and recognizable ways of moving and working. The dominant UK dance institutions and organizations, including funders, broker these programs as part of a legitimizing process that attempts to pass on perceived artistic capital via association. And to date, Jonathan Burrows, Hofesh Schechter, and Jasmin Vardimon rank among the dominant mentoring figures for HHDT artists. These conditions indicate that the choreopolicing of HHDT echoes cultural imperialism, perpetuating what the writer bell hooks (2008) described over two decades ago as a "solely white Western artistic continuum." This operates through a system that "sees and values only those aspects that mimic familiar white Western artistic traditions" (29).

Some other players in the choreopolicing scenario are also worth noting. Producers play an increasingly pivotal role in the brokerage of UK funding streams and the development of artistic legacies, including those of dance.[27] In addition, annual dance trade events such as the British Dance Edition and the British Council Showcase exert a heavy influence on the UK dance sector. Hylton calls this aspect of the dance *metaspace* "the business of the foyer," where reputations are made and where artists get a "thumbs up" or "thumbs down." He also notes the "popcorn that they are putting out with a lot of the shows [and that] legacy is being written into this ecology [where] the funding sustains certain legacies" (interview with the author, January 5, 2016).

Artistic Continuum

The prescriptive nature of the lauded artistic practices inherent in UK contemporary dance theater exerts a heavy influence on HHDT, which often relies on watered-down storylines that rehash common Western theater pieces, narratives, and staging. In many cases HHDT has been reduced to a kind of spectacle of tantalizing performance elements, reminiscent of Guy Debord's (1994) view that it "expresses the total practice of one particular economic and social formation: it is, so to speak, the formation's *agenda*" (15; my emphasis).

As an example, we might examine the decision by the UK Arts Council in 2015 to award £1,000,000 to the partnership between ZooNation and Sadler's Wells' Breakin' Convention project. Almost half of the award was given to support a nationwide tour of ZooNation show *Into the Hoods: Remixed*—a thinly disguised reimagining of Stephen Sondheim's classic hit musical *Into the Woods*—promoting their highly successful brand of West End musical Hip Hop theater as a flagship for HHDT throughout the UK.[28] The remainder of the award went toward supporting a two-year nationwide tour of the Breakin' Convention project, with the aim of developing future professional HHDT artists.

ZooNation has adopted a long-established and successful formula and applied it to the production of theater, fusing popular classical Western narratives, West End musical staging and aesthetics, and corporeally virtuosic Hip Hop dance.[29] It consistently generates revenue for producers and jobs for Hip Hop performers and attracts sell-out audiences. The original production of *Into the Hoods* (2006) was a proven commodity, in every sense the archetypal spectacle, exemplifying the linking of Hip Hop dance with capitalist concerns. The restaging of the original asset as the *Into the Hoods: Remixed* tour (2015–2017) was coproduced by Sadler's Wells Theatre, capitalizing on the success of the original sell-out show by staging a *remix*. With tickets selling at up to £49 each, we might ask why this proven commodity needed Arts Council funding, who and what it was aimed at, and what story it was trying to tell/sell.

The Arts Council heralded the funding award with a press release that recognized the partnership of the Sadler's Wells Breakin' Convention project and ZooNation— both headed by Sadler's Wells' own associate artists—as a showcase for "some of the best HHDT in the world" (Wilson in Smith 2015).[30] Here, once again, we can see choreopolicing at work in a declaration that not only signifies *Into the Hoods: Remixed* as the international epitome of HHDT, but also highlights a focus on the "professional development of emerging Hip Hop dance talent and leaders across England" (2015). *Metaspatial knowledge* therefore leads us toward the thought that The Arts Council may be developing economic rather than artistic *leaders* in order to secure the capital growth of the HHDT brand.

In this context, HHDT, as exemplified by ZooNation, is far from breaking any conventions and is simply following the conventional formula of West End theatrical production: restaging certified narratives and merely substituting one form of dance for another. Furthermore, this raises concerns about the use of dominant Western theatrical narratives in HHDT and problematizes the legitimizing nature of classic texts such as Sondheim, Dickens, and Shakespeare: "It sends a message that the hip-hop generation has no stories of its own and that in order for hip-hop to qualify as theater it must attach itself to such certified texts" (Hoch in Prickett 2013, 182). This analysis expands on the idea of the choreopolicing of HHDT that is played out and enforced through the high-level funding of projects that mimic the familiar traditions of the Western artistic continuum.

Clearly, the *metaspace* of HHDT is complex and filled with multiple intrigues, one of which is that by managing both of these funding strategies via its own associate artists, Sadler's Wells is able to establish a firm link between product and process on a nationwide scale. In a press release acknowledging the funding, Spalding praised the ability of HHDT "to continuously evolve and develop a highly original vocabulary—a language that is dynamic and current, and speaks to ever increasing numbers of young people" (Spalding in Dyke 2015). To investigate what this language is presently articulating to its institutional investors, be it economic growth, inclusion, diversity, multiculturalism, or other benefits, let us take a closer look at the discourse of Sadler's Wells Theatre.[31]

Spalding, CBE, is what Herrnstein Smith (1983) might call a "power-holding subject" in the UK contemporary dance scene.[32] In an article for the *Financial Times* (2013), Spalding identified HHDT as "arguably the dance form of the future," concluding that "in today's increasingly diversified dance world, it is likely that the next Nijinsky or Nureyev will not come from ballet but from hip-hop or tango." Spalding's language seems to mimic the Western dance canon by using two iconic male figures as examples, invoking the familiar gaze of a white imperialist artistic tradition—a tradition that hooks (2008) decries as oppressive by the very nature of its investment in canons that are linked to an aesthetic of white supremacy. The article received some provocative responses from *Financial Times* readers:

> I am pleased that the "serious" end of culture and dance in the UK takes up modern music, but I have my doubts that hip hop is the way to go for ballet. What seems like agility can when looked at more closely seem a lot clumsier than ballet might require, and crucially, hip hop artists lack the years of discipline and training needed for ballet. Nor do I wish to see ballet politicized. Whatever next? Swan Lake with machine guns? (Lucinda, July 13, 2013, quoted in Spalding 2013).

Lucinda's declamation contains the essence of many of the problems that HHDT encounters in the UK high-art setting. Sadler's Wells counts high-profile multinational financial corporations such as Bloomberg, Rothschild and Co, the executive search firm Egon Zehnder, Clifford Chance (a law firm handling and advising on major offshore capital investment), and American Express among its corporate partners, and this reflects the audience demographic that it aims to attract. I suggest that Hip Hop dance is still seen as "other" by the establishment art world and self-proclaimed dance aficionados like Lucinda, showing little understanding of the years of intense training demanded to achieve an elite level and, in Lucinda's case, demonstrating ignorance of the political history of classical dance itself. Furthermore, Lucinda's final commentary reflects a sense of disdain that adds to the perception of HHDT as a low-art form.

We can see that, to date, the Breakin' Convention project has had little impact on the yearly programming of the main Sadler's Wells stage, beyond the annual May Day bank holiday slot and the occasional visiting international company such as Wang and Ramirez, whose aesthetic invariably leans toward high-art contemporary dance. This might be read as tokenistic and symptomatic of the marginalization of HHDT to a yearly festival of fun rather than a serious platform for emerging artists. Perhaps Spalding might be seen as attempting to mediate a transition. But while funding may demonstrate that ACE has shown commitment to the "creative phenomenon that is Hip Hop culture, at a time when peace, love, unity, and fun is much needed" (Jonzi D in Dyke 2015), it can also be argued that the choreopolicing of artists via the HHDT brand compromises their artistic and political agency as well as their latent potential.

A Glimpse of the Nascent

In the environment I have outlined, the cultural and creative industries' apparatus dominates and innovation is seldom encouraged. The counter-movement to HHDT is in its infancy in the UK, and a small group of young artists whom I describe as Hip Hop dancers in the space of dance theater are attempting to navigate new routes amid the complexities of an institutionally governed framework. The members of this group can be viewed as marginal figures who work within this framework because of economic and pragmatic necessity while remaining artistically driven toward questioning the status quo, and I include among them Botis Seva (Far From the Norm), Lee Griffiths (The Company), and Kwame Asafo Adjei (Spoken Movement).

These artists are searching for their artistic-political voice through the exploration of a hybrid approach to making dance theater that draws on Hip Hop dance as a central creative element. They create experimental work that challenges binary thinking, such as being cast as HHDT or Hip Hop theater, and their work provokes debate about issues that confuse, concern, and (im)mobilize their generation, with the aim of mobilizing their generation. Yet the strategic supervision of HHDT guides their voices toward the fourth-wall staging aesthetics of contemporary dance, imposing the need to follow long-established traditions of flattened, linear choreography.[33] And all too often, because of the minimal funding and minimal time slots that HHDT platforms such as Breakin' Convention's international festival offer, the artists are only able to create bite-sized pieces that barely touch the surface of their inquiry.[34]

To date, these alternative voices remain very much underfunded and continually struggle to find the means to produce their work. As I have outlined, all too frequently support is not offered to these artists in the form of financial encouragement to research and create their own work; instead, mentorships are made available, but they perpetuate the agendas and clichés of the institutions providing the mentorships. These artists struggle to maintain their voices. This is because they are assimilated into the modern and postmodern contemporary dance canon or the formulaic patterns of West End theater via development programs that are constructed by the hierarchy of UK contemporary dance and the creative industries. They are a very small, select(ed) group, and by isolating and compromising their radical voices via funding streams, rather than dismantling the hegemony of the Western arts canon by dancing on it, as Dodds (2011) suggests, they currently dance very much within it.

The London-based HHDT artists' collective Artists4Artists, headed by Joseph Toonga and Lee Griffiths, was formed in late 2016 to debate and strategize against these prevailing conditions.[35] Artists4Artists was striving for greater autonomy so that it did not have to rely on the precarious support of Breakin' Convention, which it felt focused too much on the work of international, rather than national, HHDT artists. Yet by the close of 2018, the work of Artists4Artists had, in my opinion, shifted toward being a model of human capital because it had become an industry-driven program of activities, and in doing so had drifted away from the collective's initial independent, artistically driven agenda. Funded primarily by ACE and describing themselves as part of the UK dance industry, in 2018 the members of Artists4Artists organized workshops such as Identity, Ideas, Industry and Dance + Industry. They also offered boot camps (intensive workshops for emerging and young dancers) to upskill Hip Hop creatives with artistic and business skills needed in and out of the studio. I suggest that such output-based agendas can be linked to ACE funding and wider dialogic creative and cultural industry prerogatives.

Since becoming an organization primarily funded by ACE, Artists4Artists now appears to have assimilated an industry-driven agenda that mirrors that of Breakin' Convention, where upskilling and scratch-performance outputs dominate the agenda. The scratch format—a mode of presenting work in progress to elicit feedback—has evolved as the main output of HHDT artists owing to the minimal funding they receive and the time slots that platforms such as Breakin' Convention's International Festival and Artists4Artists scratch nights adopt. In these circumstances, HHDT artists are only able to create bite-sized pieces, which barely touch the surface of their exploration, and they continually repeat the process to produce new bite-sized work that conforms with the demands of each new scratch platform. In this demanding and underfunded environment, where trackable and observable outputs dominate the funding exchange, artists are rarely afforded the opportunity to develop their ideas fully so that they can work toward creating work of greater depth, complexity, or length.

Conclusion

The complexity of the institutional negotiation with Hip Hop dancers moving in the space of UK theater has not yet been fully engaged with on an artistic or scholarly level and raises important questions about the artists' (im)mobility and agency that involve multiple forces. Currently, these conditions suggest that HHDT constructs an imagined social category that is enacted via the interrelated forces of choreopolicing that I have discussed.

The stages of UK contemporary dance are already filled with clichés inherited from the tried and tested tropes of dance, art, and theater, and this suggests that both the performance itself and the dancers' bodies already resonate with these inherited preconceptions of what dance is and should be (Lepecki 2015, 63). Yet this in itself constitutes only one aspect of choreopolicing, and, as I have outlined, the *metaspace* that governs HHDT is inextricably bound to governmental economic imperatives. Consequently, because they are "kettled" by the dominant currency of the HHDT form/brand, artists struggle to exercise agency and to mobilize their artistic potential.

In the light of austerity and continuing widespread funding cuts to the arts, we must ask how a system that increasingly offers funding and support only through institutional collaboration impacts the ecology of emerging UK Hip Hop dance artists making theater. The prospect of institutional support in a climate of financial struggle seems a tempting proposition, but it is fraught with dangers informed by the notion of the artist as human capital (McRobbie 2016, 70). Not least of these is that without the development of *metaspatial knowledge* within their own ranks, emerging artists might be consumed by the HHDT brand, becoming packaged and contained to suit the politics and tastes of a strategically driven dance sector that is concerned with market forces rather than artistic expression. In the wake of these anxieties, it seems increasingly urgent to examine the discourse surrounding these artists, as the structure of governmental processes creates an ever-widening socioeconomic divide that directly impacts the arts. I have shown how "creativity is designated by current modes of biopolitical power" that work toward a strategic economic endgame (Harvie 2005, 38). Moreover, I have contextualized this environment through notions of choreopolicing to illustrate how the wider space of the UK arts agenda defines the space of HHDT and the form/brand itself.

By developing *metaspatial knowledge*, the realization of an alternative way of making work in the UK might be found; the space this work is done in should be free of the supervisory constraints of national economic prerogatives, where *knowledge* is strictly supervised. I argue that the corporeal versatility of Hip Hop dance is beyond question—though for aficionados like Lucinda it is strictly low art—and that Hip Hop dancers exploring the space of UK dance theater are a nascent force capable of redefining that space. And, more importantly, if they do so, they will also be capable of dismantling the hegemony of the Western arts canon (Dodds 2011). However, the HHDT form/brand prevents this from happening by guiding artists along the stabilized route of the Western arts continuum, where their voices are assimilated and packaged to suit its legitimized tastes.

It is time for practitioners and researchers to explore and challenge the complex *metaspace* that informs the choreopolitics of the moment and to question the economic model that presently shapes HHDT. We must also reach beyond the paradigms, tropes, and coercions of the canonical framework to address the choreopolicing strategies that national arts institutions perpetuate.

"We as artists have to start to rethink how we're engaging in spaces and to question whether a publicly funded space is the space for artists now. And if we are really interested in making work where we produce, market, and present ourselves, then we have to think about alternative spaces. Which, ultimately, means that we have to stop thinking about our work as a product that earns us money in the same way, and think about making work that shifts the consciousness of our audience and speaks to the sociopolitical landscape of our time, which is not necessarily about putting them into these well-known black boxes, but we have to think about working outside the black box, in order to make a real impact. We are the ones who have to change the landscape because what we are doing is working in these old, tested models that are starting to fail (Reid interview)."

This calls for a reassessment of the manner in which artists negotiate their work. They need to step away from a product-based agenda and toward a revised concept of spatiality: a radically open perspective that encourages a new way of spatial thinking where "choreography as a planned, dissensual, and nonpoliced disposition of motions and bodies becomes the condition of possibility for the political to emerge" (Lepecki 2013, 22). By increasing their *metaspatial knowledge* Hip Hop dance artists can examine new ways of negotiating the territory of UK dance theater that might lead to new ways of moving and making. This is, essentially, *knowledge* of the wider sociocultural, historical, economic, and political space in which HHDT artists move. This could lead artists to a clearer understanding of how the environment of UK dance shapes their performance and how imposed and inherited preconceptions of what dance should be circulate in this arena. What I am advocating, therefore, is that artists should have a greater awareness of the broader sociopolitical and economic conditions in which they move as a means of empowering them to move, make, and perform differently. I strongly encourage the continual development of *metaspatial knowledge* so that Hip Hop dance artists in the space of UK dance theater might negotiate a position in which they become the unfettered voice of their generation.

NOTES

1. Davis (2006); Hodges-Persley (2015); Daniel Banks (2006); Hoch (2006); Fogarty (2011); and Osborn, Kearney, and Fogarty (2015) discuss "Hip Hop theatre." Shapiro (2004) and McCarren (2015) discuss the French "Hip Hop ballet" and "Hip Hop concert dance," while Osumare (2006) discusses Rennie Harris as a "Hip Hop concert choreographer."
2. The following two examples illustrate this: Hoggard (2016), writing for the *Evening Standard*, invokes the Western art continuum via legitimized venues while summarizing the event via a "low art" comparison: "It was fascinating to see how hip-hop has embraced elements of 'high art,' while several spoken word pieces could easily have been staged at the Bush or Young Vic . . . At heart Breakin' Convention is a variety show. For the finale, *Britain's Got Talent* finalists Flawless stormed the stage with their firecracker pyrotechnics."
   Elese (2017) for the website I Am Hip Hop, London, wrote a review that lacks the critical awareness that Breakin' Convention is not autonomous and is a Sadler's Wells Theatre

project. The review also critiques elitism while proposing that HHDT follow the same path as ballet: "Breakin' Convention broke down the usually stuffy and elitist doors of Sadler's Wells Theatre for its 13th year . . . Breakin' Convention is at the vanguard of Hip Hop culture, a cultural merging point between theatre and grass roots urban culture. I really hope Hip Hop dance theatre becomes a thing like going to the ballet."

3. "Gentrification is a form of socio-spatial urban development wherein working class or lower-income residential neighbourhoods are transformed into middle-class residential or commercial neighbourhoods, resulting in the displacement and geographical reshuffling of existing residents" (Deobhakta 2014, 1).

   "Gentrifiers' consumption patterns, translated into boutiques, cafes, and bars by new retail entrepreneurs, clash with those of longtime residents, and act as both a visible sign of safe capital investment and a force of cultural displacement" (Zukin 2015, 232).

   I use the term "(im)mobility" (Pellegrino 2011, 157) to describe the notion of a dialogic interaction between corporeal and conceptual freedom and constraint. I employ the term to capture a negotiation between mobility and immobility that emerged from my own practice research with HHDT artists, where I came to realize that the two states are intricately linked and inform each other; they are causal and reciprocal, interacting and negotiating with each other. Therefore, the term "(im)mobility" captures this continuous dialogue and contains both a conceptual and a corporeal discourse.

   Culturfication is a neologism used on some online discussions to mean becoming cultured. However, I use culturfication to mean a corporate strategy, linked to globalization that produces and manufactures culture as a financial commodity. This product is closely linked to notions of cultural and financial capital aimed at tourism and international markets. It is a homogenous product designed to control and replace the diverse (vernacular) cultural sites that it consumes. Used in this way, culturfication echoes aspects of Peter K. Fallon's (1991) notion of the "Disneyfication of society" (Fallon in Kehoe 1991, 373).

4. " 'Hip-hop theatre,' coined from inside the culture by Brooklyn-based poet Eisa Davis in *The Source* magazine in March 2000, has come to describe the work of a generation of artists who find themselves defined in a new category of both prospective opportunity and limitation" (Uno 2004).

5. "Sadler's Wells is the world's leading dance house, a place where artists come together to create dance and where people of all ages and from all walks of life come to experience dance. We present, commission, produce and tour the best dance from around the world" (Sadler's Wells, 2019). Sadler's Wells is the hub for HHDT, which is supervised via Breakin' Convention, a National Portfolio Organisation that sits within Sadler's Wells's funding stream. Sadler's Wells instigates supervisory structures that are sanctioned and funded by Arts Council England. These include allocated mentorships that demonstrate an endogamous strategic governance of HHDT in the UK. Therefore, I have chosen to scrutinize the interplay between these supervisory components. For more information see "Support Us" on the Sadler's Wells website, https://www.sadlerswells.com/support-us. Accessed April 23, 2019.

6. "Choreopoliced movement can thus be defined as any movement incapable of breaking the endless reproduction of an imposed circulation of consensual subjectivity, where to be is to fit a prechoreographed pattern of circulation, corporeality, and belonging" (Lepecki 2013, 20).

7. The lens of reflection presents my perspective as a white Western male of working-class origin, with a genealogy rooted in Franco-Irish ancestry. It draws on my immersion in

politically engaged theater and dance over the past thirty-eight years, which has included Western and non-Western practices. During this time, my training, performance, and research have drawn me to work with, among other things, contemporary dance, butoh, martial arts, UK jazz dance, Northern soul, intercultural theater, and, extensively, with capoeira. I have constantly worked with artists and students in workshop scenarios, including as an assistant to Jonzi D and as a mentor at the Breakin' Convention's "Open Art Surgery." Since 1997 my artistic work and research have focused primarily on Hip Hop dance artists in the space of UK dance theater, many of whom voice dissatisfaction with the tensions between the prescribed natures of (im)mobility, agency, and access in present HHDT practice. For more information, see "About" at my website, https://paulsadot.com. Accessed June 12, 2019..

8. "The *fourth wall* is a theater term referring to the imaginary line, or wall, between the actors on the stage and the audience" (Del Seamonds 1996).

9. At the time of writing, it can be argued that a patrimonial, dialogic, and legitimizing network of four major UK venues/organizations exists that has supported, funded, and mentored the handful of HHDT companies that have secured National Portfolio Organisation status: Sadler's Wells, The Barbican, The Place (home of the London School of Contemporary Dance), and Arts Council England.

10. Intellectual property rights cover the following: "Organising, arranging and staging dance festivals and live dance exhibitions, including Hip Hop dance theatre; booking agencies for dance festivals and theatre tickets; management of dance and theatre festivals; production of entertainment shows featuring dancers and live performers; organising workshops, lectures and demonstrations on Hip Hop dance theatre; provision of dance classes; publication of printed matter relating to all the aforesaid services; information and advisory services relating to the aforesaid services" (Patent Office 2016).

11. Advertised as Breakin' Convention's "coming of age," WorX is an exclusive adult-only evening offering "titillating tales of desire and temptation through dance, circus and poetry" (Dyke, 2018). The audience must follow a smart dress-code policy to gain entry to this event. See https://www.sadlerswells.com/whats-on/2019/breakin-convention-presents-worx-/.

12. In an article for the *Guardian* website, British author and political activist Owen Jones (2014) accused the BBC of being politically biased and "stacked full of rightwingers."

13. Elisabeth Murdoch's appointment caused a backlash from arts professionals in the UK, and arts activist and academic Dr. Stephen Pritchard argued that "Elisabeth Murdoch's appointment to Arts Council England National Council is a corporate takeover of the arts—a takeover facilitated by Sir Nicholas Serota and his wife Teresa Gleadowe" (Pritchard 2017a). Much has already been written about her father Rupert Murdoch's use of family and media interests to influence political outcomes and events throughout the world (Mahler and Rutenberg 2019; Muller 2018).

14. Ryan Bukstein, chief cultural engineer at the Ace Hotel in Shoreditch, has said: "If harnessed in the right way, cultural tourism could offer huge long-term value to London and inspire and motivate more repeat travel across London. . . . Most of our clientele are cultural tourists. Our whole brand is based upon this cultural exchange" (quoted in Mayor of London 2015, 22).

15. Foucault summarizes the various forces that have an impact on institutionalized forms in the term *dispositif*: "What I'm trying to pick out with this term is, firstly, a thoroughly heterogeneous ensemble consisting of discourses, institutions, architectural forms,

regulatory decisions, laws, administrative measures, scientific statements, philosophical, moral and philanthropic propositions—in short, the said as much as the unsaid. Such are the elements of the apparatus. The apparatus itself is the system of relations that can be established between these elements" (Foucault 1980, 194).

16. Writing about constraint and improvisation, Danielle Goldman echoes Foucault's (1991) writing on practices of freedom to argue that symbiosis necessarily exists between constraint and freedom and that improvisation arises from, and moves in relation to, these circumstances. Improvised dance, Goldman (2010) argues, is "giving shape to oneself by deciding how to move in relation to an unsteady landscape" (5).

17. Human *agency* is a term that is often used in academic writing, and linguistic and sociocultural anthropologist Laura Ahearn (1999) notes that its meaning varies greatly depending upon the context of its usage (12). In the context of my research, I find Ahearn's (2001) definition of *agency* as "the socioculturally mediated capacity to act" (28) a useful anchor point. This provisional definition recognizes that, to some degree, sociocultural and political tensions inform all human actions and interactions.

18. Originally called "Olympicopolis," the name of the project changed in 2018 to East Bank, with Sadler's Wells new outpost becoming Sadler's Wells East. "The line-up is completed with Sadler's Wells, designed by ODT [O'Donnell + Tuomey] as a purplish brick shed containing a 550-seat theater and dance studios. It's topped with a sawtooth factory roofline, recalling the industrial history of the site. It is a consciously tough edifice to stand opposite the voluptuous curves of Zaha Hadid's aquatics centre and a ground-floor corner will be devoted to a community dance space, providing a shop window of cavorting bodies to lure people inside" (Wainwright 2018).

19. "Any reading of Olympic history reveals the true motives of each host city. It is the necessity to shock, to fast track the dispossession of the poor and marginalized as part of the larger machinations of capital accumulation. The architects of this plan need a spectacular show; a hegemonic device to reconfigure the rights, spatial relations and self-determination of the city's working class, to reconstitute for whom and for what purpose the city exists. Unlike any other event, the Olympics provide just that kind of opportunity" (Kumar 2012).

20. For more information about regional ethnic diversity in Newham prior to the Olympics, see the briefing from the 2011 census, "Geographies of Diversity in Newham" (2013), http:// hummedia.manchester.ac.uk/institutes/code/briefings/localdynamicsofdiversity/geog raphies-of-diversity-in-newham.pdf. There is little information that is available to date about the specific ethnic and class groups impacted by the evictions caused by the Olympic games. Readers may find Kumar's (2012) analysis useful.

21. Globalization proposes interdependence between nation states and encompasses political, cultural, and economic agendas. This raises many concerns regarding the homogenization of culture and the impact on diversity. Western culture's dominant role in this process indicates hegemonization.

22. The first phase of 259 homes sold out fast off-plan and they were priced from £375,000 for a one-bedroom flat to £985,000 for a five-bedroom house.

23. Between 2016 and 2019, I submitted freedom of information requests to ACE and the press office at Sadler's Wells to try to ascertain the structure and scope of the academy, but neither of these bodies was able to expand upon the little information that is available to the general public.

24. It is important to acknowledge that this process also implicates professional artists in the same gentrification processes that displace minoritarian communities. Artists have been recognized as an initial group that attracts gentrification schemes to an area via cultural capital, and much has been written on this subject (Pritchard 2017b; Kendzior 2014; Lees, Slater, and Wiley 2010; Zukin 2010).

25. In 2018 Seva was appointed as the 2018–2019 guest artistic director of the National Youth Dance Company (NYDC), which is run by Sadler's Wells. In 2019 Seva won the Olivier award for *BLKDOG*, commissioned by Sadler's Wells. Sadler's Wells's associate artists, Akram Khan and Matthew Bourne, also received Olivier Awards on the same night.

26. Since 2016 there has been a rapid growth in university courses in the UK that offer Hip Hop dance and HHDT modules that are linked to theater production in the UK. One such example is the London Studio Centre (2019), which in 2019 introduced a new MA Dance Producing and Management course that focuses on "business models, governance and management structures for dance production." Influential contemporary dance producers Farooq Chaudhry and Katie Prince are among the chief advisers on the course, and Hip Hop is grouped among the practices covered. It is interesting to note that in the LSC Theatre Dance BA program, Hip Hop is offered in years 1 and 2 as a peripheral/optional skills choice along with Pilates, pointe work, tap dance, and other skills. It is dropped in year 3 so that students can concentrate on one of the course's main areas—classical ballet, contemporary dance, jazz theater dance, or music theater.

27. Farooq Chaudhry can be seen as pivotal to multimillionaire choreographer Akram Khan's rise to fame. And in a wider context, Isabella Blow is said to have instigated the rise of iconic multimillionaire fashion designer Alexander McQueen, and Charles Saatchi launched the career of multimillionaire artist Damien Hirst.

28. The Royal Opera House's (2018) promotional material announced: "ZooNation creates irresistible narrative Hip Hop dance theater. The company has won nationwide acclaim with its hugely popular shows, including *Into the Hoods* and *Some Like It Hip Hop*. Playfully drawing on everything from Shakespeare to Sondheim, Artistic Director Kate Prince and her company present brilliantly exuberant dance adventures overflowing with energy and wit."

29. Kate Prince is an associate artist at the Old Vic and Sadler's Wells. In 2018 the company changed its name from ZooNation to ZooNation: The Kate Prince Company. In the same year it received ACE lottery funding and support from the Heritage Lottery Fund and the Department for Digital, Culture, Media and Sport to stage and tour *SYLVIA*, which combines "dance, Hip Hop, soul and funk" to tell the story of Sylvia Pankhurst and the suffragette movement. For more information, see "About Us" on the ZooNation website, https://zoonation.co.uk/explore/kate-prince/. Accessed June 18, 2019.

30. Joyce Wilson, the area director of London Arts Council England, said in an interview for London dance.com: "We are delighted to be able to support Breakin' Convention and ZooNation Dance Company through our Strategic touring program; it is a clear illustration of the breadth and quality of work that we value and support. These tours will not only showcase some of the best HHDT in the world, but also support the professional development of emerging Hip Hop dance talent and leaders across England (quoted in Smith 2015).

31. "Discourse generally refers to a type of language associated with an institution, and includes the ideas and statements, which express an institution's values. In Foucault's

writings, it is used to describe individual acts of language, or 'language in action'—the ideas and statements that allow us to make sense of and 'see' things" (Danaher, Schirato, and Webb 2000, x).

32. "The whole honours system stinks of class privilege and social snobbery . . . It is a relic of feudalism, with a taint of nepotism and corruption. . . . In addition, too many honours have imperial titles, such as Member of the British Empire. The Empire is rightly long gone. When it existed, hundreds of millions of people in Africa, Asia, the Caribbean and Pacific were colonised by Britain, ruled against their will, enslaved, exploited as cheap labour and had their lands stripped of natural resources. This sordid imperial history is not something worthy of commemoration with honours such as MBEs, OBEs and CBEs" (Tatchell 2016).

33. Flattened or linear choreography refers here to a generic HHDT movement style that adheres to the notion of the fourth-wall end-on staging paradigm that dominates UK dance theater. This is visible in the work of many of the young emerging artists whose work I have seen, primarily because it is the only model they have been exposed to through mentorship programs and venue-specific support, which generally requires sharing work with an audience. Consequently, these artists choreograph to suit those spaces and the expectations of mentors, a particular audience, and funders.

34. An example of how the institution shapes what the audience sees is visible in the notable changes made to the maximum time allowed on the Breakin' Convention festival's main stage. A maximum time limit of ten minutes for pieces submitted for inclusion in the program was introduced in 2011. Prior to this, artists could submit a piece of any reasonable length for consideration. Since that time, the introduction of a limited-time slot format has resulted in the emergence of a homogenized product.

35. Among the panelists at the three-day launch event were me, Kenrick Sandy (Boy Blue), Ivan Blackstock (formerly of BirdGang Dance Company), Joseph Toonga (Just Us Dance Theatre), Lee Griffiths, Yami Löfvenberg, Botis Seva, and Robert Hylton. The overall consensus that emerged from the often-heated debates was that after fourteen years of creating work, UK Hip Hop artists have made no impact on the main stage programming of Sadler's Wells and little in the wider scope of UK venues. The gathered artists felt marginalized by the long-term struggle to secure sustained support, arguing that funding was tokenistic.

References

Ahearn, L. (2001). "Agency and Language." *Annual Review of Anthropology* 30: 28–48.

Arts Council England. (2013). *Great Art and Culture for Everyone: 10-Year Strategic Framework, 2010–2020.* http://www.artscouncil.org.uk/great-art-and-culture-everyone. Accessed June 24, 2016.

Banks, D., ed. (2011). *Say Word! Voices from Hip Hop Theater.* Ann Arbor: University of Michigan Press.

Beech, D. (2015). "Incomplete Decommodification: Art, State Subsidy and Welfare Economics." *PARSE Journal* 2 (Autumn): 15–27. http://parsejournal.com/article/incomplete-decomm odification-art-state-subsidy-and-welfare-economics/.

Bevan, R. (2016). "Olympicopolis Architects on Their £1.3 Billion Vision for E20." *Evening Standard.* http://www.standard.co.uk/lifestyle/london-life/olympicopolis-architects-on-their-13-billion-vision-for-e20-a3198041.html. Accessed August 2, 2016.

Bourdieu, P. (2010). *Distinction.* Oxon, UK: Routledge Classics.

Cetina, K. K., Schatzki, T. R., and Von Savigny, E., eds. (2001). *The Practice Turn in Contemporary Theory.* London: Routledge.

Cocotas, A. (2016). Design for the One Percent. *Jacobin Magazine* https://www.jacobin mag.com/2016/06/zaha-hadid-architecture-gentrification-design-housing-gehry-urbanism/.

Collini, S. (2012). *What Are Universities For?* London: Penguin.

Danaher, G., Schirato, T., and Webb, J. (2000). *Understanding Foucault.* St. Leonards, AUS: Allen & Unwin.

Davis, E. (2006). Found in Translation. Theatre Communications Group (online). http://www.tcg.org/publications/at/julyaugust04/translation.cfm. Accessed July 26, 2016.

Debord, G. (1994). *Society of the Spectacle.* Translated by Donald Nicholson-Smith. New York: Zone Books.

Del Seamonds, L. (1996). "The Fourth Wall." *The Museletter* 9 (3).

Deobhakta, S. (2014). "Analysis of Social Costs of Gentrification in Over-the-Rhine: A Qualitative Approach." PhD diss., University of Louisville.

Dodds, S. (2011). *Dancing on the Canon: Embodiments of Value in Popular Dance,* New York: Palgrave Macmillan.

Dyke, J. (2018). "Breakin' Convention Presents: WorX." Sadler's Wells. https://www.sadlerswe lls.com/whats-on/2019/breakin-convention-presents-worx-/. Accessed June 2, 2019.

Dyke, J. (2015). "ZooNation and Breakin' Convention Secure Over £1 Million Funding from Arts Council England." Sadler's Wells. http://www.sadlerswells.com/press/news/2015/09/zoonation-and-breakin-convention-secure-over-1-million-funding-from-arts-council-england/. Accessed June 26, 2016.

Elese, M. (2017). Review: Breakin' Convention 2016 (@BConvention) |Breakin' Perception. *I Am Hip Hop Magazine*http://www.iamhiphopmagazine.com/breakin-convention-review-2016-breakin-perception/. Accessed August 5, 2016.

Foucault, M. (1997). *Ethics: Subjectivity and Truth.* Vol. 1. Edited by P Rabinow. New York: New Press.

Foucault, M. (1991). *Discipline and Punish.* Translated by Alan Sheridan. London: Penguin.

Foucault, M. (1980). "The Confession of the Flesh." In *Power/Knowledge: Selected Interviews and Other Writings,* edited by C. Gordon, 194–228. This interview was conducted by a round-table of historians.

Fogarty, M. (2011). "Dance to the Drummer's Beat: Competing Tastes in International B-Boy/B-Girl Culture." PhD. University of Edinburgh. http://hdl.handle.net/1842/5889. Accessed November 12, 2014.

Gardner, L. (2011). "When Every Edinburgh Show Gets Five Stars, Rating System Inflation Has Won." *The Guardian,* August 21. https://www.theguardian.com/culture/2011/aug/21/critics-notebook-lyn-gardner . Accessed June 10, 2016.

Goldman, D. (2010). *I Want to Be Ready.* Ann Arbor: University of Michigan Press.

Harvie, J. (2005). *Staging the UK.* Manchester: Manchester University Press.

Hansen, P., and Callison, D., eds. (2015). *Dance Dramaturgy.* New York: Palgrave MacMillan.

Heathcote, E. (2015). "Where Will London's Artists Work?" *Apollo,* December 21. http://www.apollo-magazine.com/where-will-londons-artists-work/ Accessed June 17, 2016.

Higgins, C. (2005). "Sadler's Wells Chief Unveils Strategy to Give Dance a Lift." *The Guardian,* March 7. https://www.theguardian.com/uk/2005/mar/07/arts.artsnews1. Accessed August 9, 2016.

Hill, L. (2014). "Status Quo Preserved in Arts Council's NPO Funding Round." Arts Professional (online), February 2. http://www.artsprofessional.co.uk/news/status-quo-preserved-arts-councils-npo-funding-round. Accessed August 13, 2016.

Hoch, D. (2006). "Toward a Hip-Hop Aesthetic." In *Total Chaos: The Art and Aesthetics of Hip-Hop*, edited by J. Chang, 349–363. New York: BasicCivitas.

Hodges Persley, N. (2015). "Hip-Hop Theater and Performance." In *The Cambridge Companion to Hip Hop*, edited by J. Williams, 85–99. Cambridge: Cambridge University Press.

Hoggard, L. (2016). "Breakin' Convention, Dance Review: Breakin' Good with the Hip Hop World." *Evening Standard*, May 3. http://www.standard.co.uk/goingout/theater/breakin-convention-dance-review-breakin-good-with-the-hip-hop-world-a3238831.html. Accessed August 4, 2016.

hooks, b. (2008). *Outlaw Culture: Resisting Representations*. 3rd ed. Oxon, UK: Routledge.

Huntingdon, C. S. (2007). *Hip Hop Dance: Meanings and Messages*. Jefferson, NC: McFarland.

Jones, O. (2014). "It's the BBC's Rightwing Bias That Is the Threat to Democracy and Journalism." *The Guardian*. https://www.theguardian.com/commentisfree/2014/mar/17/bbc-leftwing-bias-non-existent-myth. Accessed June 28, 2016.

Kehoe, A. (1991). *Christian Contradictions and the World Revolution: Letters to My Son*. Dublin: Glendale.

Kendzior, S. (2014). "The Peril of Hipster Economics: When Urban Decay Becomes a Set Piece to be Remodelled or Romanticised." "Opinion." *Aljazeera* online, May 28. https://www.aljazeera.com/indepth/opinion/2014/05/peril-hipster-economics-2014527105521158885.html.

Klein, N. (2001). *No Logo*, London: Flamingo.

Kumar, A. (2012). "Special Report: Want to Cleanse Your City of Its Poor? Host the Olympics." *CeasefireMagazine*, April 12. https://ceasefiremagazine.co.uk/olympics-opportunity-cleanse-city/. Accessed September 10, 2016.

Lees, L., Slater, T., and Wyley, E., eds. (2010). *The Gentrification Reader*. New York: Routledge.

Lepecki, A. (2013). "Choreopolice and Choreopolitics: or, the Task of the Dancer." *TDR: Drama Review* 57 (4): 13–27. https://muse.jhu.edu/article/526055/pdf.

Lepecki, A. (2015). "Errancy as Work: Seven Strewn Notes for Dance Dramaturgy." In *Dance Dramaturgy*, edited by P. Hansen, and D. Callison, 51–66. New York: Palgrave MacMillan.

Lepecki, A. (2016). *Singularities: Dance in the Age of Performance*. Oxon, UK: Routledge

Logan, B. (2014). "Breakin' Convention: A Comedy Critic's Verdict on the Hip-Hop Festival." *The Guardian*, May 6. https://www.theguardian.com/stage/2014/may/06/breakin-convention-street-dance-sadlers-wells-hip-hop. Accessed August 3, 2016.

London Studio Centre. (2019). MA Dance Producing and Management. Course description. https://londonstudiocentre.org/courses/ma-dance-producing-management. Accessed June 17, 2019.

Mahler, J., and Rutenberg, J. (2019). "How Rupert Murdoch's Empire of Influence Remade the World. *New York Times Magazine*, April 3. https://www.nytimes.com/interactive/2019/04/03/magazine/rupert-murdoch-fox-news-trump.html. Accessed June 17, 2019.

Martin, R. (1998). *Critical Moves*, Durham, NC: Duke University Press.

Mayor of London. (2015). "Take a Closer Look: A Cultural Tourism Vision for London 2015–2017." Retrieved January 10, 2018, from https://www.london.gov.uk/sites/default/files/cultural_tourism_vision_for_london_low_res_version.pdf.

McKenzie, J. (2001). *Perform or Else: From Discipline to Performance*. New York: Routledge.

McRobbie, A. (2016). *Be Creative*. Cambridge, UK: Polity.

Muller, D. (2018). "Media Power: Why the Full Story of Murdoch, Stokes and the Liberal Leadership Spill Needs to Be Told." *The Conversation*, April 28. http://theconversation.com/media-power-why-the-full-story-of-murdoch-stokes-and-the-liberal-leadership-spill-needs-to-be-told-103522. Accessed June 17, 2019.

Osborn, J., Kearney, D., and Fogarty, M. (2015). "The Multiple Legitimacies of Tentacle Tribe, a Dance Company" in Guerra, P. and Moreira, T. (eds) *Keep It Simple Make It Fast: An Approach to Underground Music Scenes*, 535–546. Portugal, University of Porto.

Patent Office. (2016). Intellectual Property Office: Case Details for Trade Mark Available at: https://trademarks.ipo.gov.uk/ipo-tmcase/page/Results/1/UK00002482019. Accessed September 15, 2016.

Pellegrino, G., ed. (2011). *The Politics of Proximity: Mobility and Immobility in Practice.* Farnham, UK: Ashgate.

Prickett, S. (2013). "Hip-Hop Dance Theatre in London: Legitimising an Art Form." *Dance Research* 31 (2): 174–190.

Pritchard, S. (2017a). "Artwashing and Gentrification (or the Deeply Interwoven Web of Arts and Corporate Interests)." *Colouring in Culture* (blog), March 30. http://colouringinculture.org/blog/artwashinggentrificationcomplexweb. Accessed June 18, 2018.

Pritchard, S. (2017b). "Elisabeth Murdoch's Appointment to Arts Council England National Council Is a Corporate Takeover of the Arts—a Takeover Facilitated by Sir Nicholas Serota and His Wife Teresa Gleadowe." *Colouring in Culture* (blog), December 15. http://colouringinculture.org/blog/murdochserotacorporatetakeover. Accessed June 18, 2018.

Royal Opera House. (2018). *The Mad Hatters Tea Party.* https://www.roh.org.uk/productions/the-mad-hatters-tea-party-by-various. Accessed June 14, 2018.

Shapiro, R. (2004). "The Aesthetics of Institutionalization: Breakdancing in France." *Journal of Arts Management, Law, and Society* 33 (4): 316–335.

Shapiro, R., and Heinich, N. (2012). "When Is Artification?" *Contemporary Aesthetics* 4, pp.1–16. https://digitalcommons.risd.edu/cgi/viewcontent.cgi?article=1196&context=liberalarts_contempaesthetics Accessed August 11, 2016.

Smith, B. H. (1983). "Contingencies of Value." *Critical Inquiry* 10 (1): 1–35. http://www.jstor.org/stable/1343404.

Smith, C. (2015). "News: Funding Boost for Hip Hop Dance Theatre." Londondance.com. http://londondance.com/articles/news/arts-council-england-funding-boost-for-hip-hop/ . Accessed March 5, 2016.

Soja, E. (1996). *Thirdspace: Journeys to Los Angeles and Other Real and Imagined Spaces.* Malden, MA: Blackwell.

Spalding, A. (2013). "The Diary: Alistair Spalding." *Financial Times* (online). "Life and Arts," , July 12. http://www.ft.com/cms/s/2/3678cbfa-e949-11e2-9f11-00144feabdc0.html#axzz3UNa5z3Tz. Accessed January 1, 2015.

Taşkale, A. R. (2012). "Kettling and the Fear of Revolution." *Critical Legal Thinking* (blog). http://criticallegalthinking.com/2012/03/23/kettling-and-the-fear-of-revolution/ . Accessed August 7, 2016.

Tatchell, P. (2016). "David Furnish, There's No Equality in Snobbery." *The Guardian*, April 6. https://www.theguardian.com/commentisfree/2016/apr/06/david-furnish-equality-snobbery-elton-john-honours-system. Accessed September 29, 2016.

Thornton, S. (1996). *Club Cultures: Music, Media, and Subcultural Capital*, Middletown, CT: Wesleyan University Press.

Uno, R. (2006). "Theatres Crossing the Divide: A Baby Boomer's Defense of Hip-Hop Aesthetics" in Chang, J. (ed.) *Total Chaos: The Art and Aesthetics of Hip-Hop*, 300–305. New York: BasicCivitas.

Uno, R. (2004). The 5th Element. *Theatre Communications Group*. http://www.tcg.org/publi cations/at/apro4/element.cfm. Accessed September 2, 2016.

Wainwright, O. (2018). "From Olympic Park to East Bank: How St Paul's 'Faux Pas' Led to Design Rethink." https://www.theguardian.com/artanddesign/2018/jun/05/goodbye-olympicopolis-hello-east-bank-more-plans-unveiled-for-troubled-site . Accessed October 5, 2018.

Zukin, S. (2010). "Gentrification: Culture and Capital in the Urban Core." In *The Gentrification Reader*, pp. 220–232. Oxon/New York: Routledge.

CHAPTER 24

∙∙

MAKE THE LETTERS DANCE

A Hip Hop Approach to Creative Practice

∙∙

ANTHONY "YNOT" DENARO
AND MARY FOGARTY**

*INTRODUCTION (Y)

For those who have studied the early development of Hip Hop, the culture is considered to be made up of four main "elements": DJn [deejaying], EmCee'n [MC-ing], Breaking, and Writing [Aerosol Art]. Ultimately, a fifth element was added: knowledge.[1] Hip Hop's embodiment of Knowledge is about knowing oneself, and constantly keeping an open mind to building, growing, and learning. In Hip Hop's developing years, people attached themselves to a certain art form (element) they were attracted to, and would, at times, dabble with the other mediums. It wasn't necessary for participants to partake in all the elements, even if many prominent early practitioners used Hip Hop's various art forms to express themselves.

In this chapter, we highlight these artistic elements (or disciplines) and the relationship between them as a form of practice that informs knowledge. To know oneself is to have a practice that allows you to collaborate with others, and to continue to grow and inspire. Although some may take the traditional elements of Hip Hop for granted—or perhaps as an outdated way of thinking about the culture—they are very relevant when we are thinking about Hip Hop as an actual practice that produces inspiring art.

Because I was introduced to Hip Hop through its foundational elements, I have always perceived these art forms as entities that are connected. Indeed, I now regularly integrate these different visual arts, musical expressions, and dances in my own practice.

---

* RAMM:ΣLL:ZΣΣ.

** Note: This is a collaboratively-written chapter that also acknowledges individual perspectives, with headings that indicate emphases ("Y" for YNOT, "MJ" for Mary Fogarty, and "Y&MJ" for the voices of YNOT and Mary Fogarty).

Having this multifaceted approach has given me the opportunity to travel around the world, meeting various Hip Hop practitioners. Sharing my journey inside Hip Hop culture has given me a strong interest in collaborative art-making over my last twenty years as a practitioner. I believe that the more varied the artistic mediums are, the more you see the relationship between them, thus manifesting a larger cognizance of the interaction between these art forms and their future possibilities.[2] Diversifying your range of influences across the arts in this way also promotes multidisciplinary art-making that opens up conversations that can lead to collaborations. This chapter itself is a collaboration and embodies the ethos that my practice is built on.

My central argument is that knowledge built from both individual and dialogical understandings (i.e., the relationships between the elements) offers a holistic approach to Hip Hop aesthetics. In other words, Hip Hop aesthetics are shaped by the shared characteristics across the elements, which came together at a specific moment in time to spawn Hip Hop culture. I will also share some examples of how my own practice has moved back and forth from visual practices to sonic ones to movement explorations. Although there isn't room here to consider how each of the first four elements interact, both historically and in people's practices across the globe, I will address the connection between two of them: Breaking and Writing, since both are underpinned by an understanding of rhythm.

TERMINOLOGY

The term *Breaking* was not a word I heard when I was first introduced to the dance. In the New Jersey neighborhood where I grew up, there were many people who participated in the "Hip Hop Explosion" that happened during the '80s, and most people I came into contact with referred to the dance as "Breakdancing." It wasn't until Crazy Legs schooled me that the dance's accurate terminologies and their histories became clear. He always introduced himself as a "B-boy" and said that he wanted to stay true to what the older generations had been calling themselves since the '70s. Legs was someone who was exposed to and participated in the media explosion of Hip Hop, and he said that once things got to a certain point, he felt it was his obligation to combat the media-derived label of "breakdancing" and inform the scene. Meeting him sparked my curiosity. I began to ask questions and look into the depths of the culture. I found that during Legs's era, and prior, "Burning," "Going Off," and "Rocking" were also names used to describe the dance. In the documentary *The Freshest Kids* (2002), there is a scene where Crazy Legs and Mr. Freeze are explaining how even they fell into calling it "breakdancing" for a time.

Similarly, the written form of Hip Hop also acquired a media-derived term that has gone through a series of transformations and interpretations. As the pioneering aerosol artist, Michael Lawrence Marrow (aka PHASE 2), has explained, the term "Graffiti" was latched onto the Writing movement by journalists and state authorities in the 1970s. It was a way to denounce and stigmatize their art and, thus, received criticism from certain prominent practitioners (IGTimes 1996, 7). Such practitioners thought deeply about their art form, and knew that "Graffiti" was neither what they originally called their art, nor was it a proper representation of it. Rather than being a form of vandalism, which "Graffiti" denoted, Writing was a political statement, a voice for the voiceless, and a way to get recognition among peers.

However, the Writing movement predated the concept of Hip Hop, and there were many Writers who later did not affiliate themselves with Hip Hop music or its elements. (One of DONDI's most influential pieces was based on lyrics from a Black Sabbath song.) This may confuse some people's understanding of how Writing and Breaking are connected, especially if the forms existed separately before they were brought together as part of the conceptualization of Hip Hop. This conceptualization came from Afrika Bambaataa, and many practitioners believe this connection between the arts to be the true path, following its theories and philosophies, but this often depends on how you were introduced to the culture: where, from whom, and in what time period.

Again, for many who participated in the New York subway art scene, Writing was a way to express political discontent through movement. Everyone had a unique signature—most commonly consisting of a moniker and a street number—and this was your way of marking territory, letting people know that you existed. From the stories and archived images of such penmanship, I've observed that most people wrote their names stylistically. Writing thrived and evolved in New York City, and there was a unique experience of catching tags, throw ups, and, importantly, pieces on a moving canvas, the subway train.

The subway train represented a composition with momentum. Most Writers would *lean* their letters to match the locomotion and direction of where the train was going. This was the beginning of not only having motion in your piece, but also adding movement to your letter or overall composition. These are theories about rhythm and the direction of movement that I've learned through closely following the life and career of an artist who describes himself as the equation "RAMM:ΣLL:ZΣΣ"[3] (referred to in this chapter as Rammellzee).

Rammellzee created an in-depth and influential theory about letters and their purpose, which he called "Gothic Futurism."[4] Based mostly on military theories and models, he wanted to arm letters with weapons, or for letters to become weapons themselves for protection against other symbols. According to Rammellzee, his "Ikonoklast" style also meant "symbol destroyer" and, in this way, his letters took on a broader purpose, or could carry out certain tasks.[5] He gave them characteristics and special qualities that allowed them to evolve into deconstructive forces. His approach to art was captured in an explanation by Donald White (aka "DONDI"), in the extra footage available on DVD in 2013 for the documentary *Style Wars*: "Rammellzee believed the only way to destroy a symbol is with a symbol, or the only way to destroy another symbol is to arm a symbol." (Original theatrical release, 1983, USA: Public Art Films). POPMASTER FABEL has a similar way of framing his practice, which he calls "Urban Stylized Lettering" (discussed in the "Urban Stylized Lettering" section below). For now, it's worth reiterating how important it is for artists to have their approach properly named and categorized. Otherwise, an artist can feel that their message and artistic quality are being marginalized, or that the distinctions between their approaches and the approaches of other artists are being collapsed. Learning about each artist's approach can also unleash your own creativity, as a visual artist or as a dancer (and, especially, as both).

Another influential Writer and B-boy who has theorized his work in this fashion is Jeffrey "DOZE" Green.[6] He has described his art as "intuitive movement," and explained that he progressed from stylized signatures into "Gothic Futurism," having studied with Rammellezee and Dondi. The latter was a mentor of Green and also a member and founder of the CIA (Crazy Inside Artists) Writing crew. Sharing its acronym with the Central Intelligence Agency was a clever act of defiance, given that the CIA has a long history of collecting intelligence on "many black radicals, artists, activists, and intellectuals who were targeted for surveillance" (Browne 2015, 2). Like the Black radical thinkers, such as Frantz Fanon, whom the government CIA surveilled, Writers like Green have been expressing subversive thoughts through their art and social commentary for decades. In many ways, Writers have been the biggest observers in New York City, noticing the movement of people in places and spaces. Green is a witness to his time, and this trait of watching the movements of people coming and going relates to how the B-boys take up and mime city street vignettes. Green explains the connection between the arts and his practice as he got older:

> I'll still dance, I'll still rock when the music's right and I feel it in my bones, but it's like something that I don't practice every day. What I do practice on is expanding my knowledge of things around me in the world and symbols and symbolism and different genres of art. (quoted in Chang 2006, 323)

Today, Green's artwork is mostly centered around dreams, the occult, "Afrodiasporic traces," and surreal experiences, interpreted through his experiences as a B-boy (Chang 2006, 321). In turn, Green's experience of creating paintings of crowds of people with their own stories to tell is similar to how the famous B-boy Frosty Freeze could translate different experiences and walks of life into his moves, metamorphosing and shifting shape to please the crowd.[7] There are unconscious and conscious tendencies in art practices, just as there are in the creation of dance. The connection between Afrodiasporic aesthetics, surrealism, and the Black Radical tradition has been theorized (see Kelley 2000), but there has been less attention paid to the relationship between elements within Hip Hop and their generative symbiosis in the creative process of significant Hip Hop artists.

RHYTHM IN WRITING AND DANCING (Y&MJ)

Dance and the written letter, despite being two apparently different practices, present a complementary relationship regarding space and movement. Dance performs patterns of movement and creates ephemeral forms in space, while writing and drawing, in their material substance, become static, fixed forms nonetheless created from movement. The end results may not necessarily be the same, but the vocabulary, the principles, and the processes of creation shaping both disciplines are closely related.

Some practitioners have made and continue to make specific correlations between the rhythm of Writing and rhythmic dancing. Those who have made a significant contribution include artists such as Jorge "POPMASTER FABEL" Pabon, Stephen "Mr. Wiggles" Clemente, DOZE Green, Doc TC5, DONDI, Rammellzee, Lady Pink, and Carlos "Mare 139" Rodriguez.[8] There is also a social connection between some of them: a few attended the High School of Art and Design in New York.[9] This institution, a high school for the arts, was a meeting ground not only for Writers but also B-boys and EmCees and other participants of the underground youth culture happening in New York.[10] It became a place for sharing knowledge and trying out new ideas. The legacy of art schools is relevant in the emergence of many influential Hip Hop artists, and perhaps the most valuable resource provided by art schools is time.

Movement is also at the center of the links that POPMASTER FABEL makes between Writing and dancing. In the next section, YNOT dives into his research with Fabel, whose visual art practice informs his dance, and vice versa, tying together two components of this creative art movement called Hip Hop.

URBAN STYLIZED LETTERING (Y)

In this section, I focus on my interactions with POPMASTER FABEL and his considerations of the relationship between dancing and Writing. In the second half, I expand on the principles he offers with some concrete examples and comparisons with other artists' processes from different genres. Fabel is best known as a dancer who engages in a style called Electric Boogie or Electric Boogaloo, better known as Popping.[11]

Fabel has long explored the correlation between the techniques of Popping and the written, stylized letterform. He has found them to parallel each other creatively through image and rhythmic qualities, and smooth flow. As mentioned, he describes what he does as Urban Stylized Lettering, and he expanded on the principles in my documentary short film, "Make the Letters Dance: Episode 1":

> I used to hang out with my boy Kool Keith from Ultra Mag[netic MCs] . . .—we called him "Activity". . .—we actually came up with a letter style. We were bugging out and I was like, "Oh dude [starts making sounds and matching movements to show the letter A with his arms], that's an A" . . . we spent the whole session dancing and coming up with like, letters, you know, with our movement [demonstrates] . . . After those sessions with Keith I would go out and get busy, battle dudes and consciously be like, "I'm going to throw an A and B at homeboy in a battle and I got the rest of the alphabet to smash them with in case that doesn't work," you know? . . . For the most part, it's something that happens unconsciously, you know, when I dance. I think it all becomes so much part of the same spirit that they easily sort of merge . . . They are

blurry lines between physical movement and wild style letters and other aspects of Hip Hop culture. It all connects. (YNOT 2016)

Fabel is saying the structure for his dance came from his practice as a Writer. Sometimes, his movements intentionally connected with his art but, often, these connections were unconscious. They come together to create a Hip Hop aesthetic that would be hard to separate by element. When discussing the fluidity of Popping, Fabel juxtaposed its "sharp movements and very fluid rolls." He talked about his dancing as letters "coming to life," through movement, and said that imagining the letters provided a structure for his dance.

I have applied a similarly holistic approach to my own artistic movement practice. Take the lower-case letter "t" for example. It can be comparable to the shape of the image of a body of a stick figure. When I look at dancing bodies, I think of their lines and angles, which I tend to look at from my dance experience. A dancer's "lines" or "angles" can refer to the linear imagery created by their arms, shoulders, hips, legs, and torso or spine. I visualize that the letter "t" can take on the characteristic of a dancing body, and therefore there are multiple ways that the "t" can be positioned in space. The lean and weight of the letter form can now be viewed as having a human "characteristic," giving it various sources of creative influence. In fact, any letter can then take on a human or animalistic quality. The serif of a letter can become the letter's "feet," on which now the letter can stand. With standing comes position, posture, attitude, bearing, and weight distribution, or a look inside at a letter's biomechanics. As with one's gait, the quality that brings these elements together for Fabel is rhythm: "What I've discovered is that the most common denominator is rhythm. From one 'element' to the next that is the through-line. It's all about Rhythm really" (YNOT 2016).

Breaking, inspired by knowledge of the written letter, now can give way to a more in-depth way of thinking about the body or transforming the image of the Hip Hop posture. Dance becomes an experiment in space, an embodiment of what it's like to be an object in space. Therefore, the object takes on new characteristics and knowledge of how it interacts and exists. On paper, through the practice of Writing, one can visualize the object (body) in space and experiment with visualizing the moment. Embodying the posture and its position can inform the visual manifestation of it.

Visualization is the key; it is a school of seeing motion and then directing it through sound. Being able to "see" or imagine what you want to create physically, prior to doing it, can be a powerful tool in both Writing and dance. While you practice one form you are simultaneously enhancing the other and your ability to "see." There is a mental and physical practice in both forms that requires the artist to think and do, then do and think, and that repeats constantly, at different times (Figure 24.1).

Understanding this relationship between Writing and Breaking can inform practice. As a visual thinking tool, the Hip Hop lens reveals the sorts of lines and flows that create a pleasurable aesthetic. The general principles of creating lines and shapes can be compared to other approaches to thinking about the body and empty space. For example, contemporary choreographer William Forsythe (1999) used elements

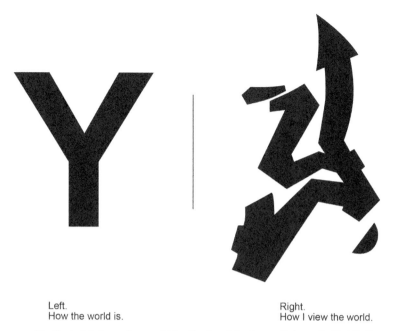

Left.
How the world is.

Right.
How I view the world.

FIGURE 24.1 To the left is how the world is. To the right (a rendition of a YNOT letter "Y") is how I see the world.

of improvisational techniques to generate a unique movement approach that creates planes that can be flattened and rotated through the body and its surrounding space. This approach involves matching lines, sliding and collapsing them, and a multitude of other combinations of movement patterns involving the creation of imaginary lines and planes. Forsythe's relationship to dancers and traditions is described by Dimitra Stathopoulou (2011):

> After working with ballet dancers for more than 15 years, Forsythe realised that ballet dancers are trained to understand chorographical movement by matching lines and shapes in space. So, he analysed dance movement into points, lines, planes, volumes and started composing choreographies by using processes such as rotation, extrusion, inscription, folding, unfolding, etc. Clarifying that there is an infinite number of possible movement combinations, restricted only by the physical structure of the human body. (13)

What's interesting is how similar Forsythe's ideas of creating points and lines through the body are to the movement ideas described by Fabel.[12]

Like Forsythe, Fabel has contributed to movement analysis of the body within space from a Hip Hop perspective, through the techniques and technologies that shape multiple disciplines. Through visualizing letters in space, and by using the empty space around the movement to make funky angles, Fabel has developed a creative process with an extended vocabulary, a way of learning and improvising on the spot. Using an aesthetic style developed through a shared community of Hip Hop practices, his dancing and Writing are part of an already happening conversation within Hip Hop about funk. Creative organizations of the body and Writing resonate with other practitioners of the tradition and cultivate shared meanings. In other words, the purpose of learning the structure of these forms isn't to be bound by a set of rules, but rather to open up spaces for creative exploration, open to individual understandings and approaches yet tied to meanings within a community.

CREATIVE PRACTICE IN THE ACADEMY (Y)

Like Forsythe (1999), in his *Tool for the Analytical Dance Eye*, I wish to expand on the idea of the body's kinesphere, and explore how all, or at least most, body movements (including the shape of the body itself) relate to geometry. To do so, I am currently producing a series of drawings to demonstrate the math that goes on inside the movement. These drawings will be arranged to give as much insight into the mechanics of the dance as possible. I am looking to make the technique of Breaking available through these images and Writings. In other words, I am translating the aesthetic of the dance to visual cues, in order to prompt understandings that are often tacit in Hip Hop culture, so that the style can be consciously understood.

The Hip Hop entrainment sometimes sees shapes and angles within empty spaces that are conceptually influenced by the music, or by a certain feeling. I am interested in the distinctive methods and forms of a Hip Hop aesthetic. There are continuous things that are influencing the B-Boy's/B-Girl's (dancer's) mind when he/she/they are submerged within the culture. For example, a dancer might embody the calligraphy of Hip Hop (Writing). It is customary to gather information that is all around you and turn it into pure inspiration and creativity.

There is great potential to draw from our everyday movement practices, such as dance or any other full-body actions, and the knowledge within those practices. For dance studies, this is often thought about as "space-consciousness," or having a consciousness or an understanding of force and time (Figure 24.2). Barbara Mettler (1947) has already discussed this at length. She suggests that there is common knowledge in the ways that dance and the visual arts approach space. We learn this through interacting with objects every day in our daily lives. Dance and other physical activities create various movements that can heighten our space-consciousness through practice. She argues that "we" then become educated through the mastery of the movement. Mettler's elitism, however, is problematic. She spends time suggesting who does and does not have access to space-consciousness, and her work is riddled with perplexing notions of "primitive" people. Her writing is thus a product of the problematic academic discourses in the fields of anthropology circulating during her time that were often incorporated into dance studies and shared with music studies. This chapter shows, through the study of and practices in everyday movement vocabularies, how

FIGURE 24.2. Bodies in space. The dancer is Jordan Reti.

access to "space-consciousness" is in fact a part of Hip Hop vocabularies, aesthetics, and cultural traditions.

Signatures of Dance (Y)

It begins as far back as your signature. This is the beginning of the choices you make in developing your "style." Those choices are based on your life, your surroundings, and, ultimately, your choices. Your style ultimately defines who you are compared to everyone else. We all have our own signature, a way of writing our name that is unique to our hand and our preference. After you develop your signature, it ultimately becomes something you draw instead of something you write. You have created your way, and now your hand flows in the way that is natural to you. I will examine this concept through the art of "Tagging," where the Hip Hop lens causes lines to do things that most common Writing techniques do not.

Tagging is Hip Hop's version of writing a signature, and once you develop your style it can become a part of everything you do. It becomes your name, your identity. The "tag" is created and develops into an expressive line of style, a stylized fashion signature influenced by Hip Hop's principles, in conjunction with our outside influences and experiences. It starts simply, like Writing your name. Learning to write your signature in school, cursively, is the beginning of understanding how to connect letters, and to begin to "flow." As a fluctuation of rhythm and timing, this fluent motion should always be evident in the name.

Flow is one of the most important components of motion; you must flow in order to continue with your idea and connect to other ideas. The quality of your line speaks to who you are as an individual. These stylized line qualities are called "isms." As in the dictionary meaning of the suffix "-ism" an "ism" means a distinctive practice, system, or philosophy; this is typically a political ideology or an artistic movement, such as surreal*ism*. In Hip Hop, "ism" also has taken on the meaning of "one's unique mannerisms." These "-isms" are also present within the dance.[13]

What if this line had a trajectory? What if it could explode and then suddenly arrow back onto itself? This is what the line of Writing does, and not coincidentally also what the movement of Breaking does. In Breaking, we expand and move through kinespheric boundaries, to then spiral back along the original path of the movement we had previously executed. There is a way of thinking that goes behind that line, a cultural context that creates this type of movement in space. Straight meets curved, bends connect to angles, extruding and protruding segments create new pathways—these visual elements are present in both practices, their movement possibilities expressing shared ideas (Figure 24.3).

Rhythm is often related to music and our experience of time. If you follow movement within dance, you grasp a rhythmical connection between music and dance because concur. When it comes to visual art, rhythm is conveyed via repetition and/or pattern. You can see the pulse or beat that is produced by the image as it guides your eye from one detail to the next. In Writing, this is often referred to as the "funk" of a letter. The funk refers to the bending and disposition of a letter form, the usage of straight lines or curves as well as varying angles and proportions. When tweaking the angle, you change the feel. There is also a sense of movement through the usage of arrows. With these arrows, an artist can also suggest motion and direction, contributing to the flow of the Writing's rhythm.

Rhythm (MJ)

Rhythm is one of the areas that has been historically undertheorized in music theory. Popular music scholar Simon Frith (1996) locates this lack of theorization within the history of colonialization and its parallels in the development of musical theory. Following Kofi Agawu (1992, 2003), Frith argues that complex African polyrhythms were undervalued and their meanings distorted. The complexities of polyrhythms were reframed by European colonialists as barbaric, as they rationalized slavery by belittling other cultures and traditions. This imperialist exercise for musical theory meant that rhythm became associated with the "body" and labeled "primitive," as opposed to

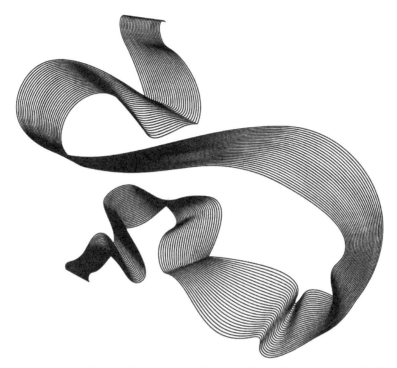

FIGURE 24.3. A vector letter *S* done in a free-flowing ribbon-like texture based off a study of gymnastic ribbon creating letter forms in space.

concepts such as harmony and counterpoint, which became identified with "civilisation" and the "mind." Similarly, complex dance forms based on polyrhythms were belittled and identified as "social" or "vernacular" dance in dance scholarship (as opposed to theatrical dance, which sometimes appropriated the arts of other cultures and often lacked the complexities found in groove articulations).[14] The relationship between complex rhythms in music, dance, and art have always been integral to Hip Hop culture, yet too often are dismissed or denigrated.

The implications of this historical-theoretical violence are profound for dance education, for example. If dance education is to work at decolonization, music needs to be considered alongside dance. This is already a common practice in some fields of study such as South Asian dance studies (see, for example, Sharma, Hutnyk, and Sharma 1996; Chatterjea 2004). Modern Dance education, however, too often devalues music to assert the autonomy of its form. Again, the Eurocentric suspicion of rhythm infiltrates even practices founded in musically embodied repetition.

The ability of researchers to think through music from a dance perspective and vice versa is thus one barometer for how these fields are doing in reconsidering and rectifying their historical implication in racialized hierarchies. From a practice-based point of view, part of the work of decolonizing popular music education, for example, demands some basic dance training. Being around dancers can help one learn how the body shapes listening, and vice versa. It is crucial to feel how the body's dynamics make and match musical accents. To illustrate: if one is teaching toprock in a Breaking class, emphasis has to be placed not only on acquisition of the dance's moves, but on how body shapes convey the rhythmic flow of the music. For example, angular, dynamic shapes can highlight accents in the music, so hitting dramatic shapes to match when the snare upbeat is on the 2 and the 4 (downplaying the 1 and 3) perform fidelity to the music. (On important and related ideas of "groove," see Durden 2009). Working on articulating this relationship between music and dance is a skill that develops with time and effort. Expressing a love of the music is one thing, but being able to <u>become</u> the music is another thing altogether. YNOT's dancing exemplifies this when he chooses to follow the throughline of a horn solo in a Jimmy Castor breakbeat[15].

To separate out the dance—without thinking about the movement or the other arts and cultural movements surrounding its birth—is to fail to embody the aesthetic of the dance we are trying to appreciate and interpret and value. Relatedly, a rethinking of specialization as a segregation of disciplines is a necessary move. In other words, if you neglect visual art as movement, or mishear the polyrhythms and grooves of the music the dance is done to, this colonizes the form to fit standards imposed from above or beyond, rather than seeking to understand how social contexts inform aesthetic practices.

Hip Hop and the Art School Continuum (Y&MJ)

Although art schools are rarely considered in the history of Hip Hop culture, they have been crucial meeting grounds for musical artists and dancers. Art schools have provided the space for cultivating relationships between high art skills and mass cultural forms: "Art schools cross these divisions in terms of both class and ideology" (Frith and Horne 1987, 2). The impact of art-school educations on important Hip Hop artists should not be underestimated because the schools provided key access points to histories of art that the students could then interact with. It may be hard to pinpoint what exactly is learned in art schools, no matter what the genre or style learned (Elkins 2001). However, they facilitate key features of a creative life—there, artists gather together, have time to contemplate and create, form networks, and can also respond to what art has been valued in society (and to reject that in the case of many). Art schools offered a productive space for members of the Rocksteady Crew, for example, even as their practice was clearly also informed by other factors.

To ignore or downplay these educational spaces—for instance, by naming only the streets—is to construct Hip Hop in a way that primarily serves a mythology, rather than fully documenting the histories of its lived practices and social realities. Mapping a false image of Hip Hop that stereotypes "ghetto" living and the "streets" often keeps the Hip Hop practitioner in a box, unable to express their ultimately expansive form.

To understand the aesthetics, sometimes you need to shift from an exoticizing gaze to attend to listening practices. Many people have misconceptions about Hip Hop artists, assuming they are not articulate about their practices. Hip Hop has always been eclectic. Many styles and ideas have influenced the movement, so the sort of eclecticism we get into here is what Hip Hop is all about: getting inspired by your surroundings and having something to say about your world and experiences, in all their diversity and complexity. In other words, understanding how Writing works to create rhythm and movement through letters can help to understand the conversation some dancers are having between bodies, how the funk gets revealed in a way that is tacit or intuitive for those immersed in it. If you don't come from the same family background, cultural upbringing, and educational influences as earlier generations, you'll have to put in time and work to feel and understand those experiences.

Final Thoughts (Y)

I hope that some of the models we have provided for creative practice in this chapter can inspire those in the education system while still foregrounding the need to be connected to Hip Hop communities and the principles that give our art its shape. I grew up in a unique environment, in which I met some important and interesting people who were a part of an underground scene that I considered an underworld, a scene that existed within another scene, like a parallel universe. These were cliques, mostly of marginalized men, due to the fact that Hip Hop, especially at that time, seemed to be a male-dominated art form in America. I didn't have the greatest relationship with my father as a youth, and now, looking back, I assume that played a role in my interest in this particular scene's players. Not having a Father figure, I was searching for my identity around male energy. I was seeking to discover my signature as a young man.

It took me some time in my life to figure out what a "proper role model" was. In the beginning, I watched the way this guy would hold a cigarette, or how that guy would interact with his girlfriend. I aligned myself with what I valued or appreciated and created my own way of being. Like most young men in America, I didn't necessarily have my father fully in my life during important developmental stages. He was a Bronx-born Sicilian yet considered to be an immigrant because he was a young boy when Italians were fighting on the opposing side in WWII. Italians didn't become "white" in the eyes of many until some years after the war. Considering what little I knew of my Dad and his personality at first, and after my understanding grew as I learned about his experiences when I got old enough, I realized why I thought the way I did. The idea of being white didn't sit well with me. I remember putting down "other" on my test one day at school, and my teacher laughed and made me change it. Although this was confusing to me for a while, it helped me to understand more who I was and also how people viewed me. This is really important knowledge I took with me on my journey of life. I learned how to "read the room," so to speak, and navigate a situation where I am a minority as well as a majority, depending on where I was. From being in New Jersey and having my Mom do her best to enroll me in private Catholic schools, to dropping out and going to public schools until I moved out on my own to Philadelphia, I had to adapt. I was obsessed with the streets and the idea of the superhero individual, the Lone Ranger type. I wasn't a person who spoke much, so "freedom of speech" wasn't something I sought out with my art; it was more like "Freedom of Thought." Later on, I realized that these ideas about ways to be were present in the energy and creative process of Hip Hop. I sampled, cut, and pasted my lifestyle, and continue to do so to this day. The early stages of this development were uncomfortable to me, and to others, I'm sure. In hindsight the process was very shaky and a bit on the dangerous side.

That artistic, creative energy in the struggle of such an art form spoke to me, from the people through to the product. The complex and contradictory construction based on the richness and fogginess of the modern experience spoke to me. I was attracted to a hybrid thought process rather than to the purist mindset that was offered by those Writing and Breaking abstractly. I prefer "both-and" to "either-or," black *and* white, and sometimes gray, to black *or* white. I realize that the idea of including everything is much harder than excluding it all. The idea is not to keep the cipher too small but to expand it, as long as knowledge and self-reflection are attached. I think Hip Hop at one point had this idea as its purpose. This idea is developed through African American and Latinx people living and sharing their ideas.

I believe in that, and create based off on this rich history within Hip Hop. My goal is to expand on the knowledge of each individual "element," and then to explore the idea of what is created from the amalgamation of them. This leads into design for function, such as architecture, industrial design, a lifestyle. Add life experience and individualism into the mix to create something the world has never seen through the Hip Hop aesthetic. That is the goal. That is how I see the world (Figure 24.5).

FIGURE 24.4. Final S chair design completed for thesis project 2017.

FIGURE 24.5. Various images of the Rammellzee (stylized RAMM:ΣLL:ZΣΣ).

Notes

1. See Murray Forman and Mark Anthony Neal's (2004) *That's the* Joint for coverage of the elements by pioneering hip hop scholars.
2. Preston (2015) demonstrates how meaning is formed between art forms in early ballet, writing: "The *Balet comique*'s chimerical structure leaps between verse, prose, and ekphrastic description, intercutting elaborate narratives with beautifully engraved images, staves of music, poetry, and prose. As a result, Beaujoyeulx's *livret* is a difficult text to follow, not only because the work crosses epistemological and disciplinary boundaries but also because it makes the crossing of categories its meaning." Similarly, the approach to Writing and Breaking covered in this work makes the intersection of elements its meaning.
3. See the *New Yorker* article, "The Spectacular Personal Mythology of Rammellzee," by Hua Hsu (2018).
4. See *RAMMELLZEE: It's Not Who But What*, A Red Bull Music Documentary, posted on YouTube, May 31, 2018. https://www.youtube.com/watch?v = PjAfVHSeIvY. Accessed January 15, 2021.
5. Rammellzee described in interviews how he was inspired by the BBC television documentary, *Civilisation: A Personal View* by Kenneth Clark. Particularly, he was inspired by fourteenth-century monks who made their work so hard to decipher that authorities couldn't make it out.
6. See Chang (2006) for an interview with Jeffrey "DOZE" Green.
7. Robin G. Kelley (2000) suggests that "surrealism served as a bridge between Marxism and the Black Radical Tradition" (p. xxi) in his foreword to a new edition of Cedric J. Robinson's (1983) *Black Marxism: The Making of the Black Radical Tradition*, originally published in 1983.
8. See Mare's https://museumofgraffiti.com for more on his projects. Accessed January 15, 2021. A representation of one of Carlos Mare's b-boy sculptures is also the cover art of this handbook and honors b-boy, Maurizio "Next One" Cannavo from Italy.
9. See Jeff Chang's (2006) interview with DOZE Green, who mentions attending the art school, a YNOT's (2016) documentary on Vimeo, "Make the Letters Dance," where Jorge "POPMASTER FABEL" Pabon discusses his attendance at the school.
10. The school also has an all-star alumni of artists such as Tony Bennet (1945), Ralph Bakshi (1956), Calvin Klein (1960), Antonio Lopez (1960), Tracy 168 (1976), Lee Quiñones (1978), and Marc Jacobs (1981), to name a few.
11. Pabon (2006) explains a bit about the history of the Lockers and the Electric Boogaloos in his chapter "Physical Graffiti: The History of Hip-Hop Dance." He suggests that Sam "Boogaloo Sam" Solomon named a combination of moves the "Boogaloo": "This form includes isolated sharp angles, hip rotations, and the use of every part of the body" (p. 23).
12. Forsythe went on to use elements of Breaking in his choreography for *A Quiet Evening of Dance* (2018).
13. We can go as far as to say you build from your own DNA to advance the genetic composition of your style.
14. See Gottschild (1996); DeFrantz (2002); McCarthy-Brown (2014, 2017); Amin (2016); and Kraut (2016) for more on this topic.
15. See "YNOT at Rock Steady Crew 30th Anniversary!!" https://www.youtube.com/watch?v= WWVUf8bJyf8 Accessed October 18, 2021.

REFERENCES

Agawu, Kofi. (1992) "Representing African Music." *Critical Inquiry* 18.2: 245–266.

Agawu, Kofi. (2003). *Representing African Music: Postcolonial Notes, Queries, Positions.* Routledge.

Amin, T. N. (2016). "Beyond Hierarchy: Reimagining African Diaspora Dance in Higher Education Curricula." *Black Scholar* 46 (1): 15–26.

Browne, S. (2015). *Dark Matters: On the Surveillance of Blackness.* London: Duke University Press.

Chang, J. (2006). "Codes and the B-Boy Stigmata." In *Total Chaos: The Art and Aesthetics of Hip-Hop,* edited by J. Chang, 321–330. New York: BasicCivitas.

Chatterjea, A. (2004). *Butting Out: Reading Resistive Choreographies through Works by Jawole Willa Jo Zollar and Chandralekha.* Middletown, CT: Wesleyan University Press.

DeFrantz, T. F. (2002). "African American Dance: An Unchecked History." In *Dancing Many Drums: Excavations in African American Dance,* edited by T. F. DeFrantz, 3–35. Madison: University of Wisconsin Press.

Durden, M. (2009). *History and Concept of Hip-Hop Dance.* New York: Dancetime Publications. Film.

Elkins, J. (2001). *Why Art Cannot Be Taught: A Handbook for Art Students.* Urbana: University of Illinois Press.

Forman, M., and Neal, M. A. (2004). *That's the Joint! The Hip-Hop Studies Reader.* New York: Routledge.

Forsythe W. (1999). *Improvisation Technologies: A Tool for the Analytical Dance Eye.* CD-ROM/ DVD. ZKM | Zentrum für Kunst und Medientechnologie Karlsruhe; Deutsches Tanzarchiv Köln. Hatje Cantz: Ostfildern.

Frith, S. (1996). *Performing Rites.* New York: Oxford University Press.

Frith, S., and Horne, H. (1987). *Art into Pop.* London: Routledge.

Gottschild, B. D. (1996). *Digging the Africanist Presence in American Performance: Dance and Other Contexts.* Westport, CT: Greenwood Press.

Hsu, H. (2018). "The Spectacular Personal Mythology of Rammellzee." *New Yorker,* May 21. https://www.newyorker.com/magazine/2018/05/28/the-spectacular-personal-mythology-of-rammellzee. Accessed January 15, 2021.

IGTimes. (1996). *Style, Writing from the Underground: (R)evolutions in Aerosol Linguistics.* Viterbo, Italy: Stampa Alternativa.

Kelley, R. D. G. (2000). Foreword to *Black Marxism: The Making of the Black Radical Tradition* by C. J. Robinson, xi–xxvi. Chapel Hill: University of North Carolina Press. (Original work by Robinson published in 1983).

Kraut, A. (2016). *Choreographing Copyright: Race, Gender, and Intellectual Property Rights in American Dance.* Oxford: Oxford University Press.

McCarthy-Brown, N. (2014). "Decolonizing Dance Curriculum in Higher Education: One Credit at a Time." *Journal of Dance Education* 14 (4): 125–129.

McCarthy-Brown, N. (2017). *Dance Pedagogy for a Diverse World: Culturally Relevant Teaching in Theory, Research and Practice.* Jefferson, NC: McFarland.

Mettler, B. (1947). "The Relation of Dance to the Visual Arts." *Journal of Aesthetics and Art Criticism* 5 (3): 195–203.

Pabon, J. (2006). "Physical Graffiti: The History of Hip-Hop Dance." In *Total Chaos: The Art and Aesthetics of Hip-Hop,* edited by J. Chang, 18–26. New York: BasicCivitas.

Preston, V. K. (2015). "'How Do I Touch This Text?' or, the Interdisciplines between Theater in Early Modern Archives." In *The Oxford Handbook of Dance and Theater*, edited by N. George-Graves. Oxford University Press.

Robinson, C. J. (1983). *Black Marxism: The Making of the Black Radical Tradition.* London: Zed Press.

Sharma, S., Hutnyk, J., and Sharma, A. (1996). *Dis-orienting Rhythms: The Politics of the New Asian Dance Music.* London: Zed Books.

Silver, T., and Chalfant, H., dirs. (1983). *Style Wars.* Documentary film. USA: Public Art Films.

Stathopoulou, D. (2011). "From Dance Movement to Architectural Form." MPhil thesis. University of Bath. https://purehost.bath.ac.uk/ws/portalfiles/portal/244434/UnivBath_MPhil_2011_D_Stathopoulou.pdf.

YNOT. (2016). "Make the Letters Dance: Episode 1 featuring POPMASTER FABEL." Vimeo, May 19. Video file. https://player.vimeo.com/video/167284096.

PART V

HIP HOP HEALTH: INJURY, HEALING, AND REHABILITATION

CHAPTER 25

HIP HOP DANCE AND INJURY PREVENTION

TONY INGRAM

DISCLAIMER: *this chapter is for informational purposes only; consult a qualified health-care professional regarding the prevention and management of injuries. Last reviewed by the author in 2015. Readers are encouraged to seek contemporary sources of information.*

INTRODUCTION

Exciting advances in our understanding of injury prevention have been made in recent years, but it is difficult to apply them to Hip Hop dance, and particularly to breaking. For instance, the majority of injury-prevention research focuses on mainstream sports like soccer or football, and dance science typically involves the study of classical dance forms. There has been little research on the incidence and type of injuries in breaking. Although b-boys and b-girls possess a considerable range of movement skills and styles, generalizing the existing literature to this population remains a challenge for dance educators, healthcare providers, and independent artists alike. The considerable gaps in our knowledge highlight the need for more Hip Hop dance injury-prevention research.

This chapter reviews the existing research on Hip Hop dance injury, as of 2015, and discusses recent sports injury-prevention research as it might apply to breaking. The current literature on the incidence of Hip Hop dance injury is also reviewed. To provide the context for these discussions, the chapter will review the physical demands of breaking. It will also present common methods of injury prevention, including protective equipment, stretching, strength training, coordination, and proprioceptive exercise, and conclude with general recommendations for breaking. As research typically involves group averages, personalizing training to meet the specific needs of individual dancers will be considered throughout. Finally, topics of further inquiry will be suggested for those planning research on this unique population of dancers.

Breaking is the focus of the chapter for several reasons: (a) it is widely regarded as the original Hip Hop dance; (b) it arguably involves the most extreme physical demands of any Hip Hop dance, or any dance period, which will be an important consideration later in the chapter; and (c) perhaps surprisingly, it happens to be the most extensively studied form of Hip Hop dance in the literature.

INCIDENCE OF INJURY IN BREAKING

Many practitioners of the dance have been confronted with the safety concerns of their friends and family. The unique, dynamic, and acrobatic movements of breaking undoubtedly prompt such inquiries. However, reliable data on the incidence and severity of breaking-related injuries are scarce. Until recently, the research has been limited to published case reports in various medical journals. Such reports began to surface early in the 1980s, shortly after the dance became internationally popular (Dorey and Mayne 1986; Goscienski and Luevanos 1984; Johnson and Jones 1986; Leung 1984; Norman and Grodin 1984; Sharma et al. 1986), and breaking was associated with such injuries as bone fractures (Dieden 1985), bursitis (Broome and Heppenstall 1985), eye trauma (Joondeph, Spigelman, and Pulido 1986), scrotal pain (Wheeler and Appell 1984), wrist pain (Gerber, Griffin, and Simmons 1986), back pain (Moses and Shannon 1985), neck pain and injury (Byun, Cantos, and Patel 1986; McBride, Lehman, and Mangiardi 1985), and brain injury (Lee and Clough 1990). If one were to search the medical literature published in the 1990s for information on breaking-related injuries, however, one might feel discouraged. The literature remained silent until the early 2000s, when case studies again began to surface, likely reflecting the renewed popularity of the dance. The new case studies associate the dance with similar musculoskeletal injuries as were found in the earlier studies (Chen et al. 2008; Khoury, Loberant, and Jerushalmi 2009; Schneider et al. 2002) and lung injury (Balfour-Lynn 2002), as well as hair loss, supposedly caused by practicing head spins (Monselise, Chan, and Shapiro 2011).

But is breaking truly dangerous? After all, injuries are a risk in any sort of physical activity, and therefore the emergence of case reports with the rise in popularity should not be a surprise. A better question is, how dangerous is breaking compared to other activities? Case reports are well-documented anecdotes, but anecdotes, plural, are not data. Even the existence of numerous case reports fails to provide important comparative data on injury prevalence or the relative distribution of injury types, and should not be considered to provide an indication of whether or not the dance is particularly risky.

In recent years, a few studies have been published that investigate more appropriately the epidemiology of Hip Hop dance injury in surveys of large groups. One of the first of these appeared in the *American Journal of Sport Medicine*, where Kauther and colleagues (2009) retrospectively surveyed 144 dancers. Interestingly, the sample was collected at the Battle of the Year World Final in Braunschweig, Germany, where 40 of the participants in the competition (referred to as "professionals") and 104 randomly chosen dancers from the audience (referred to as "amateurs") were recruited to fill out a questionnaire. The questions covered typical demographics such as age, sex, and handedness, but also information about training habits, including amount of training time, time spent warming up, stretching, and engaging in other sports activities. The questions about injuries included the number of traumatic and overuse injuries, where each was defined for the participants. Also included were questions on the use of protective equipment, whether training time was lost due to injury, and whether medical treatment was sought.

The results revealed numerous musculoskeletal injuries, such as muscle strains, ligament sprains, and bone fractures (Kauther et al. 2009). Interestingly, many of the issues that were reported in past case studies were not found in this sample, such as brain injury, ocular trauma, scrotal pain, lung issues, and more. This demonstrates the tendency of case studies to report rare and unusual occurrences that should not be generalized to an entire population. Professional dancers had more injuries and overuse syndromes than amateur dancers on a per dancer basis. However, this could be accounted for simply by the increased hours of training experienced by the professionals; the injury rate for amateurs was 5.08 injuries per 1,000 hours of dancing; while professionals demonstrated a rate of 4.66 injuries per 1,000 hours. That professionals experienced slightly fewer injuries per hour may indicate a protective effect of proper execution and technique, but the differences were not statistically significant and may have been observed due to chance. The most commonly injured parts of the body were the knee and the spine for both amateurs and professionals; shoulder, skin, wrist, and ankle injuries were moderately common; and the elbow, head, and thorax were the least injured areas. Unfortunately, the authors did not elaborate on what was meant by a spine injury, an injury type that may have been better subdivided into neck and upper- and lower-back injuries. Measuring time lost per injury type revealed that the most debilitating injuries for b-boys and b-girls were knee and wrist injuries, with an average of 14 and 10.6 training days lost per injury, respectively. In their concluding discussion, Kauther et al. (2009) noted that "breakdance should be categorized as a 'collision' or 'contact' sport, as 'the athletes purposely hit or collide with the ground with great force'" and called for further research on protective equipment, even though they had not observed a negative correlation between wearing protective gear and injury rate in their study.

Another epidemiological study was published in 2009, in the journal *Injury*, by researchers from South Korea (Cho et al. 2009). Similar to the methods reported by Kauther et al. (2009), Cho et al. surveyed 23 professional and 19 amateur dancers asking questions regarding training practices and incidence of injury. However, Cho et al. did not indicate how participants were recruited, nor did they report total training hours, preventing a calculation of an injury per hour rate. Fortunately, the authors divided spine injuries into lumbar injuries and cervical spine injuries. The most common injuries, from most common to least common, were wrist (69% of dancers having experienced such an injury), finger (61.9%), knee (61.9%), shoulder (52.4%), lumbar spine (50%), elbow (42.9%), cervical spine (38.1%), ankle (38.1%), foot

(28.6%), and hip (16.7%). This is generally in line with the data from Kauther, since combining the two spine categories in Cho would have put spine injuries at the top of their list. An interesting difference in Cho et al.'s data is the dominance of injuries of the wrist rather than the knee or shoulder. This may reflect a survivorship bias in the Kauther data, where those with current wrist injuries may not have made it to the Battle of the Year event. Indeed, wrist injuries were one of the most debilitating injuries in Kauther et al.'s data, resulting in the second greatest loss of training time after knee injuries.

More recently, two additional studies have been published, one in 2012 in the *Scandinavian Journal of Medicine and Science in Sports*, and another in 2014 in the *Journal of Sports Medicine and Physical Fitness* (Joka et al. 2014; Ojofeitimi, Bronner, and Woo 2012). Ojofeitimi et al. (2012) investigated three categories of Hip Hop dancer: "Breakers," "Popper/Lockers," and "New Schoolers." As in the Kauther and Cho studies, the dancers answered survey questions that gathered both demographic and injury information. Unlike the previous two studies however, dancers were not asked about their training habits, such as weekly hours of training and years as a dancer. Instead, experience level was determined by years, such that intermediate dancers had 5 years or less, advanced dancers had 6–9 years, and expert dancers had 10 or more years of experience. Dancers were only asked about their injuries in the last twelve months, to determine annual incidence of injuries. As in the previous studies, Breakers reported wrist, knee, and shoulder injuries as common. Unlike the previous studies, Breakers reported ankles as the most often injured body part. Poppers/Lockers and New Schoolers both experienced fewer injuries overall, and these were dominant in the lower extremities compared to Breakers. Annual incidence from this study was compared to previous research on different types of dance and gymnastics. Hip Hop dancers were shown to experience more injuries than modern, tap, or ballet dancers, but the incidence was similar to gymnasts.

Annual incidence of injury can be misleading, because it does not control for the number of hours one is exposed to the activity. This is illustrated well in the results of Joka et al. (2014), who surveyed 46 males and 16 female amateur breakers regarding their training habits and injuries. Their results revealed an injury rate of 4.02 injuries per 1,000 hours of dance training or competition in past 12 months. In line with previous studies, the three most commonly injured areas in descending order were the knee, wrist, and shoulder. There were no significant differences in injury rate between males and females, except that there was a greater tendency for females to experience more finger injuries but fewer shoulder injuries than males. When taking into account training frequency, warm-up, stretching, strength training, use of protective equipment, types of movements, and supervision, the only factor to show a statistically significant association with injury rate was amount of training time. It is rather intuitive that the more time one spends performing an activity, the more likely one is to be injured—the more times a person crosses a street, the more likely they are to be hit by a car.

Table 25.1 Injuries per 1,000 hours of exposure to selected activities
for comparison.

Activity	Injury rate	Source
Soccer (professional, 2 games/wk)	25.6	(Dupont et al. 2010)
Triathlon (competing)	18.45	(Zwingenberger et al. 2014)
Running (recreational)	10.0	(Hespanhol et al. 2013)
Soccer (youth, outdoor)	5.59	(Emery and Meeuwisse 2006)
Breaking (professional)	4.66	(Kauther et al. 2009)
Ballet (professional)	4.4	(Allen et al. 2012)
Soccer (professional, 1 game/wk)	4.1	(Dupont et al. 2010)
Breaking (amateur)	4.02 to 5.08	(Joka et al. 2014; Kauther et al. 2009)
Triathlon (training)	1.39	(Zwingenberger et al. 2014)
Ballet (pre-professional)	1.38	(Ekegren et al. 2014)
Weightlifting (powerlifting)	1.0	(Siewe et al. 2011)
Weightlifting (bodybuilding)	0.24	(Siewe et al. 2014)

Rather than raw or annual injury incidence, it is far more informative to compare injuries per hour for various sports and activities to get a sense of how risky breaking may be. Table 25.1 illustrates injury rates per 1,000 hours of exposure to various popular physical activities and sports. It should be noted that higher levels of expertise (professional vs. amateur) do not always change injury rates dramatically, whereas it appears that intensity (competition vs. training) and frequency can have a profound impact. Such details add much-needed context when comparing injury rates.

Many of the studies reported above contained warnings about the safety of the dance; Kauther et al. (2009) suggested: "Breakdancing must be considered as a potentially high-risk dancing sport," (797) and Cho et al. (2009) called for more supervision and injury-prevention education for these dancers. However, these warnings should not be taken as pejorative comments about the dance, but as calls to the healthcare community to familiarize themselves with the common risks of an art form that is growing in popularity. Ojofeitimi, Bronner, and Woo (2012) commented, "Sports and dance medicine practitioners must begin to recognize and accept these dancers as legitimate artists and athletes. They should be as familiar with the injury patterns of Hip Hop dance as they are with classical dance and other sports such as gymnastics and baseball" (353). As illustrated in Table 25.1, breaking is no more injurious an activity than the majority of popular sports, and should not be regarded as a dangerous fringe activity. That said, breaking is a relatively new dance with practitioners that may not be adequately informed about injury prevention. The remainder of the chapter will discuss injury-prevention research as it applies to breaking.

ATHLETIC DEMANDS OF BREAKING

Aside from the epidemiological studies described in the previous section, there is a severe lack of research on injury prevention for Hip Hop dancers. To this author's knowledge, no studies investigating the efficacy of any injury prevention method for b-boys or b-girls have been published in peer-reviewed journals. The only study that exists is an unpublished masters thesis (discussed in the section "Stretching" below). Given this dearth of evidence, we must turn to research on injury prevention in other sports and activities. A rational approach to this involves first establishing the athletic demands of breaking so that we can relate the research that has been done on other populations to the dance appropriately. For instance, a study investigating the effects of stretching for injury prevention in runners likely has little bearing on the efficacy of stretching for dancers because the flexibility requirements of the two activities are strikingly different. This section will therefore discuss the athletic demands of breaking and how they compare to other activities commonly studied in the existing injury-prevention literature. We will broadly characterize the movement skills, conditioning, strength, and flexibility requirements of a typical, competitive b-boy or b-girl. However, throughout this discussion we must recognize the considerable variability between individual dancers. Some dancers may require more strength, flexibility, or any other physical characteristic than others, depending on their approach to the dance. Throughout this section, it will be assumed that the reader is familiar with common terms used broadly to categorize movements in breaking such as "foundation," "toprock" or "uprock," "footwork," "power moves," and "freezes." Having established this basis, we will then review injury-prevention research, and discuss how the results may or may not apply to breaking.

On observation, it is clear that the typical, competitive b-boy or b-girl exhibits a wide variety of movement skills. Dancers perform a variety of dance steps rythmically to music while performing "toprock" or "uprock." This represents one of the major differenes between breaking and the majority of sports, where movement is not dictated by music. However, it should be noted that human movement typically relies on rythmic patterns as dictated by the neural circuitry that controls walking and many other bodily functions (Guertin 2014). Dance steps likely do not impose significantly different demands on the body compared to running due to the rhythmicity alone, for example. With respect to comparing dancing to sports that involve running: the repetitive movement of the lower limbs may be similar in terms of energetic and muscular force demands, but the variety of movement involved in dancing considerably changes the distribution and volume of these forces.

The power moves, freezes, and various acrobatic movements utilized in breaking may share considerable similarity with gymnastics and the martial arts. These movements involve powerful spins, jumps, flips, kicks, and hand balancing in a variety of positions, and are often performed near the end range of a dancer's flexibility. These dynamic movements are typically not performed in conformance to strict criteria as in gymnastics. Instead, value is placed on variation between dancers, and on slightly unrefined or "raw" movements. While this approach may be thought to increase impact forces, it could be argued that the inherent variety distributes these forces in such a way that overuse of a particular body part becomes less likely. Furthermore, it should be noted that movement variability is desirable, and that impact forces are not to be vilified; variability is important in motor learning (Herzfeld and Shadmehr 2014), and the impact forces of exercise have been shown to improve bone-mineral density (Ahola et al. 2009). Further research must clarify the biomechanical impact of breaking, and how it differs from other activities. Finally, the footwork in breaking is unique. Performing technically elaborate foot and leg patterns while close to the ground, supported by the upper extremities for extended periods of time, is unlike any other activity this author can imagine. This makes it very difficult to relate existing research on injury prevention to footwork. Overall, breaking involves a wide variety of movement skills, each with different levels of similarity to other sports and activities.

The energetic demands of breaking depend on the context in which the dancer tends to perform. Common settings include practice, competition, the cypher, or stage performance. Dancers typically autoregulate their effort during practice to ensure their conserved energy allows them to perform the movements they are focusing on. Competitions usually involve turn-based freestyle dancing lasting roughly thirty seconds, either one on one, or crew versus crew. Stage performances often involve prolonged choreography for extended periods of time. Longer performances are typically choreographed to allow dancers reasonable pacing and rest when possible. Cyphers are culturally significant Hip Hop dance circles that take place in a variety of social settings, including practices, parties, clubs, and competitions. Dancers perform one at a time with as much rest as desired; however, they will occasionally compete in unlimited rounds. Because one-on-one competitions likely represent one of the most common and physically demanding goals of a b-boy or b-girl, this discussion will assume that our dancer trains to perform well in one-on-one competitions. In such events dancers would be expected to perform their best and most demanding material in two to three 30-second rounds with an equivalent amount of rest. Dancers may compete in four to five battles over a few hours, assuming they make it to the finals.

The short bursts of intense effort involved in competitive breaking require similar energetic demands as sprinting. Sprint training is currently a hot topic in exercise science. Of particular interest in recent years is a form of exercise known as high-intensity interval training (HIIT), which consists of "all out" sprinting for 30-second work and 30-second rest ratios, repeating for five to ten minutes. HIIT has been shown to provide health and fitness benefits similar to traditional continuous, paced endurance exercise, despite significantly shorter overall training time (Burgomaster et al. 2008; Gibala et al. 2012). It should be noted that HIIT may not be suitable for sedentary individuals (Hardcastle et al. 2014), and may not confer all the same benefits of continuous endurance exercise (Keating et al. 2014). A notable difference between HIIT and breaking is that, whereas dancers may perform at full effort during their competition rounds, much of their effort likely is placed on the control of complex movements rather than on maximally contracting muscles during a simpler pattern, as in sprinting. Nevertheless, b-boys and b-girls who consistently train for one-on-one competitions demand much the same from their bodies as do sprinters compared to runners. This is an important consideration because much of the existing injury-prevention literature has utilized runners as participants.

Adequate muscular strength and power can be extremely important for the majority of advanced movements, depending on the dancer's individual style. Powermoves, freezes, and footwork require momentary to extended time supporting one's bodyweight using the upper extremities. As reflected in the high incidence of injury reported by Cho et al., wrist and shoulder mobility and strength are of utmost importance. This is especially true for those who perform dynamic movements while inverted and supported by their hands. Many dancers perform a variety of flips in their rounds, requiring considerable lower-extremity strength as well. Thus the strength and power requirements of breaking are similar to those of gymnastics. Dancers likely do not require advanced weight training to build strength beyond the ability to control their bodyweight easily. In any case, weight training is likely an ideal approach to progressively building the strength required, and continued training may be extremely important for injury prevention, as will be discussed below.

The amount of flexibility breaking requires can vary considerably from dancer to dancer. Some dancers perform incredible feats of flexibility, much as a contortionist does, in movements that are central to their individual style. However, many dancers are only modestly flexible. In fact, many b-boys and b-girls likely possess less flexibility than classically trained dancers. The range of motion with which a dancer performs likely reflects their natural abilities when they first learn to dance. Those who already possess impressive flexibility likely discover movements utilizing these abilities, and are encouraged either personally or by others to continue on such a path. Some very dedicated dancers will commit themselves to intense flexibility training to achieve particular movements. Many dancers excel at different aspects of the dance that do not require much flexibility. This variability is likely due to the fact that breaking emphasizes creativity and originality rather than mastery of a strictly defined skill set. For this discussion we will assume that most competitive dancers aim for the somewhat high degrees of flexibility that are required for most powermoves. For instance, performing a powermove called the air flare requires considerable hip mobility but doesn't necessarily require front and side splits, although such flexibility would be an asset. Comparing this with the existing injury-prevention literature, this amount of flexibility is likely similar to that needed by martial artists, gymnasts, and dancers of other forms.

INJURY-PREVENTION RESEARCH: WHAT WORKS, AND WHAT DOESN'T?

As with other sports, injury-prevention advice has traditionally been passed down to dancers by their mentors, based on anecdotal evidence. However, one cannot determine the efficacy of an injury-prevention method retrospectively. For example, if an athlete completes a training session without suffering an injury, how can they be certain it was due to stretching beforehand? Their success might be due to their warm-up, diet, or psychological readiness to perform. Perhaps they wouldn't have suffered an injury regardless of their preparation. The most appropriate research method for determining the efficacy of an intervention is a rigorously designed prospective trial.

Although controlling for confounding variables can be complicated, and a discussion of proper experimental design is beyond the scope of this chapter, the concept of such a trial is simple. Participants are typically divided into two groups: one group receives the intervention, such as stretching before training, and one is a control group, which recieves either no intervention or a different one for comparison. The two groups then carry out their activity for a period of time, often an entire sports season, and the number of injuries suffered is recorded at the end of the trial. A well-designed trial provides a far more objective assessment of the efficacy of a given injury-prevention method.

In the last couple of decades, such trials have both confirmed prior beliefs and surprisingly debunked some of the most popular methods of injury prevention. The majority of this research has focused on popular team sports such as soccer, likely for reasons of funding and ease of participant recruitment. Therefore not all of these results will be directly applicable to breaking. Having established what physical capabilities are required of an archetypical competetive b-boy or b-girl in the previous section, we can begin to review recently published injury-prevention research to consider its relevance in breaking.

Protective Equipment and Flooring

The use of protective equipment has been shown to be effective in reducing the rate of injury in some cases. Strong evidence exists for the effectiveness of ankle braces in reducing ankle sprain injury and reinjury in a variety of sports (Dizon and Reyes 2010; McGuine, Brooks, and Hetzel 2011; McGuine et al. 2012). Reductions of up to 70% fewer ankle injuries have been reported in the literature.

Knee injuries are more common in breaking and thus knee braces may be of more interest. Unfortunately, the research on knee braces is less encouraging. Knee braces do not appear to reduce injury in football players (Pietrosimone et al. 2008; Salata, Gibbs, and Sekiya 2010), nor do they impair or improve the physical capabilities of an athlete (Mortaza et al. 2012; Mortaza et al. 2013). The mechanism of knee injury likely differs significantly between football and breaking. Breaking knee injuries likely result from high-speed contact with the floor or an awkward landing; football knee injuries result from high impact contact with other players or rapid direction changes during sprinting. It is therefore difficult to determine whether knee braces are beneficial for dancers, and the wearing of them cannot be encouraged or discouraged until further research clarifies their role. With that said, knee injury incidence can be reduced through alternative methods which will be discussed below.

Dance flooring may represent an important environmental factor in preventing dance injury. Studies conducted with ballet dancers have implicated inappropriate flooring as potentially causative of lower-extremity injuries. Potential flooring issues include either excessive or inadequate foot adhesion and decreased force reduction (Hopper et al. 2014; Wanke et al. 2012). It should be noted, however, that perfect flooring might not be necessary. Research has shown that people naturally adjust their running mechanics to normalize joint forces when running on surfaces of differing stiffness (Ferris, Louie, and Farley 1998; Tillman et al. 2002). Unfortunately, no trials have been performed to demonstrate the impact of improving flooring on reducing dance injury incidence. Because breaking involves frequent body contact with the floor and is not restricted to the lower extremities, it is the opinion of this author that appropriate flooring is extremely important for preventing injury in all types of Hip Hop dance.

Stretching

Perhaps one of the most surprising results from sport and exercise science research in the last few decades has come from the research on stretching. Stretching typically refers to taking a bodily movement to its end range with the purpose of improving the muscle or connective tissue extensibility. Stretches can be performed in a variety of ways, including by holding the end point (static stretching) or being in continuous motion (dynamic stretching) while relaxing the targeted muscles (passive stretching) or contracting (active stretching) them. Static passive stretching is by far the most commonly studied form of stretching. As expected, stretching has been shown to be an effective method in increasing joint range of motion and muscle extensibility (Harvey, Herbert, and Crosbie 2002; Sainz de Baranda and Ayala 2010). Generally, static stretching has not been shown to prevent injuries in a wide variety of athletic populations (Herbert and Gabriel 2002; Lauersen, Bertelsen, and Andersen 2014; Thacker et al. 2004). Furthermore, static stretching for 45 seconds or more appears to result in 5%, 2%, and 2% reductions in muscular strength, power, and explosive performance, respectively (Simic, Sarabon, and Markovic 2013). It should be noted that most of this research was performed on participants in field sports such as soccer, or on army recruits, likely for practical reasons. Nonetheless, these results have had a powerful effect on sports and exercise science, and have led to a questioning of the conventional wisdom of including stretching in an injury-prevention program.

Since prospective trials of stretching have not been performed on dancers of any type, it is difficult to determine whether or not stretching should be recommended for the prevention of dance injury. One could argue that the results found depend on the type of athlete studied. Soccer players and army recruits likely do not require the same range of motion as a dancer, martial artist, or gymnast. Stretching may improve muscle extensibility and reduce the chances of straining a muscle in those who regularly move toward the end of their range of motion. Therefore, dancers may benefit from stretching whereas soccer players do not. This may be a valid argument; however, it should be noted that in most sports, the majority of muscle strains appear to occur within the normal ranges of motion during eccentric (lengthening under tension) muscle contractions (Garrett 1996; Shrier 2000), which tend to occur when landing a jump, breaking a fall, or in cutting maneuvers during sprinting. In dancers, excessive stretching may actually contribute to muscle strain; retrospective studies of student and professional ballet dancers have shown that up to 88% of muscle strains occur during slow stretch training, with the remainder occurring during powerful movements (Askling et al. 2002; Askling et al. 2007; Deleget 2010). Finally, muscle strains only represent one type of injury, where there are many types of injury that are unlikely to be affected by muscle flexibility; it is unlikely that ligament sprains or bone fractures occur as a result of excessively tight muscles.

The research results on stretching for injury prevention may be at odds with the experience of many athletes, particularly dancers. Many athletes simply do not feel ready to perform without first completing their routine stretching. This author would like to contend that this experience is likely due to factors independent of the efficacy of stretching in preventing injuries. Because stretching does improve flexibility, it is reasonable to assume that stretching prior to an activity requiring a large range of motion improves ease of movement. Stretching has also been shown to alter sensation, perhaps having analgesic effects on the discomfort of stretching (Weppler and Magnusson 2010). Unless they are training vigorously for increased flexibility, people typically do not stretch for 45 seconds or more, and thus likely avoid any detrimental effect on muscular strength and power. For these reasons, it is not recommended that dancers discontinue stretching because of the research results just described. The amount and type of stretching a dancer engages in should depend on the range of motion they plan to utilize. Before training or a performance, warm-up stretching should be limited to roughly 30 seconds per muscle group. If improved flexibility is a goal, stretching for longer periods per muscle group would best be done at the end of the training session. So, while dancers can and perhaps should continue to stretch, the results of the research reviewed above indicate that injury-prevention efforts should be placed elsewhere. Fortunately, research has demonstrated that other forms of physical training are indeed effective for reducing injuries.

A special consideration regarding stretching for breaking may include wrist-extension flexibility. No previous research has indicated that a lack of wrist mobility is predictive of wrist injury, but such studies have been performed. The wrist is one of the most commonly injured areas in breaking. Breaking frequently requires the wrist to extend to or beyond ninety degrees while supporting the dancer's entire bodyweight. It is possible that ensuring adequate wrist flexibility is essential to preventing wrist injuries. One unpublished master's thesis by physiotherapist and b-girl Sophie Manuela Linder (2014) investigated the effects of a combination of manual wrist therapy, strengthening, and stretching for wrist flexibility in twenty-two Spanish breakdancers. Linder demonstrated clinically and statistically significant improvements in wrist extensor range of motion in the dancers studied, along with their subjective reports of improved stability and reduced pain. This study is a promising start to Hip Hop dance injury-prevention research because it appropriately investigated a specific issue common to a specific population—wrist injuries in breakers—and established an effective and reproducable protocol. Further research should investigate whether such an intervention indeed reduces injury incidence.

Strength Training

Over the last decade, sports injury-prevention research has generally focused more on active training intervention than on passive equipment studies (McBain et al. 2012a, 2012b). This change in focus may be an outcome of the promising results being reported for exercise-based approaches. Strength training has been shown to reduce injuries by to up to 68%, making it possibly the most effective exercise-based approach to injury prevention (Lauersen, Bertelsen, and Andersen 2014). Any form of resistance training is likely beneficial; however, the literature typically prescribes strength training in the form of bodyweight exercises. Commonly strained muscles such as the hamstrings and groin muscles are often specifically targeted. It is unclear whether or not potential muscle imbalances should be targeted. Questions remain as to whether there is an optimal level of strength for preventing injuries, or whether the positive effects are due to the training itself. Many people are familiar with the idea that overuse can cause injury, but fewer may realize that underuse can also cause deterioration (Stovitz and Johnson 2006). For instance, it is known that optimal tissue loading is necessary to maintain tendon integrity (Arampatzis, Karamanidis, and Albracht 2007). It is possible that strength training increases tissue tolerance of repetitive or excessive forces, reducing the incidence of injury. Regardless of the mechanism, it is clear that regular strength training is an effective means of preventing injuries.

In their study of the etiology of injuries in amateur breakdancers, Joka et al. (2014) indicated that the majority of dancers did not partake in strength training outside their regular dance practice. Interestingly, there was no difference in injury incidence in dancers who did do some sort of strength training. This lack of effect may be due to the relatively small sample size leading to a lack of statistical power. Given that breaking requires considerable muscular strength and power, and the impressive preventative effects of strength training in other athletes, it is likely that b-boys and b-girls would benefit significantly from general bodyweight strength-training programs.

Coordination and Proprioceptive Training

Muscular strength and flexibility may have a role in preventing muscle strains, but they are unlikely to help a person who is falling to the ground or moving a joint in an abnormal direction. Some of the most devastating athletic injuries involve stressing connective tissue in directions that are not biomechanically congruent, resulting in career altering injuries such as anterior cruciate ligament (ACL) ruptures. Training programs have thus been developed to improve joint mechanics during jumping, landing, sprinting, and cutting maneuvers. Such programs typically emphasize neuromuscular control of the hips and knees during dynamic movements, so that forces are distributed favorably across the joints. For example, greater motion or force in knee valgus, where the knees drift toward midline, has been associated with increased risk of ACL injury (Hewett et al. 2005).

Training programs are designed in the hopes that developing control of these movements will reduce the incidence of injury. Such exercise has been referred to as neuromuscular training, coordination training, motor control, or proprioceptive training—the latter referring to one's sense of joint and limb position in space. Thus far, the research has been very encouraging, showing knee and ankle ligament injury reductions estimated from 50% to 85% (Gagnier, Morgenstern, and Chess 2013; Hübscher et al. 2010; Laursen, Bertelsen, and Andersen 2014; Sadoghi, von Keudell, and Vavken 2012).

Interestingly, it has been shown that classically trained dancers have considerably fewer ACL injuries than athletes involved in team sports, such as soccer (Liederbach, Dilgen, and Rose 2008). This decreased rate of injury has been attributed to the emphasis on movement quality in dancing. For instance, female athletes have been shown to land their jumps with greater peak knee valgus than male athletes; and dancers land with more favorable knee mechanics with no significant differences between sexes (Orishimo et al. 2014). Furthermore, dancers take longer to reach a level of fatigue that affects their landing mechanics detrimentally compared to athletes, regardless of sex (Liederbach et al. 2014). These results are thought to be due to the training in jumping and leaping that dancers receive; dancers are taught to land gracefully with correct knee alignment. Perhaps by practicing for more aesthetically pleasing movement, dancers serendipitously learn to move safely.

But if the research on jumping mechanics might not be directly generalizable to breaking, the importance of proper form and execution is. What is perhaps not obvious to the nonexpert observer is that there is a generally accepted technique for executing the majority of fundamental breaking movements, from which variations are derived. Advanced movements are to be executed well without "crashing," particularly in the competitive arena. This emphasis on movement quality may explain the comparatively low rate of injury in breaking relative to the explosive and abstract movements performed in the dance, compared to other sports and activities. However, b-boys and b-girls do not receive the same training with respect to landing mechanics that classically trained dancers do. Depending on the dancer's style, it may be of interest to practice coordination and proprioceptive training to improve lower-extremity control during toprock or while performing flips, for example.

The application of coordination and proprioceptive training to movement skills that are specific to breaking may be essential, and this presents an exciting avenue for future research. Footwork and the majority of powermoves are unique to breaking, and are therefore unlikely to be addressed by the current injury-prevention programs being studied. Few upper-extremity coordination exercises have been developed and studied for their efficacy in preventing upper extremity injuries, and upper-extremity injury-prevention research in general is lacking (McBain et al. 2012a, 2012b). One existing option is the upper-extremity Y-balance test (Gorman et al. 2012; Westrick et al. 2012). Because the lower-extremity version of the Y-balance test has been shown to predict lower-extremity injury (Smith, Chimera, and Warren 2015), the upper-extremity version may be an effective diagnostic or training tool for improving upper-extremity motor control. Given that two of the most common breaking injuries are those affecting the shoulder and wrist, b-boys and b-girls should perform a variety of simple exercises that involve supporting and shifting their bodyweight on their arms with the goal of improving control and stability. Future studies should strongly consider testing such exercise protocols in breakers and gymnasts to determine their efficacy in preventing upper-extremity injury.

Conclusions and Recommendations

The preceding review provides convincing evidence that effective injury-prevention methods exist. How effective these interventions are for Hip Hop dancers will remain a matter of speculation until further research is conducted. In the interim, it seems reasonable to propose that much of the existing research applies to breaking, with some special considerations. Protective equipment such as ankle or wrist braces should be utilized as required, depending on training needs and a dancer's history of previous injury. Most practice should take place in a safe area that has proper flooring. Dancers should continue to stretch as needed to perform their desired movements. Adequate wrist extension flexibility may be an essential requirement for the majority of breaking movements. Dancers should engage in coordination and proprioceptive warm-up exercises emphasizing balance, stability, and agility of the wrist, shoulder, and knee joints. Dancers should perform one to three weekly sessions of full-body strength training, with emphasis on bodyweight exercises, in addition to their regular dance training. Although little research has investigated the efficacy of endurance training in reducing injuries, fatigue has been shown to affect joint mechanics negatively, as was demonstrated by the landing mechanics research described above (in the section "Coordination and Proprioceptive Training"). Dancers should train for endurance in a manner specific to their goals. For instance, a one-on-one competition dancer should train to dance for three to five 30-second work-rest intervals. Other factors that have not been well studied through prospective trials on injury incidence should still be considered. Examples that are certain to be relevant include the effects of adequate rest, sleep, nutrition, and hydration, reducing stress and ensuring psychological readiness to perform. And all recommendations given here should be adjusted for each dancer as appropriate, based on their personal goals and individual approach to the dance.

FUTURE DIRECTIONS

This chapter attempted to review the existing injury-prevention literature to date, in consideration of its relevance to breaking. This approach is necessary given the current lack of research on injury-prevention for b-boys and b-girls. The author attempted to draw upon his own education and experience to provide reasonable recommendations, yet the occasionally surprising research results—such as those regarding stretching—indicate that even the most logical rationale must be tested. Therefore, the recommendations provided in this chapter must be confirmed or refuted by well-designed experiments. Because breaking involves a unique set of physical requirements compared to the majority of other sports and activities, prospective trials must be performed with dancers as participants.

The most commonly injured areas in breaking appear to be the wrist, shoulder, knee, neck, and lower back. Studies should investigate the effects of stretching, strength training, and coordination exercises for each of these areas, and their efficacy in reducing specific or overall injuries. Both full-body and targeted training interventions should be studied. Particular emphasis should be placed on preventing upper-extremity injuries given the lack of research on this area in general. Research on stretching has focused on static passive stretching, and therefore prospective trials must compare different types of stretching or exercise training to determine the most effective methods for dancers. Finally, because dancers differ considerably in their movement repertoires, more research is needed on individual differences in injury incidence and prevention, as well as on the particular risks of specific movements.

Successfully carrying out such a research program requires close interaction between dancers and researchers. Dancers typically do not possess the appropriate expertise in rehabilitation, sport, and exercise science to carry out well-designed experiments. By the same token, researchers unfamiliar with the dance may have misconceptions about its terminology and physical requirements. Proper subgrouping is required to take account of the wide range of Hip Hop dance styles; researchers unfamiliar with the dance may erroneously aggregate Hip Hop dancers of all types in their studies, creating heterogeneous populations and reducing the validity of the results. For example, a targeted wrist-strengthening protocol is unlikely to affect the injury rates of a dancer who rarely supports their bodyweight on their hands. However, researchers with dual expertise in experimental design and Hip Hop dance are rare, and so researchers must fill their knowledge gaps by establishing close relationships with local dance communities. Such collaboration is also likely to improve participant recruitment.

Collaboration between healthcare professionals and both dancers and researchers is also important. If healthcare professionals wish to address the individual needs of dancers, they must familiarize themselves with their craft, as they would with any other athlete. To ensure that treatment is evidence based, they must also avail themselves of the existing research literature and maintain an open dialogue with researchers. Healthcare professionals may also form a vital link between dancers and researchers, where their patients may provide a much-needed pool of research participants. Researchers should likewise avail themselves of the services of healthcare professionals to properly screen dancers for injuries so that dancers receive the best possible care while participating in a study.

Achieving these goals will require a concerted effort on the part of dancers, researchers, healthcare professionals, and any relevant supporting organizations. Dancers must be educated about the benefits of supporting such research; healthcare professionals must have access to continuing education; and researchers must be offered funding and support. To this author's knowledge, such resources are currently scarce. With the growing worldwide popularity of breaking and Hip Hop dance, it is critical that quality research be conducted. It is my hope that this chapter will provide an adequate foundation for those interested in studying Hip Hop dance injury prevention in the future.

REFERENCES

Ahola, R., Korpelainen, R., Vainionpää, A., Leppäluoto, J., and Jämsä, T. (2009). "Time-Course of Exercise and Its Association with 12-Month Bone Changes." *BMC Musculoskeletal Disorders* 10: 138. doi:10.1186/1471-2474-10-138.

Allen, N., Nevill, A., Brooks, J., Koutedakis, Y., and Wyon, M. (2012). "Ballet Injuries: Injury Incidence and Severity over 1 Year." *Journal of Orthopaedic and Sports Physical Therapy* 42 (9): 781–790. doi:10.2519/jospt.2012.3893.

Arampatzis, A., Karamanidis, K., and Albracht, K. (2007). "Adaptational Responses of the Human Achilles Tendon by Modulation of the Applied Cyclic Strain Magnitude." *Journal of Experimental Biology* 210 (Pt. 15): 2743–2753. doi:10.1242/jeb.003814.

Askling, C., Lund, H., Saartok, T., and Thorstensson, A. (2002). "Self-Reported Hamstring Injuries in Student-Dancers." *Scandinavian Journal of Medicine and Science in Sports* 12 (4): 230–235.

Askling, C., Tengvar, M., Saartok, T., and Thorstensson, A. (2007). "Acute First-Time Hamstring Strains during Slow-Speed Stretching: Clinical, Magnetic Resonance Imaging, and Recovery Characteristics." *American Journal of Sports Medicine* 35 (10): 1716–1724. doi:10.1177/0363546507303563.

Balfour-Lynn, I. M. (2002). "Break Dancer's Lung." *Archives of Disease in Childhood* 86 (3): 224.

Broome, H. E., and Heppenstall, R. B. (1985). "'Break Dancers' Bursitis." *JAMA* 253 (6): 777.

Burgomaster, K. A., Howarth, K. R., Phillips, S. M., Rakobowchuk, M., Macdonald, M. J., McGee, S. L., and Gibala, M. J. (2008). "Similar Metabolic Adaptations during Exercise after Low Volume Sprint Interval and Traditional Endurance Training in Humans." *Journal of Physiology* 586 (1): 151–160. doi:10.1113/jphysiol.2007.142109.

Byun, H. S., Cantos, E. L., and Patel, P. P. (1986). "Severe Cervical Injury due to Break Dancing: A Case Report." *Orthopedics* 9 (4): 550–551.

Chen, Y. H., Kuo, C. L., Lin, L. C., Wang, S. J., and Lee, C. H. (2008). "Stress Fracture of the Ulna in a Break-Dancer." *Journal of Sports Science & Medicine* 7 (4): 556–559.

Cho, C. H., Song, K. S., Min, B. W., Lee, S. M., Chang, H. W., and Eum, D. S. (2009). "Musculoskeletal Injuries in Break-Dancers." *Injury* 40 (11): 1207–1211. doi:10.1016/j.injury.2009.05.019.

Deleget, A. (2010). "Overview of Thigh Injuries in Dance." *Journal of Dance Medicine & Science* 14 (3): 97–102.

Dieden, J. D. (1985). "Break Dancer's Fracture of the Fifth Metatarsal." Letter to the editor. *Western Journal of Medicine* 142 (1): 101.

Dizon, J. M., and Reyes, J. J. (2010). "A Systematic Review on the Effectiveness of External Ankle Supports in the Prevention of Inversion Ankle Sprains among Elite and Recreational Players." *Journal of Science and Medicine in Sport / Sports Medicine Australia* 13 (3): 309–317. doi:10.1016/J.Jsams.2009.05.002.

Dorey, R. S., and Mayne, V. (1986). "Break-Dancing Injuries." *Medical Journal of Australia* 144 (11): 610–611.

Dupont, G., Nedelec, M., McCall, A., McCormack, D., Berthoin, S., and Wisløff, U. (2010). "Effect of 2 Soccer Matches in a Week on Physical Performance and Injury Rate." *American Journal of Sports Medicine* 38 (9): 1752–1758. doi:10.1177/0363546510361236.

Ekegren, C. L., Quested, R., and Brodrick, A. (2014). "Injuries in Pre-professional Ballet Dancers: Incidence, Characteristics and Consequences." *Journal of Science and Medicine in Sport / Sports Medicine Australia* 17 (3): 271–275. doi:10.1016/j.jsams.2013.07.013.

Emery, C. A., and Meeuwisse, W. H. (2006). "Risk Factors for Injury in Indoor Compared with Outdoor Adolescent Soccer." *American Journal of Sports Medicine* 34 (10): 1636–1642. doi:10.1177/0363546506288018.

Ferris, D. P., Louie, M., and Farley, C. T. (1998). "Running in the Real World: Adjusting Leg Stiffness for Different Surfaces." *Proceedings of the Royal Society B: Biological Sciences* 265 (1400): 989–994. doi:10.1098/rspb.1998.0388.

Gagnier, J. J., Morgenstern, H., and Chess, L. (2013). "Interventions Designed to Prevent Anterior Cruciate Ligament Injuries in Adolescents and Adults: A Systematic Review and Meta-Analysis." *American Journal of Sports Medicine* 41 (8): 1952–1962. doi:10.1177/0363546512458227.

Garrett, W. E. (1996). "Muscle Strain Injuries." *American Journal of Sports Medicine* 24 (6 Suppl): S2–8.

Gerber, S. D., Griffin, P. P., and Simmons, B. P. (1986). "Break Dancer's Wrist." *Journal of Pediatric Orthopedics* 6 (1): 98–99.

Gibala, M. J., Little, J. P., Macdonald, M. J., and Hawley, J. A. (2012). "Physiological Adaptations to Low-Volume, High-Intensity Interval Training in Health and Disease." *Journal of Physiology* 590 (Pt. 5): 1077–1084. doi:10.1113/jphysiol.2011.224725.

Gorman, P. P., Butler, R. J., Plisky, P. J., and Kiesel, K. B. (2012). "Upper Quarter Y Balance Test: Reliability and Performance Comparison between Genders in Active Adults." *Journal of Strength and Conditioning Research / National Strength & Conditioning Association* 26 (11): 3043–3048. doi:10.1519/JSC.0b013e3182472fdb.

Goscienski, P. J., and Luevanos, L. (1984). "Injury Caused by 'Break Dancing.'" *JAMA* 252 (24): 3367.

Guertin, P. A. (2014). "Preclinical Evidence Supporting the Clinical Development of Central Pattern Generator-Modulating Therapies for Chronic Spinal Cord-Injured Patients." *Frontiers in Human Neuroscience* 8: 272. doi:10.3389/fnhum.2014.00272.

Hardcastle, S., Ray, H., Beale, L., and Hagger, M. (2014). "Why Sprint Interval Training Is Inappropriate for a Largely Sedentary Population." *Frontiers in Psychology* 5: 1505. doi:10.3389/fpsyg.2014.01505.

Harvey, L., Herbert, R., and Crosbie, J. (2002). "Does Stretching Induce Lasting Increases in Joint ROM? A Systematic Review." *Physiotherapy Research International* 7 (1): 1–13.

Herbert, R. D., and Gabriel, M. (2002). "Effects of Stretching before and after Exercising on Muscle Soreness and Risk of Injury: Systematic Review." *BMJ (Clinical Research Ed.)* 325 (7362): 468.

Herzfeld, D., and Shadmehr, R. (2014). "Motor Variability Is Not Noise, but Grist for the Learning Mill." *Nature Neuroscience* 17 (2): 149–150. doi:10.1038/nn.3633.

Hespanhol Junior, L. C., Pena Costa, L. O., and Lopes, A. D. (2013). "Previous Injuries and Some Training Characteristics Predict Running-Related Injuries in Recreational

Runners: A Prospective Cohort Study." *Journal of Physiotherapy* 59 (4): 263–269. doi:10.1016/S1836-9553(13)70203-0.

Hewett, T. E., Myer, G. D., Ford, K. R., Heidt, R. S., Jr., Colosimo, A. J., McLean, S. G., and Succop, P. (2005). "Biomechanical Measures of Neuromuscular Control and Valgus Loading of the Knee Predict Anterior Cruciate Ligament Injury Risk in Female Athletes: A Prospective Study." *American Journal of Sports Medicine* 33 (4): 492–501.

Hopper, L. S., Alderson, J. A., Elliott, B. C., and Ackland, T. R. (2014). "Dance Floor Force Reduction Influences Ankle Loads in Dancers during Drop Landings." *Journal of Science and Medicine in Sport / Sports Medicine Australia* 18 (4): 480–485. doi:10.1016/j.jsams.2014.07.001.

Hübscher, M., Zech, A., Pfeifer, K., Hänsel, F., Vogt, L., and Banzer, W. (2010). "Neuromuscular Training for Sports Injury Prevention: A Systematic Review." *Medicine and Science in Sports and Exercise* 42 (3): 413–421. doi:10.1249/MSS.0b013e3181b88d37.

Johnson, S. R., and Jones, D. G. (1986). "Break Dancing: The Need for Supervision." *British Journal of Sports Medicine* 20 (2): 91.

Joka, T., Clarke, N. D., Cohen, D. D., and Delextrat, A. (2014). "Etiology of Musculoskeletal Injuries in Amateur Breakdancers." *Journal of Sports Medicine and Physical Fitness.*

Joondeph, B. C., Spigelman, A. V., and Pulido, J. S. (1986). "Ocular Trauma from Break Dancing." *Archives of Ophthalmology* 104 (2): 176–177.

Kauther, M. D., Wedemeyer, C., Wegner, A., Kauther, K. M., and von Knoch, M. (2009). "Breakdance Injuries and Overuse Syndromes in Amateurs and Professionals." *American Journal of Sports Medicine* 37 (4): 797–802. doi:10.1177/0363546508328120.

Keating, S., Machan, E., O'Connor, H., Gerofi, J., Sainsbury, A., Caterson, I., and Johnson, N. (2014). "Continuous Exercise but Not High Intensity Interval Training Improves Fat Distribution in Overweight Adults." *Journal of Obesity.* Article 834865. doi:10.1155/2014/834865.

Khoury, J. J., Loberant, N., and Jerushalmi, J. (2009). "Shoulder Pain in a Young Break-Dancer Evaluated with Bone Scintigraphy." *Clinical Nuclear Medicine* 34 (12): 916–917. doi:10.1097/RLU.0b013e3181becf53.

Lauersen, J., Bertelsen, D., and Andersen, L. (2014). "The Effectiveness of Exercise Interventions to Prevent Sports Injuries: A Systematic Review and Meta-Analysis of Randomised Controlled Trials." *British Journal of Sports Medicine* 48 (11): 871–877. doi:10.1136/bjsports-2013-092538.

Lee, K. C., and Clough, C. (1990). "Intracerebral Hemorrhage after Break Dancing." *New England Journal of Medicine* 323 (9): 615–616.

Leung, A. K. (1984). "Hazards of Break Dancing." *New York State Journal of Medicine* 84 (12): 592.

Liederbach, M., Dilgen, F. E., and Rose, D. J. (2008). "Incidence of Anterior Cruciate Ligament Injuries among Elite Ballet and Modern Dancers: A 5-year Prospective Study." *American Journal of Sports Medicine* 36 (9): 1779–1788. doi:10.1177/0363546508323644.

Liederbach, M., Kremenic, I. J., Orishimo, K. F., Pappas, E., and Hagins, M. (2014). "Comparison of Landing Biomechanics between Male and Female Dancers and Athletes. Part 2: Influence of Fatigue and Implications for Anterior Cruciate Ligament Injury." *American Journal of Sports Medicine* 42 (5): 1089–1095. doi:10.1177/0363546514524525.

Linder, S. M. (2014). "Injury Prevention of the Breakdancer's Wrist." Escuelas Universitarias Gimbernat y Tomàs Cerdà, Barcelona, Spain.

McBain, K., Shrier, I., Shultz, R., Meeuwisse, W. H., Klügl, M., Garza, D., and Matheson, G. O. (2012a). "Prevention of Sports Injury I: A Systematic Review of Applied Biomechanics and Physiology Outcomes Research." *British Journal of Sports Medicine* 46 (3): 169–173. doi:10.1136/bjsm.2010.080929.

McBain, K., Shrier, I., Shultz, R., Meeuwisse, W. H., Klügl, M., Garza, D., and Matheson, G. O. (2012b). "Prevention of Sport Injury II: A Systematic Review of Clinical Science Research." *British Journal of Sports Medicine* 46 (3): 174–179. doi:10.1136/bjsm.2010.081182.

McBride, D. Q., Lehman, L. P., and Mangiardi, J. R. (1985). "Break-Dancing Neck." *New England Journal of Medicine* 312 (3): 186.

McGuine, T. A., Brooks, A., and Hetzel, S. (2011). "The Effect of Lace-Up Ankle Braces on Injury Rates in High School Basketball Players." *American Journal of Sports Medicine* 39 (9): 1840–1848. doi:10.1177/0363546511406242.

McGuine, T. A., Hetzel, S., Wilson, J., and Brooks, A. (2012). "The Effect of Lace-Up Ankle Braces on Injury Rates in High School Football Players." *American Journal of Sports Medicine* 40 (1): 49–57. doi:10.1177/0363546511422332

Monselise, A., Chan, L. J., and Shapiro, J. (2011). "Break Dancing: A New Risk Factor for Scarring Hair Loss." *Journal of Cutaneous Medicine and Surgery* 15 (3): 177–179.

Mortaza, N., Abu Osman, N. A., Jamshidi, A. A., and Razjouyan, J. (2013). "Influence of Functional Knee Bracing on the Isokinetic and Functional Tests of Anterior Cruciate Ligament Deficient Patients." *PloS One* 8 (5): Article e64308. doi:10.1371/journal.pone.0064308.

Mortaza, N., Ebrahimi, I., Jamshidi, A. A., Abdollah, V., Kamali, M., Abas, W. A., and Osman, N. A. A. (2012). "The Effects of a Prophylactic Knee Brace and Two Neoprene Knee Sleeves on the Performance of Healthy Athletes: A Crossover Randomized Controlled Trial. *PloS One* 7 (11): Article e50110. doi:10.1371/journal.pone.0050110.

Moses, J., and Shannon, M. (1985). "Back Pain, Vomiting after Break-Dance Mishap. *Hospital Practice (Office Ed.)* 20 (3): 100K–100L, 100P.

Norman, R. A., and Grodin, M. A. (1984). "Injuries from Break Dancing." *American Family Physician* 30 (4): 109–112.

Ojofeitimi, S., Bronner, S., and Woo, H. (2012). "Injury Incidence in Hip Hop Dance." *Scandinavian Journal of Medicine & Science in Sports* 22 (3): 347–355. doi:10.1111/j.1600-0838.2010.01173.x.

Orishimo, K. F., Liederbach, M., Kremenic, I. J., Hagins, M., and Pappas, E. (2014). "Comparison of Landing Biomechanics between Male and Female Dancers and Athletes. Part 1: Influence of Sex on Risk of Anterior Cruciate Ligament Injury." *American Journal of Sports Medicine* 42 (5): 1082–1088. doi:10.1177/0363546514523928.

Pietrosimone, B. G., Grindstaff, T. L., Linens, S. W., Uczekaj, E., and Hertel, J. (2008). "A Systematic Review of Prophylactic Braces in the Prevention of Knee Ligament Injuries in Collegiate Football Players." *Journal of Athletic Training* 43 (4): 409–415. doi:10.4085/1062-6050-43.4.409.

Sadoghi, P., von Keudell, A., and Vavken, P. (2012). "Effectiveness of Anterior Cruciate Ligament Injury Prevention Training Programs." *Journal of Bone and Joint Surgery* 94 (9): 769–776. doi:10.2106/JBJS.K.00467.

Sainz de Baranda, P., and Ayala, F. (2010). "Chronic Flexibility Improvement after 12 Week of Stretching Program Utilizing the ACSM Recommendations: Hamstring Flexibility." *International Journal of Sports Medicine* 31 (6): 389–396. doi:10.1055/s-0030-1249082.

Salata, M. J., Gibbs, A. E., and Sekiya, J. K. (2010). "The Effectiveness of Prophylactic Knee Bracing in American Football: A Systematic Review." *Sports Health* 2 (5): 375–379. doi:10.1177/1941738110378986.

Schneider, F., Milesi, I., Haesler, E., Wicky, S., Schnyder, P., and Denys, A. (2002). "Break-Dance: An Unusual Cause of Hammer Syndrome." *Cardiovascular and Interventional Radiology* 25 (4): 330–331. doi:10.1007/s00270-002-1932-y.

Sharma, V., Knapp, J. K., Wasserman, G. S., Walsh, I., and Hoover, C. J. (1986). "Injuries Associated with Break Dancing." *Pediatric Emergency Care* 2 (1): 21–22.

Shrier, I. (2000). "Stretching before Exercise: An Evidence-Based Approach." *British Journal of Sports Medicine* 34 (5): 324–325.

Siewe, J., Marx, G., Knöll, P., Eysel, P., Zarghooni, K., Graf, M., et al. (2014). "Injuries and Overuse Syndromes in Competitive and Elite Bodybuilding." *International Journal of Sports Medicine* 35 (11): 943–948. doi:10.1055/s-0034-1367049.

Siewe, J., Rudat, J., Röllinghoff, M., Schlegel, U. J., Eysel, P., and Michael, J. W. (2011). "Injuries and Overuse Syndromes in Powerlifting." *International Journal of Sports Medicine* 32 (9): 703–711. doi:10.1055/s-0031-1277207.

Simic, L., Sarabon, N., and Markovic, G. (2013). "Does Pre-exercise Static Stretching Inhibit Maximal Muscular Performance? A Meta-Analytical Review. *Scandinavian Journal of Medicine & Science in Sports* 23 (2): 131–148. doi:10.1111/j.1600-0838.2012.01444.x.

Smith, C. A., Chimera, N. J., and Warren, M. (2015). "Association of Y Balance Test Reach Asymmetry and Injury in Division I Athletes. *Medicine and Science in Sports and Exercise* 47 (1): 136–141. doi:10.1249/MSS.0000000000000380.

Stovitz, S. D., and Johnson, R. J. (2006). "'Underuse' as a Cause for Musculoskeletal Injuries: Is It Time That We Started Reframing Our Message? *British Journal of Sports Medicine* 40 (9): 738–739. doi:10.1136/bjsm.2006.029975.

Thacker, S. B., Gilchrist, J., Stroup, D. F., and Kimsey, C. D. (2004). "The Impact of Stretching on Sports Injury Risk: A Systematic Review of the Literature." *Medicine and Science in Sports and Exercise* 36 (3): 371–378. doi:10.1249/01.MSS.0000117134.83018.F7.

Tillman, M. D., Fiolkowski, P., Bauer, J. A., and Reisinger, K. D. (2002). "In Shoe Plantar Measurements during Running on Different Surfaces: Changes in Temporal and Kinetic Parameters." *Sports Engineering* 5 (3): 121–128. doi:10.1046/j.1460-2687.2002.00101.x.

Wanke, E. M., Mill, H., Wanke, A., Davenport, J., Koch, F., and Groneberg, D. A. (2012). "Dance Floors as Injury Risk: Analysis and Evaluation of Acute Injuries Caused by Dance Floors in Professional Dance with Regard to Preventative Aspects." *Medical Problems of Performing Artists* 27 (3): 137–142.

Weppler, C. H., and Magnusson, S. P. (2010). "Increasing Muscle Extensibility: A Matter of Increasing Length or Modifying Sensation?" *Physical Therapy* 90 (3): 438–449. doi:10.2522/ptj.20090012.

Westrick, R. B., Miller, J. M., Carow, S. D., and Gerber, J. P. (2012). "Exploration of the Y-Balance Test for Assessment of Upper Quarter Closed Kinetic Chain Performance. *International Journal of Sports Physical Therapy* 7 (2): 139–147.

Wheeler, R. E., and Appell, R. A. (1984). "Differential Diagnosis of Scrotal Pain after Break Dancing." *JAMA* 252 (24): 3366.

Zwingenberger, S., Valladares, R. D., Walther, A., Beck, H., Stiehler, M., Kirschner, S., et al. (2014). "An Epidemiological Investigation of Training and Injury Patterns in Triathletes." *Journal of Sports Sciences* 32 (6): 583–590. doi:10.1080/02640414.2013.843018.

CHAPTER 26

"THEY COME FOR THE HIP HOP BUT STAY FOR THE HEALING"

Reflections on the Work of BluePrintForLife in Remote Indigenous Communities and Maximum-Security Youth Prisons

STEPHEN "BUDDHA" LEAFLOOR

INTRODUCTION

I am many things: a father of three, a social work activist, a b-boy named "Buddha." I have worked many frontline jobs in social work for the past thirty-five years: doing street outreach, investigating child abuse, delivering wilderness outreach programs, managing group homes; I've even been a probation officer. I love helping people, especially angry young men (a subject, you will see, that is close to my heart). Social work is an important part of my life.

But if you were to ask me what defines me as a person, who I feel I am, I would shout to the world with pride, "I am a bboy!" When I completed my Masters of Social Work (MSW) degree in 1985, my thesis was called "Hip Hop Don't Stop."

This is the lens through which I view the world.

At the time of authoring this, I'm sixty-one years old, which means I've been dancing for over forty-five years (Figure 26.1).[1] But Hip Hop is more than just a dance hobby for me. It has informed my life choices and career experience and led me to develop a full-time career doing mental health outreach through Hip Hop. To understand why this is, you have to know a bit about my background.

FIGURE 26.1. The original Canadian Floor Masters in 1985.

I was horribly bullied in high school. Having just moved with my family to a new community, I was the new kid in grade 9. I was also very small for my age. I remember many times being stuffed into garbage cans in front of five hundred laughing students in the cafeteria. I would get punched so severely by bullies that I had huge bruises on my arms. On one occasion, I was given a wedgie that was so hard, I was lifted into the air and my underwear was ripped completely off my body. Then to humiliate me further, the bullies held my underwear up like a trophy, showing it to all the young girls and throwing it down the hall.

I wanted to melt and disappear. I was so full of rage and hatred that I imagined myself killing the people who hurt me. Instead, I would suffer in silence at home. I smoked a lot of dope and got involved with break-and-enters. Not the type of ninja break-and-enters, where you try to not get caught, but the "I don't give a shit" kind, where you throw your life to chance and just kick the door in with rage.

But then I found something that I had a passion for—roller skating. Where I lived, teenagers skated almost every night at different rinks in the '70s. Plus, I was sixteen and full of teenage hormones, and I realized that I could impress the pretty girls by being the best roller skater at the rink. So I practiced over and over, spinning on one foot at high speed, jumping into a round-off back handspring and ending with a jump into the splits. I imagined myself taking this to the roller rink, shocking everyone, and pointing directly to the bullies when I finished my explosion on roller skates.

And I did! Many times. I became that defiant little skater, and it was magic—my first taste of swag.

This was, in a way, my early Hip Hop moment. I couldn't fight those guys, because they would've killed me, but I could still assert my existence in a way where no one would get hurt. I used my skill to get some street cred and acceptance. Despite all the pain and rage, looking back now, it seems clear to me that at the age of sixteen I was developing a bboy mentality: learning how to channel one's anger and negative emotions through something positive. It wasn't about size; it was about skill. It was about representing music through my body to make a statement about who I was.

This was the canvas of my early years in 1975, before bboying became known to the world outside the South Bronx, in 1983. Then in the early '80s I first saw the movie *Flashdance*. Like many old school bboys, I had to see this movie many times just to watch that famous short clip when Jennifer Beals, who is the main character, searches for personal inspiration for a dance audition and becomes inspired by the streetdancers. I remember seeing the shot of a guy spinning on his back, and I knew that I needed this. I didn't really know why, but I knew I needed it. This was the magic of early Hip Hop: to inspire and reach out to others, encouraging all of us to make it our own; to use it to express who we were and explore our own identity.

In 1983, I co-founded the Canadian Floor Masters (Figure 26.2). My crew have opened for James Brown, IceT, Black Eyed Peas, George Clinton, Public Enemy, GrandMaster Flash, and even the Kirov Ballet of Russia. The memories I have of my crew of young dancers and friends as we traveled and opened for the legends of Hip Hop are still with me. We often reflected among ourselves that we were like a gang without all the negativity—too busy "beating up" on the dance floor to get into fights and trouble. I'm not trying to overromanticize things, but when people talk about Hip Hop saving their lives because it moved them away from destructive elements, it's often true. A number of our original crew members didn't have dads, or they had moms that drank way too much. Stories of abuse in people's lives were not uncommon, and there was this rage inside many of us that was always just beneath the surface. We didn't have much, but we had each other.

In this chapter, I will describe the type of Hip Hop outreach I have developed over the past ten years through my company BluePrintForLife (https://www.blueprintforlife.ca), including details about our programming. I will not be able to go into comprehensive details on every aspect, since we have a wide variety of programs and techniques, but I will be able to give readers a sense of the range of our work, along with some concrete examples.[2] In 2006, I took my MSW degree, years of experience in social work, and love of Hip Hop, and formed BluePrintForLife. This company has grown, and now employs thirty-five of Canada's top streetdancers and youth outreach workers. Together, we have completed over a hundred week-long intensive projects in more than fifty remote Inuit and First Nations communities. We have also worked in large urban centers with youth from newly immigrated families, for example, the Sudanese in Calgary, and with gang-involved youth in maximum-security youth correctional facilities across Canada. But the work of Blueprint began in the Arctic. To describe how we integrated Hip Hop and

FIGURE 26.2. Inuit teachers participating in a Blueprint program in Inukjuak Nunavik.

traditional culture into a healing tool, we first have to examine the challenges the youth we work with face.

The people in most of the places we visit have experienced a high degree of complex trauma. In other words, they are suffering, not just from one easily identifiable traumatic event, but from many traumatic events. The chronic stress this creates results in individuals who are so tightly wound up that they often operate from a "fight or flight" frame of mind. This may be a necessary survival technique, but it takes its toll on one's mental health. Feelings of loss of identity, loss of control, and hopelessness are common. An overwhelming situation is created when traumatic events are combined with other issues like chaotic households, loss of traditional culture, and the effects of colonialism, addictions, poverty, overcrowding, family violence, bullying, and sexual abuse. Families and communities are at a loss as how to care for their children and help them survive.

In many ways, the youth we work with are at the extreme fringes of society. In my opinion, complex trauma requires many creative, complex engagement techniques that can also be flexible and customized to each community. Hip Hop allows us this flexibility, and perhaps more importantly, it's something that the youth are interested in. Hip Hop is the fun hook we use to get them involved in our programming, but I believe that they stay engaged with us because it also provides a way to connect mind, body, and spirit. Hip Hop becomes a conduit for healing.

I am not a brain specialist. But I have learned some things about the human brain when it comes to complex trauma. I once attended a conference on the intergenerational trauma that is the legacy of Canada's residential schools.[3] At this conference, the facilitator explained how complex trauma causes the brain to fire and network itself around the ancient brain (which includes the *limbic system*, specifically the *amygdala*). Historically, these older parts of the brain served us well as a species in order to survive, allowing us to go into "fight or flight" mode. But being in this state too often is problematic. It can lead to a lack of impulse control, anger, and addictive behavior, which all seem to be involved in this area of the brain. In a more balanced human brain, the complex thought processes that happen in the front of our brain (*prefrontal cortex*) help to mitigate much of this.

Even though the human brain can get stuck in repetitive and addictive types of behavior, it also has the capacity to be elastic and to heal. Medical science is catching up with what artists and indigenous cultures of the world have long known—art, music, and dance can be healing. The images from PET (positron emission tomography) scans of the brain reveal that some of the best ways to create new neural pathways are by using art, music, dance, and traditional culture, and by telling one's personal story.

We use many of these activities in our work with BlueprintForLife, and, in fact, Hip Hop encompasses these elements. My particular favorite is the oral tradition of telling one's personal story. This can be by writing a poem, or rap, or spoken-word piece, or simply by putting one's thoughts in a journal. All BlueprintForLife staff freely share our own compelling stories of struggle, as I did to open this chapter. For me it is very revealing how we were all drawn to Hip Hop for personal reasons, and how we continue to heal through our love of Hip Hop.

Our first project took place in 2006. At the time, I was a senior child-abuse investigator at a large government agency. I have a sister who had been living in Iqaluit in Canada's Arctic for many years. She is married to an Inuit man and together they have three daughters.

Canada's Inuit and First Nations communities often struggle with extremely high rates of suicide, addiction, poverty, food insecurity, and abuse, much of which is connected to the legacy of Canada's residential schools. Technology, such as satellite television, allows these remote communities to connect to the rest of the world, but at the risk of losing their traditional ways of life. Being aware of the systemic challenges of living there, I wanted to do something positive for my sister's children and the larger community.

We created a program for about a hundred youth. Fifteen of them were from the Baffin Youth Correctional Centre. The basic premise was that we would engage large groups of youth for an intense one-week period, from 9 a.m. to 5 p.m., Monday to Friday. Effectively, we became the alternative school for the week instead of their regular classes. The program would end on that Friday night with a cultural showcase and dance battle for the whole community. The programming would combine various elements of Hip Hop, traditional culture, and intense discussion about the ongoing issues in the youths' lives. This is the basic recipe for our structure, which also includes best-practice techniques discussed later.

FIGURE 26.3 Inuit youth throat singing.

A day would typically ebb and flow between different types of activities. This adaptable structure was designed to help hold the youths' interest and, at the same time, create an energy that would facilitate individual and collective healing. We designed a one-week boot camp to challenge the youth with various streetdance forms (bboying, locking, boogaloo), introduce them to DJing, and create a large graffiti mural (Figure 26.3) representing their culture by means of a message they wanted to share.

Later, as our programming grew and diversified, we would introduce storytelling, spoken word, journaling, rapping, meditation, and bucket drumming (Figure 26.4).

Hip Hop was the hook. They had all seen Hip Hop on TV, but what they were watching was gangsta rap, which often included degrading images of women. In our programming, we take the time to discuss these harmful images and how they are not a reflection of the true meaning of Hip Hop.

Although dance was a major theme throughout each day, we didn't just dance with the youth. When their bodies tired, we engaged them in conversations. The youth in the Arctic were often shy and emotionally hurt, and they felt disconnected from the rest of the world. We would start on Monday with simple topics like the history of Hip Hop and how it has been adapted by different cultures. Eventually, we would move to more difficult topics like bullying, rage, addiction, and sexual abuse.

Some of the discussions that might take place in a typical program week could be about:

1. Bringing your own culture into Hip Hop and cultural pride
2. Anger management (finding your one mic) and Buddha's story

FIGURE 26.4. Youth in Arctic Bay participate in mental health discussions.

3. Sabotaging yourself with drugs, alcohol
4. Respect and loyalty: to oneself, others, and one's environment and community; treatment of women
5. Bullying: learning to say you're sorry, rebuilding relationships, fear of trusting
6. Impulse control
7. Why not gangs? A Hip Hop perspective—getting a new *familia*
8. Healing paths: a model for a lifelong journey of healing; sexual abuse
9. Who to talk to when bad things happen; personal inventory (safety plans, outside resources)
10. How will you sabotage yourself?

During our northern projects, we also asked teachers, police officers, social workers, and elders to join the program as participants (Figure 26.5). This helps them not only to learn new and unique ways of engaging youth, but also to reconfigure their relationships with them. I call this "retraining the adult brain." By dancing side by side with the youth, we hoped to create a better means of communication between the generations.

Optics count. You can't just have adults leaning against the walls watching. Not only is this intimidating to youth (who often already feel judged), but how can we ask them to take positive risks and try new and difficult things if the adults aren't willing to do the same? It always makes me laugh when I meet a forty-year-old teacher, trying to play the age card, who says they don't dance. This is hard to do when they see my sixty-year-old

FIGURE 26.5. Incarcerated youth learning a choreo.

bones actively dancing and sweating profusely during the warm-ups! Struggling to master physical activity is a humbling experience and a great equalizer.

I have had many teachers and social workers tell me that participating in our program was the best professional development they had ever experienced, in terms of learning new ways of engaging youth and building relationships. They also comment that they learned a lot about how to engage youth in discussions on difficult topics. Relationships between service providers and the community are hard to build, especially if old ideas persist. When you see the social worker as someone who takes the babies away, it's hard to think of turning to them for counseling or support. And social workers, police officers, and other professionals are often run ragged dealing with crisis after crisis. But when they participate actively in our program, the youth quickly learn to see them in a new way—more accessible, instead of just "us" and "them." The benefit to the community is significant.

Throughout our week-long program, we also incorporate cultural activities. We ask the youth to teach us drum dancing, throat singing, or traditional Arctic games. This is intentional. We want to shift the focus away from any perception of our team as "star bboys and bgirls" from the south, and instead provide the youth with a chance to adapt Hip Hop, and to feel pride in their cultural heritage. The BluePrintForLife team acknowledges the participants as the experts.

One example shows how this approach has been successful. Some of the youth on our projects in the Arctic started combining ancient throat singing with a beatbox in a freestyle way, much the way a jazz musician improvises (Figure 26.6). This style is now known as "throat boxing," and it has spread across northern Canada. I remember being thanked by an elder in one of these communities for helping preserve their culture. She

FIGURE 26.6. Youth at Calgary Young Offenders Centre. Mask are worn to protect identities.

told us that her granddaughter had given up throat singing, but that now she was excited to continue learning it because of our program

I have seen elders in the audience at the final night's show, grinning from ear to ear when the youth created a human dog sled during the dance battle. These elders may not have understood Hip Hop, but they understood that their youth were confident, happy, and hadn't forgotten where they came from.

Another important healing technique we use is telling one's personal story (Figure 26.7). The youth are shocked when they hear about the bullying I endured. We often have from five to ten staff on our team who also talk about their own experiences in a way that resonates with the youth. A social worker can discuss sexual abuse, but it's quite a different experience when one of our team speaks emotionally about their own abuse and trauma and how they continue to heal through dance.

I'm very proud of the fearlessness of my team in opening up about their own deep hurts. Amazing things happen when youth see big, tattooed bboys sharing in this way, and comforting each other. We don't just talk about strong men crying or reaching out for help. We model it in real time.

All in all, we use about eighteen therapeutic, best-practice techniques that are highly regarded by social workers and counselors. We often present them in a Hip Hop format or in a creative, cultural way. We will do things like meditate or visualize a safe spot out on the land (often hunting or fishing). We use the following techniques in the eight programs we now offer:

Cognitive therapy and meditation
Mentorship and role modeling
Group therapy
Resiliency training
Humor and laughter therapy

FIGURE 26.7 Inuit elders try DJing.

Anger-management training, impulse-control techniques
Safety planning
Sport, play, dance, and art therapy—in a cultural context
Disclosure and healing path stories (telling one's story)
Goal setting, daring to dream
Self-regulating, self-discipline techniques
Leadership training, cooperation skills
Positive risk-taking
Inventory of strengths
Visualization
Healing ceremonies and healing circles
Journaling and poetry
Empathy-building by sharing life stories (staff and youth)

Besides these techniques, BlueprintForLife often includes cultural elements in our programs—healing circles and ceremonies, traditional smudging and prayers, drumming, oral storytelling and legends, Arctic sports and games. These are all important elements in our work with northern communities.

One moving healing ceremony we do is the "Burning of Secrets." The youth reflect quietly on someone they need to forgive. This could also be a personal reflection about an incident that they themselves need to let go of. Then they write a letter to themselves, expressing those feelings, crumple up the paper, and put it in a cardboard box. This box has been decorated by the youth with slogans such as "it wasn't my fault" or "my anger no longer defines me," often written in traditional language. We then form a circle somewhere out on the land, offering everyone the opportunity to speak if they want and share what they wrote. Some youth will want to share; others will want everything to remain private. Then the box is burned, and, symbolically, all the anger and bad memories disappear with the smoke. We have even performed this ceremony with adults, youth, and elders as part of a program developed specifically around the effects of residential schools and intergenerational trauma. These types of exercises have always been particularly powerful in our projects.

Recently, we have also started working with incarcerated youth in maximum-security correctional centers (Figure 26.8). Many are involved with gangs and have committed serious crimes, including murder. With each successful project, news of our program has spread, to the point where we have now created a nonprofit sister company, Blueprint Pathways, to grow our work with incarcerated youth. Last year, we received significant, multiyear funding through a federal government grant that also includes a research component. We believe it will be the largest study ever done on prison populations using dance anywhere in the world.

Initially, I could tell that many of the front-line security staff in these correctional centers were very nervous about the work we were going to do, and very skeptical that we could have a positive impact. Yet we persevered. And day by day, the youth went back to being kids, putting their rival-gang mentalities aside and interacting with respect, tolerance, and spontaneous laughter. By the time Friday arrived, their body language and attitudes were often transformed. Kids with full-face gang tattoos were no longer tightly wound, ready to pop off against each other in rage. In one facility, we had twenty warring gangs in the gym at the same time, and there was not even one negative incident. The corrections staff were constantly coming up to members of my team and telling them that they couldn't believe what they were witnessing. I believe the youth were so busy having fun and learning new things that along the way they also learned about respect, cooperation, vulnerability, and empathy, and that they had more in common with one another than they originally thought. Comments from many senior staff and executive directors of these facilities often told us that the program might just be the most ambitious and effective of any in the history of youth corrections. One senior staff at the Edmonton Young Offenders Centre who was helping emcee the final night's show told the audience of parents and social-service professionals: "I know it will be hard for you to believe as you weren't here—but in my 35 years of working here I have never seen anything as intense and as healing as what I witnessed this week."

When we visit incarcerated youth in correctional facilities, our approach is very similar to what we use in our projects in other communities. We give all the youth their own journals on the first day. We then introduce them to the concept of "One Mic," which is basically a metaphor we have adapted from the Rapper Nas and his song of the same name. In the music video, Nas uses music and words to help address his anger about

FIGURE 26.8. Buddha doing a street routine with a Cree youth in Saskatchewan.

the injustice he sees in the world. We ask the youth to think about positive activities they could do to deal with their anger (e.g., dance, sports, music), and then we challenge them to think of new "One Mics" that they would like to pursue in the future. This becomes their "homework" back in their cells, where they try to visualize how they will pursue this new activity and develop a plan to move toward it. We have also introduced the practice of journaling to youth in these populations, and our experience has shown that once they start doing it, journaling can become a significant, lifelong strategy that can help them deal with the chaos in their lives. For example, after our one-week intensive project in Manitoba's largest youth prison, we started working with a smaller group of twelve aboriginal young women in a spoken-word follow-up program. All of them continued to journal even after our program ended.

We have also finished a program in a maximum-security youth facility in Calgary, Alberta (Figure 26.9). It just so happened that the final night's show was going to fall on Halloween, and we wanted to do something special for all the families and probation officers who would be coming to see the youth perform. We decided to do a choreographed routine with all the kids to Michael Jackson's "Thriller." As I watched like a proud dad, the executive director pointed to one youth and said, "You see that kid right there. He is arguably one of the most difficult mental health challenges in this province's system. He has difficulty staying focused for 30 seconds at a time. And you have had him focused and fully engaged for an entire week."

FIGURE 26.9. Graffiti in Arctic Bay with Narwhales.

I love this about our work. It reaches those that are "hard to reach", and takes into account the trauma they have experienced in their lives. This type of trauma-informed care is one of the directions I believe social work and counseling needs to go in. It considers the strengths and differences of the youth, and the trauma they have experienced, yet it is also fun and engaging.

When I share my personal story with these youth on the first day of the program, I can't tell you how many of them come up to me and say it felt like I was telling their story. I work well with angry young men because I understand their rage. I was never locked up, but that could have easily been my fate.

The eight programs that we have developed over the past ten years grew organically: the more work we did, the more we saw the need for different types of programs where none existed. All of our work is rooted in Hip Hop and traditional culture. We have even started to develop a culturally sensitive Leadership Through Hip Hop program to help build local capacity, helping them to continue the Hip Hop clubs after our team leaves a community.

Currently, our eight programs are

1. Social Work Through Hip Hop (our flagship program)
2. Leadership Through Hip Hop
3. Healing Through Hip Hop
4. Respect Through Hip Hop (for younger youth, aged 8 to 13)
5. Empowerment Through Theatre
6. Share Our Spirit—an Arctic exchange program with Unity Charity in Toronto
7. Intergenerational Healing for communities affected by Residential Schools
8. They Come for the Hip Hop, but Stay for the Healing—youth prison work

It is certainly a challenge to keep any type of programming going in most remote communities, as it's very expensive to fly there. And getting ongoing adult support is often difficult because many adults struggle with their own addictions and trauma. To try and mitigate these challenges, we have often sent small teams back to a place for three days at a time to help train the youth leaders and adults on how to structure an ongoing program, detailing strategies on how to get local parents involved. We have developed a creative document as a resource around this, as well as creating a series of support videos that we leave with the community. We also encourage communities to stay in touch with our team through our Facebook group, where we post ongoing updates about our work, and articles related to our work and youth issues. Of particular note, we piloted a youth mentorship program in which we trained and paid older youth in some communities to join the Blueprint team on other projects. This mentorship program not only gave some of these young Inuit and First Nations leaders opportunities to learn skills and put them into practice, but it also helped in growing their self-confidence, which gave them the courage to be involved in their own communities. Some of our youth, such as in the community of Clyde River Nunavut, actually went on to become peer counselors, around issues like suicide, and were employed by the local wellness center, becoming part of a crisis-response team in other communities. Many of these seeds of personal growth and leadership started to germinate in the local Hip Hop clubs. We have even had Inuit moms eventually become full-time Blueprint staff as we worked in neighboring communities.

As you can see from the variety and complexity of the programs we offer, meeting two hours a week or after school is not sufficient. The type of intense engagement we offer between the staff and the participants needs to be cultivated over longer, day-to-day interaction. It takes time for youth to open their ears and hearts, and get to where they can have deeper conversations about the pain in their lives. They get to know the Blueprint team on a personal level, and then can identify more closely with the wide variety of personalities on our team, and connect with them through trust. This allows us to move much further than just being a program that builds self-confidence, which, in my opinion, represents the majority of Hip Hop outreach in the world. These programs are cool, and still important, but I believe they are limited in their reach.

We often say, *They come for the Hip Hop, but stay for the healing*—and this is true, not just for the youth, but also their communities (Figure 26.10).

THREE STORIES OF HEALING

In keeping with the power of storytelling, I offer these three examples of the incredible healing potential of dance and the community spirit that is inspired by Hip Hop. There are so many other stories of this sort, and perhaps these examples will help to explain why I have so much passion for my work.

FIGURE 26.10. Bucket drumming.

The first story is about "Frost Graffiti." After we had already visited a remote Inuit community called Pond Inlet (far above the Arctic Circle), I was home again in my office, planning a return project to work on youth leadership and healing. Then I received a phone call from a teacher in Pond Inlet who told me she had something exciting to share. The youth had created "frost graffiti" all over the *community.* " Frost graffiti?" I exclaimed, "What's that? I didn't teach them that!"

She then told an emotional story. Apparently, after we left from our weeklong project, the youth had formed a Hip Hop club, with some support from parents and teachers. The club had been meeting twice a week, and between forty and fifty youth often showed up. On one recent evening, she said, they had all gathered, but everyone was crying. One of their teenage friends had passed away. I don't know how, and I didn't ask. The teacher went on to describe how the Hip Hop club was serving as a valuable gathering spot, where the youth to go and comfort one other (Figure 26.11). In the past, when the youth were upset, they usually just suffered in silence at home. As they were crying and hugging each other, one of them announced, "I know how we can honor her life—let's do frost graffiti."

Now, in southern cities like Toronto, Montreal, or New York, it's not cold enough for the walls of the buildings to get covered with frost. But in Pond Inlet, when the conditions are right, the outside walls of everyone's homes get covered with a thick

FIGURE 26.11. Final night of the community show in Pond Inlet, Nunavut.

frost. Fifty youth went around town and spent a good part of the evening taking off their warm sealskin mitts and using the heat of their fingertips to melt positive messages into the walls. Messages about missing their friend, about not giving up on life, and about how beautiful and wonderful she was. In the morning when the community woke up, many adults didn't even go to work. They chose instead to walk around town, reading the messages of hope. And it didn't stop there. Many families in the north are poor, and often struggle just to provide the basics, like food. Well, the members of the Hip Hop club went to their own cupboards and lined up at the family home of the deceased girl, giving them cans of food, and offering their prayers and condolences.

Eventually the sun would come out over the frost graffiti, melting it forever.

Wow! I was a weeping wreck on the other end of the phone. These youth had internalized one of the great gifts of Hip Hop: creating communities, creating "something outta nothing." We had never talked about frost graffiti, but we had talked a lot about being proud of who you are and where you come from. It was something invented and shared as young Inuit teenagers put their own creative minds together in a moment of grief and caring. Invented in the Arctic—not in New York City.

My second story is from one of the most remote northern communities in the world, Grise Fiord.

We have been to this community of approximately 150 people a number of times, and had just returned to launch a new program called Healing Through Hip Hop. We realized that the youth would be more comfortable opening up about difficult issues in smaller groups. We were starting our programming on the first day when a young adult called Willy came to see what we were doing. He was cautious and kept his distance. Seeing him there, we encouraged him to come join us. We were shocked when the other youth publicly complained that he was dirty and smelled . . . and was going to kill himself soon anyway. We needed Willy to join us – for his own safety. Willy had some mental health struggles, and he lived alone, having just returned from an institution down south. With encouragement from my Blueprint team, Willy joined us and slowly began to open up. After a few days, the other youth were no longer shunning Willy, but actively encouraging him and helping him in the dance and with his poetry.

As we do in all our projects, we were going to end the week with a Friday night showcase of dance and culture. Some of the youth would present spoken word or raps they had written. The whole Grise Fiord community had assembled and was incredibly supportive and proud of their youth. And then it was Willy's turn to present his poem.

Willy went to the front with a microphone, but he struggled, stuttering and getting stuck in his nervousness. His poem was about wanting to be accepted because this was his home and community. He also talked about being deeply hurt by others and about forgiveness. But he was visibly shaking and crying. I was about to go up and support Willy, but I didn't have to because a woman named Meeka went up and hugged him. She was the Mayor. And she held Willy until he found his composure and finished his poem.

The whole community showed support for that lonely young man. They cried with him. And yet there was a feeling of hope in the room—like they knew they were stronger together.

My last story takes place in a remote Inuit community on the shores of Hudson Bay, called Inukjuaq. We have worked with physically challenged and special needs youth in many communities. I am always trying to find ways not only to include them in our program, but also to make them superstars, perhaps for the first time in their lives, to know how this magic feels. (Shout out to our good friend Lazylegz who does international work like this with his team, "ILL-Abilities.")

On this project we had the great honor of meeting Timothy. Timothy's body was malformed and twisted, and he used a wheelchair. He had limited use of his hands and arms, but every day he came in wearing his favorite Hawaiian shirt, and would battle me, using his face to dance. Yep, he looked old man Buddha straight in the eye with a sheepish grin, hitting the beats by contorting his face. Timothy was excited to be there, and was often assisted by his twin brother Nathan, who was able-bodied. Nathan helped with Timothy's basic care throughout the week.

The final night's show would have fifty youth battling another group of fifty youth for the main event. Earlier in the week, I had helped design a routine where Nathan would ride out on the back of his brother's wheelchair and juggle hats between their heads using some body-wave action (Figure 26.12). When they reached the middle of the floor, Timothy spun his wheelchair in circles. But then, Nathan lifted his brother's frail body out of the chair and placed him on the floor in the center where everyone could see. Timothy could only wiggle and shake—but the battle was won in that moment. The entire community had come out to see the show, and many of them were so touched that they started weeping, just sobbing with emotion. The hoots and hollers from the crowd and Timothy's crew were deafening. There was some kind of magical connection everyone felt with Timothy. It was the same connection we, as bboys and bgirls, share in a dance cypher. It felt like pain and struggle and hope—a necessary hope to not give up when life is difficult.

Upon reflection, it seems our work has grown in the nicest way, through word of mouth instead of marketing. This has always been the grassroots way of Hip Hop culture. For me, Hip Hop continues to be a great gift to the world. I came for the Hip Hop but stayed for the healing (Figure 26.13). This is the story for many of us. My wish for the world is that this gift continues to grow and be shared in the darkest places of despair, and that we continue to reflect deeply, as a Hip Hop community, on how we can give back. This is how I believe Hip Hop will change the world.

"Each one Teach One"

Buddha

Founder and Executive Director

BluePrintForLife.ca

Ashoka Fellow Canada.

FIGURE 26.12. Timothy and his brother Nathan work a hat routine.

FIGURE 26.13.   Blessings from Bboy Buddha.

NOTES

1. All the photos in this chapter are (c) Blueprintforlife and BluePrint Pathways. They are provided to this publication as a courtesy.
2. Further videos, documentaries, news stories, and project evaluations can be found at the BluePrintForLife website, http://www.blueprintforlife.ca.
3. An influential talk at the conference was "The Circle of Life: Understanding the Impact of Generational Trauma and Its Relationship to Behavioral and Academic Performance," by Jane Middelton-Moz, MS, and Tiffiny Hubbard, MS, on Monday January 16, 2012. The speaker I am referring to was Jane Middelton.

   - Link to residential schools - https://indigenousfoundations.arts.ubc.ca/the_residentia
     l_school_system/-

....

CAN EXPERT DANCERS BE A SPRINGBOARD MODEL TO EXAMINE NEUROREHABILITATION VIA DANCE?

....

REBECCA BARNSTAPLE, DÉBORA RABINOVICH,
AND JOSEPH FRANCIS XAVIER DESOUZA

INTRODUCTION

....

LYING on his back in the MRI, head immobilized in foam, Ken Swift listens through special MR-compatible headphones to sixty seconds of music he self-selected: Grandmaster Flash's remix of "Apache" (1973), from the Incredible Bongo Band, which has been synced over eight minutes to the MRI scans. He has performed to this track countless times, and is familiar with every shift his body registers as it plays. Visualizing his movements, he imagines how he would interpret and express the nuances of this, one of his favorite pieces of music. The scanner is noisy and confining, but in his mind, Ken is moving with the grace, power, creativity, and ease that comes from over thirty years of cultivating expertise in his chosen form (See Figure 27.1a and b).

Expertise generally requires prolonged dedication and effort devoted to the acquisition and practice of specific skills (Ericsson and Charness 1994). We now know that the acquisition of expertise is also reflected in neurophysiological changes, which relate to *neuroplasticity*, the brain's inherent ability to restructure for ever-greater efficiency, affected by learning and habit. Instead of assuming a static structure and hierarchy, brain regions communicate fastest with the areas they most often coordinate with in practiced activities. Learning a new skill, or putting in the time and effort to achieve

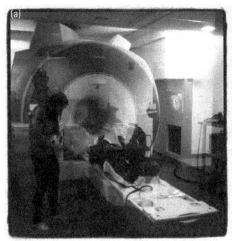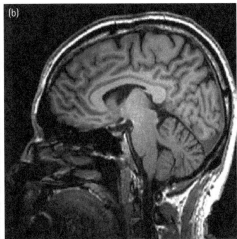

FIGURE 27.1. Ken Swift in a 3-tesla Siemens tim trio MRI scanner. Siemens Medical Systems, Erlangen, Germany. A 32-channel head coil records changes in blood oxygenation levels to various regions of his brain while he imagines dancing (Olshansky et al. 2014).

expertise, changes brain structure and function, and these differences are measurable (Hänggi et al. 2010; Olshansky et al. 2014; Giacosa et al. 2016; Burzynska et al. 2017). Expert dancers put in hours of training to develop coordination, achieving extremely high levels of performance. Some of these skills may be shared with other elite athletes, while other skills reflect specialization that accords with the particularities of the movement vocabulary, music, and style of their primary form. Studying this highly qualified expertise in dancers can increase our understanding of how our brains learn and process movement, from the simplest gesture to more intricate sequences.

Ken Swift's involvement in this neuroimaging study is an example of a relatively new field of research that investigates the effects of dance on the brain. Examples of projects within this field include efforts to understand how dancer's neural activity may differ from that of nondancers or experts in related fields, such as music (Poikonen, Toiviainen, and Tervaniemi 2018); attempts to determine the network of brain regions that are involved in aspects of dance, such as learning choreography (Bar and DeSouza 2016); and the implications of dance-related brain plasticity for health and well-being across the lifespan (Müller et al. 2017). Emerging data suggest that engagement in dance is both neuroprotective (helps preserve neuronal structure and function), and neurorehabilitative (restores structure and function; Dhami, Moreno, and DeSouza 2015). Dancing, at any age, seems to promote recovery in the nervous system, from both physical and psychological trauma. Findings in this direction are incredibly promising; as our population ages, we will need to identify treatments and activities that promote health in longevity. Instances in which dance has been used to treat complex neurodegenerative disorders are proliferating, and supporting research is already starting to demonstrate that dancing can, and will, keep us healthy longer (Houston, and McGill 2013; Westheimer et. al. 2015; Kshtriya et al. 2015). Dance programs yoked to specific conditions such as Parkinson's, an incurable and progressive neurodegenerative disease, have multiplied around the globe as participants have reported the radical difference these make in their lives. Additionally, programs are emerging that use specific elements or styles of dance that may target or build creatively off symptoms; one example of this is Popping For Parkinson's®, an international project providing free weekly classes in the United Kingdom and Italy, which specifically leverages the language and elements of Hip Hop to improve the lives of people living with Parkinson's. In this approach, described by founder Simone Sistarelli, Parkinson's becomes a starting point, not a dead end: "Parkinson's does not define a person, just like any other condition/disability should not define anyone. Parkinson's has to be acknowledged though, not disregarded or ignored or even hidden" (pers. comm., May 6, 2019). Thus, for students in Sistarelli's program, the tremor of Parkinson's becomes the Pop; slowness becomes Slow Motion style; and shuffling becomes Crazy Legs style, as symptomatic elements of PD are transformed into a creative expression. (More on this in the section "Neurorehabilitation: Dance for Parkinson's® and Popping For Parkinson's®").

NEUROSCIENCE AND
DANCE: COMMON GROUND

While the disciplines of dance and neuroscience may seem worlds apart, at heart they share vast common ground and interests, starting with the primacy of movement. The brain (and central nervous system) is predominantly occupied with coordinating responses to our surroundings, and while the senses by which we receive information are varied (vision, touch, hearing), our primary means of response is always through movement—away from, toward, in conjunction with—or the cessation of movement, as in stillness or freezing. Our brain and central nervous system do not only coordinate movement; our internal systems are themselves coordinated *by* the movements we see and make during our individual development. The vast, complex neuronal networks of our minds are organized, first, by self-relational movements (i.e., reflexes; see Buzsaki 2006), then by orienting in an environment. Brain structures and networks are built up in increasingly complex fractal patterns generated by our movement experiences. Dance, as a complex, organized form of movement, works within this substrate, shaping and being shaped by volitional action within the parameters of space and time. We can think of dance as an artistic rendering and extension of the components and mechanisms that are at the heart of how we coordinate effective and adaptive response strategies, including motor control and interpretation.

Studies of dance, and dancers, provide an ideal means to investigate phenomena fundamental to neurological structure and functioning, such as spatial awareness, timing, coordination, accuracy, and entrainment. These phenomena, along with elements of improvisation, creativity, and aesthetic judgment are honed through various dance practices. There are long associations between dance and healing (Goodill 2005, 2016); however, it is only in recent years that we can correlate participation in dance with improvements in specific symptoms associated with various disorders. It is plausible that wide-ranging benefits, such as the cultivation of "brain reserve" (increased adaptive neuroplasticity), along with improved structural and functional connectivity, can result from practicing dance. These benefits can have significant impact on quality of life as people grow older. Indeed, a vast amount of literature now supports the idea that dance can lead to improvements in balance, gait, functional mobility, and other nonmotor symptoms for people with Parkinson's disease, the elderly, or other groups of people at risk of falling. A growing number of studies report improvements in symptoms in people with PD who follow a dance-based therapeutic program, including increased endurance and reduced risk of falls, along with better executive function (Rosario de Natalea 2017). A recently published longitudinal study from our group showed that attending a weekly dance class can slow the progression of some of the most debilitating symptoms of Parkinson's (Bearss and DeSouza 2021). Positive results have also been reported for people with subacute stroke following a modified dance program based on jazz and merengue (Demers and Mckinley 2015). In more recent studies, contemporary dance was shown to improve motor function and increase brain volume in Huntington's disease (Trinkler et al. 2019), while a Greek traditional dance program that involved both healthy elderly and people with mild cognitive impairment (MCI), a forerunner of Alzheimer's disease, saw improvements in attention and executive function along with improved physical functioning and quality of life (Douka et al. 2019). How, exactly, does participation in dance facilitate improvements in pervasive and progressive conditions such as these, which are neurodegenerative and/or related to structural damage in the brain? Understanding the *mechanisms* of these reported improvements is the next step in research examining the effects of dance, in terms of both people's experience and mapping the brain-based biological changes. Advances in technologies such as neuro-imaging can provide new data on what was previously viewed as a wholly internal, and somewhat untranslatable, experience.

Neuroimaging uses various methods to acquire and generate images of the nervous system's structure and function, including fMRI (functional magnetic resonance imaging), EEG (electroencephalography), MEG (magnetoencephalography), TMS (transcranial magnetic stimulation), and others (for an overview of common techniques, see Table 27.1). Imaging is a relatively new discipline in medicine and psychology, and the data thereby acquired are unique in that they represent/present an *image* of what is happening in the brain (or another area, such as the heart) at a specific moment in time, which can be associated with an activity, such as remembering or responding to a cue. These operations often must be performed in conditions in which the subject is still (not moving in space), because movement artifacts contaminate the neuroimaging data so that portions of it cannot be used. When the researcher is investigating questions related to movement, such as dance, subjects are often asked to imagine performing the movements, as it has been determined that visualization uses

Table 27.1 Neuroimaging Techniques

Technique	How it works	Limitations
Single-cell recording	Measures action potentials from individual neurons via electrodes implanted in the brain.	Requires brain surgery; cannot be performed on humans unless they are already having brain surgery and give consent. Does not show connections to other neurons or brain areas.
fMRI Functional magnetic resonance imaging	Measures changes in oxygen levels in the blood related to BOLD signal (blood oxygenation level response) by taking many images and combining them over time.	Signal change can imply *either* excitation or inhibition, as both involve neural activity that requires oxygen. Good spatial resolution (within millimeters); temporal resolution on the order of full seconds. Requires complex statistical analysis and the combination of multiple images.
EEG Electroencephalography	Measures electrical activity of large populations of neurons near the surface of the brain (cortical) via electrodes places on the scalp.	Good temporal but poor spatial resolution; signal is generated by many neurons, sometimes in disparate regions of the brain, and is affected/diffused by passing through the scalp.
TMS Transcranial magnetic stimulation	Uses a magnetic pulse to create a temporary "lesion" in the brain (knock-out an area).	Allows for speculation about function without causing permanent changes; still limited in terms of spatial accuracy—effects populations of neurons in an area of >5mm.
PET Positron emission tomography	Measures brain activity indirectly through changes in blood flow, indicated by the introduction of a radioactive tracer.	Fairly high spatial resolution (around 1cm), very poor temporal resolution (on the order of minutes). Also requires the use of radioactive isotopes—cannot be repeated frequently on the same subject.
MEG Magnetoencephalography	Measures magnetic fields associated with large populations of neurons using magnetometers; similar to EEG. Can be combined with fMRI for greater localization specificity.	Good temporal resolution, and signal is not diffused by the scalp; however, there are problems with signal intermixing and spatial resolution is still poor.

the same or similar brain regions and processes as are used in actual engagement in the activity (Cross, de Hamilton and Grafton 2006). New methods such as MoBI (Mobile Brain-Body Imaging, which allows for EEG with moving subjects) are allowing for the investigation of motor and cognitive behavior in naturalistic conditions, but many challenges remain if we want to look at dynamic and unconstrained movement behavior such as dance (for more details on the potential for using MoBI in dance, see Barnstaple et al., 2020).

The study with Ken Swift (Olshansky, Bar, Fogarty, and DeSouza 2014) used fMRI, a technique that measures neural activation of brain region by detecting changes associated with blood flow. In this method, the subject must lie in a large, loud tube housing a powerful electromagnet (DeSouza, Ovaysikia, and Pynn 2012). Essentially, neuronal activity is accompanied by increases in blood flow; the iron in blood (deoxyhemoglobin) causes distortions in the magnetic field in comparison with oxyhemoglobin (oxygenated blood), and these differences are picked up by the scanner and localized spatially in the brain regions of interest. Functional MRI is the most commonly used means of investigating which regions of the brain are involved in a specified task, and how these areas may connect or interact with other regions; it is noninvasive, records at a high spatial resolution, and can show the entire network of brain areas engaged in a task, making it a popular choice for this kind of research.

THE DANCE NETWORK

In the Ken Swift study and other research, brain areas related to music perception, motor programming, and motor execution can be conceived of as forming a *dance network*: regions that coordinate and are active during engagement in dance-like activities (Kung et al. 2013; Zatorre, Chen, and Penhune 2007). It follows, then, that such a network would be more highly developed in expert dancers and could be observed to function more effectively in this group than in recreational dancers or people who have little dance experience. The main areas considered to be involved are the *primary sensory cortices* (auditory/visual/somatosensory), which are important during the learning of a dance through visualization when cued by music. They are also involved in music perception, mental imagery, and the processing of rhythmic patterns, melodies, and timing. The *cerebellum*, a small structure at the base of the brainstem, which makes up only 10% of a brain's volume yet contains twice as many neurons as are in all the rest of the brain, is involved in many functions, including the maintenance of balance and posture, coordination of voluntary movements, motor learning, and many aspects of cognitive function. Auditory processing and improvised generation of rhythmic and melodic structures also occur here, during imagined and perceived familiar melodies (Herholz, Halpern, and Zatorre 2012). Other cortical nodes include the superior temporal gyri, the dorsal premotor cortex, the pre-supplementary motor area (SMA), and the SMA Supplemental Motor Area (Brodmann's area 6). This latter one—SMA—is the critical region for motor planning sequences of movement (Makoshi et al. 2011; Thickbroom et al. 2000), and important for motor execution and imagery (Burianová et al. 2013; Jeannerod 1995; Lotze and Halsband 2006; Lotze et al. 1999). The SMA also mediates beat perception and reproduction (Merchant et al. 2015). Because the SMA has historically been shown to be active during the mental imagery of motor tasks and those that involve mental imagery accompanied by music (Leonardo et al.,1995; Chen, Penhune, and Zatorre 2008; Cross et al. 2006; de Manzano and Ullén 2012; Herholz Halpern, and

Zatorre. 2012; Zvyagintsev et al. 2013), it is a model region of the brain to observe when investigating the effects of music familiarity during kinesthetic motor imagery (KMI) of dance. KMI involves imagining or visualizing movement from a first-person perspective; the person goes through the motions in their mind, so to speak, as if they are engaged in the imagined activity. In our own data, we have found that the SMA seems to be the most critical region for visualizing a previously learned dance that has been performed over a season (Bar and DeSouza 2016, 2012). Our tasks allow enough time for the subject to begin imagining their specific dance, as they are doing for one full minute, giving the subject sufficient time to achieve detailed visualization (Bar and DeSouza 2016, 2012; Olshansky, Bar, Fogarty, and DeSouza 2014).

Differences in Brain Structure and Function in Expert Dancers

We compared Ken Swift's (KS) neuroimaging data with that of two other subjects, one, a professional ballet dancer, and the other, a relative novice (six months experience of beginner ballet). All were between 44 and 51 years old. There were two conditions for KMI: (1) a breaking condition, using the music provided by KS ("Apache"), and (2) a ballet condition, which used the first 60 seconds of Bach's "Fugue from Concerto in C Major" (this was provided by the ballet school, and identified as a piece they were currently learning in the apprentice program). The data from the professional ballet dancer had been collected previously and were used as a contrast in the ballet condition. The subjects were instructed to visualize themselves from an internal, first-person perspective, as if they were going to complete the movements. When they heard the music, they "danced" in their mind's eye. In our results, KS's auditory regions were noticeably less active in the breaking condition. This may reflect repetition suppression (Bergerbest et al. 2004) and stimulus expectation, because he was very familiar with the music. His SMA, however, showed greater bilateral activation across conditions than did the control subject. The SMA, as outlined in the previous section, is important for motor planning, motor execution, and imagery; our data demonstrate that this area of the brain can be enhanced by training. What this indicates is that participation in dance, and practice visualizing movement, may improve ability to carry out motor activities, even when motor capacity has been impaired. According to early research on using dance for conditions such as Parkinson's, this hypothesis may prove to be the case (for further details, see the section "Neurorehabilitation: Dance for Parkinson's® and Popping For Parkinson's®"). Dance also has affective and expressive dimensions; when subject KS visualized dancing his choreography to very familiar music, his neural circuits showed changes in activity in the cingulate cortex (Cg25; Figure 27.2a, b).

Neuroimaging data from experts can also be used to model the network of emotional links to music that can produce *flow* (Csikszentmihalyi, 1990). *Flow* is a hypothesized

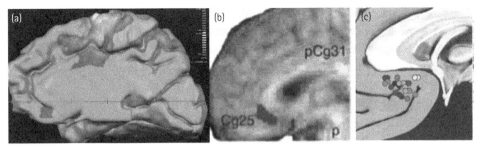

FIGURE 27.2. (a) This neural network (p <0.0001 BONF corrected for multiple comparisons) is from subject Ken Swift while visualizing dance. Most interesting is the activation of cingulate gyrus during this imagined dance (Olshansky et al. 2014). (b) Nodes of activation from Mayberg and colleagues. Green area shows the medial frontal cortex region with decreased cg25 in chronic fluoxetine from Parkinson's disease–related depression. (c) Electrical stimulation sites for deep brain stimulation (Hamani et al. 2009).

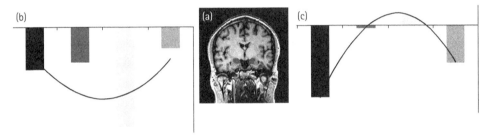

FIGURE 27.3. (a) Anatomical localization of the amygdaloid complex in both hemispheres for subject Ken Swift. (b) Signal from expert dancers in a Bar and Desouza (2016) study using the anatomical localization from Ken Swift in all five expert dancers for left hemisphere amygdala showing a modulation across learning from improvisation (blue bars) to overlearned choreography (light blue bars). (c) Same for right amygdala.

state associated with losing track of time and feeling in a state of bliss or intense focus on the task at hand. In a typical experimental setting, subjects may be asked to report if, and when, they achieve a "flow state"; this is extremely difficult because the act of reporting likely brings subjects out of the state they are meant to report! We speculated that the amygdala would be involved in the neural network of flow and examined this in our dataset of expert ballet dancers (Bar and DeSouza, 2016), hypothesizing that *flow* might be attained once they were preforming the choreography regularly on stage (32 times over 30 weeks). In comparing signal from 7 weeks of rehearsal (third bars, Figure 27.3b and c) to newly learned choreography [0 weeks (first bars) and 1 week of practice (fourth bars), there is a change in the BOLD signal from the left and right amygdala (Bar and DeSouza 2016). This same area is activated in subject KS when he is imagining performing to his chosen piece of music which is familiar and well-practiced, even when that practice is based on improvisation rather than choreography.

Deliberate practice–an intense amount of goal-directed training, preferably supervised by a qualified expert–does not only provide a lens through which to understand the development of expertise or exceptional performance. Research is showing that practice is the basis for observed anatomical changes resulting from intense physical activity. Ericsson and Charness (1994) suggest that "the study of expert performance has important implications for our understanding of the structure and limits of human adaptation and optimal learning" (725). This has clear implications, and not only for experts—when we consider the potential applications of dance in the context of debilitating, progressive, or chronic conditions, flexible adaptation and the learning of new movement strategies can have life-altering and life-enhancing effects. Although dancers share physical effort and strenuous training with other high-level athletes (Koutedakis and Jamurtas 2004), the use of memory to recall long sequences of movement is unique to dance in comparison with most other sports (Kogan 2002). In addition, coordinating movement with music, expression, and (often) other dancers requires the use of fine cognitive strategies (Bläsing 2012). Dance programs for people experiencing disabilities such as Parkinson's have produced research suggesting cognitive benefits associated with dance (Houston and McGill 2015; Westheimer et. al. 2015), and there is a growing body of literature investigating the cognitive effects of dance for an aging population (Alpert et al. 2009; Coubard et al. 2011; Kim et al. 2011; Kimura and Hozumi 2012; Kattenstroth et al. 2010, 2013; Hackney et al. 2015). Other dance-related differences in neurophysiology include differences in white and gray matter between dancers and nondancers (Hänggi et al. 2010; Karpati et al. 2017) and evidence that expert dancers create different mental representations in long-term memory, related to functional phrasing of movement (Bläsing et al. 2009); these may provide the basis for enhanced motor control. Studies such as these indicate that dance can lead to increases in functional connectivity, which is linked with better performance. This has important implications for dance-based neurorehabilitation (Lossing et al. 2016).

Neurorehabilitation: Dance for Parkinson's® and Popping For Parkinson's®

Programs involving dance for people with Parkinson's disease have sprung up around the globe recently, buoyed by reports in news outlets and journals about the power of dance to improve the lives and symptoms of those affected by this debilitating movement disorder. Parkinson's is a progressive, neurodegenerative disease, for which (at the time of publication) there is no cure (although DBS—deep brain stimulation—has shown some promise as a treatment). Symptoms progress from tremor and rigidity to general loss of control of movements in both the sympathetic and parasympathetic nervous systems. Patients may find temporary relief through pharmacology; drugs such as Levodopa can reduce symptoms for several hours at a time. However, once patients begin taking this drug, its effectiveness gradually declines, eventually leaving many without any relief. High dosages of this medication can cause unpleasant side effects, such as *dystonias* (nonvolitional movements, such as twisting or writhing). Dance seems to offer reprieve from symptoms, at least temporarily, and possibly even longer; how much longer is yet to be determined. These reported benefits have sent many sufferers in search of dance classes, which are now, as noted, offered around the world, sometimes by professional companies, such as the English National Ballet, the Houston Ballet, and the Queensland Ballet in Australia. In Toronto, a pilot study conducted by our group in conjunction with Canada's National Ballet School investigates the neurobiological correlates of improvements in motor and nonmotor symptoms for participants in the class. Based on methods developed by the Mark Morris Dance Group in New York City for the original Dance for PD® program taught by David Leventhal, participants attend a 75-minute dance class once a week. For this brief period of time, they are dance students, warming up, improvising, and learning choreography drawn from the ballet company's repertoire (Bearss et al. 2017). And for this period, according to many reports, their Parkinson's symptoms diminish, and in some cases, are even felt to have disappeared (for first-hand reports on how this happens, see the documentary *Capturing Grace*, http://www.capturinggracefilm.com/).

In our research, behavioral tests associated with this program have shown that, along with physiological improvements in balance and the ability to get up from seated position, there is a notable increase in SMA activity, evident after just 11 weeks, and even more pronounced after 15 weeks. This is with only approximately 150 minutes of dance with feedback in the NBS studio. From these results, we can hypothesize that training in dance is changing people's brains, putatively a *neuroplastic* effect, in which existing brain structures are modified and participants discover improvements in their motor abilities. These results, along with participants' reports, strongly suggest that dance contributes to a more responsive and better-equipped motor system, capable of improving performance—be it in a professional dancer, or an elderly person combating a debilitating movement disorder (Figure 27.4).

Simone Sistarelli, the Founder of Popping For Parkinson's®, uses Hip Hop vocabulary in his dance project, which offers free Popping classes to people with Parkinson's. Sistarelli describes his method and philosophy as follows:

> Popping is a dance technique born in California in the 1970s, based on the instant and voluntary contraction and release of all the muscles of the body to the music, and it is now considered an integral part of the Hip Hop dance styles and techniques, therefore of the Hip Hop Culture.
>
> Hip Hop Culture teaches you to be yourself. To fully embrace who you are.
>
> Kids in the Bronx ghetto in the 1970s, mainly Blacks and Latinos, living in poverty and surrounded by drugs and criminals, would give themselves a name/street name: they were creating their own identity, empowering themselves, trying to find an outlet for their anger and frustration of living in those terrible conditions. All they had was their creativity. The negative situation they were in became what they would rap about, turning it into gold through an artistic expressive form. That is how Hip Hop was created.

FIGURE 27.4. Simone Sistarelli of Popping for Parkinson's® with a student. Courtesy of Cath Dupuy.

So, if we apply this to people with Parkinson's, the tremor becomes the Pop, the slowness become Slow Motion style, the shuffling becomes Crazy Legs style etcetera. This is Popping For Parkinson's®.

Sistarelli suggests that dance could work as well as a pill, if taken regularly and at the right dosage—one that has no side effects (although we could also maintain that dance has side effects, all positive—social engagement, joy, physical exercise, reduced stress). Students in Sistarelli's program feel that Popping works better for them than other styles due to the specifics of the associated movements and culture, including oppositions between muscular contraction and release, the use of music with a very high groove, and the lack of a unique Popping stereotype, which students report to be incredibly freeing: "Popping teaches you that if you are yourself within the dance, you can never be wrong." While these elements are specific to his primary style of Popping, these are also shared by all forms of dance. Sistarelli goes on to say:

> The great thing about dance is that it does not care about your age, gender, sexual orientation, religion, background or anything, it embraces you. And it challenges you. And it stimulates you.
>
> Dance is a primal instinct, that needs nothing more than oneself.
>
> Hip Hop shares the same approach. What matters are your skills and your uniqueness.
>
> Everyone can dance. Everyone should dance.

Some questions that remain unanswered are whether dance is neuroprotective across the lifespan (do dancers live longer?) and is there any evidence that experience with dance contributes to a better quality of life as we age? Are the improvements observed in dance class transferable to situations in participant's everyday lives? Are reports of improvements on cognitive and memory tasks (Alpert et al. 2009; Coubard et al. 2011; Katenstroth et al. 2010, 2013) potentially neuroprotective and/or generalizable to other domains and situations?

To answer these and other questions, more research is needed. Studies are required that examine more closely various aspects of dance interventions to better understand how their parameters contribute to benefits in respect to conditions or symptoms; in some cases, these are already underway (Lossing et al. 2016). Collaborations between dancers and scientists such as Christina Soriano and Christina Hugenschmidt (Wake Forest University), or dancers-turned-scientists such as Madeleine Hackney (Emory University) are generating research designs that are better able to sustain and describe key elements of dance while allowing for clear and precise measurement of changes. One such area meriting further investigation relates to the amount of practice needed to reach desired outcomes. Most dance programs implement a once- or twice-a-week attendance regimen, and the results have been varied. Few studies have been conducted with a more intense participation scheme (everyday attendance), but those that have followed this model have shown more clearly promising results—the progression of illness was halted, and in some cases, patients reported an associated decline in symptoms (Batson 2010; Hackney and Earhart 2009; Rabinovich et al. 2017). Does this mean that higher exposure to dance leads to a more impactful neuroprotective or rehabilitative effect? More studies in this line are needed to correlate this relationship. Professional dancers, advanced amateurs, or people trying to master higher levels of dance tend to practice regularly to acquire and further finesse their technique. Level of practice seems to be a crucial factor in most domains and extremely significant in relation to physical endurance, plasticity, and increasing range of motion. In addition, the motto of many dance teachers and choreographers ("practice the steps until they become automatic") is proving to have some neuro-physiological merit. In our study with expert dancers (Bar and DeSouza, 2016), it was shown that SMA activity gradually increases while they are learning and beginning to perform a new movement sequence; this increase was most pronounced between week 1 and week 7 of learning and rehearsal. However, there was a significant decrease in SMA activity *after* that period. We interpreted this decline in SMA to be due to habituation and familiarity with the choreography. In fact, the SMA seems to be directly correlated with the anticipation, planning, and execution of a complex motor-skill sequence. As the sequence becomes more familiar, we find a decrease in SMA activation while subcortical areas may maintain their activity, particularly basal ganglia nuclei such as the caudate and putamen (Bar and DeSouza 2012). More research is needed to see if a daily dance practice can show beneficial effects in neurorehabilitation, and if so, what are the correlating networks responsible for these processes. In our recent longitudinal study following people with PD over a 3-year period, weekly dance classes had an impact on both motor and non-motor symptoms, slowing disease progression. In contrast, a PD-reference group showed the expected rate of decline in motor function and experiences of daily living (Bearss and DeSouza, 2021). This demonstrates the potential for dance to impact quality of life and support wellbeing, even in the face of disease.

Interestingly, dancers with PD have mentioned the diminished need for, and increased effectiveness of, medication while they are involved in the dance program. Given that standard medications such as Levodopa gradually lose their effectiveness over time, necessitating greater dosages, and eventually stop working putatively due to adaptation or continued degeneration of the dopamine-producing neurons, this effect could have major implications. If we can establish that dance—the right type, in the right "dose," and at the right time could prolong the time between onset of symptoms and need for medication, it would represent a huge reduction of the financial burden associated with PD, while demonstrating a clear improvement in quality of life for those diagnosed. Further research is needed to firmly establish the extent to which dance can be applied to reduce symptoms, and to maximize our knowledge of the way that specific movement interventions can facilitate this. We may indeed discover that dance can replace or support pharmacological interventions, at least for a period of time, and in some cases. Dance, it can also be noted, has little to no side effects, save for enjoyment and other positives.

Applications for an Aging Population

Dance is pleasurable, rewarding, challenging, and provides access to unique learning strategies related to neuroplasticity and rehabilitation. In comparison with exercise, dance provides an enriched environment, offers a greater degree of cognitive challenge, and shows a very high rate of adherence–people find attending a dance class to be a rewarding experience (Kshtriya et al. 2015; Barnstaple 2015; Bar and DeSouza 2012). The inclusion of social aspects and sensory elements such as touch may contribute to this enjoyment, and enhance the potential for the acquisition of new, flexible, and adaptive ways of moving in an environment. The use of imagery, memory, narrative, and imagination lift people out of current circumstances and transport them to a realm where they can experience themselves, as bodies, in an entirely new way. If we can show, through studies of experts, that dancers have actually developed differences in brain structures that make them better equipped to respond to movement cues, we have the basis for a theory that not only validates dance as a positive adaptation; we have reason to believe that learning dance, at any age, can cause improvements in one's ability to carry out motor programs. Considering that age tends to bring with it diminishing ranges of motion and abilities to carry out tasks, gradually limiting autonomy and impacting quality of life, our findings suggests that dance participation is of the utmost importance in improving people's health and happiness throughout their life span.

References

Alpert, P. T., Miller, S. K., Wallmann, H., Havey, R., Cross, C., Chevalia, T. et al. (2009). "The Effect of Modified Jazz Dance on Balance, Cognition, and Mood in Older Adults." *Journal of the American Academy of Nurse Practitioners.* 21: 108–115. doi:10.1111/j.1745-7599.2008.00392.x.

Bar, R., and DeSouza, J. (2012). "Do Neural Circuits Involved in Learning a Dance over 8 Months Continue to Show Increased Activation?" *Neuroscience Meeting Planner.* Society for Neuroscience Abstracts, Washington, DC.

Bar, R. J. and DeSouza, J. F. X. (2016). "Tracking Plasticity: Effects of Long-Term Rehearsal in Experts Encoding Music to Movement." *PLoS One* 11 (1): Article e0147731.

Barnstaple, R. (2015). "Movement in Mind: Dance, Self-Awareness and Sociality: An Investigation of Dance as Treatment/Therapy." MA thesis. York University.

Barnstaple R., Protzak J., DeSouza J. F. X. and Gramann K. (2020). "Mobile Brain/body Imaging (MoBI) in dance: A dynamic transdisciplinary field for applied research." *European Journal of Neuroscience,* special issue – *Time to move: Brain dynamics underlying natural action and cognition.*

Batson, G. (2010). "Feasibility of an Intensive Trial of Modern Dance for Adults with Parkinson Disease." *Complementary Health Practice Review* https://doi.org/10.1177/1533210110383903.

Bearss, K. A., Mcdonald, K. C., Bar, R. J., and Desouza, J. F. X. (2017). "Improvements in Balance and Gait Speed after a 12-Week Dance Intervention for Parkinson's Disease." *Advances in Integrative Medicine* 4: 10–13. https://doi.org/10.1016/j.aimed.2017.02.002.

Bearss, K. A. and DeSouza, J. F. X. (2021). "Parkinson's Disease Motor Symptom Progression Slowed with Multisensory Dance Learning over 3-Years: A Preliminary Longitudinal Investigation." Brain Sciences 11: 895. https://doi.org/10.3390/brainsci11070895

Bergerbest, D., Ghahremani, D. G., and Gabrieli, J. D. E. (2004). "Neural Correlates of Auditory Repetition Priming: Reduced fMRI Activation in the Auditory Cortex." *Journal of Cognitive Neuroscience* 16: 966–977. doi:10.1162/0898929041502760.

Bläsing, B., Tenenbaum, G., and Schack, T. (2009). "The Cognitive Structure of Movement in Classical Dance." *Psychology of Sport and Exercise* 10 (3): 350–360.

Bläsing, B., Calvo-Merino, B., Cross, E. S., Jola, C., Honisch, J., and Stevens, C. J. (2012). "Neurocognitive Control in Dance Perception and Performance." *Acta Psychologica* 139 (2): 300–308. doi:10.1016/j.actpsy.2011.12.005.

Burianová, H., Marstaller, L., Sowman, P., Tesan, G., Rich, A. N., Williams, M. et al. (2013). "Multimodal Functional Imaging of Motor Imagery Using a Novel Paradigm." *Neuroimage* 71: 50–58. doi:10.1016/j.neuroimage.2013.01.001.

Burzynska, A. Z., Finc, K., Taylor, B. K., Knecht, A. M., Kramer, A. F., and Anya, M. (2017). "The Dancing Brain: Structural and Functional Signatures of Expert Dance Training." *Frontiers in Human Neuroscience*, 11. https://doi.org/10.3389/fnhum.2017.00566.

Buzsaki, G. (2006). *Rhythms of the Brain*. New York: Oxford University Press.

Chen, J. L., Penhune, V. B., and Zatorre, R. J. (2008). Listening to Musical Rhythms Recruits Motor Regions of the Brain." *Cerebral Cortex* 18: 2844–2854. doi:10.1093/cercor/bhn042.

Coubard, O., Duretz, S., Lefebvre, V., Lapalus, P., and Ferrufino, L. (2011). "Practice of Contemporary Dance Improves Cognitive Flexibility in Aging." *Frontiers in Aging Neuroscience* 3: 13. doi:10.3389/fnagi.2011.00013.

Cross, E. S., Hamilton, A. F. D. C., and Grafton, S. T. (2006). "Building a Motor Simulation de Novo: Observation of Dance by Dancers." *Neuroimage* 31: 1257–1267. doi:10.1016/j.neuroimage.2006.01.033.

Csikszentmihalyi, M. (1990). *Flow: The Psychology of Optimal Experience*. New York: Harper and Row.

de Manzano, Ö., and Ullén, F. (2012). "Activation and Connectivity Patterns of the Presupplementary and Dorsal Premotor Areas during Free Improvisation of Melodies and Rhythms." *Neuroimage* 63: 272–280. doi:10.1016/j.neuroimage.2012.06.024.

Demers, M., and Mckinley, P. (2015). "Feasibility of Delivering a Dance Intervention for SubAcute Stroke in a Rehabilitation Hospital Setting." *International Journal of Environmental Research and Public Health* 12: 3120–3132. https://doi.org/10.3390/ijerph120303120.

DeSouza, J. F. X., Ovaysikia, S., and Pynn, L. (2012). "Correlating Behavioral Responses to FMRI Signals from Human Prefrontal Cortex: Examining Cognitive Processes Using Task Analysis." *Jove: Journal of Visualized Experiments* (64). doi:10.3791/3237.

Dhami, P., Moreno, S., and DeSouza, J. F.X. (2015). "New Framework for Rehabilitation— Fusion of Cognitive and Physical Rehabilitation: The Hope for Dancing." *Frontiers in Psychology* 5: 1478.

Douka, S., Zilidou, V. I., Lilou O., and Tsolaki, M. (2019). "Greek Traditional Dances: A Way to Support Intellectual, Psychological, and Motor Functions in Senior Citizens at Risk of Neurodegeneration." *Frontiers in Aging Neuroscience* 11 (6). doi:10.3389/fnagi.2019.00006.

Ericsson, K. A., and Charness, N. (1994). "Expert Performance: Its Structure and Acquisition." *American Psychologist* 49 (8): 725–747. http://dx.doi.org/10.1037/0003-066X.49.8.725.

Giacosa, C., Karpati, F. J., Foster, N. E. V., Penhune, V. B., and Hyde, K. L. (2016). "Dance and Music Training Have Different Effects on White Matter Diffusivity in Sensorimotor Pathways." *Neuroimage* 135: 273–286. doi:10.1016/j.neuroimage.2016.04.048.

Goodill, S. W. (2005). *An Introduction to Medical Dance/Movement Therapy: Health Care in Motion*. London: Jessica Kingsley.

Goodill, S. W. (2016). "Dance/Movement Therapy and the Arts in Healthcare: The First 50 Years." *American Journal of Dance Therapy* 38: 293–296. https://doi.org/10.1007/s10 465-016-9235-z.

Hackney, M. E., and Earhart, G. M. (2009). "Short Duration, Intensive Tango Dancing for Parkinson Disease: An Uncontrolled Pilot Study." *Complementary Therapies in Medicine* 17 (4): 203–207. https://doi.org/10.1016/j.ctim.2008.10.005.

Hackney, M. E., Byers, T., Butler, G., Sweeney, M., Rossbach, L., and Bozzorg, A. (2015). "Adapted Tango Improves Mobility, Motor-Cognitive Function, and Gait but Not Cognition in Older Adults in Independent Living." *Journal of the American Geriatric Society* 63: 2105–2113. doi:10.1111/jgs.13650.

Hamani, C., Mayberg, H., Synder, B., Giacobbe, P., Kennedy, S., and Lozano, A. M. (2009). "Deep Brain Stimulation of the Subcallosal Cingulate Gyrus for Depression: Anatomical Location of Active Contacts in Clinical Responders and a Suggested Guideline for Targeting." *Journal of Neurosurgery* 111 (6): 1209–1215.

Hänggi, J., Koeneke, S., Bezzola, L., and Jäncke, L. (2010). "Structural Neuroplasticity in the Sensorimotor Network of Professional Female Ballet Dancers." *Human Brain Mapping* 31: 1196–1206.

Herholz, S. C., Halpern, A. R., and Zatorre, R. J. (2012). "Neuronal Correlates of Perception, Imagery, and Memory for Familiar Tunes." *Journal of Cognitive Neuroscience* 24: 1382–1397. doi:10.1162/jocn_a_00216.

Houston, S., and McGill, A. (2013). "A Mixed-Methods Study into Ballet for People Living with Parkinson's." *Arts and Health: An International Journal for Research, Policy and Practice* 5 (2): 103–119.

Jeannerod, M. (1995). "Mental Imagery in the Motor Context." *Neuropsychologia* 33: 1419–1432. doi:10.1016/0028-3932(95)00073-C.

Kaltsatou, A. C., Kouidi, E. I., Anifanti, M. A., Douka, S. I., and Deligiannis, A. P. (2014). "Functional and Psychosocial Effects of Either a Traditional Dancing or a Formal Exercising Training Program in Patients with Chronic Heart Failure: A Comparative Randomized Controlled Study." *Clinical Rehabilitation* 28 (2): 128–138. https://doi.org/10.1177/026921551 3492988.

Karpati, F. J., Giacosa, C., Foster, N. E. V., Penhune, V. B., and Hyde, K. L. (2017). "Dance and Music Share Gray Matter Structural Correlates." *Brain Research* 1657: 62–73. https://doi.org/ 10.1016/j.brainres.2016.11.029.

Kattenstroth, J. C., Kolankowska, I., Kalisch, T., and Dinse, H. R. (2010). "Superior Sensory, Motor, and Cognitive Performance in Elderly Individuals with Multi-Year Dancing Activities." *Fronties in. Aging Neuroscience* 2: 1–9. doi:10.3389/fnagi.2010.00031.

Kattenstroth, J. C., Kalisch, T., Holt, S., Tegenthoff, M., and Dinse, H. R. (2013). "Six Months of Dance Intervention Enhances Postural, Sensorimotor, and Cognitive Performance in Elderly without Affecting Cardio-Respiratory Function." *Frontiers in Aging Neuroscience* 5 (5). doi:10.3389/fnagi.2013.00005.

Kim, S. H., Kim, M., Ahn, Y. B., Lim, H. K., Kang, S. G., and Cho, J. H. (2011). "Effect of Dance Exercise on Cognitive Function in Elderly Patients with Metabolic Syndrome: A Pilot Study." *Journal of Sports Science and Medicine* 10: 671–678.

Kimura, K., and Hozumi, N. (2012). "Investigating the Acute Effect of an Aerobic Dance Exercise Program on Neuro-Cognitive Function in the Elderly." *Psychology of Sport and Exercise* 13: 623–629. doi:10.1016/j.psychsport.2012.04.001.

Kogan, N. (2002). "Careers in the Performing Arts: A Psychological Perspective." *Creativity Research Journal* 14 (1): 1–16. http://dx.doi.org/10.1207/S15326934CRJ1401_1.

Koutedakis, Y., and Jamurtas, T. (2004). "The Dancer as a Performing Athlete: Physiological Considerations." *Sports Medicine* 34 (10): 651–661.

Kshtriya, S., Barnstaple, R., Rabinovich, D., and DeSouza, J. F. X. (2015). "Dance and Aging: A Critical Review of Findings in Neuroscience." *American Journal of Dance Therapy* 37: 81–112. http://dx.doi.org/10.1007/s10465-015-9196-7.

Kung, S. J., Chen, J. L., Zatorre, R. J., and Penhune, V. B. (2013). "Interacting Cortical and Basal Ganglia Networks Underlying Finding and Tapping to the Musical Beat." *Journal of Cognitive Neuroscience* 25: 401–420.

Leonardo, M., Fieldman, J., Sadato, N., Campbell, G., Ibañez, V., Cohen, L. et al. (1995). "A Functional Magnetic Resonance Imaging Study of Cortical Regions Associated with Motor Task Execution and Motor Ideation in Humans." *Human Brain Mapping* 3: 83–92. doi:10.1002/hbm.460030205.

Lossing, A., Moore, M., and Zuhl, M. (2016). "Dance as a Treatment for Neurological Disorders." *Body, Movement and Dance in Psychotherapy* 12 (3): 170–184. https://doi.org/10.1080/17432979.2016.1260055.

Lotze, M., and Halsband, U. (2006). "Motor Imagery." *Journal of Physiology-Paris* 99: 386–395. doi:10.1016/j.jphysparis.2006.03.012.

Lotze, M., Montoya, P., Erb, M., Hülsmann, E., Flor, H., Klose, U. et al. (1999). "Activation of Cortical and Cerebellar Motor Areas during Executed and Imagined Hand Movements: An fMRI Study." *Journal of Cognitive Neuroscience* 11: 491–501.

Makoshi, Z., Kroliczak, G., and van Donkelaar, P. (2011). "Human Supplementary Motor Area Contribution to Predictive Motor Planning." *Journal of Motor Behavior* 43: 303–309. doi:10.1080/00222895.2011.584085.

Merchant, H., Grahn, J., Trainor, L., Rohrmeier, M., and Fitch, W. T. (2015). "Finding the Beat: A Neural Perspective across Humans and Non-Human Primates." *Philosophical Transactions of the Royal Society B: Biological Sciences* 370 (1664): 20140093-20140093. doi:10.1098/rstb.2014.0093.

Müller, P., Rehfeld, K., Schmicker, M., Hökelmann, A., Dordevic, M., Lessmann, V. et al. (2017). "Evolution of Neuroplasticity in Response to Physical Activity in Old Age: The Case for Dancing." *Frontiers in Aging Neuroscience* 9: 56. doi:10.3389/fnagi.2017.00056.

Olshansky, M. P., Bar, R., Fogarty, M., and DeSouza, J. F. X. (2014). "Supplementary Motor Area and Primary Auditory Cortex Activation in an Expert Break-Dancer during the Kinesthetic Motor Imagery of Dance to Music." *Neurocase* 21 (5): 607–617.

Poikonen, H., Toiviainen, P., and Tervaniemi, M. (2018). "Naturalistic Music and Dance: Cortical Phase Synchrony in Musicians and Dancers." *Plos One* 13 (4): Article e0196065. https://doi.org/10.1371/journal.pone.0196065.

Rabinovich, D. B., DeSouza, J. X. F., Arakaki, T., Rodriguez Quiroga, S., Litvak, V., Firmani, J. M. et al. (2017). "Intensive Short-Term Dance Intervention in Parkinson's Disease." 21st International Congress, Parkinson and Movement Disorders. Vancouver, BC.

Thickbroom, G. W., Byrnes, M. L., Sacco, P., Ghosh, S., Morris, I. T. et al. (2000). "The Role of the Supplementary Motor Area in Externally Timed Movement: The Influence of Predictability of Movement Timing. *Brain Research* 874: 233–241. doi:10.1016/S0006-8993(00)02588-9.

Trinkler, I., Chehere, P., Salgues, J., Monin, M.-L., Tezenas du Montcel, S., Khani, S., et al. (2019). "Contemporary Dance Practice Improves Motor Function and Body Representation in Huntington's Disease: A Pilot Study." *Journal of Huntington's Disease* 8 (2019): 97–110. doi:10.3233/JHD-180315.

Westheimer, O. et.al. (2015). "Dance for PD: A Preliminary Investigation of Effects on Motor Function and Quality of Life among Persons with Parkinson's Disease (PD)." *Journal of Neurological Transmission*. Published online April 3.

Zatorre, R. J., Chen, J. L., and Penhune, V. B. (2007). "When the Brain Plays Music: Auditory-Motor Interactions in Music Perception and Production." *Nature Reviews Neuroscience* 8 (7): 547–558.

Zvyagintsev, M., Clemens, B., Chechko, N., Mathiak, K. A., Sack, A. T., and Mathiak, K. (2013). "Brain Networks Underlying Mental Imagery of Auditory and Visual Information." *European Journal of Neuroscience* 37: 1421–1434. doi:10.1111/ejn.12140.

AFTERWORD: DANCE, HIP HOP STUDIES, AND THE ACADEMY

JOSEPH SCHLOSS

WITHOUT dance, Hip Hop culture would not exist.

This is an axiomatic statement for Hip Hop scholarship—or at least it should be. After all, every history of Hip Hop culture acknowledges that dancing bodies were the driving force behind the birth of Hip Hop music. The first Hip Hop deejays cut up breakbeats—and thus gave birth to a new musical form—for the express purpose of making people move. The process of developing Hip Hop's radical new musical aesthetic was, for all intents and purposes, exactly the same thing as figuring out what made people dance. A few years later, dance was also the first element of Hip Hop to fully emerge into the commercial mainstream, through movies like *Flashdance*, *Breakin'*, and *Beat Street*.[1] Without dancers, those movies would not have attracted worldwide audiences, and Hip Hop might never have expanded beyond what Jeff Chang (2005) has called its "seven-mile circle" in New York City (109). To this day, groove remains the ultimate measure of Hip Hop quality. If people feel a Hip Hop record in their bodies, then it is a good record. If it clears the dance floor, then—pretty much by definition—it is not.

Dance has indisputably been central to Hip Hop culture for its entire history, and dancers have consistently served as Hip Hop's innovators, curators, ambassadors, and advocates. So why has so little been written about them?

How is it possible that this extraordinary anthology is the first collection of academic writings on Hip Hop dance, an Afro-diasporic cultural tradition that has been evolving for over a half-century and is now practiced around the globe?[2] The answer to that question says far more about the priorities of Hip Hop scholarship than it does about the value of the dance itself. In fact, I suggest that an important step toward fully appreciating the voices represented in these pages is to think seriously about why so many of them have been absent from the academic discourse around Hip Hop up to this point. The chapters themselves suggest a variety of answers to that question. But in the end, the common thread is simply that dance isn't relevant to most of the issues that Hip Hop studies—as a field—has historically addressed. But that is not dance's weakness; *that is its strength.*

As I will discuss, a variety of academic pressures, cultural assumptions, and political concerns—many of which are perfectly legitimate on their own terms—have come to-gether to marginalize Hip Hop dance in the academy. This is not so much the result of any conscious resistance to dance as it is a reflection of a confluence of pressures that have shaped the field of Hip Hop studies in a particular way, making it naturally better suited to address some issues than others. As a result, Hip Hop dance has come to seem less important than it is, simply because the discourse has not been equipped to handle it. But that is precisely the reason dance is important: Hip Hop dance scholarship can bring those often-invisible constraints into the light. The study of Hip Hop dance thus offers a valuable opportunity to rethink Hip Hop studies itself. By asking how and why our preconceptions may have obscured the value of Hip Hop dance, we also enable our-selves to ask what *other* experiences and perspectives may have been hidden by those same assumptions. This handbook not only helps us to understand the present shape of the field with more depth and perspective; it also gives us the opportunity to plot a more sophisticated and nuanced course for the future.

But putting aside for the moment what Hip Hop dance may be able to contribute to our understanding of Hip Hop culture in general, it is, also - *of course* - important in its own right. Hip Hop dance forms have been continuously and rigorously refined for over fifty years. Their artistic vocabularies, aesthetic principles, conceptual frameworks, and pedagogical systems are as sophisticated as those of any artistic form anywhere in the world. Moreover, those vocabularies, principles, and frameworks are deeply rooted in a wide range of historical experiences across the African Diaspora and on the continent itself. It should go without saying that Hip Hop dance forms are worth studying for these reasons alone.

In this afterword, I draw out some of the common themes that have emerged in the handbook with regard to the study of Hip Hop dance and its place in Hip Hop studies more generally. Taken collectively, what can the perspectives in this handbook teach us about Hip Hop dance as a cultural practice? What can they teach us about the way we think about Hip Hop culture in general? And how can they help us to develop a more productive approach to the relationship between the two?

I became interested in Hip Hop dance through my research on Hip Hop's sampling practices, which led me back to a repertoire of songs that were revered by the first Hip Hop deejays for their ability to rock a crowd (Schloss 2004, 17–39). What initially intrigued me was not just that the Hip Hop community recognized these songs— "Apache," "It's Just Begun," "Give It Up or Turn It a Loose," "The Mexican," "Listen to Me," and others—as being historically significant, but also that they felt so strongly about it that b-boys and b-girls were still dancing to those exact same songs some thirty years later. And the more I listened to these records, the more I could see why; or more pre-cisely, the more I could *feel* why. I wanted to be able to dance to them too. So I started to learn. And that was basically my introduction to Hip Hop dance. Which is all to say that I came to dance from the broader Hip Hop culture, rather than vice versa, and so I was attracted to the movements as a response to the music more so than as impressive acro-batic feats. That perspective gave me a particular appreciation of the fact that Hip Hop music and dance evolved together, and an interest in the multiple ways that this relationship has influenced both to this day.

In the early seventies, deejays were playing records for teens in working-class Black and Latino neighborhoods in New York City, competing for their attention and loyalty. In that context, recorded music had a serious deficit when compared to live music: a record sounds basically the same no matter who plays it, so a deejay's only competitive advantage lay in either having records that others didn't have or somehow finding a way to play them differently from other deejays. And the success of either strategy would be judged by whether or not people danced. The birth of Hip Hop can be understood as an extraordinarily successful embrace of both strategies.

Deejays applied these strategies in several ways. By searching for obscure records that expressed a youthful, intense energy, they drew a youthful, intense audience whose music could not be heard elsewhere. By choosing records that combined African American and Latino rhythms, they encouraged their audiences to combine African American and Latino dances. By prioritizing songs that emphasized the break, they prioritized *dances* that emphasized the break, particularly the emerging Afro-Latino fusion known as "rocking." And by extending the break, they pushed the dancers to focus on the part of the dance that was associated with that part of the song, especially the startling floor moves known as "down rock."

As the breaks got longer, the down rock became more elaborate. This, in turn, inspired the deejays to make the breaks an increasingly central part of the performance. And because manipulating records in this way was far more labor-intensive than just letting them play, the deejays now had less time to attend to their other duties, such as announcing records and working the crowd. They delegated this job to the first MCs, who soon started to use rhymes as part of their presentation.

In retrospect, it's easy to forget that the deejays didn't have to do this. They could have easily decided that cutting up breaks for the dancers wasn't worth the trouble. But the dancers *were* worth the trouble, and that trouble became Hip Hop.

Besides hyping up the dancers, the rhymes also made the breaks interesting for people who didn't want to dance. This allowed deejays to serve both parts of the crowd simultaneously, without having to prioritize one group at the expense of the other. They could play more breaks. Which led to more floor moves, which led to more breaks, which led to more rhymes, which led to a billion-dollar industry.

When the first commercial Rap recordings were made in 1979, they featured MCs rhyming over breakbeats played by live bands. Knowing what we know now, that may seem like an obvious choice, but it was not so obvious at the time. In fact, I would argue that if one tries to understand the origins of the genre in purely musical terms, it makes absolutely no sense at all. There is no strictly musical logic that would motivate a transition from performing original Funk songs to repeating short sections of other people's songs and then talking over them. That development—the birth of Hip Hop music— only makes sense if you see it as an attempt to imitate the sound of a live experience that had dance at its core.

I learned this story from people in the Hip Hop dance community. And the reason I was able to do that is because it had been carefully passed down through the decades via a complex apprenticeship system that included an oral tradition of its own history. As a result, students were not only introduced to the narrative itself; they were also taught a culturally specific methodology and ideology for understanding and transmitting that narrative. These intellectual approaches are themselves part of a larger body of conceptual, aesthetic, and practical knowledge that is passed down from teacher to student under the general rubric of "foundation." As Ken Swift and Yarrow Lutz, [3] B-boy Storm, and others discuss in this handbook, foundation includes actual dance moves, battle strategy, aesthetic theory, history, and other tools for a dancer's development. Given that this highly sophisticated and traditional body of knowledge is central to the practice of Hip Hop dance, and that dance is central to Hip Hop culture, it stands to reason that the study of dance offers Hip Hop scholars a unique opportunity to engage with the core values of Hip Hop culture. So why have they so rarely done so?

* * *

In my estimation, dance's almost total absence from the Hip Hop studies discourse up to this point is largely the result of three structural issues in the academy: (1) Hip Hop dance culture's ideological incompatibility with many of the scholarly frames that are typically used to understand Hip Hop; (2) the perceived impracticality of studying Hip Hop dance; and (3) the marginalization of Hip Hop dance scholars due to their disciplinary affiliations.

The first explanation—Hip Hop dance's incompatibility with the theoretical concerns of many Hip Hop scholars—is reflective of a larger blindness to the cultural value of Hip Hop dance and its community. Simply stated, it often just doesn't occur to Hip Hop scholars to talk about dance. This, I would argue, is not an individual oversight so much as it is the result of interactions between several larger factors, including the way the Hip Hop studies discourse itself is framed conceptually, the fact that traditional Hip Hop dances have had very little media presence since the 1980s (and are thus less amenable to being analyzed as pop culture), a lack of scholarly access to the cultural spaces where the dance discourse has developed, and a general discomfort with centering the body in discussions of Afro-diasporic art due to a long history of racist stereotypes.

Conventional academic approaches to Hip Hop culture are also inconsistent with the internal conceptual world of Hip Hop dance in specific ways. One of these ways is that, as the chapters in this handbook demonstrate, Hip Hop dance tends to complicate many of the foundational binaries that often underlie Hip Hop scholarship: mind versus body, African American versus multicultural, authentic versus commercial, and even masculine versus feminine. For many practitioners of Hip Hop dance, these concepts do not stand in ideological opposition to each other in the same way they might in other forms of Hip Hop. As a result, to the degree that any given framework for understanding Hip Hop is based on these binaries, that framework may not work well for dance. And that incompatibility may then make it appear as though dance itself is simply not a good subject for analysis.

In the current volume, DeFrantz speaks to this issue indirectly, warning of accepting frameworks and categories that have emerged more from the history of scholarship than from the experiences of the people in the relevant communities. Though he is specifically referring to boundaries between dance forms, I would suggest that his advice could also be productively applied to the categories that separate dance from other areas of Hip Hop that are studied in the academy. In other words, we should let the *experience of dancing* lead us to the best tools for the job, rather than choosing the tools first and then finding appropriate applications:

> Maybe we can write toward the tiny adjustments of energy and encounter that produce recognizable differences, and think outward from those noticings toward speculative assessments of moving and its implications . . . We can tell stories about how we danced, when and where, and what our shared recalling of those gestures means to us now that we aren't dancing . . . *Maybe what we needn't do, though, is try to fix these dances by overdefining them, policing them, or restricting them.* (DeFrantz, this volume; emphasis added)

Another way that dance is inconsistent with conventional approaches to Hip Hop has to do with the nature of academic disciplines themselves. The lines between departments and schools reflect a scheme for the categorization of knowledge that has developed over the last several hundred years in response to social, cultural, historical, and economic forces in the academy. Hip Hop as a field of study has naturally been categorized according to the disciplines that pioneered it, and thus assigned a body of theory and methodology that was appropriate to those disciplines. If Hip Hop is viewed primarily as a form of political poetry, as it often has been, then it makes sense to use the tools of literary theory to interpret it. But literary theory may not provide the best tools to study dance. And for people who are trained in literary theory, that disjuncture may make dance seem like a less promising subject for study than it actually is. It may also make disciplines that *do* study dance seem too distant to reasonably collaborate with. This schism may be further reinforced by the fact that dance programs in many colleges and universities are organized around a conservatory model and thus perceived to be more concerned with practical instruction than with theoretical analysis. Whether that is actually true or not in any given case, the perception itself may still tend to isolate the study of dance from other fields.

In describing the students in her dance class, for example, grace shinhae jun notes, "Many of them describe Hip Hop as a form of expression and see the course as extracurricular" (jun, this volume). These students clearly value Hip Hop dance (after all, they voluntarily chose to take the course), yet they still place it in a separate category from their other classes. A similar dynamic may apply at the faculty level. Existing academic conversations around Hip Hop culture may not seem relevant to dance, or vice versa, and so a scholar might preemptively abandon dance research as a dead end.

The second reason for dance's marginalization within Hip Hop studies has to do with its perceived practicality as a research topic. Dance-related topics may not have seemed practical to Hip Hop studies researchers, either in terms of their general feasibility as projects or their ultimate value to an academic career in their particular discipline. Social geography may also contribute to this dynamic. Some aspects of Hip Hop culture can be studied at a distance, particularly those meant to be experienced through the mass media in the first place. But generally speaking, dance is not such an aspect; dance can only be experienced in specific social spaces. And to the degree that's the case, a researcher's access to the dance would naturally be mediated by their access to those spaces.

Even on a more abstract level, the theorization of the researcher's personal relationship to the social space in which Hip Hop takes place, as an evolving process that fundamentally shapes their research as it develops, is crucial to the study of Hip Hop dance. Johnson's contributions to the current volume address this issue across multiple axes. Though she specifically addresses the experience of women ethnographers, the larger analytical framework she describes—in which an individual's perceived identity will profoundly influence the nature of their research experience—is applicable to Hip Hop dance researchers regardless of gender. As a result of this dynamic, Hip Hop dance researchers tend to be drawn from disciplines—mainly ethnographic—where critical engagement with such issues is fundamental to the methodology. But such questions of embodied research experience are just not part of the methodology of many of the disciplines that have historically been used to study Hip Hop culture, and this makes it difficult to use those disciplines to study dance. And if one believed that those disciplines are the only ones available, then it would be difficult to study dance at all.

The third reason that dance may be underrepresented in Hip Hop Studies is that even when scholarly works on Hip Hop dance have been produced, they often do not become part of the mainstream discourse of Hip Hop scholarship. This has primarily affected two categories of researchers. The first is those who have worked in fields not traditionally associated with the Hip Hop studies mainstream, including—as Andy Bennett (this volume) notes—dance studies, sports science, health studies, contemporary history, and globalization studies). The second is those who work outside the academy. It is not an accident that scholars from both of these groups are well represented in the current volume. The editors are well aware that they are an essential part of the Hip Hop dance studies conversation.

The marginalization of the first group is connected to the issues around academic disciplines I have just discussed. The structure of the academic world has created a false distance between disciplines that are suited to the study of different aspects of Hip Hop culture. But I think that the second group is particularly important to emphasize here.

Hip Hop dancers (along with some nondancers who nevertheless are part of the culture) have produced many works of scholarship and documentation that remain unknown to most Hip Hop studies scholars. These include books such as Alien Ness's, *The Art of* Battle[4]; Mabusha "Push" Cooper's *Push Hip Hop History, Vol. 1, The Brooklyn Scene*; Martha Cooper and Nika Kramer's *We B*Girls*; Luis De Jesus's *The Kings of*

Dance; Willie Estrada's *The Dancing Gangsters of the South Bronx*, and Thomas "T-Bopper" Guzman-Sanchez's *Underground Dance Masters: Final History of a Forgotten Era*; documentaries such as Ana "Rokafella" Garcia's *All the Ladies Say* and Jorge "Fabel" Pabon's *Apache Line: From Gangs to Hip-Hop*, many instructional videos that provide historical information from credible sources, and countless online interviews and minidocumentaries. This work often has a different agenda from that of academic research, but that's precisely why it's valuable—because it can alert us to approaches and concepts that may not have occurred to us in the academy. Even beyond its immediate value, the absence of an entire branch of Hip Hop research from the discourse should be concerning just as a matter of general principle. By bringing these issues to the surface, this handbook does not only offer us the opportunity to ask what dance can contribute to the broader field of Hip Hop studies, it goes a long way toward answering that question.

It is important to note that all three of the possibilities I have outlined here involve the leveraging of real power in academic institutions: ideological power, economic power, social power, and cultural power. As a result, any attempt to analyze or mitigate these forces is, to some degree, a critique of that power. In that spirit, I would like to look at some common themes that emerge from the chapters in this anthology, and give some thought to what these themes can tell us about what dance can contribute to Hip-Hop Studies.

* * *

Many years ago, when Break Easy (Breaking in Style crew) taught me the six-step, he noted that each position had distinctive qualities that offered a unique set of options. The six-step was a cycle unto itself, but it was also a six-way fork in the road that led to a potentially infinite number of other paths. Similarly, the content of the handbook naturally seems to fall into six general categories. Like the six-step, these categories form a complete 360-degree cycle when taken together, but each category in its turn also represents a chance to break out of that cycle, to explore new aesthetic, methodological, and theoretical moves.

The first category involves the articulation of a Hip Hop dance *aesthetic*. What are the principles of the dance, and what are the implications of those principles? The second category involves *pedagogy and transmission*. How are the principles preserved and passed along to others? How does the form of this system affect its content, and vice versa? The third category concerns the *history and historiography* of the dance. How did the dance develop? What is the relationship between that history and the current shape of the dance? What has been left out of this narrative? Which voices have been centered, and which marginalized? The fourth category concerns *practical information* for practitioners and others. What should a Hip Hop dancer know in order to perform the dance safely and effectively? How can they maximize the dance's value in their lives? How can Hip Hop dance serve other goals beyond pure artistic expression? The fifth category is *context*—social, cultural, economic, and political. How has the dance influenced and been influenced by the worlds in which it lives? The final category is *ontology*. How do we frame Hip Hop dance conceptually? What are its defining characteristics generally, and what characteristics define individual forms? And how did those particular characteristics come to be significant?

* * *

The first category is aesthetics. Just the fact that Hip Hop dance forms are based on coherent and articulable principles may come as a revelation to many people. But in reality, the question is not whether a fifty-year-old dance form is based on definable principles that are consciously embodied by its practitioners. Of course it is. The real question is why anyone would think that it wasn't. Hip Hop generally deals with that question by ignoring it, thereby shifting the burden of proof onto Hip Hop's challengers and freeing up intellectual energy for more important things. I would suggest that this is actually a battle tactic. Hip Hop defends itself by refusing to be defensive. In that sense, not only are the aesthetic discussions in the handbook important documents of a deep cultural philosophy, but the ways in which that philosophy is presented are themselves manifestations of that philosophy.[5] The chapters by Storm, YNOT and Fogarty, and Swift and Lutz exemplify Hip Hop's internal discourse in this regard. Ken Swift, Storm, and YNOT are well respected b-boys who have each played a historical role in the development of the dance. It should not, therefore, be surprising that they all have very extensive and detailed ideas about how the dance should be performed. Yet it is noteworthy that none of the three present their chapters as their personal vision for what a Hip Hop dance aesthetic *should be*—which they could have easily done given their status—but as their take on what the Hip Hop dance aesthetic *is*. This suggests a deep respect, not only for the tradition itself, but—perhaps more importantly—for the *idea* of tradition.

Though he is too modest to acknowledge it, Ken Swift, in particular, is uniquely qualified to make authoritative statements about the building blocks of the dance— he was responsible for codifying many of them. In Swift's case, it is also significant that his chapter with Lutz emphasizes the relationship between the dance and its cultural context as a crucial aspect of the dance's internal artistic agenda. Many of the other scholars in this collection make arguments about that relationship—especially in terms of its politics (cf. the chapters by Bragin, Roberts, and Osumare and Ofosu, among others)— so Swift and Lutz's foregrounding of that relationship provides all the more support for those arguments. It demonstrates that these ideas are part of the practitioners' discourse, not something being projected onto the community by sympathetic outsiders. Many of these analyses hinge on the relationship between individual and community. In the current volume, Bragin discusses how political power manifests itself not only in slogans and mass movements, but also in physical bodies. And to the extent that dance is about finding freedom for individual bodies in the context of a collectively negotiated aesthetic, it can not only model liberation but also begin to enact it.

Roberts's chapter similarly explores the intrinsic politics of the Hip Hop dance aesthetic, in this case along racial lines: "This examination necessitates sensing into the microlevel Black and Brown physical performances of culture to ask what they reveal about macrolevel social injustices. Put another way, what knowledge has accumulated in acts of containment, and when it is released, what is revealed? And what of the macro (social systems of injustice) is contained in the micro (bodily movement practices)?"

Though the connection might not be immediately apparent, it is worth viewing Storm's contribution in this light as well. Storm positions himself as a member of the international b-boy community who happens to be from Germany, as opposed to a representative of a distinctively German style of breaking. Though, of course, dancers from Europe do reflect their own individual and collective experience in their dance, that experience is framed as part of a larger global dance culture with a fundamentally unified history. This is a perfect example of how political organizing may be implicit in the aesthetic principles of an artistic community. How do your personal artistic goals connect to the deeper shared aesthetics of the dance? How does that aesthetic connection articulate—or even create—a social connection?

This is not a mere abstraction. As Osumare and Ofosu detail in their chapter, this process has enabled Hip Hop dance to be both global *and* distinctively Afro-diasporic at the same time. At its core, Hip Hop dance embodies many social, aesthetic, and even spiritual approaches that mark it clearly as a cultural expression of the African diaspora. Yet this identity does not prevent it from being embraced by individuals from other cultural backgrounds. If anything, it facilitates that process, ultimately producing what Osumare calls the "intercultural body." This has substantial and wide-ranging implications for social interaction and political change. As the authors write, "Hip Hop dance is movement *text* [original emphasis] that speaks to these global and local forces within the context of the ancient Africanist circle that we call the cipher. Today, the global Hip Hop dance cipher is a spiritual 'outlaw space,' where dominant narratives are simultaneously reinforced and subverted."

Another example of how dance provides a space for individuals to define their relationship to the collective is in the realm of gender. Many if not most of the scholars represented in these pages have consciously decentered masculinity in such a way as to make it both more visible and less conventional. This approach simultaneously reflects actual gender politics in the Hip Hop dance community and also theorizes the way gender works as part of the academic discourse. In that sense—like many of the writings here—it is *about* politics and also political in itself.

YNOT's chapter with Fogarty connects the dance aesthetic to the graffiti aesthetic, not only as parallel elements of Hip Hop culture, but also in their shared goals, visual language, rhythm, and relationship to physical and conceptual space. These common threads not only connect the art forms themselves; they also connect the practitioners to each other and to the larger Hip Hop community. As a practitioner, YNOT also speaks to the idea that the artists themselves consciously frame Hip Hop as a series of shared aesthetic commitments. It is not merely the projection of academics.

In their respective chapters, Shapiro and Sadot explore the implications of presenting the Hip Hop dance aesthetic in the context of the theatrical stage. Implicit in both discussions is a detail so obvious that it often goes unstated: not only was Hip Hop dance not designed to be presented on stage, in many ways it was specifically designed to *resist* being presented on stage. As I have written elsewhere, there is a tendency to view such aesthetic disjunctures between Hip Hop and supposed "high art" as failings on Hip Hop's part, when in reality, they are often intentional critiques of the racial or class politics inherent in the concept of "high art" itself:

> The idea that Hip Hop lacks a coherent set of aesthetic principles often reflects a logic that assumes that any disparity between Hip Hop and mainstream ideologies necessarily can only reflect a deficiency on Hip Hop's part. Since much of the Hip Hop aesthetic was intentionally designed by marginalized groups to challenge mainstream society's ideologies about cultural production, this critique quickly becomes circular: Hip Hop's rejection of mainstream culture can't be taken seriously because it rejects mainstream culture. Marginalized groups should be marginalized because they are marginalized. By its very construction, this logic implicitly rejects the possibility that the Hip Hop aesthetic could include a legitimate critique of contemporary social and cultural norms. It leaves only the conclusion that Hip Hop is—and is meant to be—a nihilistic violation of those norms. From this point of view, sample-based Hip Hop producers can't create an alternative approach to intellectual property; they can only steal other people's music. Graffiti writers can't challenge the use of state power to restrict access to public space; they can only trespass and vandalize. B-boys and b-girls can't create new competitive dance forms based on traditional Afro-Diasporic cultural and spiritual principles; they can only spin on their heads. MCs cannot challenge conventional poetic forms; they can only fail to be poets. (Schloss 2017, 186)

This is one of the reasons it is important to document the aesthetic principles of Hip Hop dance: not necessarily to defend the Hip Hop community's choices so much as to defend their *right to make those choices* in the first place. That right—and its integration into the substance of the dance at the deepest level—means that the aesthetic principles of various Hip Hop dance forms in various contexts almost universally embody a politics of critique.

* **

The second of the six categories is pedagogy. It is noteworthy that a substantial portion of this handbook is devoted to analyzing the way Hip Hop dance is taught. That would likely not be the case for most other art forms, but pedagogy is a crucial component of the experience of Hip Hop dance, and it is understood as such by the community. As noted above, Hip Hop's traditional dance forms are most often passed from teacher to student through an apprenticeship system. As with any such system, the line between cultural transmission and cultural construction is often blurry; the genealogy of apprenticeship reinforces historical narratives, schools of thought, and concepts of authenticity. The pedagogical system is designed to serve the aesthetic content, but once it is established, it naturally tends to shape it as well. Perhaps the most revealing aspect of this process is the concept of "foundation" (which provided the title of my own 2009 monograph on breaking).

Foundation refers to a body of basic knowledge—practical, cultural, and philosophical—that any b-boy or b-girl should know, in order to be considered a legitimate exponent of the tradition. Beyond the actual information, foundation—as a concept—is an important pedagogical tool in itself, since it defines the aesthetic as a coherent body of knowledge that can be transmitted from one person to another and which confers certain responsibilities in return. In terms of its content, it also serves to represent what any given teacher considers to be important (which is often a reflection of their lineage). This in turn raises important questions about the politics of cultural maintenance: What are those responsibilities? What are the advantages of continuity? What are the implications of change? Interestingly, several chapters of this anthology address these questions by focusing on the relationship between the abstract idea of foundation and the practical context in which it is taught.

Storm, for example, sets out in his chapter to write a history of the breaking aesthetic, but since this evolution occurred in the context of specific moves being taught and learned, it naturally blurs into a history of Hip Hop pedagogy. His contribution can thus be seen as a history of the social processes through which Hip Hop dance was transmitted at different times. Petchauer also focuses on context, though he takes as his subject the role of music as a framework for the educational process:

> A great deal of this education concerns how to relate with the music and the aesthetic forms—like flow, layering, and ruptures—that are common across Hip Hop elements . . . People learn to dance in, around, and in relation to the music, responding to what they hear and feel: how to break on the break. This education also concerns how to present oneself in the midst of this music, and with respect to its sonic qualities. Breaking certainly involves learning to do things with the body and learning about the historical context of the dance. But the relationship between the dance (moves, steps, movements etc.) and music is integral to what it means to be a b-boy or b-girl.

This suggests that a relationship to music is not only an important component of the dance on a practical level; it is also significant in the abstract. It can serve to create a sense of space, narrative, and tone. Moreover, Petchauer presents these artistic concerns not only as *objects* of study and teaching, but as part of the teaching process itself. Again we see the dynamic relationship between the content and process of teaching.

As part of her oral history of b-girls in New York in the 1990s, Park focuses on transmission as a gendered process. Gender identity influences who has access to certain information and relationships, how that access is granted, and how the information is presented. Taken together, these analyses suggest that Hip Hop dance pedagogy is embedded in a very rich set of relationships between context and content in any specific moment.

* * *

The third general category of analysis in this handbook is critical historiography, which takes several forms. The most obvious is the history of specific dance communities in different geographical areas: Armenia (Aprahamian), New Orleans (Miller), New York

City (Park), the United Kingdom (Sadot), and France (Shapiro). Aprahamian's work has much to offer, both in terms of his methodology and also in terms of how he frames his inquiry conceptually. But perhaps the most significant contributions are the connections that arise between those two aspects. Like virtually all histories of Hip Hop dance, his history of the breaking community in Armenia had to be constructed via ethnography and oral history, simply because there are no other reliable sources for this information. But these methodologies also provide opportunities to let individual speakers locate their own experience in the broader context of post-Soviet Armenia. In this way, not only does a collective experience gradually emerge, but so does a shared context for that experience. Similarly, Miller's chapter on twerking and p-popping in New Orleans locates specific developments in the context of a larger social history that provided an environment that was friendly to the practice, not only in terms of social space, but also in terms of cultural history and even the movements themselves.

In her analysis of the New York City breaking scene of the 1990s, Park frames her history not only geographically, but also in terms of era and gender, focusing specifically on the experiences of women. This specificity allows these voices not only to present their individual stories, but also to provide a multidimensional perspective on the areas in which they overlap. Her use of oral-history methodologies allows her subjects to construct their own contexts in such a way that—like Aprahamian—the overlap between the individual narratives creates a collective one. Moreover, this approach also raises the question of how an academic oral history approach might intersect with existing internal historical methodologies in the Hip Hop community. In fact, many well-respected dancers conducted themselves as historians long before they had any formal contact with the academic world, and to this day, they regularly debate the implications of different historical methodologies. This process has implicitly informed virtually every chapter of the present volume, and it is explicitly analyzed in Johnson's discussions of women-identified Hip Hop researchers, who are primarily scholar-practitioners, and who thus credit the community for their foundational training in streetdance research. Contrary to what many may assume, this is not only true from a methodological standpoint; it is also true in regard to many aspects of its theoretical framing.

In her discussion of Hip Hop dance forms in France, Shapiro argues that although Hip Hop culture started in the United States, it was well suited to merge with certain long-standing aspects of French culture. Specifically, she notes that the idea of a dance "troupe" was a close parallel to the Hip Hop concept of the "crew," which allowed crews to fit into a preexisting role in French social life. In this sense, Hip Hop dance could be simultaneously global *and* local, new *and* old. This is a surprisingly common—and vastly underappreciated—pattern. As folk-music scholar Elijah Wald has noted, "We often talk about musical roots. And that's a terrific metaphor that's always misused. People talk about musical 'roots,' meaning what came before something else. But roots don't come before plants. Roots are what grow down as the rest of the plant is growing up. And that, in fact, *is* how we [use] history" (Wald 2013). In this case, Hip Hop dance grew its roots down into the fertile soil of French culture, and this gave it tremendous power as a tool for social change there. And this dynamic is not unique to France; grace shinhae jun similarly notes that one way in which Hip Hop has become part of the Asian American experience is that traditional Asian dance groups have incorporated Hip Hop dance into their preexisting practices (jun).

Sadot's history of the institutionalization of Hip Hop dance in the United Kingdom also uses oral history and ethnography, but it uses these individual experiences to not only construct a collective history, but to locate that history in the larger context of the mechanics of institutionalization. The implications of Hip Hop dance in any institutional context can also be seen in jun's analysis, which also uses ethnographic methodologies to effectively develop a shared social context for her subjects.

Another historical thread in this anthology concerns the development of Hip Hop dance forms themselves, a form of analysis which often also includes critical approaches to the methodologies that have been used to document and recover that history. Scrambleock discusses the strengths and weaknesses of archiving streetdance footage and, particularly, the value of independent community-based archives versus academic archives. In the case of Hip Hop dance, the most important archives are often the personal collections of practitioners. Moreover, these collections tend to combine informal field recordings with videos that were produced for commercial sale, and the line between the two is sometimes blurry. In both cases, it is useful to view the recordings as being cultural products in themselves and therefore reflective of social and cultural processes in both form and content. This means that, unlike traditional field recordings, which generally strive to be objective documents of an event, these recordings are often intentionally designed to reflect the aesthetic principles of Hip Hop dance in their cover art, editing, conceptual approach, soundtracks, and other areas. They also, both intentionally and unintentionally, reflect processual issues related to the creation and distribution of the recording, which can also be useful data for analysis. For example, before the rise of the Internet, many Hip Hop dance videos that were produced as commercial products were still sold exclusively at battles and jams, by their own subjects. They could only be accessed by people who were already part of the community, via face-to-face interactions with the artist. (See Fogarty [2006] for extensive discussion of how this process influenced the development of international social networks among dancers.) As a process, this exchange—though still undoubtedly capitalist—was quite different from a typical corporate distribution model.

Lakewood discusses the politics of early documentation via photography, particularly how the performative nature of dance reflected a deeper community consciousness of being observed—often with suspicion—and all that that entails. And Durden connects Hip Hop dance history to a larger dance heritage, both within the African American community and also across the African diaspora in general. In doing so, he draws an important distinction between a history of practices and a history of meaning. Can you have one without the other? If so, how does that affect the nature of the continuities that ensue? This is a particularly complex question for Hip Hop since, as he notes, it evolved in the context of white supremacy, which actively worked to obscure threads of meaning in the African American community, even if the practices themselves were able to continue. This is particularly true for connections to Afro-diasporic traditions that were not African American, where additional linguistic and cultural transitions come into play.

* * *

The fourth of the six categories consists of practical information for dancers, which roughly falls into two subcategories: how to be a more effective dancer, and how to apply dance to other areas of life. Though these subjects may seem out of place in the context of an academic anthology, this approach is actually deeply connected to both the nature and context of Hip Hop dance. Simply stated, there is a thin line between scholarship and advice because there is a thin line between scholars and practitioners. And that thin line is itself an important cultural element of Hip Hop dance. The chapters by Bragin, Sadot, Storm, and Swift, and Lutz could all be viewed in this light, and several are explicitly framed this way: the aesthetic is discussed for analytical purposes, but also as a guide for dancers.

On a similarly practical level, Ingram's chapter on Hip Hop dance and injury prevention also works as both advice and analysis. The chapter reviews the implications for breakers of the latest research on athletic injuries generally and presents strategies to minimize risk and damage. On its own terms, it is a practical guide for dancers seeking to avoid injury. But in the context of the handbook as a whole, it also serves as an analysis of the *concept* of physical risk as an element of breaking culture. This is a concern that is close to the hearts of virtually all dancers in this tradition, all the more so for those who derive income from it. At the same time, it often goes unacknowledged, possibly out of a fear of speaking it into existence. As a result, the way that the risk of physical injury may influence aesthetic choices in different contexts, not to mention the collective cultural implications of these choices, is rarely discussed as an influence on the aesthetic of the dance. This, then, is an important contribution to the discussion, not only in terms of its specifics, but also as an illustration of how some forces that influence a culture may go unspoken in spite of their significance.

With regard to strategies for applying dance concepts to other areas of life, Stephen "Buddha" Leafloor's discussion of the work he does to bring healing to underserved communities through his program BluePrintForLife is exemplary. The program does not simply use Hip Hop dance as a platform for ideas that are ultimately derived from other places. Rather, Buddha consciously set out to use the healing philosophies and strategies that were *already part of Hip Hop culture* as a way to structure the program. Issues of power and social geography that may not be recognized by other programs naturally come to the surface when one is thinking in Hip Hop terms. To take just one example, the BluePrintForLife policy of expecting institutional authority figures, such as school principals, to participate in the program on equal terms with students rather than observe from the sidelines as bystanders is clearly built on the conceptual foundation of the cypher.

Barnstaple, Rabinovich, and DeSouza address the way that prolonged experience with Hip Hop dance affects the structure and functionality of the brain, and then explore the implications that this may have for the treatment of neurodegenerative disorders such as Parkinson's disease. Though, strictly speaking, this is not part of the internal discourse on Hip Hop dance, this study does connect with dancers' collective experience on a broad conceptual level and provides support for the idea that these forms can produce positive change in individuals that is not only social or psychological, but actually neurological.

Hip Hop dance conveys these insights in a community-centered environment that is designed to bring the best out of the individual, help them avoid pitfalls, and maximize the benefits for all concerned. Taken together, these chapters do not only provide advice; they explore the nature and significance of advice itself as a component of Hip Hop dance culture.

* * *

The fifth category is context: How does Hip Hop dance reflect the social, economic, physical, and political spaces in which it lives? To what extent and in what ways is this process a conscious part of Hip Hop dance practice? Virtually every chapter in this handbook touches on this issue in some respect, and as a general proposition it is not unique to Hip Hop dance. That said, Hip Hop dance is particularly concerned with placing the moving body in context, even as compared to other dance forms. As a battle dance that developed in urban spaces that were not particularly conducive to dance—such as hallways, rooftops, and playgrounds—breaking emphasized adaptability to the environment as a fundamental building block of its aesthetic (as did the West Coast forms, albeit in slightly different ways). If one was challenged, one had to respond at that moment, *in that space*. Anything else would be considered a loss. As a result, not only was it philosophically important to develop a consciousness of one's surroundings, but it was also strategically essential. Over time, the aesthetic philosophy and the strategic imperative reinforced each other, creating an increasingly abstract set of approaches that had applications far beyond the world of dance. How was Hip Hop's development in specific cultural and physical spaces connected to the larger social and economic forces that led those particular individuals to be in those spaces in the first place? To what extent and in what ways is dancing on concrete related to living on concrete?

These issues are most evident in the aforementioned history of Hip Hop dance communities outside of the United States, which naturally tend to frame the appeal of Hip Hop to particular populations in terms of the preexisting social, cultural, and economic histories of those communities. In many cases, these histories are manifested in spatial terms, which is not unexpected when population demographics are part of the history, as they often are in the cases discussed here. Given that Hip Hop was created to fight against various restrictions faced by its community, it is not surprising that Hip Hop would be attractive to other groups in other parts of the world whose movements were similarly restricted. This is true of Hip Hop culture in general, but it is particularly central to dance, since dance is an art form that literally takes physical motion as its medium. To look at issues of social space and cultural circulation is thus an important component of the analysis of Hip Hop dance, with regard to both its global spread and its roots in the United States.

Eric Pellerin's consideration of the influence of Kung Fu films on breaking, for example, addresses multiple aspects of that relationship, but issues of space and circulation are particularly central to his analysis. Specifically, he notes that the economics of the distribution of Kung Fu films in the 1970s and 1980s tended to place them in the same spaces as the blaxploitation films of the same era, setting the stage for a crossover influence. Even on a purely geographical level, these films tended to play in the dilapidated theaters of New York City's vice district of 42nd Street and Times Square, a setting that had multiple implications. Because of its central midtown location, Times Square was widely accessible to people from all parts of the city by public transportation, while the area's sleazy reputation invested it with an air of intrigue and danger that made it irresistible to teenage breakers. Partially for this reason, the neighborhood already provided an important space for Hip Hop generation socialization for other reasons, even aside from the films' appeal. As Pellerin notes, the act of seeing these films was easily integrated into the other social activities that people were already exploring in the neighborhood. This may not have been the case if the films had played in more far-flung locations.

Sadot explores the growing institutionalization of Hip Hop Dance Theater through the concept of "metaspatial knowledge," which he defines as the "*knowledge* [original emphasis]of the wider sociocultural, historical, economic and political space in which [Hip Hop dance theater] artists move." By framing his analysis in this way, he is able to talk about both the broader implications of these developments for the Hip Hop community and the academic value of the concept of metaspatial knowledge itself. That concept in particular connects to many of the other discussions in this anthology, being yet another acknowledgment of Hip Hop dance's ability to use its aesthetic to comment on its own place in the world. In particular, it connects to arguments made by both Swift and Lutz and Bragin that Hip Hop dance not only responds to its social context, like other artforms, but actually holds the *idea* of context as an important component of its aesthetic foundations.

* * *

The sixth and final category is a bit more abstract than the others, though no less fundamental, and is accordingly addressed in this volume somewhat more obliquely. This is the question of what defines Hip Hop dance as a general concept, what defines its particular forms, and how we can know such things. Such definitional issues arise in all art communities, but in Hip Hop dance they tend to be invested with a particularly wide-ranging significance that can determine everything from personal authority as a practitioner to the historical legitimacy of entire dance forms. As the sociologist Howard Becker (1998) notes, "An object is constituted by the way people are prepared to act toward it . . . So giving names, saying that something is or isn't something, is a way of saying how that thing ought to be acted toward or, if the name sticks, will be acted toward" (158).

What distinguishes Hip Hop dance from many other arts communities in this regard is that such intentions are often explicitly stated by dancers. As a result, when the scholarship presented here addresses definitional questions, it is generally understood to be a commentary on questions of access, significance, and the distribution of resources, even if that is not specified in the chapter. In fact, Sadot's aforementioned discussion of the institutionalization of Hip Hop dance makes this phenomenon the centerpiece of his analysis, casting these kinds of arguments as an integral part of the institutionalization process, rather than as a byproduct of them. As a practical matter, he asks, how does the Hip Hop community define and maintain its standards of authenticity, and what are the implications of these choices?

Similarly, there is no doubt that the performances of the Fly Girls—the dancers who were featured throughout each episode of the early 1990s sketch-comedy television show *In Living Color*—are among the most widely and regularly viewed representations of Hip Hop dance ever. But though they are sometimes mentioned in discussions of Hip Hop's general emergence into the world of popular culture, the Fly Girls are almost always discussed in terms of the image they presented in the media. Their historical significance *as dancers* is made to seem almost beside the point. Leah McKesey, Diana Reyes and Mary Fogarty address this oversight by centering the dance in their analysis and then viewing other important elements of the Fly Girls' influence through that lens. As dancers who were personally inspired and influenced by the Fly Girls, Reyes and McKesey's own histories prove that these televised performances played an important role in the larger history of Hip Hop dance. So why have they not received more attention for that contribution? First and most obviously, the social dynamic being discussed here is that of women influencing other women, a realm of experience often assumed to be *ipso facto* marginal to the masculine enterprise of Hip Hop. Second, and partially as a result of those gender assumptions, the specific influences that they detail don't necessarily fit the narrative that many want to promote about Hip Hop dance or Hip Hop culture. McKesey and Reyes specify that the Fly Girls were central to their own experiences as dancers in several areas, including their media presence, fashion choices, choreography, the role of family as a social context for dance education, and what they characterizes as "homage"—essentially, the way the Fly Girls served as role models to younger dancers. In doing so, the authors make visible many assumptions of the Hip Hop discourse that might otherwise be overlooked. For example, by emphasizing the significance of choreography, they implicitly question the assumption that Hip Hop dance should primarily be improvisational. In doing so, they also center the role of the professional choreographer, a role that—not incidentally—is often filled by women.

Miller's analysis of twerking and p-popping raises several related issues in this regard: first, what is the relationship between so-called party dances and Hip Hop dance generally, especially since many of these dances are also performed to non–Hip Hop music? And second, if these dances *are* part of Hip Hop, why are they often marginalized in that context? As Kyra Gaunt (2015) has noted, variations of these dances often exist in cultural environments that are not specific to Hip Hop and in some cases that actually predate Hip Hop (253). At the same time, as Miller demonstrates, there is no question that in contemporary New Orleans culture, these dances are clearly part of the Hip Hop experience. I would compare this issue to arguments about the historical role of graffiti in Hip Hop culture; the practice is known to predate the birth of Hip Hop, and many graffiti pioneers contend that the relationship between their art form and Hip Hop cul- ture was minimal at best (at least initially). Some even argue that it was not part of Hip Hop at all. At the same time, nobody doubts that graffiti is part of Hip Hop now.

The point here is the question itself. By arguing about this issue—or by choosing not to argue about it—we are implicitly making claims about the conceptual boundaries of Hip Hop culture. Similarly, the broader question of how and why party dances are often marginalized in the Hip Hop dance discourse is often an indicator of deeper issues about the essential character of Hip Hop culture—or, at least, what any given speaker believes that essential character *should* be. Sexuality, respectability politics, personal morality, gender, and class are all implicit in these conversations. Similarly, by placing Hip Hop dance forms in the context of larger traditions, Durden implicitly raises the question of where those traditions end and where Hip Hop begins, or if that distinction is even a meaningful one at all. And, if it is meaningful, how and why is that the case?

DeFrantz makes the question of boundaries and their significance the centerpiece of his discussion of the relationship between Hip Hop and house dance. Given that they emerged in similar social circumstances, why should they be considered separate dance genres, and what are the implications of that distinction? What, if any, cultural principles does Hip Hop dance share with graffiti writing or turntablism that it does not share with house dance? What can that tell us about the way that both dance communities have constructed their identities—or had their identities constructed for them? And what can it tell us about how those borders have affected the way we conceive of both forms?

CONCLUSIONS

To return to the analogy I mentioned earlier, the six-step is a foundational move in its own right, but it may be more significant for the opportunities it provides to develop "transitions." Though transitions are generally among the least flamboyant moves, they are arguably the most vital. Experienced Hip Hop dancers will tell you that any move, no matter how expertly performed, has not been mastered until the dancer knows multiple ways to get into and out of it. The concepts that emerge in each of the six areas described here can be seen as the deep connective tissue that offers a range of intellectual options, and I want to conclude by thinking about exactly what that offer entails. In other words, to return to my initial question: What commonalities emerge from these chapters, and what can those common issues contribute to Hip Hop studies in general?

Perhaps the most fundamental of the insights this handbook offers is simply that there *are* principles to Hip Hop dance. Contrary to popular stereotype, it is not just "kids spinning on their heads." This, in turn, suggests a second point: the development of these principles—and the Hip Hop dance aesthetic they support—was a project that was intentionally undertaken by specific individuals and groups, in specific times and places. Moreover, the details of those contributions are known to history. It may seem odd that something like that even needs to be said, but it is common in both scholarly and popular writing about Hip Hop to view its artistic innovations as the collective expression of a folk culture rather than the work of individual innovators. To be sure, there certainly were cultural imperatives at work, but they were not impersonal forces driving a nameless mass of ethnic archetypes. They were the hopes and dreams of actual human beings, some of whom have contributed chapters to this anthology. The Hip Hop dance discourse thus calls attention to the broader fact that looking at Hip Hop as a folk culture is an ideological position, not a self-evident reality. And in the context of a broader white supremacist environment, such a choice has deep and complex implications. I would suggest that similar issues also apply to Hip Hop studies more generally.

Another important concept that connects these chapters is the idea that Hip Hop aesthetics and Hip Hop communities are mutually constitutive. Now more than ever, the lived relationship between aesthetics and social space is an essential one for Hip Hop studies to consider. This issue is at the heart of Bennett's chapter, which suggests a range of strategies for locating Hip Hop practices in social spaces. In doing so, he helps to create a theoretical basis for understanding not only what the social context of any given act *is*, but what it *does*. This, in turn, helps us to ask how that context influences identity, geography, history, politics, and many other issues discussed elsewhere in the book. Of course, this would be a valuable endeavor for any social or cultural inquiry, but it is particularly relevant to Hip Hop dance for two reasons. First, as Bennett notes, the construction of social space has always been one of the central processes in the Hip Hop experience. And second, as noted throughout the chapters of the handbook, this process is explicitly theorized by dancers themselves as part of their art. Bragin and Sadot, in particular, speak to the nature of this spatial awareness, particularly with regard to the application of Hip Hop dance principles to other endeavors. As their and other chapters amply demonstrate, the relationship between movement and context is an intentional and significant component of the dance's aesthetic strategy. In fact, the idea of placing this dance in context borders on redundancy. It places *itself* in context, in many ways and on multiple levels—physically, aesthetically, pedagogically, and historically. It is clear that part of the goal of Hip Hop dance as an art form is to help people develop an abstract understanding of their own relationship to social space.

Hip Hop dance also theorizes the balance between a central tradition and distinctive local expressions of that tradition. As much as Hip Hop dance prizes individual innovation, the internal discourse emphasizes that these innovations are to be understood within the larger context of a fundamentally unified form. The transitional New York style known as Electric Boogie, for example, is a branch of a larger history of popping that began in California. Korean breakers may integrate uniquely Korean movements into their dance, but their larger conceptual framework is the same as that of breakers in Morocco or the United States.

The experience of Hip Hop dance also reiterates the significance of pedagogy and its relationship to cultural maintenance in different contexts. This is massively understudied in other aspects of Hip Hop. For all that has been written about Rap music, how many studies have been written about how people *learn* to Rap?

Finally, one of the most fundamental commonalities that becomes apparent across these chapters is that, on both practical and conceptual levels, gender is fundamental to Hip Hop dance—not secondary or tertiary. It shapes the historical narrative (both actively and by omission), the aesthetic (again, both actively and by omission), the pedagogical system (on many levels), and even the relationship between Hip Hop dance and commercialism.

With all of these ideas in mind, I would like to offer a few preliminary thoughts on what the study of dance can offer the study of Hip Hop generally. Unlike other areas of Hip Hop studies that tend to frame Hip Hop as a set of media texts, the study of Hip Hop dance focuses on the analysis of Hip Hop as an *activity*. This perspective has two major implications. The first is that it emphasizes participant observation, and all of the theoretical questions that go along with such methodologies. The second is that on a more general level, ability and credibility are deeply linked. The better you are at an activity—as judged by the community—the more right you have to talk about or analyze it. Needless to say, this is not always an accepted convention in the academic world, and it might not be useful in all cases, but it is worth thinking about some of its implications. The foundation of this approach is that skill is a strong gauge of an individual's seriousness about their art. In other words, it is not the skill itself that necessarily conveys intellectual credibility, but the time, energy, and commitment that were necessary to gain the skill in the first place. Second, it is a measure of the respect that the individual receives from other members of the culture. To the extent that the criteria for what constitutes "skill" are subjective, the fact that an individual is perceived as fulfilling those criteria reflects their subjective relationships with both the community itself and its standards. In circumstances where institutional authority is either not available or not accepted, alternative forms of intellectual authority come into play, and we would do well to understand their structures.

A second important concept offered by Hip Hop dance is the idea of battling as a framework for understanding intellectual interaction. Approaching discussions of Hip Hop philosophy as though they were battles is the norm in breaking culture and present to varying degrees in other elements. In this context, aesthetic principles, historical information, personal experience, and social context all become resources to be strategically deployed in battle. The most important potential benefit of this idea for academics is that it reconciles Hip Hop's political discourse with its aesthetic discourse by making both of them tools to be used by the Hip Hop community in the same venue, and thus subject to the same rules of engagement. These often unspoken rules guide the discourse and are essential to understanding the knowledge that discourse produces. For example, I have observed multiple instances in which a dancer has learned of a new source or piece of historical information that was previously unknown to the broader community. Rather than immediately reveal it, they will often hold it back until it can be deployed to maximum effect. From a conventional academic standpoint, the idea of uncovering evidence that would support your argument, but then hiding it, is hard to understand. But from a battle standpoint, this makes perfect sense; why would you waste your best move on an opponent you could easily defeat through other means? On a more general level, the idea that all discourse happens in a social context is also an important part of Hip Hop dance philosophy. The idea that one's arguments should be strategically deployed, not only in terms of their content and logic, but also in terms of the social context in which they are being made, is absolutely essential for understanding Hip Hop's internal conversations.

Perhaps the single most important contribution of this handbook is that it provides multiple models of how to integrate the idea of *Hip Hop as activity* into one's analysis. Methodologically, virtually all the contributors to this volume—at least those who make specific claims about the nature of Hip Hop dance culture—have used some combination of participant observation, ethnography, and oral history. We can draw several conclusions from this. First, from a practical standpoint, this is the best—and sometimes the only—way for a scholar to access information about most issues in Hip Hop dance. Second, this is the methodology that has been favored by the culture's internal scholars for decades, so their work can be integrated with academic scholarship that was also done this way relatively readily.

Third, it naturally situates researchers' analysis in the context of their own social experience, which not only has specific benefits for the research itself, but also makes that aspect available for critique by the community. Along similar lines, the use of participant observation tends to locate experience in the context of the body, which is obviously useful when studying dance. On a more abstract level, just the idea that such an inquiry can be framed this way is valuable to the general enterprise of Hip Hop scholarship.

An important part of this framing is that it also brings experiences of gender to the forefront, creating a framework that is not only valuable for its own sake and for the sake of critique, but also because it allows researchers to make theoretical connections between their gendered institutional experience in the academy and their gendered field experience in the community.

Johnson's contributions foreground all of these issues. Perhaps the most powerful and far-reaching aspect of her analysis lies not only in its detail, but in the way it is framed. As she notes, women have been the most significant voices in academic scholarship on Hip Hop dance. Consequently, any discussion of women's experiences in this regard is de facto a discussion of the normative experience for researchers in the field and is significant for that reason alone. In other words, the experience of *not being a woman* is anomalous for Hip Hop dance researchers and should be framed as such. This is not only a valuable perspective for its own sake, but it is also emblematic of the way that Hip Hop dance can challenge the accepted frameworks of Hip Hop scholarship, which often center masculinity as normative without acknowledging that they are doing so.

* * *

Hip Hop dance offers fresh voices, fresh methodologies, and fresh perspectives on Hip Hop culture. Redefining Hip Hop studies in such as way as to include dance is thus valuable not only because of that inclusion, but also because it would require us to break down the conceptual, social, cultural, and institutional barriers that have tended to exclude dance in the first place—including those within our own minds. Centering dance necessarily requires us to reflect on problematic assumptions about theory, methodology, gender, race, and institutional power. This is important because the forces that have excluded dance have almost certainly excluded a lot of other important things too. The voices of Hip Hop dance studies are not those of conventional Hip Hop scholarship, much less mainstream cultural scholarship in general. They are more often women, Latinx, LGBTQ+, working class, and non-academic. Their methodologies—battling, critical historiography, participant observation—remain rare in Hip Hop studies. As scholar-practitioners, they often blur the line between documenting and defining, intrinsically challenging the framing of academic scholarship itself. But, in my opinion, if we had a discourse that focused on the continuums and connections raised by Hip Hop dance praxis, we would be better able to appreciate the richness of the unique resources that we each bring to the table, to more creatively use those resources to create new analyses and opportunities, and to more effectively help each other to make the most of them.

Many b-boys and b-girls will tell you that their first real experience of Hip Hop dance consisted of being shoved into the cypher by a friend who refused to accept their hesitant attitude. It is my hope that this anthology will provide a similar service for Hip Hop studies itself.

NOTES

1. Though the immense commercial success of the Sugarhill Gang's "Rapper's Delight" did predate the breakdancing fad by several years, I would argue that most listeners at the time perceived the song as a one-of-a-kind disco novelty rather than a representation of a new musical genre or a cultural movement.

2. A note on terminology: Generally speaking, the term *Hip Hop dance* refers to both the East Coast and West Coast dance forms that are conventionally considered part of Hip Hop culture as well as the choreographed and party dances that are associated with Hip Hop music and its environments (though perhaps not exclusively). However, since many of the ideas about culture and community discussed in this handbook tend to cluster more specifically around what could be called Hip Hop's "traditional" dance forms—rocking, breaking, popping, and locking—I use the term *Hip Hop dance* to refer specifically to these forms and the cultures associated with them. The most prominent of these forms is known by several names, including "breakdancing," "breaking," "b-boying," and "b-girling," each of which has multiple, sometimes conflicting, implications. The term "breakdancing" is generally viewed as an artifact of the dance's moment as an '80s fad, and is now almost universally rejected by dancers on that basis. "B-boying" was the standard term when I was doing my research in the early 2000s; it was generally counterposed to breakdancing in an "authentic versus inauthentic" binary. "B-girling" was introduced as a counterpoint to the gender specificity of the term b-*boying*, but it struck most people as mannered and is still rarely used. Even many b-girls refer to what they do as "b-boying." More recently, as reflected in this text, the community seems to be moving toward the term "breaking," presumably because it is neither gender specific like b-boying nor symbolic of inauthenticity like breakdancing. For the purposes of this afterword, I will use the term "breaking," That said, there were several

instances in which "b-boy" or "b-boying" felt like the more appropriate word, as in phrases like "b-boy attitude" or "b-boy culture." My rule for those cases was that if I felt that masculinity was a significant part of the concept in question then I would use the term "b-boy." But my reason for making that choice is simply to acknowledge that a cultural relationship between the concepts of masculinity and authenticity does exist, not to take a position on whether or not it should.

3. Though Ken Swift and Yarrow Lutz coauthored the chapter, it is written in the first-person singular and presents itself as an expression of Ken Swift's unique personal experience and perspective. For the sake of clarity, when referring to the chapter itself, I refer to both authors, but when referring to the experience and perspective it contains, I will refer to them as being Swift's alone.

4. In the interest of full disclosure, I wrote the introduction for this book.

5. Academic scholars who are committed to defending the value of Hip Hop sometimes find themselves at a loss when Hip Hop artists themselves decline to do so. Contrary to what some may believe, the reason is not that they don't believe that their art is valuable. It is that they refuse to accept the terms of the argument in the first place. Understanding the social context of a conflict has been a fundamental element of battle strategy in all Hip Hop art forms since their earliest days. Battling in someone else's neighborhood, for example, is different from battling in your own neighborhood, and it requires different tactics. When I was researching sample-based Hip Hop production in the late nineties, I was initially surprised by how many serious Hip Hop producers seemed to accept the notion that Hip Hop wasn't music. I soon realized, however, that what they were really saying was that if someone's definition of the word "music" didn't have room for Hip Hop, it probably wasn't worth your time to try to change their mind, and that the most sophisticated response in that scenario was simply to refuse to get drawn into a patently unfair argument. In other words, it was a strategic decision. But the social and cultural history that had informed that strategic decision was, in its own right, an extremely rich legacy to explore, and offered multiple profound ideological (and political) lessons of its own.

References

Alien Ness, (2015). *The Art of Battle.* New York: Self-Published.

Becker, H. (1998). *Tricks of the Trade.* Chicago: University of Chicago Press.

Chang, J. (2005). *Can't Stop Won't Stop.* New York: St. Martin's Press.

Cooper, M. (2003). *Push Hip-Hop History.* Vol. 1: *The Brooklyn Scene.* New York: Self-Published.

Cooper, M., and Kramer, N. (2005). *We B*Girls.* New York: PowerHouse Books.

De Jesus, L. (2013). *The Kings of Dance.* Miami: WakeUpWrite.

Estrada, W. (2016. *The Dancing Gangsters of the South Bronx.* New York: Latin Empire.

Fogarty, M. (2006). "'What Ever Happened to Breakdancing?' Transnational B-Boy/B-Girl Networks, Underground Video Magazines and Imagined Affinities." MA thesis. Brock University.

Gaunt, K. D. (2015). "YouTube, Twerking and You: Context Collapse and the Handheld Co-presence of Black Girls and Miley Cyrus." *Journal of Popular Music Studies* 27 (3).

Guzman-Sanchez, T. (2012). *Underground Dance Masters: Final History of a Forgotten Era.* Santa Barbara, CA: Praeger.

Schloss, J. G. (2004). *Making Beats: The Art of Sample-Based Hip-Hop.* Middletown, CT: Wesleyan University Press.

Schloss, J. G. (2009). *Foundation: B-Boys, B-Girls and Hip-Hop Culture in New York.* New York: Oxford University Press.

Schloss, J. G. (2017). "Culture, Ethnicity and the Inherent Theater of Hip-Hop." In *Theater and Cultural Politics for a New World*, edited by C. Thelwell. New York: Routledge.

Wald, E. (2013). "Sing Out! Broadsides and Banjos: The Folk Music Revival." Presentation. New York Public Library Rhapsodic City series. YouTube video. https://youtu.be/7ybB8Hur4HA Accessed 5/20/2018.

Index

For the benefit of digital users, indexed terms that span two pages (e.g., 52–53) may, on occasion, appear on only one of those pages.

Note: Tables and figures are indicated by *t* and *f* following the page number

Abeni, Cleis, 349–50, 352, 353, 354, 359
Abramson, Michael, 48
Accra dance crews, 273–74
Accrorap, 63–64, 419
Adams, Tony, 153
Adler, Bill, 204–5
Adowa. dance, 88
Adzogbo dance, 274
aesthetic of Hip Hop, 540–43
"Aesthetics in Action" (Bordwell), 100
African American Hip Hop. 271–72, 281,
    290, 304, 315–18, 537–38, *See also* Black
    aesthetics in streetdancing,
  Africanist aesthetics within breaking, 297
  B-Girls in, 120
  on campus, 282–83, 283*t*
  as cultural form, 172–73
  dance culture of, 243, 252, 374, 402, 536,
    546–47
  expressive practices, 81, 82–83, 84–85
  heritage of, 84–85, 88
  kung fu film audiences and, 102–3, 104–5
  In Living Color and, 386
  local movement subjectivities, 297
  origins of, 308–9, 312–13
  popping and, 374, 375, 376
  stereotypes, 320
  street culture of, 180–81
  twerking and, 308–9, 310–14, 315–18,
    320–21
  waacking/whacking, 390
The Africanist Aesthetic in Global Hip Hop
    (Osumare), 261
Afrika Bambaataa, 81–82, 136, 204–5

Afro-Caribbean influences, 85–86, 91–92,
    271–72, 315, 367–80
Afrodiasporic connection, 5–7, 84–85, 92, 194,
    263, 348, 460, 534, 535
Afrofuturism, 246
aging populations and Hip Hop, 528–29
Ahearn, Charlie, 50–51, 204–5
Airchair, 65–66, 78*f*
Airflare, 70, 78*f*
Air Mail Special (1941), 83–84
air moves, 15, 25–26, 28–29
Aktuel Force, 61, 63–64, 410
Aleksanyan, Garik, 295–96, 302
Ali, Muhammad, 20
Alim, H. Samy, 218
All the Ladies Say!, 248
American Broadcasting Corporation (ABC),
    46–47
American Journal of Sport Medicine, 478–79
American Koreans, 70
American photojournalism, 41
America's Best Dance Crew (TV show), 351
Andreasyan, Sargis "B-Boy Flash," 294–98
animal dances, 85–86
anterior cruciate ligament (ACL) injury, 488–89
Apfelbaum, Erika, 365–66
Aprahamian, Serouj, 120
Aragones, Fabrice "Gemini," 213–14
Armenian Hip Hop
  Andreasyan, Sargis "B-Boy Flash," 294–98
  B-Boys in, 300–3
  development of, 303–5
  internet generation in, 298–305
  introduction to, 292–94

Armenian Karate Federation, 301
around the worlds, 22
artification, 424, 430
artistic genre of Hip Hop, 413
Artists4Artists, 445
art school continuum, 468–69
Arts Council England (ACE), 432, 445
art transit, 42–43
Asafo marching dances, 274
Asian Americans in Hip Hop
    campus demographics, 282–83, 283*t*
    dance teams, 284–86
    introduction to, 280–82
    summary of, 290
Asia One, 335
Aspects of Performance: Graffiti Rock
    exhibition, 36
Associated Press, 41
Astor, Patti, 50–51
athleticism, 66, 68–71, 270, 300, 301–2, 482–84
Atkins, Charles "Cholly," 87–88, 94
Atomic style six-step, 59–60
Attou, Kader, 419
aural kinesthesia, 352
autoethnography, 153
Autoethnography as Feminist Method
    (Ettorre), 153

Baby Freeze, 23, 27–28, 60, 77*f*
Back 2 Da Underground, 397
"Back in Love Again" (L.T.D.), 13
backrock, 22
Backslide, 93
back spins, 23–24, 194
Back Swipe, 72
badass femininity, 292–93, 332–33
Bailey, Bill, 93
Baker, Greg, 313
Bakoko dance, 317
ball culture, 82–83
ballet in French Hip Hop, 411–12, 415
Banes, Sally, 43, 45, 46, 49, 54, 136, 137, 149
Baraka, Amiri, 348, 433–34
Battle of the Year (BOTY), 421–22
battles
    B-Boys/B-Girls and, 189, 252–53, 336–39
    crew battles, 17

culture of, 82–83, 121, 189, 252–53, 336
dance-battle-turned-stop-and-arrest, 49–50
in French Hip Hop, 411–12, 420–22
healing potential of Hip Hop outreach and, 513
International Battle of the Year event, 62
moves for, 196
as organized competition, 62
Battle Squad, 63, 74
B-Boy Azo, 302–3
B-Boy & B-Girl Dojo platform, 199–200
B-Boy Cico, 69
B-Boy Dyzee, 397
B-Boy Focus, 65
B-Boy Midus, 123
B-Boys
    in Armenian Hip Hop, 300–3
    breaking and, 117–19
    as foundation of Hip Hop, 61
    invention of dance terminology, 73–74
    kung fu films and, 97, 99, 102
    "new school" b-boy style, 270
    personal signature moves, 62
B-Boys/B-Girls
    air moves, 25
    battle culture and, 189, 252–53, 336–39
    Breaking paradigm and, 59
    crew routines, 17–18
    cyphers and space for practice, 195–98
    distinction in dancing styles, 332–33
    footwork importance to, 22
    foundations of, 14, 16–17, 62
    freezes, 28
    gender identity and, 327–28
    individuality of, 16
    introduction to, 4, 326–27
    music in educative culture, 191
B-Boy Summit, 206–7, 212, 213
Beat Street (1984), 37, 51, 106, 110–11, 176, 252–53,
    260, 284, 294, 296–97, 534
Beebish, 331–32
BeFLYCreate, 398–99
Bell, Lee Anne, 369
Berki, Farid, 414
Berlatsky, Steve, 322
Bernal, Martin, 229–30
Berry, Fred, 212
Beyoncé, 309, 379

B-Girls, 116–17, 123–24
  defined, 133
  gender and identity, 327–28
  introduction to, 326–27
  labeling struggles, 329–39
  presentation of, 334–36
  research design, 328–29
B-Girl Honey Rockwell (Ereina, Valencia), 133,
    134–35, 139–40, 142–44, 145–46
B-Girl Rokafella, 133, 135–36, 139, 140–42,
    144–46
B-Girl Terra, 123
Bhabha, Homi K., 368–69
The Big Boss (1971), 110–11
Big Freedia, 309, 318, 319–21, 322
Biter, defined, 65
*Bitter Fruit: The Politics of Black-Korean
    Conflict in New York City* (Kim), 286–87
Black aesthetics in streetdancing
  grimes, d. Sabela, 350, 354–57
  introduction to, 347–51
  jacking, 360–61
  Néné, Nubian, 357–58
  popping, 352–53
Black American English, 82–83
Black Belt Theater, 97, 102–3, 111
Black Blanc Beur, 414
*The Black Dancing Body: A Geography from
    Coon to Cool* (Gottschild), 374
The Black Dragon (1974), 104–5
Black dysfunction, 49
Black Feminist Thought (Collins), 219
Black hypersexuality stereotype, 316–17
*Black Noise: Rap Music and Black Culture in
    Contemporary America* (Rose), 2–3, 149–51
Black political project, 230
Black people and Hip Hop. *See also* African
    American Hip Hop
  Blackness in popular media, 48–49
  body aesthetic in twerking, 316–17
  ghetto youths, 273
  monetizing Black creativity, 253–54
  popular culture and, 247–49
  power dances, 245
  slang in kung fu films, 104–5
  social congregation, 49
  social dancing, 243–44

Black Star, 41
Blak Kat, 390–91
blaxploitation, 105
Blige, Mary J., 394, 398–99
BluePrintForLife, 499–500, 501
Bochner, Arthur, 153
body genre, 97–98, 110
Boogaloo, 92, 93
Boogie Woogie, 86
Bop dance, 94
Bordwell, David, 99–100
Botis Seva, 432, 439
*Bounce: Rap Music and Local Identity in New
    Orleans* (Miller), 310
bounce style, 309, 310
Bourdieu, Pierre, 273, 276
brain structure/function in expert dancers,
    522–24
Braithwaite, Fred (Fab 5 Freddy Love), 36
breakdancing *(la danse au sol),* 413–14
breaker, defined, 15
breaking
  athletic demands on breaking, 482–84
  B-Boys and, 117–19
  exploitation era of, 59–60
  gender studies on, 116–17
  injury incidence, 478–81, 481*t*
  introduction, 1
  masculinity, 117–18, 121, 122–24
  origin of terminology, 458
  overexposure of, 110–11
  paradigm, 59
  sexualized gestures, 119–20
breaking fundamentals. *See also* technical
    developments in breaking
  air moves, 25–26
  combinations, 28–29
  components of, 15, 16–18
  drops/dropping, 21
  education styles, 18–19
  footwork, 17–18, 21–23, 29–30
  freezes, 17–18, 27–28
  go downs, 21
  introduction to, 13–15
  spins/spinning, 17–18, 23–24
  summary of, 29–31
  Top Rock, 17–18, 19–21

Breaking in Style (BIS), 131
"breaksploitation" films, 50–51
bridge freeze, 23
British Council Showcase, 441
British Dance Edition, 441
bronco move, 26
Brooklyn rock, 267–68
Brown, James, 87–88, 208
Brown, Mike, 248
Browne, Simone, 51–53
Browning, Barbara, 378–79
Bruce Lee and Kung Fu Mania (1993), 104–5
Bryant, Rebecca, 94
Bryant, Willie, 94
bullying, 498–99
the Bump, 16
Burning, 18–19
burns/burners, 18, 120
Burrows, Jonathan, 441
Bus Stop, 16
Bust Down, 310–11
Butler, Judith, 264–65, 276
butt spins, 23

Cakewalk, 94
California backspin, 24
Camel Walk, 88–89
Campbell, Don, 85
Campbell, Luther "Luke Skyywalker," 311, 313
Campbellocking, 85, 211–12
Canadian Floor Masters, 499, 500f
Candelario, Wanda "WandeePop," 132
Can't Stop Won't Stop (Chang), 46
Capoeira moves, 59
Cassanova, Ralph "King Uprock," 131
Castle, Irene, 85–86
Castle, Vernon, 85–86
celebrity culture, 53–54
Centre for Contemporary Cultural Studies (CCCS), 178–80
Chair Freeze, 23, 27–29, 60, 66, 77f
Chakravorty, Gayatri, 153–54
Chalfant, Henry, 36, 42–43, 44, 136
Chan, Jackie, 109–11
Chang, Jeff, 46, 107, 136
Chang Cheh, 101
Charleston, 86

Charleston Basic, 93
Cheeky Blakk, 309, 311
Chen Kuan Tai, 109
Chicago Defender, 102
Chicken Noodle Soup, 94
Chicken Scratch, 92
Chion, Michel, 101
   choreography/choreographing, 63–64, 68, 285, 355–56
   Rock Steady Crew and, 106–8
   urban choreography, 285, 286
choreopolicing, 440, 441
Chung, Brian, 351
church jams, 14
CIA (Crazy Inside Artists) Writing crew, 460
cipher. *See* dance cipher
"Cité Danse" in Suresnes, 63–64
Citizen Shaw (1980), 101
civil rights movement, 245
Clark, Dick, 88–89
classical music in French Hip Hop, 414
clean choreography, 355–56
Clemente, Deena "Snapshot," 131–32
Clemente, Stephan "Mr. Wiggles," 132, 366–67, 370–80
clichéd masculinity, 117–18
Clief, Ron Van, 104–5
Coffee Grinder, 71
Cohn, Nik, 309
collective performance body, 377
Collins, Patricia Hill, 219
Colon, Richie "Crazy Legs," 204–5
commercialized Hip Hop, 268, 281, 347
common movement vocabulary, 67–68
community trust, 224
competitive plausibility, 229–30
Concord Productions, 103
Condry, Ian, 270
Conference on the Folk Culture of the Bronx (1981), 46
connective marginalities of young people, 304
consistency, 67
context of Hip Hop, 540–41, 548–49
continuous backspin, 24, 107
controlled aggression, 196
Conzo, Joe, Jr., 204–5
Cooper, Martha, 136, 137.

Blackness in popular media, 48–49
  in broader public sphere, 40–43
  challenges with, 43–46
  hypervisibility, 36–37
  introduction to, 32–36, 33*f*, 34*f*, 35*f*
  law enforcement and, 53–54
  overview of photographs, 32–40, 33*f*, 34*f*,
    35*f*, 39*f*, 40*f*
  performance under arrest, 49–50
  projections of, 50–53
  racializing surveillance, 51–53
  ritual warfare, 46–47, 47*f*
  summary of, 54–55
coordination in injury prevention, 488–90
core strength, 69
Cornelius, Don, 88–89
Cornell Hip Hop Collection, 204–5
corporate Hip Hop, 267, 275–76
corporealities of identity, 158–63
corporeal orators, 84–85
corporeal orature, 280
cosmopolitanism, 122–24
Count Basie, 83–84
COVID-19 pandemic, 3, 209–10, 231–32
crab move, 29
Crazy Commandos, 59
Crazy Legs, 53–54, 59–60, 81, 104, 107. *See also*
  Rock Steady Crew
creative practice approach
  art school continuum, 468–69
  introduction to, 457–58
  movement and, 464–70, 465*f*
  rhythm in writing and dance, 460–61
  signatures of dance, 465–66
  summary of, 469–70, 470*f*, 471*f*
  terminology, 458–60
  urban stylized lettering, 461–64, 463*f*
creativity as signature, 65–66
crew battles, 17
crew routines, 17–18
Crichlow, Tara, 133
Criner, Terry, 86–87
critical ethnography, 219
Crocker, Frankie, 83
Crossover Step, 62
Crunk Feminist Collective, 387–88
Cuban Rumba, 87

cultural appropriation, 81–82, 90, 308
cultural heritage, 82–83
cultural scenes of Hip Hop, 175–78
cultural-social-symbolic expectations, 347–48
Curran, Sean, 374
cyphers, 195–98
Cyrus, Miley, 308–9, 320–23

Dafora, Asadata, 93
dance and Hip Hop
  aesthetic of Hip Hop, 540–43
  common themes, 540–41
  context of Hip Hop, 540–41, 548–49
  defining as general concept, 549–51
  history and historiography of Hip Hop,
    540–41, 544–47
  introduction to, 534–37
  pedagogy and transmission of Hip Hop,
    540–41, 543–44
  practical information for dancers, 540–41,
    547–48
  summary of, 551–55
dance-battle-turned-stop-and-arrest, 49–50
dance cipher, 261–63
Dance Delight in Japan, 90
dancers as embodied researchers, 152
dance schools, 53–54, 301
Dance Spirit Magazine, 133
Dance Studies Association, 3–4
dance teams, 6, 281–83, 284–86, 288–90
Daniels, Jeffrey, 93
Dark Matters: On the Surveillance of Blackness
  (Browne), 51–53
Darling-Wolf, Fabienne, 276
David Letterman Show, 59–60
Davis, Sammy, Jr., 89
Dazl, 390–91
dead man freeze, 27
Debord, Guy, 442
Dee, Jimmy, 106
Dee, Jonathan, 312
definitive guides to Hip Hop, 54–55
défis, defined, 421
DeFrantz, Thomas, 280, 356, 386
deindustrialization, 48, 182
DeNaro, Anthony "YNOT," 190–91, 194,
  366–67

Desmond, Jane, 260–61
Desser, David, 103
Detours (2002), 293
dialectic method, 68
digitization of streetdance footage, 207–8, 209–11
disco, 173–74, 245–47, 249, 257, 398
Distinction: A Social Critique of the Judgement of Taste (Bourdieu), 273
ditty bop walk, 90
DIY (do-it-yourself) of cultural production, 176
Djemad, Jean, 410
DJ-Gestapo, 71
DJ Hollywood, 81–82. *See* Holloway, Anthony "DJ Hollywood"
DJ Ill Literate, 188–89
DJing/DJs (deejays)
    birth of Hip Hop and, 536
    live DJ, 191–92
    music in educative culture, 191–94
DJ Kool Herc, 81–82, 190
DJ Renegade, 214–15
DJ Rusty Lazer, 322
donkey move, 26
Douglas Projects, 14
Down Rock, 62–64, 70
Doze Green, 106–7
dozens game, 83
dreadlocks hairstyle, 89–90
dressing for Hip Hop dancing, 154–58
Drop Charleston, 92
drops/dropping, 21
DuBois, W. E. B., 369
Durden, E. Moncell, 286, 353, 366–67
Durham, Aisha, 153
dursi tgherk (street kids), 295
Duteil, Patrick, 409
DVDs, 207–8, 209, 210
Dvorak, Petula, 313
Dynasty Rockers, 131
DysFunkShn, 338–39

Edison, Thomas, 88
Ed Sullivan Show, 87–88
éducation populaire, 411
educative process

future of space and sound, 199–201
introduction to, 188–89
music in, 189, 190–95
space in, 195–99
Effect Records, 310–11
eight-count linear counting, 356–57
Eisenstein, Sergei, 100
elbow rock, 22
Elbow Spin, 60–61
Electric Boogaloos, 132
Elgato Video Capture, 209–10
Elite Force Crew, 89–90
Elkins, Doug, 374, 416
Ellis, Carolynn, 153
Englert, John, 46–47
Enter the Dragon (1973), 103
Esch, Kevin, 105
ethnography, defined, 152
Ettorre, Elizabeth, 153
Eurocentric hierarchies in dance, 85–86
everyday life concept, 183
Evolution Dancers, 269–70
exploitation era of Breaking, 59–60

Facciuto, Eugene Louis, 86
family and streetdance community, 226–30
family trope, 160–61
Far East Coast in the House (1998), 90
Farmer in House, 94
Farrow, Kenyon, 281–82
fashion and image, 71, 154–58
female masculinity, 332–33
Fensterstock, Alison, 321
Firestyle Dance Crew, 301
First Nations communities, 501–7, 502f, 503f, 504f
Five Fingers of Death (1973), 104
Five on the Black-Hand Side (Russell), 83–84
Flares, 60–61
Flashdance (1983), 26, 106, 110–11, 175, 252–53, 260, 284, 294, 499, 534
flexibility requirements in breaking, 484, 486–87
Flip Rock, 61
Float Committee, 139
floats, 26, 206
Flo Master, 120–21
Floormasters Dancers, 99

flow, in motion, 466
Floyd, George, 3–4
Fly Girls
    as fashion inspiration, 389–90
    firsthand accounts of, 390–404
    Fly Lady Di, 393f, 393–95, 395f, 400–2, 401f,
        403–4, 404f, 405f
    impact of, 388–90, 550
    introduction to, 384–88
    McKesey, Leah "McFly Waackeisha," 387–88,
        390–93, 391f, 397–400, 399f, 401f, 402–3,
        404f, 405f
    role of routines, 389
Flying Steps, 63, 298–99
Fly Lady Di, 393f, 393–95, 395f, 400–2, 401f,
    403–4, 404f, 405f
Fogarty, Mary, 101–2, 197–98, 298–99, 396f,
    396–97
Fon-Ewe-Yoruba, 314–15
footwork, 17–18, 21–23, 29–30
foreign dancing, 272
Forman, Murray, 195–96
Forsythe, William, 462–63, 464
Foster, Jimmy "Scoo B Doo," 358–59
Foster, Susan, 153
Foucault, Michel, 436
foundation in Hip Hop, 543–44
Four Step Brothers, 86–87
the Freak, 16
Freakmasters, 20
freedom of movement, 440
freedom of speech, 469–70
Freestyle Session, 212
freestyling, 18–19, 265, 272
freezes, 17–18, 27–28, 62–64
"freeze to please," entertaining style, 121–22
Freire, Paolo, 349
French Hip Hop
    ballet and, 411–12, 415
    battles and, 411–12, 420–22
    defining practice of, 412–14
    displacement, 414
    festivals and, 418
    intellectualization of, 419–20
    introduction to, 408
    la danse Hip Hop, 412–13, 422–23
    organization of, 415–17

    professionalization of, 417–18
    roots of, 420–22
    singularization of, 418–19
    smurf/smurfers and, 408–10, 413
    summary of, 422–24
French National Dance Center, 415–16
Frere-Jones, Sasha, 319–20
fresh, defined, 81
The Freshest Kids (2002), 458
Fresh (George), 81
The Fresh Prince of Bel-Air (TV show), 389,
    392–93
Frosty Freeze (Wayne Frost), 20, 26, 32, 40f,
    46–47, 121–22, 137
funk, 66, 87, 196, 246–47
funky, defined, 191–92
Funky Charleston, 93
Funky Monsters Crew, 302
FUSION, 280–82

Ganaway, George "Twist Mouth," 92
gang culture, 82–83
gang origins of Hip Hop, 54, 249–50
gang violence, 48
Garcia, Ana "Rokafella," 133
Garcia, Roger, 107–8
Gardner, Lyn, 430–31
Gateward, Frances, 100
Gaunt, Kyra, 84–85, 359–60, 387–88
Gaze Afar, 93
gender, defined, 327–28
gendered stereotypes, 118–19, 165–66
gender identity and B-Girls, 327–28
gentrification, 438
Gervais, Thierry, 41
Ghana tradition, 262–76
ghetto connotations, 173
GhettOriginal Dance Company, 63–64, 142
GhettOriginal Productions, 137
Gibbard, Ben, 319
the Gigolo, 16
Gilmore, James, 84
Gilmore, Ruth Wilson, 231–32, 354
Gindi Theatrical Management, 138
Gladys Knight and the Pips, 87–88
Global Hip Hop Nation (GHHN), 267–71,
    276–77

global Hip Hop underground, 304
globalization of Hip Hop, 261–63
    Ghana tradition, 262–76
    Global Hip Hop Nation, 267–71, 276–77
    Hawaiian tradition, 263–71
    introduction to, 260–61
    summary of, 276–77
go downs, 21
Going Off, 66–67
Golden Harvest Kung Fu films, 25
Golden Harvest studio, 101, 103
Goldman, Danielle, 436
Gomez, Michael, 314–15
Google Trends, 308
Gothic Futurism, 459–60
Gottschild, Brenda Dixon, 316–17, 348, 374
graffiti, origin of term, 458–59
Graffiti Rock event, 44
graffiti writing, 42, 458–60
Gramsci, Antonio, 420
Grandmaster Flash, 81–82, 100, 192–93
Grandmaster Flowers, 84
Green, Jeffrey "DOZE," 460
Green, Tony, 314
Griffiths, Lee, 432, 439, 445
grimes, d. Sabela, 350, 354–57
grindhouse distribution of kung fu films, 97,
    98, 102–4
groupie label, 156–57, 162

habitus, 264–65, 273
Hager, Steven, 44
Hai Jumping Crew, 296
Hall, M. Morton, 84
hand-clapping games, 84–85
hand glide spin, 24
Hansen, Chadwick, 316
Harlem Lite Feet, 94
Harlem Shake, 93–94
Harlem Twist, 92
Harris, Jossie, 394
Harris, Rennie, 80, 366–67
Harvie, Jen, 431
Hawaiian tradition, 263–71
Hawes, Bessie Lomax, 85
hazing, 221–22, 223
Hazzard-Donald, Katrina, 367–68

headache move, 29
head spin, 23, 24, 60–61
healing potential of Hip Hop outreach
    for incarcerated youths, 505*f*, 506*f*, 507–9
    in Inuit and First Nations communities,
        501–7, 502*f*, 503*f*, 504*f*, 508*f*, 509*f*
    storytelling case studies, 510–14, 511*f*, 512*f*,
        514*f*, 515*f*
heartbeats, 17–18
Hecht, David, 275
heightened performative sensibility, 53
Heinich, Nathalie, 418–19
helicopter, 22, 25, 28–29, 71
Hellenic Telecommunications Organization, 298
Henderson, Douglas "Jocko," 83
heritage, defined, 81. *See also* history and
    heritage
Higgins, James "OG Skeeter Rabbit," 350, 358–59
high-intensity interval training (HIIT),
    483–84
high swipe, 25–26
High Times Crew, 36–37, 45, 46–47, 49–50
Hinds, Princess Samantha "Shayla," 397–98
Hip Hop: The Illustrated History (Hager), 44, 48
Hip Hop Congress Armenia, 301
    Hip Hop dance theater (HHDT) in the UK,
        430–32, 444–45
    institutional framework, 434–36
    metaspatial knowledge, 436–45, 446–47
    pioneers in, 432–34
    strategic agenda of UK arts and, 440–41
    summary of, 445–47
Hip Hop feminists, 150, 166, 387
Hip Hop Files: Photographs 1979-1984
    (Cooper), 36, 37–38
"Hip Hop's Two-Pronged Bodily Text"
    (Osumare), 265, 266*f*
The Hiplife in Ghana (Osumare), 261, 271
history and heritage
    as continuum of cultural heritage, 82–83
    corporeal orators, 84–85
    cultural appropriation and, 81–82, 90
    cultural identity and migration, 89–90
    in dance categories, 540–41, 544–47
    Eurocentric hierarchies in dance, 85–86
    introduction to, 80–81
    lineages of moves and music, 86–87

locking, 85, 87–89
rhythm and rhyme, 83–84
social dances and, 92–94
summary of, 91–92
Hitch-Hike, 93
HIV/AIDS, 231–32
Holder, Geoffrey, 93
Holloway, Anthony "DJ Hollywood," 83
homology, 182
Honey Rockwell (Ereina, Valencia), 133, 134–35, 139–40, 142–44, 145–46, 334–36
hooks, bell, 48, 441
horror genre, 97–98, 105
house and Hip Hop
    Black popular culture and, 247–49
    disco and, 245–46
    feminine house, 255
    funk and, 246–47
    gang origins of Hip Hop, 249–50
    house, defined, 243–44
    introduction to, 243
    masculine house, 255
    neoliberalism and, 253–54
    nervous system of, 255–56
    scholarship of, 256–58
    sex/sexuality and, 252–53
Hovakimyan, Lia, 301
Hsiao Ho, 107–8, 109–10, 112f
Hunt, Leon, 97–98
the Hustle, 16, 87–88
hustle culture, 82–83
hybridity, 276
Hylton, Robert, 432, 433–34
hype, defined, 191–92
hypersexualization in Hip Hop, 285

Icey Ice Six-step, 59–60
iconicity, 172
identity
    corporealities of, 158–63
    cultural identity and migration, 89–90
    gender identity, 327–28
    sociocultural significance, 178–82
    sociocultural significance of Hip Hop, 178–82
    triangulation of urban dance identity, 286–89, 287f

women ethnographers of Hip Hop dances, 158–63
imperialism, 219, 441
improvisational dance, 18, 265, 326
incarcerated youth outreach programs, 505f, 506f, 507–9
independent Hip Hop labels, 314
individuality, 65–66, 292–93
individuation in Black vernacular dancing, 353
industrialization of UK arts, 431
Injury, 479–80
injury/injury prevention
    athletic demands on breaking, 482–84
    in Breaking, 122
    coordination and proprioceptive training, 488–90
    effectiveness of advice, 484–90
    flooring requirements, 486
    future directions in, 490–92
    injury incidence, 478–81, 481t
    introduction to, 477–78
    protective equipment, 485–86
    recommendations, 490
    strength training, 488
    stretching in, 486–87
In Living Color (TV show), 384–85, 386, 388, 389, 391–92, 550
Inside Subculture: The Postmodern Meaning of Style (Muggleton), 179–80
insult game, 83
International Battle of the Year event, 62
internationalization of Hip Hop. See globalization of Hip Hop
Internet Relay Chat (IRC) client, 207
Inuit communities, 501–7, 502f, 503f, 504f
Irish Hornpipe, 93
Iron Fists and Kung Fu Kicks (Ou 2019), 100
Iton, Richard, 46

jacking, 360–61
Jackson, Janet, 269, 393–94
Jackson, John L., 366
Jackson, Jonathan David, 349–50
Jackson, Michael, 93, 205, 208, 249–50, 394, 398–99
Jackson, Ronald, 48
The Jacksons, 87–88

Jamaican Ska dance, 92
James, Leon, 93–94
Jam on the Groove (JOTG), 132, 138f, 138,
    140–41, 143
Jam Style & Da Boogie, 298–99
Japanese dancers, 89–90
jazz dance, 386, 413
*Jazz Dance: The Story of American Vernacular
    Dance* (Dafora, Holder), 93
jerks, 18, 92
Jim Crow era, 315
jive slang in kung fu films, 105
Johnson, Imani Kai, 195–96, 270, 292–93
Jones, Ansley Joye, 120
Jonzi D, 432, 433, 439
Josiah-speak, 270
Journal of Sports Medicine and Physical Fitness,
    480

Kaba Modern, 284
Käfig, 418, 419
Kai Johnson, Imani, 352
Kajikawa, Loren, 193
Karima, 329–30
Katey Red (Kenyon Carter), 319
KeepRockinYou Toronto B-girl Movement, 337
Keil, Charles, 359–60
Kelley, Robin D. G., 369
Kelly, R., 394
Kid Creole, 193
Kid n' Play Kickstep, 93
Kim, Claire, 281, 286–87
kinesthetic expression, 66, 117
kip up, 26, 71
"Kissing My Love" (Withers), 84
K-Mel, 120–21
knee injuries in breaking, 485
knee rock, 22
knee spin, 24
knowledge in Hip Hop culture, 431–32, 457–58
Kool Herc, 387
Kugelberg, Johen, 204–5
Kundum dance, 274
Kung Fu Cult Masters (Hunt), 97–98
kung fu films
    grindhouse distribution of kung fu films, 97,
        98, 102–4

introduction to, 97–99
overexposure of, 110–11
remastering of, 108–10
Rock Steady Crew and choreography, 106–8
sound design of, 101–2
summary of, 111–12
trailers and marketing, 104–6
visceral impact of, 97–98, 99–100
Kwikstep, 145
KWON, 99

la danse Hip Hop, 412–13, 422–23
Lady Jules, 336–38
Lantern laws, 52–53
Lathan, Stan, 176
Lau Kar Leung, 107–8
law enforcement and breaking mediatization,
    53–54
Leah McFly. *See* McKesey, Leah "McFly
    Waackeisha"
Lee, Bruce, 20, 103, 104–5, 110–11
Lee, Jimmy, 106
Lefebvre, Henri, 195
Legends of Hip Hop (Harris), 80
legend status, 80, 119
legwork, 22
Lennox, Annie, 322
Lepecki, André, 431
Les Rencontres de la Villette, 416–17
Leventhal, David, 524–25
Levitin, Daniel, 84–85
LGBTQ+ participants, 124, 166
Li, Jet, 112
Life magazine, 41
The Light Brothers, 25
Lil' Lep, 107
Lindy Hop, 86, 92, 173–74
lineages of moves, 86–87
Lipsitz, George, 287
Listening Guide (Gilligan), 370
Liu, Gordon (Kung Fu Leung), 102, 108, 109
live DJ, 191–92
local scene, 177
The Lockers, 213
Locking, 85, 87–89, 211–15, 480
Locking4Life movement, 213–14
lofting, 131

London School of Contemporary Dance, 433
Lopès, Bruno, 409
Louie New Wave, 139
Lu Chin-ku, 104–5

Ma, Jessie, 289
Mackey, Nathaniel, 348
Mad Force Crew (MFC), 293, 295–96
Madison, D. Soyini, 219
Mad Monkey Kung Fu (1979), 20–21, 107–8, 109–10
Malik, Rachel, 40–41
Malta Guinness Street Dance Competition, 275
Mapouka dance, 317
Market, Catherine, 52–53
Mark Morris Dance Group, 524–25
Marrero, Yolanda, 313
Marrow, Michael Lawrence, 458–59
Martel, Diane, 89–90
Martin, Randy, 260–61, 366
Martin, Trayvon, 248
masculinity, 117–18, 121, 122–24, 250, 326–31, 542
Mashed Potato, 88
Massey, Doreen, 173
Mathews, Edith, 92
Matson, Andrew, 319
McClarin, Boogie, 360–61
McKesey, Leah "McFly Waackeisha," 387–88, 390–93, 391*f*, 397–400, 399*f*, 401*f*, 402–3, 404*f*, 405*f*
McQueen, Hanifa "Hanifa Queen," 329–30
McQuirter, Marya, 349
meaning making, 110, 369–70
Melamed, Jodi, 354
Melle Mel, 16, 193
melodrama genre, 98
Merzouki, Mourad, 412, 419
metaspace, 441, 443, 446
metaspatial knowledge, 436–45, 446–47
Mia X, 312
Mike Douglas Show, 86–87
military dance culture, 274
Milking the Cow, 93
Miller, Percy "Master P.," 314
Milliot, Virginie, 409–10, 415
Minetta Lane Theater, 138, 142–43
Minns, Al, 93–94

Mirando, Richie "Seen," 204–5
Mismatched Couples (1985), 111
misogyny, 151, 253, 267, 397
Mitterand, François, 410
modern choreography, 285
monetizing Black creativity, 253–54
Monroe, Raquel L., 355–56
Moore, Colleen "Miss Twist," 131–32, 133
Moore, Madison, 269
MOPTOP, 390–91
moral panics, 178–79
Morel, Gaëlle, 41
Morgan, Joan, 387–88
Motivated On Precision Towards Outstanding Performance (Mop-Top), 89–90
motor learning, 482–83
Mr. Wave, 61, 248
MuchMusic, 206
Multi-Asian Student Association (MASA), 280
Murray, Charles, 375–76
music/musicality. *See also* rap music
    classical music in French Hip Hop, 414
    in educative process, 189, 190–95
    future of space and sound, 199–201
    lineages of, 86–87
    technical developments in breaking, 66–67
mythology and Hip Hop, 81

naming moves, 72–73
National Audio-Visual Institute (INA), 412–13
National Dance Center (CCN) of La Rochelle, 419
National Geographic magazine, 41
National Portfolio Organisations' (NPO), 432, 434–36
Neal, Mark Anthony, 49, 122–23
neck move, 23
Néné, Nubian, 357–58
neoliberalism, 253–54, 304, 351
neurorehabilitation and Hip Hop
    aging populations, 528–29
    brain structure/function in expert dancers, 522–24
    commonality of, 518–21, 520*t*
    dance network and, 521–29
    introduction to, 516–18, 517*f*
    Parkinson's disease, 518–20, 524–28

Nevins, Jason, 206
New Amsterdam, 102
New Jack Swing Era, 284
New Orleans Jazz and Heritage Festival, 320
New Orleans twerking scene
   increased exposure, 319–22
   introduction to, 308–9, 310–14
   p-popping, 309, 310–11
   roots of, 314–18
   sissy rappers, 311, 319
   spread of, 318–19
   summary of, 322–23
"new school" b-boy style, 270, 480
Newsweek, 110–11
Newton, Esther, 157
New York City Breakers (NYCB), 61, 107
The New Yorker, 319–20
New York Marathon, 67
New York Post, 37–40
New York Ricans from the Hip Hop Zone
   (Rivera), 5, 136–37
New York subway art scene, 459
New York Times, 41, 85–86
New York Times Magazine, 309, 312
Nicholas Brothers, 386
Ninja Freeze, 72–73
No Limit Records, 314
Notargiacomo, Marcel, 410
Notorious B.I.G., 394
Notz, Cindy, 86–87
Nuissier, Gabin, 410, 412
Nu-Style, 90

Obsessive Funk (2005), 213–14
Ofusu, Terry Bright Kweku, 5–7
Okumura, Kozo, 90
"old school" style, 15
Once upon a Time in China (1991), 112
One-Hand 1990 move, 69
one-shot head spin, 24
Ongiri, Amy Abugo, 102–3
oral history of B-Girls, 131–46, 326–27
   introduction to, 131–46
organic intellectuals, 420
Oritz, Hector, 50
Osumare, Halifu, 5–7, 132–33, 136–37, 261, 262,
   265, 267, 268, 297, 304

outreach efforts. *See* healing potential of Hip
   Hop outreach

Pabon, Jorge "PopMaster Fabel," 132, 204–5
Paniccioli, Ernie, 204–5
Paris Olympics (2024), 1
Parkinson's disease, 518–20, 524–28
park jam (block party), 16
Parliament-Funkadelic family, 208
patting juba, 84–85, 93
pedagogy and transmission of Hip Hop, 540–
   41, 543–44
Pellerin, Eric, 112*f*, 113*f*
Perez, Rosie, 385–86, 389–90, 393–94, 403–4
performance/performativity, 264–65, 268, 366
permits for dancing, 53
personal signature moves, 62
Peters-Muhammad, Jamilah Y., 312
Pick Up technique, 62
Pizarro, Victor, 320
Pizza, Pizza Daddy O (1968), 85
Playing Bones, 85
Playing Spoons, 85
playing the dozens, 83
Poe One, 65
pop cultural hegemony, 264
Pope, Greg "Campbellock Jr.," 87–88
Popin' Pete, 352–53
PopMaster Fabel, 132, 461–64, 463*f*
popping
   aesthetics of, 367–80
   Clemente, Stephan "Mr. Wiggles," 366–67,
      370–80
   ethnic and racial tension in, 378–80
   hiphopography and, 222
   as influence, 92
   injury incidence, 480
   introduction to, 365–67
   learning movements, 370–75
   overview of, 309, 310–11
   written, stylized letterform and, 461–64
Popping For Parkinson's, 517–18, 524–28, 526*f*
Pop-up, 71
Portelli, Alessandro, 133
Postal Service, 319–20
power-*versus*-style debate, 270
p-popping. *See* popping

practical information for dancers, 540–41, 547–48
practice of freedom, 441
practitioner-researched divide, 227–28
presumption of criminality, 46
primary sensory cortices, 521–22
Prince (artist), 204–5, 208
Prince of Soul, 84
Proctor, Tyrone, 390–91
proprioceptive training in injury prevention, 488–90
Public Enemy, 71, 82, 385
public-housing projects, 48
punk, 172–73, 175, 178, 182, 197–98, 251
pushing head spin, 24
python style top rock, 20–21

Queen Latifah, 249–50
queer studies, 269–70
Quiñones, Lee, 51

racial bias in academia, 233–35
racial-gender assumptions, 350
racialized stereotypes, 118–19, 541–42
racializing surveillance, 51–53
racism, defined, 231–32
Rack Daddy, 93
Raimist, Rachel, 5
Rainey, Ma, 88–89
Rammellzee, 36, 459–60
rap music
    appropriation of kung fu films, 104
    authenticity and, 167–68
    impact of, 46–47, 172, 260
    as oral poetry, 132–33
    pedagogy and, 552
    research on, 2–3, 45–46
    rise of, 53–54
    twerking and, 310, 311, 314, 318
"Rappin' to the Beat" (20/20), 46–47
Ras AKA Ray, 99
Rastus, Joe, 88
R & B and funk, 246
RCA, 20
Reagan, Ronald, 49, 61
Récital (Käfig), 418
Reck n' Shop Live from Brooklyn (Martel), 89–90

Red Bull sponsor, 199–200, 298
Reed, Lenard, 94
reflexive modernity, 182
Reggie Rockstone (Reginald Ossei), 272
Reid, Benji, 432, 433
Rencontres de danses urbaines (Urban Dance Meetings), 416
Rentie, Jerry, 367–68
researcher-researched divide, 228
research intensive institutions, 439
Revolver technique, 62
Reyes, Diana "Fly Lady Di," 387–88
rhythm and rhyme, 83–84, 460–61, 466–68, 467f
Riley, Teddy, 284
riot-in-progress, 50
ritual warfare, 46–47
Rivera, Raquel, 5
roach move, 29
Roberts, Dorothy, 369
Roberts, Shauna, 390–91
Robinson, Lisa, 46–47
rock/rocking
    backrock, 22
    Brooklyn rock, 267–68
    Down Rock, 62–64, 70
    elbow rock, 22
    Flip Rock, 61
    knee rock, 22
    overview of, 16, 18–19
    python style top rock, 20–21
    Top Rockin, 17–18, 19–21, 62–64, 72–73, 93, 482
    Uprock, 18–19, 482
Rock Steady Crew. See also Crazy Legs
    battle culture and, 121, 336
    B-Girl affiliations, 132
    choreography and, 106–8
    cypher dance and, 32, 35f, 40f, 46
    Hawai'i chapter of, 270–71
    impact of, 20
    Swift, Ken, 69
Rockstone, Reggie, 264
Roger Rabbit, 93
Rojas, Frank, 87–88
Rokafella, 133, 135–36, 139, 140–42, 144–46, 332–33

Ron AKA DJ Groove, 188
Rose, Tricia
    ethnographic studies by, 149
    Hip Hop feminism, 387–88
    Hip Hop's Black coded images, 288
    impact of, 2–3, 5, 49
    love of Hip Hop, 150
    sociocultural significance of Hip Hop, 172
Ross, Diana, 249–50
rowboat move, 29
Rud, Casanova Rud, 88
Ruffin, Nadine "Hi-Hat," 93
Run DMC, 82, 206
Russell, Charlie, 83–84
Russian move, 29
Russian Taps, 71
Ryder, Katie, 319–20
RZA (rapper), 105–6, 108

sacred dances, 274
Sadler's Wells' project Breakin' Convention,
    432, 434–35, 442–44
Sadler's Wells Theatre, London, 431
Samba, 93
Sammo Hung, 110–11
Santiago, Richard "Breakeasy," 131
sass, 247–48
Savoy Ballroom, 83–84
Scandinavian Journal of Medicine and Science
    in Sports, 480
Schechter, Hofesh, 441
Schloss, Joseph, 5–7, 97, 100, 136–37, 190, 281
Scissor Kick Charleston, 92–93
Scott, Anna, 348
Scott, James, 365–66
Seattle Times, 319
Seize Crew, 293
self-presentation, 154–58
Sellers, Caleaf, 353
sensual connectivity, 359
sexism, 223
sexism in Breaking, 141
sex/sexuality, 119–20, 252–53
sexual advances, 157, 158, 159–60
Sgalambro, Emilio, 74
Shabba Doo, 212, 358–59
Shahinyan, Vanush "B-Boy Booble," 299–300

Shanghai Tang Yong Kung Fu Collection, 109
Shaolin and Wu Tang (1983), 102
Shaviro, Steven, 97–98
Shaw Brothers studio, 25, 101, 103, 110–11
Sherrow, Pauline, 133
shimmy, 93–94, 317–18
Shim Sham, 94
Shipley, Jesse, 264
shoeshine routine, 17–18
shoulder spins, 23, 24
side-to-side step, 20
signatures of dance, 465–66
Simone, Maliqalim, 275
sissy rappers, 311, 319
Sistarelli, Simone, 525–27, 526f
Six-step, 59–60, 61, 75f, 540
Skate step, 94
Skeme, 193
skill acquisition, 64–65
the Slop, 88
Sly and the Family Stone, 208
Smarth, Marjory, 366–67
Smith, Ernie, 84
Smith, Herrnstein, 443
Smith, Linda Tuhiwai, 219
smurf/smurfers, 408–10, 413
social dances/dancing, 92–94, 222, 243–44
social justice, 365–66, 369
sociocultural significance of Hip Hop
    body studies in, 182–83
    cultural scenes, 175–78
    identity and, 178–82
    introduction to, 171–72
    space and place, 172–75
    summary of, 184
socioeconomic marginality, 179–80, 378–79
solo jazz dances, 86
Solomon, Sam "Boogaloo Sam," 92
Sondheim, Stephen, 442
soul period, 87
SoulSeek, 207
Soul Train Line, 88–89
Soul Train (TV show), 212–13
Source magazine, 370–71
South Korea, 70
space-consciousness, 464–65
spaghetti westerns, 105

Spalding, Alistair, 433, 434, 443
Spann, Hank, 83, 84
Spartanic Rockers, 63
Spencer Davis Group, 191
spider move, 29
spins
    back spins, 23–24, 194
    butt spins, 23
    California backspin, 24
    continuous backspin, 24, 107
    Elbow Spin, 60–61
    hand glide spin, 24
    head spin, 23, 24, 60–61
    knee spin, 24
    one-shot head spin, 24
    overview of, 17–18, 23–24
    pushing head spin, 24
    shoulder spins, 23, 24
    tapping head spin, 24
    Turtle spins, 60–61, 72
    Zulu spins, 22
the Stab, 60, 66, 76f
Starchild La Rock, 104
Stathopoulou, Dimitra, 462–63
static stretching, 486
Stearns, Jean, 386
stomach roll, 24
storytelling approach, 17
strategic essentialism, 153–54
streetdance archives and collections
    current directions, 208
    digitization of, 207–8, 209–11
    introduction to, 204–5
    Locking footage, 211–15
    organization directions, 209
    origins of, 205–7
streetdance community hiphopography. See also
    women ethnographers of Hip Hop dances
    critical hiphopography, 218–20
    family and, 226–30
    hiphopography, defined, 218–19
    institutional power and, 230–35
    introduction to, 217–18
    racial bias in academia, 233–35
    "show and prove" attitude, 221–26
    summary of, 236–37
    thematic analysis, 220–35

streetdancers/streetdances. See also Black
    aesthetics in streetdancing
    casual and informal nature of, 163
    culture of, 2–3
    fashion and, 154–58
    studies on, 2, 8, 152
strength training, 488
Stretch, Buddha, 82, 348–49, 351
stretching in injury prevention, 486–87
studio-based learning, 349
Style Elements, 120–21
Style Wars (1983), 137
Subway Art (Cooper and Chalfant), 42–43
Suicidal Lifestyle, 298–99
suicide move, 26
Suidiata Keita Cha-Jua, 103
Superfly (1972), 103
Super Lover Cee, 88
Suresnes Cités Danse festival, 417, 418
the Sweep, 71
Swift, Ken
    B-Boys/B-Girls competitions, 338
    Breaking skills, 118–19, 120–22
    impact of Hip Hop on, 304–5, 541
    kung fu films and, 101–2, 105–6, 107–8, 113f
    neurorehabilitation and Hip Hop, 516, 517f,
        517–18, 521–22, 523f
    teaching materials, 206–7
    technical developments in breaking, 59–60,
        69, 87
Swift Kids, 99
swordplay film, 97–98

Tacky Annie, 94
tagging, 465–66
Tamet, Christian, 417–18
tap dance, 86–87, 93
tapping head spin, 24
Taylor, Diana, 349
technical developments in breaking
    adopted terms, 71
    Airchair, 65–66, 78f
    Airflare, 70, 78f
    athleticism, 68–71
    Baby Freeze, 23, 27–28, 60, 77f
    battle as organized competition, 62
    Chair Freeze, 23, 27–29, 60, 66, 77f

technical developments in breaking (*cont.*)
  character of, 72
  common movement vocabulary, 67–68
  consistency, 67
  craftsmanship, 64–65
  creativity, 65–66
  demand for more knowledge, 73–74
  fashion, 71
  individuality, 65–66
  introduction to, 58
  learning process, 70–71
  musicality, 66–67
  naming moves, 72–73
  One-Hand 1990 move, 69
  Six-step, 59–60, 61, 75*f*
  the Stab, 60, 66, 76*f*
  summary of, 74–75
  theater productions, 63–64
  trends, 58–62
  the Windmill, 60–61
Temptations, 94
"tenaxis" challenges, 348
TeN (Justin Alladin), 267–69
Teo, Stephen, 97–98
The 36th Chamber of Shaolin (2007), 105–6
theater productions, 63–64
Théâtre Contemporain de la Dance
      (Contemporary Dance Theater), 417
Thicke, Robin, 321
Thien-Bao Thuc Phi, 281
Thompson, Robert Farris, 262–63, 271
throw back flip, 17–18
Time Inc., 41
Times-Picayune, 313
Tip, Tap & Toe, 86–87
together-dancing, 359–60
Tolliver, Denny, 88
Tolstoy, Leo Nikolaevich, 91
Tool for the Analytical Dance Eye (Forsythe),
      464
Toonga, Joseph, 445
Top Rockin, 17–18, 19–21, 62–64, 72–73, 93, 482
translocal scene, 177
Tribalat, Frédéric, 410
truck driver step, 20
Tru Essencia Cru (TEC), 131–32, 133
turf wars, 173–74

Turner, Javae, 311–12
Turtle spins, 60–61, 72
Tutting, 94
20/20 (ABC program), 46–47, 47*f*
twerking, 308–9, 310–14
the Twist, 92
Twist Step, 92
2 Live Crew, 313, 318

UDEF/Pro Breaking Tour, 199–200
UK Arts Council, 442
UK B-Boy Championships, 298–99
underground art movements, 42
United Kingdom (UK) Hip Hop. *See* Hip Hop
      dance theater (HHDT) in the UK
United Street Artists (USA), 139
"Unity and Respect" dance event (2006),
      86–87
Universal Zulu Nation, 180–81
upright dance (*la danse debout*), 413–14
Uprock, 18–19, 482
urban choreography, 285, 286
urban dance, 285, 286–89
Urban Movement event, 269, 270–71
urban space, 173–74
urban stylized lettering, 461–64, 463*f*

Valencia, Ereina "Honey Rockwell," 131–32, 133
Valme, Nedge "Blak Kat," 397–98
VanBuren, Sylvia, 312–13
Vardimon, Jasmin, 441
Vaudeville era, 88
Velvet Revolution in Armenia, 303
VHS rips, 207, 209–10
Village Voice, 43, 45
virtual scene, 177
visceral impact of kung fu films, 97–98,
      99–100
visual expression, 66

waacking/whacking, 390
Walker, Aida Overton, 386
walking the dog move, 29
Wallace, Michael, 48
Wang, Oliver, 281
Warner Bros studio, 101, 103, 105
warrior image, 71

Washington, Alesha Dominek, 384
Washington, Booker T., 248
Wayans, Keenan Ivory, 384–85
Wayne, Teddy, 309, 322
We Aren't Cheap Brands (On n'est pas des
   marques de vélo) (2002), 409
weepie genre, 97–98
Whip Nae Nae, 94
White, Donald, 459–60
white Hip Hop, 251
Wiggins, Jack, 94
wildfire popular diffusion, 54
Wild Style (1982), 50–51, 52f, 106, 110–11, 192–93
Wilkins, Walter, 88
Williams, Linda, 97–98, 100
Willis, Chuck, 88–89
Willis, Paul, 99
Wilson, Jackie, 87–88
Windmill, 24, 72
the Windmill, 60–61, 107
Wing step in the House, 94
Withers, Bill, 84
women ethnographers of Hip Hop dances.
   See also streetdance community
   hiphopography

boundaries and, 154–58
identity and, 158–63
intimacy and, 154–58
introduction to, 149–51
methodological approach, 151–54
self-presentation and, 154–58
setting boundaries, 158–63
summary of, 168
thematic analysis, 154–68
Wray, Ama (Sheron), 88
Wreckz-n-Effect, 390
Writing movement, 458–60
Wu Tang Clan, 71, 102–3, 111, 206

Y-balance test, 489–90
Yen, Donnie, 111
Ying Yang Twins, 314
youth cultural landscape, 180–81
Youth Olympic Games, 199
Yuan, Peipei "Peppa," 332
Yuen Wo Ping, 100, 111

ZooNation, 442–43
Zulu Nation, 136
Zulu spins, 22